The Social Ecology of Resilience

Michael Ungar

Editor

The Social Ecology of Resilience

A Handbook of Theory and Practice

 Springer

Editor
Michael Ungar
Killam Professor of Social Work
Dalhousie University
Halifax, NS, Canada
michael.ungar@dal.ca

ISBN 978-1-4614-0585-6 (hardcover)   ISBN 978-1-4614-0586-3 (eBook)
ISBN 978-1-4614-8092-1 (softcover)
DOI 10.1007/978-1-4614-0586-3
Springer New York Heidelberg Dordrecht London

Library of Congress Control Number: 2011935367

Acknowledgements

To bring together a volume of this scope requires the efforts of many committed individuals. I have to thank dozens of research assistants and colleagues affiliated with the Resilience Research Centre who helped to organize events that brought together many of the authors who appear in this book, and who also helped introduce me, during my travels, to the people doing the most innovative work on resilience in the world. It is the vast network across dozens of countries that the RRC sustains that makes a volume like this possible.

I also owe a debt of gratitude to my codirector at the RRC, Linda Liebenberg, who helped with many of the logistical supports that made this book possible, and Dorothy Bottrell for her helpful review of my own contributions.

Finally, a sincere thank you to my support team at Springer.

Contents

Biographies of the Contributors

Derrick Armstrong is the Deputy Vice Chancellor (Education) and Professor of Education at the University of Sydney, Sydney, Australia.

Kate M. Bennett is a Senior Lecturer at the Institute of Psychology, Health and Society, at the University of Liverpool, England, United Kingdom.

Peter Berliner is professor in Community Psychology, DPU, Department of Education, University of Aarhus, Copenhagen, NV, Denmark.

Theresa S. Betancourt is Assistant Professor in the Department of Global Health and Population at the Harvard School of Public Health (HSPH), and directs the Research Program on Children and Global Adversity (RPGCA) at François-Xavier Bagnoud Center for Health and Human Rights.

Dorothy Bottrell is a Lecturer of teaching and learning in the Faculty of Education and Social Work, University of Sydney, Sydney, Australia.

Arn Chorn-Pond is a former child soldier in Cambodia, and an internationally recognized human rights leader. He is the founder and, at present, the spokesperson for Cambodian Living Arts.

Ronald Chung is a Senior Research Assistant in the Department of Pediatrics at McMaster University in Hamilton, Canada.

Heather D'Antoine is Associate Director of Aboriginal Programmes, Menzies School of Health Research, in Casuarina, Northern Territory, Australia.

Gonwo Dahnweih has been a field worker for the project "A Services Approach to Preventive Mental Health for Adolescent Refugees" at the UIC College of Medicine, Department of Psychiatry.

Stéphane Dandeneau is Franco-Métis from St-Boniface, Manitoba and is currently the Professor of social psychology at the Université du Québec à Montréal where his research focuses on uncovering the underlying processes of social-cognitive resilience.

Jack Demick is an Adjunct Professor Department of Education, Center for the Study of Human Development, Brown University, Providence, Rhode Island, USA.

Pat Dolan is joint founder and Director of the Child and Family Research Centre and Director of the Higher Diploma/Masters Degree in Family Support Studies at the University of Galway, Ireland.

Kimberly DuMont is a Research Scientist for New York State's Office of Children and Family Services (OCFS) Bureau of Evaluation and Research, Rensselaer, NY, USA.

Vicki Durrant is the Director of The Youth of Today Society that operates a community run shelter and drop-in center for homeless and street-involved youth in Whitehorse in northern Canada.

Mark Eggerman is Research Fellow of the Macmillan Center for International and Area Studies at Yale University, New Haven, USA; and Assistant Editor (Medical Anthropology section) of the interdisciplinary journal *Social Science & Medicine.*

Susan Ehrhard-Dietzel is a Research Support Specialist with the Center for Human Services Research at State University of New York, Albany, New York.

Petra Engelbrecht is Professor of Education in the Education Research Directorate, Faculty of Education, Canterbury Christ Church University, Canterbury, United Kingdom.

Leonce Hakizimana has been a program officer in Burundi and a field worker for the project "A Services Approach to Preventive Mental Health for Adolescent Refugees" at the UIC College of Medicine, Department of Psychiatry.

Rebecca Harvey is an Assistant Professor and Marriage and Family Therapy Program Director at Seton Hill University. She maintains a private practice specializing in couples and sexuality issues.

Jean Hine is Reader in Criminology at De Montfort University in the United Kingdom. She directs the UK research network "Pathways into and out of Crime: Risk Resilience and Diversity."

Nan Henderson is the President of Resiliency In Action, a training, consulting, and publishing company in Southern California.

Katrina D. Hopkins is a Ph.D. candidate and recipient of an Australian Postgraduate Award, Curtin University of Technology Postgraduate Scholarship, and a Stan & Jean Perron Award for her doctoral research in resilience in Aboriginal youth.

Morgan Kahentonni Phillips (Kanien'kehá: ka/Mohawk) is a researcher for the Network for Aboriginal Mental Health Research (www.namhr.ca) and McGill University's Faculty of Medicine specializing in Indigenous health and wellness.

Martha Kent serves as Clinical Neuropsychologist at the Carl T. Hayden Veterans Affairs Medical Center in Phoenix.

Kristen Kirkland is a Research Scientist at the New York State Office of Children and Family Services Bureau of Evaluation and Research, Rensselaer, New York.

Laurence J. Kirmayer is the James McGill Professor and Director, Division of Social and Transcultural Psychiatry, McGill University; Director, Culture and Mental Health Research Unit, Lady Davis Institute, Jewish General Hospital; and Codirector, National Network for Aboriginal Mental Health Research.

Silvia H. Koller is a Professor at the Department of Developmental and Personnality Psychology, Institute of Psychology, Federal Universidade do Rio Grande do Sul, Porto Alegre, Rio Grande do Sul, Brazil.

Line Natascha Larsen is a Ph.D. fellow, Department of Psychology, University of Copenhagen, Denmark.

Renata M. C. Libório is a Professor, Department of Education, Faculty of Science and Technology, Julio de Mesquita Filho São Paulo State University, Presidente Prudente, São Paulo, Brazil,

Elise Levin is a sociocultural anthropologist with a background in public health who works as a research manager at UIC College of Medicine, Department of Psychiatry with an interest in behavioral and social underpinnings of health practices and outcomes, sub-Saharan Africa, and social justice.

Linda Liebenberg is the Codirector of the Resilience Research Centre and adjunct Professor of Social Work at Dalhousie University, Halifax, Canada.

Lewis P. Lipsitt is Professor Emeritus of Psychology, Medical Science, and Human Development, and Research Professor of Psychology at Brown University, Providence, Rhode Island, USA.

Macalane Malindi resides in Bethlehem in the Free State Province of South Africa and is a Senior Lecturer in the Department of Education at North-West University.

Elizabeth Marshall is the Director of the Treaty Beneficiary Association and Community researcher, Eskasoni, Nova Scotia, Roots of Resilience Project.

Robyn Munford is Professor of Social Work and Social Policy, School of Health and Social Services at Massey University in Palmerston North, New Zealand.

Kate Murray is a postdoctoral fellow in the Comprehensive San Diego State University-University of California, San Diego Cancer Center Comprehensive Partnership, USA.

Orit Nuttman-Shwartz is Associate Professor, Chairperson, The Israeli National Council for Social Work and the Dean, School of Social Work, Sapir College, Israel.

Catherine Panter-Brick is Professor of Anthropology, Health, and Global Affairs at the Jackson Institute and at the Department of Anthropology, Yale University, New Haven, USA; and Senior Editor (Medical Anthropology section) of the interdisciplinary journal *Social Science & Medicine.*

Jennifer Puig is a Ph.D. candidate at the Institute of Child Development at University of Minnesota.

Michael Rutter is Professor of Developmental Psychopathology at the Social, Genetic, and Developmental Psychiatry Centre, Institute of Psychiatry, King's College London, London, United Kingdom.

Jackie Sanders is Senior Researcher, School of Health and Social Services at Massey University in Palmerston North, New Zealand.

Ingrid Schoon is a Professor of Human Development and Social Policy at the Institute of Education, University of London, London, UK.

Neerja Sharma is Associate Professor, Department of Human Development and Childhood Studies, Lady Irwin College, University of Delhi, Delhi, India.

Rekha Sharma Sen is Associate Professor, Faculty of Child Development, School of Continuing Education, Indira Gandhi National Open University, Delhi, India.

Jude Simpson is a Family Violence Prevention Advocate with Presbyterian Support Northern in New Zealand.

Elena de Casas Soberón is Senior Lecturer, Department of Psychoeducation, University of Cuauhtémoc, Aguascalientes, Mexico.

L. Alan Sroufe is the William Harris Professor Institute of Child Development and Department of Psychiatry, University of Minnesota, Minneapolis, MN, USA.

Bill Strickland is the Chief Executive Officer of Bidwell Training Center in Pittsburg, USA.

Laura M. Supkoff is a Ph.D. candidate at the Institute of Child Development at University of Minnesota.

Catherine L. Taylor is an Associate Professor at the Curtin Health Innovation Research Institute; and the Director of the Centre for Developmental Health Telethon Institute for Child Health Research, Population Sciences Division in Perth, Australia.

Linda C. Theron is a Professor of Educational Psychology in the School of Educational Sciences, North-West University, Vaal Triangle Campus, Vanderbijlpark, South Africa.

Piotr Trzesniak is a Professor at the Department of Physics and Chemistry, Institute of Sciences, Federal University of Itajubá, Itajubá, Minas Gerais, Brazil.

Michael Ungar is a Killam Professor of Social Work at Dalhousie University, Halifax, Canada.

Randall Waechter is a researcher in cognition and coinvestigator of a longitudinal study of child welfare-involved adolescents, along with Dr. Christine Wekerle, at McMaster University in Hamilton, Canada.

Froma Walsh is Professor Emerita, School of Social Service Administration and Department of Psychiatry, and Codirector, Chicago Center for Family Health, at the University of Chicago, Chicago, IL, USA.

Stevan M. Weine is a Professor of Psychiatry and Director of the International Center on Responses to Catastrophes at the University of Illinois at Chicago.

Christine Wekerle is an Associate Professor in the Department of Pediatrics at McMaster University in Hamilton, Canada; and a Research Associate at the Centre for Research on Violence Against Women and Children.

Joanna Welford is Research Fellow at De Montfort University in the United Kingdom.

Karla Jessen Williamson is Assistant Professor, Educational Foundations, University of Saskatchewan.

Gill Windle is a Research Fellow at the Dementia Services Development Centre, Institute of Medical and Social Care Research at Bangor University, in Wales, United Kingdom.

Alex Zautra is Arizona State University Foundation Professor of Clinical Psychology, and codirects ASU's Resilience Solutions Group.

Stephen R. Zubrick is a Professor at the Curtin Health Innovation Research Institute, Centre for Developmental Health Telethon Institute for Child Health Research, Population Sciences Division, in Perth, Australia.

Introduction to the Volume

Michael Ungar

Since 2002, the Resilience Research Centre at Dalhousie University (RRC – http://www.resilienceresearch.org) has explored culturally and contextually sensitive ways of studying resilience among children, youth and families on six continents. That work has shown that the resilience of individuals growing up in challenging contexts or facing significant personal adversity is dependent on the quality of the social and physical ecologies that surround them as much, and likely far more, than personality traits, cognitions or talents. As the authors in this volume show, *nurture trumps nature* when it comes to explaining why many children do well despite the odds stacked against them.

More than two decades after Rutter (1987) published his summary of protective processes associated with resilience, researchers continue to report definitional ambiguity in how to define and operationalize positive development under adversity. The problem has been partially the result of a dominant view of resilience as something individuals *have*, rather than as a *process* that families, schools, communities and governments facilitate. Because resilience is related to the presence of social risk factors (we can only speak of resilience in the presence of at least one stressor),

there is a need for an ecological interpretation of the construct that acknowledges the importance of people's interactions with their environments.

This perspective is still young. Talking about cultural differences in how resilience is expressed, or the complexity of interactions between elements of our environment, makes the science of resilience messy. Suddenly there are many more variables to consider. Simple associations between traits like emotional regulation or an internal locus of control and positive development become less determined as we ask questions like, 'In what context does this trait contribute to resilience?' and 'What role does culture play with regard to whether a particular attribution style is valued as something that protects children or adults from problems?'

This understanding of resilience extends the discourse concerning positive human development under adversity, suggesting that social ecological factors such as family, school, neighbourhood, community services, and cultural practices are as influential as psychological aspects of positive development when individuals are under stress. An abundance of research in the field of genetics, cognition, human development, family processes, community responses to disaster and trauma studies (reviewed in the chapters that follow) provide a solid basis for a definition of resilience that explicitly accounts for the disequilibrium between vulnerable individuals who lack opportunities for growth and the influence of environments that facilitate or inhibit resilience-promoting processes.

M. Ungar (✉)
Killam Professor of Social Work,
Dalhousie University, Halifax, NS, Canada
e-mail: michael.ungar@dal.ca

M. Ungar (ed.), *The Social Ecology of Resilience: A Handbook of Theory and Practice*,
DOI 10.1007/978-1-4614-0586-3_1, © Springer Science+Business Media, LLC 2012

Each chapter in this volume provides evidence for this ecological understanding of resilience in ways that help to resolve both definition and measurement problems. As well, by positioning authors from both western and non-western contexts in this volume, my hope is to challenge the discursive bias of western scientists and mental health practitioners. That bias has tended to favour individual-level variables and culturally homogenized notions of the interaction between risk factors and aspects of positive development in threatening social and physical ecologies. The voices in this text are, therefore, not uniform. Most texts on resilience have tended to invite authors well known in the west doing research that conforms to standards set by western-trained psychologists. Although many of the chapters and their authors meet these standards, many others do not. In particular, I have included five interviews with individuals from the United States, Canada, South Africa, Cambodia and New Zealand, who grew up facing great adversity and not only survived, but thrived. Their stories, in Part Two, are offered as a means to ground the discussion in the other chapters by reminding us what we are really talking about: lives as they are lived and the way social and physical ecologies make resilience possible.

To these interviews are added more than two dozen chapters that help explain why lives are lived successfully despite the threats people experience to their healthy psychosocial development. As the editor, I purposefully sought out authors who were both world leaders in the study of resilience as well as those writing on the margins of the resilience field, or from the perspectives of cultures and contexts very different from my own. In many cases, I was their student, learning about South African school children orphaned because of the death of their parents from AIDS, Brazilian children who work as domestic labourers, Aboriginal youth in western Australia, gay, lesbian, bisexual, transgendered and queer youth in the United States, and communities in Greenland facing drastic cultural changes. To these voices are added more recognizable studies of children in child welfare systems in western countries, studies of the neurology of resilience, resilience

in schools, the science of post-traumatic growth, the resilience of children who face violence and ways in which young people's contributions (engagement) protects them.

The authors may not all be well known in the field of resilience, but all are well established researchers from Western and non-Western countries, recognized for their work on child development, family processes and community engagement in their respective fields of Psychiatry, Social Work, Sociology, Child and Youth Studies, Education, Anthropology and Psychology. In many cases, they bring a fresh perspective to this field of research and its application to practice.

The chapters that follow build on the groundbreaking contributions of other volumes that have contributed to our understanding of resilience. Though less ecologically focused, all have hinted at the importance of social ecologies when considering the developmental trajectories of children, youth and adults. In particular, readers of this volume may want to also consider reading Reich, Zautra, and Hall's *Handbook of Adult Resilience* (2010). Likewise, two excellent volumes that helped set the stage for this present work are Luthar's *Resilience and Vulnerability* (2003) and Lester, Masten and McEwen's *Resilience in Children* (2006).

My work in this field, including the *Handbook for Working with Children and Youth: Pathways to Resilience Across Cultures and Contexts* (Ungar, 2005), like that of my colleagues, has been influenced by recent reports on important research related to the study of resilience. A short list of these works includes Sroufe, Egeland, Carlson and Collins (2005) wonderful volume on the Minnesota Study of Risk and Adaptation from Birth to Adulthood titled *The Development of the Person*; Schoon's (2006) *Risk and Resilience: Adaptations in Changing Times* that provides support for a temporal, historical perspective of resilience; and work by Elliott et al. (2006) who reported on studies of neighbourhoods in Denver and Chicago in their book titled *Good Kids from Bad Neighbourhoods: Successful Development in Social Context*.

Related works that would be of interest to readers include Brown's (2008) edited volume

Key Indicators of Child and Youth Well-being; Wong and Wong's (2006) *Handbook of Multicultural Perspectives on Stress and Coping*; Kagitçibasi's (2007) *Family, Self, and Human Development Across Cultures*; Peters, Leadbeater and McMahon's (2005) *Resilience in Children, Families, and Communities;* and Jenson and Fraser's (2006) *Social Policy for Children & Families: A Risk and Resilience Perspective.*

With this foundation in mind, *The Social Ecology of Resilience* provides access to innovative research throughout the following chapters.

Part 1: Introduction to the Theory

In this chapter, I present an ecological approach to the study of resilience and its application to practice and policy. The chapter begins with a detailed expression of resilience that defines it as a set of behaviours over time that depends on the opportunities that are available and accessible to individuals, their families and communities. Building on the research of other scholars and the RRC, I show the importance of understanding resilience as a contextually and culturally embedded construct and the need to capture what people mean when they say 'doing well when facing adversity'.

Next, Sir Michael Rutter, in his chapter titled *Resilience: Causal pathways and social ecology,* distinguishes resilience from concepts of positive psychology and competence by showing that there is heterogeneity in how humans respond to environmental hazards, whether those are physical or psychological (Rutter, 2006). His goal is to explore these different responses in order to discover the causal processes that relate to resilience. His chapter shows the wisdom that comes with more than four decades of research in this area.

The third chapter in Part 1 seeks coherence between more individually focused understandings of resilience and an ecological perspective. In their chapter, titled *Theory and measurement of resilience: Views from development,* Lewis Lipsitt and Jack Demick in the US explore the relationship between the construct of resilience and other concepts such as invulnerability, stress

resistance, hardiness and protective factors. To advance an explanation of the construct, they present two developmental approaches to the study of resilience. The first, based on developmental learning theory, argues that the behavioural seeds of resilience inhere in the predisposing capabilities of the newborn infant. The second, grounded in a holistic/systems developmental perspective, proposes that the *telos* of development entails a differentiated and hierarchically integrated person-in-environment system with the capacity for flexibility, self-mastery and freedom. Although the two approaches differ in some ways, Lipsitt and Demick show that they share theoretical and methodological assumptions.

Finally, the fourth contribution to Part 1 is a challenging discussion of resilience by Piotr Trzesniak, Renata Libório and Silvia Koller titled *Resilience and Children's Work in Brazil: Lessons from physics for psychology.* The chapter begins with a discussion of resilience itself, borrowing concepts from physics to better understand what resilience means. They conclude that resilience is not 'reality' but a 'convenient way' to describe a phenomenon in which children cope with adversity. They show the application of this understanding of resilience and the cognitions that accompany it to a discussion of working children in Brazil.

Part 2: Five Interviews

Part 2 changes the focus from theory to the phenomenon of resilience as illustrated through the narratives of individuals who have experienced challenging contexts. To show the interaction between individuals and their social ecologies, I conducted five interviews with very special people from very different backgrounds.

The first is with Macalane Malindi, a lecturer in education at North-West University in South Africa. We spoke together about his upbringing and the impact that education and social policy had on him during the apartheid and post-apartheid eras.

The second interview is with Bill Strickland, a community activist and social entrepreneur in

Pittsburgh who has started a network of adult educational facilities to lift people out of poverty in urban America. Having grown up facing the same disadvantage as many of his students, Strickland shows how when we build prisons, we create prisoners and criminals. But when we build schools we nurture citizens.

The third interview is with a remarkable woman from New Zealand named Jude Simpson who, despite a history of abuse and gang involvement, has become a leading advocate for safe families and communities.

The fourth interview changes continents again. This time, I went to Canada's north and spoke with Vicki Durrant, a single parent who started a program for high-risk Aboriginal youth who spend most of their time on the street. The innovative program she runs engages hard to reach youth by providing food, shelter, and training to young people with few other resources.

The final interview is with Arn Chorn-Pond, an internationally recognized peace activist and former child soldier from Cambodia. His work now focuses on the revival of traditional music and art after the Khmer Rouge. His story of his own survival shows how important the arts can be to young people's ability to cope with extreme adversity and recover later from the trauma of war.

Part 3: The Individual (In Context)

Martha Kent's chapter begins Part 3 that focuses on individual factors and their interaction with social ecologies. Her chapter is titled *From neurons to social context: Restoring resilience as a capacity for good survival.* It examines the neurobiological mechanisms that facilitate adaptation. The chapter provides a brief overview of the basic brain, endocrine and behavioural mechanisms that are related to resilience at a biobehavioural level. A number of concepts are reviewed such as homeostasis, affiliation as an anti-stress system, brain circuits and their responsivity to context, mirror neurons, social neural networks and the nature of personal agency.

The next chapter by Laura M. Supkoff, Jennifer Puig and Alan Sroufe is titled *Situating resilience in developmental context.* The authors

link the theory of resilience to principles of general development and show that resilience is similar to other outcomes. They show that the 'hierarchical' or 'cumulative' feature of human development is particularly relevant to the study of resilience, with adaptation over time the product of a child's current circumstances and the supports and challenges that are present. They show that when children overcome adversity or recover following exposure to trauma, their success is the result of earlier positive supports and experiences of positive adaptation.

In the third chapter, *Temporal and contextual dimensions to individual positive development: A developmental-contextual systems model of resilience,* Schoon introduces a developmental-contextual model of resilience that takes into account developmental and contextual influences on individuals' manifest adaptation under adversity. Building on her research reviewing historical cohort data sets in Britain, Schoon describes multiple contextual factors and their influence on individual functioning over the life course. Her work shows that early experiences in childhood do not necessarily predict negative development later and that assumptions of developmental constancy are overstated.

The fourth chapter of Part 3, *Girls' violence: Criminality or resilience?* by Jean Hine and Joanna Welford, examines girls' violence and considers whether it is a risk factor or part of a strategy by some youth to sustain resilience. Hine and Welford show that violent behaviour by girls is 'doubly condemned' as violence and an unfeminine expression of identity. Using narratives from girls themselves, Hine and Welford show that within gendered spaces that marginalize young women, violence can sometimes be a rational response that helps girls cope when there are limited choices.

Part 4: The Family

Leading off Part 4 on the family, Froma Walsh presents *Facilitating family resilience: Relational resources for positive youth development in conditions of adversity.* As one of the innovators of the concept of family resilience, Walsh's work shows us that a social ecological understanding of resilience recognizes the important contributions of family and social networks, community services and cultural influences on young people. The chapter offers relational and systemic perspectives on resilience, first considering how key family bonds in the multigenerational network of relationships can nurture children's resilience. It then addresses resilience in the family as a functional unit, from ecological and developmental perspectives. It describes Walsh's (2006) research-informed family resilience framework developed for clinical and community-based practice to strengthen children and families facing adversity and the key processes in family resilience, culled from findings from research on resilience and effective family functioning.

The next chapter by Christine Wekerle, Randall Waechter and Ronald Chung explores *Contexts of vulnerability and resilience: Childhood maltreatment, cognitive functioning and close relationships.* Wekerle and her colleagues examine the problem of childhood maltreatment and its relationship to resilience. Specifically, they discuss two elements of resilience, those external to the child like close/romantic relationships and the care received from child welfare caseworkers, and internal ones such as neurocognitive processes. They argue that following disclosure of abuse, there is much that can be done to improve individual development. They propose several strategies that may be helpful creating a coherent sense of self that buffers the impact of maltreatment. These include strategies such as cognitive re-appraisal, contextualizing the maltreatment event, dealing with shame and guilt, and authoring an accurate and self-compassionate narrative.

These same themes are discussed in very different ways by Kimberly DuMont, Susan Ehrhard-Dietzel and Kristen Kirkland in their chapter *Averting child maltreatment: Individual, economic, social and community resources that promote resilient parenting.* Understanding resilience as an ecological construct, they show that a mother's parenting behaviours help nurture the healthy development of her child and protect the child from maltreatment. But they also argue that to this parent–child understanding of resilience must be added a more contextualized appreciation for the child-rearing environment that influences the ability of caregivers to nurture their children. Reporting on a study with a sample of mothers who face a great deal of adversity and were at risk of neglecting or abusing their children, the chapter identifies which factors are likely to predict poor outcomes and who defines the nature of risk.

Gill Windle and Kate M. Bennett then broaden the focus to a discussion of caregiving in their chapter *Caring relationships: How to promote resilience in challenging times.* They argue that the burden of care provision within a family (whether to a child, spouse or parent) poses considerable risk to psychosocial outcomes. However, as not all caregivers are affected negatively, Windle and Bennett examine the factors that are likely to predict the resilience of adult caregivers.

In the fifth chapter in Part 4, Jackie Sanders, Robyn Munford and Linda Liebenberg write about *Young people, their families and social supports: Understanding resilience with complexity theory.* They take the innovative approach of exploring the way complexity theory can help us understand resilience among young people. The chapter uses a case example to apply three aspects of complexity theory to practice, demonstrating how complexity theory is congruent with an ecological understanding of the supports (family and otherwise) that make resilience more likely.

Part 5: The School

Part 5 explores the considerable influence school environments have on human development. The first contribution is by Dorothy Bottrell and Derrick Armstrong whose chapter, *Local resources and distal decisions: The political ecology of resilience,* examines the resilience of young people as they cope with processes of school exclusion, placement as students with emotional and behavioural difficulties, and interactions with the criminal justice system. They report findings from a qualitative study in the UK called 'Pathways Into and Out of Crime: Risk, Resilience and Diversity' that showed the links between criminality, school experiences and coping.

The next chapter switches the discussion to South Africa where Linda Theron and Petra Engelbrecht discuss the role of educators. Their chapter, titled *Caring teachers: Teacher–youth transactions to promote resilience* shows that when communities are challenged by AIDS-related losses, divorce and violence, teachers become particularly important as 'agents of resilience'. They use stories collected from non-white South African youth who face significant challenges to show how caring teachers that are accessible to children provide an ecological source of hope, optimism and mentorship.

The following chapter by Neerja Sharma and Rekha Sharma Sen shifts the focus to India and *Children with disabilities and supportive school ecologies.* They focus specifically on children with disabilities and the disadvantages they face inside and outside educational institutions. Even for those fortunate enough to receive formal education, Sharma and Sen show that children's experiences vary greatly. Reporting on their own research, they discuss how schools can play a role mitigating the risks children with disabilities face. Their work is as applicable to western contexts as it is to India, identifying the physical, socio-cultural and systemic features of schools that serve protective functions and promote positive development.

Nan Henderson next discusses *Resilience in schools and curriculum design,* building on her successful work as a lecturer on school resilience. She shows through case examples how important schools are to fostering resilience among children and youth. The nature of that school environment will influence everything from a child's academic success, to the safety they experience, and their capacity for social and emotional well-being.

Part 6: The Community

In Part 6, the focus widens even further to community factors that influence resilience. Steven Weine, Elise Levine, Leonce Hakizimana and Gonwo Dahnweigh in their chapter *How prior social ecologies shape family resilience amongst refugees in U.S. resettlement*, discusses the experiences of refugee families during resettlement and how they overcome the multiple adversities that result from exposure to war, forced displacement and long periods of internment in refugee camps and the stressful resettlement process that follows. While the stressors are complex, Weine et al. shows that refugee families bring with them family and community resources that buffer the impact of resettlement. Their work builds on results from an ethnographic study of 73 Liberian and Burundian refugee adolescents in the US. Much of what predicts a family's ability to cope depends on the capacity of its community to help the family find or build new churches, secure adequate living space and share parenting responsibilities with other adults. The implications for policy and resettlement programs is discussed.

In the next chapter, Rebecca Harvey discusses her own personal and professional experience as a queer family therapist/supervisor. She provides case examples of a variety of youth who identify as queer, an umbrella term for lesbian, gay, bisexual, transgendered and queer. Her work, titled *Young people, sexual orientation and resilience*, is a kaleidoscope of images of young people and the multiple ways they cope when marginalized in their communities, including the role that mentors, therapists, schools and families play in nurturing these young people's resilience.

The following chapter by Kate Murray and Alex Zautra is titled *Community resilience: Fostering recovery, sustainability and growth.* In their chapter, they define community resilience and identify the components that predict it will occur. Three dimensions are highlighted: recovery, sustainability and growth. Their discussion focuses on communities like those of Sudanese refugees who have experienced forced migration, emphasizing the importance that community plays to future adaptation. They show through their report on their research that community collaboration, shared identity and empowerment increase bonding and bridging capital that promote the well-being of people under stress. They argue that an emphasis on community resilience places value on the social connections, policies, programs and community context necessary for resilience in different cultures and contexts.

The next chapter of Part 6 is by Theresa S. Betancourt and focuses on war-affected youth in the context of Sierra Leone. Her work, titled *The social ecology of resilience in war-affected youth: A longitudinal study from Sierra Leone*, reports on findings from a mixed methods longitudinal study. Betancourt shows that a developmental and ecological perspective on the lives of children affected by armed conflict helps us to see the role environment plays in how well children cope during and after exposure to violence. Individual factors interact with family and community factors to bolster well-being, securing for children the cultural and community resources necessary for mental health while addressing the problems of stigma and alienation.

The final chapter related to community is by Pat Dolan from Ireland and is titled *Travelling through social support and youth civic action on a journey towards resilience*. In it, Dolan explores the connection between resilience and social support and how each is affected by individual, family and wider ecological factors that can be addressed at the level of social policy. The focus is on concepts of social support networks and how resilience can be built at multiple levels through youth civic action. Several short vignettes are presented that show how good policy can affect young people and the programming required to make this happen.

Part 7: Culture

Part 7, which discusses the links between culture on resilience, begins with a chapter by Catherine Panter-Brick and Mark Eggerman entitled *Understanding culture, resilience, and mental health: The production of hope*. Reporting on their multidisciplinary and longitudinal studies of Afghan families that included paired interviews with adolescents and adult caregivers, the authors argue that cultural values are the 'bedrock' of resilience: they underpin the meaning attributed to great suffering, hope for the future and a sense of emotional, social and moral order to ordinary and extraordinary aspects of life. Remarkably, they show that war-related trauma is not the principal driver of poor mental health: traumatic experiences are linked to fractured family relationships and a failure to achieve personal, social and cultural milestones. Resilience, meanwhile, rests upon a demonstration of family unity. In the context of structural disadvantage that includes poverty, crowded living conditions and exposure to violence, Panter-Brick and Eggerman also show that cultural dictates come to entrap Afghans in the pursuit of honour and respectability, a core facet of psychosocial resilience. Their chapter highlights linkages between psychosocial and structural resilience, cautioning against a simplistic view of culture as a set of protective resources. Instead, they discuss the ramifications of social policies that raise not just hope, but undue expectations without sufficient resource provision.

The next chapter by Peter Berliner, Line Natascha Larsen and Elena de Casas Soberón provides a case study of Greenland's Paamiut Asasara, a program to promote community resilience using local values. This chapter shows how one community facing high rates of crime, violence, suicide, drug abuse and child neglect were able to address these social problems by strengthening community-wide resilience. Interventions included the revitalization of the local culture, shared activities, the building of social networks, and opening up opportunities for creative self-expression. The chapter reports at length on the participants' descriptions of the changes they experienced and describes differences in the community at large.

The following chapter by Laurence J. Kirmayer, Stéphane Dandeneau, Elizabeth Marshall, Morgan Kahentonni Phillips and Karla Jessen Williamson shifts the focus once again. It is titled *Toward an ecology of stories: Indigenous perspectives on resilience*. Kirmayer and his colleagues, well-known researchers in the area of resilience among Aboriginal people in Canada and Australia, argue for more attention on how people cope outside the US and UK. They show that indigenous peoples have their own unique cultures and contexts, and that their historical rootedness can help them cope with the profound disadvantages caused by colonization and the political oppression and bureaucratic control that followed. In this chapter, the authors incorporate material from collaborative work in Cree, Inuit, Mohawk, Mi'kmaq and Métis communities to explore how cultural ideologies, institutions and practices sustain processes associated with resilience.

The next chapter in Part 7 is by Orit Nuttman-Shwartz from Israel and is titled *Macro, meso and micro perspectives of resilience during and after exposure to war*. In it, she explores the role that sense of belonging to one's family, community and nation plays in buffering the impact of the stress and trauma related to war. Reporting on a sample of Israeli young people living on the border with Gaza, she suggests that feelings of national identity and sense of belonging help people to cope and are associated with the meaning people make from their experiences of violence. This work, like the rest of the chapters in Part 7, help us to think more broadly about the socio-political ecologies that shape resilience, no matter which side of a war we are on.

In the last chapter by Katrina D. Hopkins, Catherine L. Taylor, Heather D'Antoine and Stephen R. Zubrick, *Predictors of resilient psychosocial functioning in Western Australian Aboriginal young people exposed to high family-level risk*, the authors review results from a study in Western Australia of stress exposure and resilience among Aboriginal children and young people who come from families where there is violence. The findings are provocative given the social and economic marginalization the youth face. Results show that the youth who are the most resilient are those who report *less* adherence to their culture and come from *lower* rather than higher socioeconomic households.

Next Steps

Combined, these chapters offer a unique compilation of perspectives on resilience that emphasizes the social ecologies that make resilience more likely to occur. Each part provides a sampling of some of what we already know. More importantly,

each part hints at what more is possible. There continues to be large gaps in our knowledge of how social ecologies influence resilience, even though it is obvious that individual oriented understandings of the resilience construct overlook many of the factors that shape successful development under stress. What we need now is more research, both qualitative and quantitative, to capture indigenous knowledge, practice-based evidence and narratives of success, as well as empirical cross-sectional and longitudinal studies that explore homogeneity and heterogeneity among children, youth, families and communities at-risk. This is the goal of the RRC and its partners worldwide.

References

Brown, B. V. (Ed.). (2008). *Key indicators of child and youth well-being*. New York: Taylor & Francis.

Elliott, D. S., Menard, S., Rankin, B., Elliott, A., Wilson, W. J., & Huizinga, D. (2006). *Good kids from bad neighborhoods: Successful development in social context*. New York: Cambridge University Press.

Jenson, J. M., & Fraser, M. W. (Eds.). (2006). *Social policy for children and families: A risk and resilience perspective*. Thousand Oaks: Sage.

Kagitçibasi, C. (2007). *Family, self, and human development across cultures: Theory and applications* (2nd ed.). Mahwah: Lawrence Erlbaum.

Lester, B. M., Masten, A. S., & McEwen, B. (Eds.). (2006). *Resilience in children*. Boston: Blackwell.

Luthar, S. (Ed.). (2003). *Resilience and vulnerability: Adaptation in the context of childhood adversities*. Cambridge: Cambridge University Press.

Peters, R. D., Leadbeater, L., & McMahon, R. J. (Eds.). (2005). *Resilience in children, families, and communities: Linking context to practice and policy*. New York: Kluwer.

Reich, J. W., Zautra, A. J., & Hall, J. S. (Eds.). (2010). *Handbook of adult resilience*. New York: Guilford.

Rutter, M. (1987). Psychosocial resilience and protective mechanisms. *American Journal of Orthopsychiatry, 57*, 316–331.

Rutter, M. (2006). Implication of resilience concepts for scientific understanding. In B. M. Lester, A. S. Masten, & B. McEwen (Eds.), *Resilience in children* (pp. 1–12). Boston: Blackwell.

Schoon, I. (2006). *Risk and resilience: Adaptations in changing times*. Cambridge: Cambridge University Press.

Sroufe, L. A., Egeland, B., Carlson, E. A., & Collins, W. A. (2005). *The development of the person: The Minnesota study of risk and adaptation from birth to adulthood.* New York: Guilford.

Ungar, M. (Ed.). (2005). *Handbook for working with children and youth: Pathways to Resilience across cultures and contexts.* Thousand Oaks: Sage Publications.

Walsh, F. (2006). *Strengthening family resilience* (2nd ed.). New York: Guilford.

Wong, P. T. P., & Wong, L. C. J. (Eds.). (2006). *Handbook of multicultural perspectives on stress and coping.* New York: Springer.

Part I

Introduction to the Theory

Social Ecologies and Their Contribution to Resilience

Michael Ungar

In the physical sciences, resilience refers to a quality of a material or an ecosystem (Walker & Salt, 2006). A trestle of steel is more or less resilient depending on its capacity to recover from load bearing and return to its previous state unchanged. A natural environment that sustains an industrial disaster and recovers also demonstrates resilience. The term began to appear with frequency in the psychological sciences in the 1980s and was a metaphor for the ability of individuals to recover from exposure to chronic and acute stress. In the language of human cybernetics (Bateson, 1972; von Bertalanffy, 1968), individuals return to a state of homeostasis (recovery to a previous level of functioning) or, in rare cases, experience change and growth (morphogenesis) following exposure to a toxic environment. These processes, like the environments in which they take place, were theorized as predictable and measurable phenomena that could be manipulated through interventions within neatly nested ecological levels.

A simple example of this positivist epistemology in the study of resilience was Anthony's (1987) notion of psychoimmunization in which early or current experiences of stressful events, when combined with high social support, were shown to be less likely to be pathogenic. The individual was thought to develop an "invulnerability" to later risk exposure. Recovery from trauma could be stimulated by engaging the individual in a process that promoted his or her expression of latent coping capacity. Resilience was reified in psychological discourse as something intrapersonal even if it was dependent on the resources, or structures, of the wider environment for its realization. Anthony suggested that "what are needed are objective measures regarding such structures and the degree of the individual's participation in them" (p. 7). Almost always, early studies of resilience focused on the individual as the locus of change. The environment (a family, school, institution, or community) was assessed for its influence on individual developmental processes but it was still the qualities of the individual, not the environment, which intrigued researchers. Self-efficacy (Bandura, 1977), sense of coherence (Antonovsky, 1987), self-esteem (Brown & Lohr, 1987), prosociality (Dovidio, Piliavin, Schroeder, & Penner, 2006), and other individual qualities associated with resilience have been hypothesized as more or less amenable to protection from the negative influence of environmental stressors and the health-promoting function of supports (Murphy & Moriarty, 1976; Werner & Smith, 1982).

By implication, within this individually focused view of resilience (what I'll term "the first interpretation of the resilience research"), those who are disadvantaged are expected to exercise personal agency in regard to accessing opportunities in their environments in order to increase their psychological functioning. This approach, mirroring materials science, suggests latent capacity of the

M. Ungar (✉)
Killam Professor of Social Work, Dalhousie University, Halifax, NS, Canada
e-mail: michael.ungar@dal.ca

M. Ungar (ed.), *The Social Ecology of Resilience: A Handbook of Theory and Practice*,
DOI 10.1007/978-1-4614-0586-3_2, © Springer Science+Business Media, LLC 2012

individual. It focuses attention less on processes of social production that create conditions of risk and growth than it does on the individual's temperament that makes him or her amenable to change. This discourse of individualism embodied by western psychological sciences (and reflecting a cultural narrative of the rugged individual who "beats the odds") is changing as evidence gathers for a more contextualized understanding of human development (Lerner, 2006). Studies of individual qualities limit our understanding of psychological phenomena to a fraction of the potential factors that can explain within and between population differences. It was for this reason that groundbreaking work by Rutter (1987) helped shift our understanding of resilience as the result of individual traits that predicted coping under stress to processes that included reducing risk exposure, developing adequate self-esteem, preventing the negative impact of risk factors on developmental trajectories, and opening new opportunities for development by shaping the child's environment.

In this chapter, I summarize our emerging understanding of the relationship between individuals and the social and physical ecologies that make resilience more likely. Resilience is defined as a set of behaviors over time that reflect the interactions between individuals and their environments, in particular the opportunities for personal growth that are available and accessible (Ungar 2010a, 2010b, 2011b). The likelihood that these interactions will promote well-being under adversity depends on the meaningfulness of these opportunities and the quality of the resources provided. This understanding of resilience distinguishes between strengths within a population and the role strengths play when individuals, families, or communities are under stress. In this chapter I show that resilience results from a cluster of ecological factors that predict positive human development (more than individual traits), and that the effect of an individual's capacity to cope and the resources he or she has is influenced by the nature of the challenges the individual faces. This interactional, ecological understanding of resilience is supported by brief discussion of two studies being done by the Resilience Research Centre (RRC) at Dalhousie University

in Canada (of which I am the Principal Investigator and Co-Director), one mixed methods and one qualitative. Both are international in scope.

An Ecological Perspective of Resilience

Arguing against a paradigm of individualism, Lerner (2006) and other human developmentalists emphasize a more contextualized understanding of children as reflected in the work of Vygotsky (1978) that explores the scaffolding of experience that supports human development. This shift to a position that I will term "ecological" is an important part of the arguments made by all the authors of the chapters in this volume. An interactional, environmental, and culturally pluralistic perspective provides a second way to understand resilience. It builds on the process oriented arguments of Rutter (1987) and Lerner (2006). Its proponents are showing that environments count a great deal more than we thought, perhaps even more than individual capacity, when we investigate the antecedents of positive coping after individuals are exposed to adversity. Whether mapping the effect of schools on individuals (Chapter 21), or the shaping of neuron networks that result from healthy attachments (Chapter 11), a more ecological understanding of resilience suggests complexity in reciprocal person–environment interactions. The goodness of fit between elements of the mesosystem (interactions between family, school, and community systems; Bronfenbrenner, 1979) predicts positive growth in suboptimal conditions. As individuals or environments change, the factors most likely to correlate with positive developmental outcomes also change. Luthar, Cicchetti, and Becker (2000) suggest that successful adaptation is properly operationalized when it reflects high fidelity to the way good development is theorized for a particular sample of at-risk individuals in a particular context. Of course, which interaction is most likely to be a catalyst for resilience depends in part on which outcomes are chosen as the measures of good functioning under stress. In few instances are *a priori* assumptions of positive outcomes negotiated with research participants to ensure contextual relevance. More often, those studying resilience impose a standard set of outcome measures that are reasoned to be relevant to a population but may overlook indigenous coping strategies that are adaptive in contexts where there are few choices for other forms of adaptation (Castro & Murray, 2010; Gilgun & Abrams, 2005; Ungar 2010a, 2010b). The child who works, for example, may according to a number of researchers (International Union of Anthropological and Ethnological Sciences, 2002; Liborio & Ungar, 2010; Liebel, 2004) argue that his or her burdensome employment brings several advantages with regard to sense of self-worth, hope for the future, and respect from others for the contribution he or she makes to his or her family. While not an argument for complete relativism (not all outcomes desired by a specific population are necessarily advantageous long-term), an ecological understanding of resilience positions these negotiations for control of meaning and the resources that support growth as an integral part of all studies of resilience and their application to practice.

I've termed this contextualized approach to the study of resilience a social ecological one (Ungar, 2008, 2011a). Whereas proponents of an individual interpretation of capacity under stress still emphasize personal qualities as the *sine quo non* of developmental outcomes, interactionists posit individual gains as the consequence of congruence between individual needs and environments that facilitate growth. A social ecological perspective on resilience that evolves from this interactional perspective results in more focus on the social and physical environment as the locus of resources for personal growth. As the authors in this volume show, the individual and ecological positions are neither mutually exclusive nor antagonistic. They simply emphasize different aspects of the processes associated with resilience, whether those processes are compensatory, protective, or promotive (Luthar et al., 2000). For example, the capacity to avoid delinquency despite early experiences of deprivation may be attributable to individual traits like attachment to a caregiver, a lack of genetic predisposition towards antisocial behavior, self-regulation, or gender (Henry, Caspi, Moffitt, Harrington, &

Silva, 1999; Moffitt, 1997; Rutter, 2008), or be a consequence of structural factors like neighborhood stability, access to employment, and avoidance of discrimination (Elliott et al., 2006; Law & Barker, 2006; Sampson, 2003). Ecological interpretations of resilience make clear the complexity inherent in the processes that contribute to growth. Even in optimal neighborhoods a child's capacity to avoid delinquency may still depend on early attachments with caregivers (Sroufe, Egeland, Carlson, & Collins, 2005) and epigenetic processes that moderate the effects of genes that predispose a child from a criminogenic home from repeating patterns of antisocial behavior (Hudziak & Bartels, 2008; Moffitt, Caspi, Rutter, & Silva, 2001).

The problem is not the complementarity of individual and ecological approaches to the study of resilience, but the oversight that results when ecological aspects of resilience are de-emphasized (individual resilience is seldom overlooked in psychological research). Understood in this complex, multidimensional way, resilience is as, or more, dependent on the capacity of the individual's physical and social ecology to *potentiate* positive development under stress than the capacity of individuals to exercise personal agency during their recovery from risk exposure. A broader ecological understanding of resilience is more likely to produce interpretive models that explain how people navigate through adverse environments over time (Schoon, 2006).

Ecological Opportunity Structures and Resilience

An intervention by Bierman et al. (2004), members of the Conduct Problems Prevention Research Group, provides support for this ecological interpretation of resilience. Based on a survey of 10,000 kindergarten students in four high-risk neighborhoods (Durham, NC; Nashville, TN; Seattle, WA; rural central Pennsylvania), 891 children were identified as being at risk for future conduct problems. Using random assignment to intervention and control groups, a 10-year intervention was performed that included parent behavior management training, child social cognitive skills training, reading support, home visiting, mentoring and changes to classroom curriculum. Assessment of the children over time suggests that programming with multiple elements can have a significant impact on children's development, but that the impact varies by an individual's level of risk (based on assessments during kindergarten) and the intensity of the services provided. Fast Track, as the program was known, "had a statistically significant and clinically meaningful positive effect on preventing childhood and adolescent externalizing psychiatric disorders and antisocial behavior, but only among the highest risk subgroup of kindergarteners" (p. 1259). Notably, it was the combination of long term developmentally appropriate services that focused on children's cognitive skills, peer relationships, parenting practices and the quality of the school climate that accounted for changes in expected child functioning. Youth who experienced the greatest fidelity to the intervention, and were at the highest risk for conduct disorder when first assessed, were those most likely to benefit from the intervention. Youth at little risk of conduct disorder showed little change from their matched controls.

The study tells us three things about resilience. First, resilience depends on clusters of factors that influence individual, relational, and broader social factors. Second, it is the intervention, and its intensity (a change in the child's social ecology), more than individual motivation that accounts for the greatest amount of variation in outcomes (Bierman et al., 2004). In other words, the locus of change is the intervention. The quality of its design and implementation determine whether children do well. Very little individual level change is attributable to personal traits. Motivation to attend and the exercise of personal agency to do so may have been a contributing factor to Fast Track's success, but the ability of the program to attract youth and families was likely more important to its overall effectiveness.

Third, a protective process like an intervention to prevent conduct disorder may have little promotive effect on a population as a whole, but instead interacts with the risk factors that are present to produce changes in those most at-risk. Though individual level variables are important and may co-vary with changes to the environment, more change can be accounted for by environment-level variation than by individual factors (Ungar, 2011b). In other words, an individually focused interpretation of resilience could overlook the cause for much of an individual's change over time (Laub & Sampson, 2003). Furthermore, protective processes are most likely to affect those who face above average levels of risk but may have no effect at all on individuals who are already better resourced.

Distinguishing Resilience from Assets

The Fast Track example illustrates how factors associated with resilience are different than strengths or assets. Despite definitional ambiguity among proponents of positive youth development, assets are best defined as characteristics shared by a population regardless of level of risk exposure (Lerner, Dowling, & Anderson, 2003; Moore, Lippman, & Brown, 2004). Their function is assumed to be always positive, with a greater number of internal and external assets correlating with an individual's capacity to resist (in the case of youth) delinquency, drug abuse, early sexual initiation, and school dropout (Benson, 2003; Larson, 2006). Martin and Marsh (2006, 2009), for example, are explicit with regard to this difference when they define "academic buoyancy," their construct for the everyday "cumulative enabling factors" (p. 358) that all students use to buffer normal educational stress. Assets (and the processes associated with their acquisition) are, however, more or less protective depending on the individual's level of exposure to adversity. As Zautra, Hall, and Murray (2010) explain, there is an interaction between factors associated with positive development (common across a population) and factors that suppress the impact of risk (specific to those who are vulnerable). This more complex interpretation of our "psychological economy"

(p. 10) suggests that well-being is more than the absence of disorder and the profusion of internal and external strengths. It is the active engagement in processes that promote well-being even when disorder is present. A program like Fast Tracks changes social structures and provides assets that interact with levels of disorder to change developmental pathways. The potential for disorder is still there, but the adapted social ecology changes the likelihood negative qualities get expressed (much as genes get triggered by environmental stressors). An intervention that assesses only assets and not risk is likely to miss the complex interchanges in which assets become protective factors and contribute to what is understood as patterns of behavior associated with resilience when risk is present.

Social and Physical Ecologies Potentiate Resilience

Conceptualizing this ecological understanding of resilience requires that elements of temporality, opportunity, and meaning be accounted for. Where there is potential for exposure to significant adversity, resilience is both the capacity of individuals to *navigate* their way to the psychological, social, cultural, and physical resources that build and sustain their well-being, and their individual and collective capacity to *negotiate* for these resources to be provided and experienced in culturally meaningful ways (adapted from Ungar, 2011b). These dual processes of navigation and negotiation are important. They emphasize that individuals engage in processes that demonstrate resilience when they take advantage of the opportunities they have and do better when they exercise influence over what those opportunities are and how they are provided. While individual agency is a component of one's ability to navigate to resources, it remains the role of families, communities, and governments to make those resources available in culturally meaningful ways that reflect the preferences of those who need them. Therefore, resilience is a shared quality of the individual and the individual's social ecology, with the social ecology likely more important than

individual factors to recovery and sustainable well-being for populations under stress.

These negotiations are clear when we look at the co-construction of deviance. Crime, for example, is construed situationally, with certain behaviors judged to be criminal in some contexts but not others (Latimer & Foss, 2005; Lesko, 2001). An individual's motivation to commit a crime arises because of interactive processes between individuals and their environments in which the costs and benefits of antisocial behavior are assessed with delinquency seeming to be worthwhile when other opportunities are unavailable or inaccessible (Gilgun & Abrams, 2005; Wikström, 2005). Understood this way, behaviors that are perceived as delinquent by some may be thought of as functional or even prosocial by others, though often these decisions lack self-reflexivity and are instead reflections of broader meaning systems that support or discourage particular actions (Bottrell, Armstrong, & France, 2010). Resilience shares much the same quality, with positive outcomes negotiated within discursive spaces that influence our judgment of what is and is not experienced as an indicator of well-being under stress in different contexts.

To illustrate, an individual personality trait like the ability to act independently, resisting the need to participate in delinquent behavior and remain an outsider to a peer group, requires that the skills of resistance be seen as active and empowering. A positive self-concept should reasonably precede their expression. Murray (2010) notes that young people who resist offending behaviors are not doing nothing (resistance as a passive coping strategy). They are demonstrating "active resilience" by preventing themselves from engaging in problem behaviors that change life trajectories. According to Murray, youth use several strategies, such as "othering" offenders, avoiding offending peers, and thinking about their future as ways to avoid the potential risk impact posed by peers. These are active intelligible strategies responsive to very specific ecological stressors that result in individuals experiencing a sense of personal efficacy. Suggesting that these young people simply do nothing diminishes their experience of their own power. In this regard, the process of participating in a social discourse that values their resistance skills (an ecological process) is likely to make youth who resist delinquency more self-satisfied as a result of the recognition their actions bring. As a number of qualitative studies have shown, however, denying children participation in a discourse that supports their active coping strategies will make it more likely that they participate in delinquent activities to satisfy their need to feel powerful (Bottrell, 2009; Hecht, 1998; Munford & Sanders, 2005; Ungar, 2007).

The same processes of navigation and negotiation occur at the level of mesosystemic interactions between the family and other systems. For example, Driscoll, Russell, and Crockett (2008) have shown that while authoritative parenting is just as effective with Mexican immigrant youth as it is for White Americans, other aspects of family functioning carry different meaning depending on the degree of family acculturation. In this case, studies of acculturation processes suggest that acculturation can pose a risk to mental health and is associated with negative behaviors among Latino youth such as smoking cigarettes, using drugs, and alcohol related problems. It is thought that the emphasis in American culture on independence and autonomy undermine cultural expectations for family ties, mutual support and social obligations. In fact, US born Mexican-American parents are more likely to be permissive than their authoritative immigrant parents. By the third generation, acculturation and the relinquishing of traditional values brought from the family's country of origin result in the adoption of dominant cultural values. The result is that children of more recent immigrants have better mental health than children of parents who are fully acculturated. The benefits, however, show a complex pattern. Third generation youth with problem behaviors report higher self-esteem (possibly an artifact of their acceptance of dominant cultural values), though depression levels are stable across all three generations and lower than the national mean. In this case, parenting styles, the transmission of values, and processes of acculturation exert a direct influence on measures of personal functioning associated with mental health and conduct. From the point of view of an ecological interpretation of resilience, one can see that resources like family ties and values may, or may not, be protective depending on cultural and temporal factors. In this case, Latino families that argue against acculturation (and are privileged in the social discourse that defines the antecedents of mental health among immigrants) need to have their voices privileged.

Beyond the family, socioeconomic factors account for significant amounts of the variance between populations. Parke et al. (2004) examined economic stress, parenting, and child adjustment in Mexican-American and European-American families. Similar to the results from Driscoll et al. (2008), Mexican-American families who were the least acculturated and had the lowest annual incomes experienced the least economic stress. Parke et al., speculate that their results suggest that less acculturated families who engage in the dual processes of resisting dominant culture and promoting indigenous values and beliefs avoid the threats to well-being that accompany social comparison.

This shift in focus to a contextually-relevant understanding of resilience de-centers the individual as the primary unit of analysis. Instead, the role played by the individual's social and physical ecology is emphasized and patterns of coping that are synonymous with resilience are identified (Dawes & Donald, 2000). To illustrate this point further, we can look critically at the work of Masten and Obradović (2006) who, building on Murphy's (1962) work, distinguish two types of coping. Coping I, referring to internal integration, and Coping II, external adaptation. Both represent aspects of individual competence and reflect a degree of personal agency. One might also imagine, however, Coping III, the adaptation of the environment to the individual in order to moderate exposure to risk, mitigate the consequences of exposure when it does occur, or suppress risk altogether. Changing the environment potentiates the long-term positive development among children who are at-risk. This view of resilience starts with the premise that individuals do not need to demonstrate internal integration or external adaptation if the environment is sufficiently modified to remove conditions that threaten development.

One way to show this is to examine the compounding effect of ADHD and peer rejection on educational achievement (as a proxy measure for resilience) over time. Mikami and Hinshaw (2006) worked with an ethnically diverse sample of girls aged 6–13, assessing them at baseline and 5 years later. One hundred and forty participants with ADHD and 88 without were included in the study. Ninety-two percent of the original sample was retained. Interestingly, they found that ADHD and peer rejection in childhood does not contribute to internalizing and externalizing behaviors 5 years later, but does contribute to decreased academic achievement. Notably, children with self-perceived academic competence in childhood had lower levels of adolescent externalizing and internalizing behavior. This effect held for both children with ADHD and those without, meaning self-perceived competence was a promotive factor that also buffered the impact of ADHD when present. The findings suggest that "self-perceived scholastic competence buffers against externalizing behavior and substance use through the mediator of keeping adolescents connected to school and away from deviant peer groups" (pp. 835–836). The results suggest that the risks girls with ADHD face are cumulative, and that processes associated with resilience change children's experiences of their social ecologies. While both risk factors (one individual, the other relational) threaten children's developmental paths, it is the maintenance of a school attachment (and the facilitative environment of the school which makes this attachment possible) that contributes to positive development regardless of the risks the child faces.

Resilience is, therefore, the ecologically complex (multi-dimensional) processes that people engage in that makes positive growth possible (e.g., engaging in school, resisting prejudice, creating networks of support, attending religious institutions), all of which are dependent upon the capacity of social and physical ecologies to provide opportunities for positive adaptation (preferably in ways that express prosocial collective norms). When

resilience is measured as an outcome, individual traits, behaviors and cognitions are always outcomes that result from positive developmental processes that have been made possible by an individual's wider ecology. Higher self-esteem may result from success with peers, family cohesion, or success at school (Kidd & Shahar, 2008). Secure attachment results from adequate caregiving (Beckett et al., 2006). Efficacy is the result of opportunities to make a meaningful contribution to others or find other ways to control one's world (Bandura 1977; Emond, 2010). Delayed sexual initiation has been attributed to cultural factors, peer associations and opportunities to experience self-esteem (Shoveller, Johnson, Langille, & Mitchell, 2003; Spencer, Zimet, Aalsma, & Orr, 2002). And positive peer relations depend on neighborhood characteristics to provide children with a selection of choices (Barber, 2006; Chauhan, Reppucci, Burnette, & Reiner, 2010). Outcomes from each of these experiences will depend more on the quality of the environment (its capacity to meet the needs of vulnerable individuals) than individual competence. The error of attribution in many studies of resilience is to measure personal agency and ignore the larger influence of sociopolitical, economic and cultural factors that shape developmental paths.

An Ecological Expression of Resilience

To account for this complexity, I borrow from Kurt Lewin's (1951) work in the early 1950s, his expression $B = f(P, E)$ which says that behavior is a function of the person in interaction with his or her environment. The expression can be modified to describe a more ecological understanding of resilience (Ungar, 2011b) – in the context of exposure to significant adversity:

$$R_{B(1,2,3,\ldots)} = \frac{f(P_{SC}, E)}{(O_{Av}, O_{Ac})(M)}.$$

In the expression, R_B refers to resilience as a set of observable behaviors associated with adaptive outcomes in contexts of adversity. These behaviors (functional outcomes that we can measure or observe like high school graduation, association with prosocial peers, and description of one's feelings of self-esteem) can be assumed as proxies for internal integration and external adaptation that makes individual coping more likely. As longitudinal studies of resilience and risk show, these patterns of behavior are temporal, changing over time as new horizontal stressors (normative developmental challenges that occur over the lifespan) and vertical stressors (acute or chronic challenges that transect the developmental life course and negatively skew growth) influence the individual's capacity to cope and the resources available (Laub & Sampson, 2003; Schoon, 2006; Werner & Smith, 1992). At different points in a child's development, there are windows of opportunity that maximize the potential for positive growth or change (Masten & Wright, 2010).

Behaviors we associate with resilience (like staying in school, or associating with non-delinquent peers) are a function of the person (P) and his or her strengths and challenges ($_{SC}$), expressed within a complex ecology (E). The emphasis on both strengths and challenges makes explicit findings from studies of resilience that show it is a combination of personal advantages and disadvantages that influence life trajectories. It is easy to assume, for example, that intelligence would be a strength, while intellectual delay would be a challenge in most contexts. The nature of the interaction between strengths and challenges, however, is more complicated when the risk posed by the environment is also considered. To illustrate, Tiet et al. (1998) showed in their analysis of data from a household survey in four geographic areas of the United States that IQ affects coping positively for high-risk children but has less effect on the coping skills of children at lower risk.

A similar pattern is evident in the work of Obradović, Bush, Stamperdahl, Adler, and Boyce (2010) who showed that among primary school children, stress reactivity (when measured using biological markers like cortisol levels) biologically predisposed sensitive children to feel emotional slights and be prone to anxiety that decreased school performance when in a threatening environment such as one where bullying is prevalent.

These same children, however, will outperform their less anxiety-prone peers when there is little stress in their environment. Such children are not only more likely to do better academically, they are also likely to be creative, expressive individuals, and it's those characteristics that endear them to their parents and teachers. The differences in performance are situational, not child-dependent. The child who is not reactive, not anxious, who can seem aloof or even aggressive, may be the child who survives better in a stressful environment, outperforming the more sensitive child whose talents cannot be properly used when he or she feels threatened. The advantage that the less reactive child experiences, however, is only seen in stressful environments where the child is stressed. The above expression of an ecological model of resilience is meant to capture these nuances in protective processes and suggest their interaction with individual differences.

Further updating Lewin, the E here refers to ecology rather than environment. Human cybernetics (Bateson, 1972) and even theories of human ecology (Bronfenbrenner, 1979) reified an understanding of the environment that was progressive a half century ago. Advances in the physical sciences have shown, however, that the assumptions of environmentalism differ from those of ecology (Naess, 1989). Environmentalism reflects a positivist orientation towards systems that emphasize causality, hierarchy and disciplined processes of change. Environments can be manipulated. They serve the purpose of meeting the needs of one part (typically individual humans) and reflect the values of colonization, extraction, and endless growth. Ecology is a post-positivist interpretation of the relationship between elements of an ecosystem, where emphasis is placed on the intrinsic worth of each part regardless of its perceived utility (Drengson, 2000). Even those elements of an ecology that are noxious, or apparently redundant, have value in and of themselves. Relationships are complex and outcomes non-teleological (there are no assumptions that one set of outcomes are necessarily better than another). The subjectivity of the observer is accounted for in what is taken to be a valued aspect of one ecology and not another.

By theorizing resilience as a social ecological construct, this same post-positivism and subjectivity can be accounted for. Thinking ecologically, researchers studying resilience acknowledge variability in the definition of what constitutes the individual's environment (does the researcher include measures of family functioning, school engagement, community cohesion, neighborhood stability, or political empowerment?). The individual's strengths and challenges are also understood as contextually dependent for their definition as they are expressions of culturally embedded values that influence the co-construction of what is meant by successful coping and risk (Dawes & Donald, 2000; Ungar et al., 2007).

Opportunity

All of this depends on two aspects of the individual's social and physical ecology, represented by elements in the denominator of the expression. The capacity of the social and physical ecology to provide resources for internal integration and external adaptation is constrained by the opportunity structure (O) that surrounds the individual. Opportunity structures are a quality of the social and physical ecology, not the individual. As the research discussed above shows, opportunity dramatically influences developmental trajectories by making resources available ($_{Av}$) and accessible ($_{Ac}$). Processes associated with resilience (whether characterized by adaptive or maladaptive coping) (Bottrell, 2009) are always dependent upon the factors that trigger and sustain them. At the most individual level, that of one's genetic profile, studies of epigenetics suggest that resilience is triggered by aspects of the environment that bolster the expression of latent individual capacity, just as noxious environments can trigger dysfunctional self-regulatory processes (Caspi, Taylor, Moffitt, & Plomin, 2000). Likewise, immunity to future adversity can develop through exposure to manageable amounts of stress earlier in life (Lemery-Chalfant, 2010). In other words, the opportunity structures that surround an individual will shape the individual's capacity to experience resilience when facing adversity. The locus for

change, however, is within the social and physical ecology that shapes the individual's behavior. For example, Laub and Sampson (2003) provide evidence in their longitudinal study of elderly men who were once delinquent boys that those who formed secure bonds with an intimate partner (i.e., married well) were more likely to desist from problem behaviors. In other words, a fortuitous relationship provides the former delinquent with available and accessible supports that promote positive behavior and prevent the continuation of growth along negative life trajectories (incarceration, drug abuse, unemployment).

It can be difficult to predict the influence of an opportunity without understanding both the context in which it becomes available, as well as the strengths and challenges of those who access it. To illustrate, Sloboda et al. (2009) conducted a randomized field trial of a substance abuse prevention program delivered to all students in 83 school clusters (high schools and their feeder schools). They showed that over a period of 5 years post-intervention that universal school-based substance abuse prevention targeting tobacco, alcohol and marijuana can have a negative effect on baseline non-users of tobacco and alcohol. The opportunity afforded by this kind of intervention makes it more likely students who were baseline non-users will use substances later. However, students who were baseline marijuana users seemed to take advantage of the opportunity presented by the intervention and were more likely than controls to reduce or avoid drug use later. The intervention used Drug Abuse Resistance Education (D.A.R.E.) officers who delivered ten lessons during seventh grade and seven "booster" sessions in grade nine. Contrary to expectations, "Of those who did not use alcohol or smoke cigarettes at baseline, a statistically significantly higher proportion of treatment than control students drank or smoked in the past 30 days when in grade 11" (pp. 6–7). There were, however, no differences between controls and intervention group on marijuana use suggesting great specificity in how an opportunity like a drug and alcohol prevention program influences a process such as resisting substance use which is often associated with resilience.

Sloboda and his colleagues also found gender and race/ethnicity differences, suggesting that individual personality differences may be less important than macrosystemic contextual variables related to social location. In regard to gender, males in the treatment condition had higher rates of alcohol use than females, while female students who participated in the intervention were more likely to binge drink and smoke. When the participants were stratified by race/ethnicity (white and non-white in order to get cell frequencies large enough for analysis) the white students who participated in the intervention had higher risk ratios for all the substance use categories, though the differences were not statistically significant. Only with regard to cigarette use were non-white students more likely than controls to report significantly higher levels of use (risk ratio 1.23). Among white students, the intervention group was more likely to binge drink, use alcohol, get drunk, and smoke when compared to the controls.

Interestingly, students who were already substance users at baseline showed significant and positive treatment effects, reporting declining rates of substance use 5 years later. These findings demonstrate an iatrogenic effect for a universal program of substance abuse prevention. Only those youth were already users were likely to benefit. The intervention appears to create school wide shifts in access to information about drugs, alcohol and tobacco and "may increase interest in substance use" (p. 8). Thus, as reflected in the above expression of R, in and of itself, the amount of risk a child faces, and the amount of protection afforded a child by a resource (like an alcohol and drug prevention program) cannot be predicted without also accounting for the nature of the child's strengths and challenges (including behavior) and the opportunities that are available.

Meaning

The last element of the expression is the M, the meaning systems to which individuals and their communities adhere. It is this meaning which determines the decisions people make with regard to which resources (opportunities) they value and

access and which resources their family, school, community and nation provides. Meaning depends on cultural constructions of the factors that influence well-being. The concept is multidimensional. At the level of individuals, values and beliefs (reflecting socialization processes like acculturation) shape individual discrimination of experiences as either facilitative of growth or posing a barrier to personal development. As shown above, a drug and alcohol prevention program, an intimate relationship, or resistance to acculturation, can either help or hinder resilience depending on what the resource means to those using it. A resource like prevention programming is a value laden opportunity. One could equally imagine harm reduction workshops for teenagers or the decriminalization of alcohol consumption as a status offence (removing the notion of underage drinking). While both strategies could do more harm than good, what is interesting is that those intervening have preferred to focus on programming that promotes abstinence without questioning the culturally embedded bias and historical context that influences their perspectives with regard to what is appropriate behavior by an adolescent. One could also imagine (and find) a society where limited substance use is not seen as a social problem, but a normative rite of passage which contributes to an adolescent's self-esteem. In moderation, and under the influence of a different meaning system, well-defined alcohol use might be an opportunity for a young person to show he or she is becoming a responsible adult (a rite of passage).

At the level of the collective, families, schools, communities, and governments take action and invest in resources that are meaningful based on negotiations to decide policy and resource allocation (Leadbeater, Dodgen, & Solarz, 2005; Lyons, 2004). This is one dimension of the relationship between meaning and resilience. The meaning we attribute to aspects of our social and physical ecology shape the opportunities that we create (Ungar, 2005). For example, do we support workfare that forces single parents to work and put their children in daycare, or do we support social assistance that is adequate to allow economically disadvantaged parents time at home with their pre-school aged children? The ability of people to navigate to resources is based on the preferences of those in power.

A second dimension of meaning as it relates to resilience is the relative power of each individual in the social discourse to influence the definition of what resilience looks like. Our sense of who we are, our identity as resilient or vulnerable, depends on these processes of co-construction and negotiation (see Bruner, 1997). The self is both what we learn from the statements of others, as well as self-generated meaning-making within culturally diverse social spaces that provide varying opportunities for accessing the resources we need to experience resilience. Just as we are influenced by the meaning systems of others, so too do we participate in their co-construction which reflexively determines who we think we are, what we value, and how we behave (Walsh & Banaji, 1997). To see ourselves and our patterns of coping as resilient, both must be vested with positive regard by ourselves and others. This is particularly evident in gendered constructions of resilience (Leadbeater & Way, 2007) and those by racialized minorities (Blackstock & Trocmé, 2005) where meaningful patterns of resistance to dominant norms may be adaptive for individuals but viewed as antisocial by cultural elites when the patterns of those facing significant adversity do not conform to conventional norms. An interesting, albeit potentially dangerous, example of this is the pro-ana movement in which people diagnosed with anorexia nervosa argue that their "disorder" is a coping strategy that sustains their sense of well-being.

The co-construction of what is a meaningful expression of resilience, then, reflects the relative power of those involved to argue for the legitimacy of their experience. For example, Nguyen-Gillham (2008), reporting results from a qualitative inquiry with 321 Palestinian youth, explains resilience as social suffering. "The Palestinian concept of *samud* – a determination to exist through being steadfast and rooted to the land – is at the heart of resilience. Within a Palestinian context, suffering and endurance have to be interpreted at both an individual and collective level. The construct of resilience goes beyond

an individualistic interpretation: resilience is (re) constituted as a wider collective and social representation of what it means to endure" (p. 292). Observations of Israeli youth present a different understanding of resilience, one focused on selfless contribution and defense of nationhood, a meaning system no less powerful than that expressed by the Palestinians (Ungar, 2007).

This meaning which is attributed to a particular coping strategy is not just an artifact of language, but shapes behavior at multiple levels, even down to the level of neural functioning. Though there is little work that links brain physiology to resilience as a process (studies of neuroplasticity have tended to only focus on individual capacity to heal brain physiology after trauma and subsequent behavioral change), there is evidence that resilience can be compromised by the effect of risk exposure on brain functioning. For example, Lewis, Granic, and Lamm's (2006) work on aggression in children has shown that "reduced neural activity related to emotion regulation corresponds with an overall decrease in behavioral flexibility in children with aggressive behavior problems" (p. 165). Significantly, this pattern of brain development is directly attributable to parenting and socialization which stimulates reactive self-regulation. Changing the family's capacity to socialize the child not only changes the child's behavior, helping him or her inhibit aggression (Nagin & Tremblay, 1999), it also changes brain physiology. How a family chooses to socialize their child, however, is a function of what they believe to be in the child's best interest and reflects a meaning system that reinforces those beliefs.

An ecological expression of *R* can also be used to deconstruct aspects of risk that, by extension, help identify the processes that are necessary to create resilience. To illustrate, Chauhan et al. (2010) used data gathered from 141 girls aged 13–19 recruited from a juvenile correction center in Virginia. The youth were 50% black, 38% white, and 12% from other ethnoracial groups. The girls did not differ in regard to severity of previous criminal charges, violence, or delinquency, with 79% of the total sample having at least one prior charge for violence such as assault, attempted murder or armed robbery. Eighty percent of the group was re-contacted 6 months after they left the correctional center. Using rearrest data and geo-coding of neighborhood census tracts, disadvantage was calculated as the percentage of people below the poverty line, households on public assistance, female headed households (sole parents), and rates of unemployment. Though both black and white girls self-reported rates of offending post-discharge that were not significantly different, black girls were more likely to be rearrested, especially for nonviolent crimes. These black girls were also the youth most likely to live in disadvantaged neighborhoods. Logistic regressions were run to examine the relationship between neighborhood disadvantage, race, rearrest overall, and nonviolent rearrest. Race was significantly associated with overall rearrest but not neighborhood disadvantage. Furthermore, race was not significantly related to rearrest for nonviolent crime once neighborhood disadvantage was accounted for. "A standard deviation increase in neighborhood disadvantage increased the odds of being rearrested for a nonviolent crime by about a tenfold" (p. 537). The authors conclude that one can show that while both black and white girls are just as likely to commit the same crimes (there is no differential involvement between the two racial groups), differences in where the girls live, and how their neighborhoods are policed, results in different rates of arrest (there is differential selection based on the social ecology of the girls' neighborhoods). While black girls were no more likely to reoffend than their white peers, they were much more likely to be caught. The issue is not race as much as it is neighborhood disadvantage which results when minorities are marginalized in poorer communities with differences in expressions of state control like policing and arrest patterns.

Over time, then, the opportunities presented by an economically advantaged community interact with personal strengths and challenges (like a pattern of delinquency, or status as a ethnoracial minority). The disproportionately high numbers of black girls in detention is the result of social ecological factors more than individual factors

that distinguish them from white girls their same age. Race and neighborhood disadvantage combine to change opportunity structures. Arguably, engaging delinquent girls in processes to bolster resilience would be most effective if they focused on positive aspects of development in specific social ecologies. However, unless interventions also address the unfair treatment of black girls in their communities, the clinical intervention is unlikely to be effective. Environment may trigger personal predispositions (Moffitt et al., 2001), but it is structural constraints on development that make a child more or less resilient over time (i.e., time in jail skews future opportunities for life success)(Blackstock & Trocmé, 2005). Patterns of individual maladaptive coping (delinquency) and their consequences are contextually dependent. In the previous example, individual qualities may predict recidivism, but they do not predict the outcomes that follow such as rearrest or changes in a child's capacity to cope with disadvantage. A youths' experience is more a function of contextual variation (and the value laden responses that address the risks children face) than individual disposition.

A Program of Research

To explore the social ecologies that make resilience more likely to occur, the RRC has conducted a number of interrelated studies across different cultures and contexts. These studies have helped to both innovate and validate theory. A summary of findings from two of these studies is presented here in order to demonstrate how a social ecological understanding of resilience informs the expression presented above.

Multiple Service Users, Risk, and Resilience

The Pathways to Resilience (PTR) study is a mixed method, multi-year study that began in Atlantic Canada and has since expanded to South Africa, Colombia, China and New Zealand. The study seeks to understand how youth ages 13–19 experience multiple mandated services (child welfare, corrections, mental health and special education) and less formal community programming (recreation centers, community programming by NGO's) and informal family and community supports. The study examines service and support use patterns in relation to risk mitigation and the processes associated with resilience. Phase One of the study included 531 urban and rural youth using at least 2 mandated services and a comparison group of 91 youth who rely on non-mandated community services provided by an organization that supports street-involved youth and their families. The study included questions that explored ecological complexity (differences in individual, family, peer, school, community and cultural resources). All participants were referred to the study by their service providers, or in the case of the comparison group, staff at community programs. Although the sample was not random, care was taken to conduct the study in regions and communities throughout Atlantic Canada that would contribute to the rural, urban and cultural diversity of the sample.

Each of the main study variables (service use, risk, and resilience) was assessed as follows. Service use comprised a composite score assessing service use history (i.e., has the youth ever used a service, and if so, how often) of mental health, child welfare, youth corrections (including contact with the police), and educational supports beyond regular classroom programming. Youth were provided with a list of possible services and scored themselves on lifetime use. Scores for each service type were standardized with a minimum score of zero and a maximum score of 10. Higher scores indicated greater involvement with service providers.

Risk was assessed through measures of both community dangers and personal characteristics associated with acute or chronic adversity. Specifically, delinquency was assessed using the *Delinquency* sub-scale of the 4HSQ (Phelps et al., 2007; Theokas & Lerner, 2006). The 12-item version of the Centre for Epidemiological Studies Depression Scale (CES-D-12-NLSCY) (Poulin, Hand, & Boudreau, 2005) was included to assess levels of depression among participants.

A composite score was also computed for sense of community danger using items from the Boston Youth Survey (BYS), a biennial, survey of high school students in Boston Public Schools.

Resilience was measured using the four subscales of the Child and Youth Resilience Measure (CYRM) (Ungar, Liebenberg, Boothroyd, & Duque, 2008). The CYRM is a 28-item instrument validated with a purposeful sample of 1,451 youth growing up facing diverse forms of adversity in 11 countries (Canada, USA, Colombia, China, India, Russia, Palestine, Israel, Tanzania, the Gambia, and South Africa). Items measuring individual characteristics (Individual) include "I cooperate with people around me," "I try to finish what I start," "I am aware of my own strengths," and "I know how to behave in different social situations." The alpha coefficient in the first phase study was 0.795.

Items measuring relationships with parents or primary caregivers (Relationships A) include "My caregiver(s) watch me closely," "My caregiver(s) know a lot about me," and "If I am hungry, there is enough to eat." The alpha coefficient was 0.793.

Items measuring relationships with peers and mentors (Relationships B) include "I feel supported by my friends," "My friends stand by me during difficult times," and "I have people I look up to." The alpha coefficient was 0.751.

Items measuring contextual characteristics (Context) include "Spiritual beliefs are a source of strength for me," "I think it is important to serve my community," "I have opportunities to develop skills that will be useful later in life (like job skills and skills to care for others)," "I am proud of my ethnic background," and "I am treated fairly in my community." The alpha coefficient for the present sample was 0.785.

Results of the study have shown that contextual characteristics measured by the CYRM and other aspects of the youths' environment combine to provide the best prediction of functional indicators of positive development such as school engagement. For example, using a hierarchical regression analysis to examine the effects of risk, resilience and service use on degree of school engagement, results show that resilience, service use and three risk variables (engagement in delinquent behavior, depression, and perceived danger within one's community) provided a model that could account for 32% of the variance in school engagement within the sample. Only the context subscale of the CYRM ($t(475) = 3.426$, $p = 0.001$) was significant. Engagement in delinquent behavior ($t(475) = -6.675$, $p = 0.000$), participation in correctional mandated services ($t(475) = -2.567$, $p = 0.011$), and risk of depression ($t(475) = -2.644$, $p = 0.008$) all have a significant and inverse association with school engagement. The findings show that specific patterns of service provision (availability) and use (accessibility) affect school engagement. Furthermore, contextual factors related to culture, participation in religious activity, nationalism and rites of passage, appear to influence functional outcomes like a child's school attendance, thoughts about school, and feelings of belonging when at school.

A Visual Methods Study in Five Countries

A methodologically different study by the RRC, The Negotiating Resilience Project (NRP), conducted 16 case studies of 13–16-year-olds in 5 countries (Canada, China, Thailand, India, and South Africa) (Theron, Ungar, & Didkowsky, 2011). The study's goal was to identify culturally embedded patterns of adaptive coping among youth who face significant chronic stress. Local researchers assembled advisory committees who then referred young people to the study. Selection criteria included youth who faced a chronic stressor understood to cause children developmental problems in each country context, as well as being a child "out of place" but still "doing well" on functional behavioral indicators associated in the resilience literature with positive development in adverse circumstances. The out of place signification was used to maintain homogeneity across the sample by identifying young people with a common experience of being different from their peers, even though these differences varied by context. These differences included: youth with

physical disabilities in mainstream schools or communities where they were marginalized; Aboriginal youth living in urban environments; youth displaced because they were orphaned, political refugees or economic migrants. While qualitative case studies cannot produce generalizable theory regarding the nature of children's coping strategies, they were useful identifying meaningful patterns of resilience relevant to youth who experience some disadvantage. Between 2008 and 2009, one boy and one girl were chosen from eight matched sites: Vaal Triangle, South Africa and Halifax, Canada; Chiang Mai, Thailand and Vancouver, Canada; Jinan, China and Saskatoon, Canada; and Meghalaya, India and Montreal, Canada. Doing well was understood as variable by context. In China a child's focus on his or her studies outside of school was considered important. In Thailand, a child's ability to cope with minimal parental supervision was considered a sign of positive development. For Aboriginal youth in Saskatoon, local advisors emphasized the young people's resistance to gang involvement.

Data collection included three types of qualitative data. Youth were asked nine catalyst questions during open-ended interviews that were recorded, transcribed and translated (as required). Questions included: "What would I need to know to grow up well here?" "What do you do when you face difficulties in your life?" and "Can you share with me a story about another youth who grew up well in this community despite facing many challenges?" Next, a video-recording was made of one full day in the life of each participant, beginning when the youth woke and ending later that same evening. In all but two cases, filming took place during a non-school day. Following the filming, each youth was invited to participate in a phase of photo elicitation (Croghan, Griffin, Hunter, & Phoenix, 2008). Each was provided a disposable camera and asked to take pictures of aspects of their lives that helped explain their coping with chronic adversity. Finally, focal interchanges from the recording of a day in the life of each youth were selected by the research team, and shown to the participant for feedback. Focal interchanges from another youth in the matched site were also shared with the youth to engage them as co-researchers in the interpretation of the data. During the final interview, all the data, including the photos the youth had taken, were discussed.

Findings have suggested a number of unique contextually relevant patterns youth use to cope. For example, the data show two distinct but interrelated patterns to the way participants contribute to the welfare of their families, and in return secure for themselves a powerful identity and sense of personal and social efficacy. Youth contributions were either "precocious" (synonymous with processes of adultification in relationships with caregivers) or developmentally "appropriate" (reflecting culturally sanctioned expectations). Precocious development was expected in situations where the family faces adversity and requires help from its children to cope. Examples included inverting hierarchies and having children assume responsibility for instrumental tasks like domestic chores and childcare. Flattened hierarchies included children in these same tasks but positioned them in a more peer-like relationship with a parent without the youth assuming full responsibility for any other family member. Developmentally appropriate contributions were negotiated as culturally meaningful. A youth might work as part of a family business, or be responsible for the care of a younger sibling temporarily while parents are occupied. They might be expected to navigate between home, school, and activities in their community themselves, or share money they earn with family members in order to ensure everyone's financial security. Depending on the context, these contributions were distinguished as either culturally normative or exceptional.

Conclusion

If the concept of resilience has struggled to gain credibility, it may be that it has tended simply to replicate studies of individually-focused factors that contribute to growth under stress (Kaplan, 1999). Resilience, however, is more than just a proxy for attachment, self-efficacy, self-esteem,

neuroplasticity, positive peer relationships, or any of a number of other protective factors that are centered on an individual's traits or behavior. It is the complex interactive processes embedded in social and physical ecologies that contain levels of risk that exceed the norm (Wyman, 2003). These compensatory, promotive and protective processes contribute most to successful coping when individuals, families and communities face significant exposure to adversity. A carefully designed program of research should focus on individuals and fully explore the ecologies that shape the opportunities they experience for positive development.

The study of resilience is necessarily contextual because it always involves the presence of risk. Unlike the study of strengths or assets which are promotive regardless of the presence or absence of stress, processes associated with resilience are dependent upon opportunity structures and meaning systems for their influence on how people navigate and negotiate for resources associated with well-being. As the chapters in this volume show, to understand resilience we must explore the context in which the individual experiences adversity, making resilience first a quality of the broader social and physical ecology, and second a quality of the individual. To invert this order is to misattribute the cause of successful coping to individual traits like motivation or self-esteem which can account for only a small portion of the difference within a population.

A comprehensive and ecological study of resilience helps to explain why, for example, studies of neglected children's psychosocial development have shown that early deprivation thwarts development, but that certain strengths have a disproportionately large impact on future growth depending on the nature of the child's early experience and wider context (Beckett et al., 2006). The greater the risk exposure, the more beneficial a secure attachment (Sroufe et al., 2005), school engagement (Dotterer, McHale, & Crouter, 2009), or intervention (DuMont, Widom, & Czaja, 2007) becomes later in life. This is the significance of the concept of resilience. It theorizes factors and processes as contextually dependent, interacting with social and physical ecologies to create unique outcomes. This focus on process also opens the door to a far less teleological interpretation of lives lived well. No single factor can be assumed to predict in every instance a positive outcome when we account for differences in opportunities and meaning. For example, while there is generally consensus that the parentification of children places them at risk, and that demands for children to provide emotional and instrumental support to their caregivers that invert family hierarchies may disadvantage children, there is contrary evidence that shows that in resource poor environments parentification may in fact be protective (Hooper, Marotta, & Lanthier, 2008; Jurkovic, Morrell, & Casey, 2001; Maratta & Lanthier, 2008). It can provide children with few opportunities to sustain a sense of positive self-worth a means to experience themselves as competent. This is especially true when the child's community or extended family relationships (and the child's parent) acknowledge the parentified child's role as important to the welfare of others. Not only does this finding suggest complexity when we seek to understand protective processes, individual behavior and functional outcomes, it also supports a view of resilience as including heterogeneous processes that can be atypical of what we assume will be the normative developmental pathways employed by children, youth and adults (Ungar 2010a, 2010b, 2011b). Furthermore, it lends support to the argument in this chapter that opportunities and meaning are both aspects of resilience that depend for their influence on the capacity of individuals under stress to navigate to the resources they need, and negotiate with others for what they define as meaningful and supportive.

A social ecological interpretation of resilience points to the need to encourage exploration of the transactional effects of individual traits and chaotic, non-causal environments. This will challenge us to deconstruct individual discourse that remains dominant in the work of those seeking to understand both psychopathology and resilience. For example, Rutter (2008) asks us to consider "What are the causal mechanisms involved in

individual differences in responses to stress and adversity?" (p. 18). The question is a good one. To answer it, we will also need to ask whether changing an individual's ecology can increase the likelihood that resilience will result regardless of individual traits. It is like turning a pair of binoculars around and looking at the world differently. It is this inversion of our thinking that is transforming the study of resilience from attention to the capacities of individuals to a more complex understanding of the capacity of social and physical ecologies to potentiate the protective processes that contribute to what we define as functional outcomes associated with resilience in contexts of adversity.

References

Anthony, E. J. (1987). Children at high risk for psychosis growing up successfully. In E. J. Anthony & B. J. Cohler (Eds.), *The invulnerable child* (pp. 147–184). New York, NY: Guilford.

Antonovsky, A. (1987). The salutogenic perspective: Toward a new view of health and illness. *Advances, Institute for Advancement of Health, 4*(1), 47–55.

Bandura, A. (1977). Self-efficacy: Toward a unifying theory of behavioral change. *Psychological Review, 84*, 191–215.

Barber, J. G. (2006). A synthesis of research findings and practice and policy suggestions for promoting resilient development among young people in crisis. In R. J. Flynn, P. M. Dudding, & J. G. Barber (Eds.), *Promoting resilience in child welfare* (pp. 418–429). Ottawa, ON: University of Ottawa Press.

Bateson, G. (1972). *Steps to an ecology of mind*. New York, NY: Ballantine Books.

Beckett, C., Maughan, B., Rutter, M., Castle, J., Colvert, E., Groothues, C., et al. (2006). Do the effects of early severe deprivation on cognition persist into early adolescence? Findings from the English and Romanian adoptees study. *Child Development, 77*(3), 696–711.

Benson, P. L. (2003). Developmental assets and asset-building community: Conceptual and empirical foundations. In R. M. Lerner & P. L. Benson (Eds.), *Developmental assets and asset-building communities: Implications for research, policy, and practice* (pp. 19–46). New York, NY: Kluwer Academic/Plenum.

Bierman, K. L., Coie, J. D., Dodge, K. A., Foster, E. M., Greenberg, M. T., Lochman, J. E., et al. (2004). The effects of the Fast Track program on serious problem outcomes at the end of elementary school. *Journal of Clinical Child and Adolescent Psychology, 33*, 650–661.

Blackstock, C., & Trocmé, N. (2005). Community-based child welfare for Aboriginal children: Supporting resilience through structural change. In M. Ungar (Ed.), *Handbook for working with children and youth: Pathways to resilience across cultures and contexts* (pp. 105–120). Thousand Oaks, CA: Sage.

Bottrell, D. (2009). Understanding 'marginal' perspectives: Towards a social theory of resilience. *Qualitative Social Work, 8*(3), 321–340.

Bottrell, D., Armstrong, D., & France, A. (2010). Young people's relations to crime: Pathways across ecologies. *Youth Justice, 10,* 56–72.

Bronfenbrenner, U. (1979). *Ecology of human development*. Cambridge, MA: Harvard University Press.

Brown, B. B., & Lohr, M. N. (1987). Peer-group affiliation and adolescent self-esteem: An integration of ego-identity and symbolic-interaction theories. *Journal of Personality and Social Psychology, 52*(1), 47–55.

Bruner, J. (1997). A narrative model of self-construction. In J. G. Snodgrass & R. L. Thompson (Eds.), *The self across psychology* (pp. 145–161). New York, NY: New York Academy of Sciences.

Caspi, A., Taylor, A., Moffitt, T. E., & Plomin, R. (2000). Neighborhood deprivation affects children's mental health: Environmental risks identified in a genetic design. *Psychology Science, 11*(4), 338–342.

Castro, F. G., & Murray, K. E. (2010). Cultural adaptation and resilience: Controversies, issues, and emerging models. In J. W. Reich, A. J. Zautra, & J. S. Hall (Eds.), *Handbook of adult resilience* (pp. 375–403). New York, NY: Guilford.

Chauhan, P., Reppucci, N. D., Burnette, M., & Reiner, S. (2010). Race, neighborhood disadvantage, and antisocial behavior among female juvenile offenders. *Journal of Community Psychology, 38*(4), 532–540.

Croghan, R., Griffin, C., Hunter, J., & Phoenix, A. (2008). Young people's constructions of self: Notes on the use and analysis of the photo-elicitation methods. *International Journal of Social Research Methodology, 11*(4), 345–356.

Dawes, A., & Donald, D. (2000). Improving children's chances: Developmental theory and effective interventions in community contexts. In D. Donald, A. Dawes, & J. Louw (Eds.), *Addressing childhood adversity* (pp. 1–25). Cape Town, SA: David Philip.

Dotterer, A. M., McHale, S. M., & Crouter, A. C. (2009). Sociocultural factors and school engagement among African American youth: The roles of racial discrimination, racial socialization, and ethnic identity. *Applied Developmental Science, 13*(2), 61–73.

Dovidio, J. F., Piliavin, J. A., Schroeder, D. A., & Penner, L. A. (2006). *The social psychology of prosocial behaviour*. Mahwah, NJ: Lawrence Erlbaum Associates.

Drengson, A. (2000). Education for local and global ecological responsibility: Arne Naess's cross-cultural, ecophilosophy approach. *Canadian Journal of Environmental Education, 5*(Spring), 63–76.

Driscoll, A., Russell, S. T., & Crockett, L. J. (2008). Parenting styles and youth well-being across immigrant generations. *Journal of Family Issues, 29*(2), 185–209.

DuMont, K. A., Widom, C. S., & Czaja, S. J. (2007). Predictors of resilience in abused and neglected children grown-up: The role of individual and neighborhood characteristics. *Child Abuse & Neglect, 31,* 255–274.

Elliott, D. S., Menard, S., Rankin, B., Elliott, A., Wilson, W. J., & Huizinga, D. (2006). *Good kids from bad neighborhoods: Successful development in social context*. Cambridge, UK: Cambridge University Press.

Emond, R. (2010). Caring as a moral, practical and powerful endeavour: Peer care in a Cambodian Orphanage. *British Journal of Social Work, 40*(1), 63–81.

Gilgun, J. F., & Abrams, L. S. (2005). Gendered adaptations, resilience, and the perpetration of violence. In M. Ungar (Ed.), *Handbook for working with children and youth: Pathways to resilience across cultures and contexts* (pp. 57–70). Thousand Oaks, CA: Sage.

Hecht, T. (1998). *At home in the street: Street children of Northeast Brazil*. Cambridge, UK: Cambridge University Press.

Henry, B., Caspi, A., Moffitt, T. E., Harrington, H., & Silva, P. (1999). Staying in school protects boys with poor self-regulation in childhood from later crime: A longitudinal study. *International Journal of Behavioral Development, 23*(4), 1049–1073.

Hooper, L. M., Marotta, S. A., & Lanthier, R. P. (2008). Predictors of growth and distress following childhood parentification: A retrospective exploratory study. *Journal of Child and Family Studies, 17,* 693–705.

Hudziak, J. J., & Bartels, M. (2008). Genetic and environmental influences on wellness, resilience, and psychopathology: A family-based approach for promotion, prevention, and intervention. In J. J. Hudziak (Ed.), *Developmental psychopathology and wellness: Genetic and environmental influences* (pp. 267–286). Washington, DC: American Psychiatric Publishing.

International Union of Anthropological and Ethnological Sciences. (2002). *Studies of integrated holistic programmes with children and youth: Child labour in Nepal*. New York, NY: IUAES.

Jurkovic, G. J., Morrell, R., & Casey, S. (2001). Parentification in the lives of high-provile individuals andthier families: A hidden source of strength and distress. In B. E. Robinson & N. D. Chase (Eds.), *High performing families: Causes, consequences, and clinical solutions* (pp. 129–155). Alexandria, VA: American Counseling Association.

Kaplan, H. B. (1999). Toward an understanding of resilience: A critical review of definitions and models. In M. D. Glantz & J. L. Johnson (Eds.), *Resilience and development: Positive life adaptations* (pp. 17–84). New York, NY: Kluwer/Plenum.

Kidd, S., & Shahar, G. (2008). Resilience in homeless youth: The key role of self-esteem. *The American Journal of Orthopsychiatry, 78*(2), 163–172.

Larson, R. (2006). Positive youth development, wilful adolescents, and mentoring. *Journal of Community Psychology, 34*(6), 677–689.

Latimer, J., & Foss, L. C. (2005). The sentencing of Aboriginal and non-Aboriginal youth under the young offenders act: A multivariate analysis. *Canadian Journal of Criminology and Criminal Justice, 47*(3), 481–500.

Laub, J. H., & Sampson, R. J. (2003). *Shared beginnings, divergent lives: Delinquent boys to age 70*. Cambridge, MA: Harvard University Press.

Law, J. H. J., & Barker, B. K. (2006). Neighborhood conditions, parenting, and adolescent functioning. *Journal of Human Behavior in the Social Environment, 14*(4), 91–118.

Leadbeater, B., Dodgen, D., & Solarz, A. (2005). The resilience revolution: A paradigm shift for research and policy. In R. D. Peters, B. Leadbeater, & R. J. McMahon (Eds.), *Resilience in children, families, and communities: Linking context to practice and policy* (pp. 47–63). New York, NY: Kluwer.

Leadbeater, B., & Way, N. (Eds.). (2007). *Urban girls: Resisting stereotypes, creating identities*. New York, NY: New York University Press.

Lemery-Chalfant, K. (2010). Genes and environments: How they work together to promote resilience. In J. W. Reich, A. J. Zautra, & J. S. Hall (Eds.), *Handbook of adult resilience* (pp. 55–80). New York, NY: Guilford.

Lerner, R. M. (2006). Resilience as an attribute of the developmental system: Comments on the papers of Professors Masten & Wachs. In B. M. Lester, A. S. Masten, & B. McEwen (Eds.), *Resilience in children* (pp. 40–51). Boston, MA: Blackwell.

Lerner, R. M., Dowling, E. M., & Anderson, P. M. (2003). Positive youth development: Thriving as the basis of personhood and civil society. *Applied Developmental Science, 7*(3), 172–180.

Lesko, N. (2001). *Act your age: A cultural construction of adolescence*. New York, NY: Routledge Falmer.

Lewin, K. (1951). Defining the "field at a given time". In D. Cartwright (Ed.), *Field theory in social science* (pp. 43–59). New York, NY: Harper & Brothers.

Lewis, M. D., Granic, I., & Lamm, C. (2006). In B. M. Lester, A. S. Masten, & B. McEwen (Eds.), Behavioral differences in aggressive children linked with neural mechanisms of emotion regulation. (pp. 164–177). Boston, MA: Blackwell.

Liborio, R., & Ungar, M. (2010). Children's perspectives on their economic activity as a pathway to resilience. *Children and Society, 24*, 326–338.

Liebel, M. (2004). *A will of their own: Cross cultural perspectives on working children*. London, UK: Zed Books.

Luthar, S. S., Cicchetti, D., & Becker, B. (2000). The construct of resilience: A critical evaluation and guidelines for future work. *Child Development, 71*(3), 543–562.

Lyons, J. S. (2004). *Redressing the emperor: Improving our children's public mental health system*. Westport, CT: Praeger.

Martin, A. J., & Marsh, H. W. (2006). Academic resilience and its psychological and educational correlates: A construct validity approach. *Psychology in the Schools, 43*(3), 267–281.

Martin, A. J., & Marsh, H. W. (2009). Academic resilience and academic buoyancy: Multidimensional and hierarchical conceptual framing of causes, correlates and cognate constructs. *Oxford Review of Education, 35*(3), 353–370.

Masten, A. S., & Obradović, J. (2006). Competence and resilience in development. In B. M. Lester, A. S. Masten, & B. McEwen (Eds.), *Resilience in children* (pp. 13–27). Boston, MA: Blackwell.

Masten, A. S., & Wright, M. O. (2010). Resilience over the lifespan: Developmental perspectives on resistance, recovery, and transformation. In J. W. Reich, A. J. Zautra, & J. S. Hall (Eds.), *Handbook of adult resilience* (pp. 213–237). New York, NY: Guilford.

Mikami, A. Y., & Hinshaw, S. P. (2006). Resilient adolescent adjustment among girls: Buffers of childhood peer rejection and attention-deficit/ hyperactivity disorder. *Journal of Abnormal Child Psychology, 34*, 825–839.

Moffitt, T. E. (1997). Adolescents-limited and life-course-persistent offending: A complimentary pair of developmental theories. In T. P. Thornberry (Ed.), *Developmental theories of crime and delinquency* (pp. 11–54). New Brunswick, NJ: Transaction Publishers.

Moffitt, T. E., Caspi, A., Rutter, M., & Silva, P. A. (2001). *Sex differences in antisocial behaviour*. Cambridge, UK: Cambridge University Press.

Moore, K. A., Lippman, L., & Brown, B. (2004). Indicators of child well-being: The promise for positive youth development. *Annals of the American Academy of Political and Social Science, 591*, 125–145.

Munford, R., & Sanders, J. (2005). Borders, margins and bridges: Possibilities for change for marginalized young women. *Community Development Journal, 42*, 317–329.

Murphy, L. B. (1962). *The widening world of childhood: Paths toward mastery*. New York, NY: Basic Books.

Murphy, L. B., & Moriarty, A. E. (1976). *Vulnerability, coping, and growth from infancy to adolescence*. New Haven, CT: Yale University Press.

Murray, C. (2010). Conceptualizing young people's strategies of resistance to offending as 'active resilience'. *British Journal of Social Work, 40*(1), 115–132.

Naess, A. (1989). *Ecology, community and lifestyle: Outline of an ecosophy* (D. Rothenberg, Trans.). Cambridge, UK: Cambridge University.

Nagin, D., & Tremblay, R. E. (1999). Trajectories of boys' physical aggression, opposition and hyperactivity on the path to physically violent and non-violent juvenile delinquency. *Child Development, 70*, 1181–1196.

Nguyen-Gillham, V. (2008). Normalising the abnormal: Palestinian youth and the contradictions of resilience in protracted conflict. *Health & Social Care in the Community, 16*(3), 291–298.

Obradovi, J., Bush, N. R., Stamperdahl, J., Adler, N. E., & Boyce, W. T. (2010). Biological sensitivity to context: The interactive effects of stress reactivity and family adversity on socioemotional behavior and school readiness. *Child Development, 81*(1), 270–289.

Parke, R. D., Coltrane, S., Duffy, S., Buriel, R., Dennis, J., Powers, J., et al. (2004). Economic stress, parenting, and child adjustment in Mexican American and European American families. *Child Development, 75*(6), 1632–1656.

Phelps, E., Balsano, A. B., Peltz, J. S., Zimmerman, S. M., Lerner, R. M., & Lerner, J. V. (2007). Nuances in early adolescent developmental trajectories of positive and of problematic/risk behaviors: Findings from The 4-H study of positive youth development. *Child and Adolescent Psychiatric Clinics of North America, 16*(2), 473–496.

Poulin, C., Hand, D., & Boudreau, B. (2005). Validity of a 12-item version of the CES-D used in the National Longitudinal Study of Children and Youth. *Chronic Diseases in Canada, 26*(2/3), 65–72.

Rutter, M. (1987). Psychosocial resilience and protective mechanisms. *The American Journal of Orthopsychiatry, 57*, 316–331.

Rutter, M. (2008). Developing concepts in developmental psychopathology. In J. J. Hudziak (Ed.), *Developmental psychopathology and wellness: Genetic and environmental influences* (pp. 3–22). Washington, DC: American Psychiatric Publishing.

Sampson, R. J. (2003). The neighbourhood context of well-being. *Perspectives in Biology and Medicine, 43*(3), S53–S64.

Schoon, I. (2006). *Risk and resilience: Adaptations in changing times.* Cambridge, UK: Cambridge University Press.

Shoveller, J. A., Johnson, J. L., Langille, D. B., & Mitchell, T. (2003). Socio-cultural influences on young people's sexual development. *Social Science & Medicine, 59*, 473–487.

Sloboda, Z., Stephens, R. C., Stephens, P. C., Grey, S. F., Teasdale, B., Hawthorne, R. D., et al. (2009). The Adolescent Substance Abuse Prevention Study: A randomized field trial of a universal substance abuse prevention program. *Drug and Alcohol Dependence, 102*, 1–10.

Spencer, J. M., Zimet, G. D., Aalsma, M. C., & Orr, D. P. (2002). Self-esteem as a predictor of initiation of coitus in early adolescents. *Pediatrics, 109*(4), 581–584.

Sroufe, L. A., Egeland, B., Carlson, E. A., & Collins, W. A. (2005). *The development of the person: The Minnesota study of risk and adaptation from birth to adulthood.* New York, NY: Guilford.

Theokas, C., & Lerner, R. M. (2006). Observed ecological assets in families, schools, and neighbourhoods: Conceptualisation, measurement and relations with positive and negative developmental outcomes. *Applied Developmental Science, 10*(2), 61–74.

Theron, L., Cameron, A., Lau, C., Didkowsky, N., Ungar, M., & Liebenberg, L. (2011). A 'day in the lives' of four resilient youths: Cultural roots of resilience. *Youth and Society.* DOI: 10.1177/0044118X11402853.

Tiet, Q. Q., Bird, H. R., Davies, M., Hoven, C., Cohen, P., Jensen, P., et al. (1998). Adverse life events and resilience. *Journal o the American Academy of Child and Adolescent Psychiatry, 37*(11), 1191–1200.

Ungar, M. (2005). Pathways to resilience among children in child welfare, corrections, mental health and educational settings: Navigation and negotiation. *Child and Youth Care Forum, 34*(6), 423–444.

Ungar, M. (2007). *Playing at being bad: The hidden resilience of troubled teens.* Toronto, ON: McClelland & Stewart.

Ungar, M. (2008). Resilience across cultures. *British Journal of Social Work, 38*(2), 218–235.

Ungar, M. (2010a). Researching culturally diverse pathways to resilience: Challenges and solutions. In H. M. McCubbin, K. Ontai, L. Kehl, L. McCubbin, I. Strom, H. Hart, & J. Matsuoka (Eds.), *Multiethnicity and multiethnic families* (pp. 253–276). Honolulu, HI: Le'a Press.

Ungar, M. (2010b). What is resilience across cultures and contexts? Advances to the theory of positive development among individuals and families under stress. *Journal of Family Psychotherapy, 21*(1), 1–16.

Ungar, M. (2011a). *Counseling in challenging contexts: Working with individuals and families across clinical and community settings.* Belmont, CA: Brooks/Cole.

Ungar, M. (2011b). The social ecology of resilience. Addressing contextual and cultural ambiguity of a nascent construct. *American Journal of Orthopsychiatry, 81*, 1–17.

Ungar, M., Brown, M., Liebenberg, L., Othman, R., Kwong, W. M., Armstrong, M., et al. (2007). Unique pathways to resilience across cultures. *Adolescence, 42*(166), 287–310.

Ungar, M., Liebenberg, L., Boothroyd, R., Kwong, W. M., Lee, T. Y., Leblanc, J., et al. (2008). The study of youth resilience across cultures: Lessons from a pilot study of measurement development. *Research in Human Development, 5*(3), 166–180.

Von Bertalanffy, L. (1968). *General system theory: Foundations, development, application.* New York, NY: Brazilier.

Vygotsky, L.S. (1978). *Mind in society: The development of higher psychological processes.* Cambridge, MA: Harvard University Press.

Walker, B., & Salt, D. (2006). *Resilience thinking.* Washington, DC: Island Press.

Walsh, W. A., & Banaji, M. R. (1997). The collective self. In J. G. Snodgrass & R. L. Thompson (Eds.), *The self across psychology* (pp. 193–214). New York, NY: New York Academy of Sciences.

Werner, E. E., & Smith, R. S. (1982). *Vulnerable but invincible: A longitudinal study of resilient children and youth.* New York, NY: McGraw-Hill.

Werner, E. E., & Smith, R. S. (1992). *Overcoming the odds: High risk children from birth to adulthood.* Ithaca, NY: Cornel University Press.

Wikström, P. H. (2005). The social origins of pathways in crime: Towards a developmental ecological action theory of crime involvement and its changes. In D. P. Farrington (Ed.), *Integrated developmental & life-course theories of offending* (pp. 211–246). New Brunswick, NJ: Transaction Publishers.

Wyman, P. A. (2003). Emerging perspectives on context specificity of children's adaptation and resilience: Evidence from a decade of research with urban children in adversity. In S. S. Luthar (Ed.), *Resilience and vulnerability: Adaptation in the context of childhood adversities* (pp. 293–317). Cambridge, UK: Cambridge University Press.

Zautra, A. J., Hall, J. S., & Murray, K. E. (2010). Resilience: A new definition of health for people and communities. In J. W. Reich, A. J. Zautra, & J. S. Hall (Eds.), *Handbook of adult resilience* (pp. 3–34). New York, NY: Guilford.

Resilience: Causal Pathways and Social Ecology

Michael Rutter

During recent years, there has been a marked tendency for researchers, clinicians, and policy-makers to shift their focus from risk to resilience (Mohaupt, 2008). Part of the motivation for their shift was a wish to emphasize the positive, rather than always concentrating on maladaptive outcomes or psychopathology. The aim was to be the fostering of success, instead of treating failure. The emergence of positive psychology as a major movement represents this goal most clearly (Seligman & Csikszentmihalyi, 2000). In the UK, Layard's (2005) "happiness" agenda constitutes an extreme example of the same concern. Several points need to be made. First, it fits firmly into the "risk" paradigm; it merely concentrates on the positive, rather than the negative, pole. Insofar as that is so, it mainly constitutes a relabeling. Instead of studying the risks associated with family conflict, the protective effects of family harmony can be the focus. Instead of investigating depression, happiness is studied. Of course, the shift would be real and not just semantic, if it could be shown that the influences fostering positive outcomes were not just the opposite of those predisposing to negative outcomes. However, few such examples have been found. In their absence, there is the

real risk of trivializing the public and private health importance of serious mental disorder.

Many would argue that there can be little justified interest in whether this person without mental disorder is, or is not, happier than some other person without mental disorder. In addition, the focus runs straight into all the empirical and methodological problems associated with "positive mental health" in an earlier era (Jahoda, 1959). How do we differentiate hedonistic pleasure and excitement from the quiet satisfaction of a job well done? Should Italian President Berlusconi's alleged preoccupation with young girls and with paid call girls be viewed as a positive attribute because it gives him pleasure? What about former US President Bush and British Prime Minister Blair's seemingly smug, satisfied, guilt-free complicity in torturing prisoners and invading Iraq on a lie? Is a positive personal outcome something to be deplored or welcomed in these circumstances?

Another, somewhat different, concept is that of psychological and social competence (Masten et al., 1999). That is different in the sense that it is potentially quantifiable. However, it suffers from three important limitations. First, it assumes that the causal influences will be the same in the nonstressed general population as in those suffering adversity. That could turn out to be true, but it has to be tested and not assumed. Secondly, it assumes that the outcomes will be explicable on the basis of the balance between risk and protective factors; in other words, the concept is firmly based in the risk tradition. Third, it assumes that

M. Rutter (✉)
The Social, Genetic and Developmental Psychiatry Centre, Institute of Psychiatry, King's College London, London, UK
e-mail: camilla.azis@kcl.ac.uk

M. Ungar (ed.), *The Social Ecology of Resilience: A Handbook of Theory and Practice*,
DOI 10.1007/978-1-4614-0586-3_3, © Springer Science+Business Media, LLC 2012

all individuals will respond in the same way to the same degree.

For all these reasons, resilience differs fundamentally from concepts of positive psychology and of competence. Its starting point is quite different in that it begins with the universal finding from all research, naturalistic and experimental, human and other animals, that there is huge heterogeneity in the response to all manner of environmental hazards, physical and psychological (Rutter, 2006). It is argued that systematic investigations of the causes of this heterogeneity should not just throw light on the specifics of different responses to a specific hazard but, in addition, might throw light on a broader range of causal processes. As we shall see, this concept necessarily brings with it several other differences.

Definition of Resilience

It is generally accepted that resilience is defined as a relative resistance to environmental risk experiences, the overcoming of stress or adversity, or a relatively good outcome despite risk experiences (Rutter, 2006). In other words, it is an interactive concept in which the presence of resilience has to be inferred from individual variations in outcome in individuals who have experienced significant major stress or adversity. The inference of resilience requires a demonstration that the effects differ from those found in the absence of such stress/adversity. Note that this concept means that resilience cannot be viewed as a trait that is open to direct measurement.

Does This Mean That Resilience Can Be Reduced to the Finding of a Statistically Significant Interaction Effect?

There are three main reasons why this is not justifiable. First, a statistical interaction requires variations in both variables and not just one. The importance of this point is that some environmental hazards are population-wide. Thus, in the parts of the world in which malaria is endemic,

everyone is subject to a broadly similar exposure. Nevertheless, some are relatively resistant and many are not. That would not be detectable through a statistical interaction because there is so little variation in malaria exposure. Exactly the same applies to hay fever in the UK. More or less everyone receives the same exposure to pollens in the spring but some individuals are resistant to hay fever, whereas others are not. That is a biological gene-environment interaction, albeit not a statistical one.

Is Resilience Merely Another Word for Successfully Coping?

Certainly, resilience and coping are closely connected concepts. In particular, unlike most risk research, the emphasis is on an active *process* and not static traits. Nevertheless, the two are not synonymous because coping is essentially an *individual* feature, and moreover one that implies some overt action. As we shall see, that is an important component of resilience but it is not all. In particular, it ignores the social context and social influences, both of which can be very influential.

Insofar as Resilience Involves Coping, Is It More Likely That There Will Be Substantial Continuity Over Time and Place?

Of course, a degree of continuity is expectable on the basis of the role of individual traits. Nevertheless longitudinal studies of temperament and personality show only moderate continuity (Caspi & Shiner, 2008). Also, if social context or life situation change, there are likely to be impacts on resilience. More directly, empirical studies (discussed below) show that the genetic affects on environmental susceptibility to the same hazard (child abuse) differs according to whether or not the outcome being studied is depression or antisocial behavior. For obvious reasons, it is implausible that the resilience to infections, to cancer, to heart disease, and to maltreatment will involve identical mechanisms.

Even with the Same Hazard and the Same Outcome, Can Resilience Be Reduced to a Unitary Factor?

It cannot be so reduced because resilience may show itself in the form of either resistance to stress/adversity or "steeling" effects in which individuals are actually strengthened by a bad experience. Although possible, it is not likely that these two different outcomes will involve exactly the same causal processes.

Can Resilience Be Reduced to the "Chemistry" of the Moment?

It cannot be considered just as something that applies at a single moment of time. That is because resilience may derive from factors operating before the environmental hazard occurs, from those acting during the experience, and from circumstances years later that affect recovery. A lifetime perspective is essential and resilience is best considered as a dynamic process rather than the occurrence of an event.

Is Resilience No More Than a Fancy New Name to Re-label the Well-Established Traditional Concepts of Risk and Protection?

No, because the two are fundamentally different in both their starting point and their assumptions. The concepts of risk and protection focus on group differences predicated on the assumption that, broadly speaking, all individuals will respond in much the same way. Accordingly, the causal factors will be found to reside in the balance, and severity, of individual risk and protective factors, and these will apply to the whole population.

By contrast, resilience starts with the assumption (firmly based on good empirical evidence) that, given the same dose and pattern of stress/adversity, there will always be marked heterogeneity in response. Analyses, therefore, focus on the range of possible influences giving rise to that heterogeneity. The expectation is that the answers will be informative on the causes of these individual differences and the hope is that these findings will be more broadly applicable to the causal process more generally.

Does This Mean, Therefore, That We Should Abandon Research into Risk and Protective Factors, and Instead Focus Just on Resilience?

Certainly not! The reason is that the whole approach to the study of resilience has to start with a careful, rigorous quantified measurement of risk and protection. That is because an essential methodological requirement is that the reality of major risk has been firmly established and quantified in order to ensure that the heterogeneity of response is examined in relation to a standard baseline. It needs to be added, in addition, that a substantial proportion of individual differences *does* reflect the balance between risk and protective factors. The concept of resilience does not deny that but, rather, adds an additional crucially important element. A further requirement is that research should have established that the risk is truly environmentally mediated. The concept of resilience is equally applicable to genetic risks but, in this review, the focus will be strictly on environmental hazards.

Does the Concept of Resilience Have to Apply to Individuals; Can There Be Resilient Communities?

Although there could be resilient communities (and an example will be discussed) it is difficult to know what *community* outcome could be used as an index. It is certainly appropriate to conceptualize *influences* at a community level, but resilience as an outcome is still better viewed in terms of individual outcomes, and that is the approach used here.

Steeling Effects

With these background concepts in mind, attention needs to be focused on the occurrences of "steeling" effects – meaning circumstances in which individuals are actually strengthened by the experience of challenge, stress, or adversity. Conceptually, it needs to be recognized that coping with challenge is a normal feature of development. Biologically speaking, it would make no sense to seek to rear children with the aim of a total avoidance of environmental hazards. The medical example of resistance to infections constitutes the best example. Good physical health is not fostered by avoiding all contact with infectious agents. Rather it is fostered by encountering such agents and dealing with them successfully (the acquisition of natural immunity), or by immunization in which a controlled dose of a modified version of the pathogen is administered (thereby providing induced immunity).

The key question is whether something comparable applies to psychological stresses. Perhaps, although not as extensively studied as would be desirable, the most direct parallel is provided by the physiological adaptations found in experienced parachute jumpers (Ursin, Badde, & Levins, 1978). Novices, not surprisingly, show high arousal immediately prior to jumping. By contrast, experienced jumpers show a different, adaptive, physiological response well before jumping. There is no obvious social contextual influence but, of course, there is a protective camaraderie in being part of a cohesive group of successful "experts."

The second contextual effect is seen more clearly in the high morale shown by soldiers working in conditions of extreme danger in the Vietnam War but undertaking a crucially important task and taking pride in doing so well (Bourne, Coli, & Datel, 1968; Bourne, Rose, & Mason, 1967). In this instance, although not experimentally tested, it seems reasonable to conclude that their resistance to the stresses of severe danger derived from the particular features of their social group.

A rather different example stems from Elders' longitudinal analyses of the California cohorts going through the economic depression of the 1920s and 1930s (Elder, 1974). In brief, the relevant finding was that whereas younger children tended to fare poorly, adolescents were sometimes strengthened by the experience. The proposed explanation was that those of greater maturity and experience were better able to take on new social responsibilities, and finding that they could do this successfully made them more resilient.

The early finding that children who experienced happy separation from their parents (such as by staying with grandparents or having "sleepovers" with friends) tended to cope better with the stresses of hospital admission (Stacey, Dearden, Pill, & Robinson, 1970). Of course, admission to hospital involved multiple stressful events other than separation. Nevertheless, the acquired social confidence and self-efficacy deriving from successful social experiences seemed to foster resilience.

Yet another example is provided by the evidence that, for girls raised in group care institutional conditions, success at school (usually not academic, but including success in positions of responsibility or in sport or in music) left them with a feeling of control over their lives that was sorely lacking in most of the institution-reared group (Quinton & Rutter, 1988).

Two points need to be emphasized. First, the findings are necessarily somewhat speculative in their implications. Second, it would be quite wrong to suppose that all steeling effects necessarily involve social contextual influences. The best example of one that does not is to be found in Levine et al.'s rodent studies (Levine, 1956; Levine, Chevalier, & Korchin, 1956). Physical stress was experimentally induced by putting the animals in a centrifuge that spun them around. Counter to expectations, this unpleasant experience had both structural and functional effects on the neuroendocrine system that were associated with an enhanced resistance to later stresses.

Only the most tentative inferences are possible on the qualities associated with "steeling" effects.

But such evidence as there is suggests that physio logical adaptation and psychological habituation are both involved and that successful coping with the challenge or environmental hazard is more likely when there is a sense of self-efficacy, the acquisition of effective coping strategies and a cognitive redefinition of the negative experience.

Communities Fostering Resilience

Three community examples serve to make the same point. First, the Chicago study undertaken by Sampson, Raudenbush, and Earls (1997) showed that crime was highest in geographical areas showing social disorganization and a lack of collective efficacy. In other words, area differences in crime were not mainly a result of noxious influences pushing individuals into crime but rather reflected a lack of a positive social ethos in the community that, when it was present, protected individuals in a high risk area from engaging in crime. The more recent study by Odgers et al. (2009), although using rather different measures and a quite different type of sample, similarly identified collective efficacy as the quality seeming to foster resilience.

The third example was different yet again, but despite this, pointed to similar mechanisms. Bruhn and Wolf (1979, 1993) noted that in a small town, Roseto, in Pennsylvania the death rate from heart disease was roughly half that in the United States as a whole and about a third of that in two apparently similar towns also largely made up of hardworking European immigrants. The differences did not appear to stem from variation in diet, exercise, or family history. What they found was that the Rosetons had created a powerful protective social structure, which was egalitarian in helping the unsuccessful and discouraging the wealthy from flaunting their success. In a town of just under 2,000 people there were 22 separate civic organizations, many multigenerational homes in which the grandparents were respected, a cohesive Catholic church group and a tendency for people to visit one another, stopping to chat in Italian on the street or cooking for one another in

their backyards. This constituted a powerful, but highly unusual, example of collective efficacy that seemed to foster both physical and mental health (Gladwell, 2009).

Opportunity, Practice, and Multiplier Effects

Gladwell (2009) has brought together an important set of concepts and findings on outstanding economic success. Although that is far from synonymous with psychosocial resilience, it nevertheless provides three key messages that do apply to resilience. First, there is the role of some unexpected opportunity. Gladwell drew attention to the observation that a surprisingly high proportion of ice hockey stars were born in the first 3 months of the year. The cut-off for selection to a junior squad who received special coaching was January first. This means that those who were oldest, and therefore physically most mature, had a big advantage within the 1 year cohort over those who could be up to 12 months younger – a huge age gap in preadolescence. A comparative effect is also evident in scholastic success (Bedard & Dhuey, 2006).

The striking aspect of this age advantage phenomena is its remarkable persistence (see Misch & Grondin, 2001). This is because the initial opportunity led on to a markedly superior experience – the crucially important multiplier effect. In addition, this led to a much greater duration of practice. This led to the so called "10,000 rule" – the notion that an outstanding expert performance is only possible with an extraordinary duration of deliberate practice (see Ericsson, Krampe, & Tesch-Römer, 1993). This was most closely examined in the fields of sport and music but perhaps the same may apply in the field of social functioning.

Family Fostering of Talent

Many people have a strong belief in the importance of native ability, as indexed by IQ, in predicting world success. The most famous example of a study designed to examine this notion was Terman's longitudinal study if 730 young boys with a measured IQ of at least 140 (ranging up to 200) (Minton, 1988; Seagoe, 1975; Shurkin, 1992). In adult life, about a fifth of these Termites (as they came to be known) were outstandingly successful by any criterion, but a fifth were strikingly unsuccessful. A third of the latter group dropped out of college and most were struggling in their work. Strikingly, the successes and failures did not differ in IQ. The differentiation lay in the fact that the former overwhelmingly came from upper middle class families whereas the latter did not (indeed about a third had a parent who dropped out of high school before the eighth grade). Did the difference reflect genetic or cultural advantages/disadvantages? We do not know, but a very small scale qualitative study of third graders provides possible clues. Lareau (2003) made a differentiation between families that provided what she called "concerted cultivation" and "accomplishment of natural growth." The former involved active parental scheduling of the children's activities, an expectation that children talk back to adults in order to negotiate and question, and a fostering of a sense of entitlement. The latter were equally caring but differed in having a style that let children grow and develop on their own. Children were expected to be compliant and obedient and there was no fostering of active entitlement. The design allowed no testing of causation but the suggestion was that success involved not only the ample provision of active learning opportunities but also a style of encouraging curiosity and an expectation of being respected and listened to.

Value of Meaningful Work

There are striking national differences in mathematics and science achievements as shown by the TIMSS comparative study (see Gladwell, 2009). These differences parallel similar contrasts on the willingness to work hard over long hours. But for work to be satisfying, meaningful, and worthwhile, it seems also necessary for there to be autonomy, complexity, and a clear connection between effort and reward. Although, once again,

whether these associations reflect causal influences, the experience of successful immigrants does to appear to show these features.

Schooling

The studies of effective schooling (Rutter, Maughan, Mortimore, Ouston, & Smith, 1979) add further dimensions. It is clear that the sheer number of hours spent at school overall (roughly estimated as 15,000 h) makes it evident that there is ample opportunity for schooling to make an important impact on young people's progress. Comparison of effective and less effective schools (as judged by pupil success) showed the value of an appropriate academic emphasis and of high expectations, but the findings also pointed to the crucial role of social experiences. Children fared better when treated well, given responsibility and multiple opportunities for success in varied fields, and the teachers provided models of conscientious behavior and an interest in and positive response to pupils' work and other activities. Academic success tended to be associated with good attendance and good behavior, and the qualities already noted in relation to post-school employment (autonomy, complexity, and rewards) apply equally in the school environment. The findings show that the school ethos *will* affect social functioning simply because it constitutes a social group as well as a pedagogic institution. It is not a matter of schools choosing to target social functioning; rather the issue is whether the social group (both in terms of teachers and pupils, and the mix of the peer group) will have a beneficial or damaging effect. However, it is also relevant that upper SES children tend to progress during the long summer vacation, whereas lower SES children do not (Alexander, Entwisle & Olson, 2001). This suggests an important compensatory role of schooling.

Turning Points in Adult Life

Resilience is often seen as something that develops in childhood but two examples illustrate the importance of turning point effects in adult life.

Both also show the value of combining quantitative and qualitative research strategies. Hauser, Allen, and Golden (2006) followed into adult life 67 young people who were patients in an inpatient psychiatric unit when adolescent. The qualitative study compared nine who showed outstanding resilience and seven with "ordinary" outcomes. The researchers argued that those who showed the expected poor outcomes were likely to be less informative. Three key elements appeared to characterize resilience: (1) personal agency and a concern to overcome adversity; (2) a self-reflective style; and (3) a commitment to relationships.

The second example is provided by Laub and Sampson's (2003) following up to age 70 years of the Glueck's sample of 500 incarcerated adolescent delinquents and 500 matched nondelinquents. Quantitative data showed positive turning point effects leading to resilience associated with military service, marriage, and employment. The interview responses pointed to human agency exercising focused choice. Given all the horrors of war, one may well ask why, in a disadvantaged delinquent group, this proved protective? The two main explanations seemed to lie in the U.S. G.I Bill that provided college education for those serving in the army. This opened up crucial opportunities for a group who had often opted out of schooling. This went along with a postponement of marriage – a postponement that meant the widening of marital choice beyond the individuals' own delinquent peer group. Marriage proved even more protective (see Sampson, Laub, & Wimer, 2006). It might be supposed that this just derived from a loving relationship but the interviews showed that the protective elements also lay in social support and commitment, the informal social control provided by wives, the change in routines, lifestyle activities and peer group, a residential change, and the birth of children with their consequent effects on responsibilities and the need for regular paid employment.

Putting these multiple social context studies together, the pathways to resilience seemed to lie in the combination of a new opportunity that served to knife off a disadvantaged past, a sense of active agency to make the most of the opportunity, and a multiplier effect that served to strengthen and reinforce the change for the better. The personal protective qualities that seemed important included good scholastic achievement, a secure selective attachment, multiple harmonious relationships, a sense of self-efficacy, a range of social problem solving skills, a positive social interactional style, and a flexible, adaptive approach to new situations. Positive school influences fostered these qualities by, amongst other things, giving ample opportunities for both success and responsibility, as well as appropriate models of behavior. Community influences added the dimension of collective efficacy and community cohesiveness.

Gene-Environment Interactions (GxE)

In this chapter so far, attention has been mainly paid to social psychological features that appear to have an environmentally mediated effect serving to foster resilience. This must be balanced by the strong evidence that genetic influences have a strong role in moderating the effects of risk environments (probably through an impact on environmental susceptibility and not just on responses to adverse circumstances). For example, pioneering epidemiological/longitudinal studies by Caspi, Moffitt, and their colleagues using the Dunedin cohort have shown that a polymorphism of the serotonin transporter promoter gene moderated the effect of child maltreatment on the liability to depression (Caspi et al., 2003) and that a polymorphism of the MAOA gene does the same in relation to the liability to antisocial behavior (Caspi et al., 2002). Risch et al. (2009) have expressed doubts about these statistical interactions but their review was flawed (Uher & McGuffin, 2010) and there are many epidemiological replications, as well as biological support from both animal models and human experimental studies (Rutter, Thapar, & Pickles, 2009). The precise mechanisms are not known but the implication is that the environmental effects may be operating on the same biological pathway as the genetic effects. Uher (2008) has suggested that the findings may have useful therapeutic implications, but these have yet to be put to the test.

Finally, we should recognize that the very important findings on GxE do *not* mean that the genetic effects irrevocably *determine* outcome. The effects are probabilistic and this potential lies in the possibility of understanding both the genetic and environmental causal pathways, and not in any supposed fixed effect.

Some Caveats and Concerns

The focus in this chapter has been strictly on the phenomenon of resilience: namely, that, even with the most extreme adversities, some individuals nevertheless function well and a few appear strengthened by their negative experiences. As discussed, there is good evidence that the phenomenon is real and, clearly, it provides an important element of hope. On the other hand, it is crucial that we do not assume that abuse, neglect, and torture are a "given" that must be accepted. To the contrary, it is essential that all appropriate steps be taken to reduce their occurrence. That is at least as important as resilience but, because the policy and practice implications are different, it is outside the scope of this chapter. In addition, it would be misleading to assume that all individuals could become resilient. That is implausible. Moreover, although there is a wealth of promising intervention initiatives to foster resilience, very few have been subject to rigorous tests of their efficacy. We have yet to determine what works best for which individuals, what mechanisms mediate efficacy, and why some individuals fail to show a beneficial response. These issues remain a research challenge.

Some people working in the resilience field have urged that we "depathologize" post-traumatic stress disorders and other responses to severe stress and adversity. Presumably, this argument is based on recognition that it is "normal" to show such responses. In my view, that is a mistaken way of conceptualizing the issues. It involves a return to an outmoded mind-body dualism. There is good evidence that stress and adversity have measurable effects on brain and neuroendocrine structure and function (see Arnsten, 2009) and that some of these effects are maladaptive (and therefore "pathological").

We do not depathologize cancer and heart disease because environmental factors play a major role in etiology. Why, therefore, should we seek to do so with mental disorders? Perhaps, however, the plea is based on recognition that not all stress disorders require treatment. Quite so, but the same applies to grief and bereavement. Not all bereaved people need treatment but some do; hence the development of bereavement counseling. Professional responses should be shaped by need and not by invalid notions of pathology.

One other issue concerns the uncertainty regarding the mechanisms involved in the helpful effects of social support. Humans are social animals and, as such, social relationships are very important – as noted in some of the studies discussed in this chapter. Nevertheless, we should avoid the assumption that the security provided by a good loving relationship is all that matters. Self-efficacy is more important than high self-esteem (Bandura, 1997) – and also relationships may be important because they play a role in the development of goals, ambitions, and a sense of personal agency.

Biological Limitations on Resilience

There are optimistic messages in the resilience findings but it is important to appreciate that, not only do we have a limited understanding of how to foster resilience, but also there are limitations on resilience brought about by the enduring biological effects of some very seriously adverse environments (Rutter & Sonuga-Barke, 2010) and possibly some more ordinary environmental variations operating through epigenetic mechanisms (Meaney, 2010). Just because environments have biological effects does not mean that the effects are necessarily irreversible but there needs to be caution about the extent of resilience.

Conclusion

Resilience is a process and not a trait; moreover, it operates throughout the lifespan – before, during, and after adverse experiences. It involves a range of individual qualities that include active agency, flexible responses to varying circumstances, an ability to take advantage of opportunities, a self-reflective style making it easier to learn from experiences, and a commitment to relationships. Family influences, both environmentally and genetically mediated, are important, but so are effects of the school and peer group, and community cohesion and efficacy.

References

Alexander, K. L., Entwistle, D. R., & Olson, L. S. (2001). Schools, achievement and inequality: A seasonal perspective. *Education Evaluation & Policy Analysis, 23*, 141–191.

Arnsten, A. F. T. (2009). Stress signalling pathways that impair prefrontal cortex structure and function. *Nature Reviews: Neuroscience, 10*, 410–417.

Bandura, A. (1997). *Self-efficacy: The exercise of control*. New York: Freeman.

Bedard, K., & Dhuey, E. (2006). The persistence of early childhood maturity: International evidence of long-run age effects. *Quality Journal of Economic, 121*, 1437–1472.

Bourne, P. G., Coli, W. M., & Datel, W. E. (1968). Affect levels in 10 special forces 'A' team members under threat of attack. *Psychological Reports, 22*, 363–366.

Bourne, P. G., Rose, R. M., & Mason, J. W. (1967). 17-OHCS levels in combat: Data on 7 helicopter ambulance medics. *Archives of General Psychiatry, 17*, 104–110.

Bruhn, J. C., & Wolf, S. (1979). *The Roseto story*. Norman: University of Oklahoma Press.

Bruhn, J. C., & Wolf, S. (1993). *The power of clan: The influence of human relationships on heart disease*. New Brunswick: Transaction Publishers.

Caspi, A., McClay, J., Moffitt, T. E., Mill, J., Craig, I. W., Taylor, A., et al. (2002). Role of genotype in the cycle of violence in maltreated children. *Science, 297*, 851–854.

Caspi, A., & Shiner, R. L. (2008). Temperament and personality. In M. Rutter, D. Bishop, D. Pine, S. Scott, J. S. Stevenson, E. Taylor, & A. Thapar (Eds.), *Rutter's child and adolescent psychiatry* (5th ed., pp. 182–194). Oxford: Wiley-Blackwell Publishing.

Caspi, A., Sugden, K., Moffitt, T. E., Taylor, A., Craig, I. W., Harrington, H., et al. (2003). Influence of life stress on depression: Moderation by polymorphism in the 5-HTT gene. *Science, 301*, 386–389.

Elder, G. H. (1974). *Children of the great depression*. Chicago: University of Chicago Press.

Ericsson, K. A., Krampe, R. T., & Tesch-Römer, C. (1993). The role of deliberate practice in the acquisition of expert performance. *Psychological Review, 100*, 363–406.

Gladwell, M. (2009). *Outliers: The story of success*. New York: Little, Brown, and Co.

Hauser, S., Allen, J., & Golden, E. (2006). *Out of the woods: Tales of resilient teens*. Cambridge: Harvard University Press.

Jahoda, M. (1959). *Current concepts of positive mental health*. New York: Basic Books.

Lareau, A. (2003). *Unequal childhoods: Class, race and family life*. Berkley: University of California Press.

Laub, J., & Sampson, R. (2003). *Shared beginnings, divergent lives: Delinquent boys to age 70*. Cambridge: Harvard University Press.

Layard, R. (2005). *Happiness: Lessons from a new science*. New York: Penguin Press.

Levine, S. (1956). A further study of infantile handling and adult avoidance learning. *Journal of Personality, 25*, 70–80.

Levine, S., Chevalier, J. A., & Korchin, S. J. (1956). The effects of early handling and shock on later avoidance behavior. *Journal of Personality, 24*, 475–493.

Masten, A. S., Hubbard, J. J., Gest, S. D., Tellegen, A., Garmezy, N., & Raimerz, M. (1999). Competence in the context of adversity: Pathways to resilience and maladaptation from childhood to late adolescence. *Development and Psychopathology, 11*, 143–169.

Meaney, M. J. (2010). Epigenetics and the biological definition of gene x environment interactions. *Child Development, 81*, 47–79.

Minton, H. L. (1988). *Lewis M. Terman: Pioneer in psychology testing*. New York: New York University Press.

Misch, J., & Grondin, S. (2001). Unequal competition as an implement to personal development: A review of the relative age effect in sport. *Developmental Review, 21*, 147–167.

Mohaupt, S. (2008). Review article: Resilience and social exclusion. *Social Policy and Society, 8*, 63–71.

Odgers, C. L., Moffitt, T. E., Tach, L., Sampson, R., Taylor, A., Matthews, C. L., et al. (2009). The protective effects of neighborhood collective efficacy on children growing up in deprivation: A developmental analysis. *Developmental Psychology, 42*, 942–947.

Quinton, D., & Rutter, M. (1988). *Parenting breakdown: The making and breaking of intergenerational links*. Farnham: Avebury.

Risch, N., Herrell, R., Lehner, T., Liang, K. Y., Eaves, L., Hoh, J., et al. (2009). Interaction between the serotonin transporter gene (5-HTTLPR), stressful life events, and risk of depression: A meta-analysis. *Journal of the American Medical Association, 301*, 2462–2471.

Rutter, M. (2006). Implications of resilience concepts for scientific understanding. *Annals of the New York Academy of Sciences, 1094*, 1–12.

Rutter, M., Maughan, B., Mortimore, P., Ouston, J., & Smith, A. (1979). *Fifteen thousand hours: Secondary schools and their effects on children*. Cambridge: Harvard University Press.

Rutter, M., & Sonuga-Barke, E. J. (Eds.), (2010). Deprivation-specific psychological patterns: Effects of institutional deprivation. *Society for Research in Child Development Monograph, 75*(1), 48–78.

Rutter, M., Thapar, A., & Pickles, A. (2009). From JAMA: Commentary on paper by Risch et al. (2009) – gene-environment interactions: Biologically valid pathway or artefact? *Archives of General Psychiatry, 66*(12), 1297–1289.

Sampson, R. J., Laub, J. H., & Wimer, C. (2006). Does marriage reduce crime? A counterfactual approach to within-individual causal effects. *Criminology, 44*, 465–508.

Sampson, R. J., Raudenbush, S. W., & Earls, F. (1997). Neighborhoods and violent crime: A multilevel study of collective efficacy. *Science, 277*, 918–924.

Seagoe, M. V. (1975). *Terman and the gifted*. Los Altos: William Kaufmann.

Seligman, M. E. P., & Csikszentmihalyi, M. (2000). Positive psychology: An introduction. *American Psychology, 55*, 5–14.

Shurkin, J. N. (1992). *Terman's kids: The groundbreaking study of how the gifted grow up*. New York: Little, Brown & Co.

Stacey, M., Dearden, R., Pill, R., & Robinson, D. (1970). *Hospitals, children and their families: The report of a pilot study*. London: Routledge & Kegan Paul.

Uher, R. (2008). The implications of gene-environment interactions in depression: Will cause inform cure? *Molecular Psychiatry, 13*, 1070–1078.

Uher, R., & McGuffin, P. (2010). The moderation by the serotonin transporter gene of environmental adversity in the etiology of depression: 2009 update. *Molecular Psychiatry, 15*, 18–22.

Ursin, H., Badde, E., & Levins, S. (1978). *Psychobiology of stress: A study of coping men*. New York: Academic.

Theory and Measurement of Resilience: Views from Development

4

Lewis P. Lipsitt and Jack Demick

Theory and Measurement of Resilience: Views from Development

From its early appearance in the psychological literature (e.g., Garmezy, 1973; Werner, 1971) through the present (e.g., Diehl & Hay, 2010; Masten, 2007), the construct of *resilience* has met both theoretical and methodological obstacles. We believe those impediments to be surmountable. Investigators have debated, but not resolved, the relationships of the construct of resilience to other concepts such as *invulnerability, stress resistance*, and *protective factors,* and they have proposed a variety of methods for the measurement of resilience and related concepts. To provide an explication of the construct, we first briefly review these obstacles and then outline two developmental approaches, with which we each have long been associated, for the study of resilience. These approaches, we believe, have the capacity to advance the science of resilience significantly.

Overview of Resilience Science

Masten (2007) has provided a comprehensive review of what she considers to be the history of resilience science as embodied in four waves of research with resilience typically defined as "good outcomes in spite of serious threats to adaptation or development" (Masten, 2001, p. 228). Simply stated, the first wave was descriptive and sought to define and measure resilience in different populations using developmental psychopathologies, particularly schizophrenia, as starting points and then expanding to include a wide range of groups such as children of the Great Depression (cf. Elder, 1974) and children of immigrants (cf. Garcia Coll & Marks, 2009) and to identify the correlates of resilience with *isolated variables* related to child, family, and/or environmental characteristics (e.g., Masten, 1999). The second wave attempted to uncover the *processes* accounting for the correlates of resilience such as the roles of psychobiological stress reactivity and self-regulation systems (e.g., Cicchetti & Curtis, 2006) or of psychosocial attachment relationships (e.g., Davies & Cummings, 2006) and/or social support (e.g., Rutter, 1985) in fostering resilience over time. The third wave consisted of experiments designed to promote resilience through *prevention and intervention programs* (e.g., Weissberg, Kumpfer, & Seligman, 2003). The fourth and current wave consists of the analysis of *multilevel dynamics* or the ways in which resilience is shaped by interactions across levels of analysis (e.g., Luthar, 2006).

While we applaud Masten's (2007) attempt to organize relevant work on resilience, we were surprised to learn that relevant research has had such a long and variegated history that studies may be neatly categorized into one of four waves.

J. Demick (✉)
Department of Education,
Center for the Study of Human Development,
Brown University, Providence, RI, USA
e-mail: Jack_Demick@Brown.edu

M. Ungar (ed.), *The Social Ecology of Resilience: A Handbook of Theory and Practice*,
DOI 10.1007/978-1-4614-0586-3_4, © Springer Science+Business Media, LLC 2012

From our perspective, we see a number of thorny issues associated with such a strategy. We contend that the four waves of research bring us to a tsunami of extreme confusion – despite repeated attempts to weather the storm (e.g., Luthar, Cicchetti, & Becker, 2000; Rutter, 2006). We try here to examine the nature of resilience in terms that do not capitalize merely on retroactive reconstructions, but seek to comprehend how resilience as a psychological construct can help us understand its origins and consequences. Our hope is that this approach will bring further clarity to the theoretical conceptualizations underlying the concept and provide methodological advisories for consideration.

Theoretical Conceptualization

A small number of authors (e.g., Masten, 1994; Richardson, 2002; cf. Luthar et al., 2000) have advocated distinguishing between *resiliency,* reflecting traits of individuals leading to more general "steeling" or "inoculating" functions in future adverse situations, and *resilience,* referring to dynamic processes leading to favorable outcomes for individuals following adversity. However, this distinction can be faulted by the following lay and academic observations. First, numerous if not all dictionaries consider *resilience* and *resiliency* synonymously (http://dictionary.reference.com). Second, in the first phase of an ongoing large-scale study of age differences in laypersons' conceptions of resilience (here employing undergraduates), Demick and Rodriguez (2011) have found support for the notions that: (a) virtually all individuals in this sample did not distinguish between resilience and resiliency; (b) while one-third of the sample reported that resilience applies only to human beings, the remaining two-thirds acknowledged that resilience may also be applied to other entities (in descending frequency: animals, institutions, inanimate objects, plants, communities, and neighborhoods but there was no mention of dyadic relationships or families); and (c) resilience is most often construed as an individual trait characterized by, for example, "an ability to

bounce back" or "perseverance." In line with this, the study also uncovered significant positive correlations between participants' performance on a task of *trait resilience* and both their *emotional intelligence* and *learning style characterized by active experimentation.* These findings supported a trait conceptualization of resilience and implicated social relationships and (novel) activity as underlying processes.

Third, a computerized literature review of PsychArticles (journals published by the American Psychological Association and allied organizations) uncovered that 42 articles related to this problem area have been published in 2010 alone: of these, only two (4.7%) have employed the term *resiliency* rather than *resilience* in the proposed sense while the remaining 40 articles have employed *resilience* to refer to either a trait or a process. For us, this makes the distinction between terms almost useless and suggests the need for continued, perhaps heightened, focus on clarifying the nature of resilience and its accompanying uncertainties.

Further, an in-depth analysis of the 2010 published articles on resilience – all of which did not fall neatly within Masten's fourth wave of research and/or even within the first three – uncovered both old and new theoretical and methodological controversies. Synoptically, these included:

- Whether, and if so how, resilience differs theoretically from other psychological constructs both internal (e.g., *vulnerability, risk, and protective factors*) and external (e.g., *ego resilience, hardiness, stress resistance*) to resilience research (cf. Wright & Masten, 2006, vs. Seifer, 2011).
- Whether resilience refers specifically to an individual trait or to more general dynamic processes (cf. Rutter, 2006).
- Whether resilience applies to "extraordinary" individuals or to "ordinary" individuals and/or groups of individuals (cf. Hou, Law, Yin, & Fu, 2010, on cancer survivors), leading to consideration of Masten's (2001) assertion of the normative (vs. nonnormative) function of human adaptation.
- Whether a risk factor (a negative characteristic that predicts a negative outcome) needs to be

major or can be regarded as minor (cf. Taylor, Hulette, & Dishion, 2010, on the negative role of children's imaginary companions in adaptation).

- Whether a favorable outcome following adversity can and should be measured in single or multiple domains, as in the Cicchetti and Garmezy (1993) recommendation to differentiate positive adaptation into more circumscribed terms such as *educational resilience*, *emotional resilience*, and *behavioral resilience* so as not to imply that positive adaptation occurs across all levels of functioning.
- Whether resilience constitutes a one- or a multitime phenomenon (cf. Seery, Holman, & Silver, 2010, on cumulative lifetime adversity and resilience).
- Whether resilience is manifest similarly in disparate cultural groups and/or contexts (cf. Ungar, 2004).
- Whether resilience constructs can be generalized from the subfield of developmental psychology to other subfields such as clinical psychology (cf. Braverman, 2001, on the direct application of resilience concepts to the prevention of adolescent substance abuse vs. Richardson, 2002, on the less direct and useful application of resilience research to patient processes in psychotherapy).
- Whether resilience science can be framed more comprehensively within a unifying approach.
- Whether some methods of probing and some research designs are more conducive to the explicative study of resilience.
- Whether resilience should be measured immediately, intermittently, or long following adversity.
- Whether, and if so how, intervention studies may be designed to help shed light on various of the above issues, especially to determine whether the presumed antecedents of "resilience" do indeed have follow-through effects on developmental outcomes.

Many of these interrelated issues, but especially the last four, have figured to some degree in our own work and will be elaborated below.

To make advances in resilience science, we believe that such theoretical and methodological imprecision must be constantly addressed and refined in light of accumulating evidence and ultimately eliminated as "scholars who advocate for scientific parsimony contend that the notion of resilience adds nothing to the more general term 'positive adjustment' and argue that the focus on resilience does not augment developmental theory" (Luthar et al., 2000, pp. 553). This constitutes a major issue for both our field and the lay public. For example, researchers (e.g., Amato, 2001; Eschleman, Bowling, & Alarcon, 2010) have begun to conduct meta-analyses on empirical studies of resilience and related constructs, which become meaningless if theoretical and methodological differences are not noted and clarified. Further, as is the case in the real world popularization of any psychological construct, resilience science and the disciplines it represents may be left wide open for unnecessary skepticism and criticism. To date, parents and teachers have already been bombarded by popular psychological material (e.g., Brooks & Goldstein, 2007; Cefai, 2008), which has promised to help them raise "resilient children." If general audiences interpret these materials as suggesting that the focus of change resides only in children and that the only change agents are parents and, to a lesser extent, teachers, we run the serious risk of impeding individuals at all stages of life and the social policies that need to be enacted to enhance their development.

In concert with this, we believe our respective (Lipsitt and Demick, 2011) developmental approaches to the study of resilience, although starting from very different theoretical traditions and interests in age groups, but sharing some major underlying assumptions nonetheless, have the potential to eliminate confusions and make recommendations for future resilience research based on sound developmental science. Together, our developmental approaches lead us to view resilience as a specific phenomenon, positing theoretical notions to explain the phenomenon and to suggest the most effective means of data collection in attempts to support our conceptualization. Following brief explications of our approaches – which have been employed to study the paradigmatic problems of Sudden Infant Death Syndrome and person-in-environment transitions across the life span respectively – the commonalities between our approaches will be delineated to provide the broad brush strokes for a comprehensive theory of resilience and its measurement.

Developmental Learning Theory, SIDS, and Resilience

Sudden Infant Death Syndrome or SIDS (alternatively referred to as *crib death* in North America and *cot death* in South Africa, Australia, India, and the United Kingdom), the sudden death usually during sleep of an infant under 1 year of age that is unexpected by history and unexplained after an autopsy and death scene investigation, and from which more infants die in developed countries than from all other causes combined, remains frightening and mysterious to this day. This is because the cause of SIDS is largely unknown.

Numerous studies have long identified biologically based prenatal (e.g., maternal alcohol and drug use, inadequate prenatal care and nutrition) and postnatal (e.g., low birth weight, premature birth, anemia) risk factors for SIDS, which is also more likely to occur in males and in Native and African Americans. However, given this research, there has been surprisingly little understanding of the syndrome's precise biological cause(s). Further, although infant behavior may explain some of these deaths, scant attention has been paid to work that has addressed the behavioral and/or biobehavioral characteristics of babies who die without medical explanation at least until more recently.

Any explanation of SIDS must account for the fact (Lipsitt, 2003) that most SIDS deaths occur between 2 and 5 months of age. Acknowledging that a protective mechanism must spare infants before 2 months but then disappear, Lipsitt reasoned that the respiratory occlusion reflex serves as an initial defense against smothering and thus can provide such an explanation. For example, McGraw's (1943) classic work on the orderly developmental course of neuromotor capacity has demonstrated that infantile reflexes wane after providing opportunities for learned responses to be acquired. Given her well-documented neurobe-

havioral transition from subcortical to cortically mediated responding occurring in the 2- to 5-month age range (which she described as a period of confusion in which "the baby doesn't know whether he is supposed to be a reflexive creature or a learned organism"), Lipsitt reasoned that some infants, viable for the first 2 months, become especially vulnerable to SIDS if they fail to acquire sufficiently strong learned defensive behaviors needed to prevent occlusion after the waning of the life-preserving reflex.

Lipsitt supported his position with data from the National Institute of Child Health and Human Development: back-to-sleep directives that infants sleep on their backs to avoid smothering (*American Academy of Pediatrics*, 1992) led to a 50% decline in U.S. SIDS cases from 1992 to 2000. This has implied that the state of back-sleeping somehow leaves infants to fend more easily for themselves should they become confronted with a respiratory challenge (e.g., occlusion, threat of oxygen deprivation) and that this fending process is essentially behavioral. Further, he has recommended that, in addition to back-sleeping, parents should provide infants with: ample exercise in the prone position when awake that may generalize to maneuvers for keeping respiration clear from obstruction while asleep; and deliberate practice in resisting respiratory occlusion so that, during the period when the respiratory defense reflex wanes, they are more likely to engage in behaviors aimed at removing offending objects. Finally, he has also advocated for enhanced programs of developmental research with longitudinal designs that assess interacting conditions (e.g., maturation, learned behavior, environmental hazards) rather than single antecedents of SIDS.

This work on SIDS (Lipsitt, 2003) as a biobehavioral phenomenon has direct applicability to the study of resilience. For example, the approach assumes that the behavioral seeds of resilience inhere in the predisposing capabilities of the newborn infant. Viable human babies have reflexes, in some more intense than in others, and these approach and avoidance behaviors are of life-saving merit. The congenital reflexes of the newborn are "coaxed" by environmental stimuli concordantly with the growth of neuromyelin tissue and dendrite proliferation. *Resilient infants* are those in whom the migration to cortically mediated learned behavior, from subcortical reflexes, is successful. Nonresilient infants who succumb to SIDS during the critical 2- to 5-month period are those in whom the transition has been incomplete or unsuccessful. These nonresilient infants are not capable of learned psychomotor strategies which, in resilient infants, can save the child's life from respiratory occlusion.

This resilience, which is put to the test in the first few months of life, is assumed to continue over the course of the life span whereby infant experience influences child development and, in due course, adult outcomes. Over the course of ontogenesis, *behavioral misadventures* (Lipsitt, 1989), defined as any or all injuries that are not the result of illness such as accidents, suicide, drug and alcohol consumption, risky sexual behavior, and possibly SIDS, result from individuals learning destructive ways of getting their needs met through failures of the brain hedonic system that lead to failures in learning.

Lipsitt (1988) has speculated that such failures of the hedonic system that lead to failures in learning have their early origins when a baby: (1) lacks the hedonic mediating mechanisms which inform and reinforce appropriate behavior, (2) has not been presented with challenges or perturbations from the reduction of which learning could occur, or (3) does not have in its response repertoire the appropriate motor behaviors to enable the variety of actions from which some will be rewarded more than others. In all events, there is a failure of the hedonic system to be effectively paired with patterns of behavior that reduce stress and enhance reward (p. 178).

Thus, the theory posits that behavioral misadventures later in life result from a deficit in learning about how to protect oneself from harm. This learning involves a complex interchange between neurobehavioral predispositions and environmental feedback beginning in infancy. In neurotypical and psychologically "usual" development, the child becomes more reliant on learned behaviors than on reflexes (cf. Lipsitt's theory about the final pathway to SIDS that involves the neu-

robehavioral transition from subcortical to cortically mediated responding, or from reflexes to learned behaviors, in the 2- to 5-month-old period when human infants are most vulnerable).

Later behavioral misadventures often occur during other stressful transitions, for example, in adolescence, following stressful life events and periods of adaptation to trauma. As Lipsitt (1989) has summarized:

> Accidents, adolescent suicide, excessive drinking, and chemical abuse are due, often, to self-deprecatory non-caring patterns of behavior that were acquired in the context of adverse environmental conditions. Both social and antisocial behavior are learned, and are embellishments of self-protective approach and avoidance responses. The socialization and disciplining of children are mostly matters of training such self-protective responses as the search for pleasure under conditions of restraint and caring – and all of it begins at birth. (p. 214)

In essence, individuals are all born with natural defenses against harm and it is through exchange processes with the environment (e.g., infant and child attachment) that they learn how to self-regulate and to develop coping strategies, which keep themselves protected. In terms of the problem at hand, resilient individuals who avoid behavioral misadventures are those who are born with greater elicitability and strength of natural defenses that lead to better self-regulation and coping strategies under stress. It is interesting to note that this is consistent with some resilience research (e.g., Leipold & Greve, 2009) that has viewed resilience as a conceptual bridge between coping and development.

Holistic/Systems-Developmental Theory, Life Transitions, and Resilience

Holistic/systems-developmental theory (HSDT) is an elaboration and extension of Heinz Werner's (1957) organismic-developmental theory. The original theory and its elaborations are *organismic/holistic* insofar as psychological part-processes (cognition, affect, valuation, action) are considered in relation to the total context of human activity and *developmental* in that they employ a systematic principle describing developmental progression and regression so that living systems may be compared with respect to their formal organizational features.

Applied most extensively to the analysis of developmental life transitions (e.g., Demick, 2003), the elaborated approach is:

(a) *Holistic* with respect to the unit of analysis, *the person-in-environment system,* which is assumed to be an integrated system whose parts may be considered in relation to the functioning whole.

(b) *Systems oriented,* acknowledging that the person-in-environment system includes three aspects of the person – *biological, intrapersonal,* and *sociocultural* – and three analogous aspects of the environment – *physical, inter-organismic,* and *sociocultural.*

(c) *Developmental,* assuming that progression and regression may be assessed against the ideal of development embodied in the *orthogenetic principle* with its assumption of developmental change from dedifferentiated to hierarchically integrated person-in-environment functioning toward flexibility, self-mastery, and freedom. Development, according to this mode of analysis, is seen as progression in ontogenesis in several domains, for example, microgenesis, pathogenesis, and ethnogenesis.

Corollary assumptions include: (a) *transactionalism:* the person, the environment, and their respective aspects mutually define, and cannot be considered independent of, one another; (b) *multiple modes of analysis* including structural or part-whole analysis and dynamic or means-ends analysis; and (c) *constructivism:* the person-in-environment system actively constructs his or her experience of the context in which the person is behaving. The interested reader is referred to Demick (2002) for a more complete discussion of these and other of the theory's assumptions.

How do these assumptions help us conceptualize resilience science? First, against the backdrop of the holistic/systems assumptions, the approach advocates that a complete understanding of the factors involved in resilience must include consideration of a wider range of variables and their interrelations than has typically been the case. For example, risk and protective factors may reside in the physical (e.g., age, sex, race), intrapersonal (e.g., intelligence, personality, values) and sociocultural (e.g., socioeconomic status, religion, roles) aspects of the person and the physical (e.g., physical locations such as home), inter-organismic (e.g., people, pets), and sociocultural (e.g., community, sociohistorical context) aspects of the environment.

Although some more recent resilience research has notably moved from being empirically driven to more theoretically based with the conceptual recognition of the importance of multiple contexts in individuals' development, such work has often failed to consider the range of variables and/or processes relevant to the particular condition of adversity under study. For example, Garcia Coll et al.'s (1996) integrative model for studying minority youth has posited eight major constructs relating to the development of minority children, namely, *social position variables, racism, segregation, promoting/inhibiting environments, adaptive culture, child characteristics, family values,* and *developmental competencies.* While these constructs are salient in and often unique to the lives of minority youth, one might wonder – from the lens of HSDT – whether certain other relevant variables and/or processes have been overlooked (e.g., children's and family members' physical health, intelligence, motivations, and roles; marital/family quality and stability; legal concerns; media influences). Further, consistent with Ungar's (2004, 2011) social ecological model of resilience that argues that social ecological practices such as family context, community services, and cultural practices are also essential components contributing to resilience, HSDT emphasizes consideration of the person-in-environment system as the appropriate unit of analysis and has social ecological processes inherently built into each and every psychological analysis.

Second, while resilience researchers have more recently also advocated for the assessment of the interactions of resilience processes across levels of organization (cf. Masten, 2007), relatively few have delineated the formal organizational features of systems to characterize these various interrelationships (e.g., as an exception, see Luthar, 1993, for discussion of the differences among *protective, protective-stabilizing, protective-enhancing,* and *protective but reactive processes*). HSDT in contrast has posited several frameworks for capturing these interrelationships. First, based on Wapner's (1969) analysis of the relations among cognitive processes and Demick and Wapner's (1990) analysis of the relationship between individuals and societies, the relationships between adversity and adaptation may be conceptualized as *supportive* (e.g., youth living in the inner city and peer acceptance), *antagonistic* (e.g., youth living in the inner city and school achievement), or *substitutive/vicarious* (e.g., youth living in the inner city substituting the good of society for their own desires).

Second, Wapner and Demick's (1998) application of the orthogenetic principle to self-world relationships, characterized by different modes of coping, might also be applied to developmental outcomes in resilience research, namely, *dedifferentiated person-in-environment system state* characterized by accommodation, *differentiated and isolated person-in-environment system state* characterized by disengagement, *differentiated and in conflict person-in-environment system state* characterized by nonconstructive ventilation (e.g., expression of extreme anger only), and *differentiated and integrated person-in-environment system state* characterized by constructive assertion. Use of such category systems may help to lead resilience research toward both overarching developmental conceptualization and much needed parsimony.

Third, the HTSD approach also has heuristic potential for the conduct of research on resilience. For example, Donalds and Demick (2011) are currently conducting an experiment aimed at delineating an HTSD conceptualization of the nature of resilience. We are attempting to demonstrate the credibility of a concept of resilience as consisting of the psychological traits of flexibility (e.g., mobility of cognitive style) and strength (e.g., hardiness) mediated by the use of controlled (vs. automatic) empathy. Using these measures, preliminary analyses provide support for the generalization that, respectively, resilience and nonresilience encompass higher and lesser amounts of both cognitive and emotional differentiation/

integration. Such research makes inroads into identifying more general processes inherent in the construct of resilience and puts us in tune with recent attempts (e.g., Bonanno, Papa, Lalande, Westphal, & Coifman, 2004; Westphal, Seivert, & Bonanno, 2010) to identify flexibility as one such process.

Commonalities Across Our Approaches: Directions for Resilience Theory and Measurement

Although the two approaches we have put forth here differ in fundamental ways, they share on the most general level (a) the theoretical assumption that resilience may be seen as constitutional traits of individuals' development as they flexibly negotiate changing situational demands; and (b) the methodological assumption that the concept of resilience may best be assessed proactively through experimental methods. The first assumption is illustrated in Lipsitt's view that the behavioral seeds of resilience inhere in the predisposing capabilities of the newborn infant and in Demick's view that an individual's resilience (or lack thereof) is related to a biologically based cognitive style as reflected in greater (or lesser) cognitive and emotional differentiation/integration.

Although we both see resilience as a constitutional characteristic residing with the person, we also believe that persons are constantly faced with the necessity of flexibly negotiating situational demands with cross-situational consistency across the life span. This can be seen in Lipsitt's view of a variety of developmental transitions faced by the infant, child, and adolescent and involving the integration of biological, behavioral, and environmental processes, which may or may not lead to behavioral misadventures. This notion, sometimes referred to as *reciprocal determinism,* implies that sets of factors – those relating to the person and to the environment – mutually influence one another. This may also be seen in both Lipsitt's and Demick's underlying transactional worldview whereby aspects of persons and aspects of environments cannot be considered independent of one another. Thus, both approaches advocate that there is not only room for, but a pervasive need to, consider and integrate systematically both person variables (e.g., traits) and more general dynamic processes within resilience research.

The second assumption concerning methodology is demonstrated by our joint belief that a fundamental relatively unexplored strategy in resilience science involves the delineation of causal explanations to understand better the relationships between adversity and adaptation and that these explanations may be best obtained through controlled laboratory investigations. Agreeing with the criticism that it is often difficult to determine in any given study whether all participants viewed as resilient experienced comparable levels of adversity, we propose that the use of the experimental method not only has the potential to inform us about cause-effect relationships underlying resilience but also to eliminate the potentially confounding variable of uncertainty in risk measurement.

Lipsitt has specifically called for an enhanced program of governmentally sponsored research on the reflexive behavior of infants in the early months of life with special focus on the transitional stage marked by the 2- to 5-month critical period associated with SIDS. As he has written, "Studies of learned reactions in the first 6 months of life, the neuromuscular maturation of the infant, and environmental hazards that may contribute to inadequate responsiveness by the baby must be carried out using research designs that acknowledge interacting conditions rather than single antecedents as causing the tragic deaths of 1,000 of infants" (Lipsitt, 2003, p. 170). Such a prospective study has the potential more specifically to resolve the mystery behind crib death since there is no posited approach other than Lipsitt's biobehavioral theory that accounts for why infants up to about 2 months of age are "immune" and after 5 months are "home free."

In his work on life transitions, Demick has been concerned with the transition into and out of the college setting, described by some (e.g., Steinberg, 2011) as paralleling the transition from elementary to secondary school with similar if not greater amounts of stress. Thus, laboratory studies over the course of students' college careers (e.g., manipulating frustration as in Orne's, 1959 classic work on demand characteristics of experiments) have the potential to shed light on the processes underlying resilience across the college experience with a heightened focus on two potentially difficult transition points within a relatively short period of time. In these ways, prospective studies that assess the antecedents of resilience will complement and elucidate prior retrospective studies through the use of laboratory studies with both relatively short-term and long-term longitudinal designs.

There are also other ways in which our two approaches share commonalities. First, we are advocates of holistic research espousing relationships among biological, psychological, and environmental or sociocultural processes. Second, we both honor the active nature of the individual as exemplified by Lipsitt's learning approach whereby the infant acquires strong defensive behaviors and Demick's HSDT whereby the person-in-environment system actively constructs or construes his or her experiences. Third, we collaboratively view development as involving organizational changes over time toward a more efficient end state, for example, toward optimal livelihood with minimal behavioral misadventures (Lipsitt) and toward freedom, self-mastery, and flexibility as required by the individual's goals, capabilities, and disparate environmental demands (Demick). Fourth, we both acknowledge central processes inherent in human functioning (e.g., Lipsitt with transitions, learning, and coping and Demick with transitions, cognitive/emotional flexibility, and coping). Fifth, we share the belief about the importance of praxis derived from all research, even from basic research, that moves individuals to optimal states of functioning (see Lipsitt on behavioral interventions to decrease SIDS and Demick on ways to foster person-environment congruence during life transitions). Sixth, as we hope to have demonstrated here, we believe strongly that our respective approaches and their commonalities have viable implications for the study of resilience and its development.

In sum, comparison of our approaches has suggested that future studies on resilience would benefit first from the elaboration of developmental theories, which integrate the trait and process foci of previous research with an eye toward delineating central processes in resilience that cut across persons and the broadly defined contexts that they inhabit. Not only does this recommendation align us with the central theme of this volume, namely, the social ecology of resilience, that represents the full complexity of the everyday life situation but it also proposes a theoretical conceptualization of resilience that advances the construct of "positive adjustment." Further, future studies on resilience would be strengthened through heightened laboratory investigations on antecedent-consequent relations between prior adversities and later recovery or adaptation as mediated by various coping strategies and fortuitous events. In these ways, resilience research – which to date has explored such diverse areas as psychopathology, families, violence, poverty, optimism, and rational cognition – may ultimately illustrate the ways in which the theory and methodology from one subfield of psychology may advance the theory and methodology of another. Consistency among our theories and methods will help lead us to a more unified discipline of psychological science.

Acknowledgements An ongoing Study Group on "Development, Adversity, and Resilience" and the work described herein were supported by the Brown University Wayland Collegium Fund for the 2009–2010 academic year. We wish to thank the Wayland Collegium as well as our dedicated colleagues who attended the Study Group meetings.

References

Amato, P. R. (2001). Children of divorce in the 1990s: An update of the Amato and Keith (1991) meta-analysis. *Journal of Family Psychology, 15*(3), 355–370.

Bonanno, G. A., Papa, A., Lalande, K., Westphal, M., & Coifman, K. (2004). The importance of being flexible: The ability to both enhance and suppress emotional expression predicts long-term adjustment. *Psychological Science, 15*(7), 482–487.

Braverman, M. T. (2001). *Applying resilience theory to the prevention of adolescent substance abuse. 4-H Center for Youth Development Focus* (pp. 1–11). Davis: University of California Davis.

Brooks, R., & Goldstein, S. (2007). *Raising a self-disciplined child: Helping your child become more responsible, confident, and resilient.* New York: McGraw Hill.

Cefai, C. (2008). *Promoting resilience in the classroom: A guide to developing pupils' emotional and cognitive skills.* London: Jessica Kingsley Publishers.

Cicchetti, D., & Curtis, W. J. (2006). The developing brain and neural plasticity: Implications for normality, psychopathology, and resilience. In D. Cicchetti & D. J. Cohen (Eds.), *Developmental psychopathology: Vol. 2. Developmental neuroscience* (2nd ed., p. 64). Hoboken: Wiley.

Cicchetti, D., & Garmezy, N. (Eds.). (1993). Milestones in the development of resilience [Special issue]. *Development and Psychopathology, 5*(4), 497–774.

Davies, P. T., & Cummings, E. M. (2006). Interpersonal discord, family process, and developmental psychopathology. In D. Cicchetti & D. J. Cohen (Eds.), *Developmental psychopathology: Vol. 3. Risk, disorder, and adaptation* (pp. 86–128). Hoboken: Wiley.

Demick, J. (2002). Stages of parental development. In M. Bornstein (Ed.), *Handbook of parenting: Vol. 3. Being and becoming a parent* (2nd ed., pp. 389–413). Mahwah: Lawrence Erlbaum Associates.

Demick, J. (2003). Holistic, developmental, systems-oriented approach. In J. R. Miller, R. M. Lerner, L. B. Schaimberg, & P. M. Anderson (Eds.), *The encyclopedia of human ecology* (Vol. 1, pp. 363–365). Denver: ABC-CLIO.

Demick, J., & Rodriguez, C. (2011). *Laypersons' conceptions of resilience.* Manuscript in preparation. Brown University, Providence, RI.

Demick, J., & Wapner, S. (1990). Role of psychological science in promoting environmental quality. *American Psychologist, 45*(5), 631–632.

Diehl, M., & Hay, E. L. (2010). Risk and resilience factors in coping with daily stress in adulthood: The role of age, self-concept incoherence, and personal control. *Developmental Psychology, 46*(5), 1132–1146.

Donalds, R., & Demick, J. (2011). *Cognitive style, hardiness, and controlled empathy as determinants of resilience.* Manuscript in preparation. Brown University, Providence, RI.

Elder, G. H. (1974). *Children of the great depression: Social change in life experience.* Chicago: University of Chicago Press.

Eschleman, K. J., Bowling, N. A., & Alarcon, G. M. (2010). A meta-analytic examination of hardiness. *International Journal of Stress Management, 17*(4), 277–307.

Garcia Coll, C., Lamberty, G., Jenkins, R., McAdoo, H. P., Crnic, K., Wasik, B. H., et al. (1996). An integrative model for the study of developmental competencies in minority children. *Child Development, 67,* 1891–1914.

Garcia Coll, C., & Marks, A. K. (2009). *Immigrant stories: Ethnicity and academics in middle childhood.* New York: Oxford University Press.

Garmezy, N. (1973). Competence and adaptation in adult schizophrenic patients and children at risk. In S. R. Dean (Ed.), *Schizophrenia: The first ten Dean Award Lectures* (pp. 163–204). New York: MSS Information Corp.

Hou, W. K., Law, C. C., Yin, J., & Fu, Y. T. (2010). Resource loss, resource gain, and psychological resilience and dysfunction following cancer diagnosis: A growth mixture modeling approach. *Health Psychology, 29*(5), 484–495.

Leipold, B., & Greve, W. (2009). Resilience: A conceptual bridge between coping and development. *European Psychologist, 14*(1), 40–50.

Lipsitt, L. P. (1988). Stress in infancy: Toward understanding the origins of coping behavior. In N. Garmezy & M. Rutter (Eds.), *Stress, coping, and development in children* (pp. 161–190). New York: McGraw-Hill.

Lipsitt, L. P. (1989). Development of self-regulatory behavior in infancy: Towards understanding the origins of behavioral misadventures. In S. Doxiadis (Ed.), *Early influences shaping the individual* (pp. 207–215). New York: Plenum Press.

Lipsitt, L. P. (2003). Crib death: A biobehavioral phenomenon? *Current Directions in Psychological Science, 12*(5), 164–170.

Lipsitt, L. P., & Demick, J. (2011). Resilience Science comes of age: Old age that is. *PsycCRITIQUES, 36*(26), DOI: 10.1037/a0023900.

Luthar, S. S. (1993). Annotation: Methodological and conceptual issues in the study of resilience. *Journal of Child Psychology and Psychiatry, 34*, 441–453.

Luthar, S. S. (2006). Resilience in development: A synthesis of research across five decades. In D. Cicchetti & D. J. Cohen (Eds.), *Developmental psychopathology: Vol. 3. Risk, disorder, and adaptation* (pp. 86–128). Hoboken: Wiley.

Luthar, S. S., Cicchetti, D., & Becker, B. (2000). The construct of resilience: A critical evaluation and guidelines for future work. *Child Development, 71*(3), 543–562.

Masten, A. S. (1994). Resilience in individual development: Successful adaptation despite risk and adversity. In M. C. Wang & E. W. Gordon (Eds.), *Educational resilience in inner-city America: Challenges and prospects* (pp. 3–25). Hillsdale: Lawrence Erlbaum Associates.

Masten, A. S. (1999). Resilience comes of age: Reflections on the past and outlook for the next generation of research. In M. D. Glantz, J. Johnson, & L. Huffman (Eds.), *Resilience and development: Positive life adaptations* (pp. 289–296). New York: Plenum Press.

Masten, A. S. (2001). Ordinary magic: Resilience processes in development. *American Psychologist, 56*(3), 227–238.

Masten, A. S. (2007). Resilience in developing systems: Progress and promise as the fourth wave rises. *Development and Psychopathology, 19*, 921–930.

McGraw, M. B. (1943). *The neuromuscular maturation of the human infant*. New York: Columbia University Press.

Orne, M. T. (1959). *The demand characteristics of an experimental design and their implications*. Paper presented at American Psychological Association annual meeting, Cincinnati.

Richardson, G. E. (2002). The metatheory of resilience and resiliency. *Journal of Clinical Psychology, 58*(3), 307–321.

Rutter, M. (1985). Resilience in the form of adversity: Protective factors and resistance to psychiatric disorders. *The British Journal of Psychiatry, 147*, 598–611.

Rutter, M. (2006). Implications of resilience concepts for scientific understanding. *Annals of the New York Academy of Science, 1094*, 1–12.

Seery, M. D., Holman, E. A., & Silver, R. C. (2010). Whatever does not kill us: Cumulative lifetime adversity, vulnerability, and resilience. *Journal of Personality and Social Psychology*, Advance online publication. doi: 10.1037/a0021344.

Seifer, R. (2011). *Is resilience the vestigial organ of the body of risk research? Lessons from young children with mentally ill parents*. Unpublished manuscript, Department of Psychiatry and Human Behavior, Warren L. Alpert School of Medicine at Brown University, Providence.

Steinberg, L. (2011). *Adolescence* (9th ed.). New York: McGraw-Hill.

Taylor, M., Hulette, A. C., & Dishion, T. J. (2010). Longitudinal outcomes of high-risk adolescents with imaginary companions. *Developmental Psychology, 46*(6), 1632–1636.

Ungar, M. (2004). A constructionist discourse on resilience: Multiple contexts, multiple realities among at-risk children and youth. *Youth and Society, 35*(3), 341–365.

Ungar, M. (2011). Social ecologies and their contribution to resilience. In M. Ungar (Ed.), *The social ecology of resilience*. New York: Springer.

Wapner, S. (1969). Organismic-developmental theory: Some applications to cognition. In J. Langer, P. Mussen, & N. Covington (Eds.), *Trends and issues in developmental theory* (pp. 35–67). New York: Holt, Rinehart and Winston.

Wapner, S., & Demick, J. (1998). Developmental analysis: A holistic, developmental, systems – oriented perspective. In W. Damon (Series Ed.) & R. M. Lerner (Vol. Ed.), *Handbook of child psychology: Vol. 1. Theoretical models of human development* (5th ed., pp. 761–805). New York: Wiley.

Weissberg, R. P., Kumpfer, K. L., & Seligman, M. E. P. (2003). Prevention that works for children and youth: An introduction. *American Psychologist, 58*, 425–432.

Werner, H. (1957). *Comparative psychology of mental development*. New York: International Universities Press.

Werner, E. E. (1971). *The children of Kauai: A longitudinal study from the prenatal period to age 10*. Honolulu: University of Hawaii.

Westphal, M., Seivert, N. H., & Bonanno, G. A. (2010). Expressive flexibility. *Emotion, 10*(1), 92–100.

Wright, M. O., & Masten, A. S. (2006). Resilience processes in development. In S. Goldstein & R. B. Brooks (Eds.), *Handbook of resilience in children* (pp. 17–38). New York: Springer.

Resilience and Children's Work in Brazil: Lessons from Physics for Psychology

5

Piotr Trzesniak, Renata M. C. Libório, and Silvia H. Koller

In this chapter, we explore the contribution physics can make to our understanding of resilience, showing how the concept can be understood and the need to pay careful attention to the context in which it is found. To examine the application of this understanding of resilience, we will discuss the case of child and adolescent labor in Brazil. Controversially, we show that child labor is not always a sign of significant adversity for all working children, but instead, in specific contexts, may be a contributor to children's capacity to function normally. A clearer defintion of resilience, building on principles from physics, makes it much clearer how this can be the case.

Science, in its broadest sense, is our way of understanding the universe, both human and natural. These words have been chosen carefully: science is indeed not what the universe *is*, it is just our way to make its behavior meaningful to us. The human mind seeks for order, logical structure, and causal patterns which will allow us to anticipate and control the future. Resilience, as a scientific concept, is one of the pieces involved in this task. Our first concern will be to try to establish at which level of the scientific description of the "real world" *resilience* best fits.

There are two general aspects of science that we must keep in mind to complete this first proposed task. The first one is that our scientific discourse is predominantly *verbal*: it relies on verbalized *concepts*. In a mature area of knowledge, concepts are well established, clear, rigorous, and shared by the whole research community. This kind of precise and objective communication is actually an *essential* ingredient for discussion, knowledge building, and exchange and comparison of research results. On the other hand, a confused and controversial conceptual framework, in which each researcher understands the same words in a different way, *hinders* scientific progress. Arguably, the concept of resilience lacks precision, with multiple verbalizations available.

The second general characteristic is that no *concept* (verbalization of some aspects of a phenomenon) *is* reality. It is just the *most convenient way to describe* something, where *most convenient* means the most simple, transparent, and logical way which will allow us to control the phenomenon toward the desired result, within a previously established approximation. Therefore, the question to be answered is not *what resilience is*, but *what is the most convenient way to look at it*.

As a building piece in the description of the universe, resilience has to attend to both requirements. The first step toward this goal is identifying the *level of description* in which it best fits.

P. Trzesniak (✉)
Department of Physics and Chemistry, Institute of Sciences, Federal University of Itajubá, Itajubá, Minas Gerais, Brazil
e-mail: piotreze@gmail.com

M. Ungar (ed.), *The Social Ecology of Resilience: A Handbook of Theory and Practice*,
DOI 10.1007/978-1-4614-0586-3_5, © Springer Science+Business Media, LLC 2012

Four Hierarchical Levels to Describe the Universe

The understanding of the universe involves four hierarchical levels. The first, and closest to "real life" is the *phenomenological* level. A phenomenon is any interesting temporal evolution of the universe – anything that happens and that elicits someone's interest. *Frequency of occurrence* and *importance to well-being* are criteria we might use to assess why a particular phenomenon becomes worthy of our attention.

Strictly speaking, the phenomenological level is not a description, but rather *reality as perceived by human senses*: phenomenon is what a person sees, hears, smells; it is the (interesting) temporal evolution of the universe in its full complexity. Therefore, a phenomenon is actually a collection of nonverbal neurophysiological interpretations of impressions, something that is impossible to accurately express in words: no verbal description can be a complete representation of the reality it is supposed to depict. However, if a person puts the neurophysiological interpretations in words in a fairly complete way, this may be regarded as a description at the phenomenological level, and will be the first step from the "real" universe to the "abstract" (i.e., built on verbal concepts) science.

The next step toward abstraction is the *process* level. A process is also a description of an interesting temporal evolution of the universe, but intentionally leaving out what is (considered) irrelevant and keeping only what is (considered) important. It is at this point that concepts start to be proposed, because a specialized and agreed-upon terminology starts to be necessary to accurately describe the observed behavior of the phenomenon.

After multiple observations of the corresponding process, the description of a phenomenon eventually reaches the level of *mechanism*. Well-established *concepts* and *relationships* among them (*scientific models*) will then allow science to make predictions about the future behavior of the universe. The investigation of the mechanism associated with a phenomenon starts with "What will happen if I do that?" *open* questions and ends with "If I do that, then…" *definite* answers.

A careful reading of the history of the concept of resilience illustrates this evolution from phenomenological interpretations of children's lives, which turned out much better than expected, to the identification of generic processes observed across populations at risk, and finally models that explain positive development under stress (Ungar, 2011).

Eventually, some of the concepts that appear at the mechanism level may show qualitative or quantitative variation. These will be the *parameters* and the *variables* of the phenomenon, and only they can be measured. So, one has to reach the mechanism level *and* have a clear conceptual framework to be able to speak about measurement; *it does not make sense to speak about measuring phenomena, processes, or mechanisms*.

In which of these four levels should we locate resilience to get the most of its descriptive power? Our proposal here is that the idea of resilience is most useful if regarded as a constructive piece at the *phenomenon/process* level.

Looking at Resilience

An immediate consequence of this view is that *resilience cannot be directly measured*, since only variables and parameters can be subject to that form of inquiry. However, due to the hereditariness existing among the descriptions levels, variables and parameters actually contain *partial* information of the more general process. Thus, it has become *natural* to speak about *measuring resilience* when only some specific variables related to the resilience process are being measured. Even if one could measure *all* variables related to the resilience process, one is still not measuring resilience, but just the *set of variables* associated with the process.

To advance the idea of resilience further, we will need to borrow the concept of *system* from the natural sciences. In the sense that it is used in that domain, a system is the most convenient *entity*, the part of the universe one is interested in when performing a study. It can be a *person*, a *group of persons* (family, school peers, racial minority, etc.), or an *object*. However, it is a requirement of the concept that it must be always *absolutely clear* whether *any* part of the universe does or does not belong to the system.

Besides the system, everything else in the universe is called the *environment*. A system that interacts with its environment is called *open*; otherwise, it said to be *insulated*.[1] The combination of *environment* and *interactions* constitutes the *context* of the system.

Although, in principle, a statistical sample can be considered a single system, it is generally more fruitful to regard it as a set of systems of the same kind.

We can now state that, to understand resilience, we must start considering an *open system* that undergoes a *process* (but not just that). Conditions that may vary, but are eventually *fixed* under particular circumstances, are the *parameters* of the process. Other measurable descriptive aspects that *actually vary* during the process are *variables*. Whether they describe the *system*, the *environment*, or some feature of the *dynamics* of the process, parameters and variables receive the corresponding denomination *system variables*, *system parameters*, and so forth. Variables and parameters that describe (exclusively) system characteristics are sometimes called *traits*.

A Concept for Resilience

So, what is *the best way to look* at resilience (as opposed to defining resilience)? To answer this question, we have to go to a concept formulation technique, which requires (Dib, 1974):

- Identifying the *critical dimensions* of the concept of resilience.
- Discriminating the concept against others, which present almost all of its critical dimensions.

The full technique involves a third step, *generalization of the concept*, which means identifying it even when it is camouflaged due to the presence of one or more noncritical aspects (besides the critical ones). At its current stage of development, resilience has not yet reached the necessary maturity to be generalized in this sense.

Critical Dimensions and Some Light on Resilience from Physics

A concept establishes a class of ideas, objects, or entities fulfilling a certain unique set of conditions or attributions, which are called its *critical dimensions*. Any object presenting this set of attributes is an *instance* of the concept. There cannot be another concept presenting *exactly* the same set of attributes. The task we are proposing for this chapter is to identify the *critical dimensions*, the conditions *sine qua non*, that have to be present for a phenomenon-process to be identified as *resilience*.

Borrowing again from the field of physics, we can ask "How does *resilience* compare to other concepts close to it?" What are the critical dimensions that make resilience unique against, for instance, rigidity, elasticity, plasticity, flexibility, and hysteresis? All six involve responding to an external stress, but each one describes a different response. Careful examination of each of these physics terms can provide a deeper understanding of resilience and its specific application to psychology.

Essentially, all six apply to *materials* (like, wood, glass, iron, asphalt, …), but one has to consider *at least* a *body* (i.e., a limited amount of the material in question, with a more or less defined shape) to verify if the property exists or not. As we will see later, for some of the properties, verification involves bodies attending specific requirements. A *system*, as we defined earlier in this chapter, may be just a single body or a set of them. In the latter case, the bodies may be *constrained* among themselves, forming a *structure*.

Rigidity is the simplest of the six terms to understand: a rigid *system*, *body* or *material* simply will

---

[1] In Physics, the terminology *closed* is used for a system that can exchange energy, but not matter, with its environment; an *insulated* system cannot exchange either one. In the resilience context, what is mainly exchanged is *information*, which is closer to energy than to matter. Therefore, our preference for *insulated* instead of *closed*.

not change under any stress. It neither deforms nor bends, a behavior that, in psychology, may correspond to what has been described as *invulnerability* (Anthony, 1987). A body made with a rigid material will obviously be rigid, but a structure of rigid bodies may be rigid or not, depending on the nature of the constraints.

An *elastic material* will change its form under stress, but will return exactly to its previous condition when the stress is removed, and will not retain any memory of the episode. *Hysteresis* shares some critical dimensions with elasticity, but (1) the deformation pattern when the stress is gradually removed is different from when it is applied, and (2) the material may keep some nonimmediately apparent changes (a memory) from the stress after going back to its original state; for instance, there may be microstructural changes that only become apparent under specific testing.

This leaves us with *plasticity*, *flexibility*, and, of course, *resilience*. A body made of a *plastic material* will show a form change after stress. It may show some elasticity when the stress is removed, but it never recovers totally. *Flexibility*, in its turn, is the capacity to accept bending without breaking. It may be shown by elastic as well as by plastic materials, but requires a body with a length much larger than its transversal dimension, like a rod or a wire. Both plasticity and flexibility seem to be very similar to the idea of resilience. Why, then, is there the need for another concept?

The answer is that resilience accounts for a behavior that is not described by any of the other five properties. To be tested, resilience requires a system (a body, a structure, or a device) with an *expected behavior*, a *purpose* or *finality*; *it is not* just a process of deformation and recovery. Resilience considers *functioning* of the system: the system goes on functioning *as expected*, *within the boundaries of normality*. Elasticity, plasticity, or the shapes that the system takes on before and after stress are relatively unimportant; what actually matters is that the system goes on *functioning normally*. This is what attention to resilience helps us to observe.

Attending to purpose is everything. A process has a resilient ending if, even partially destructed by stress, the undergoing system is still able to fulfill its purpose. An informal illustration would be the killer robot in the first movie of the *Terminator* series (Cameron, Hurd, & Wisher, 1984): just a few of its parts remain together and barely working at the end, but it still goes on trying to accomplish its mission. That is resilience! One may even (very carefully) say that *the robot is resilient*. This does not mean, however, that the robot has something inside called resilience, but that it was built *strengthening certain internal characteristics* and *avoiding specific internal weaknesses* in a way that would make it keep working *normally*, *as expected*, or *intended*, even under significant stress and despite consequent damage.

Resilience in a Psychological Context

Borrowing from physics an understanding of the basic properties of materials and systems helps us to establish a fundamental critical dimension of the concept of resilience: *functionality*. The system has to remain capable of working in an acceptable (sometimes called *normal*) way, bound by the standards it was designed to meet. In human systems, this can be translated as *functioning in a socially and culturally acceptable way* or *in accordance with socially accepted rules*. This functionality within social processes is reflected in Ungar's (2011) definition of resilience:

> In the context of exposure to significant adversity, resilience is both the capacity of individuals to navigate their way to the psychological, social, cultural, and physical resources that sustain their well-being, and their capacity individually and collectively to negotiate for these resources to be provided in culturally meaningful ways. (p.10)

Our perception is that this definition supports our above proposition that a system fulfills its purpose when it functions normally under stress and, therefore, shows resilience. However, for the purpose of our discussion, we will re-state Ungar's definition in a shorter, but equivalent way: In the context of exposure to significant adversity, resilience is the capacity of individuals to function normally.

This shorter statement contains the critical dimensions of the concepts of resilience:

1. Context
2. Exposure to adversity
3. *Significant* adversity
4. The capacity
5. Of individuals
6. Functioning normally

The more compact phrasing leaves us with six elements. Although we listed these six elements in order of appearance in the statement, discussion will follow a more convenient way to clarify our view of the concept.

We start with *individuals*. Our belief is that the concept of resilience should be useful to more than just individuals. We may, for instance, apply it to *groups*, where *collective* ways of *functioning normally* do not correspond to just the sum of individual ways, but may exhibit totally unexpected qualitative attributes (like having life from a specific combination of atoms). Examples of such groups of individuals are family, ethnic groups, political parties, school peers, and so on, and all are *systems* in the way we previously defined. In principle, each can show resilience regarding their properties and behavior *as a group*, and, since an *individual* can also be looked at as a *system*, we suggest substituting the former with the latter.

Our second point of discussion is the phrase *the capacity*. Strictly speaking, although not being a trait, resilience is indeed *a* capacity of the system. But is it *the* capacity? Our view is that, under the *same conditions*, systems can undergo a resilient process due to *different sets* of internal skills, resources, and abilities, as well as due to *not presenting* some weaknesses. Posed this way, resilience may be *the* capacity if you focus *only on the result*. But more accurately, it is *a* capacity that *can be built in several distinct ways inside the system*. In other words, the capacity of resilience is not an entity; it is just a manifestation of other ones, more fundamental, which we will call *strengths and weaknesses*. We, therefore, propose to replace *the capacity* in the definition. It should instead read as *resilience is a nonunique combination of strengths and weaknesses of a system allowing it*… and so on.

There are *three* sources of time-dependent influences on a resilient process (or, alternatively, on the resilience mechanism): the *system*, the *environment and* the *interactions* between both. The term *context* introduces the latter two in the definition. *Exposure to adversity*, a necessary resilience condition, requires the context of the system to be unfriendly or even hostile. Some discussion can be raised here concerning who is deciding that a context is adverse. Is it an external judgment or is it the way the context is perceived (received?) by the system? In the latter case, the introduction of the word *perceived* would help. Whether we include the word raises the same question posed earlier: is it more convenient to look at resilience by considering an *internal* or an *external* evaluation of *adversity*? Our feeling is that the external view would orient research towards more social implications of psychology and to *populations* under adverse conditions (favoring intervention), while the internal view would apply more to *individual* instances (clinical psychology).

We have chosen to discuss the term *significant* separately from adversity because this adjective allows one to distinguish a resilient process from adaptation, adjustment, or other coping processes. Further conceptual refinement may lead to the conclusion that resilience is a particular case of the latter, and that they can be arranged in a clear, logical hierarchical structure, or that all (or part) of them have unique critical aspects, which would make these totally independent concepts. But this is not the problem here: we are looking for something unique concerning resilience, and this is undoubtedly the *significance* of the adversity. Why do certain processes (like resilience) raise research interest? *Due to their unexpectedness*! Under the observed circumstances of *significant* stress, the expectation was that *most* of the exposed systems would collapse, or *stop functioning normally*. The fact that some of them (including persons) went on *functioning normally*, the *exceptions*, raises questions about the possibilities of coping under such significant stress.

Systems in general and individuals in particular are constantly subjected to some kind of (harder or softer) stress. However, they are able to deal with it most of the time, without surpassing the limits of normality long enough to reach a pathologic state. Only some eventually surpass that limit. Therefore, the regular stresses of "daily living" do not qualify as conditions that help define a process or system as resilient. For an *adversity* to be *significant*, it is necessary that the *majority* of similar systems exposed to it *cease to function normally*.

With these points in mind, we can restate Ungar's definition of resilience as:

> In the context of exposure to (or perception of) significant adversity, resilience is a nonunique combination of strengths and weaknesses of a system that allows it to function normally.

The remaining sections of this chapter provide an illustration of our proposal-concept in practice, showing how a good concept helps to clarify the view of the phenomenon as well as how difficult it is to assess the variables, concepts, and constructs associated with resilience. We conducted an investigation regarding child and adolescent labor in a medium size Brazilian city. Contrary to expectations, our findings show that labor is not always a *significant adverse condition* for children, but may instead be a potential contributor to their *normal functioning* and well-being. These results suggest that *child and adolescent labor* is a poor quality variable, because its presence has antagonistic effects on the outcome of the process. The real variables to be taken into account are *the working conditions* children's experience, and their *perceptions* of their labor.

Child Labor as a Resilience Variable in the Brazilian Context

Child labor is a worldwide problem, and Brazil is not an exception. Between 1970 and 1980, due to the rate of population growth and to structural changes in the Brazilian economy, there was a significant expansion in child work in Brazil (i.e., work done at ages below those which the law permits). However, in the 15 years from 1992 to 2007, according to the 2007 National Survey by Domicile Sampling conducted by the Brazilian Institute of Geography and Statistics (IBGE, 2008), the percentage of working children aged 5–17 decreased from almost 20% to less than 11% – an impressive 45% reduction (see Fig. 5.1). Important factors contributing to this change were the passing of the Children and Adolescents Statute (1990) and the Program for Eradication of Child Labor (which has the acronym PETI in Portuguese), which was created in 1996 by the federal government. The figures can be further understood as a result of an increasing engagement in social causes during the 1990s, due to the action of local and national NGOs, which started (and maintained) discussion about the need for programs to fight poverty, to enhance children's quality of life, and to promote fundamental human rights.

Despite these changes, the IBGE (2008) report tells us that there are still 4.8 million working

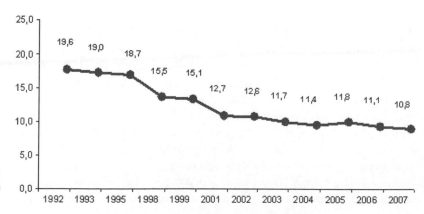

Fig. 5.1 Percentage of persons with age between 5 and 17 years occupied in the week of data collection (IBGE, 2008)

children in Brazil, a number well above tolerable limits. Specifically:

- Absolute numbers (in millions) by age is: 0.157 (5–9); 1.1 (10–13); 1.3 (14–15); 2.3 (16–17).
- The fraction working 40 or more hours-per-week by age is: 30.5% (5–17); 6.6% (5–13); 46.6% (16–17).
- The fraction working without a salary by age is: 60% (5–13); 39.1% (14–15); 21.3% (16–17).
- Most working children were male (65.7%) and Afro-descendents (59.5%).
- About one in five were living in homes in which the per capita income was less than 25% of the national minimum salary (approximately US$300 in 2007).
- Their most frequent occupations were agricultural and domestic activities.

This overall picture was confirmed by an investigation conducted in Presidente Prudente, a municipality (município) with a population of 207,000 in the far west of São Paulo State. Child labor still persists, with children and adolescents working on the street or doing household activities, at their own, or at another person's house. Their economic activities were reported as purposeful efforts, aiming to sustain themselves and their families financially, as well as to fulfill their personal consumption, aspirations, and needs (Liborio & Ungar, 2010). Despite the potential for limited benefits, child labor is viewed as a violation of children's rights that exposes them to conditions that can harm their physical, social, and psychological development. International organizations (International Labour Organization and UNICEF) and various authors (Alberto, 2004, 2005; Campos & Francischini, 2003; Cosendey, 2002; Moreira & Stengel, 2003; Silva, Junior, & Antunes, 2002) regard it as a risk factor for the development of children and adolescents, and continue to seek its eradication.

However, in Brazil, as well as internationally, there are researchers that question the interpretation of child labor as an *absolute* risk to human development (Alves-Mazzotti, 1998; Alves-Mazzotti & Migliari, 2004; Dauster, 1992, in Moraes, 2007; Liborio & Ungar, 2010; Liebel,

2003, 2007; Martinez, 2001; Sarmento, 2005; Woodhead, 1999, 2004). They argue that much of the research on child labor has disregarded cultural characteristics and subjectivity aspects of the working children themselves, attributing to child labor the status of a homogeneous variable when in fact, children's experiences of labor are complex and heterogeneous. Controversially, research suggests that under some circumstances, children and adolescents may derive benefits from their work, even when involved in higher risk forms of labor, like working in the street (Grover, 2004; Invernizzi, 2003), sexual exploitation (Montgomery, 1998; Rubenson, VanAnh, Hojer, & Johanson, 2004; Taylor, 2005), and armed conflict (Baldwin, 2006; Betancourt, 2008; Blattman & Annan, 2007; Cortes & Buchanan, 2007).

These controversies tell us that *child labor* is not a good variable for study since it is ambiguous concerning its effects on the child (the system). To see that, we just have to ask: *What can we conclude about the development of a child from the information that she/he works regularly?* Strictly speaking, we cannot conclude anything, because the answer seems to be *it depends on the circumstances, on the local culture, and on the subjective perception of the child.* Therefore, it is necessary to abandon child labor as a variable *per se*, and either qualify it, adding adjectives like *deleterious* or *healthy*, or substituting for it with other variables that are more descriptive of the circumstances, culture, and the children's own perceptions of their work, as well as an assessment of whose values will establish clearly and unambiguously the benefit or the harm of labor to children's development.

The poor quality of child labor as a variable to study risk and resilience can be illustrated by another finding of the 2007 National Survey (IBGE, 2008). Although school attendance among the whole population between 5 and 15 years of age was 94% and increasing, it was approximately 80% and *decreasing* among child laborers. At first glance, it seems obvious that child labor is a risk factor to children's psychosocial development. However, the actual harm to development is their *not attending school.*

As children's pattern of work clearly threatens school engagement, what is the difference?

The way the argument is developed is very important. If our system of interest (as we defined it earlier) is the *whole population*, we might say that if school attendance among nonworkers is about 94%, and falls to 80% among working children, *there is* about 14% less development among the latter group. We might, therefore, conclude that child labor is a *group* risk factor. But it *is not* an *individual* one. This is because it does not apply if our system is *a single person*. No *individual* working child or adolescent will have a 14% lower development than her/his nonworking counterpart. This figure is an average effect. *Those who are not attending school will experience a 100% effect on their individual systems*, while *those attending will experience a 0% effect* on their development. Fully 80% of all working children may, as individuals, derive positive benefits from their employment when we analyze their experience independent of the overall population of all children (regardless of their disadvantage and exposure to adversity).

Research Goals and Characterization of the Participants

With this distinction in mind, we now turn to our own research. Our investigation had as its goal to explore the characteristics of children and adolescents in any kind of working activity (domestic or nondomestic) and to understand the meaning they attribute to their occupation. Seven hundred and two children ranging in age from 9 to 14 years old, living in neighborhoods with high social exclusion indices (Sposito et al., 2002) answered a 61-question survey of mostly multiple-choice questions. Initially, we randomly selected schools located in parts of the municipality presenting the highest rates of complaints to child protection services regarding child work. The first five municipality-maintained and the first five state-maintained schools that agreed to participate in the survey were visited by a researcher and classes randomly selected. Students of these classes who volunteered and signed the consent were then interviewed.

In a first general, descriptive quantitative analysis, 20% of the participants said they do some kind of work. Detailed examination of the answers of these 20% allowed us to select 16 children and adolescents for more detailed study. Eight were involved in domestic work, and another eight in nondomestic work.[2] All 16 were informal workers in the sense that they were working without any protection of law. In Brazil, youth under 14 years of age cannot legally work.

A semi-structured interview was conducted with each of the 16 participants, searching for subjective perceptions of their roles as workers, how they make sense of their roles, and if they identify work activities as a risk or as a protective factor. Interviews were recorded and transcribed, and were subsequently analyzed through the creation of meaningful categories and content analysis.

All 16 participants have parents. Only three of their mothers do not work outside the home. Among the fathers, one is retired and the others are either self-employed or factory or informal workers. Therefore, thirteen families have two providers and three have just one. All 16 participants were attending elementary school, except one of the domestic working group, who was in high school. Concerning *gender*, there were seven female participants in the domestic group and three in the nondomestic one. *Age distribution* was very similar in both groups, with two participants in the 9–11 and six in the 12–14 years range. With respect to *working conditions*, participants of the domestic group were working every day, at their own homes, and were exclusively responsible for all tasks; two reported that they were verbally or even physically punished if they did not accomplish all assigned activities.

---

[2] All these 16 children were directed to the PETI Program in Presidente Prudente at the beginning of 2008.

Of the nondomestic group, seven were working Monday to Friday and one only on weekends. Two were involved in potentially dangerous activities (electric services and packing coal). The others were selling products, dealing with cattle, and taking orders and/or cleaning in restaurants and supermarkets.

Study Results

Resilience researchers like Martineau (1999), Pesce, Assis, Santos, and Oliveira (2004), Ungar (2004), and Yunes and Szymanski (2001) point out that a person's interpretation of what harms (or does not harm) their development may differ and even be distinct from researchers' assumptions. To assess a condition as an absolute risk factor may actually be a mistake: it is necessary to take into account its evaluation by the individual. This implies that researchers may be unaware of the risk associated with a certain condition that is actually affecting individuals. The contrary is also possible: a condition (like children working) may be seen as a risk by researchers even though it does not negatively affect, or is even positive, to individuals. This is related to the *quality* of the involved condition as a *variable*: the less ambiguous or incomplete it is in terms of the information it is supposed to carry, the less *additional* information one needs to understand its meaning, and the higher its *quality*.

These considerations justify the choice of *positive and negative attributions* as an analytic category in our study. As a variable, child labor can represent a risk to certain children because they perceive that their lives are hindered in some way due to their work; others see the working condition as a positive dimension of their lives, because they feel useful, valued, and responsible, aspects that favor their self-esteem. Still others, however, may have positive and negative perceptions simultaneously (Woodhead, 2004). To better understand these patterns of attribution, our analysis separates the participants that work at home from those performing other kinds of activities.

Domestic Work: Positive and Negative Perceptions

Of the eight participants who were performing domestic work, four presented positive perceptions associated with their roles as housekeepers in their own homes. Specifically, they mentioned they were positively influenced by:

- Motivation, stimuli, and praise given by parents and grandparents.
- Satisfaction with being able to help their mother, who comes home tired after working elsewhere all day.
- Acknowledgment, by family and friends, of the importance of the work done.
- The importance given to "taking care of home" by others in the child's family and community.
- Expectation to be rewarded in the future.
- Feeling that their work has an important social function in the family, being useful and not replaceable.
- Development of responsibility and of a sense of solidarity among family members.

One of the participants mentioned more than once the satisfaction she felt "helping the neighbor." This behavior was also described by Jensen (2007), who observed that children and adolescents might feel great satisfaction due to the gratitude they receive in response to taking care of a family member who faces a limit on functioning (e.g., an elder who becomes physically ill). In the case of some participants, cultural valorization of the kind of work they do promotes positive feedback and an attribution that their work is important.

All these statements should not be confused with a romantic defense of, or support for, the inclusion of children and adolescents in domestic work. Our findings simply challenge the general belief that such activity represents *only* a risk to development: we are suggesting instead that it is mistake to affirm that child labor is *always* a risk to the development of children and adolescents, because this identification also depends on the *perception* of the working child (besides circumstantial and local cultural aspects, that must also be taken into account). It is, therefore, not possible to make an *a priori* assessment that child labor is harmful to *all* children and adolescents.

In support of this variability in perceptions, four interviewees reported some dissatisfaction with the domestic work they performed. The associated *negative* meanings were:

- Imposition of the work as an obligation by the family.
- Body pain and fatigue, which would be the reason for poor school performance.
- Punishment for not doing their work.
- Lack of recognition of the effort taken.
- Devaluation of the work, causing dissatisfaction.

Authors like Alves-Mazzotti (1998), Woodhead (2004), and Montgomery (1998) point out that one of the elements that most affect the quality of the attributions made to the meaning of work is the degree of valuation by family and the wider community. In this regard, children's experiences of their work are likely to be influenced by broader contextual and cultural factors. One of the female participants reported that family devaluation of the work done did interfere with both her identity and self-esteem. According to Woodhead (2004), this is a point that has to be taken into account when trying to understand whether child work represents a significant risk to healthy development.

Nondomestic Work: Positive and Negative Perceptions

An important theme that emerged in our study was the relationship between *work* and *dignity*, an idea that was implicitly present in the statements of some participants. Campos and Alverga (2001) warn that "even if it is exercised in an unworthy manner, work is seen as a supreme value, formation of the spirit, educator" (p.230). Various forms of work may bring with them educational and rehabilitation benefits. As they explain, "both families and other sectors of society add reasons of a subjective nature to economical justifications to stimulate and to encourage the early engagement of children into some productive activity" (p.228).

Positive meanings associated with work found in the statements of the interviewees were reflections of *subjective reasons* (they mostly decided for themselves that they wanted to work) and to *economic reasons* (to have money to buy things for themselves and, to a lesser extent, to directly help their families financially) associated with feelings of independence and autonomy. The engagement of any daughter or son in some kind of work also represented an *indirect* help to the family, due to the spending relief correspondent to this particular child. Working children and adolescents in this study saw this as a positive aspect of their work, which brings with it a sense of autonomy that they develop in their relationships with their parents. A similar finding is also present in the studies of Alves-Mazzotti (2002) in Brazil, Hugerland, Liebel, Lisecke, & Wihstutz (2007) in Germany, and Invernizzi and Tomé (2007) in Portugal.

Most respondents reported that, although working, they still had free time, which they used to perform a variety of activities. There was just one exception, a female interviewee who complained that the work left her tired, impairing her school attendance and academic achievement.

One remarkable finding was that, with the exception of the adolescent who was working in a coal factory, all others were working with their family members (parents, uncles, or brothers). Also, seven of the participants received payment for work done (at the time of the survey, their monthly payments were between 25 and 60 American dollars). Of these children, six reported that they were using the money to defray personal expenses (buying clothes, makeup, cell phones) and were also directly helping with family expenses. Three interviewees reported that they were being encouraged by family members to continue working.

With regard to negative aspects, interviewees reported that payment was irregular, occuring according to the will of parents or employers; two adolescents reported exposure to activities and locations that could harm them physically (such as handling poisons); and others were performing tasks dealing with tools (hoes and electrical equipment) and objects (recycleable garbage) that may pose risks to their health

(Forastieri, 1997). Nevertheles, despite having identified the physical risks present at work, they still reported valuing their work as something important and enriching for their self-esteem.

Invernizzi and Tomé (2007) say that children's relationships with their work activities have four dimensions: *economic*, *social* (sociability), *leisure*, and *identity* (personal identity and competence). In our research, we saw these dimensions clearly. We observed that many children go to work to earn money sometimes for the sustenance of the family, sometimes to buy what they want for themselves; we also found that some of them like work as a distraction from routine, while others reported benefits such as knowing more people, work as fun, or as an opportunity to experience playfulness unavailable at home. Finally, some participants mentioned the association between their work and self-esteem and autonomy.

Concluding Remarks

In this chapter, we presented a definition of resilience and some theoretical concepts borrowed from physics that help us to understand its application in psychology. The following points emerged from our discussion:

- Resilience is a concept at the phenomenon/process level that cannot be directly measured.
- Resilience, in psychology, should apply not just to individuals, but also to groups of humans; therefore, we prefer to say that it applies to *systems*.
- As a concept, resilience has six critical dimensions. It concerns (1) *systems* that, due to (2) *a nonunique set of internal resources*, are able to (3) *function normally*, although exposed to a (4) *context* of (5) *significant* (6) *stress*.
- Measurements related to the resilience process can be made specifying their characteristic through quantitative parameters and variables; the more complete and unambiguous the information these parameters and variables contain, the better is its quality.
- Qualitative date, complementarily, provides us with an understanding on the (un)ambiguity in how resilience, its context, and its variables are perceived.

- As the nature of the system of interest changes, it is almost certain that new variables and parameters will be needed to interpret resilience; rather then studying any of the latter specifically, it is more useful to establish *effects and properties* of the variables and parameters, describing them as *categories*. For example, classifying them as *risk factors*, *protection factors*, *vulnerabilities*, etc.

The empirical part of this chapter focused on child labor as a resilience variable, assessing its quality. Reflecting the principles of resilience named above, it was found that:

- Child labor *per se* is an ambiguous and even contradictory variable, requiring qualification to eventually become meaningful.
- The meaning child labor has in the lives of our research participants is undefined, since we found both positive and negative aspects, sometimes both occurring simultaneously. This implies that, for some participants, work is perceived as a risk factor, while for others it functions as a protection factor. For others, work is both a risk factor *and* a protective factor at the same time.
- The positive perceptions associated with work by most of our participants suggests that the conclusion that a carefully established and correctly administrated "dose of work" *can* favor the resilience process in a social ecology where that work receives social valorization, promotes the autonomy of the child, and strengthens the sense of solidarity and responsibility of the child towards family members (Liborio & Ungar, 2010).

Although there have been significant changes in recent years, Brazil is a country with a history of generating poverty contexts and social inequalities, including widespread expressions of structural violence that still characterize its society. Such conditions have a great potential to harm children and adolescents, especially if, due to the lack of efficacy of public policies, the latter cannot fulfill their consumption wishes and access the services necessary to their well-being. While we are not seeking to collude with those who promote conditions of social exclusion, we recognize that in circumstances with little access to other resources exists, doing some kind of work is the best option for some children and adolescents to enhance their self-esteem, their feelings of self-efficacy, their relationships with significant others, and their social valorization. In this regard, work becomes, in the absence of socially acceptable alternatives and social inclusion, a viable pathway to resilience. This interpretation of children's work results from a systemic understanding of resilience and from the nature of what is understood as *normal functioning under stress*.

References

Alberto, M. F. P. (Ed.). (2004). *Trabalho infanto-juvenil e direitos humanos*. João Pessoa: Editora Universitária.

Alberto, M. F. P. (2005). *O trabalho infantil doméstico em João Pessoa – Paraíba: um diagnóstico rápido à luz das piores formas de trabalho infantil*. João Pessoa: OIT.

Alves-Mazzotti, A. J. (1998). Trabalho infanto-juvenil: Representações de meninos trabalhadores, seus pais, professores e empregadores. In A. S. P. Moreira & D. C. Oliveira (Eds.), *Estudos interdisciplinares de representação social* (pp. 285–302). Goiânia: AB Editora.

Alves-Mazzotti, A. J. (2002). Repensando algumas questões sobre o trabalho infanto-juvenil. *Revista Brasileira de Educação (ANPED), 19*, 87–98.

Alves-Mazzotti, A. J., & Migliari, M. F. B. M. (2004). Representações sociais do trabalho infantil: Encontros e desencontros entre agentes educativos. *Revista de Educação Pública, 13*(23), 149–166.

Anthony, E. J. (1987). Children at high risk for psychosis growing up successfully. In E. J. Anthony & B. J. Cohler (Eds.), *The invulnerable child* (pp. 147–184). New York: Guilford.

Baldwin, H. (2006). *Fighting to survive in Rwanda: War, agency and victimhood*. Unpublished doctoral dissertation, Boston College, Boston, MA. Available (for purchase) at http://proquest.umi.com/pqdlink?Ver=1& Exp=08-05-2016&FMT=7&DID=1251850071&RQ T=309&attempt=1&cfc=1.

Betancourt, T. S. (2008). Child soldiers: Reintegration, pathways to recovery and reflections from the field. *Journal of Developmental & Behavioral Pediatrics, 29*(2), 138–141.

Blattman, C., & Annan, J. (2007). *The Consequences of Child Soldiering*. Retrieved Aug 1, 2011, 19:50 GMT, from http://www.hicn.org/papers/wp22.pdf.

Cameron, J., Hurd, G. A., & Wisher, W., Jr. (1984). *The terminator*. London: Hemdale Film Corporation & Los Angeles.

Campos, H. R., & Alverga, A. R. (2001). Trabalho infantil e ideologia: Contribuição ao estudo da crença indis-criminada na dignidade do trabalho. *Estudos de Psicologia, 6*(2), 227–233.

Campos, H. R., & Francischini, R. (2003). Trabalho infantil produtivo e desenvolvimento humano. *Psicologia em Estudo, 8*(1), 119–129.

Cosendey, E. M. V. M. (2002). O trabalho infanto-juvenil: Características e malefícios. In M. E. Marques, M. A. Neves, & A. C. Neto (Eds.), *Trabalho infantil: A infância roubada* (pp. 47–53). Belo Horizonte: Editora da PUC-Minas.

Cortes, L., & Buchanan, M. J. (2007). The experience of Columbian child soldiers from a resilience perspective. *International Journal for the Advancement of Counseling, 29*(1), 43–55.

Dauster, T. (1992). Uma infância de curta duração: trabalho e escola. *Cadernos de Pesquisa* (São Paulo), *82*, 31–36. Retrieved Aug 6, 2011, 20:30 GMT, from http://educa. fcc.org.br/pdf/cp/n82/n82a03.pdf.

Dib, C. Z. (1974). *Tecnologia da educação e sua aplicação ao ensino da física*. São Paulo: Pioneira.

Forastieri, V. (1997). *Children at work: Health and safety risks*. Geneva: International Labour Office.

Grover, S. (2004). Democratizing education: A theoretical case example of innovative pedagogy with street children. *Journal of Children and Poverty, 10*(2), 119–130.

Hugerland, B., Liebel, M., Lisecke, A., & Wihstutz, A. (2007). Paths to participatory autonomy: The meanings of work for children in Germany. *Childhood, 14*(2), 257–277.

IBGE. (2008). *Pesquisa Nacional por Amostra de Domicílios – 2007*. Retrieved Aug 1, 2011, 19:48 GMT, from http:// www.ibge.gov.br/home/presidencia/noticias/noticia_ visualiza.php?id_noticia=1230&id_pagina=1.

Invernizzi, A. (2003). Street working children and adolescents in Lima: Work as an agent of socialization. *Childhood, 10*(3), 319–341.

Invernizzi, A., & Tomé, S. (2007). O trabalho dos adolescentes no Algarve: Um estudo sobre as suas motivações, organização familiar e práticas de socialização. *Análise Social, 42*(184), 875–898.

Jensen, K. B. (2007). *Child domestic workers in Dhaka: a geographical study of discourses, work and education*. Unpublished doctoral dissertation, Pennsylvania State University, PA. Retrieved Aug 1, 2011, 19:42 GMT, from http://etda.libraries.psu.edu/theses/approved/ WorldWideFiles/ETD-2190/FinalMaster.pdf.

Liborio, R. M. C., & Ungar, M. (2010). Children's perspectives on their economic activity as a pathway to resilience. *Children and Society, 24*(4), 326–338.

Liebel, M. (2003). Working children as social subjects: The contribution of working children's organizations to social transformations. *Childhood, 10*(3), 265–285.

Liebel, M. (2007). Paternalism, Participation and Children's Protagonism. *Children, Youth, and Environments, 17*(2), 56–73.

Martinez, A. M. (2001). Trabajo infantil y subjetividad: Una perspectiva necesaria. *Estudos de Psicologia, 6*(1), 235–244.

Martineau, S. (1999). *Rewriting resilience: a critical discourse analysis of childhood resilienc and the politics of teaching resilience to "kids at risk"*. Unpublished doctoral dissertation, The University of British Columbia, Vancouver, CA. Retrieved Aug 1, 2011, 19:35 GMT, from https://circle.ubc.ca/bitstream/handle/2429/10174/ubc_1999-389413.pdf?sequence=1.

Moraes, R. V. (2007). *A produção acadêmica sobre trabalho infantil: um olhar nos periódicos científicos brasileiros (1981–2004)*. Unpublished master thesis, UNESP, Marilia Campus, SP. Retrieved Aug 1, 2011, 19:30 GMT, from http://www.athena.biblioteca.unesp.br/exlibris/bd/bma/33004110042P8/2007/moraes_rv_me_mar.pdf.

Moreira, M. I. C., & Stengel, M. (Eds.). (2003). *Narrativas infanto-juvenis sobre trabalho doméstico*. Belo Horizonte: Editora da PUC-Minas.

Montgomery, H. (1998). Children prostitution and identity: A case study from a tourist resort in Thailand. In K. Kempadoo & J. Doezema (Eds.), *Global sex workers: Rights, resistance and redefinition* (pp. 139–150). New York: Routledge.

Pesce, R. P., Assis, S. G., Santos, N., & Oliveira, R. V. C. (2004). Risco e proteção: Um equilíbrio promotor de resiliência. *Psicologia Teoria e Pesquisa, 20*(2), 135–143.

Rubenson, B., VanAnh, N. T., Hojer, B., & Johanson, E. (2004). Child domestic servants in Hanoi: Who are they and how do they fare? *The International Journal of Children's Rights, 11*(4), 391–407.

Sarmento, M. J. (2005). Trabalho infantil em Portugal: Controvérsias e realidades. In A. Matos, C. Vieira, A. M. Seixas, M. P. Lima, M. Vilar, & M. R. Pinheiro (Eds.), *Ensaios sobre o Comportamento Humano: Do diagnóstico à intervenção contributos nacionais e internacionais* (pp. 95–116). Coimbra: Almedina.

Silva, J. L. T., Junior, L. F. N., & Antunes, M. M. (2002). Trabalho infantil: realidade, diretrizes e políticas. In M. E. Marques, M. A. Neves, & A. C. Neto (Eds.), *Trabalho infantil: A infância roubada* (pp. 17–41). Belo Horizonte: PUC Minas.

Sposito, E. S., Guimarães, A. A., Almeida, A. L. J., Chagas, E. F., Martin, E. S., Melazzo, E. S., Guimarães, R. B., Pizzol, R. J., & Magaldi, S. B. (2002). *Sistema de informação para a tomada de decisão municipal, fase II*. Partial Research Report, Faculdade de Ciências e Tecnologia da UNESP, Presidente Prudente Campus, SP (88 pp). Retrieved Aug 1, 2011, 19:20 GMT, from http://www.fct.unesp.br/Home/Pesquisa/CEMESPP/Relatorio%20Parcial%20Fapesp%20Fase%20II%20-%20Marco%202002.pdf.

Taylor, L. R. (2005). Dangerous trade-offs: The behavioral ecology of child labour and prostitution in rural northern Thailand. *Current Anthropology, 46*(3), 411–423.

Ungar, M. (2004). A constructionist discourse on resilience: Multiple contexts, multiple realities among at-risk children and youth. *Youth and Society, 35*(3), 341–366.

Ungar, M. (2011). The social ecology of resilience: addressing contextual and cultural ambiguity of a nascent construct. *American Journal of Orthopsychiatry 81*(1), 1–17. Retrieved Aug 1, 2011, 19:00 GMT, from http://onlinelibrary.wiley.com/doi/10.1111/j.1939-0025.2010.01067.x/full.

Woodhead, M. (1999). Combatting child labour: Listen to what children say. *Childhood, 6*(1), 27–49.

Woodhead, M. (2004). Psychosocial impacts of child work: A framework for research, monitoring and intervention. *The International Journal of Children's Rights, 12*, 321–377.

Yunes, M. A. M., & Szymanski, H. (2001). Resiliência: Noção, conceitos afins e considerações críticas. In J. Tavares (Ed.), *Resiliência e educação* (pp. 13–42). São Paulo: Cortez.

Part II

Five Interviews

An Interview with Macalane Malindi: The Impact of Education and Changing Social Policy on Resilience during Apartheid and Post Apartheid in South Africa

Macalane Malindi and Michael Ungar

Macalane Malindi, Ph.D., was born in 1967 in Lindley, in the Free State Province of South Africa. Despite the death of his parents and then an elder brother who looked after him, he still managed to graduate from high school in 1988. When his elder brother died, his sister-in-law and uncles helped him attend university where he completed a Bachelor of Arts in Education and a Bachelor of Arts in Psychology, then a Postgraduate Diploma in Education and finally his Ph.D. in 2009. He now resides in Bethlehem in the Free State Province and is a senior lecturer in the Department of Education at North-West University where he built on his experience as an educator and guidance consultant in the community prior to starting his doctoral studies.

Malindi's story, from his father's conflict with his boss of the farm where he worked (he bought a car and his boss fired him) to Malindi being forced to leave school to support himself and his family, unfolded against the backdrop of the Apartheid system and the changes it went through. As a successful young academic, Malindi gives much back to his community and is involved in research projects concerned with the study of resilience in South Africa. His own story informs what resilience means to him. That includes fulfilling one's obligations toward one's family, the

importance of faith, and the necessity for changes in social policy (specifically, policies related to education) that promote social justice. All these things, Malindi suggests, are necessary to make it more likely that children will do well.

This interview was recorded in January, 2010.

Macalane: Mine is a family of five. I have 3 daughters. My eldest daughter is 14. The second one is 10, and the third one is 8. My wife is an elementary school teacher in Lindley in the Free State Province where I was born. I teach at North-West University, Vaal Triangle Campus, in the school of Educational Sciences. I'm a Zulu-speaking South-African. My father was a farm worker, but he lost his job. The main reason was that he managed to buy a car for 600 Rand, which is about 90 dollars.

Michael: I don't understand. How did that cause him to lose his job?

Macalane: Because he bought the car, tension developed between him and the farm owner. Perhaps the farm owner was jealous that one of his black workers bought a car. Then one afternoon my father was told to pack and go because "…jy dink jy is nou baas" meaning "…you think you are the boss now." But my father was very proud of what he had done. My father always told us this story with a little bit of embarrassment. Embarrassment that he lost

M. Ungar (✉)
Killam Professor of Social Work,
Dalhousie University, Halifax, NS, Canada
e-mail: Michael.Ungar@dal.ca

M. Ungar (ed.), *The Social Ecology of Resilience: A Handbook of Theory and Practice*,
DOI 10.1007/978-1-4614-0586-3_6, © Springer Science+Business Media, LLC 2012

his job and he was the bread-winner. But he was also very thankful because although he lost his job, he was able to go to a semi-urban area where he was able to send us to school. When my brother and I went to school, we already knew how to read and my father was the one who taught us how to read.

Michael: How old were you when you began school?

Macalane: I was already 8, and my brother was 11 when we went to school for the first time.

Michael: What education did your father have?

Macalane: My father had primary education. He could only go up to Standard Four at that time. Then he had to leave school because my grandfather passed away and my father had to go and work on the farm so that he could support the family.

Michael: In the late 1970s, there was no education for children on the farms?

Macalane: There were schools on some farms. Even today, some farms do not have schools but children on such farms attend school on neighboring farms. In the small town where my father went, there was only one school and many learners. The school couldn't accommodate everybody, so churches were sometimes used as classrooms. My sub-standard A [Grade 1] classroom was a church building. The church was divided into two. Grade one faced north and Grade 2, which was my elder brother's class, faced south. So each teacher taught on their side of the same church building. Sometimes it would be difficult to hear everything since both teachers taught at the same time.

Michael: Did you have textbooks?

Macalane: Yes, but not enough. This school was, as I said, very big. We actually sat on benches, with no tables, and if we had

to write, we would kneel down and use the same bench we sat on as a desk. We would share books. For example, 2 or 3 pupils shared one book. Educational resources were unequally and inequitably distributed among schools serving children from different race groups. This was in line with the policy of Apartheid.

Michael: Were your teachers well enough trained?

Macalane: Yes, some of the teachers were qualified. Some of these teachers were only teaching with their standard 8 or standard 10 qualifications. But, again, I think it was a question of a shortage of teachers at the time. Even those who were qualified had received poor training at colleges of education designed only for Africans.

Michael: And your father, from his perspective, he thought this was a good educational experience that he could give you?

Macalane: Yes. Not many parents were literate enough to be able to evaluate the system. Parents used to motivate children to go to school because it was clear that education was needed anyway.

Michael: So your father found work in the city. And your mother?

Macalane: Actually, my mother and father separated when I was very young, but I stayed with my father.

Michael: Is this different from most families when there's a break-up?

Macalane: I'm not sure whether it was culturally accepted at that time, but it did happen, not only in my family, but in a few other families I knew of. In my family, my brother and I were left with my father and then my grandmother took care of us from then on. That is until my father remarried a year before I went to school.

Michael: I see.

Macalane: I didn't know my mother very well until I was much older. By then my father had remarried. I think a year before I went to school. At that time, he was working as a construction worker and then he learned about land surveying. He also learned about engineers. He actually wanted me to become a land surveyor. My brother was what we call a "gifted child" these days. His IQ was superior and he could read on his own. Most of the things that a teacher would want to teach he already knew. For example, he would read the Bible on his own and especially in high school, he read widely on his own.

Michael: But your father really wanted you to get an education?

Macalane: Yes, he motivated us a lot. In fact, when he looked at our results, he would be so proud that his children had the highest marks in class. And he would point at me and say, "One day you are going to become a land surveyor" and point at my brother and say, "You are going to be an engineer." So we grew up with this idea that we would become somebody even if we couldn't pronounce the words or understand what those people did.

Michael: Did your father ever talk about what motivated him to ensure his children got an education?

Macalane: I just knew that my father wanted me to be something that sounded very, very, very good. So although we didn't know anything about what he meant, we did know that we should become someone very important. We would be very important people if we became what my father wanted us to be. He actually passed away when I was 15 due to Tuberculosis. After he passed away, my step-mother had to start working to support the family. She had to take over and become the bread-winner. She worked as a domestic worker, earning 85 Rand per month. My grandmother was still alive then, but she was very old. She was 83. Her pension and the money that my step-mother was earning were barely enough to take care of all our needs. Then, in 1983, my grandmother passed away and the situation got even more difficult for our step-mother. So in 1984, my brother and I had to drop out of school because there wasn't enough money to pay for our school fees and to buy the books that we needed.

Michael: Your step-mother and grandmother were able to keep you in school, even after your father died and money was scarce?

Macalane: Yes, but it was not easy at all. This was very important to them just as it had been for our father. My brother and I dropped out of school at the end of 1984. I was 17. We had to go and look for work because my stepmother could not afford to keep us in school. This was a year after my grandmother passed away.

Michael: What grade did you leave?

Macalane: I had passed standard 7, which is grade 9 and my brother had just passed standard 8, which is grade 10, both of us with flying colors. I was employed before my brother, as a construction worker, like my father. I worked around people who were older than me and a lot of them had not had opportunities to go to school and qualify. So I was the second highest qualified employee. The other person had only finished standard 8, so we were the only ones who could read, write, understand English, and Afrikaans. So we used to interpret quite a lot for others.

Michael: Could you earn enough money to save and go back to school?

Macalane: No. I was paid fortnightly. I used to earn 118 Rand and 2 cents.

Michael: So every 2 weeks you'd earn 118 Rand…

Macalane: and 2 cents, yes.

Michael: So every 2 weeks you'd earn about $18. Less than $500 a year. Did I just do the math right?

Macalane: It wasn't enough to be able to save anything. Towards the end of 1985, my brother was employed as a police officer. There was political instability all over the place, so the government was recruiting more people to serve as police officers attached to municipalities. The reason was to deal with riots and the violent political activities that were taking place at that time. Houses belonging to people suspected of being spies or informers were being torched, police officers' houses and those of councilors' were being torched. Although my elder brother joined the police, he didn't want to become a police officer. Anyway, he decided to join the police since he did not have many employment choices.

Michael: Even though he was a very bright man?

Macalane: Yes. Soon after he joined the police force in October 1995, I decided to stop working as a construction worker and go back to school to finish my education and he was very excited about that. So I went back and I finished my Standard 8, my Standard 9, and my Matric. My brother was able to finance my studies. Other things also changed. The government put more money into educating us black, young South Africans and parents did not have to buy text books anymore. It became easier for many parents to educate their children because they only had to buy stationary. Still, some children dropped out of school. The law that children had to be in school was there, but it wasn't applied very strictly when it came to black South Africans.

Michael: I see.

Macalane: When I was in Standard 10, I told my brother that I wanted to become a lawyer, not just a land surveyor as my father had wished. And he agreed to support me but he died as a result of an accident in 1988. The car he was driving overturned and he died later in hospital. That actually set me back a little bit again.

Michael: I would imagine.

Macalane: But I was very fortunate because my brother's wife knew exactly what I wanted to be and she said, "Your brother wanted to educate you. He has passed away. I am going to take over." I had already been admitted to university. She was also a police officer. So she sponsored my university education. My cousin also contributed. My undergraduate studies depended heavily on the bursary which I received. Although I didn't become a lawyer, I had an opportunity to study and qualify as a teacher. My cousin and sister wouldn't have been able to finance my law studies.

Michael: You've done very well in the field of education.

Macalane: I received my degree in 1992. And I got married in 1995.

Michael: Can you talk about how you met your wife? Often our relationships are significant to what we do in life.

Macalane: Yes. I was a footballer [soccer player], and the football team for which I played, was semi-professional, run by teachers and ordinary members of the community. One of these people was a reverend. His house actually served as our clubhouse. He had a niece and each time I went there I would look at her and…

Michael: He was a reverend?

Macalane: Yes…

Michael: The reverend's daughter!

Macalane: He treated her like his own daughter. I actually thought she was his daughter at first. He didn't know. Nobody knew. But since I was the team captain I went to his house more often.

His niece and I became acquainted and I think I fell in love with her.

Michael: Oh, this is lovely.

Macalane: My uncles negotiated with her family for her hand in marriage.

Michael: Your father's brothers…

Macalane: Yes.

Michael: …went and negotiated with her family, the reverend…

Macalane: Yes, yes.

Michael: …for the marriage.

Macalane: Yes, for her hand in marriage.

Michael: Did you have enough money to marry?

Macalane: Yes, I was a teacher at that time. I was able to pay *amalobolo*?

Michael: What's *amalobola*?

Macalane: It's part of my culture. Long ago, I think even before my grandfather was born, if a young man wanted to marry a young girl, the young man's family would actually take cattle to the family of the young lady as a sign of appreciation for the good work they had done by bringing this girl up. It is a symbolic gesture to join the two families. But since people lost cattle, they now use money. It's actually a phrase: *izinkomo zamalobolo*. In other words, these are the cattle, money in my case, that my family sends to my fiancé's family in order for us to get married.

Michael: I appreciate your story very much. But how do you account for your success?

Macalane: For me and many other young boys the community was there. There were people in the community who served as role models who guided us. This played a role in our development. And our extended families played a role too. If a father in one particular family passed away, uncles supported the family to the best of their abilities. Even though parents passed away, or were working in other cities away from home, there were still father and mother figures for us. In my case, the

mother figure was my grandmother after the divorce of my parents. When I think of my grandmother, she played a very, very important role as a mother figure during my childhood. I miss her a lot, especially these days, because I'm sure she would be very proud to see what I have become.

Michael: Can you talk a little about how she influenced you?

Macalane: Yes. She gave me my initial religious upbringing and I have kept it throughout my life. I'm still a very religious person. And she taught me everything: norms, values. She was very strict though. I realized the reason why my father was such a responsible man. It is probably because of the strict upbringing that she gave him.

Michael: What were some of the other values that she gave you?

Macalane: After my father and mother separated, we were left in her care. She played every role that my mother would have played if my mother and father hadn't separated. She gave us all the love that we needed. She gave us all the care that we needed and she actually supervised our behavior. She taught us respect. She motivated us to go to school, although she had forgotten how to read and how to write at that time. There is an interesting story of how she would wake us up very early in the morning. Sometimes, on Saturday, she'd forget that it was Saturday and she would very quickly wake us up and ask us to get ready for school. And we would have to tell her, "Grandma, it's Saturday. It's not Monday, It's not Friday. It's Saturday." She wouldn't even laugh at herself. She would just say, "Okay, sleep then."

Michael: And your church? How big a force is the church in your life?

Macalane: My church played a pivotal role in my life as a child. My grandmother would not let us stay home on Sunday without going to church. I had difficulty playing football because sometimes we would go and play football on a Sunday afternoon, and my grandmother would say, "You can't go and play football on that day." But the team that I played for was run by teachers among others and they made sure that all the children who were in their care in the community as members of the football team were well behaved. They made sure that we didn't smoke. They made sure that we didn't drink. They made sure that we didn't do drugs and, in fact, they went out of their way to tell us about the dangers of all these things.

Michael: Really?

Macalane: So our team was a very special team in the sense that the children that played for this team, all of us never smoked, all of us never drank until later in life. Although there were other football teams in the township where I grew up, ours was very special. That was why we were able to grow so strong and disciplined as children. And what is interesting is that when I look back at my peers who played football with me, some of them became teachers. My role model is also a teacher who was actually my football coach at school. He's still alive at the moment and I got an opportunity to say thank you to him for being my mentor after I got my Ph.D.

Michael: And your church?

Macalane: My church is the Methodist Church and I have been in this church since I was born. I learned that there is another higher power and that person is actually in charge of our lives, that our lives are actually meaningful because He is there for us. I have never been able to separate my life as a footballer, my life as a teacher, and my other roles as parent or husband, from my faith.

Michael: What you are telling me is very profound. I know you study resilience

too, and what I'd like to ask you is what do you think actually makes a difference when a child faces adversity?

Macalane: Using myself as a case study, I would say those children who believe that they have the potential to become someone, coupled with other people around them who make them believe that they can become someone. I think those are the strong forces that propel us.

Michael: So it was really the people around you, and your church, that helped you get through. I'm curious, did your teachers play a role too?

Macalane: Yes. Our teachers used to tell us that we had limited opportunities, looking at the political situation in our country at that time. But they always made sure that there was no police officer listening. They always told us that because of the political system in the country we had limited options, but if we didn't have some kind of education, our options were going to be even more limited. They taught us that even under difficult circumstances, education, even bad as it was, could be one's salvation, if I may use that religious concept. Salvation lay in us being able to obtain some kind of education, even though it meant limited career opportunities. They motivated us a lot.

Michael: What would have happened if the police were listening?

Macalane: They could have been arrested and detained.

Michael: Which part of what they said was the illegal part?

Macalane: It could be interpreted as a political statement.

Michael: That you have limited options?

Macalane: Yes, because that was true.

Michael: But you weren't allowed to say that you had limited opportunities.

Macalane: Well, the Apartheid system was designed to make sure that we didn't have enough options in life as Africans, so making a statement like that would amount to a political statement. It was very, very dangerous.

Michael: Can you tell me more about how the Apartheid system put limits on you.

Macalane: We can start with the school system itself. You'd find schools which did not have a curriculum for math and science. In other words, the children who matriculated at that school only would have one curricular option. History being the main one, followed by, for example, biology and geography or biblical studies. The school where I matriculated was like that. There was no science curriculum at matric level. So that means you can't become anything which requires science subjects if you follow a curriculum like that. That practice had a long history starting from the time of Hendrik Verwoerd, the Apartheid Prime Minister who was assassinated 6 years after he miraculously survived an earlier assassination attempt. Let me read you what he said [his words are quoted in Brian Lapping's *Apartheid*: *A History* (1987)]: "There is no place for [the Bantu] in the European community above the level of certain forms of labor … What is the use of teaching the Bantu child mathematics when it cannot use it in practice? That is quite absurd. Education must train people in accordance with their opportunities in life, according to the sphere in which they live." It seems we were not supposed to be educated to very high meaningful levels of education. That's why there were jobs that we wouldn't even think of doing. Nevertheless, many Africans managed to reach high levels of education and we admired them.

Michael: Can you give me some examples?

Macalane: There was an act called the Job Reservations Act, which meant that some skilled jobs were reserved for whites. This Act was supported by the Education Act which meant that Africans were not to receive good, quality education that would enable them to hold certain high positions. The education of African children was aimed at ensuring that they could serve their own people in line with Apartheid. The Act was aimed at eliminating what was considered unfair competition.

Michael: What happened after 1994 and the end of Apartheid?

Macalane: 1994 gave a lot of people hope that things were going to be different. But I don't think we realized the magnitude of the task of changing everything that needed to be changed. I grew up in a shack which meant that housing was a problem for Africans. Townships were severely underdeveloped and we did not have access to clinics, for example. We didn't have enough hospitals too. These and other amenities were segregated according to race. Our schools, hospitals and few clinics were not as well resourced as those that served other population groups, especially whites. We had schools that were built of mud and even those didn't have enough classrooms. That legacy persists since we still have schools where children are educated in temporary buildings or old dilapidated school buildings. And then we have schools where they don't have proper toilet facilities, especially in rural areas. Others don't have libraries. Those are some of the imbalances that we still have at the moment. But I think life will surely improve because we see our housing program has speeded up. We see infrastructure being developed, especially in rural areas. But the problems are being made worse by the fact that a lot of people are moving away from rural areas to urban areas. So urbanization, which couldn't happen before because of the Group Areas Acts and the Pass Laws, is now causing problems. The influx control legislation was aimed at keeping people in what were called their "homelands."

Michael: Thinking about your own daughter now who's 14, what are your thoughts for her future as a postapartheid child?

Macalane: At the moment, opportunities are available. I put her in one of the best schools in the country. I always tell her that "I educate you so that you can be independent, so that you don't have to depend on someone else to make a living." My daughter tells me that she wants to become an architect.

Michael: This is an opportunity that is open now?

Macalane: Yes, opportunities are there. My university education is an opportunity too. I went to university in 1989. The Vaal Triangle where my university was situated was politically unstable at that time. There was a lot of political violence and the government was unable to contain it. The African National Congress and Inkatha Freedom Party were at loggerheads and many people lost lives due to the violence that resulted. If one was suspected of belonging to the ANC one could be executed very easily. In the township, you could be shot dead, you could be banned, because of, for example, suspicion that you belong either to one group or the other. You could be killed or burned alive. Some people were mysteriously killed during night vigils or in their homes. In spite of these occurrences, the fight for freedom did not stop, pointing to the resilience of South Africans of all colors who opposed Apartheid. I lived in this township and I used to commute to the university. One night, our house was attacked while I was studying for my psychology test the following day, but to this day we are not sure who attacked us. Not much

damage occurred and no one was injured at all.

Michael: What motivated the attack?

Macalane: I think it was political. My sister-in-law was a police officer. So the police officers were actually targets of the ANC-aligned youth. In this case, we were surely mistaken for the "enemy." We were able to resolve whatever was the problem and lived peacefully in the township afterwards.

Michael: Sounds very dangerous.

Macalane: When I was in my final year this violence actually intensified, especially in June while I was writing my semester exams. The ANC-aligned youth would round us up so that we could help patrol the streets, "to make sure that our mothers" as they put it, "and our sisters were not attacked." As I said, people were attacked and killed at night in their homes. So there I was, in the middle of exams, I was supposed to be studying, and instead I was patrolling the streets in the night in the area. A lot of youth were carrying machine guns and weapons such as knives. And there I was, patrolling with them with only my fists and nothing else. I couldn't refuse to go. Politically the country was very ungovernable at that time.

Michael: And in 1994, how did things change?

Macalane: Before 1994 we did feel like, "Wow, with all these political negotiations taking place, we are being liberated," but I think the actual liberation took place when we cast our ballots. I was very excited.

Michael: Had you not voted before? There was no voting at all for blacks?

Macalane: No, no, no. Not for us Africans. We couldn't vote at all, so for all of us it was a very exciting day when we voted on the 27th of April, 1994. We really felt that we were citizens of this country. I made sure that I voted in every election since then.

An Interview with Bill Strickland: How Community-Based Adult Educational Facilities Can Lift People Out of Poverty in Urban America

Bill Strickland and Michael Ungar

Bill Strickland grew up in Manchester, an inner-city neighborhood of Pittsburgh in the United States. His life changed from that of a potential high school drop out to CEO of a thriving educational institution when he became inspired by his high school art teacher, Frank Ross, a skilled artisan on the potter's wheel. That relationship helped Strickland envision the Manchester Craftsmen's Guild which began as an after-school arts program in a donated North Side row house that Strickland secured while still a college student at the University of Pittsburgh. When he graduated in 1969 with a bachelor's degree in American history and foreign relations, the decline of the steel industry in Pittsburgh had created widespread unemployment. As a result of Strickland's success with the Guild, he was asked to assume leadership of the Bidwell Training Center (BTC) which would become, under his guidance, a model vocational and arts training institution. His dedication to arts training would later earn him the MacArthur Fellowship "Genius Award." His story is chronicled in his recent book *Make the Impossible Possible*.

BTC helps the poorest, least educated individuals in Strickland's community get the training they need for immediate employment. It is a formula for community-wide social change achieved through partnerships with businesses, government officials, and the individual learners who share Strickland's vision. Today, BTC and the Guild offer accredited associate degree and diploma programs in fields as varied as culinary arts, chemical laboratory technologies, health careers, horticulture, and office technology. With mentorship from individuals like Jeffrey Skoll, former president of eBay, and James L. Heskett at Harvard University's Graduate School of Business Administration, Strickland has set himself the goal of establishing 200 similar centers around the world. Almost a dozen are already built or being designed.

Strickland's work is unique, in that he has called for a change in how education for adults and children is delivered. He shows an enduring optimism for people's potential to be lifted out of poverty. A lot of his success has to do with the environment that Strickland helps to create for his students. Though built adjacent to one of Pittsburgh's poorest, most violent neighborhoods, BTC is a place where people are respected. There are no armed security guards and fresh flowers from their own greenhouses adorn the premises. Students and the wider community feel an ownership for the Center. According to Strickland, it is this model of vocational training and community development which has created the conditions for people to realize their resilience.

M. Ungar (✉)
Killam Professor of Social Work,
Dalhousie University, Halifax, NS, Canada
e-mail: Michael.Ungar@dal.ca

M. Ungar (ed.), *The Social Ecology of Resilience: A Handbook of Theory and Practice*,
DOI 10.1007/978-1-4614-0586-3_7, © Springer Science+Business Media, LLC 2012

This interview was recorded in October, 2009.

Michael: Can you tell me about your work?

Bill: I run a Center that I created called Manchester Bidwell Corporation. It was started in 1968 as the BTC and Manchester Craftsmen's Guild, two separate entities. But a couple of years ago we combined them both together. Bidwell vocational school focuses on unemployed adults, under-employed adults, people who have been kind of left behind in the social order. We provide a tuition free education to people to get them connected with employment, career opportunities, jobs and give them the tools to get themselves out of poverty. We've done this with some success working with companies like Bayer and Calgon Carbon, PPG, and the University of Pittsburgh Medical Center. We've gotten very good at creating customized training for poor folks who normally would not be exposed to that kind of training.

Michael: What's the difference between what you do and other regular colleges and training programs in the Pittsburgh area?

Bill: A lot of the people we train actually get work. And they get out of poverty.

Michael: How does your Center do that?

Bill: Well, one thing that we focus on is making sure the curriculum meets the employers' needs. So we spend a lot of time with employers developing curriculum before we teach it, which is generally not done by educational institutions that have a tendency to talk to themselves but not to the employment market. So a number of years ago we had the idea, before we start teaching folks, let's go find out what the employers need. Our curriculum is very current and very customized specific to our constituency. We really focus on recovering people who have not been considered assets in their community. We work with the population that nobody else seems to be interested in working with. People like welfare moms, unemployed individuals, poor people. We've created an environment, a world class facility that really creates motivation by allowing students to understand that they are valuable. The facility tells them that we consider them assets, not liabilities. Our environment, the quality of our technology, the value proposition of our faculty, and the customized training that we've developed with industry make us a very unique brand. That's the difference.

Michael: I see.

Bill: Starbucks and Caribou, both are coffee companies, but if you ask them they would say that their values are very different from each other even though they have the same product.

Michael: What are some of the barriers that people bring with them?

Bill: Well most of these people have very poor academic skills. They don't read well, they don't do math well. Many of them have never graduated from high school. If they have, they haven't been very successful with their lives up to the point when they come to the Center. A lot of them are poor. They have been on welfare for generations, and they have very low self-esteem and almost no confidence in their ability to learn. Some of them have drug issues, some of them have criminal records. So they bring a lot of baggage with them when they come.

Michael: How do you engage them despite all those barriers?

Bill: First, because we want to. You have to start there. You have to want to do this and a lot of educational institutions are running the other way. They don't want to deal with these high-risk individuals who bring all this baggage with them. It's difficult, unpleasant work sometimes. There's not a lot of funding that supports this stuff even though we think it's valuable. So in order to be successful you need to have a positive attitude and feel good about the work you do. That gets communicated to the students.

But if they feel that you're in despair and have contempt for them or their circumstances, that comes across very clearly. You don't profit, and certainly they don't profit either.

Michael: Are you able to get around the barriers of lower levels of literacy and numeracy?

Bill: We have academic programs that can get people trained to read and do math. We are very good at it. We can get them to high school equivalency in less than a year's time. Then we can put them in accelerated training programs and get them work.

Michael: Do people find you, or do you find them?

Bill: Well a lot of people find their way to us through successful graduates who become great public relations for the Center. If you're running a program that is successful and has a history of being successful, is well run, managed properly, and gets results, people will hear about you and they'll find their way to your door. Now we also of course go out to unemployment centers, social service agencies, and so forth to promote what we do. But a lot of our students get here through word of mouth and because of our reputation.

Michael: Can you give me an example of somebody that stands out? Someone for whom you've managed to provide that bridge from chronic unemployment and poverty to good employment?

Bill: I'm thinking of one young woman who was selected to be our graduation speaker. She was a culinary student. She told us that at Christmas time she was in the county jail for drug offences and I suspect other related things as well. As she tells it, she was at the bottom of her life and lost hope. She heard about Bidwell while in jail. The counseling program down there apparently had a brochure about us. She not only finished the program, she's got a job working in industry. She said during her brief presentation that she wanted to ask her children for forgiveness. They were in the audience celebrating her graduation. She said, "I want to ask of you forgiveness because when I was in jail I was feeding my drug habit, I wasn't feeding you. And I want to ask if you would allow me to re-establish myself as your mother." Well they came up on stage, at the podium, and gave her a hug and forgave her.

Michael: That's very moving. I get the sense that you and your staff saw her potential.

Bill: Yeah. I feel that way about every student that walks across the threshold. That's why we're here. That's why we built this place.

Michael: I understand from the pictures I've seen that Bidwell is quite unique, even in the way you've set up the physical space.

Bill: I was very impressed early on with Frank Lloyd Wright's architecture. And I decided that I wanted to do something that used his architecture for an educational facility. So a number of years later I hired one of his students to build Bidwell. It's fulfilled, maybe exceeded, my expectations in terms of creating a warm, nurturing, healthy environment. For people who have been neglected, what we've discovered is that if you build wonderful, nurturing spaces for them, they have a tendency to take on the characteristics of the environment where they are. So if you build productive, innovative environments, the students have the tendency to be productive and innovative. If you build prisons, they have a tendency to become prisoners.

Michael: That's a very powerful statement.

Bill: We're absolutely convinced that aesthetics, the physical plan, actually alters behavior in very powerful and positive ways.

Michael: Now, this Center is located in what kind of neighborhood. Does it fit in well or does it stand out?

Bill: Well it's in an industrial park, next to the neighborhood where I was born. Yeah, it stands out. But other companies are moving their facilities here. So one of the outcomes has been that we've created an economic development engine for the area.

Michael: Am I understanding right, from what I've read, that unlike many academic training institutions, you don't have a lot of security in the building?

Bill: No cameras, no metal detectors, no bars on the windows. We normally have no guards in the building at all except one guy comes in to check people in and out of the building at night. There are no hall monitors, no security apparatus of any kind. And over 24 years, we've never had a drug or alcohol incident, a fight, theft, or a police call. And we're in the middle of a neighborhood with one of the highest crime rates in Pittsburgh.

Michael: What have you learned that other communities need to know?

Bill: Well you have to set very high standards and you have to live the philosophy rather than preach the philosophy. Living it is critical. That's how people learn. We have learned how to alter poor people's behavior. Most people think if you build beautiful facilities poor people will tear them up. Well, they won't if you stick around to run the place and let people know you mean what you say. There needs to be a process of communication. We've found that most people will respond to our positive message if we are consistent over a long period of time. We're not in the miracle business. This is mainly hard work.

Michael: How do you involve the community? Build trust?

Bill: Well first of all, the community is the student body. So literally, as you begin to get successful graduates, they become part of your fan club in the community. You build a reputation that way. Then the students become the police force in the Center. They have decided they want to protect this place for themselves and their fellow students. That's very important. We need to get to that level of trust and confidence. We've really built an educational community as opposed to just a program.

Michael: What kinds of programs do you provide?

Bill: Well there's two parts. The vocational school is Bidwell, and we provide a culinary arts training experience. We also train pharmaceutical technicians and medical coders and medical billing people. We train chemical technicians for the chemical industry. We have a horticultural program where we train people for the horticultural industry. So we have these very market specific training programs that put people to work. All of which are completed by the students in less than 12 months. Then there's the arts program. Manchester Craftsmen's Guild works with public school kids, grades 8 through 12. We provide them with experience working with ceramics, photography, and digital imaging. And we've been very successful graduating a substantial number of these kids from high school. Many of them go on to college as a result of what they learn in the arts.

Michael: I've heard that your own story begins with the arts as well.

Bill: Yeah, a public school teacher, a guy named Frank Ross, helped me to get my life refocused. He taught me ceramics when I was in high school. I got pretty good at it. He said "You know? Your life is too important to waste on the streets so you're going to college." He helped me apply to the University of Pittsburgh. That's where I graduated from and where I now serve as a trustee.

Michael: Would you have dropped out without having become involved with the arts?

Bill: Oh probably. I was 16-years-old in tenth grade. And I worked with Frank Ross that year and in my senior year. That's when things really started to take hold.

Michael: Were you a good student up until then?

Bill: No, I was a very mediocre student. Not well motivated, not really focused on much of anything. The arts really provided the spark that got me engaged with education.

Michael: I see. If I can broaden this a little, how do you define resilience? What does that word mean to you given your life history?

Bill: Well, our value proposition basically is focused on resilience. That is the ability to rejuvenate, reconstitute, and reconfirm your life and your value proposition that accompanies your life. And the ability to do that is the measure of resilience in my view. I've been very skilful in creating an environment that is energizing for all the people who come there to learn. They feel positive about life. They feel encouraged about what they do. They receive energy from the experience of being in this place. Whether it is from the quality of the food, or the quality of the art work on the walls, or the sunlight streaming in, or the orchids that are on the desk at the reception, orchids we grow in our own gardens. In fact, we have flowers around the entire building. We create an engaging, energetic, positive environment for students. We have learned that what we do creates and sustains resilience on the part of the students, and on the part of the faculty, and the administration too, I might I add.

Michael: It almost seems that it's the environment that makes it more likely that someone, even if they are coming in with lots of challenges, will flourish. That you've created the right social and physical space for them to grow.

Bill: That's exactly the point of the story. That's why I'm building more places like Bidwell around the country and eventually around the world. We have discovered that environment alters behavior. Like I said before, you build beautiful environments, you get beautiful people. You build prisons, you get prisoners. It's as simple to read that story as Dick and Jane. We've discovered ways, methods, strategies to alter the behavior of people who are considered incapable of altering their behavior in a positive way.

Michael: How do you respond, then, to people who say resilience is more about the individual and whether the individual wants to change? Like Will Smith in *The Pursuit of Happyness*.

Bill: Unfortunately, you hear that in churches all the time because the minister in many cases stands up and gives this lecture about how the individuals sitting in the pews have got to incorporate God, embellish this, embellish that, go on faith, and do it all as an individual. And what I'm arguing is that there is no one individual that by themselves can sustain a value proposition in a vacuum. You have to do it in a community. That's where you draw your resilience, and your energy, and your confirmation from. The Bidwell philosophy isn't focused just on the individual. It is a philosophy that focuses on the community that benefits the individual. That's very fundamental to everything that we do. There's shared responsibility, there's shared ownership, there's an expectation of contribution on the part of all that are here at the Center. Whether it's a student in a classroom, the maintenance department, or the CEO of the place, each of us is expected to contribute something.

Michael: What's been the response from local churches when you say what you just said?

Bill: Interestingly enough, some of them are starting to listen to me. There's a church in Vancouver that wants to start a center like ours.

Michael: Isn't that interesting.

Bill: A minister heard my speech and invited me to speak with his congregation. Then the minister told people that this is how they can express their faith, by sponsoring a center. And we've got maybe another church interested too. The Bishop of the Episcopal Diocese of Tanzania showed up here a couple of weeks ago and was so taken with the story of what we're doing that he's promised us land in Tanzania to build a center.

Michael: I sometimes hear people say that it's the individual who needs to pull themselves up by their own bootstraps. Sometimes I hear that from people in government or business. What's been the reaction from those people to your message? That it takes a community to help people.

Bill: Well the government tends to be very slow in terms of comprehending anything other than what it's already doing. So you can't look to government for innovation. That's just not in the cards. We may create a strategy that lets them participate in the innovation but they're not going to be the ones who sponsor it. I think if you're waiting for that to happen you'll die a slow and painful death. I've decided that the only way we can get a change is to create it ourselves. And to then try to make the case with government and philanthropy and corporate leadership. We've got a good story to tell and they can be a part of that story. It's a philosophy that really emphasizes cooperation, not confrontation. It's a very different approach to social change.

Michael: How have you managed to get business on board?

Bill: Practically speaking, I've trained competent employees for them. We can start right there and that gets people's attention.

Michael: I'll bet it does.

Bill: And as we save them money, they get to check off the affirmative action box on their hiring policy. But, you know, many of these companies are very image conscious and very community minded. We're a great asset to be associated with. There's great press that comes from their supporting what we do. So it's kind of a win-win situation. And we tend to emphasize this as a training center, not a charity. It allows businesses to relate to us based on what they do rather than having to think like us to work with us.

Michael: That's interesting. You're each getting what you need from this alliance.

Bill: Nothing wrong with self-interest.

Michael: So, let me ask you, how do you know when someone is succeeding?

Bill: Number one, some guy has no work, is on welfare, then gets a job and pulls himself out of poverty. That's not real complicated. Number two, we take an at-risk kid that is probably going to drop out of high school. That kid goes to college. That's pretty measurable. You know the fact we've had no fights or drug incidents in 24 years of operation, that's a very measurable thing too. So if you start looking at the facts, you'll know what you're doing is working. But if you're spending a fortune on prison's, and drug rehabilitation programs, and people with bullets in their heads in the emergency room, and public school systems that don't seem to be able to teach people how to read, then something isn't working. A center like ours can do much more for substantially less money and is getting three, four times the results of other programs. That's how we should look at success. I mean, you would have

Michael: to be pretty uninformed to not at least listen to the arguments for a training Center like Bidwell.

Michael: Given what you know, what would you do differently in our high schools?

Bill: Rebuild them. That's what we should be doing differently. Most of them don't work and you've got to engage in partnerships with community-based organizations that do work. We can unite around the common goal of trying to improve the lives of the kids who are in the high schools. You have to stress innovation and change rather than maintaining the same old programs that have gotten us into this mess.

Michael: Concretely, what would that look like?

Bill: Well, more centers like ours. I'm building them around the country as we speak. We've got three open, Grand Rapids, Cincinnati, Frisco, and eight more being planned. Same issues, same problems everywhere. The goal is to build 200. One hundred in the US, 100 around the world.

Michael: That's an amazing goal. And interesting because many of the kids I work with are victims of de-streaming. We've taken away the vocational programs for them in school which means they finish high school without any specific skills.

Bill: That's a mistake

Michael: Ten, 15 years ago, we wanted to take away the stigma of a vocational education. But I often hear from young men and women that school has become completely irrelevant to them. They get pushed up grade after grade, but basically they're still reading at grade levels 5, 6, 7, or 8, well below the grade they're actually in. And I just can't help but think this is a terrible way to abuse their self-respect.

Bill: That's all wrong, in my view. We're not all built the same. We have different aptitudes, different interests. We're not stamping out McDonalds hamburgers. We're talking about human beings. And we need to customize a lot of the training, and have value propositions based on what each person needs.

An Interview with Jude Simpson: Growing Beyond a Life of Abuse and Gang Involvement in New Zealand

8

Jude Simpson and Michael Ungar

Jude Simpson lives in Mount Maunganui, New Zealand, a beautiful small town that seems a long way from the world of family violence in which she works. Her self-published biography "*Lost and Found*" tells her story of growing up neglected and abused and then her years of involvement with criminal gangs. Now a Family Violence Prevention Advocate with Presbyterian Support Northern in New Zealand, Jude works tirelessly to help families avoid the mistakes she made. In her public talks, and in her work directly with families, Jude brings her own personal experiences of abuse as a child, and the wisdom that comes with having overcome her violent past and grown into a successful woman in her late 40s. She explains how family violence had altered her life course and how it instilled in her troubling beliefs about herself. As she says, "Carrying an incorrect negative belief about yourself can lead you into places that are not healthy and nurturing and loving but painful and scary and sad."

Her life would have been very different if she hadn't met a counselor she was mandated by the courts to see. It was through that relationship that she gained a new outlook on her life and the motivation to reconnect with her own children. In this regard, Jude's life is a testimonial to the power of relationships that change life trajectories. Her resilience, difficult to have seen beneath the troubling

behaviors of her youth, was periodically visible to those who knew her and appreciated that Jude was doing the best she could to survive in an environment that offered her few choices.

The following interview took place in April 2009.

Michael: Jude, can you give a sense of what you experienced growing up? What were some of the challenges that you faced?

Jude: I have to say, one of the first things and most important things I experienced was I had the love of one parent, which was my dad and he became a rock for me for most of my life. His love was absolutely paramount for me. It was the only thread I had to hang on to. I hate to think what would have happened if I didn't have that love of a parent. Surrounding me there was so much rejection and abuse. But I always had him. I realize now how resilient I was. That I could be subjected to so much hurt and pain, but the love I had for my father was my absolute strength.

Michael: Did you live with him?

Jude: Yes, when I was very young I lived with my four older siblings and my parents. But my mother didn't want to have me, she didn't want to carry me at birth, she didn't want to be pregnant with me, and then at birth she didn't want anything to do with me. She completely rejected me. So I grew up in a family where there was a divided line. There was my

M. Ungar (✉)
Killam Professor of Social Work,
Dalhousie University, Halifax, NS, Canada
e-mail: Michael.Ungar@dal.ca

M. Ungar (ed.), *The Social Ecology of Resilience: A Handbook of Theory and Practice*,
DOI 10.1007/978-1-4614-0586-3_8, © Springer Science+Business Media, LLC 2012

mother and siblings on one side and my father and I on the other. And I used to often look at my mother and siblings and wonder what I did wrong? Why doesn't she like me? That's why my father's love was so important. If I didn't have that, I wouldn't have had anything.

Michael: How did he show you that love?

Jude: That is an interesting question. Men back then didn't really express their love. He wasn't an affectionate man. He didn't verbalize his feelings, and I now realize that I can't actually say how I knew he loved me because he never told me and he never hugged me. But I knew he did. Maybe it was because he was kind, and he was very gentle, and he always spoke to me nicely.

Michael: And, in contrast, what did you experience with your mother?

Jude: She was never physically abusive or horrible to me, but she just never liked me. She just never wanted anything to do with me. She spoke to me if she had to. I remember walking down the main street of town 1 day and we were going to cross the main road. I was four, and I tried to hold her hand and she wouldn't hold my hand. The day my mother died, when I was 16, the last words she said to me were, "Your father not's even your real father."

Michael: That sounds awful.

Jude: I don't know what that was about. My mother used to do things with other men. And I wonder, even to this day, why she would say such a thing to me, knowing that she was going to die and that was the last thing she left with me.

Michael: Where did your life go after that, given these experiences with your mother?

Jude: In my early years, I lived with a huge sense of rejection. And confusion. I grew up wondering what was wrong with me. But then I had that love for my dad, except later when I was nine, my parents divorced. Then my father got a girlfriend and she absolutely hated me.

That's when the abuse started. Physical abuse, verbal abuse, psychological abuse. My father was working and she was at home with me. She was absolutely terrifying. It didn't take long for her to have full power and control over me. I couldn't tell my father of course. If I did, then look out when he goes to work the next day and I was home alone with her again.

Michael: What would she do, while your dad was gone?

Jude: First, there was a lot of verbal abuse. She'd tell me I was a piece of trash, that I was scum, that I was unlovable. And she used to say, "Even your own mother couldn't love you." After 5 years of having that said to me, I took it as the truth and it became a very entrenched belief for me. I walked with that for the next 30 years. Keeping it all inside. The results were absolutely devastating. My self-esteem just plummeted. There was lots of other psychological abuse too. She used to spit in my dinner. I'd watch her do it, then she would put it in front of me and make me eat it. I was just hurting all the time. I was confused. I was sad. I didn't understand. Then I began getting angry. To me the world was such an ugly, horrible place. It was cruel. But then, I believed that I was just a piece of scum.

Michael: And where did that take you?

Jude: When I was 14, I left my father to live with my mother and because I had no sense of belonging or feeling of love for her, or maybe because I was separated from the only love I knew, which was my dad, I went out on the streets and started looking for love. And I became very promiscuous. I substituted sex for love. I thought boys would make me feel loved. You know, it was like I was desperate. It was like I was on the hunt for food, for someone to make me feel that I was okay. "Please someone, be nice to me. Please someone make me feel loved." You know?

I ended up getting pregnant at 14 and had a termination, and then got pregnant at 16 and got married because that was what was expected. I married this poor boy who didn't want to be married, but his family made him marry me and it was just destructive. Then to make things worse, while I was pregnant, my father was killed in a car accident. Four months later, my mother died of cancer.

Michael: That's a lot to have happen at one time.

Jude: It was devastating to lose my father. I got involved with drugs and alcohol and left my husband and took my baby. And then I got involved with one of the most notorious gangs in New Zealand which was the Mongrel Mob. And my daughter and I entered the gang world. And we got involved with all sorts of terrible, terrible things. That's when my husband took me to court and got custody of my daughter. He took her to live with him and his family and I stayed in the gang world and got really involved in gang life. Drank lots, got involved with organized crime, things like that. Those people are very brutal, very vicious.

Michael: Inside the gang, you experienced more violence?

Jude: Extremely so. But by this time in my life I'm very used to it. It was very normal for me. And in fact, if I weren't in that situation, I probably would have thought there was something wrong. Isn't that a bizarre way to think?

Michael: I've heard the same thing from young people who have experienced a lot of abuse.

Jude: What's strange, though, is that even though I was in that incredibly abusive and ugly world, I still felt a sense of belonging. And that was what I was searching for.

Michael: What was it about the gang that gave you that sense of belonging?

Jude: They were like a family. We were all alike. Ninety-nine percent of the gang members were from incredibly dysfunctional homes where they'd felt no sense of belonging. It was different in the gangs. There we could feel like we belonged.

Michael: That makes sense.

Jude: It was the same for me. It was abusive, but as horrific as it was, in their own distorted way, they look after their own. They care about you like you are family.

Michael: Did you go on to have more children?

Jude: Yes. I have a son with a man from the Mongrel Mob. But I left the Mob when he was 9 months old after my partner tried to cut my throat. It was quite normal, except that time it was more vicious. I had to leave my son, though. If I had tried to take him with me, his father would have killed me. So, I had a choice. To either stay and continue to be brutalized, or leave my son. I chose to leave my son, which I regret because he's suffered a great deal. He is a broken man.

Michael: Where did you go?

Jude: I ran away to the South Island. But within a week of being there I got myself into an identical relationship. I felt absolutely desperate. When I left the Mob I felt so alone. There was no place where I could belong. And for me, I was always trying to find that with a man. I needed a man to make me feel loved. So, within a week, I was back in an incredibly violent relationship and the cycle started all over again. I had another child, a little girl. When she was 15 months old, my partner went away for a week and I went down to a local pub and met another man and he was from another gang in New Zealand called the Highway 61s. And we got talking and he said to me, "You know Jude, if you don't get out of that relationship you're going to be murdered." It was the right timing. I truly believe in timing, I don't think anyone will move us if we are not quite ready to move. So I left and I took my daughter and that man in the pub and me became involved and 11 years later we decided to have our own child together. We never lived together but we had an on-off relationship. I've had four children to four different men. But when I was in the early stages of that fourth pregnancy there was a knock on my door one evening and it was the police who told me my partner was one of New Zealand's most wanted criminals. He was an armed robber and I was being taken into custody and locked up and charged with three counts of armed robbery and one charge of harboring an escaped prisoner. And I was facing 10 years in prison if convicted.

Michael: Did you go to jail?

Jude: No, I was held in jail for a while, then the judge released me to give birth to my daughter. I ended up being found not guilty on three charges and dismissed on one other. During that time my partner told me that he was already married, and that he was leaving me to do his prison term in a jail closer to where she lived. So he left me after 11 years, pregnant. It was one of the biggest betrayals I'd ever experienced in my entire life.

Michael: How did you ever leave this life behind?

Jude: It was a person. I got sent to a course by my worker at income assistance, which is a government social service department. She was the facilitator. Deb Chase is her name. I had to go to the course, otherwise I would have had my benefits stopped. She had the ability and the wisdom to know what she was seeing in me. I had quite a bad attitude and I wasn't a very nice person. And she challenged me, and she said to me, "You know, if you could lose that bad attitude of yours, and if you would let me help

you, you could turn your life around, and then you could use what you been through to help others." And that's exactly what we did. She's been helping me for the last 10 years now.

Michael: Did other people extend you a hand before that? Other social workers, police?

Jude: No. I was never involved with any social workers, never. And as for the police, there wasn't really any help like there is today. Domestic violence wasn't a huge issue. There wasn't the awareness that there is now. Even when I was arrested, no social service agencies came to find out what was happening to me and my children. No one came near me. Not one person.

Michael: Was there something special about the way Deb approached you? What did she do that captured your attention? Was it the course content?

Jude: I just felt her sincerity. I knew she didn't have any hidden agendas. She just openly cared. And I got that. People like me know when people are real or they aren't real. I knew she was real. She was the first person ever to believe in me.

Michael: After your father.

Jude: After my father. Yeah, she was just amazing.

Michael: And the course Deb was offering? Was that important?

Jude: The course was really irrelevant.

Michael: Well you've just trashed hundreds of human service programs! If I hear you, what you're saying is we have to put nice people in front of wayward children. That's it, isn't it? You're saying something very profound. It's so easy to forget that the programs professionals offer are often secondary to the relationships that are formed.

Jude: Absolutely. The course was for solo parents to try to help them to get back into the work force because the government wanted us off benefits.

Michael: Do you think Deb saw herself as doing something different from what she was supposed to be doing?

Jude: I think she was there to deliver a program. But you could tell she wanted people to have the best in life that they could have. She came from a place that was 100% heart. The content of what she was delivering was good, but it was how she delivered it that mattered.

Michael: What happened after that? After you got inspired to make some changes in your life?

Jude: Deb helped me get a job with the same company that she was working with. In fact I ended up delivering the same program to parents. I wanted to be around her as much as possible. She was helping me create a new belief system. She kept telling me that it was never true that I was a piece of trash. It was never true that I was unlovable. I could walk with that.

Michael: Could you have heard this same message a decade or two earlier if you'd met her then?

Jude: I don't really know. I believe in the perfect timing of things. I often have wondered, did other people present opportunities to me like this one and did I just not see them?

Michael: After you started working with Deb, what happened with your own children?

Jude: It was interesting because my children were starting to repeat the same life I'd lived. My third daughter got pregnant very young and was in a bad relationship. She was becoming dependant on benefits. You know, exactly the same stuff I'd experienced. But then she watched me slowly start to turn things around and develop a new attitude. She did the same. Now she works full time.

Michael: And your other children?

Jude: My daughter, she's coming up on 33. She was angry with me until she was 30-years-old. Because I had abandoned her, and left her with a gang member. But she came to me when she was 30 and said to me, "I've been angry at you for so long now, I just can't stay angry any more." We have a very good relationship now, which is wonderful. But my son, unfortunately, he grew up in a very abusive, destructive place and he became an addict. He's been clean for the last 2 years and has come back into my life. His father died a few years ago. I think he felt more comfortable to come to me after that. My four children came together for the first time earlier this year. It was absolutely fantastic to watch all of them. I sat there looking at all of them quite astounded and quite overwhelmed at how they seemed to fit together.

Michael: Jude, this term resilience, if I say it to you, what do you think it means?

Jude: Resilience? I find it absolutely intriguing. I guess it's how we hang in there when the odds are so overwhelming. How we overcome, even as a child.

Michael: I hear you saying that resilience is about something inside us that helps us cope. And yet, in your story, I hear you talking about not only the importance of your father, but also Deb. And the way you are influencing your own daughters. Is resilience all about what's inside us or is it also about what is outside?

Jude: Absolutely. It's a combination. Who we are and the other people we meet. I don't believe I could be where I am today without the people that have been influential in my life. There's not many of them, but the ones who have been there for me were so important to helping me get through situations. Except it hasn't been just about getting through. I hear people say, "I am a survivor of abuse," but they aren't really living. They might be physically living, but they are caught up in ways of thinking that hold them back. Resilience has to be more than that.

Michael: That's interesting you say that.

Jude: I could have just survived. But I'm very blessed. I'm not just in any job. I have work I'm passionate about. That I just love so much. And I'm giving back.

Michael: I know you work for a religious organization. I'm curious is religion or belief in God or spirituality a part of what makes you resilient?

Jude: I am a Christian, but I didn't go to Presbyterian Support Services because of that. They actually approached me and created a job for me.

Michael: Oh.

Jude: I truly believe that in the last 3 years that God has been watching over me. I was brought up believing in God. My brothers and sisters and I, we all went to Sunday school. My parents never came, but I always believed in God, always.

And when I was going through all those years of hurt and turmoil. I never stopped believing in Him. I just never went near him because I was doing everything that I knew he wouldn't like.

Michael: I see.

Jude: It wasn't until years later when all these wonderful things kept happening for me that I started to think, I am making all these good things happen. And I realized, this is God. And from that day on I committed my whole life to Him. And that's exactly what I've done. And it's just gone from strength to strength to strength. But I don't talk very much about my Christian faith. It shuts people down. That's not what I want to do at all. I want to help them, like others helped me.

An Interview with Vicki Durrant: Creating a Community Program for High-Risk Aboriginal Youth in Canada's North

9

Vicki Durrant and Michael Ungar

Vicki Durrant is the Director of The Youth of Today Society which operates a community run shelter and drop-in center for homeless and street-involved youth in Whitehorse, a city of 25,000 in Canada's Northern Yukon Territory. She has worked for a decade to establish a program that provides access to shelter, food, and adult mentors for Aboriginal youth who would otherwise be fending for themselves. Her understanding of what high-risk youth need is profound, growing out of her practical experience running a program that engages youth who are difficult to involve in services.

Durrant herself knows much about thriving in a tough situation. A single parent, she survived on social assistance while establishing the Center, cajoling local businesses to donate space and service clubs to help with money for food and art supplies. The Center now operates with a budget of $380,000 a year, and is poised to become a model for other programs across the Yukon.

Durrant understands that resilience is both a young person's inner qualities and the services and supports that make it possible for that young person to do well. She talks about parents, professionals, and her wider community as all having important roles to play in helping young people realize their full potential. The Center she started is remarkable for the way it helps meet the needs of the most disadvantaged youth in a small urban setting where there are few resources. It is Durrant's creativity and multidimensional approach to programming that makes Angel's Nest stand out as an exemplar of resilience-promoting support in a community setting.

The following interview took place in August, 2009.

VICKI: When we set up Angel's Nest [a program operated by The Youth of Today Society] there wasn't really much in Whitehorse to support high-risk youth, and so, there was a lot of youth getting into crime and doing things that put them at risk. Our social service system has care in place and the government does a good job making sure there is childcare for young people up to the age of 12. Then at 12 they are basically left on their own. Subsidized childcare ends and parents can't really afford to continue paying to have people care for their kids. We realized that these kids from the age of 12–18, even 20, are on their own but the investment that has been put into them – making sure they are healthy, safe – ends at the age of 12. And between 12 and 16, even older, a lot of things happen. Peer pressure is extreme, and a lot of young people make choices that are not in their best interest.

M. Ungar (✉)
Killam Professor of Social Work,
Dalhousie University, Halifax, NS, Canada
e-mail: Michael.Ungar@dal.ca

M. Ungar (ed.), *The Social Ecology of Resilience: A Handbook of Theory and Practice*,
DOI 10.1007/978-1-4614-0586-3_9, © Springer Science+Business Media, LLC 2012

MICHAEL: Right.

VICKI: So, what we felt was missing was continuing care. We don't, of course, promote it as childcare, but, it really is a kind of extended care from the age of 12–24. And then we noticed that these young people are in need of different kinds of programming. They are needing less support in the sense of physical support, but they need moral support; they need someone there to open opportunities for them, to help them experience things they would not be able to do on their own. So we set up our program to meet their needs, to have a safe place for them to come together and socialize with their peers, with an adult supervising. Or just caring, being mentors in their lives. We work with the highest risk youth in Whitehorse. A lot of them are in government care or have ran away from home.

MICHAEL: How do they find you? Are they referred?

VICKI: No, it's just word of mouth. It's set up like a home. The youth are involved in making a lot of the decisions. The basic program is a feeding program. We try to address basic human needs first. You know, shelter, food, moral support. And then we have an employment and training program. We employ youth too. We target the highest risk of the high-risk youth, the ones that are putting themselves physically at risk, or the ones that are on the street, that have no shelter.

MICHAEL: And when you say you target them, how do you do that? How do you make yourself relevant to them so that they come to the program?

VICKI: The way our program is set up is that it is a drop-in center. So the youth are welcome to come and we have a feeding program, and that really seems to build a trusting relationship, respect. They are very appreciative that we're here for them and we provide a meal. We provide one meal a day. It's a full course meal. Very nutritious. And we also hire some of the youth to become involved in the feeding program. They work with one of the feeding program managers to gain cooking skills. They go grocery shopping, they plan the budget, they learn everything they need to learn about managing the kitchen. And then of course they serve each other. It's quite like a family. Everybody has their place.

MICHAEL: Can you describe the centre itself?

VICKI: It's a big nine-bedroom house: nine rooms, five bathrooms. We've set the main floor up with computers, a pool table, a separate room for watching TV, a games room, and then another separate room with extra computers where they can put resumes together, you know, anything they need. And then we have another separate area for our creative side – arts and music. We provide easels and all the supplies a young person who is artistic needs. Or, we've also got in that area musical instruments. Some of the youth will not express themselves through words. But they will go into the arts center and paint a picture about something that has been bugging them for a long time. It's just a space for them to express themselves in positive ways because they are going to express themselves, somehow. Through the centre, some youth have discovered they are amazing artists. Some of them have actually gone on to arts school or study music.

MICHAEL: Where does your funding come from?

VICKI: It's project funding. What we do is put together a proposal and find a funder with criteria that fits the project. It's actually pretty difficult to find funding for a specific project. But here in the North I think we are very lucky because our community is so small. And our government has acknowledged the importance of prevention work. I think because of our isolation we are quite a bit ahead of the rest of Canada in regards to the amount of funds that the government is providing for social programming.

MICHAEL: I see. Who works in the Center? You mention that the youth sometimes help out with the dinners. Who else?

VICKI: If we have the funding, we can have lots of projects. Last year we hired 17 high-risk youth. And then we have the managers. The feeding program has its own manager, but even that is based on project funding. The same with all our staff:. Nobody's job is secure. Though at this point we are negotiating with the government. They've asked us to set up another youth center. We're at a very positive place right now in regards to funding because they're seriously considering giving us secured funding. That's going to alleviate a lot of problems with regards to running the Center.

MICHAEL: How many youth come in on a given evening?

VICKI: It varies. The average is about 20, and then some days we get 35 kids. In the winter it's really busy because it's cold outside. But we have at this moment 63 youth who are members. Of that 63, 25–30 are regulars.

MICHAEL: And other professionals who are mandated to serve the needs of high-risk youth, how much does your Center become a place where they can connect with these youth?

VICKI: Within our community, our program has served a very important role in regards to opening access to these youth. I mean the high-risk youth we work with are very difficult to engage. They are not going to go to government programs. The role we serve is to work in partnership with many other organizations. Like government run drug and alcohol services, probation officers, health and social services. We have a very close relationship and important relationship with many of the organizations that provide services for high risk youth.

MICHAEL: How do professionals engage with the youth who come to the Center?

VICKI: The number one priority is that the youth who come here feel safe. And yes, we understand that a lot of them have very negative attitudes toward government services so we are very sensitive when we open up our doors to other organizations. We actually involve the youth in organizing the visits. For instance, drug-and-alcohol services will have one of the youth we've employed work side-by-side with a professional from the organization. Peers talking to peers.

MICHAEL: When I visited the Centre, what struck me was that these professionals were in the kitchen cooking. They weren't just offering workshops.

VICKI: Yes. Absolutely. It's about building relationships. The youth have a hard time trusting people. They've come through situations where they really don't trust adults much. And, of course, part of gaining trust is to earn it. For example, we had a counselor from drug and alcohol services in the kitchen cooking and it was hard for her because she was so used to working out of her office. But when she was working in the kitchen, she would also be having conversations with the youth and those conversations would focus on drugs and alcohol. The youth would start asking questions, but it was all done in a way that left them in their comfort zone. Some of them were pretty bold and wanted to deal with their drug and alcohol issues. Others would kind of skirt around the issue and then eventually go deeper. But we focused most on the relationship.

MICHAEL: What's the demographic make-up of the kids you serve and what are some of the challenges they face?

VICKI: I'd say 99% are First Nations. Aboriginal. And they come from all over the Yukon. Whitehorse is the capital of the Yukon, so a lot of the kids who run away from their communities end up in Whitehorse. Sixty percent of our youth are male. Their number one problem is lack of family support. Here in the Yukon we are still experiencing the effects of residential schools. So many of the young people who were in the residential schools back in the 60s and 70s, that had experienced a lot of trauma and abuse, they were never taught how to parent. So then when they started having kids of their own, they neglect them. A lot of our youth come from families where there is neglect, alcohol and drug abuse, physical abuse, emotional abuse. When they reach the age of about 14 or 15, if they haven't been apprehended by child welfare services, then they run away from home.

MICHAEL: What do you provide that makes the difference for these young people?

VICKI: We really focus on giving them a home environment. And a support system that will nurture their growth. Which means love, food, shelter....

MICHAEL: All the things that a home provides.

VICKI: Exactly. So we're kind of like their extended family.

MICHAEL: Even though they've had long periods of deprivation and neglect, what have you seen in terms of the effects of the program you provide?

VICKI: Well, our youth are very resilient in the sense that they are amazing human beings who are very strong. Once they see that there is hope…

MICHAEL: They respond to that?

VICKI: Absolutely. They make choices based on their environment. So we try to provide a healthy environment. Between the ages of 15 and 20, there is so much change happening within a young individual. If we can provide a safe environment for them with all the tools and everything that is needed for them to make it through those times, it's amazing how well they adjust and thrive. We don't have professional counselors that work out of the Centre, but if a youth is wanting one, there are lots of resources in Whitehorse that we can refer them to.

MICHAEL: So you become a gatekeeper.

VICKI: Basically. Though many of them seem to heal on their own. I don't know, love is pretty powerful.

MICHAEL: Would they heal without you?

VICKI: To be truthful, I think a lot of them wouldn't. Many of them told us that they would have killed themselves had we not been here for them. We've been here for 10 years now. Many of the older youth are still a part of what we are doing here. They're even employed here. We're hoping one day that the youth who we began working with years ago will actually take over the whole program and run it just as we have.

MICHAEL: I'm curious: in the context of Whitehorse, how do you define "doing well?"

VICKI: Well, say a young person comes in, and as we get to know them, they start sharing how they are feeling about life. We've had many that when they come in they are really depressed and suicidal, and chose drugs and alcohol to help them cope with the demons they are dealing with. So when they come in, they share all of that with us and we encourage them to hang in there. We provide them with support and hope. A lot of them open up and become very vulnerable because this is a safe place.

MICHAEL: So that would be part of doing well? When youth are able to be much more open about what they need. And connect.

VICKI: Yes. And see they have other options besides ending their life or staying on drugs and drinking. When they get to the point where they say, "Hmm, okay, maybe there is hope for me and a better life." Our program provides them with the support to think that way. Nobody else provided them with options other than the alcohol and the drugs. They come from environments where the only way to cope is to get drunk, to get high.

MICHAEL: How much would you say change is the result of individual factors in the child? And how much is the result of the environment that you create for that child?

VICKI: It's a little bit of both. But even the weakest individual becomes stronger because of the environment at the Centre. I'd say 99% of them excel just because they see there is hope. You need to remember, we're not an institution. That's why the Centre works. Institutionalized programming doesn't work, and running a program like an institution doesn't work either. We've done that and we've seen the negative results. From our school system to the justice system to health and social services. Running programs like an institution will only create individuals that adapt to being institutionalized. We try to get back to the basics. I think as a society we've lost what is basic to human beings. Love, being there for one another.

MICHAEL: Get people back to those basics.

VICKI: Then just fill in the gaps. Like what happened for this one young woman. She moved to Whitehorse when she was 17 from the Northwest Territories. She was basically on her own. She was addicted to crack and alcohol and was living a very at-risk lifestyle. When she first started coming to the Centre, she was very, very angry and she expressed this. But she was also an amazing artist, and she expressed her anger in her paintings. When I discussed it with her and I asked her exactly what the paintings meant to her, she would share grotesque stories about her feelings. Eventually we hired her because we try to target the ones most at-risk and we saw that she was one of them.

MICHAEL: What does she do?

VICKI: We have an employment and training program. Part of our programming is that we run a sign company. We teach the kids graphic design. Some of them actually go out and do sales as part of our fundraising. It depends on the individual and what they are naturally gifted at. Of course, she was an artist which was very useful. We also do other projects in the community with the youth. We do murals to cover up the graffiti, which is a real problem in Whitehorse, though we know from working with youth that graffiti is their way of speaking out. They are angry. They put their mark on our town whether it's positive or negative. It's as if they are saying, "I'm here." What we do is use that energy and direct them in positive ways. We'll hire maybe ten youth and find a business that has been, you know, dealing with a lot of graffiti and we'll get the kids painting murals. That's youth putting their mark on the city in a positive way. We've done probably 10 or 15 murals in the last 10 years. Not one of our murals, not one of the businesses that the kids have painted, have been graffitied.

MICHAEL: So in a sense you're helping these youth become part of the community. Making a contribution rather than causing problems.

VICKI: Yes. As they're walking around the city, they share what they've done with their grandma and uncles and aunties. Here in the Yukon, one youth could have hundreds of relatives. If you're First Nations, you can have a huge extended family. So the youth are very proud when they do something positive for the community. But we use Tough Love as well. I mean, encouraging them to spend money on something positive instead of crack. That young woman we hired, the first check she got she spent it on crack. So after that we refused to give her her check. We would give her an hour to go out and window shop for something to spend her money on before she got the money. And when she got her check, we would give her time off to go shopping. We paid her to do that. And she came back very excited and high on the fact that she felt so good about buying things and spending her money on something positive. Then we helped her put her portfolio together as an artist. Just this year she was accepted at a prestigious art school in Victoria. That's an amazing change in just four years.

MICHAEL: It's interesting that you're an informal organization doing this. What is it about government services that make them less likely to perform these roles?

VICKI: I think governments are run like institutions. They have forgotten the basics. They never have to worry about where their funding is coming from, so the pressure to adapt to what the community needs isn't really there. They can get really stuck in their ways.

MICHAEL: Is there something about what you're providing that fits particularly well for Aboriginal youth?

VICKI: It's unfortunate that the Aboriginal people of the Yukon are the ones that have had the hardest time. Any human being that had gone through the same circumstances that they've gone through would have had the same negative effects on them. So it's not about the youth being First Nations. We also do a lot of negotiating with First Nations governments, and we have their support which then puts a little more pressure on the territorial government to help young people.

MICHAEL: I see.

VICKI: It's all about power and control.

MICHAEL: I'm also curious about your own story. How did you come to be doing this work?

VICKI: I was originally from Saskatchewan. When I was four, my mom died and my dad had ten kids. Social Services thought that, being a man, he wasn't capable of taking care of kids. So they took all of us away. I was one of the younger ones and they put us into group homes. They split up the family and put us into foster care. Some of brothers were put into juvenile hall because they didn't have any place else to put them. My dad fought for a year to try and get us all back. Being that he was White, he had the right to go and fight for us. And he of course got us all back. At that same time, you need to remember, First Nations children were being taken away from their families. They didn't have the rights we had because of their skin color. For me, I could never understand that. And then when I moved to the Yukon, I noticed that the social environment was so unhealthy. I ran a day-care in Saskatchewan for 10 years, and then I set one up here and noticed that 50% of the kids at my day-care were on Ritalin. That was another shock. They were using Ritalin as a means to control the kids.

MICHAEL: I understand what you're saying.

VICKI: And I thought, there are so many people on the street, the homeless people. And then seeing the youth. There was nothing here for them, no support in place. That's where the idea came from. At my daycare I would have my kids until they were 12. They were wonderful, healthy, happy young people and then I'd meet them when they were 15, 16 and was like "What happened to you in 2 years?" They were on their own and then they got into trouble.

MICHAEL: How did you get the money to start the Center? What's your budget now?

VICKI: Well, the first year I was on welfare. We raised maybe $1500. We did a lot of lobbying. The first step was to get community support. Even if we didn't have a building or anything, we got the community behind the idea of the program. And then after that we got amazing support. The people here in the Yukon are awesome. They will do whatever they can to help. Our first building was donated by a bar owner here in Whitehorse who heard we wanted to set up our program. All we had to do was raise enough money to pay for the utilities. I was the only staff when we started. We now have a budget this year of $380,000. Service groups from the Yukon were a huge part of our funding at the beginning. Like the Elks and the Rotary Club. Today, the government is a little more open-minded, but it's still a struggle.

MICHAEL: You've created something very special.

VICKI: What we do is to appreciate, celebrate, and encourage each individual to be like a part of an entire body. Our community, too. I mean, our body parts work together. They don't fight amongst themselves. If we have cancer, the entire body dies. When it works in harmony, each cell, each organ doing its part and appreciating the other, the entire body survives. We need to encourage every youth to do what they're meant to do.

MICHAEL: That's the trick to your success?

VICKI: Absolutely.

An Interview with Arn Chorn-Pond: Helping Children in Cambodia Through the Revival of Traditional Music and Art

Arn Chorn-Pond and Michael Ungar

Arn Chorn-Pond is a survivor of the Khmer Rouge Killing Fields in Cambodia, a former child soldier, and an internationally recognized human rights leader. Currently he is the founder and spokesperson for Cambodian Living Arts, an organization dedicated to helping young people by reviving traditional arts and supporting their contemporary expression. He is also the subject of the Emmy-nominated documentary, *The Flute Player.*

Chorn-Pond was born into a family of performers and musicians who also operated a small theater in Cambodia's second-largest city, Battambang. After the Khmer Rouge came to power in 1975, Chorn-Pond was sent to a children's work camp. He escaped death by execution and starvation by learning to play revolutionary songs on the flute for the camp's leaders. In 1979, while being forced to fight against the Vietnamese, Chorn-Pond fled across the border to Thailand. It was in a refugee camp that Chorn-Pond was found, and later adopted, by Peter Pond, an American Lutheran minister and aid worker.

Once educated in the United States, Chorn-Pond began a series of community rebuilding projects and founded several organizations, including Children of War, Cambodian Volunteers for Community Development, Peace Makers (a U.S.-based gang-intervention project for Southeast Asian youths) and Cambodian Living Arts.

Chorn-Pond is the recipient of the Reebok Human Rights Award, the Anne Frank Memorial Award, and the Kohl Foundation International Peace Prize.

This interview was recorded in January, 2010.

ARN: In 1974 I was a boy in a small province called Batdambang

MICHAEL: How old were you then?

ARN: I was about 9 years old, and my brother and I were sent to the temple to be temple boys serving Buddhist monks and to learn the Cambodian language. I didn't even know that my family owned a theater company. I was too small. I didn't even know there was a war going on. But then the Khmer Rouge came in 1975 and they came with a truckload of kids, almost my own age. They had guns and frowned a lot and they were all wearing black. They screamed, "We beat Americans and now we are going to have peace." But as you may know it wasn't true. Three days later they kicked us out of our home and they started killing everybody. Or they forced people to work in the camps. They forced us to walk miles and miles through the countryside.

M. Ungar (✉)
Killam Professor of Social Work,
Dalhousie University, Halifax, NS, Canada
e-mail: Michael.Ungar@dal.ca

M. Ungar (ed.), *The Social Ecology of Resilience: A Handbook of Theory and Practice,*
DOI 10.1007/978-1-4614-0586-3_10, © Springer Science+Business Media, LLC 2012

They killed whoever they thought were pro-American. I was separated from my family and forced to live in a temple area that they converted into a killing place. Seven hundred kids my age or a little older than me were forced to work from 5 o'clock in the morning to 12 o'clock at night with no food. We were starving. I remember that we were not prisoners but we were forced to live there. And 3 or 4 or 5 times a day they would kill people and force us all to watch. I was forced to push people into graves. If you didn't do what the Khmer Rouge said, they'd kill you too.

During my time at the temple, in the middle of all the killing the Khmer Rouge forced us to play music for their revolutionary song. They told us they were going to start a music class and asked who would like to play. So I raised my hand because I knew if I became a musician they might give me more food. And I knew that I had a special skill. I learned faster than any of the other kids. The three kids that didn't learn well, they ended up in the Orange Grove, like tens of thousands of other people the Khmer Rouge killed. And my master, my first master, whose name I didn't even know, he was allowed to teach us for 5 days. He also ended up in the Orange Grove. Lucky for me, they didn't force me to kill him. Because the Khmer Rouge played games, they played games with people. They killed people only with axes and sticks. Most of the victims had their liver and spleens taken out and many times they used to fry those and lure us to eat them. I lived in that temple for 2 years and I calculated that probably 16,000 people were slaughtered there. Only about 50 or 60 kids survived after 2 years from the 700 I came with.

Then in 1979, the Vietnamese took over Cambodia and I was given a gun by the Khmer Rouge like thousands of other kids. And I was told to fight against the Vietnamese. I was 12 probably, 12 or 13. Imagine kids getting guns without training. We were used as human shields against the Vietnamese. I was in that war, full blown war, probably for about a year and then I ran away into the jungle of Cambodia, and across the border to Thailand. I was on my last leg, I was very thin, I had malaria. Many of my friends died, shot near the border. I was unconscious in the bush when five or six girls that lived along the Thai border found me and carried me into a refugee camp. And then my dad stepped on me, literally, he stepped on me trying to rescue people from a flood. It was 1980 and I don't know what happened next. I didn't speak English at all. He took me in the trunk of a car from Thailand and somehow I ended up in New Hampshire that fall.

MICHAEL: Sorry, he took you in the trunk of a car?

ARN: Out of the refugee camp in the trunk, to Bangkok. Then out of Bangkok. I found out later that the reason he did that is because the queen of Thailand knew his mother and the queen gave him three wishes. So he took two other kids, three of us, quietly from the camp. We were the first three children to leave Cambodia and go to New Hampshire. The day after I got to America he took me to the mall and to McDonalds and I asked for rice, and he said, "No rice in America." But I liked ketchup.

MICHAEL: What I'm trying to understand is what made the difference for you? Why did you do so well in life starting off from such difficult circumstances?

ARN: As soon as I got out of Cambodia and arrived in America, that started another part of a difficult life. It's a different world here. New Hampshire is another jungle. America. I didn't know what was in store for me. I think the environment, like you say, does a lot to you. If that environment is snowing, I will be cold. If the condition is like Cambodia, the environment is hot, I get hot. It's the same thing for psychological effects. I didn't understand then but I understand now that it took close to 7 years after arriving in America and feeling I couldn't survive until I finally felt better. I often got angry and I didn't know why. I got angry at myself, or confused, or got angry at the world. I blanked out a lot of the time. I wanted to kill myself. I wanted to kill other people. I wanted to pull my English teacher's hair, and I wanted to swear at my principal in high school. I felt cornered. I felt like nobody understood, nobody understood me. Kids were making fun of me in high school. I went to the wrong bathroom, whatever. Everywhere, there was confusion. I ran away from home. I got arrested.

The turning point, I think for me, was realizing the love I felt for my foster father. I can say the word love now. My foster father Peter Pond, and my foster mother Shirley Pond, were always there for me. And many times when I did something wrong I expected them to kill me like the Khmer Rouge did. The Khmer Rouge would not have given me any chances. I would have been dead. I expected my mom and dad to kill me but they didn't. They kept saying, "There is nothing wrong with you." They kept saying that every morning. Both of them saying, "What you have went through is not your fault." But I didn't believe them. I didn't speak English in fact.

But after a while, they kept saying that same thing every morning over many years. And they'd hug me. They'd kiss me. I didn't want them to. It was strange to me that these people were doing that because I had never, never felt a hug from anybody. There were other hugs too, later on, like from Judith Thompson, who co-founded the Children of War with me in 1984. When she heard me speak for the very first time in a big cathedral, she gave me a big, big hug afterwards.

MICHAEL: How old were you then?

ARN: I was about 17, or maybe 16.

MICHAEL: How did it come about that you were speaking at that church?

ARN: They heard me speak at a small church in New Hampshire and I appeared in a newspaper in New Hampshire. That was when I started speaking out. My dad said, "You know, you must speak about your own life because if you start speaking about your life, many Americans, especially young people, will care about your cause and we will be able together to bring more of your friends from the camps." So I bought it. I didn't want to speak. Because I thought, "American kids they are all making fun of me." I never thought they would care about Cambodia or about my story. Peter encouraged me to do it and I said let's try. I memorized the words. "My name is Arn Chorn-Pond, I was 8 years old when the Khmer Rouge came and my parents and my family died. I saw so many people die during the Khmer Rouge. Pol Pot."

MICHAEL: What was it like having an audience that appreciated what you said?

ARN: That was the first time in the church.

MICHAEL: Did you go to church when you were growing up with your foster family?

ARN: My foster dad, he's a reverend.

MICHAEL: Oh I see.

ARN: Now remember, we were the first three Cambodians allowed to come to the United States from Thailand. And there was a little girl who came to me after I spoke at the church, she was almost 12 years old, almost the same age that I was when I left Cambodia. She looked at me and said, "I'm sorry for what happened to you and your family and your sister, your brother" and she gave me a dollar. She said, "A dollar, that is what I have. I appreciate you sharing your story and I wouldn't want any American children to go through what you went through. I'm very lucky." Then they made a row, all 15 people in the church. A line to come and hug me. I think I felt very strange, but I felt kind of good too. I was willing to do it, to start fundraising. Then I went back to the Thai border with Cambodia and I started to give that money to people who needed it.

MICHAEL: You seem to be describing two very different people. Who you were before you started speaking out, and who you have become after you started speaking out.

ARN: It started that day in the church. That was the beginning for me.

MICHAEL: How did the speaking out change how you see yourself?

ARN: You know, I had a sister die slowly in the jungle. I watched her die slowly and rot to death. And I still feel guilty that I didn't have a chance to share my luck with anybody. Two or three years after I got to America, even my own dad didn't know what I went through. He kind of understands it a little. He went to Thailand. But my mom had no clue about what the Cambodians went through. Nobody knows. In my head I really

sort of turned around with the caring, especially from that little girl in the church. Until then, I didn't think anybody would care, especially the white kids.

MICHAEL: Is there something about the act of speaking out that is healing? Or is there something about knowing there is a community around you? Gaining the recognition from others? I'm trying to understand what it is that would be important to help other children fleeing from war.

ARN: I'm not sure. I don't feel I understand, even today. But people, they all have a little different story and they probably heal through different things. I can only speak about me. Some gang members I work with, I talk to those kids only 1 or 2 or 3 times, and they change. Of course, some kids never change at all. They die, they get killed in the streets. Maybe it's much easier for me to hear those kids talk, and for them to hear me.

MICHAEL: What you went through with your sister tells me a lot about your strength as a person.

ARN: I don't know. I told you the love from my dad was strong, unconditional. And then meeting others too. All these years they never gave up on me, you know?

MICHAEL: Can you talk a little bit more about what that means? Having that kind of support? What should people do when they meet a child who's really having trouble?

ARN: There were people always there for me in America. When I called them, they found time for me. And they listened. They cried when I spoke and said, "Arn, I never heard anyone share a story like you so would you join me to start an organization that can bring people like you from all over the world to America." I never felt used. It took a long time for me to believe that they wanted to help. I'm still with these people. I think I chose the right people in my life.

MICHAEL: They seemed to have showed you a lot of respect.

ARN: And they were willing to listen to me. They were willing to cry with me. Before I didn't trust people easily. I worried they were like the Khmer Rouge. The Khmer Rouge also said to me, "Don't worry, Arn, we're not going to kill you." And then they started killing my friends, they started killing other people who I knew. Or maybe these people in America would be like the Japanese who came to the refugee camp and they wanted to help us, they wanted to take me to Japan. But then I found out that they wanted to sleep with us. So in my life I don't trust people easily. Then here were people who were saying the same thing, "Don't worry, we love you," and all of that. Except these people, like Judith and my adopted family, they just wanted to hug me.

MICHAEL: You said something that caught my attention. Something I hear from other children that I work with. You said you never felt like these people were using you for their own ends.

ARN: No, no.

MICHAEL: I guess that's always the danger, that people will use you.

ARN: I learned not to trust people easily. But the four or five people that I chose to be my brothers and sisters over the years, they continue to help me with the work I do in Cambodia. When I call them, they have time for me. When I go visit them, they give me advice. I hug them, we cry together when we talk and we talk about life and about our commitment to peace around the world. And they know I am committing my life

to peace. And when I see them I feel even more compassion, more love, growing out of them and being given to me.

MICHAEL: Does it help that you have a passion in life, a vocation to help others? Is that something that helps make your life better?

ARN: Yes. Because I have a sort of confidence in myself. I understand what I went through. I understand why there's suffering around the world. I wouldn't be able to know that and live through that without the hope I hear from other children. I've met them and shared stories with them.

MICHAEL: Let me ask you, then, about some other things that may have been helpful in your life. Could you comment on the role of the education you got after you came to America. You have a bachelors degree from Providence College.

ARN: At that school I didn't learn much about other people's suffering or anything like that. I took international relations but I learned only about European governments.

MICHAEL: Oh no!

ARN: I learned almost nothing about other people, about the war, about the genocide. I heard much about the Jewish Holocaust and all of that but not very much about many other places.

MICHAEL: Did you feel that the education was not relevant to you?

ARN: It took me 7 years to finish high school, and seven more years to finish college. Everybody told me how important it is to go to college, so I just did it, learned things, especially English. I learned English through my mom when I was in high school. We got up at four every morning to learn English. English was important to me because I think if not for learning the language

I would have killed myself. I think my anger would have exploded if I didn't speak English and I couldn't express myself.

MICHAEL: You went 7 years through college. What was it that kept you engaged? That kept you going?

ARN: I almost thought I couldn't do it. I kept asking myself, "Why study?" I was first at Brown University for 2 years. It's an Ivy League school. Former president Jimmy Carter wrote me a recommendation when he heard me speak at Emory University. He heard about my story and he cried and we hugged each other and he wrote a recommendation for me. He even got Amnesty International to invite me as a keynote speaker. I've been with Amnesty for 15 years. I went on to join Amnesty International's Reebok Concert Tour when I was at Brown University. But I was also asked, even forced, to see a psychiatrist when I was at Brown and at Providence College because I behaved sometimes not very good. I'm not sure how I broke a school window. Sometimes, I used to do things like that. Maybe that's why I like to help people in gangs. I have a lot of anger myself. I was even arrested by the police because they thought I was with the gang, and the gang shot at me because they thought I was working for the police. But I was also able to form a group called Peacemaker and they got five million dollars from Clinton. I like to take pride in that. And it's still running.

MICHAEL: Am I hearing you say, then, that setting up these organizations, these nongovernmental organizations, that was helpful to you?

ARN: I don't know. The thing is that when they asked me to see a psychiatrist, they also forced me to stay in school, to finish school. They said to me, "School is important Arn." But at the same time I snuck out of school and went to speak about my own life. To raise money and raise awareness. I knew I couldn't survive in school if I didn't do all that stuff. That's why I got into trouble in school because I told them I didn't go anywhere but the next day I was in *The New York Times* and *Boston Globe*. I couldn't hide it.

MICHAEL: You have a wonderful spirit.

ARN: I did it mostly on my own. That's how people got to know me and got to know my name.

MICHAEL: And people like Jimmy Carter, they noticed you and offered you very tangible assistance. This was important? That people really went out of their way to help you.

ARN: Yes. I didn't know who he was, the President. But people kept asking me to speak and I never got money for what I did. How many years? 15 years and I never charged money to tell my story.

MICHAEL: How did you support yourself?

ARN: I live on a shoestring. I've never had a bank account until 2 years ago. I mean I lived here 25 years and I never thought of getting an account. I never buy any stuff on my own.

MICHAEL: How did you afford university?

ARN: I got a full scholarship, a Presidential Scholarship at Providence College. That's how I survived.

MICHAEL: Your father was a minister. I'm curious, is the church important to resilience in children? What would you say?

ARN: It's part of it. It's part of the healing if you get support from it. But, you know, I get a lot of support, true support, from the kids that I work with who are gang members. They will even risk their lives for me, like the kids in the jungle in Cambodia. When I reflect on my own path, I remember there were many kids who would run through bullets for me in the jungle in Cambodia. And then I start thinking, why did they get killed for me? Why did those kids give up their lives for me? I think so that I would have a chance in life. To teach others.

MICHAEL: You're doing some amazing work. You haven't just helped yourself, you have reached out to help others. Could you describe briefly what you're doing in Cambodia and speak to why it makes a difference in people's lives. How does it make young people become better able to survive?

ARN: I went back to Cambodia for the first time in 1989. I was scared to go back. I couldn't find many members of my family. They were all killed, but I met a former teacher who taught me how to play the flute, which I did during my time with the Khmer Rouge. He was still alive, cutting hair and drunk and nobody cared about him. And I met other masters of the arts. Household names like Cambodia's last opera singer. He was drunk on the street, and nobody cared about any of them. They told me about my family, that my family owned a theater company in the past. That's why they were killed by the Khmer Rouge. Ninety percent of all the performers were killed. So I realized my country's culture is down the tube. And I started to reflect on my life. It was music that saved my life. The Khmer Rouge wanted to kill me but the music I played for them, their revolutionary song, that saved me. When I came back from Cambodia to America, I heard my old master calling me, "Arn, please come back and

help me to play music again." So in 1998 I started Cambodia Living Arts with a few of these old masters. I didn't know what was going to happen.

MICHAEL: That's wonderful.

ARN: In 1998 *The New York Times* wrote about me. That Arn Pond went back to Cambodia to try to save the art and culture of Cambodia. I didn't tell them it wasn't true. I was just trying to pay my respect to the art and the culture. Not to save it.

MICHAEL: Had art and music been a big part of your life here in North America?

ARN: I played the flute and a lot of people liked it. They liked it very much. I made everybody cry but I never thought I was a musician.

MICHAEL: How will the old masters recreating the arts in Cambodia help young people? Can you explain the link?

ARN: It's very simple. The young people are now starting to do hip hop and watch MTV. They talk about sex and violence too. They get hooked on anything that is from the West. In the 60s, if people sang American songs, they got killed by Pol Pot. But now, they are behaving really badly. They drink more, they have sex earlier, and they disrespect older people. They act confused, just as I did in the past. They need to learn about their own culture, their own traditions, so those traditions won't die out. I tell them, "It's you, the masters and the traditional instruments, and your culture, all of it is you. If it dies, you will die too. Trust me, because it's true." On top of that we are not only teaching them the music. Many of these old masters are about to die, and the young people's grandparents are going to die too. Some young people don't believe that Pol Pot even existed.

MICHAEL: That's horrible.

ARN: And then I talk to them about it. I explain to them that I lost my family, and they say, "Is it true Arn?" I say, "Yeah." Some of them stop drinking and the girls stop prostituting themselves. They come to play music instead. And we have a stipend for them. We give them not only music classes but also have to be practical. We give them computers, we give them English lessons, we tell them, "You have freedom. You have the future."

MICHAEL: How do you find these kids, or how do these kids find you?

ARN: Cambodians are so confused. They don't know whether they are Americans or Korean or Vietnamese or Chinese or Cambodian. If you don't know where you came from, and you most likely don't know who you, you're not going to know where you're going in your life.

MICHAEL: So these masters are providing not just some support, some stipends, some training, they're also connecting these young people back to their identity, their culture, their sense of being Cambodian. They are helping young people take some pride in that.

ARN: That's their soul. Music and art helps us learn about ourselves. From the day you're born to the day you die, music and dance exist. We need it. I can see these girls who become prostitutes. You know, they are very scared. They're on the street and I know they don't want to sleep with guys 10 times a day. It destroys their self-esteem. When they start dancing I can see they don't even know what's happening to them. They have no way to explain who they are. But when I ask them to dance for the kids that I have brought from America, kids their own age, 12 years old, 13 years old, from high

school, then I can see them put their heads up high and smile. When they start dancing there's confidence. Other good things will happen if you have confidence in yourself. And these girls have confidence.

MICHAEL: It sounds beautiful.

ARN: I asked them why they were crying, the kids from America. And they said the dancers have nothing but they wanted to us their dances. And the American kids feel they are so very lucky to be living in America. Both sides win. American kids need to cry and Cambodian kids need to smile. Art is so powerful

MICHAEL: How many kids do you help in Cambodia?

ARN: Cambodian Living Arts is the organization I started 10 years ago. I started with 30 kids. It's now grown to 80,000 members who support us. When Cambodian Living Arts started we had just two or three masters. Now we have about 15 masters in 10 provinces and about 500 or 600 students learning professionally about their own culture and developing musical skills. And we help get kids off the street and out of prostitution. We teach them to speak English and create informal schools for them in the slums.

MICHAEL: How are the children selected? How do you choose which children get to participate?

ARN: There are so many of them. The masters chose certain ones, but sometimes we just help whoever comes. Cambodian kids are not difficult at all. If anybody gives them an opportunity they just grab it. American kids are harder to work with because they get so blinded by the mall and by material things that they don't take opportunities when they have them. With a Cambodian kid, if I give them one opportunity in their life, they know that it's probably the last one they'll get and they grab it. So it's not hard to find the kids. They want to change their lives. They want to do something for the world.

MICHAEL: Arn, your lived expertise is so beyond mine. What, then, does resilience mean to you? What makes a child become resilient, or able to survive great hardship? What is it that makes the difference in a child's life, between a child who doesn't survive great hardship and a child who does?

ARN: I think if he's still alive at all, he needs a person, two persons, or a whole community, or the nation, or the world to just keep looking at who he is, in his heart, and just keep telling him, "You are a child, you didn't do anything wrong, you were forced to do what you were forced to do, or had done to you. We love you no matter what." It was 15 years, until I started believing that and was able to separate myself from the suffering that was in me. I was lucky to travel around the world and meet other children like me, and hear their stories, stories that are even worse than mine. I was able for the first time to cry for someone else, to hear someone else's story besides my own.

MICHAEL: So sharing stories makes us more resilient.

ARN: Yes. When I began to know that I can cry for someone else, and know my suffering is also shared by other people who suffer. But that takes time. A lot of time.

MICHAEL: Time, sharing in a community of others, people who really believe in you…

ARN: I can't explain it. But that worked. I proved to the Khmer Rouge that they didn't get me. I don't act like they forced me to act. I did what I did then because I was afraid that

they were going to kill me. But now I can give them the finger and say they're not bringing me down. I don't do what they do.

MICHAEL: So at the time you kept going because of fear, but now, looking back, it's the people you found, and who found you, the ones who care for you, that's what's healing.

ARN: I get my revenge on the Khmer Rouge by not doing the things they do. When I heard that America bombed Cambodia against international law, that made me think I'll get revenge. We are now lobbying and it's going to happen in 2012. It's an historic event with Cambodian Living Arts. We're going to have 70 artists, the masters and the students themselves, come to Carnegie Hall to perform for Americans and get them laughing and smiling and clapping. I will drop artists in Manhattan, not terrorists, not bombs like they did to us.

MICHAEL: So this being different from the Khmer Rouge is one aspect of your resilience. What about the fact that someone rescued you? Or that you had food and safety and someone gave you support. The scholarship you received to go to school. Are all of those material things also important for resilience?

ARN: Yes, yes. Those mean love too. But not as much as, you know, physical or mental caring. Being assured that you are someone's brother or sister and that they love you and are not going to give up on you, that's what's important.

MICHAEL: So in other words we could provide a child with food and safety and family, but those instrumental things aren't enough unless the people around the child also gave him time, a sense of community, a sense of purpose, stand by the child, don't give up on the child.

ARN: Yes, all of those things are what a child needs.

MICHAEL: Make it personal.

ARN: There are Arn Chorn-Ponds everywhere. Just love them, don't judge them. Love them as you would your own kid. Care for them. I cannot stress that enough. Some people take more time than other people to respond. Children, they are all flowers. Some flowers smell good, some don't smell good. Some flowers don't look good, but they are all flowers. Love them all. Don't judge them. Don't say, "This is my child and this is my race. You are not of my race, you are not my child, so I don't love you." No, every child is your child, every race is your race. Love them all. Look them in the eye and say, "We love you. You didn't do anything wrong. No matter what, we will love you because you are the future. You are us."

Part III

The Individual (in Context)

From Neuron to Social Context: Restoring Resilience as a Capacity for Good Survival

Martha Kent

The qualities of good survival in extreme situations have inspired the search for the neurobiological mechanisms supporting adaptation in extreme environments. The goal of this chapter is to provide a brief selective historical review of basic brain, endocrine, and behavioral mechanisms that constitute resilience at a biobehavioral level. The processes to be reviewed include concepts of homeostasis, affiliation as an antistress system, brain circuits that respond to features of context, mirror neurons and social neural networks, and the nature of agency in resilient adaptation.

Resilience does not occur in isolation. It is an interactive process that requires someone or something to interact with. It is dependent upon context or environment, including our most important relationships. How are individuals and their brains resilient in their social environment? The short answer is that our neurophysiological constitutions find viable ways of being in our worlds. Understanding the neurobiological mechanisms supporting resilience is a recent development, indeed is emerging as technology advances.

Localization of Brain Functions: The Disease and Accident Model

The brain as a socially responsive organ of the human anatomy did not appear as a concept until 1990 when Leslie Brothers (1990) coined the expression "social brain" to refer to primate cognitive processes that detect the intentions of others. These "social cognitions" were related to neural activity that could be investigated. Brothers arrived at this position after an extensive review of the literature on primate social signals, the discovery of primate "social" neurons, and a review of human impaired social cognition in autism, recognition of faces, frontal lobe surgeries, and temporal lobe stimulation. Human brain disorders and experimental animal models provided the decisive clues to Brothers' recognition of the brain's role in social processes.

An interval of 130 years separates Brothers' social brain hypothesis and the first scientific demonstrations locating higher human functions in the brain, notably Paul Broca's work of the 1860s that localized speech in the left frontal cortical area. This period represents a time of unparalleled growth in scientific methods and models of observation that expanded the scope and depth of inquiry into brain functions.

The nineteenth century opened with Franz Joseph Gall's model of the brain in which he hypothesized that the convolutions of the head

M. Kent (✉)
Phoenix VA Healthcare System, Phoenix, AZ, USA
e-mail: markent@ix.netcom.com

corresponded to organs beneath the skull that controlled particular mental functions. Each of the 27 organs represented a particular function such as affection, vanity, and others. Phrenology spread widely, placing its books in many homes, and applying its methods to the evaluation of many prominent leaders. In 1822, the Académie Français commissioned Pierre Flourens to test Gall's theory. Flourens proceeded by destroying varying amounts of cortex in chickens, frogs, and other animals. He found that the destruction of one part of the cerebrum affected all functions. All parts of the cortex were responsible for each of the faculties, thus appearing to falsify Gall's mosaic of cortical organs and associated faculties.

However flawed, phrenology did point to the brain as the place to look for human faculties. The idea of cortical localization gained particular ascendancy through discoveries concerning impaired speech. Passionate discussions and dramatic demonstrations on speech and the brain took place in Paris in mid-nineteenth century. Jean-Baptiste Bouillaud had collected hundreds of cases where loss of speech was associated with anterior lobe injury. He offered a price to anyone who could contradict this finding. Bouillard lost the wager. Simon Aubertin described a case of a man who had shot himself in the head. The injury had exposed his brain, allowing Aubertin to apply degrees of pressure to the anterior cortex, thereby stopping or reinstating the patient's speech. A few days after Aubertin's presentation in 1861, Paul Broca presented the case of "Tan," the only word his patient had uttered. On autopsy, Tan's brain showed a prominent left anterior cortical lesion, a finding immortalized as Broca's area and Broca's aphasia. Two years later, using many cases, Gustav Dax demonstrated left hemisphere dominance for speech. Thus began the intense activity over localizing the functions of the brain, present to this day, and cast in its modern version in the varieties of imaging studies (for a detailed historical review see Finger, 2000).

To this localization tradition based on disorders and injury belongs the case of Phineas Gage, the foreman of a crew building the Burlington Northern Railroad. While tamping the explosive, premature ignition of the powder shot the tamping iron through the left side of Gage's jaw and through the top of his skull. Gage survived but was much changed: used profanity, acted impulsively and childlike, and was irresponsible. Gage was no longer Gage; an astonishing discovery showing that damage to his frontal lobes had changed his personality (Harlow, 1848).

How Hormones, Neurotransmitters, and the Internal Milieu Relate to the Environment

Stress Hormones and Neurotransmitters

While the brain-focused approaches increasingly uncovered cortical faculties, the body demonstrated the necessity of adapting to and taking the environment into account in ways that sustained life. Thus, the importance of the environment or context entered through the back door of the body with the *milieu intérieur* of Claude Bernard (Gross, 1998). Bernard noted that extracellular fluid constituted the immediate internal environment. The stability of this cellular milieu protected warm-blooded mammals in their ability to survive freely and independently in many different environments. The "external variations" of the environment were compensated for by "the conditions of life in the internal environment" (Gross, p. 383). Bernard's concept had little impact for over 50 years until it came to influence the work of Walter Cannon.

The study of how the body coordinated physiological processes in order to maintain steady states under conditions of challenge and rest became Cannon's life work. He called this process of mobilization of resources during challenge and restoring resources during rest *homeostasis* (Cannon, 1929). How the body automatically corrected physiological parameters under these conditions was controlled by the autonomic nervous system (ANS). The sympathetic nervous system (SNS) maintained homeostasis and was engaged quickly during challenges, as it mobilized the energies of the body through the secretion of epinephrine and norepinephrine (adrenaline and noradrenaline), which in turn released glucose and fatty acids, increased the heart rate and blood pressure, and rushed energy to muscles for fight–flight action, and away from organs and activities not needed for emergency response, such as digestion. The parasympathetic nervous system (PNS) preserved body energies and functioned in a restorative manner by promoting digestion, growth, reproduction, and immune responses. It was engaged when threats had subsided. In major ways the two branches of the ANS, the sympathetic and parasympathetic, are said to act in opposition to each other. When one is engaged, the other is reduced in its activation.

In his early studies, Cannon examined, with the use of X-rays, the influence of SNS on the movements of the stomach and intestines in cats. The movements stopped with strong emotional stimuli and returned when the animal was relaxed or asleep, thus demonstrating the decreased activation of the SNS during digestion. He examined the role of the SNS in maintaining homeostasis during various bodily disturbances, as in hemorrhages, hypoglycemia, low and high body temperature, muscle exercise, and others. He found that the SNS acted promptly, mobilized energies quickly, and had a widespread effect that acted in a coordinated response in one direction, such as fight–flight.

Cannon viewed behavior itself as a homeostatic mechanism. Homeostatic mechanisms of temperature regulation were evident in shivering, seeking shelter, and putting on a coat. He even suggested that some "social homeostatic" mechanism was needed "to support bodily homeostasis" and thereby expanded Bernard's idea of self-regulation of bodily fluids in the wider social environment. Cannon summarized his positive view of the body's adaptive abilities in his book, *The Wisdom of the Body* (1932).

While Cannon was the first to recognize the role of the SNS and the role of epinephrine and norepinephrine in the acute stress response, Hans Selye (1956) pioneered its glucocorticoid component and the role of glucocorticoids in chronic stress, the best known of these being cortisol. In his search for the next new hormone, Selye injected rats with a variety of hormones and found that they all had the same effect on the organism. Even other toxins and challenges of heat, cold, or pain had the same effect. He called this pattern of responses *general adaptation*

syndrome (GAS). When chronically stressed by crowding, noise, or fighting, the animals died. On autopsy they had enlarged adrenal glands, enlarged pituitary glands, shrunken thymuses, and stomach ulcers. Selye attributed these findings to an excess of adrenal hormones. He thought these hormones formed a signaling system that involved the pituitary, the adrenal cortex, and the release of glucocorticoids, parts of a system known today as the hypothalamic–pituitary–adrenal (HPA) axis.

McEwen writes of Selye's work: "Most conspicuously absent was a demonstrable link connecting the emotions, the stress response, and the brain…the scientists of Selye's day did not accept the brain as the master coordinator of the stress response" (McEwen, 2002, p. 40). McEwen aptly observes that the emotions were not considered to be a function of the brain either. Indeed the brain was not considered an "emotional organ" until Paul McLean's identification of the limbic system in the 1950s. The 1980s changed this state of affairs, first with the conceptualization of *allostasis* (Sterling & Eyer, 1988) and McEwen's formulation of *allostatic load* (McEwen & Stellar, 1993), and second, with the studies of oxytocin as a social/affiliative antistress hormone and neuropeptide.

Sterling and Eyer proposed the concept of *allostasis* for maintaining stability through finely tuned changes that matched resources and needs, such as the cardiovascular system at rest and active states. McEwen (McEwen & Stellar, 1993) extended the concept of allostasis to other physiological mediators, notably cortisol, catecholamines (epinephrine and norepinephrine), age as a mediator, and others. McEwen also proposed that inefficiencies in allostasis over a longer period of time could result in accumulated negative effects, or *allostatic load*. This process resulting in allostatic load is more comprehensive than chronic stress in that it covers more facets that affect adaptation: genes, early development, life style, diet, exercise, smoking, alcohol, and other inefficiencies (McEwen & Seeman, 1999). Cannon's relatively simple concept of homeostasis has become a much more nuanced and complex process connecting organism and environment in richly textured ways.

The Affiliative Hormone and Neuropeptide

At last we arrive at an endocrine and neuropeptide system that is social and affiliative and is said to function as an antistress system. If there is an entity such as Cannon's "social homeostasis," a possible candidate might be the oxytocin affiliation system. This work began with the study of the monogamous prairie vole *Microtus orchogaster* during the early 1980s (Getz & Carter, 1980), 50 years after Cannon's seminal work on *homeostasis* and 100 years after Bernard's formulation of the *milieu intérieur*. The starting point for Getz and Carter was not the brain or physiological mechanisms that were in need of explanation, but the particular social arrangement of monogamy in these voles. The question as to the possible brain mechanisms that could differentiate between the monogamous voles and polygamous montane voles, or *Microtus montanus*, emerged from questions about a social arrangement. Getz and Carter identified the difference between monogamous and polygamous voles in the number and distribution of oxytocin receptors in the brain. These two strains of voles quickly became a powerful animal model for the study of the role of oxytocin in social behavior through methods of injecting oxytocin directly into the animal's brain. Since oxytocin did not cross the blood–brain barrier, peripheral oxytocin could not be taken to reflect comparable levels of central oxytocin. Injection of oxytocin directly into the brains of voles resulted in increased social behavior, pair bonding, attachment, sexual behavior, exploration or approach to novelty, and decreases in stress and pain. Oxytocin could also be released by social interaction, touch, warm water, massage, sexual behavior, and lactation (Carter & DeVries, 1999).

Uvnaes-Moberg and colleagues (Uvnaes-Moberg & Roberta, 2005; Uvnaes-Moberg, 1998) call the oxytocin affiliative response pattern the "calm and connection" pattern, which is physiologically supported by the vagal PNS and compliments the fight–flight stress response. When the vagal PNS is activated, sympathetic system activities are reduced. Characteristic parasympathetic activities emerge, such as increased digestion, relaxed muscles, lower cardiovascular activity, and lower cortisol that are accompanied by feelings of calm, well-being, and positive social interaction. In this parasympathetic mode, energy is used for the purposes of growth and restoration rather than for muscular activity. The calm and connection pattern can be evoked by calming sensory stimulation of touch and warmth and by environmental and psychological positive interaction. Feelings of calm and connection are slower to emerge in contrast to the immediate reactions of fight–flight.

Oxytocin thus functions as a multifaceted endogenous system for buffering stress.

Circuits in the Brain Respond to the Environment: The Fear Circuit

As the study of the brain deepened from gross cortical structures to neurotransmitters, it simultaneously expanded to questions about how brain circuits responded to the threats and rewards posed by the environment. Animal models could manipulate context, lesion areas of the brain, and empirically measure the responses of the lesioned organism. Joseph LeDoux did exactly that: he manipulate context and lesioned the brains of rats in his hunt for the brain's fear circuit.

To elicit fear reliably, LeDoux turned to fear conditioning, a well-established experimental model in which foot shock elicited fear in rats while sound alone did not elicit fear. By pairing the neutral sound with mild foot shock, the neutral sound came to elicit fear when the sound was presented alone. The sound was no longer neutral but became a cue for foot shock and impending danger. At a physiological level the sympathetic response releases stress hormones and mobilizes energy in preparation for fight–flight.

To find the fear network, LeDoux (1996; LeDoux & Phelps, 2000) followed "the natural flow of information through the brain" (1996, p. 151). He started at the highest part of the brain, or the cortex, and moved to interior and lower areas.

He lesioned the relevant auditory cortex. This had no effect on the fear response. He lesioned the next lower level, the auditory part of the thalamus. This did prevent fear conditioning. The sound stimulus did have to enter the thalamus, the station for all sensory input. LeDoux then disconnected the auditory thalamus from the amygdala. This also prevented conditioning. The essential fear circuit consisted of the thalamus and the amygdala, a circuit that could transmit fear signals without going through the cortex. LeDoux called this path the "low road" as compared to the "high road" in which the fear circuit took the longer route through the auditory cortex. The thalamus–amygdala, or low road, was faster but less accurate in that the thalamus provided rough details of a potential threat. The thalamo-cortico-amygdala path, or high road, was slower but more accurate and detailed in identifying danger. LeDoux thus demonstrated that emotional learning about danger in the environment could bypass the neocortex and higher processing activities of the brain and take the quicker short route through the thalamic-amygdala path, a route with distinct survival advantage. Better to be wrong and alive than right and dead.

Brain-Environment Dimensions

We have encountered one biobehavioral dimension in the form of the ANS and its sympathetic branch responsive to threat with fight–flight capacities and the parasympathetic branch engaged during digestion and restorative functions. Since Cannon, investigators have proposed a number of broad brain–behavior–environment dimensions. In an interesting paper Schneirla proposed that biphasic processes supported "how animals generally manage to reach beneficial conditions and stay away from the harmful, that is, how *survivors* do this" (1959, p. 1). Approach was defined as coming nearer to a stimulus source and withdrawal as increasing the distance to a stimulus source.

The main principle supporting this biphasic approach–withdrawal was intensity of stimulation. Schneirla argued that in all organisms low intensities of stimulation evoked approach reactions while high intensities of stimulation evoked withdrawal reactions. Low-energy stimulation led to food or other benefits, including no harm, while high-energy stimulation led to harm or death: "stimulative energy fundamentally dominates the approach and withdrawal responses of all animals" (p. 7). Low-intensity stimulation brought about vegetative changes through the parasympathetic system while high-intensity stimulation produced interruptive changes through activation of the sympathetic system and adrenalin secretion. Schneirla believed that his approach–withdrawal concepts summarized a broad biobehavioral evolutionary adaptive mechanism grounded in the works of Darwin, Cannon, Sherrington, and others.

An entirely different conception of approach–withdrawal evolved from the study of emotional concepts, one common method being the study of words representing emotions. Here investigators asked for judgments about emotional states and emotional objects. The goal was to identify the basic features of emotions. Results uncovered fundamental conceptual dimensions, the most common being two-dimensional ones of pleasant vs. unpleasant and activated vs. deactivated (e.g., Russell, 1979, 1980; Russell & Feldman Barrett, 1999). Russell proposed a "circumplex" model in which mood words could be arranged around the perimeter of a circle, segmented by two basic dimensions.

Subsequent investigations confirmed the two-dimensional structure (Watson & Tellege, 1985). However, more recently, Watson and colleagues (Watson, Wise, Vaidya, & Tellegen, 1999) concluded that the model did not fit the data closely. They identified two unipolar constructs of Negative Activation and Positive Activation that functioned independently as two basic biobehavioral systems of activation evolved for key adaptive tasks.

Taking a more psychobiological approach, Gray (1981, 1982) proposed two general motivational systems as the basis of behavior and affect, namely the behavioral inhibition system (BIS) that inhibits behavior leading to aversive outcomes and the behavioral activation system (BAS) that leads to reward. According to Gray (1987), the BIS focuses maximal attention on the environment, to analyzing it and its novel and dangerous stimuli through "stop, look, listen" activities. BIS promotes vigilant scanning for threat. BAS is seen as an appetitive system of approach to pleasant and rewarded results. It is based on incentive motivation rather than pain avoidance. These concepts were further elaborated by the BIS/BAS Scales of Carver and White (1994).

Additional support for the neurobiological basis of the BIS and BAS systems came from the work of Richard Davidson. He and his colleagues had applied electroencephalographic (EEG) measures to demonstrate prefrontal hemispheric asymmetry in a number of studies (Davidson, 1992; Davidson & Tomarken, 1989) In subsequent work they related hemispheric asymmetry to the BIS and BAS systems, showing greater left prefrontal activation associated with higher levels of BAS and greater right prefrontal activation associated with reported higher levels of BIS strength. (Sutton & Davidson, 1997).

A related dimension is proposed by Panksepp in his seeking and rage or aggression circuits. Panksepp proposes that these two neural circuits express mutually inhibitory interactions (1998). The mechanism that turns seeking into rage/aggression resides in the expectancy of the seeking system, where frustration of expectancy triggers rage/aggression. Panksepp locates the seeking behavioral system in the brain dopamine circuit, or reward circuit of the brain. Electrical stimulation of the ascending dopamine circuit evokes vigorous exploration and search, feelings of engagement, being able to do things, and feelings of excitement, a circuit that corresponds to the seeking behavioral system. According to Panksepp, the seeking system investigates and explores the environment with intense interest, engaged curiosity, eager anticipation, and invigorated feelings. It is not surprising that the seeking system interacts with higher brain mechanisms of the prefrontal cortex that generate plans and with higher-order information processing.

Mirror Neurons and Shared Action Representation

We arrive at the latest discovery that is revolutionizing our understanding of the brain and its deep social nature, namely the discovery of mirror neurons at a time that overlapped with Leslie Brothers' "social brain" proposal. Since then, research into the social brain and social neuroscience as well as affective neuroscience has exploded. This is reflected in the increasing number of major publications: the edited volume *Foundations of Social Neuroscience* (Cacioppo et al., 2002); *Social Neuroscience: A New Journal* (2006); the *Wisconsin Symposium on Emotions* dedicating its 12th annual symposium to "Order and Disorder in the Social Brain;" Panksepp's *Affective Neuroscience* (1998); and Davidson, Scherer, and Goldsmith's *Handbook of Affective Sciences* (2003). A review is beyond the scope of this chapter. Instead, we will focus on studies of mirror neurons that have lent significant energy and enthusiasm to these developments.

In a series of detailed neuroanatomical studies, Giacomo Rizzolatti and colleagues (di Pellegrino, Fadiga, Fogassi, Gallese, & Rizzolatti, 1992; Gallese, Fadiga, Fogassi, & Rizzolatti, 1996; Rizzolatti & Craighero, 2004) reported their findings on mirror neurons in macaque monkeys. These investigators had implanted electrodes into individual neurons of area F5 of the premotor cortex, in humans the homologous area of the left prefrontal speech area (identified earlier in this chapter as Broca's area). In macaques, this area was known to be involved in actions of the hand in grasping, holding, tearing, and bringing to the mouth. The investigators discovered that these neurons were not only activated by the grasping actions of the monkey's hand but also by the monkey simply observing an experimenter picking up an object. Thus, performing the action and observing someone else perform the same action produced the same activation in the neurons of area F5 in the monkey. Perception of action and performing an action were identical. Seeing and doing were the same, a surprising finding since action and vision were thought of as different abilities and as located in separate brain areas.

Early findings by the Rizzolatti group established that mirror neurons were activated by particular kinds of grasps the monkey made: a precision grip made for grasping a small object (raisin) with two fingers, a whole-hand grip for large objects (apple), or actions that achieved a similar goal but the grasping was for a broader range of objects. Of note is that these mirror neurons were not activated when the actions involved the same muscles or when actions did not have an object, such as in scratching an arm. Mirror neurons were thus involved in *object-oriented* action. Other neurons were called *canonical* neurons, since they responded to the sight of objects graspable with a precision grip or whole-hand grip. The type of object did not matter, only size did.

Of note is also that mirror neurons were activated when monkeys recognized the actions of others but were unable to see the action sequence fully, such as when the experimenter reached for an object behind a screen which the monkey had previously seen the experimenter place there (Umilta et al., 2001). These neurons were multimodal in that they were also activated by sounds of action (Kohler et al., 2002). Mirror neurons were even sensitive to experience, being more activated in experienced pianists listening to piano music as compared to inexperienced ones (Seung, Kyong, Woo, Lee, & Lee, 2005).

Investigators set out to explore the functions of mirror neurons. The main findings affirm that mirroring the actions of others helps to understand the actions of others by extracting the goal and meaning of those actions (Rizzolatti, Fogassi, & Gallese, 2001). Resonance reveals the outcome of the action and, thus, the goal of action (Gallese, Keysers, & Rizzolatti, 2004). The mirroring of action becomes a mechanism for simulation in order to know goals, intentions, and the minds of others.

In identifying a similar mirroring system in humans, a number of studies have used imaging approaches: including functional magnetic resonance imaging (fMRI; Buccino et al., 2004), positron emission tomography (PET; Rizzolatti et al., 1996), transcranial magnetic stimulation (TMS; Fadiga, Fogassi, Pavesi, & Rizzolatti, 1995), and magnetoencephalography (MEG; Hari & Salmelin, 1997). Studies have identified three brain areas particularly activated when observing the actions of others: (1) inferior frontal area corresponding in part to Broca's area (monkey ventral premotor area F5), (2) inferior parietal lobule, (3) middle temporal gyrus in humans (in the monkey, the superior temporal sulcus, STS).

Keysers and Gazzola (2006; Keysers et al., 2004) propose that shared activation is also evident in sensations such as pain and in perceiving emotions such as disgust and fear. They propose that the shared circuits for action, sensations, and emotions are established through Hebbian learning and through anatomical connections between the frontal, parietal, and temporal mirror neuron nodes, summarized in the well-known expression "neurons that fire together, are wired together."

The work on mirror neurons has become important to our understanding of resilience and trauma and to the development of a Resilience Building Model (BRiM), to be discussed in the concluding part of this chapter. From this vantage point, we would like to propose an additional function for mirror neurons, namely that they represent the structure of action as a unitary entity comprised of the actor, the action performed by the actor, and the object at which the action is directed, a structure or unit designated here as Actor-action-Object (AaO). The process by which this takes place may be through encoding this structure in a modular way as a single unit. It is unclear whether this unity is achieved through an inherent property of mirror neurons, through a network resulting from Hebbian learning, as Keysers and Gazzola suggest, through mirror neurons reflecting a small segment of such a network, or through some as yet unidentified mechanism. Several factors point to the existence of such an action structure:

1. In the case of macaques, mirror neurons require that the action be directed at an object. Otherwise the neurons will not fire. Also of note is that mirror neurons are not activated by pantomime in macaques, such as opening and closing the hand in a dumb-show performance (Umilta et al., 2001). In humans, mirror neurons are activated by transitive actions directed at objects and intransitive actions without objects, demonstrating a capacity to distinguish between whether an action has an object or not.

2. In real life the unity of Actor-action-Object is ubiquitous. In our everyday activities action is not disembodied. Take the example of "kicking." At a minimum, "kicking" requires effectors of legs that do the kicking. The legs, too, are not disembodied but require to be attached to a body. The body, too, cannot be disembodied but must enact the action. Thus, there is no "kicking" happening on the sidewalk without legs, without the legs attached to a body, without the body enacting the kicking, and without the actor. Nor is "kicking" happening on the sidewalk without an object being kicked. Kicking the air would appear strange, abnormal, raising concerns about something being wrong with the person doing the kicking. Thus, actions DO NOT require us to search for the Actor performing that action among myriad actors or to grope for the Object at which the action is directed among the countless objects surrounding us. However, these elements can be thus disorganized in various abnormal conditions, such as psychoses, deliriums, or identity confusion in schizophrenia. By contrast, our social world has remarkable coherence and is orderly, well organized, and remarkably smooth in the countless interactions taking place every moment around the globe. Our narratives relate stories about protagonists acting and interacting with objects and others in countless intricate ways, across many centuries, in different cultures, and in different languages.

3. Another area supporting the AaO unity is language. The AaO structure is captured in the structure of most languages, be it in syntax or through grammar. The subject and object of a sentence can be identified through the order in which subject and object occur in a sentence (e.g., English), or through grammatical endings added to nouns identifying them as subject or object (e.g., German). No matter how different the languages are, they have ways of identifying the actor and what the actor is doing with what or to whom or whether the doing is transitive or intransitive. In linguistics and in robotic simulations of language this is the universality of the predicate or predicate-argument of who does what to whom or what (Steels, 2007).

4. Another aspect of language supporting the AaO structure comes from a class of words, namely emotion terms, such as fear or anger. These words often represent the three elements of AaO in a unitary way: (a) the agent, (b) a particular action readiness state of the agent, and (c) a target or object outside of the agent. Emotion words are actually good examples that treat AaO as a unitary entity, such as the single word "fear" or "afraid" where such an action tendency implies an agent and an object outside of the agent.

5. The structure AaO stands in sharp contrast to experiences of trauma. Here the traumatized individual is actually the Object of someone else's AaO enactment. For the traumatized person the order of the action unit or structure is inverted into OaA, such that he is the Object and not the Actor/Agent/Initiator of the action. He re-experiences the traumatic event in intrusive thoughts, stimulus reminders, and nightmares; is hypervigilant; and avoids social contacts and other situations.

What happens to the mirroring of perceived action when the person is an Object? Is the action of the Object the result of a mirror neuron simulation mechanism that re-enacts the abuse perpetually and unstoppably? Or is there some other process driven by emotional mechanisms, such as the amygdala and sympathetic arousal and related actions? Grezes and de Gelder (2008) state the issue pointedly, "It is, however, an open question whether the critical factor for understanding actions with an emotional component is the activity within motor-related areas as such (the mirror system) or the interaction between the emotion-processing areas and an action related network" (p. 72). They offer one explanation. Emotions prepare the organism for a response to the environment. Perception of fear, for example, would trigger a fear reaction that was based on a fear motor program in subcortical and cortical circuitry. This fear circuitry does not involve the mirror neurons. Mirror mechanisms and emotional processing are coactivated in motor resonance or detecting intentions. However, mirror mechanisms may be dissociated from socio-affective capabilities, such as in autism.

Grezes and de Gelder's position is important in that they distinguish mirror mechanisms from emotional processes. The OaA unit in trauma may incorporate both mirroring or resonance in cases where the Object is inflicting self-abuse and mirroring the actions of the perpetrator, while the unit also represents the emotional fear reaction or a relevant sympathetic response to the perpetrator's treatment. The fear response may dissociate the fear circuit amygdala hyperactivity from the prefrontal cortical areas involving mirror neuron mechanisms that are not resonating with the perpetrator's actions. Thus, both mirroring/resonance of perpetrator's actions and fear of those actions and of the perpetrator may be involved, thus holding the victim doubly captive. At the same time, experiencing himself as an Agent in these situations is simply not in his brain, is not represented in his brain circuitry or neuroendocrine response. What is doubly represented is that of the object status and the emotional reaction of stress.

Agency and Adaptation

Our own work on brain functions and social context began several years ago with a review of good survival in extreme situations. Not all experiences of extreme situations lead to extreme stress and trauma. Indeed, the more prevalent response is one of resilience (McFarlane, 1996). Our study began with a view of resilience as a naturally occurring response to threat, one that naturally ameliorates or terminates distress. This endogenous resilience capacity would appear to be an excellent candidate for treating post-traumatic stress disorder (PTSD), as it is aimed at what Yehuda and Davidson (2000) target for treatment, "PTSD develops from an inadequate termination of a stress response…reducing the distress would be of paramount importance in the treatment of PTSD" (p. 1).

Treating distress and the reminders associated with PTSD have been the core object of mainstream psychological therapies for PTSD over the past 30 years. The main therapeutic approaches evolved out of contemporaneous psychological theories of classical and operant conditioning and of cognitive psychology, leading to empirically efficacious treatments for PTSD (Foa, Keane, Friedman, & Cohen, 2009) represented by exposure therapy (ET) and cognitive behavior therapy (CBT). New directions in therapeutic approaches have increasingly turned to the development of capacities and skills stunted in patients suffering from anxiety and mood disorders. Linehan (1993) incorporated Zen practices of acceptance and toleration of dysphoric affect in her treatment of borderline personality disorder. Recognizing the lack of effective treatment for complex PTSD associated with childhood abuse, Cloitre, Koenen, Cohen, and Han (2002) developed a skills training model. The emerging interest in capacity-building and resilience models (Kent & Davis, 2010) reflect the growing trend in "new wave therapies" (Hayes, 2004). Our own interests in resilience grew out of the recognition that the main qualities of resilience were lost or compromised in traumatic responses to threat. Over the past 6 years, we have sought to identify core resilience qualities, to develop well-articulated treatment approaches that would restore resilience in individuals suffering from PTSD, and to test their efficacy in clinical trials.

To identify resilience characteristics, this study began with naturalistic examples of good survival in extreme situations, as described in printed autobiographies by survivors themselves, in biographies, and in histories. In this informal literature, two features repeatedly characterized good survival: an attitude of approach and engagement and of social relatedness. The examples extended from Eugenia Ginzburg (1967) chanting poetry while in solitary confinement in the Gulag; a boy playing his violin whenever his city was bombed (Leet, 1984. Personal communication); a boy in Chauchilla, California, helping his schoolmates escape from a collapsing cave and kidnapping (Terr, 1979); and an inmate in a Nazi concentration camp who survived 6 years in that camp by resolving not to hate but to love and be helpful (Ritchie, 1978). In the large developmental research literature on resilience of

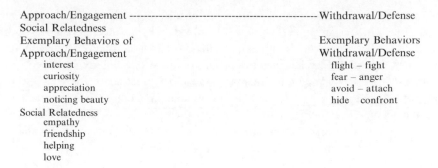

Fig. 11.1 Behavioral response tendencies of approach/engagement and withdrawal/defense

Approach/Engagement -- Withdrawal/Defense
Social Relatedness
    parasympathetic (Cannon)   sympathetic (Cannon)
    seeking (Panksepp)   rage/anger (Panksepp)
    left hemisphere (R. Davidson)   right hemisphere (R. Davidson)
    ventral vagus (Porges)   HPA axis (McEwen)
    oxytocin (Carter)   cortison, (Selye, McEwen)
    prefrontal cortex (Luria, Fuster)   amygdala (LeDoux)
    mirror neurons (Rizzolatti)   stress loop (Sousa, Dias-Ferreira)
    (Broca's area)   (amygdala vs. prefrontal cortex)

Fig. 11.2 Psychobiological dimension supporting action tendencies of approach/engagement and withdrawal/defense

children growing up in adversity, two characteristics emerge when describing resilience and positive adaptation. These are a close relationship with one or more adults and self-efficacy or being effective in their environments. These particular two qualities are replicated in numerous studies with remarkable consistency (Masten, Best, & Garmezy, 1990; Luthar, 2006).

Our wide-ranging review pointed to two prominent characteristics of good survival in the survivor literature and the resilient positive adaptation in the developmental research: (1) approach and engagement in the person's circumstances in ways that kept him or her well, and (2) social relatedness and maintaining connections with others. Figure 11.1 summarizes the main behaviors associated with approach/engagement and the response tendencies of withdrawal/defense. These two response tendencies are frequently found concurrently in low stress situations. They can become dichotomous in extreme situations of threat and challenge in which one or the other tendency prevails.

A third characteristic of good survival is an efficient stress response. The neurobiological literature on stress has long recognized an efficient stress response as essential for good adaptation, as first articulated by Cannon's (1938) fight–flight response, by Selye's (1956) GAS, and reflected in the conceptions of allostasis (Sterling & Eyer, 1988) and allostatic load (McEwen & Seeman, 1999). It is the biological literature that has long postulated a dimension of contrasting and opposing functions of approach/engagement and withdrawal/defense, as represented by the work of Panksepp (1998), Davidson (2000), Carter (1998) and Uvnaes-Moberg (1998), Porges (2001), Luria (1980), Fuster (2008), Sousa and colleagues (Sousa et al., 2000), Dias-Ferreira and colleagues (Dias-Ferreira et al., 2009), and others. Figure 11.2 summarizes this physiologically supported action dimension.

We are endowed with these major physiological mechanisms and related behaviors to interact with the environment and to do so with sensitivity to environmental contingencies. Adaptation is smooth when the environment is mainly a contingent one and what we do has an effect on it. Resilience and traumatic stress come to the fore in noncontingent environments, where what we do

Fig. 11.3 Model for
building resilience through
resilient action change

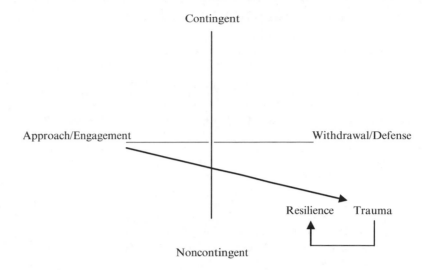

has little effect and where resilience and traumatic stress exhibit quite contrasting qualities, with resilience showing approach/engagement, social relatedness, and an efficient stress response while traumatic stress appearing to be characterized by a dysregulated stress response and the symptom triad of PTSD that includes re-experiencing, avoidance, and hyper-reactivity.

Our goal was to restore the three resilient qualities of approach/engagement, social relatedness, and an efficient stress response in conditions in which these were lost or compromised, such as PTSD, depression, and chronic illnesses. We did this by basically simulating and recreating experiences of resilience qualities (approach/ engagement and social relatedness) and then taking these into past stressful or traumatic experiences in ways that dissipated the distress and transformed stress/trauma into resilience. With this method we simulated resilience in stressful/ traumatic experiences that had lacked resilient responses. At the same time, we fundamentally changed agency. Participants did not return to past stress/trauma as objects and victims of those past experiences but as agents and initiators of resilient responses that were already part of their experiences. Changes in affect, in symptoms, and in cognition happened concurrently with the change in action. Figure 11.3 summarizes the BRiM model.

We developed a manualized program that covers the restoration of resilience strengths. It has evolved into four modules and is adapted to treat outpatient PTSD, depression, mixed Axis I groups, inpatient and outpatient addiction, sexual assault, chronic illnesses including chronic pain, fibromyalgia, and cancer. Depending on the type and severity of the disorder, the manualized program is adapted to extend from 4 to 12 weeks and is conducted in a small-group format. The sessions cover key components of resilience. Beginning modules cover the restoration of individuals' resilience strengths that include approach/engagement and social relatedness. These capabilities are subsequently drawn on as patients revisit the life episodes associated with distress. In a subsequent resolution module, participants practice the use of restored strengths by returning to challenging experiences in ways that disarmed the stress. The final module encourages individuals to consider the question "What is a good life?" as a means of helping them reweave their life narratives into ones that bring their strengths forward and that help to consolidate treatment gains.

The program begins with components of resilience experiences instead of traumatic ones. Participants are asked to place stressful/traumatic episodes "on hold" or to set them aside until the

Table 11.1 Modules for the building resilience model (BRiM)

Introduction. The body sense. The brain registers states of stress and calm in body states. This introduction serves to improve awareness of bodily states of calm energy and strength in body map exercises. Trauma is first experienced in the body, is physiologically maintained, and needs to leave bodily states.
Module I. Approach/engagement proactive orientation. It covers experiences of interest, appreciation, noticing beauty. It is regained by reexperiencing past episodes of childhood and early adulthood times that are formative. Participants are asked to describe each episode, indicate where in the body the respective qualities (of interest curiosity etc.) are, and to make a visual representation (method and materials of their choosing such as collages sculptures etc.). Approach is a basic vital response of all living organisms to approach what sustains them.
Module II. Social relatedness. It covers experiences of empathy, affiliation, friendship, bonds, love. Participants are asked to reexperience and reinstate past affiliative episodes by describing them, making the body connection, and making a visual representation. Affiliation is vital for reproduction and rearing of all mammals.
Module III. Trauma/stress resolution. It integrates the reestablished approach and relatedness experiences of Modules II and III with traumatic and stressful life events. Stressful experiences are revisited in a graded manner with practiced resilience strength experiences. Again participants are asked to describe this resilience-based return to trauma, make dividing underline the body connection, and make a visual representation.
Module IV. The future with resilience. It asks the question, what is a good life. It explores a view of the future that participants can look forward to rather than one they dread.

integration phase of Module III. They are asked to find an episode from formative years of childhood and early adult years in which they are cherished and loved or they cherished and loved someone or something else. They are asked to turn to this episode when stressed during the course of the study, rather than remain in their stressful state. The emphasis throughout the program is on the rebuilding of resilience-related strengths that are richly interconnected to neuroendocrine, neurophysiological, psychological, and cognitive functions of the individual. Each module is described in Table 11.1.

Didactic materials for each module include sample readings, photographs, and brief film excerpts. Modules also include brief and simple descriptions and illustrations of relevant brain, neurophysiological, and neuroendocrine functions, such as the fear circuitry and executive functions, the fight–flight response, cortisol and oxytocin, with an emphasis on experience-dependent brain plasticity. The brain can be changed, and related biological functions can be changed through a change in experience that is resilience-based.

A current test of this model with PTSD participants shows strong declines in symptoms of PTSD, depression, and anxiety; gains in well-being, social role and vitality; and increased memory and executive functions (Kent, Davis, Stark, & Stewart, in press).

Conclusion

The study of the brain started with Broca's area in 1861 with the discovery of the localization of speech. Today the intense interest in neuroscience has returned full circle to Broca's area in the discovery of mirror neurons and their role in intentional action. An area once considered primarily devoted to language is now treated as fundamental to the joint execution and perception of action in which language is seen as an adaptation or modification of functions carried out by action. Action has become adapted to the purpose of communication in ways that may have started with hand gestures and evolved to communication with sounds, as proposed by Rizzolatti and Arbib in their paper whimsically entitled "Language Within Our Grasp" (1998). Through their mirroring function, mirror neurons in Broca's area and related areas demonstrate that we are profoundly social beings in ways that allow us to experience each other's actions, intentions, and emotions. We are resilient when we maintain agency and approach/engagement in the face of adversity. We can restore agency when it is derailed by overwhelming experiences and hyper-reactivity of the stress response. Agency can be restored through an approach of simulated resilience that restores homeostasis and activates related neurocortical areas of resilience (Pardo, 2010).

References

Brothers, L. (1990). The social brain: A project for integrating primate behavior and neurophysiology in a new domain. *Concepts in Neuroscience, 1*, 27–51.

Buccino, G., Lui, F., Canessa, N., Patteri, I., Lagravinese, G., Benuzzi, F., et al. (2004). Neural circuits involved in the recognition of action performed by non-conspecifics: An fMRI study. *Journal of Cognitive Neuroscience, 16*, 1–14.

Cacioppo, J. T., Berntson, G. G., Adolphs, R., Carter, C. S., Davidson, R. J., McClintock, M. K., et al. (Eds.). (2002). *Foundations in social neuroscience.* Cambridge: MIT Press.

Cannon, W. B. (1929). Organization for physiological homeostasis. *Physiological Review, 9*, 399–431.

Cannon, W. B. (1932). *The wisdom of the body.* New York: Norton, 1963 [1932].

Carter, C. S., & DeVries, A. C. (1999). Stress and soothing: An endocrine perspective. In M. Lewis & D. Ramsay (Eds.), *Soothing and stress* (pp. 13–18). Mahwah: Erlbaum.

Carter, C. S. (1998). Neuroendocrine perspectives on social attachment and love. *Psychoneuroendocrinology, 23*, 779–818.

Carver, C. L., & White, T. L. (1994). Behavioral inhibition, behavioral activation and affective responses to impending reward and punishment: The BIS/BAS scales. *Journal of Personality and Social Psychology, 67*, 319–333.

Cloitre, M., Koenen, M. C., Cohen, L. R., & Han, H. (2002). Skills training in affective and interpersonal regulation followed by exposure: A phase-based treatment for PTSD related to childhood abuse. *Journal of Consulting and Clinical Psychology, 70*, 1067–1074.

Davidson, R. J. (2000). Affective style, psychopathology and resilience: Brain mechanisms and plasticity. *American Psychologist, 55*, 1193–1214.

Davidson, R. J., Scherer, K. R., & Goldsmith, H. H. (2003). *Handbook of affective sciences.* New York: Oxford University Press.

Davidson, R. J. (1992). Anterior asymmetry and the nature of emotion. *Brain and Cognition, 20*, 125–151.

Davidson, R. J., & Tomarken, A. J. (1989). Laterality and emotion: An electrophysiological approach. In F. Boller & J. Grafman (Eds.), *Handbook of neuropsychology* (pp. 419–441). Amsterdam: Elsevier.

Dias-Ferreira, E., Sousa, J., Melo, I., Morgado, P., Mesquita, A. R., Cerqueira, J. J., et al. (2009). Chronic stress causes frontostriatal reorganization and affects decision-making. *Science, 325*, 621–625.

Di Pellegrino, G., Fadiga, L., Fogassi, L., Gallese, V., & Rizzolatti, G. (1992). Understanding motor events: A neurophysiological study. *Experimental Brain Research, 91*, 176–180.

Fadiga, L., Fogassi, L., Pavesi, G., & Rizzolatti, G. (1995). Motor facilitation during action observation: A magnetic stimulation study. *Journal of Neurophysiology, 73*, 2608–2611.

Finger, S. (2000). *Minds behind the brain: A history of the pioneers and their discoveries.* New York: Oxford University Press.

Foa, E. B., Keane, T. M., Friedman, M. J., & Cohen, J. A. (Eds.). (2009). *Effective treatments for PTSD: Practice guidelines for the International Society for Traumatic Stress Studies* (2nd ed.). New York: Guilford Press.

Fuster, J. (2008). *The prefrontal cortex* (4th ed.). London: Academic.

Gallese, V., Keysers, C., & Rizzolatti, G. (2004). A unifying view of the basis of social cognition. *Trends in Cognitive Science, 8*, 396–403.

Gallese, V., Fadiga, L., Fogassi, L., & Rizzolatti, G. (1996). Action recognition in the premotor cortex. *Brain, 119*, 593–609.

Getz, L. L., & Carter, C. S. (1980). Social organization in Microtus ochrogaster. *The Biologist, 62*, 56–69.

Ginzburg, E. S. (1967). *Journey into the whirlwind* (P. Stevenson & M. Hayward, Trans.). New York: Harcourt Brace Jovanovich.

Gray, J. A. (1987). *The psychology of fear and stress.* Cambridge: Cambridge University Press.

Gray, J. A. (1982). *The neuropsychology of anxiety: An enquiry into the functions of the septo-hippocampal system.* New York: Oxford University Press.

Gray, J. A. (1981). A critique of Eysenck's theory of personality. In H. J. Eysenck (Ed.), *A model for personality* (pp. 246–276). Berlin: Springer.

Grezes, J., & de Gelder, B. (2008). Social perception: Understanding other people's intentions and emotions through their actions. In T. Striano & V. Reid (Eds.), *Social cognition: Development, neuroscience and autism* (pp. 67–78). Oxford: Blackwell.

Gross, C. G. (1998). Claude Bernard and the constancy of the internal environment. *The Neuroscientist, 4*, 380–385.

Hari, R., & Salmelin, R. (1997). Human cortical oscillations: A neuromagnetic view through the skull. *Trends in Neuroscience, 20*, 44–49.

Harlow, J. M. (1848). Passage of an iron rod through the head. *Boston Medical and Surgical Journal, 39*, 389–393.

Hayes, S. C. (2004). Acceptance and commitment therapy and the new behavior therapies: Mindfulness, acceptance, and relationship. In S. C. Hayes, V. M. Follette, & M. M. Linehan (Eds.), *Mindfulness and acceptance: Expanding the cognitive-behavioral tradition* (pp. 1–29). New York: Guilford Press.

Kent, M., & Davis, M. (2010). The emergence of capacity-building programs and models of resilience. In J. W. Reich, A. J. Zautra, & J. S. Hall (Eds.), *Handbook of adult resilience* (pp. 427–449). New York: Guilford Press.

Kent, M., Davis, M. C., Stark, S. L., & Steward, L. A. (in press). A resilience-oriented treatment for posttraumatic stress disorder: Results of a preliminary randomized clinical trial.

Keysers, C., Wicker, B., Gazzola, V., Anton, J. L., Fogassi, L., & Gallese, V. (2004). A touching sight: SII/PV activation during the observation and experience of touch. *Neuron, 42*, 335–346.

Keysers, C., & Gazzola, V. (2006). Towards a unifying neural theory of social cognition. *Progress in Brain Research, 156*, 379–401.

Kohler, E., Keysers, C., Umilta, M. A., Fogassi, L., Gallese, V., & Rizzolatti, G. (2002). Hearing sounds, understanding actions: Action representation in mirror neurons. *Science, 297*, 846–848.

LeDoux, J., & Phelps, E. A. (2000). Emotional networks in the brain. In M. Lewis & J. M. Haviland-Jones (Eds.), *Handbook of emotions* (2nd ed., pp. 157–172). New York: Guilford Press.

LeDoux, J. (1996). *The emotional brain: The mysterious underpinnings of emotional life*. New York: Simon & Schuster.

Linehan, M. M. (1993). *Cognitive behavioral treatment for borderline personality disorder*. New York: Guilford Press.

Luria, A. R. (1980). *Higher cortical functions in man* (2nd ed.). New York: Basic Books.

Luthar, S. S. (2006). Resilience in development: A synthesis of research across five decades. In D. J. Cohen & D. Cicchetti (Eds.), *Developmental psychopathology* (2nd ed., pp. 739–795). Hoboken: Wiley.

Masten, A., Best, K. M., & Garmezy, N. (1990). Resilience and development: Contributions from the study of children who overcame adversity. *Development and Psychopathology, 2*, 425–444.

McEwen, B. S., with Lasley, E. N. (2002). *The end of stress as we know it*. Washington: Joseph Henry Press.

McEwen, B. S., & Seeman, T. (1999). Protective and damaging effects of mediators of stress: Elaborating and testing the concepts of allostasis and allostatic load. *Annual New York Academy of Sciences, 896*, 30–47.

McEwen, B. S., & Stellar, E. (1993). Stress and the individual: Mechanisms leading to disease. *Archives of Internal Medicine, 153*, 2093–2101.

McFarlane, A. C. (1996). Resilience, vulnerability, and the course of posttraumatic reactions. In B. A. van der Kolk, A. C. McFarlane, & L. Weisaeth (Eds.), *Traumatic stress: The effects overwhelming experience of mind, body, and society* (pp. 155–181). New York: Guilford Press.

Panksepp, J. (1998). *Affective neuroscience: The foundations of human and animal emotions*. New York: Oxford University Press.

Pardo, J. V. (2010). Neurobiology of resilience to trauma. *International Society for Traumatic Stress Studies 26th Annual Meeting: Translation, Collaboration and Mutual Learning*. Montreal, Canada, 11-4-2010.

Porges, S. W. (2001). The polyvagal theory: Phylogenetic substrates of a soial nervous System. *International Journal of Psychophysiology, 42*, 123–146.

Ritchie, G. G., with Sherrill, E. (1978). *Return from tomorrow*. Grand Rapids: Baker Book House.

Rizzolatti, G., & Craighero, L. (2004). The mirror-neuron system. *Annual Review of Neuroscience, 27*, 169–192.

Rizzolatti, G., Fogassi, L., & Gallese, V. (2001). Neurophysiological mechanisms underlying the understanding and imitation of action. *Nature Review Neuroscience, 2*, 661–670.

Rizzolatti, G., & Arbib, M. A. (1998). Language within our grasp. *Trends in Neurosciences, 21*, 188–194.

Rizzolatti, G., Fadiga, L., Matelli, M., Bettinardi, V., Paulesu, E., Perani, D., et al. (1996). Localization of grasp representations in humans by PET: 1. Observation versus execution. *Experimental Brain Research, 111*, 246–252.

Russell, J. A. (1979). Affective space is bipolar. *Journal of Personality and Social Psychology, 37*, 345–356.

Russell, J. A. (1980). A circumplex model of affect. *Journal of Personality and Social Psychology, 39*, 1161–1178.

Russell, J. A., & Feldman Barrett, L. (1999). Core affect, prototypical emotional episodes, and other things called *emotion*: Dissecting the elephant. *Journal of Personality and Social Psychology, 76*, 805–819.

Schneirla, T. C. (1959). An evolutionary and developmental theory of biphasic processes underlying approach and withdrawal. *Nebraska Symposium on Motivation* (pp. 1–42). Lincoln: University of Nebraska Press.

Selye, H. (1956). *The stress of life*. New York: McGraw-Hill.

Seung, Y., Kyong, J., Woo, S., Lee, B., & Lee, K. (2005). Brain activation during music listening in individuals with or without prior music training. *Neuroscience Research, 52*, 323–329.

Sousa, N., Lukoyanov, N. V., Madeira, M. D., Almeida, O. F. X., & Paula-Barbosa, M. M. (2000). Reorganization of the morphology of hippocampal neurites and synapses after stress-induced damage correlates with behavioral improvement. *Neuroscience, 97*, 253–266.

Steels, L. (2007). *The recruitment theory of language origins. SONY Computer Science Laboratory – Paris. AI Laboratory Vrije Universiteit Brussel*. Cited in Lambda the Ultimate: The Programming Languages Weblog.

Sterling, P., & Eyer, J. (1988). Allostasis: A new paradigm to explain arousal pathology. In S. Fisher & J. Reason (Eds.), *Handbook of life stress, cognition and health* (pp. 629–649). New York: Wiley.

Sutton, S. K., & Davidson, R. J. (1997). Prefrontal brain asymmetry: A biological substrate of the behavioral approach and inhibition system. *Psychological Science, 8*, 204–210.

Terr, L. C. (1979). Children of Chowchilla: A study of psychic trauma. *The Psychoanalytic Study of the Child, 34*, 547–623.

Umilta, M. A., Kohler, E., Gallese, V., Fogassi, L., Fadiga, L., Keysers, C., et al. (2001). I know what you are doing: A neurophysiological study. *Neuron, 31*, 155–165.

Uvnaes-Moberg, K., translator Roberta, F. (2005). *The oxytocin factor: Tapping the hormone of calm, love, and healing*. Amsterdam: Elsevier (original); Cambridge: Da Capo Press. (available through Perseus Books, translation copy).

Uvnaes-Moberg, K. (1998). Oxytocin may mediate the benefits of positive social interaction and emotions. *Psychoneuroendocrinology, 23*, 819–835.

Watson, D., & Tellege, A. (1985). Toward a consensual structure of mood. *Psychological Bulletin, 98*, 219–235.

Watson, D., Wise, D., Vaidya, J., & Tellegen, A. (1999). The two general activation systems of affect: Structural findings, evolutionary considerations, and psychobio-logical evidence. *Journal of Personality and Social Psychology, 76*, 820–838.

Yehuda, R., & Davidson, J. (2000). *Clinician's manual on posttraumatic stress disorder*. London: Science Press.

Situating Resilience in Developmental Context

12

Laura M. Supkoff, Jennifer Puig, and L. Alan Sroufe

Since 1975, the Minnesota Longitudinal Study of Risk and Adaptation (MLSRA; Sroufe, Egeland, Carlson, & Collins, 2005) has been following 180 children from 3 months prior to birth into the adult years. In the course of this study, we have documented cases of children thriving despite birth into poverty and associated stress, as well as children functioning well following a period of struggle.

The term "resilience" has been aptly applied to both such groups. It is a descriptive term to convey adaptive functioning beyond expectations based on the presence of a developmental risk factor in a population. However, the term can be misleading when implying something unusual about these children in their inherent characteristics or in the processes that govern their development. This, in fact, may indicate a simple failure to provide an explanation for positive outcomes. For example, without such an explanation, it may initially seem reasonable to say that some abused children do not show behavior problems *because* they are resilient, while simultaneously referring to other abused children as resilient because they *do not* show behavior problems. On further consideration, however, it becomes clear that this explanation is quite circular and fails to actually explain any differences in functioning. Thus, the assumption that there is something unusual about children we refer to as resilient cannot be justified by the mere presence of individual differences in the face of adversity, even if contemporaneous associated characteristics are found (Sroufe, 2009). In fact, our prospective, longitudinal data have impressed us with the coherence and lawfulness of this phenomenon when factors beyond the risk circumstances are taken into account.

Like other authors in this volume, we have been impressed with the role of contextual factors in explaining resilience, and in particular the importance of changes in life stress, social support, and parental depression. However, our long-term study has also led us increasingly to view resilience as a developmental process, no different in underlying principles from any other developmental phenomenon, be it social competence, psychopathology, or brain growth (Sroufe, 2009). Like any developmental phenomenon, resilience is seen as a product of the cumulative history of the organism as well as the current surrounding circumstances. A prominent role of developmental history, beginning in the earliest months and years, distinguishes this viewpoint. Even later stresses and supports themselves are in part created by, interpreted, and reacted to by the individual based on his or her own history. Thus, we argue that developmental history itself is a critical contextual factor for explaining resilience.

The study of resilience emerged from the study of psychopathology, as researchers studying children at risk noticed that some were doing surprisingly well. This observation drew attention to

L.A. Sroufe (✉)
Institute of Child Development and Department of Psychiatry, University of Minnesota, Minneapolis, MN, USA
e-mail: Srouf001@umn.edu

M. Ungar (ed.), *The Social Ecology of Resilience: A Handbook of Theory and Practice*,
DOI 10.1007/978-1-4614-0586-3_12, © Springer Science+Business Media, LLC 2012

aspects of positive functioning and maintenance of competence despite risk or adversity, as opposed to an entirely problem-focused view (Luthar, 2006). When this concept was originally recognized, the success of the children doing well in the face of risk was initially attributed to a static trait of the individuals in question, with certain children thought to be "invulnerable" (Anthony & Cohler, 1987). Over time, the term resilience usurped invulnerability, with an increased understanding that this phenomenon is best conceptualized as the mobilization of resources, both external and internal to the individual, in the service of successful adaptation and functioning, rather than an exclusively individual trait. With the growth of this area of research, the change in terminology has also reflected an increased understanding that individuals should not be considered to be resilient in an absolute or unchanging sense. While invulnerability implies that the individual must consistently maintain positive adaptation at all points in time, resilience allows for more flexibility, as the individual can behave in a more or less adaptive fashion as circumstances change.

The evolution of the concept of resilience can be understood as a movement toward a process view. We view our work as supporting this shift in perspective (Egeland, Carlson, & Sroufe, 1993; Sroufe, 2009; Yates, Egeland, & Sroufe, 2003). However, there remains ambiguity as to whether and when resilience may be considered a characteristic of the person. Three main views capture thoughts that have existed in the field as to how resilience should be conceptualized. The first view, as represented by early positions about invulnerability, suggests that resilience is entirely a trait or set of traits attributable to the person (Anthony & Cohler, 1987). In its modern form, this is seen in the view that resilience arises in part due to individual characteristics, such as cognitive abilities, easy temperament, good self-regulation, self-efficacy, and a positive outlook (Parritz & Troy, 2010). The second view portrays resilience as a process which can be described and understood by measurement and understanding of contextual factors without the need to localize any factors within the individual

(Sameroff, 2000). According to this view, once all contextual risk and protective factors are understood, there is nothing left to explain. The third view of resilience, the one that we embrace, emphasizes the importance of process but also acknowledges that in time it is reasonable to describe some individuals as more resilient than others (Ellis, Shirtcliff, Boyce, Deardorff, & Essex, 2009). The personal and contextual features of resilience can be reconciled by viewing the developmental process as continuing over time. As supports accumulate, it becomes reasonable to talk about *individuals* as resilient, because their acquired attitudes, expectations, and capacities to marshal resources enable them to cope better with the additional challenges they may face. This viewpoint is well captured by Bowlby's developmental pathways model (Bowlby, 1969, 1973), which concludes that the longer individuals follow a pathway, the more resistant they will become to change and diversion away from that pathway. Developing individual capacities can be conceptualized as risk and protective factors that individuals carry with them as they move forward through time, encountering new challenges and relationships. However, this position is distinct in viewing characteristics often simply ascribed to individuals (e.g., temperament and positive expectations) as being developmental outcomes. Thus, it is through a developmental process that all supports for resilience are acquired, and yet individual assets become part of the developmental process as they are obtained.

Both positive and negative change can continue to occur as stresses, challenges, and supports wax and wane over the life course. Still, at any given time, some individuals will be more or less resilient because of their accumulated history. Early history can itself thus be seen as a context in which resilience is seeded, as it can alter the way individuals engage with their environment, the reactions individuals will elicit from that environment, and the way individuals will interpret their environment once engaged with it. In this way, history is cumulative and the interaction between the individual and the environment continues having a lasting effect over time. Though we must understand the process by which the characteristics associated with resilience become incorporated into the individual, eventually it becomes reasonable to talk about the resilience of the individual at a particular point in time.

In this chapter we will first outline what is meant by a developmental viewpoint and then provide research examples that illustrate the joint roles of current developmental context and developmental history in accounting for resilience in each phase of life, from early childhood to emerging adulthood. In so doing it will become clear that explaining resilience is in no fundamental way different from explaining individuals who develop well in general, those who do not thrive in the face of adversity, or those who show maladaptation in what appear to be advantaged circumstances. In all cases, developmental outcomes are the result of cumulative history and current supports and challenges.

The Nature of Development

Development is orderly, directional, and cumulative (Sroufe, Cooper, & DeHart, 1992). Orderly means that there is lawfulness to the timing and sequences of development. Directional means that development moves toward increasing complexity and organization over time. Finally, cumulative implies that development should be seen as building upon the foundations of earlier development, a process wherein earlier development both remains critical and is transformed in subsequent contexts. The organizational view of development (Cicchetti & Sroufe, 1978; Sroufe & Waters, 1977) suggests the importance of viewing development as more than a progression through time. It is neither a simple additive process, wherein new experiences are stacked upon older experiences in a linear fashion, nor a process of overwriting older experiences with new. Recognition of the lawfulness of development requires an appreciation of the concept of continuity, however complex or heterotypic it may be. The cumulative nature of development

means that we cannot fully understand the functioning of an individual without considering the complexity of dynamic interactions between environmental inputs and the individual over time.

A useful example when considering this view of development has been described by Sroufe (2009). The development of a chick embryo can be altered by removing a bit of tissue from the base of the leg and placing it at the tip of the wing bud. Depending on the timing of the transfer, different outcomes result from the same process. If completed early, tissue that would have become part of a thigh will become indistinguishable from the rest of the wing tip because of the influence of the surrounding cells. If completed slightly later, at a very particular moment in development, the tissue quite surprisingly forms into a claw. This outcome demonstrates the importance of both current context, as demonstrated by the influence of the surrounding cells, which induce the tissue to become part of a tip, as well as the influence of previous development, which is enough to prevent the tissue from becoming anything other than a part of a leg. Finally, if the transfer is performed even later, the tissue grows into nothing more than anomalous flesh at the tip of the wing. At this point, too much previous development has already occurred. The tissue cannot be induced by the current context of the surrounding cells to become a tip or a part of a wing, as previous development has committed the tissue to becoming part of the base of a leg.

Development also follows a potentially malleable pathway, building upon previous development while continuously influenced by additional inputs. The effect of context plays a crucial role in determining outcomes both directly, as is demonstrated by the formation of a normal wing tip, and through interaction with previous development, as can be seen by the formation of the claw. Eventually, however, with additional development, it becomes difficult to move the tissue off its prior developmental pathway. Patterns such as this demonstrate the cumulative nature of development.

This organizational view of development was elaborated in the study of developmental psychopathology (Sroufe & Rutter, 1984); however, just as employing a developmental perspective is necessary to understand mechanisms, process, and meaning of psychopathology, the same can be said about positive adaptation and resilience. As this view of development has grown in acceptance in the field of developmental psychopatho -logy, there has also been increasing interest in the study of resilience (Cicchetti & Garmezy, 1993). Maladaptation, adaptation, and resilient functioning must all be seen in dynamic transaction with forces within the individual and the environment, not as static states. In fact, one role of developmental psychopathologists is to try to understand the factors that inhibit competence or resilience (Cicchetti, 1989; Cicchetti & Garmezy, 1993). It has been suggested that mechanisms and processes which lead to resilience inform both our understanding of normal development and of psychopathology (Cicchetti & Garmezy, 1993).

Understanding resilience as a developmental process, with prior development as a context for later lawful development, allows current functioning to be predicted as an outcome of previous development and to serve as a predictor of future development. Examining this process over time is especially critical for understanding how individuals are able to maintain positive adaptation despite the presence of some or many of the risk factors or experiences of adversity that we currently understand to distract from the process of successful adaptation and development.

Longitudinal studies demonstrate important influences on development over time. If we appropriately assess and capture the wide range of inputs that contribute to the functioning of the individual, outcomes that might seem surprising based on limited amounts of information will no longer seem so exceptional. When all relevant factors are taken into account, the organizational view of development suggests that development should indeed be lawful and understandable, with resilience posing no exception to this rule despite the concept's origination from the observation of better-than-expected functioning despite the presence of threats.

The Minnesota Longitudinal Study of Risk and Adaptation

In 1975 recruitment began for what, at the time, was expected to be a short-term prospective longitudinal study examining predictors of child abuse. Thirty-six years and thousands of variables later, this project is one of the most in-depth continuous studies of human development in the field of psychology. A poverty sample of first-time mothers was targeted for participation. More than 200 women receiving care from the Minneapolis Public Health Clinic between the years 1975 and 1977 agreed to participate (Sroufe et al., 2005). Selection criteria were geared toward identifying a group of women who were expected to face more parenting difficulties than the general population. However, the characteristics of this population were such that they encountered more adversity than that associated even with poverty and the challenges of new motherhood. At the time of their children's births, 62% of the mothers were sole parents and 50% were teenagers, with an age range from 12 to 34 (Egeland, 2007). More specifically, 35% of our sample began parenthood as unmarried teen mothers. Further risk factors included low educational attainment (42% of the mothers had not completed high school) and health problems (15% had a sexually transmitted infection and 37% were malnourished; Sroufe et al., 2005). The effects of these multiple risk factors were compounded by the dearth of support these mothers had at their disposal when their children were young. For example, only 13% of the biological fathers were living in the same home as their children by the time they had reached 18 months of age (Egeland, 1997; see Table 12.1 for a selective listing of cumulative risk factors).

As one might expect, the children in our study went on to experience their own difficulties. During childhood, 80% were enrolled in some form of special education. Some of these services may have been due to psychopathology, as a full 20% received scores in the clinical range ($T \geq 62$) on the internalizing and externalizing subscales of the Child Behavior Checklist (Achenbach &

Table 12.1   Cumulative risk among children born into poverty

	Number of risk factors				
	0	1	2	3	4
Percentage (N)	20 (52)	29 (74)	22 (58)	23 (59)	6 (16)

Risks include: single mom, teen mom, no high school degree, and mother malnourishment
Total N = 259

Edelbrock, 1986; Egeland, 1997). Fifty-one children were identified as having problems with antisocial behavior in childhood, and of these children, 38 went on to have life-course persistent antisocial behavior problems (Aguilar, Sroufe, Egeland, & Carlson, 2000). By the time they had reached adolescence, 46% met criteria for at least one mental illness as assessed with the Schedule for Affective Disorders and Schizophrenia, Child Version (K-SADS; Egeland, 1997; Puig-Antich & Chambers, 1978).

However, like many other longitudinal studies of at-risk youth, we also found numerous signs of resilience despite the considerable adversity into which these children were born. For example, teacher reports indicated that 15% of the children in our sample were ranked among the most interpersonally competent in their class during middle childhood (Egeland, 1997). Two groups in our sample that were identified as being particularly at risk for maladaptation included those individuals who had experienced maltreatment as children and those who were predicted to drop-out of high school. Thirty-seven children in our study had early histories of maltreatment and were later assessed for psychopathology in adolescence. These assessments revealed that the majority of our maltreated subsample had multiple psychiatric diagnoses; yet four did not meet criteria for even a single DSM-III diagnosis (American Psychological Association Committee on Nomenclature and Statistics, 1980; Egeland, 1997). Similarly, we identified 35 people who were expected to drop out of high school based on cumulative early adversity; still, 10 of these individuals went on to graduate high school on time (Englund, Egeland, & Collins, 2008).

Just as easily as one can point to the multitude of risk factors that place children on a pathway to maladaptation, one can identify those promotive and protective factors that keep children on adaptive pathways, with outcomes deemed "resilient" when the child has also faced adversity. At all stages of development, the MLSRA has studied these factors and amassed a body of research that supports the notion that maladaptation and resilience are lawfully governed by the same rules of development and are simply different aspects of the same developmental process. Our three decades of uninterrupted data on developmentally appropriate competence allow us to examine competence, maladaptation, and resilience throughout childhood and into adulthood. The following sections will summarize, in parallel, findings related to maladaptation and resilience in two developmental periods, childhood/adolescence and emerging adulthood.

Resilience and Maladaptation in Childhood and Adolescence

Neither resilience nor maladaptation arise de novo in the individual. They are both the product of a developmental history and both begin as adaptations to current situations. For example, a key premise of attachment theory (Bowlby, 1969) is that in a context of sensitive, responsive care the infant can flexibly organize behavior around a caregiver, achieving a balance between proximity seeking and exploration of the surround that maximally supports development. In contrast, infants who experience inconsistent care or chronic rejection can still achieve some degree of closeness to their caregivers (and therefore protection) but only at the expense of exploration on the one hand or direct expression of need on the other. Through their histories of interaction, all children not only form behavioral adaptations, but also representations of themselves and others that are carried forward to influence responses to future situations (Sroufe, 2007).

Behavior becomes maladaptive when the individual brings to new situations now inappropriate expectations that lead to inflexible and counterproductive behavioral responses. For example, a distressed child who has had a history of resistant attachment may find it difficult to be reassured by a teacher when comforted. Likewise, a child with an avoidant attachment history may fail to even turn to a teacher when distressed. However, as we will discuss, a history that is marked by other positive experiences can provide the individual with expectations from which he or she can produce adaptive responses to current adversity that would not have been otherwise expected (Egeland et al., 1993).

The early years of our participants' lives were marked by intensive data collection at multiple levels of analysis focusing on many aspects of each child's experience, including measures of temperament, language and cognitive development, problem solving, social and emotional behavior, quality of care, and the family context. In total, participants and their mothers were assessed 20 times from their third trimester of gestation until the age of 11, then every 2 or 3 years after that. The constructs assessed during childhood and throughout the study can be interpreted as both outcomes and predictors of future competence and maladaptation. Many were designed to assess transactions between individual and environment that contribute to the completion of salient developmental tasks (Sroufe et al., 2005).

Some of our earliest measures did not assess characteristics of the child at all, but instead focused on the child's early environment, including characteristics of the parents and their social and economic circumstances. For example, one of our strongest predictors of competence in the preschool years is maternal life stress. Our primary measure of life stress is the Life Events Schedule (LES), a 39-question interview that assesses the amount of stress the participant has endured in the past 12 months (Egeland & Brunnquell, 1979). One factor derived from this measure, personal stress, captures family relationship transitions, family violence, and chemical dependency, and is consistently a strong predictor of child outcomes (Pianta, Egeland, & Sroufe, 1990).

Closely related to the family relationship transitions component of the personal stress factor, and highly predictive of maladaptation, is our measure of family stability. This variable was rationally constructed from the verbal account of family constellation given by the mother, and reflected the extent to which the mother was involved with the same partner during her child's preschool years (age 2–5.5). Two groups were identified: the "intact" group, composed of mothers who were involved with the same supportive partner over this 3-year period, and the "chaotic" group, composed of mothers who were involved in relationships that were constantly changing and unstable even if the same partner was coming and going (Pianta, Hyatt, & Egeland, 1986). Children from intact families displayed higher quality mother–child interactions during a series of teaching tasks when the children were 42 months old. These children were more persistent, enthusiastic, compliant, and affectionate towards their mothers. Conversely, children from the chaotic family group were more negative towards and avoidant of their mothers. Not surprisingly, the mothers' behavior towards their children was also lawfully predicted from the quality of their relationships with their partners. Mothers with intact relationships had more respect for their children's autonomy, were better at structuring the tasks, and were more confident in their interactions with their children than mothers who had chaotic relationships with their partner(s).

While assessment of maternal characteristics and the children's home environment are important predictors of resilience and markers of risk, our study has always paid special attention to the relational context of development as a predictor of later outcomes. As early as 3 and 6 months of age, the quality of the interactions between the mother and child were assessed through the observation of feeding and play in the participants' homes (Egeland, Pianta, & O'Brien, 1993; Sroufe et al., 2005). At these assessments, the mother–child relationship was also coded on Mary Ainsworth's 9-point caregiving sensitivity scales, which were the same as those used to provide external validity for attachment classifications as assessed by the Strange Situation

Procedure (Ainsworth & Bell, 1974; Sroufe et al., 2005). The quality of the attachment relationship itself was assessed at two ages in this sample, 12 and 18 months (Egeland & Farber, 1984). Subsequently, we observed that the degree of caregiver support for the child in toddlerhood was directly related to the quality of care received in infancy. These ample measures of early care, along with the contextual measures of life stress and social support to the mother throughout her child's development, provided us with a strategic vantage point for exploring our view of resilience as a developmental process.

Changes in Context and Resilience

Like other investigators in this volume, we found that positive surrounding circumstances in part account for resilience, both explaining how some children may function well in the face of adversity and, especially, how some children rebound from a period of difficulty. For example, in an early phase of our study we found that some children who had shown an anxious pattern of attachment at age 12 months were then securely attached at 18 months, while most continued to manifest anxious attachment (Vaughn, Egeland, Sroufe, & Waters, 1979). These two groups were distinguished by a greater reduction in experienced life stress reported by the mothers of those whose attachments improved during this interval. Likewise, while anxious attachment at 18 months predicted behavior problems at age 5, there were exceptions; some formerly anxiously attached children were functioning well. Note also that this is despite the general poverty status of our sample. This change to positive functioning, this resilience, was dramatically impacted by increasing social support available to the mother during this interval (Erickson, Sroufe, & Egeland, 1985). Subsequently, it was found that children with behavior problems in the preschool years who were problem-free in first grade were part of families with dramatically lower life stress than were those who showed continuous problems (Egeland, Kalkoske, Gottesman, & Erickson, 1990). Further, positive changes in functioning in later childhood

and adolescence are also in part accounted for by changes in life stress (Sroufe, Carlson, Levy, & Egeland, 1999; Sroufe et al., 2005). We have found repeatedly that these two variables, life stress and social support, account for positive changes in functioning that can be captured by the term resilience. Of course, the converse is also true: child functioning tends to deteriorate when family stress increases and/or family social support decreases.

Developmental Foundations of Resilience

The lawfulness and coherence of resilience, however, entails more than just changing circumstances. Prior experience and prior adaptation may also provide a foundation for coping with adversity or recovery from problems. For example, in an analysis by Egeland and Kreutzer (1991), early competence was a protective factor buffering the deleterious effects of concurrent maternal life stress. The construct of early competence was defined by both the child's relationship history as well as his or her self-regulatory capacity. Specifically, secure attachment classification at 12 and 18 months, as well as successful completion of the aforementioned tool/teaching tasks at 24 and 42 months were used to define this protective factor. If the salient developmental task during the preschool period is guided self-regulation that later becomes internalized, then it follows that children who had higher quality interactions with their mothers and who were better able to complete the challenging tasks presented to them at age 3 would have a foundation for later competence despite concurrent adversity.

The results of this study were consistent with these hypotheses. In general, considerable maladaptation was associated with high concurrent maternal life stress for our participants in the first grade. These children were rated among the lowest by their teachers in terms of emotional health and popularity when compared to other children in their class. They had the most adjustment and behavior problems and received low achievement scores on tests in a variety of academic domains.

However, even in this context of high stress, those children with early positive foundations functioned well across domains in first grade. Thus, their resilience in the face of adversity was a coherent outgrowth of their earlier histories.

In our most rigorous demonstration of early supports for resilience, two groups of children were defined by the quality of their care and adaptation in the first 2 years, based on three assessments (Sroufe, Egeland, & Kreutzer, 1990). One group had consistently positive experiences during this period, while the other had consistently negative experiences. Members of both groups, however, showed consistently poor functioning across the three assessments between ages 42 and 54 months. It would be argued by some that at this later age there is really only one group because they are behaving comparably and presumably the advantages of protective earlier experience, along with the experience itself, is now erased (Kagan, 1984; Lewis, 1997). However, longitudinal data can address this argument and also shed light on the process of resilience by answering the question: "When competence is assessed at a later age, will the groups be different?" Indeed, those with early positive histories were dramatically more competent in Grades 1–3 than those with early negative histories. Had the study begun in the preschool period, the improved functioning of many children – their resilience – would have appeared mysterious or may have been attributed to some inherent characteristic of the child. The longitudinal data allow us to see the developmental foundation for recovery from the period of difficulty (Sroufe et al., 1990).

In other analyses, we found that both changes in stress and early positive foundations in the history of care accounted for individuals' recovery in adolescence from a period of problem behavior in middle childhood (Sroufe, 1999). Using logistic regression we were able to show that the combination of these developmental factors accounted for 80% of the cases identified as resilient. Thus, little is left to mystery with adequate developmental data. Our research has found, time and time again, that resilience is not simply a function of good outcomes despite bad experience, but also an example of prior good experience facilitating the mobilization of resources to promote competence in the face of adversity. Furthermore, our research provides empirical support for the developmental conceptualization of resilience as a process in which early protective factors buttress later competence that undergirds resilience (Egeland, 2007; Egeland et al., 1993; Yates et al., 2003).

Parallels in Developmental Processes Underlying Resilience and Maladaptation

From the outset we have argued that from a developmental point of view there is no fundamental difference in the processes underlying resilience and those explaining other patterns of functioning, including continuous maladaptation and changes from positive functioning to maladaptation. In every case, according to Bowlby (1973), behavior is a function of the current circumstances in which an individual finds him or herself, and the entire history of the individual up to that point. Just as resilience is built upon the history of the individual, so too is negative change.

An excellent illustration of this parallel process comes from our work examining the role of early attachment history in promoting continuity and change in functioning from middle childhood to adolescence (Sroufe et al., 1999). Four groups of children were created based on attachment history. Group one had been assessed as securely attached at both 12 and 18 months, group two as insecurely attached at both ages, and groups three and four as secure then anxious or anxious then secure. Children were later assessed as functioning well or poorly across grades 1–3 in terms of behavior problems and teacher rankings of emotional health and peer competence. First, we compared all children who were functioning poorly in middle childhood, but differed in attachment history, examining each group's outcomes in late adolescence, including psychopathology symptoms at age 17.5, and competence in terms of work/education, social relationships, and personal integration at age 19. We found that children with histories of secure attachment had lower scores on psychiatric symptoms and higher scores on overall competence at age 19 than did children with histories of anxious attachment, despite the fact that they had shown comparable problem behavior in middle childhood. This is a standard demonstration of resilience, showing the importance of early positive foundations.

Second, we examined the effects of different attachment histories on the late adolescent outcomes of individuals who functioned well in the middle childhood assessments. In a complete mirror image of the previous findings, those with histories of insecure attachment were now functioning more poorly than those with histories of secure attachment despite comparable functioning in middle childhood. "Looking across all four groups, level of functioning in adolescence appeared to depend on both earlier and later experience. The children who had secure histories and were functioning well in middle childhood were consistently significantly higher in their competence ratings" (Sroufe et al., 1999, p. 8). Children with insecure histories *and* behavior problems in middle childhood showed the poorest adaptation in adolescence, while the two groups with mixed histories (secure infant attachment, middle childhood behavior problems; insecure attachment history, well-functioning in middle childhood) showed intermediate adolescent outcomes.

The substantial individual differences found among our sample in trajectories and competence outcomes are striking. Given that the levels of risk experienced by our participants in early life run the gamut from less-than-optimal parenting to confirmed cases of child abuse, the substantial degree of problem behavior we see at various ages is to be expected. Still, given excellent quality of care provided by some of our parents, and the other supports at times available to them by grandparents and others, the resilience shown by some of the children is also expected. Our review of the risk and resilience findings from the MLSRA support the viewpoint that an individual's functioning at any point in time is a product of both current context and past history.

This is not to rule out certain circumstances in which the individual's coping abilities have been pushed to the limit. For example, in a study of the differential effects of cumulative risk in early and middle childhood, Appleyard, Egeland, van Dulmen, and Sroufe (2005) found that early risks predict both externalizing and internalizing problems in adolescence above and beyond the cumulative effect of middle childhood risk. Furthermore, this relationship was linear and additive, meaning the more risk factors the children experienced in childhood the more severe their behavior problems in adolescence. Conversely, as we have shown above, a consistently positive early history can help children function well in the face of childhood stress and/or recover from a period of difficulty. These parallel sets of findings highlight the predictable, lawful nature of maladaptation and resilience when seen through a developmental lens. In the broader view of development portrayed in these analyses, resilience no longer appears to be a special case.

Resilience in Emerging Adulthood

Much of the literature on risk, resilience, and competence has focused on childhood and adolescent years. However, despite the fact that developmental trajectories tend to stabilize over the years, it is clear that change remains possible (Sroufe et al., 2005). Resilience and maladaptation are lifespan phenomena. While an important goal of resilience research may be to predict good adjustment and well-being in adulthood, there is nothing in developmental theory to suggest that resilience is childhood-limited or that adults with a prior history of maladaptation cannot subsequently do well, though the challenge may of course be greater with a greater accumulation of negative history. In the same spirit as our childhood assessments, we have focused our data collection in the emerging adulthood years on functioning in developmentally relevant domains including education, interpersonal relationships, and mental health. As our participants progress further into adulthood, issues such as intergenerational patterns of parenting, occupational functioning, and physical health are becoming increasingly important areas of inquiry. In the following section, we will present findings from our study indicating that resilience does extend into adulthood and that it is predictable based on both early and later experience. Finally, we will end by suggesting areas of inquiry for resilience research in adulthood.

The Enduring Effect of Early Experience

Adults have an immense array of attitudes, motivations, and beliefs that guide their behaviors and that need to be accounted for when examining individual differences in resilience. When one considers these factors from a developmental perspective (i.e., by viewing current functioning as a combination of experiences past and present guided by internalized schemas of the self and the world) it is no wonder that resilience researchers focus on children whose brief life histories are more easily accounted for and whose schemas are more malleable. Furthermore, the internalization of early experience adds another level of complexity to the study of resilience in adulthood, as the systems that guide the behaviors, cognitions, and emotions comprising the individual's response to adversity may operate on an unconscious level that cannot be articulated in a self-report. To be sure, changing supports and opportunities in adulthood will also have their impact, but the mature person often has more established patterns of interpreting such events. Prospective longitudinal data is the only way to account for the developmental process of resilience in adulthood because, unlike the reconstructed memory of the participants, the data's memory is veridical. We have capitalized on this characteristic to uncover the developmental antecedents of risk and protective factors that have been hypothesized to affect adjustment in adulthood.

An interesting example of available research that can be used to explore the concept of resilience in adulthood lies at the crossroads of resilience and attachment research. This research examines the phenomenon of "earned secure"

adult attachment. Traditionally, someone who is classified as "earned secure" is able to coherently, and with balance, describe their relationship with their parents despite the fact that they are describing a characteristically negative relationship history (Pearson, Cohn, Cowan, & Cowan, 1994). These people were assumed to have had an insecure attachment to their parents in infancy and yet were able to forge secure representations in adulthood, thus suggesting a manifestation of resilience in the area of interpersonal relationships. Research from our study has addressed the problems associated with taking retrospective reports of childhood experiences at face value when making the "earned secure" classification. Roisman, Padron, Sroufe, and Egeland (2002) found that individuals who were classified as "earned secure" at age 19 through negative retrospective accounts of their childhood actually had highly supportive caregiving and were frequently securely attached as infants. These individuals also enjoyed high quality romantic relationships in adulthood. Thus, while it is possible that the parent–child relationship may have deteriorated in middle childhood, they often had early positive care as well as support in early adulthood. Further characteristics that distinguished this group from other securely attached individuals was the fact that they endorsed more severe internalizing symptoms and were more likely to have depressed mothers, which may have colored their reports of childhood relationships. Therefore, although these individuals did not necessarily show resilience in the domain of attachment as expected based upon retrospective report, they were resilient in the face of psychopathology, presumably drawing on past positive experience to promote current relationship functioning despite high levels of depression and anxiety.

Additionally, it is worth noting that resilience in interpersonal relationships was also observed among some individuals who were classified as "earned secure" in the originally intended sense (i.e., individuals who were directly observed to be anxiously attached in infancy but had secure representations in adulthood). These individuals also enjoyed high quality romantic relationships and were no more likely to experience internalizing symptoms than other secure individuals (Roisman et al., 2002). It appears that the later relationship experiences helped to transform their generalized attachment representations.

Changes in Context and Resilience in Emerging Adulthood

The changes in context associated with emerging adulthood are among the most important that people experience, as they involve the assumption of adult roles and responsibilities. One theory that indirectly refers to resilience during this developmental period is Moffitt's (1993) prediction that some individuals who increase their delinquent behavior in late adolescence will terminate these behaviors upon assuming adult responsibilities in emerging adulthood. The lawful process of resilience predicts that because these individuals had an early history of supportive care, they are better able to avoid the serious consequences of delinquent behavior and are more prepared to assume adult responsibilities. In addition, changes in support or stress during emerging adulthood should also account for the recovery of some of these individuals.

In line with such predictions, our study has examined three subtypes of antisocial behavior among our sample: never antisocial (NA), adolescent onset (AO), and early onset persistent (EOP; Aguilar et al., 2000). Initial results suggested the presence of significant risk factors in the early lives of the EOP group. We found that these individuals were more likely to have experienced psychologically unavailable, neglectful, and abusive care than AO and NA youth. Furthermore, EOP youth had mothers who experienced more life stress and were more likely to be avoidantly attached than NA children. Members of the AO group faced a number of concurrent adversities and experienced more life stress and more internalizing symptoms than their EOP and NA peers (Aguilar et al. 2000). These initial analyses were completed when the participants were 16 years old.

Participants were assessed again at age 23 to determine if they followed theoretically predicted pathways (Roisman, Aguilar, & Egeland, 2004). At age 23 AO adults were more likely to have desisted from their antisocial behavior than EOP adults (Roisman et al. 2004). These findings suggest that they were better able to capitalize on past and current positive experiences in order to terminate deviant behavior. Despite experiencing more life stress in adolescence and continuing to engage in deviant behavior at greater rates than NA youth, the AO group was able to bounce back from these difficulties. Preliminary analyses from the year 28 assessment largely indicate that AO adults have less difficulty engaging in the developmental tasks of adulthood (i.e., work, relationships, and parenting) than their EOP counterparts (Alink & Egeland, 2010).

Although many in the EOP group continue to engage in antisocial activities, some desisted in adulthood (Roisman et al., 2004). Compared to those who continued to manifest a high level of problem behavior, those who desisted had formed stable romantic relationships and a more stable employment history. Thus, even for these persistently troubled youth, positive opportunities in adulthood were able to influence change and promote resilience.

Adulthood as the Next Frontier of Resilience Research

Resilience in its multiple definitions is readily apparent in emerging adulthood. Evidence ranges from individuals engaging in adaptive romantic relationships despite internalizing problems, to adaptive engagement in developmental tasks after a period of delinquent behavior. As the lives of our participants become more complex and varied, so too do the opportunities for growth and adaptation. In our original sample, we identified many mothers who were supportive and sensitive caregivers despite significant life stress and depressive symptoms (Pianta & Egeland, 1990). We now have the opportunity to see the same resilience in their children as they assume the role of parent for a third generation of participants. In the area of work, evidence of resilience in the domains of school and interpersonal relationships may lay a foundation for occupational competence. The MLSRA has collected extensive data on job satisfaction, job continuity, and work ethic that may be especially relevant to the study of resilience in the face of economic crisis. Finally, our study has maintained a consistent focus on the relation between risk factors associated with poverty and mental health outcomes in both our participants and their mothers. As our participants approach middle age, we are also becoming increasingly interested in the association between these risk factors and physical health. Through this connection, the substantial literature on resilience can be brought to bear in the area of health psychology, as health behaviors, treatment adherence, and prognosis may be affected by early experience and thus aid health professionals understand why some people fare better than expected. In sum, the possibilities for adaptive functioning despite adversity are multitudinous throughout development. Unfortunately, so too are the possibilities for maladaptation. However, both are the lawful, probabilistic result of prior history and current context. Data from the MLSRA shows that this is as true of development in childhood as it is in adulthood.

In the next phase of our own research, we see a convergence of resilience research with research on "turning points" (Laub & Sampson, 1993). There is great interest currently in opportunities for major change in adaptation (e.g., marriage, the birth of a child). Our developmental process view, of course, leads us to consider individual variations in the ability to capitalize on such opportunities, which we refer to as "potentiation effects." Not everyone shows improved adaptation upon forming a new relationship or encountering a new educational or vocational opportunity; only some do. We expect again that these differences will be accounted for by contextual factors, with developmental history being prominent. In one preliminary example, we found that we could distinguish between those who recovered from depression in adulthood following formation of a romantic partnership from those who did not

recover after partnering on the basis of different histories of infant attachment (Sroufe, Coffino, & Carlson, 2010).

Discussion and Conclusion

As described, on numerous occasions over the course of our longitudinal study we have found evidence that compels us to attend to both concurrent and prior influences on functioning and to try to understand their complex and dynamic interaction. This can be best achieved if we conceive of resilience in the same way that we conceptualize other developmental phenomena. The developmental conceptualization of maladaptation provides a useful guide to understanding resilience as a developmental process. The developmental pathways framework for understanding disturbance, as described by Sroufe (1997), outlines five implications that can be easily reinterpreted to describe resilience with little need for imagination. The implications are as follows: (1) resilience as a product of development over time, (2) multiple pathways to similar manifest outcomes, (3) different outcomes of the same pathway, (4) change is possible at many points, and (5) change is constrained by prior adaptation. First, resilience, or positive adaptation despite threats, can be understood as maintenance of normal developmental trajectories over time. The usefulness of the concepts of equifinality and multifinality (for discussion see Cicchetti & Rogosch, 1996), which are described by implications two and three, are also quite appropriate for understanding resilience. Even if two individuals appear to demonstrate the same functioning at a particular moment, they may indeed be understood as moving along very different pathways if other relevant influences are recognized. For example, two individuals who have both faced similar risk may be expected to diverge in their pathways if one has had additional assets in the past and can more easily capitalize on new assets when they become available. Likewise, an individual with positive functioning despite risk factors may appear similar to one who has never faced risk or adversity, but may be expected to face more difficulty or compromised functioning when further challenges arise. As suggested by empirical evidence described above, change is indeed possible at many points, both toward and away from positive functioning. However, said change is in part predictable by considering earlier histories of adaptation.

Though we have already come to accept maladaptation as a lawful developmental phenomenon, this does not negate the usefulness of developmental psychopathology as a specific area of study. It has been important to see maladaptation as agreeing with what we know about the processes of development in general. Resilience too can be thought of in this way, with special importance placed on the desire to understand what keeps humans on positive trajectories and what can knock us off course. This is of particular interest as we pursue interventions that can promote resilience. The study of resilience and developmental psychopathology both ultimately have a similar practical goal of understanding and promoting positive adaptation and competence. The more explicable these concepts become, as facilitated by developmental thinking, the better we will be able to utilize this knowledge to promote well-being. There is no benefit to resilience being treated as unique to particular individuals. We should prefer resilience to be explainable, as this opens the doorway to attempts at providing the assets that we understand to promote resilience to those who do not naturally have them available.

The field of resilience research has already made much progress since its first emergence. The shift to the current conceptualizations of resilience has entailed many changes in thinking. Factors outside the individual have gained acceptance as influential in promoting resilient outcomes, and there has been a changing conceptualization of the range of factors outside the individual likely to have an impact. We now understand that some of the most important influences are simply the functioning of basic adaptive systems (see Masten, 2001). Additionally, there has been a shift to better accommodate understanding individuals as resilient at some, but not all points in time, as influenced by changes

in classification of risk, adversity or competent functioning. However, there remains confusion in the field due to the use of conflicting definitions of resilience utilized by different researchers across studies. Although many consider it to be reasonable to use different definitions depending on the context of the study and the proposed questions, this has raised concerns regarding the validity of the construct of resilience as currently defined. Utilizing a developmental view of resilience, we think differing definitions pose no difficulty for the validity of resilience as a construct. In fact, thinking developmentally can explain why various definitions have surfaced. Recognition of the reasons for the conceptual difficulties may actually help facilitate an understanding of the inter-relatedness of adaptation and maladaptation under conditions of risk and adversity.

The specific parameters under which resilience has been studied in any particular investigation play a large role in interpretation of meaning. Definitions ascribe resilience to some kind of stressor(s) or measurable risk(s) with respect to some particular outcome(s) in a particular domain or set of domains. Though all researchers must wrestle with the difficulty of conceptualizing dynamic movement over time toward and away from functioning that demonstrates resilience, some studies acknowledge this vacillation, while others ignore the issue (Masten & Wright, 2010; Rutter, 2007). In our developmental view, this movement simply reflects an appreciation of the coherence of individual pathways after taking all influences into account. It becomes clear too, that though conceptual struggles and conflicting decisions made in characterization of resilience across the literature certainly reflect the complexity of the construct, their presence does not suggest that resilience is simply an incoherent and useless construct. Questions about how to understand and define risk, adversity, competence, and movement toward and away from functioning that demonstrates resilience do not in fact need to be answered in one particular fashion to maintain a coherent theory of development and resilience. The answers depend upon the individual trajectory in the area of interest, as resilience is not a singular entity. It is not contradictory to examine multiple influences and outcomes in a variety of domains, and it does not negate the usefulness of the concept to find individuals doing well in some areas and not in others, or moving back and forth from adaptive to maladaptive functioning. Arguably, each individual's development is dynamic. There is no need to label development as reflecting a trajectory that exclusively demonstrates maladaptation or resilience. Both are important to understand how development proceeds and how it can be influenced by naturally occurring contextual variables, as well as variables that can be introduced (with important implications for prevention and intervention efforts). Both can co-occur at one point in time in different domains, or change over time in a particular domain for a single individual.

Though there has been much movement towards a view of resilience as process, confusion remains as to where resilience resides. This confusion is understandable, as the compelling quality of the process view cannot fully eradicate our sense that some individuals themselves seem to show more capacity for resilience. However, it has been one of our goals in this chapter to make it clear that these views do not need to conflict. By adopting a developmental pathway understanding of resilience, the process view can retain importance even as the ability to maintain competence becomes more internalized in the individual and less likely to be altered over time. Though contextual influences become internalized over time as child competence and general coping ability, it remains important to measure more than concurrent variables and functioning. Even if it were possible to measure functioning in a manner that captures all previously internalized influences thus providing all information required to predict future functioning and resilience, this ability to predict would not negate the need to understand process. We do not simply want to know whether an individual at any given point will remain resilient or begin to show resilient functioning. Rather, we also want to understand the process by which he or she reached that current level of functioning. Without thinking

developmentally in a way that emphasizes the importance of process, it is much more difficult to make use of what we learn about resilient functioning to maximize prevention and intervention efforts. We do not only care what will happen next at any given point in time, but rather how to best intervene along the way as a child develops and grows.

Others who have argued for a developmental conceptualization of resilience have acknowledged common objections to this view. Luthar, Cicchetti, and Becker (2000) describe several reasons that resilience is a useful construct to retain in addition to simple positive development even when viewing resilience through a developmental framework. One reason suggested is that the developmental conceptualization of resilience differs from classical theories in that it suggests that "adaptation can occur through trajectories that defy 'normative' expectations" (p. 553). This may appear true at a basic level based upon a consideration of risk factors alone. However, this statement should not be taken to imply that if one knew the total cumulative history of risks and supports that trajectories would continue to defy normative expectations. The more we know about full histories and the full range of current circumstances, the less we will see the violation of our expectations. Outcomes associated with resilience, though surprising in their hopefulness, should not be surprising in terms of our ability to predict them if we are able to measure all relevant variables over the course of development. Expectations are defied only because we have failed to measure all relevant influences that would allow us to form accurate normative expectations. At our current state of knowledge, however, it is certainly the case that there are some individuals that defy our expectations. Studying these individuals provides us with the next set of clues to understanding the process of positive adaptation despite extensive risk or adversity.

The pathways model that summarizes an organizational view of development is best able to serve us in understanding the phenomenon of resilience. We must consider both current context as well as history, accepting the potential for ongoing change with variation in circumstances, yet recognizing that this potential becomes more constrained by history over time. Developmental history is thus a fundamental part of the broader context for resilience. Viewing resilience at one point in time is like viewing snapshots instead of an entire movie. With a continuous view, the picture of how an individual is functioning makes sense to us in a more coherent way. Lack of knowledge of what occurred earlier in an individual's life can obscure our understanding of what occurs later.

References

Achenbach, T. M., & Edelbrock, C. S. (1986). *Child behavior checklist. Manual for teachers report form and teacher version of the child behavior profile.* Burlington, VT: Department of Psychiatry, University of Vermont.

Aguilar, B., Sroufe, L. A., Egeland, B., & Carlson, E. (2000). Distinguishing the early-onset/persistent and adolescence-onset antisocial behavior types: From birth to 16 years. *Development and Psychopathology, 12*(2), 109–132.

Ainsworth, M. D. S., & Bell, S. M. V. (1974). Mother-infant interaction and the development of competence. In K. Connolly & J. Bruner (Eds.), *The growth of competence* (pp. 97–118). New York, NY: Academic Press.

Alink, L., & Egeland, B. (2010). *Developmental process associated with different trajectories of antisocial behavior.* Unpublished manuscript.

American Psychiatric Association Committee on Nomenclature and Statistics. (1980). *Diagnostic and statistical manual of mental disorders* (3rd ed.). Washington, DC: American Psychiatric Association.

Anthony, E. J., & Cohler, B. (1987). *The invulnerable child.* New York, NY: Guilford.

Appleyard, K., Egeland, B., van Dulmen, M. H. M., & Sroufe, L. A. (2005). When more is not better: The role of cumulative risk in child behavior outcomes. *Journal of Child Psychology and Psychiatry, 46*(3), 235–245.

Bowlby, J. (1969). *Attachment and loss. Vol. 1: Attachment* (2nd ed.). New York, NY: Basic Books.

Bowlby, J. (1973). *Attachment and loss. Vol. 2: Separation* (2nd ed.). New York, NY: Basic Books.

Cicchetti, D. (1989). Developmental psychopathology: Past, present, and future. In D. Cicchetti (Ed.), *Rochester symposium on developmental psychopathology: Vol. 1. The emergence of a discipline* (pp. 1–12). Hillsdale, NJ: Erlbaum.

Cicchetti, D., & Garmezy, N. (1993). Prospects and promises in the study of resilience. *Development and Psychopathology, 5*(4), 497–502.

Cicchetti, D., & Rogosch, F. A. (1996). Equifinality and multifinality in developmental psychopathology. *Development and Psychopathology, 8*(4), 597–600.

Cicchetti, D., & Sroufe, L. A. (1978). An organizational view of affect: Illustration from the study of Down's syndrome infants. In M. Lewis & L. Rosenblum (Eds.), *The development of affect* (pp. 309–350). New York, NY: Plenum.

Egeland, B. (1997, August). *Risk and resilience in infants and young children.* Paper presented at the meeting of the American Psychological Association, Chicago, IL.

Egeland, B. (2007). Understanding developmental processes and mechanisms of resilience and psychopathology: Implications for policy and practice. In A. Masten (Vol. Ed.), *The Minnesota Symposium on Child Psychology: Vol. 34. Multi-level dynamics in developmental psychopathology: Pathways to the future* (pp. 83–118). Hillsdale, NJ: Lawrence Erlbaum and Associates.

Egeland, B., & Brunnquell, D. (1979). An at-risk approach to the study of child abuse. *Journal of the American Academy of Child Psychiatry, 8*(2), 219–235.

Egeland, B., Carlson, E. A., & Sroufe, L. A. (1993). Resilience as process. *Development and Psychopathology, 5*, 517–528.

Egeland, B., & Farber, E. A. (1984). Infant-mother attachment: Factors related to its development and changes over time. *Child Development, 55*(3), 753–771.

Egeland, B., Kalkoske, M., Gottesman, N., & Erickson, M. F. (1990). Preschool behavior problems: Stability and factors accounting for change. *Journal of Child Psychology and Psychiatry and Allied Disciplines, 31*(6), 891–909.

Egeland, B., & Kreutzer, T. (1991). A longitudinal study of the effects of maternal stress and protective factors on the development of high risk children. In E. M. Cumming, A. L. Greene, & K. H. Karrakar (Eds.), *Life-span developmental psychology: Perspectives on stress and coping* (pp. 61–85). Hillsdale, NJ: Lawrence Erlbaum Associates.

Egeland, B., Pianta, R. C., & O'Brien, M. A. (1993). Maternal intrusiveness in infancy and child maladaptation in early school years. *Development and Psychopathology, 5*(3), 359–370.

Ellis, B. J., Shirtcliff, E. A., Boyce, W. T., Deardorff, J., & Essex, M. J. (2009, April). *Biological sensitivity to context: Stress reactivity moderates the effect of parental supportiveness on pubertal maturation.* Paper presented at the biennial meeting of the Society for Research in Child Development, Denver, CO.

Englund, M. M., Egeland, B., & Collins, W. A. (2008). Exceptions to high school dropout predictions in a low-income sample: Do adults make a difference? *Journal of Social Issues, 64*(1), 77–93.

Erickson, M. F., Sroufe, L. A., & Egeland, B. (1985). The relationship between quality of attachment and behavior problems in preschool in a high-risk sample. *Monographs of the Society for Research in Child Development, 50*(1), 147–166.

Kagan, J. (1984). *The nature of the child*. New York, NY: Basic Books.

Laub, J. H., & Sampson, R. J. (1993). Turning points in the life course: Why change matters to the study of crime. *Criminology, 31*(3), 301–325.

Lewis, M. (1997). *Altering fate*. New York, NY: Guilford.

Luthar, S. S. (2006). Resilience in development: A synthesis of research across five decades. In D. Cicchetti & D. J. Cohen (Eds.), *Developmental psychopathology: Vol. 3. Risk, disorder, and adaptation* (2nd ed., pp. 739–795). New York, NY: Wiley.

Luthar, S. S., Cicchetti, D., & Becker, B. (2000). The construct of resilience: A critical evaluation and guidelines for future work. *Child Development, 71*(3), 543–562.

Masten, A. S. (2001). Ordinary magic: Resilience processes in development. *American Psychologist, 56*(3), 227–238.

Masten, A. S., & Wright, M. O. D. (2010). Resilience over the lifespan: Developmental perspectives on resistance, recovery, and transformation. In J. W. Reich, A. J. Zautra, & J. S. Hall (Eds.), *Handbook of adult resilience* (pp. 213–237). New York, NY: Guilford.

Moffitt, T. E. (1993). The neuropsychology of conduct disorder. *Development and Psychopathology, 5*(1–2), 135–151.

Parritz, R., & Troy, M. (2010). *Disorders of childhood*. Belmont, CA: Wadsworth.

Pearson, J. L., Cohn, D. A., Cowan, P. A., & Cowan, C. P. (1994). Earned-and continuous-security in adult attachment: Relation to depressive symptomatology and parenting style. *Development and Psychopathology, 6*(2), 359–373.

Pianta, R. C., Egeland, B., & Sroufe, L. A. (1990). Maternal stress and children's development: Prediction of school outcomes and identification of protective factors. In J. Rolf, A. Masten, D. Cicchetti, K. Nuechterlein, & S. Weintraub (Eds.), *Risk and protective factors in the development of psychopathology* (pp. 215–235). Cambridge, MA: Cambridge University Press.

Pianta, R. C., Hyatt, A., & Egeland, B. (1986). Maternal relationship history as an indicator of developmental risk. *Journal of Orthopsychiatry, 56*(3), 385–398.

Puig-Antich, J., & Chambers, W. (1978). *The schedule of affective disorders and schizophrenia for school aged children*. New York, NY: New York Psychiatric Institute.

Roisman, G. I., Aguilar, B., & Egeland, B. (2004). Antisocial behavior in the transition to adulthood: The independent and interactive roles of developmental history and concurrent experiences. *Development and Psychopathology, 16*(4), 857–871.

Roisman, G. I., Padron, E., Sroufe, L. A., & Egeland, B. (2002). Earned-secure attachment status in retrospect and prospect. *Child Development, 73*(4), 1204–1219.

Rutter, M. (2007). Resilience, competence, and coping. *Child Abuse and Neglect, 31*(3), 205–209.

Sameroff, A. J. (2000). Developmental systems and psychopathology. *Development and Psychopathology, 12*(3), 297–312.

Sroufe, L. A. (1997). Psychopathology as an outcome of development. *Development and Psychopathology, 9*(2), 251–268.

Sroufe, L. A. (1999, March). *Changing the odds: The development of resilience*. Paper presented at the annual meeting of the American Association for the Advancement of Science, Anaheim, CA.

Sroufe, L. A. (2007). The place of development in developmental psychopathology. In A. Masten (Vol. Ed.), *The Minnesota Symposium on Child Psychology: Vol. 34. Multi-level dynamics in developmental psychopathology: Pathways to the future* (pp. 285–299). Hillsdale, NJ: Lawrence Erlbaum and Associates.

Sroufe, L. A. (2009). The concept of development in developmental psychopathology. *Child Development Perspectives, 3*(3), 178–183.

Sroufe, L. A., Carlson, E. A., Levy, A. K., & Egeland, B. (1999). Implications of attachment theory for developmental psychopathology. *Development and Psychopathology, 11*(1), 1–13.

Sroufe, L. A., Cooper, R. G., & DeHart, G. (1992). *Child development: Its nature and course* (2nd ed.). New York, NY: McGraw-Hill.

Sroufe, L. A., Egeland, B., Carlson, E. A., & Collins, W. A. (2005). *The development of the person*. New York, NY: Guilford.

Sroufe, L. A., Egeland, B., & Kreutzer, T. (1990). The fate of early experience following developmental change: Longitudinal approaches to individual adaptation in childhood. *Child Development, 61*(5), 1363–1373.

Sroufe, L. A., & Rutter, M. (1984). The domain of developmental psychopathology. *Child Development, 55*(1), 17–29.

Sroufe, L. A., & Waters, E. (1977). Attachment as an organizational construct. *Child Development, 48*(4), 1184–1199.

Sroufe, L. A., Coffino, B., & Carlson, E. A. (2010). Conceptualizing the role of early experience: Lessons from the Minnesota Longitudinal Study. *Developmental Review, 30*(1), 36–51.

Vaughn, B., Egeland, B., Sroufe, L. A., & Waters, E. (1979). Individual differences in infant-mother attachment at twelve and eighteen months: Stability and change in families under stress. *Child Development, 50*(4), 971–975.

Yates, T. M., Egeland, B., & Sroufe, L. A. (2003). Rethinking resilience: A developmental process perspective. In S. S. Luthar (Ed.), *Resilience and vulnerability: Adaptation in the context of childhood adversity* (pp. 243–266). Cambridge, UK: Cambridge University Press.

Temporal and Contextual Dimensions to Individual Positive Development: A Developmental–Contextual Systems Model of Resilience

13

Ingrid Schoon

In this chapter a developmental–contextual model of resilience is introduced, taking into account multiple contextual influences, ranging from the micro- to the macro-context, and their interactions with individual functioning over time. It is argued that adaptive responses to adverse circumstances are probalistically determined through reciprocal interactions between individual and context. The model challenges the assumption of necessary developmental constancy as well as the idea that experiences in early childhood set up an invariant life path. Change for better or worse can occur across the entire life path, shaped by continuous interactions between a developing individual and a changing socio-historical context.

The crux of the model are the interdependent transactions between individual and context and the assumption that individual and context mutually constitute each other through processes of co-regulation. Resilience is a dynamic and relational concept and can only be understood by examining person×environment interactions over time.

This chapter has three sections. First, I give a definition of resilience, focusing in particular on its developmental aspects. Then the developmental–contextual systems model will be introduced, describing its key assumptions and implications for

a better understanding of the temporal and contextual dimensions of individual adjustment. Finally, the implications of the model for a better understanding of the multiple influences and heterogeneity in pathways and outcomes are discussed.

Conceptualising Resilience

The notion of resilience generally refers to the process of avoiding adverse outcomes or doing better than expected when confronted with major assaults on the developmental process (Luthar, Cicchetti, & Becker, 2000; Masten, 2007; Rutter, 2006). Although individuals may manifest resilience in their behaviour and life patterns, resilience is not a personality characteristic. Adaptive functioning in the face of adversity is not only dependent on characteristics of the individual but is greatly influenced by processes and interactions arising from significant others and the wider social context.

Resilience is defined by the constellations of risk exposure and the manifestation of effective functioning in the face of that risk. The term is conceptualized as a probabilistic concept, based on expectations of successful vs. problematic adjustment in response to risk factors that are assumed to affect individual adaptation. Pioneering studies following the lives of people thought to be at risk for unfavourable outcomes, such as children growing up with mentally ill parents (e.g. parents suffering from schizophrenia), and those who have been abused, neglected, or exposed to poverty

I. Schoon (✉)
Institute of Education, University of London,
London, UK
e-mail: I.Schoon@ioe.ac.uk

M. Ungar (ed.), *The Social Ecology of Resilience: A Handbook of Theory and Practice*,
DOI 10.1007/978-1-4614-0586-3_13, © Springer Science+Business Media, LLC 2012

and socio-economic disadvantage, observed great variations in functioning, including cases of positive adaptation despite the experience of even severe adversity (Anthony, 1987; Garmezy, 1974; Rutter, 1979; Werner & Smith, 1982). These observations of unexpected positive development in the face of adversity, which were confirmed in many subsequent studies, led to a paradigmatic shift in how researchers of human development began to view the causes and course of development.

Historically, most studies of development of at-risk individuals tried to understand adjustment problems as reflected in ill health or mental disorder, academic failure, behavioural problems, or motivational deficits. These pathogenic or deficit models failed to recognise (a) the strengths and resources available to at-risk populations, and (b) the larger social system in which development takes place. Trying to understand the processes and mechanisms that enable individuals to beat the odds, to succeed in the face of adversity, led to a change of focus from deficits to the possible assets and strengths within individuals and communities. It also led to investigations of the reciprocal person×environment transactions enabling positive adjustment despite the experience of adversity (Antonovsky, 1979; Cicchetti & Garmezy, 1993; Sameroff, 1983).

Moving away from the constancy model portraying human development as being determined either through the effects of genetics or the long-term consequences of early experiences, the research evidence pointed to the plasticity of human development. Plasticity describes the capacity for change, and is characterised by non-linearity, and in contrast to the group average, by some degree of unpredictability of individual life paths (Clarke & Clarke, 2003; Sroufe & Rutter, 1984). Human plasticity is however not limitless, and is influenced by past events, specific characteristics of the individual, and current conditions (Brim & Kagan, 1980; Lerner, 1984). The malleable and unmalleable go hand in hand, and both constancy and change impact on human development. Furthermore, the potential for change exists across the life course and is the result of reciprocal transactions between a changing individual and a changing socio-historical context (Baltes, 1987; Sameroff, 1983, 2009).

Positive Adaptation

Resilience is generally understood as a dynamic process, depending on the ongoing interactions between individual and context. Adaptive functioning has been conceptualised as appropriate responses to developmental tasks encountered at different life stages (Masten, 1994; Masten & O'Dougherty Wright, 2009). The developing individual has to master and negotiate different developmental demands, comprising processes of physical, cultural, and psychosocial maturation, that represent benchmarks of adaptation in different domains expected at specific developmental periods (Masten & Coatsworth, 1998). Every developmental period has its own developmental challenges resulting from specific constellations of biological changes, role transitions, and common life events (Erikson, 1959; Havighurst, 1948/72; Heckhausen, 1999; Levinson, 1986). These tasks can comprise learning to walk or talk during infancy, succeeding at school, establishing stable relationships, or accepting physical decline in old age. Coping adequately with these changing developmental demands is considered in many studies as a measure of adaptive functioning. The criteria and levels used to identify effective functioning are however culturally determined and differ between developmental and historical contexts (Kaplan, 1999; Ungar, 2004a). For example, while 30 years ago the majority of young people in the UK left school at compulsory minimum school leaving age (age 16) to enter full-time employment, today nearly all 16-year-olds aspire to continue in further or higher education (Schoon, 2010b). The identification of positive adjustment is tied to normative judgments relating to particular outcomes, and can comprise aspects of internal or external adaptation, or both (Masten, 2001). As such, they reflect the multiple tasks of a living system to maintain internal functioning (e.g. feeling competent about one's capabilities) and at the same time same time to respond to normative respond to normative expectations regarding developmentally appropriate behaviour (i.e. general school leaving age) and adjust to their environment (e.g. select an environment that enables the realisation of one's skills and abilities).

It is now widely accepted that successful adaptation under adverse circumstances does not require extraordinary characteristics or resources but results from "ordinary", normative functions such as cognitive reasoning, self regulation, and access to social networks (Masten, 2001). However, effective functioning might be defined and interpreted differently in different cultures and contexts (Ungar, 2004a). Besides cultural variations, the identification of resilience should also take into account the seriousness of the risk exposure, not only the level of functioning (Luthar & Zelazo, 2003).

Risk Exposure

The notion of risk used in resilience research stems from epidemiological research, identifying expected probabilities of maladjustment (Cicchetti & Garmezy, 1993; Rutter, 2009). Risk or adversity can comprise genetic, biological, psychological, environmental, or socio-economic factors that are associated with an increased probability of maladjustment (Luthar et al., 2000). Fundamental to the idea of risk is the predictability of life chances from earlier circumstances. Adversities such as socio-economic disadvantage, material hardship, and family breakdown increase the risk for developmental adjustment problems later on, such as increased risk of educational failure, behaviour problems, psychological distress, or poor health.

While early studies on resilience focused on a single risk factor, such as maternal psychopathology or experience of a stressful life event like divorce, it soon became apparent that individual risk factors do not exert their effect in isolation but interact with other influences. The relationship between any single risk factor and subsequent outcomes tends to be weak, and usually many variables are involved in determining an outcome (Garmezy, 1991; Rutter, 1981, 2009). Serious risk emanates from the accumulation of risk effects. It is the accumulation of risk factors, their combined effect, and the timing and dura-

tion of exposure that exerts a deleterious impact on developmental outcomes (Schoon, 2006; Schoon, Cheng, & Jones, 2010).

Risks tend to co-occur and accumulate over the life course, and it is important to consider aspects of severity and chronicity in risk exposure, as there might be a dose–response gradient. Moderate levels of risk or controlled risk exposure sometimes entail "steeling" or inoculation effects that make it easier to respond to subsequent risk exposure, while severe levels of risk can overpower the coping abilities of the individual (Rutter, 2006). Furthermore, a developmental perspective is important in assessing risk effects, as the developmental timing and persistence of risk exposure matters. For example, risk experiences in early childhood can set up a vicious cycle of cumulating disadvantage across domains, although this does not necessarily have to be the case (Clarke & Clarke, 1976; Rutter, 1998). It might also be that individuals show resilience at one particular time point but not at another, pointing to the so-called "sensitive" or "critical" periods of development.

In identifying risk exposure, one has to assess whether a particular risk or constellation of risks is a potential cause or precursor for a specified outcome. Risks describe probabilities and not certainties, and it has been argued that we have to clearly differentiate between statistical vs. actual risk (Richters & Weintraub, 1990). Individuals exposed to particular adverse life circumstances are often treated as homogenous groups, despite possible variations in the degree to which their lives are actually shaped and how they respond to the particular risk exposure. It could be possible, for example, that a person identified by a researcher as "being at-risk" might not consider this label appropriate to describe him or herself. There are indeed serious concerns regarding stigmatisation, predetermining the failure of individuals exposed to severe hardship (Ungar, 2004b).

There is, furthermore, evidence to suggest that specific risk factors might have differential effects on specific outcomes. For example, poverty shows generally strong effects on the cognitive development of young children, while family disruption is more salient for emotional and behavioural adjustment (Conger et al., 1993; Linver, Brooks-Gunn, & Kohen, 2002; Schoon et al., 2010). As a result, we need to know more about the configurations of risk factors and their impact on specific outcomes. Furthermore, there is evidence of variations in response to environmental influences, i.e. some individuals are affected more than others, a phenomenon also described as differential susceptibility to risk exposure (Belsky et al., 2007). It might also be the case that a specific risk factor poses a significant risk at one life stage but not another, or that the negative effects do not manifest immediately but only later in life, so called sleeper effects (Rutter, 2006).

A Developmental–Contextual Systems Model of Resilience

Because resilience unfolds over time in a developing individual, it is essential to adopt a developmental perspective in order to understand the processes underlying effective functioning in the face of adversity. The very definition of resilience comprises time variant patterns of adaptation, ranging from resistance to stress or adversity as implicated in (i.) continued positive or effective functioning in adverse circumstances, (ii.) recovery after a significant trauma, (iii.) normalisation following accelerated or delayed development, or (iv.) developmental transformation (Masten & O'Dougherty Wright, 2009). Adopting a developmental–contextual perspective allows us to recognise the dynamic nature of resilience, uncovering lasting, modifiable, or unchangeable patterns of adjustment. It also helps us to acknowledge the role of the immediate and wider social context in shaping individual levels of adjustment and their interpretation.

The model to be introduced is based within an ecological systems framework for the study of human development, taking into account multiple interacting levels of influence (Bronfenbrenner, 1979, 1986, 1989), human plasticity (Lerner, 1984, 1996), developmental co-regulation (Sameroff, 1983, 2010), and the role of the wider socio-historical context in which development

takes place (Elder, 1994, 1998). It is assumed that both individuals and their environments are potentially malleable, whereby individuals actively shape their environment, which in turn influences them (Schoon, 2006). The ecological perspective provides a heuristic for understanding how multiple levels of influence contribute to individual development and adjustment in a changing context.

Structural Aspects

Human development cannot be separated from the social context. Individual and context are understood to mutually constitute each other through processes of co-regulation (Sameroff, 2010). Indeed, the notion of resilience is defined by variations in individual functioning in response to adverse risk situations (Rutter, 1985, 2006). Within a bio-ecological model (Bronfenbrenner & Ceci, 1994), human development is considered to be shaped by the interaction of genetic, biological, psychological, and socio-economic factors in the context of environmental support and constraints. Overlapping and interacting biological, psychological, and social aspects of the self interact with other interlinked systems of the wider socio-cultural context. Development occurs through ongoing reciprocal transactions among these different constituents (Sameroff, 2010).

The biopsychological self system interacts with the many interlinked structures of the immediate and wider context which it inhabits. Different aspects of the context such as culture, neighbourhood, and family are conceptualised as nested spheres of influence varying in proximity to the individual and ranging from the micro- to the macro-context. The developing child is rooted within many inter-related systems, such as families, schools, and neighbourhoods, as well as the wider socio-historical context. Bronfenbrenner's (1979, 1989) conceptualisation of context differentiates between the proximal environment, which is directly experienced by the individual (as for example the family environment), and more distal cultural and social value systems that have an indirect effect on the individual are often mediated by the more proximal context.

Another important aspect of the ecological system is time – the chronosystem – which takes into account the dynamic and ongoing transactions between individual and context (Bronfenbrenner, 1986). Time is often treated as synonymous with chronological age, providing a frame of reference for the study of change over time. As children get older, they may react differently to environmental risks and may be more able to determine and evaluate how that change will influence them. The chronosystem comprises individual aspects such as the physiological changes that occur with ageing, as well as aspects of the wider social context that are external to the individual like normative expectations regarding the timing of developmental transitions (e.g. school entry, entry into the labour market, retirement), or chance events such as a parent's death which might trigger developmental change. Other aspects to be considered are the cumulative effects of an entire sequence of developmental transitions over an extended period of time (i.e. the entire life course) and the embeddedness of individual development in a specific socio-historical context (Elder, 1974/1999; Elder & Caspi, 1988). Opportunities and constraints for individual development are shaped by the kind of sociocultural conditions that exist in a given historical period, and by how these evolve over time.

A basic principle of the life course is that human development extends over the entire life span and is embedded in a changing socio-historical context. Behaviour cannot be fully explained by restricting analysis to specific life stages, such as mid-childhood, adolescence, or old age (Baltes, 1987; Elder, 1998). It is only by following individuals from birth into and through the adult years that we can chart their developmental trajectories and pathways. Individual differences in the experience of negotiating a transition are associated with a variety of conditions, including development before the transition, the timing of the transition, and the wider socio-historical context in which the transition occurs with its opportunities and constraints.

The potential for development is shaped by the reciprocal influences of person–environment interactions that differ in terms of timing (onset, duration, termination), combination, direction, order, and the socio-historical context in which they take place. The developmental impact of events is contingent on when they occur in a person's life and which particular aspect of the developing system is affected. Furthermore, the influence of an event at a particular life stage is shaped within the context of personal biography. It has been argued that understanding how individuals navigate developmental transitions and choices is the crux of understanding risk and resilience across the life span (Graber & Brooks-Gunn, 1996). The conceptualisation of the multiple spheres of influence and the transactional interchanges between individual and context at different transition stages and over time has become increasingly influential in guiding and informing studies of resilience in at-risk populations (Cicchetti & Toth, 2009; Masten & O'Dougherty Wright, 2009; Rutter, 2006, Sameroff, 1993).

Developmental Processes

Within resilience research, current adaptive patterns are viewed as the product of transactional process between the person and the environment (Cicchetti & Garmezy, 1993; Egeland, Carlson, & Sroufe, 1993; Masten, 2009; Rutter, 2006; Sameroff, 1983) which, in turn, become predictors for future developmental outcomes. The assumption of such hierarchical integrative processes asserts consistency and coherence of individual development as it implies that future developmental outcomes can be predicted from knowledge of earlier adaptation patterns (Sroufe, 1979). For example, a child performing poorly in primary school is often expected to also manifest problems in later educational settings. Yet, the very definition of resilience predicates changes in trajectories and deviation from predicted relationships. It might, for example, be possible that school performance had become disrupted due to the experience of a family trauma or parental divorce coinciding with school entry, only to return to "normal" levels of adjustment after some time. To capture such dynamics in adjustment, it is necessary to understand why certain individuals succeed to maintain positive functioning or return to "normal" behaviour despite exposure to a significant adversity. What is needed is a model of development that takes into account both consistency and change. Key aspects of such a probabilistic epigenetic model of resilience comprise nonlinearity, multi-dimensionality, hierarchical integration and differentiation, and most crucially, processes of developmental co-regulation (i.e. co-action between different layers of influence).

Nonlinearity and Multi-directionality

Human development has been conceptualised by two contrasting positions, describing development either as a continuous growth process or as a discontinuous series of stages, where each stage requires a qualitative reorganisation of the previous one (Gottlieb, 1992; Werner, 1957). While the continuous model assumes that development is predetermined from the outset, the discontinuous model recognises the possibility of novel and emergent developmental patterns. Both models have been used to describe the processes by which individual organisms develop from fertilisation to adulthood. While some argue that the organism is preformed from the outset, persistent empirical evidence points to emergent properties through reciprocal interactions among all parts of the organism, including organism×environment co-actions (Gottlieb, 1992). Within such an epigenetic, nonlinear, and staged model of development, the emergence of new structures has been characterised as experience dependent (Sameroff, 2010), taking into account transactions between a developing individual and a changing context.

Stages can be used as a descriptive concept, focusing attention on average achievements at a particular age (Erikson, 1959; Havighurst, 1948/1972; Levinson, 1986), or as a theoretical concept, conceptualising a developmental stage as a period of stability of functioning following the transition from a structurally different period of stability (Sameroff, 2010). There are reasons to be weary of staged process models when they imply an invariant sequence. Evidence from previous research suggests substantial variations among persons or among subgroups in the population regarding the ordering, timing, and duration of adjustment to changing developmental tasks, as is shown, for example, in studies examining the transition from adolescence to independent adulthood (Garrett & Eccles, 2009; Osgood, Ruth, Eccles, Jacobs, & Barber, 2005; Schoon, Ross, & Martin, 2009). Moreover, what sometimes looks like self-generated stages of adjustment or coping may represent a sequence determined by external demands and constraints (Lazarus & Folkman, 1984).

In this regard, the notions of equifinality and multifinality, derived from systems theory, are relevant to a better understanding of risk and resilience processes. Equifinality refers to varied pathways leading to similar outcomes, and multifinality assumes that a single component or risk factor may act differently depending on the organisation of the system in which it operates (Bronfenbrenner, 1979, 1989; Cicchetti & Rogosch, 1996; von Bertalanffy, 1968). Multiple pathways can lead to similar manifest outcomes, or different outcomes may spring from the same pathway. Changes in development are possible at many points across the life course, illustrating the potential diversity in ontogenetic outcome, regardless of similarity in the risks that are experienced (Cicchetti, Rogosch, Lynch, & Holt, 1993; Lerner, 1996).

Hierarchical Integration and Differentiation

Developmental adaptation can be considered as the progressive and mutual accommodation between a developing individual and the changing properties of the immediate and wider socio-cultural context (Bronfenbrenner, 1979). Development comprises evolving states of being, where outcomes or consequences are themselves precursors to subsequent experiences and events. Functioning well in age salient developmental tasks during one developmental period establishes the foundation for doing well in future tasks (Masten, 2007). Moreover, there is evidence of developmental cascades, where achievements or failures in adaptation spread over time, from one domain to another, and potentially even across generations (Masten & Cicchetti, 2010; Any point in the life span can be understood as the consequence of past experience and as the launch pad for subsequent experiences and conditions, although developmental cascades can also alter the course of development. Life-long development may involve processes that do not originate at conception, birth, or early childhood but in later periods. The nonlinear nature of human development is characterised by the reorganisation and differentiation of behaviour and experience, leading to the emergence of new structural and functional properties and competencies which result as a consequence of ongoing interactions between the multiple structures or spheres of influence described above.

Multi-dimensionality

In his ecological systems theory Bronfenbrenner (1979) emphasises the need for the non-reductionist analysis of individual development requiring the simultaneous description of several spheres of influence, thereby moving beyond simple cause and effect explanations of behaviour. Living systems are understood as a unified whole, comprising genetic, biological, emotional, cognitive, behavioural, and social aspects, where each level is interrelated and characterised by self-activity and historicity.

Human development thus occurs across multiple domains. It is possible for a person to be competent in one domain, but not in another, to manifest resilience in response to one specific risk factor but not to others, and to manifest resilience at one time point but not another. Not all individuals respond to adversity in the same way. For example, it is possible that a child experiencing socio-economic hardship shows good academic performance and behaviour adjustment, but at the same time develops emotional problems (Schoon, 2006). Unless multiple domains of adjustment are assessed, only a partial picture of adaptation can be formulated (Cicchetti & Garmezy, 1993). However, success in a particular domain cannot be assumed to generalise to other

spheres as resilience is not an all-or-nothing phenomenon. Defining resilience as doing well across multiple tasks can lead to the reification of the concept and convey a static rather than dynamic characterisation of resilience (Masten, 2009). Such an approach also has limitations, as it might curb the understanding of specific processes that may play a unique role for a particular domain of adaptation, or a particular constellation of risk factors (Schoon et al., 2010). Thus, to gain a better understanding of overall functioning, multiple domains have to be considered and the role of specific risks within each domain.

Developmental Co-regulation

Living systems strive actively to continue functioning, i.e. surviving, under various conditions by purposively changing the environment and themselves (Bronfenbrenner, 1989; von Bertalanffy, 1968; Sameroff, 1983). The notion of self-regulating developing systems, which are open to and interact with their environments, has been specified by Ludwig von Bertalanffy in his formulation of systems theory. Systems theory itself has been informed by theoretical biology and was conceptualised as a holistic and organismic counterpoint to mechanistic preconceptions of development (von Bertalanffy, 1968).

The goal-directedness of self-active systems is historically situated in time and space, and includes the adaptation to and accommodation of external conditions and internal needs at the same time (Schoon, 2007). Within a systems view of resilience, the multilevel dynamics and transactions between individual and context can be conceptualised as aspects of co-regulation or co-action (Masten, 2007). Since environment and individual are in transaction, it follows that developmental outcomes at particular points in time not only reflect previous levels of adaptation but also intervening environmental inputs. Sameroff (2010) has used the term "other regulation" to highlight the crucial role of regulation provided by others within the proximal or wider social context in shaping individual differences in regulatory capacities. It is however also important to take into account co-regulation over time, accounting for influences of the chronosystem which can comprise age-graded or history-graded influences, as lives are shaped by the timing of encounters with historical forces, such as the experience of an economic recession or boom, peace, or war (Baltes, 1987; Elder & Caspi, 1988). The landmark study by Glen Elder on the children of the great depression in the 1930s, for example, has shown that younger children are more vulnerable to family economic stresses than older children, and that younger age cohorts were more adversely affected by the experiences of the economic recession than older age cohorts experiencing the same event, yet at a different stage in their lives. Changes in the level of adaptation can be explained based on changes within the individual, changes in the environment, changes guided by active individual choice, changes instigated by others, and by the wider socio-historical context which can of course include chance events. Through the co-action of interacting spheres of influence, a reorganisation or new kind of organisation and differentiation is brought into being.

Models of Resilience

Within the context of resilience research, the adoption of a developmental–contextual systems perspective means that different processes that can promote effective adaptation despite the experience of adversity can be understood as processes of developmental co-regulation. Through previous empirical research, different processes have already been identified, comprising compensatory, protective, or steeling effects (Garmezy, Masten, & Tellegen, 1984; Luthar et al., 2000; Masten, 2001), as well as resilient integration (Kumpfer, 1999). Conceptualising these processes as aspects of developmental co-regulation emphasises the relational and interactive nature of resilience. This means moving away from a focus on individual characteristics, or personality traits, towards a better understanding of person × environment interactions bringing about positive adaptation in the face of adversity. Furthermore, the developmental–contextual perspective acknowledges that resilience is a process that extends over time, involving many spheres

of influence, ranging from the molecular level to the wider socio-historical context.

Compensatory models. The compensatory model of resilience accounts for the availability of resources within the individual and the context that can counterbalance or neutralise the negative effects associated with risk exposure. Resource factors, or developmental assets, can include characteristics of the individual such as self-regulation, life planning, self-esteem, or cognitive competences; as well as characteristics of the family and wider social context, such as parenting skills, supportive social networks, neighbourhood characteristics, or social policies (Lerner & Benson, 2003; Masten, 2007). These resource factors show an equally beneficial effect for those who are exposed and those who not exposed to adversity, and show their beneficial effect in low- as well as high-risk conditions. According to a cumulative effect model (sometimes also referred to as main effects or additive effects model), the accumulation of assets or resources will outweigh the risks. Increasing the protective resources in quality or number could theoretically offset the negative effects of risk or adversity, or improve positive adjustment in general.

Moderating effect models. Within a moderating effect or protective model of resilience, exposure to a protective factor or process should have beneficial effects only for those individuals who are exposed to the risk factor, but not benefit those who are not exposed (i.e. there should be an interactive relationship between the protective factor, the risk exposure, and the outcome; Rutter, 2006). For example, there is evidence to suggest variability in response to childhood maltreatment based on the gene encoding the neurotransmitter-metabolising enzyme monoamine oxidase A (MAOA) (Caspi et al., 2002). Children with high levels of MAOA are less likely to develop antisocial problems, suggesting that genotypes can moderate children's sensitivity to environmental insults. However, resilience is not just a feature of gene × environment interactions. Adaptive response to adverse situations can be triggered by numerous other circumstances. For example, in a study examining processes promoting academic resilience in the face of economic adversity, parental involvement with the child's education as well as social integration were identified as protective factors, in addition and above academic ability or parental education, that were particularly important for children growing up in a high-risk environment characterised by low parental social status, rented accommodation, overcrowding, and lack of access to household amenities (Schoon, 2006). Moreover, it has been argued that behavioural and morphological phenotype change can be instigated by change in developmental conditions, such as changes in rearing styles or shifts in the physical or psychosocial environment (Gottlieb, 1992). More generally, within interactive or moderating effect models of resilience protective factors show a buffering or ameliorative influence, and are especially important if the risk level is high. Moderating influences may lead to a reduction of risk effects and prevent negative chain reactions, instigate a positive chain reaction, or create opportunities to experience self-efficacy (Rutter, 1990).

Challenge models. The challenge model of resilience suggests that resistance to risk may come from exposure to low level risk, or risk exposure within controlled circumstances rather than avoidance of risk altogether. Exposure to low level risk experiences, or controlled risk exposure, may have beneficial or steeling effects, providing a chance to practice problem-solving skills and to mobilise resources (Elder, 1974/1999; Garmezy et al., 1984; Rutter, 1987). The risk exposure must be challenging enough to stimulate a response, yet must not be overpowering. The crux of the challenge model is that moderate levels of risk exposure open up the opportunity to learn how to overcome adversity. From a developmental perspective, the challenge model can also be considered as a model of inoculation preparing the developing person to overcome significant risks in the future (Rutter, 2006).

Resilient integration. To describe successful adaptation after a prolonged period of disruption or stress, the term "resilient integration" has been used (Kumpfer, 1999). The capacity for resilience is seen as developing over time, through the integration of constitutional and experiential factors in the context of a supportive environment (Egeland et al., 1993). Certain attributes or circumstances that are generally associated with positive adjustment may not necessarily show immediate benefits, but may be predictive of positive adaptation later in life. Similar to the notion of "sleeper effects", where beneficial effects are not detected until a period of time has elapsed, resilient integration requires protective attributes or circumstances to be stored up for later use. Such a developmental "reserve capacity" is not normally utilised but can be drawn upon when required (Baltes, 1987), as for example to overcome a potentially problematic transition such as early school leaving (Sacker & Schoon, 2007; Schoon & Duckworth, 2010), or early parenthood (Schoon & Polek, 2011), or to maintain functioning in old age (Staudinger, Marsiske, & Baltes, 1993).

Turning points. Delayed recovery may also stem from positive adult experiences or "turning point" experiences in adult life (Elder, 1998; Rutter, 2006). Substantial and enduring change in life course development often occurs during transition periods, such as entry into school, work, or family formation. These events are characterised by the assumption of new social roles and change of context. For example, in a follow-up study of teenage delinquents growing up in low income areas in Boston, Laub and Sampson (2003) showed that the step into a supportive marriage can instigate a beneficial turning point effect. It is however not only just one factor, such as the effect from a secure intimate relationship that made a difference, but the associated influences of a new extended family network and friendship groups, as well as the informal controls exerted by the spouses that prevented contact with the delinquent peer group. It is this complex mix of influences that contribute to positive adjustment in the face of adversity, which also was apparent in Glen Elder's study of young people growing up in Oakland, California, during the Great Depression of the 1920s. The evidence of turning points in human lives illustrates the potential for plasticity which can occur across the entire lifespan (Schoon, 2006; Schoon & Duckworth, 2010; Schoon & Polek, 2011). Increasing age imposes constraints on potential responsiveness and one's ability to act upon the environment, yet there is persistent evidence of individual capability to meet and handle adversities and to maintain or regain levels of effective functioning even in old age (Staudinger et al., 1993).

Meaning-making and sense of coherence. Individuals are not passively exposed to external risk experiences – they interpret and process the information, bringing order and meaning to a changing world, and produce a set of expectations about how experiences fit together. The power of meaning for human life in the face of overwhelming suffering has been described by Victor Frankl in his account of daily life in a Nazi concentration camp (Frankl, 1946/1984). Frankl identified the "will to meaning" as the primary motivational force to sustain efforts to survive in horrific circumstances. The wish for meaning and coherence of what is going on in the world and one's own, often contradictory experiences of the world, has also been conceptualised as "sense of coherence" (Antonovsky, 1987). Sense of coherence comprises three dimensions: comprehensibility (the extent to which an individual perceives a situation as meaningful and predictable); manageability (the degree to which an individual perceives his or her own resources to be sufficient to meet demands); and meaningfulness (the degree to which an individual feels that life is meaningful and that problems are perceived as challenges rather than hindrances). The cognitive restructuring involved in meaning-making requires considerable capacity for thinking and reflection and is more likely to be important as people grow older (Masten & O'Dougherty Wright, 2009). However, as Ungar argues, when resilience is viewed through a constructionist lens, the way individuals create meaning of their behaviour and the context in which this takes place are key aspects of a resilient response at any age (Ungar, 2004a). Similarly, Rutter (1990) considers variations in cognitive processing and appraisal, leading to acceptance rather than denial of challenges, as a crucial protective mechanism.

Is the Potential for Resilience Unlimited?

The notion of resilience generally evokes a very optimistic outlook regarding the possibility of surviving even severe adversity or trauma. Yet, the potential for resilience and human plasticity is not unlimited. Not all individuals are able to maintain or regain positive functioning, especially in the face of continued assaults on their development. Although there is evidence to suggest stability in adjustment among at-risk children followed over time (Cowen et al., 1997; Egeland et al., 1993; Masten et al., 1999; Werner & Smith, 1982), some researchers point out that although a significant percentage of at-risk individuals show positive adjustment at a particular point in time, many falter subsequently (Coie et al., 1993; Kaplan, 1999). It has also been shown that competence over time can be displayed within but not necessarily across domains (Luthar, 1997), and it is generally acknowledged that resilience is not a static state (Cicchetti et al., 1993; Coie et al., 1993; Egeland et al., 1993). For example, evidence from the American Head Start and other competence-enhancement and prevention programmes suggest that longer periods of intervention are more effective than shorter ones (Pianta & Walsh, 1996). Similar findings are reported regarding early intervention programmes in the UK, such as Sure Start (Melhuish, Belsky, Leyland, Barnes, & National Evaluation of Sure Start Research Team, 2008); Melhuish, Belsky & Barnes, (2010), suggesting that support has to be maintained to create sustainable effects.

Despite continuous evidence regarding the malleability of individual functioning, research results should be evaluated with caution. All too often, individuals or families with the greatest need receive the least support (Schoon & Bartley, 2008). Furthermore, many individuals are crushed by the experience of continuous adversity, especially poverty and disadvantage. Children born into relatively disadvantaged families are more likely to accumulate risks associated with that disadvantage throughout their life than children born into more privileged families. This accumulation begins early in life and its consequences can continue into adulthood, and even into the next generation. The experience of early hardship weakens individual adaptation and this detrimental effect is then carried forward to the future. Subsequent experiences of adversity add to the deterioration of already reduced resources. Evidence from the UK cohort studies, for example, has shown that children from relatively disadvantaged family backgrounds who demonstrated early academic resilience did not maintain their performance to the same extent as their more privileged but academically less able peers (Schoon, 2006). Furthermore, the role of cognitive abilities in gaining academic qualifications has declined for more recently born cohorts (Schoon, 2010a), suggesting that children from disadvantaged backgrounds, starting their schooling with a high level of cognitive ability, are falling behind in their course of education, and are leaving school with lower levels of achievement than their less able peers from more privileged backgrounds.

Conclusion

Over the entire life span, humans are confronted with different events and changes that challenge successful adaptation. The notion of resilience has been introduced to describe individual variations in response to these challenges, and as a framework to examine effective adaptation under adverse life circumstances. Resilience is defined through constellations of risk and individual functioning in response to this risk. Individuals differ in the extent to which they are exposed and susceptible to different risks (Belsky et al., 2007) and in the way risk constellations are appraised and dealt with (Lazarus & Folkman, 1984; Ungar, 2004a). The outcomes following early adversity are quite diverse, with long-term effects depending on the nature of subsequent life experiences (Clarke & Clarke, 2003; Clarke & Clarke Ann, 2000; Rutter, 1989). Supportive and protective experiences occur and are effective well past early childhood. This means it is never too early or never too late for appropriate interventions (Schoon & Bynner, 2003). The process of devel-

opment necessarily involves a complex mix of both continuities and change (Lerner, 1984), and only long-term longitudinal studies can provide evidence of the dynamic nature of resilience.

Adopting a developmental–contextual systems model enables the researcher to account for the multiple influences and heterogeneity in pathways and outcomes. The developmental–contextual perspective avoids the reification of resilience as a personality trait and highlights its relational and interactive nature, emphasising malleability of both person and context, and the dynamic nature of evolving processes. Appropriate support at different life stages and key transition points can reduce the risk of adjustment problems and promote a society that looks after its most vulnerable. As has been pointed out by Uri Bronfenbrenner (1979) "It is the growing capacity to remold reality in accordance with human requirements and aspirations that, from an ecological perspective, represents the highest expression of development" (p. 10).

Acknowledgements Findings presented in this chapter are based on research funded by the Nuffield Foundation and the UK Economic and Social Research Council (ESRC) grant number RES-594-28-0001.

References

Anthony, E. J. (1987). Risk, vulnerability, and resilience: An overview. In E. J. Anthony & B. J. Cohler (Eds.), *The invulnerable child* (pp. 3–48). New York, NY: Guilford.

Antonovsky, A. (1979). *Health, stress and coping* (1st ed.). San Francisco, CA: Jossey-Bass.

Antonovsky, A. (1987). *Unravelling the mystery of health: How people manage stress and stay well* (1st ed.). San Francisco, CA: Jossey-Bass.

Baltes, P. B. (1987). Theoretical propositions of life-span developmental-psychology – On the dynamics between growth and decline. *Developmental Psychology, 23*(5), 611–626.

Belsky, J., Bakermans-Kranenburg, M. J., & Ijzendoorn, M. H. (2007). For better and for worse. Differential susceptibility to environmental influences. *Current Directions in Psychological Science, 16*, 300–304.

Brim, O. G., Jr., & Kagan, J. (1980). Constancy and change: A view of the issues. In O. G. Brim, Jr. & J. Kagan (Eds.), *Constancy and change in human development* (pp. 1–25). Cambridge, MA Harvard University Press.

Bronfenbrenner, U. (1979). *The ecology of human development: Experiments by nature and design.* Cambridge, MA: Harvard University Press.

Bronfenbrenner, U. (1986). Ecology of the family as a context for human development: Research perspectives. *Developmental Psychology, 22,* 723–742.

Bronfenbrenner, U. (1989). Ecological systems theory. In R. Vasta (Ed.), *Six theories of child development: Revised formulations and current issues* (pp. 187–250). Greenwich, CT: JAI Press.

Bronfenbrenner, U., & Ceci, S. J. (1994). Nature-nurture reconceptualized in developmental perspective – A bioecological model. *Psychological Review, 101*(4), 568–586.

Caspi, A., McClay, J., Moffitt, T. E., Mill, J., Martin, J., Craig, I. W., et al. (2002). Role of genotype in the cycle of violence in maltreated children. *Science, 297*(5582), 851–854.

Cicchetti, D., & Garmezy, N. (1993). Prospects and promises in the study of resilience. *Development and Psychopathology, 5,* 497–502.

Cicchetti, D., & Rogosch, F. A. (1996). Equifinality and multifinality in developmental psychopathology. *Development and Psychopathology, 8*(4), 597–600.

Cicchetti, D., Rogosch, F. A., Lynch, M., & Holt, K. D. (1993). Resilience in maltreated children – Processes leading to adaptive outcome. *Development and Psychopathology, 5*(4), 629–647.

Cicchetti, D., & Toth, S. L. (2009). The past achievements and future promises of developmental psychopathology: The coming of age of a discipline. *Journal of Child Psychology and Psychiatry, 50*(1–2), 16–25.

Clarke, A. M., & Clarke, A. D. B. (Eds.). (1976). *Early experience: Myth and evidence.* London, UK: Open Books.

Clarke, A. M., & Clarke, A. D. B. (2003). *Human resilience: A fifty year quest.* London, UK: Jessica Kingsley.

Clarke, A. M., & Clarke, A. D. B. (2000). *Early experience and the life path.* London, UK: Jessica Kingsley.

Coie, J. D., Watt, N. F., West, S. G., Hawkins, J. D., Asarnow, J. R., Markman, H. J., et al. (1993). The science of prevention. A conceptual framework and some directions for a national research-program. *The American Psychologist, 48*(10), 1013–1022.

Conger, R. D., Conger, K. J., Elder, G. H., Lorenz, F. O., Simons, R. L., & Whitbeck, L. B. (1993). Family economic stress and adjustment of early adolescent girls. *Developmental Psychology, 29,* 206–219.

Cowen, E. L., Wyman, P. A., Work, W. C., Kim, J. Y., Fagen, D. B., & Magnus, K. B. (1997). Follow-up study of young stress-affected and stress-resilient urban children. *Development and Psychopathology, 9*(3), 565–577.

Egeland, B., Carlson, E., & Sroufe, L. A. (1993). Resilience as process. *Development and Psychopathology, 5*(4), 517–528.

Elder, G. H. (1974/1999). *Children of the great depression: Social change in life experience.* Bolder, CO: Westview Press.

Elder, G. H. (1994). Time, human agency, and social change: Perspectives on the life course. *Social Psychology Quarterly, 57,* 4–15.

Elder, G. H. (1998). The life course as developmental theory. *Child Development, 69*(1), 1–12.

Elder, G. H., & Caspi, A. (1988). Human development and social change: An emerging perspective on the life course. In N. Bolger, A. Caspi, G. Downey, & M. Moorehouse (Eds.), *Persons in context: Developmental processes* (pp. 77–113). Cambridge, UK: Cambridge University Press.

Erikson, E. H. (1959). *Identity and the life cycle: Selected papers.* New York, NY: International Universities Press.

Frankl, V. (1946/1984). *Man's search for meaning.* New York, NY: Washington Square Press. (Original work published 1946).

Garmezy, N. (1974). The study of competence in children at risk for severe psychopathology. In E. J. Anthony & C. Koupernik (Eds.), The child in his family: Children at psychiatric risk (Vol. 3, pp. 77–97).

Garmezy, N. (1991). Resiliency and vulnerability to adverse developmental outcomes associated with poverty. *The American Behavioral Scientist, 34*(4), 416–430.

Garmezy, N., Masten, A. S., & Tellegen, A. (1984). The study of stress and competence in children – A building block for developmental psychopathology. *Child Development, 55*(1), 97–111.

Garrett, J. L., & Eccles, J. S. (2009). Transition to adulthood: Linking late-adolescent lifestyles to family and work status in the mid twenties. In I. Schoon & K. R. Silbereisen (Eds.), *Transitions from school to work: Globalisation, individualisation, and patterns of diversity* (pp. 243–264). Cambridge, UK: Cambridge University Press.

Gottlieb, G. (1992). *Individual development and evolution.* Oxford, UK: Oxford University Press.

Graber, J. A., & Brooks-Gunn, J. (1996). Transitions and turning points: Navigating the passage from childhood through adolescence. *Developmental Psychology, 32,* 768–776.

Havighurst, R. J. (1948/1972). *Developmental tasks and education.* New York, NY: David McKay.

Havighurst, R. J. (1953). *Human development and education,* New York: Longmans.

Heckhausen, J. (1999). *Developmental regulation in adulthood: Age-normative and sociostructural constraints as adaptive challenges.* Cambridge, UK: Cambridge University Press.

Kaplan, H. B. (1999). Toward an understanding of resilience: A critical review of definitions and models. In M. D. Glantz & J. L. Johnson (Eds.), *Resilience and development: Positive life adaptations* (pp. 17–83). New York, NY: Kluwer Academic.

Kumpfer, K. L. (1999). Factors and processes contributing to resilience: The resilience framework. In M. D. Glantz & J. L. Johnson (Eds.), *Resilience and development: Positive life adaptations* (pp. 179–224). New York, NY: Kluwer Academic.

Laub, J. H., & Sampson, R. J. (2003). *Shared beginnings, divergent lives. Delinquent boys to age 70*. Cambridge, MA: Harvard University Press.

Lazarus, R. L., & Folkman, S. (1984). *Stress, appraisal, and coping*. New York, NY: Springer.

Lerner, R. M. (1984). *On the nature of human plasticity*. Cambridge, UK: Cambridge University Press.

Lerner, R. M. (1996). Relative plasticity, integration, temporality, and diversity in human development: A developmental contextual perspective about theory, process, and method. *Developmental Psychology, 32*(4), 781–786.

Lerner, R. M., & Benson, P. (2003). *Developmental assets and asset-building communities*. New York, NY: Kluwer Academic.

Levinson, D. J. (1986). A conception of adult development. *The American Psychologist, 41*, 3–14.

Linver, M. R., Brooks-Gunn, J., & Kohen, D. E. (2002). Family processes as pathways from income to young children's development. *Developmental Psychology, 38*(5), 719–734.

Luthar, S. S. (1997). Socioeconomic disadvantage and psychosocial adjustment: Perspectives from developmental psychopathology. In S. S. Luthar, J. A. Burack, L. Chisholm, & J. R. Weisz (Eds.), *Developmental psychopathology: Perspectives on adjustment, risk, and disorder* (pp. 459–485). Cambridge, UK: Cambridge University Press.

Luthar, S. S., Cicchetti, D., & Becker, B. (2000). The construct of resilience: A critical evaluation and guidelines for future work. *Child Development, 71*(3), 543–562.

Luthar, S. S., & Zelazo, L. B. (2003). Research on resilience: An integrative view. In S. S. Luthar (Ed.), *Resilience and vulnerability. Adaptation in the context of childhood adversities* (pp. 510–549). Cambridge, UK: Cambridge University Press.

Masten, A. (1994). Resilience in individual development: successful adaptation despite risk and adversity. In M. C. Wang & E. W. Gordon (Eds.), *Educational resilience in inner-city America: challenges and prospects* (pp. 3–25). Hillsdale, N.J.: L. Erlbaum Associates.

Masten, A. S., & Coatsworth, J. D. (1998). The development of competence in favorable and unfavorable environments - Lessons from research on successful children. *American Psychologist, 53*(2), 205–220.

Masten, A. S., Hubbard, J. J., Gest, S. D., Tellegen, A., Garmezy, N., & Ramirez, M. (1999). Competence in the context of adversity: Pathways to resilience and maladaptation from childhood to late adolescence. *Development and Psychopathology, 11*(1), 143–169.

Masten, A. S. (2001). Ordinary magic – Resilience processes in development. *The American Psychologist, 56*(3), 227–238.

Masten, A. S., & Powell, J. L. (2003). A Resilience Framework for Research, Policy, and Practice. In S. S. Luthar (Ed.), *Resilience and vulnerablity : adaptation in the context of childhood adversities* (pp. 1–25). Cambridge: Cambridge University Press.

Masten, A. S. (2007). Resilience in developing systems: Progress and promise as the fourth wave rises. *Development and Psychopathology, 19*(3), 921–930.

Masten, A. S. (2009). Ordinary Magic: Lessons from research on resilience in human development. *Education Canada, 49*(3), 28–32.

Masten, A. S., & O'Dougherty Wright, M. (2009). Resilience over the lifespan. Developmental perspectives on resistance, recovery, and transformation. In J. W. Reich, A. J. Zautra, & J. S. Hall (Eds.), *Handbook of adult resilience*. New York, NY: Guilford.

Masten, A. S., & Cicchetti, D. (2010). Developmental cascades. *Development and Psychopathology, 22*(3), 491–495.

Melhuish, E., Belsky, J., Leyland, A. H., Barnes, J., & National Evaluation of Sure Start Research Team. (2008). Effects of fully-established sure start local programmes on 3-year-old children and their families living in England: A quasi-experimental observational study. *The Lancet, 372*(9650), 1641–1647.

Osgood, D. W., Ruth, G., Eccles, J. S., Jacobs, J. E., & Barber, B. L. (2005). Six paths to adulthood. In R. A. Settersten Jr., F. F. Furstenberg, & R. G. Rumbaut (Eds.), *On the frontier of adulthood. Theory, research and public policy* (pp. 320–355). Chicago, IL: The University of Chicago Press.

Pianta, R. C., & Walsh, D. J. (1996). *High-risk children in schools: Constructing sustaining relationships*. London, UK: Routledge.

Richters, J., & Weintraub, S. (1990). Beyond diathesis: Toward an understanding of high-risk environments. In J. Rolf, A. Masten, D. Cicchetti, K. H. Nuechterlin, & S. Weintraub (Eds.), *Risk and protective factors in the development of psychopathology* (pp. 67–96). Cambridge, UK: Cambridge University Press.

Rutter, M. (1979). Protective factors in children's responses to stress and disadvantage. In M. W. Kent, & J. E. Rolf (Eds.), *Primary prevention of psychopathology: Social competence in children* (pp. 49–62). Hanover, NH: Universty Press of New England.

Rutter, M. (1981). Stress, coping and development – Some issues and some questions. *Journal of Child Psychology and Psychiatry and Allied Disciplines, 22*(4), 323–356.

Rutter, M. (1985). Resilience in the face of adversity – Protective factors and resistance to psychiatric-disorder. *The British Journal of Psychiatry, 147*, 598–611.

Rutter, M. (1987). Psychosocial resilience and protective mechanisms. *The American Journal of Orthopsychiatry, 57*(3), 316–331.

Rutter, M. (1989). Pathways from childhood to adult life. *Journal of Child Psychology and Psychiatry and Allied Disciplines, 30*(1), 23–51.

Rutter, M. (1990). Psychosocial resilience and protective mechanisms. In J. Rolf, A. S. Masten, D. Chichetti, K. H. Nuechterlin, & S. Weintraub (Eds.), *Risk and protective factors in the development of psychopathology* (pp. 181–214). Cambridge, UK: Cambridge University Press.

Rutter, M. (1998). Developmental catch-up, and deficit, following adoption after severe global early privation. *Journal of Child Psychology and Psychiatry and Allied Disciplines, 39*(4), 465–476.

Rutter, M. (2006). Implications of resilience concepts for scientific understanding. *Annals of the New York Academy of Science, 1094*(1), 1–12.

Rutter, M. (2009). Understanding and testing risk mechanisms for mental disorders. *Journal of Child Psychology and Psychiatry, 50*(1–2), 44–52.

Sacker, A., & Schoon, I. (2007). Educational resilience in later life: Resources and assets in adolescence and return to education after leaving school at age 16. *Social Science Research, 36*(3), 873–896.

Sameroff, A. J. (1983). Developmental systems: Contexts and evolution. In W. Kesson, & P. H. Mussen (Eds.), *Handbook of child psychology* (Vol. 1). New York: Wiley.

Sameroff, A. J. (Ed.). (2009). The transactional model of Development. How children and contexts shape each other. Washington, DC: American Psychological Press.

Sameroff, A. J. (2010). A unified theory of development: A dialectic integration of nature and nurture. *Child Development, 81*(1), 6–22.

Schoon, I. (2006). *Risk and resilience. Adaptations in changing times*. Cambridge, UK: Cambridge University Press.

Schoon, I. (2007). Adaptations to changing times: Agency in context. *International Journal of Psychology, 42*(2), 94–101.

Schoon, I. (2010a). Childhood cognitive ability and adult academic attainment: Evidence from three British cohort studies. *Longitudinal and Life Course Studies, 1*(3), 241–258.

Schoon, I. (2010b). Planning for the future: Changing education expectations in three British cohorts. *Social Historical Research, 35*(2), 99–119.

Schoon, I., & Bynner, J. (2003). Risk and resilience in the life course: Implications for interventions and social policies. *Journal of Youth Studies, 6*(1), 21–31.

Schoon, I., & Bartley, M. (2008). The role of human capability and resilience. *Psychologist, 21*(1), 24–27.

Schoon, I., Cheng, H., & Jones, E. (2010). Resilience in children's development. In K. Hansen, H. Joshi, & S. Dex (Eds.), *Children of the 21st century: From birth to five years* (pp. 233–248). Bristol, UK: Polity Press.

Schoon & Duckworth, (2010). Leaving school early and making it! Evidence from two British birth cohorts. *European Psychologist, 15*(4), 283–292.

Schoon, I., & Polek, E. (2011). Pathways to economic wellbeing among teenage mothers in Great Britain. *European Psychologist, 16*(1), 11–20.

Schoon, I., Ross, A., & Martin, P. (2009). Sequences, patterns, and variations in the assumption of work and family related roles. Evidence from two British birth cohorts. In I. Schoon & K. R. Silbereisen (Eds.), *Transitions from school to work: Globalisation, individualisation, and patterns of diversity* (pp. 219–242). Cambridge, UK: Cambridge University Press.

Sroufe, L. A. (1979). The coherence of individual development: Early care, attachment, and subsequent developmental issues. *The American Psychologist, 34*, 834–841.

Sroufe, L. A., & Rutter, M. (1984). The Domain of Developmental Psychopathology. *Child Development, 55*(1), 17–29.

Staudinger, U. M., Marsiske, M., & Baltes, P. B. (1993). Resilience and levels of reserve capacity in later adulthood – Perspectives from life-span theory. *Development and Psychopathology, 5*(4), 541–566.

Ungar, M. (2004a). A constructionist discourse on resilience. Multiple contexts, multiple realities among at-risk children and youth. *Youth & Society, 35*, 341–365.

Ungar, M. (2004b). *Nurturing hidden resilience in troubled youth*. Toronto, ON: University of Toronto Press.

Von Bertalanffy, L. (1968). General system theory: Foundations development applications. New York: Braziller.

Werner, H. (1957). The concept of development from a comparative and organismic point of view. In D. B. Harris (Ed.), *The concept of development*. Minneapolis, MN: University of Minneapolis Press.

Werner, E. E., & Smith, R. S. (1982). *Overcoming the odds: High risk children from birth to adulthood*. Ithaca, NY: Cornell University Press.

Girls' Violence: Criminality or Resilience?

14

Jean Hine and Joanna Welford

Violent behaviour by girls has been the focus of much media and policy attention in recent years. Statistics for women dealt with by the criminal justice system for violence show large proportionate increases that have been a cause for concern in many countries (Australian Institute of Criminology, 2007; Kon & AuCoi, 2008; Ministry of Justice, 2009; Poe-Yamagata & Butts, 1996). This behaviour is doubly condemned: once because violence is generally abhorred, and again because such behaviour is seen as "unfeminine". Reporting often accepts that such behaviour is criminal and gives little attention to the function that engaging in this violence can play in the lives of women and girls.

This chapter addresses this issue by considering the violent behaviour of girls from the perspective of girls themselves. We explore the gendered social and environmental context within which it occurs, and show how these actions can help girls to cope in difficult circumstances, achieving what they present as positive outcomes – indeed, as resilience: "[T]he notion of resilience focuses attention on coping mechanisms, mental sets, and the operation of personal agency. In other words, it requires a move from a focus on external risks to a focus on how these external risks are dealt with by the individual" (Rutter, 2006, p. 8).

Our research revealed that these violent behaviours are far from the homogeneous activity often represented.[1] This sample present important differences between and within individuals in terms of type of and motivation for violence – demonstrating personal agency in their attempts to take control of their lives, where family, social and economic circumstances have a significant impact upon their behaviour. Their discourse reveals how violent behaviour is their way of coping and doing well in difficult circumstances – demonstrating (albeit hidden) resilience (Ungar, 2004). The girls we spoke to show how violent behaviours are not at odds with, and indeed can enhance, their feminine identity. This behaviour often has no criminal intent, yet adult involvement and response to violence by girls can lead to the criminalisation of many young women (Welford & Hine, 2010) with the potential for long-term negative consequences.

Violence by girls and young women is a complex issue. On one hand, it is seen as an increasing and worrying concern for those responsible for policing young people's behaviour – schools, families and the criminal justice system. On the other hand, studies are increasingly demonstrating the *value* of violence to girls in certain social contexts (Batchelor, 2007; Ness, 2004). This chapter discusses the role of violence in the lives of young girls living in disadvantaged neighbourhoods in

---

[1]The authors have papers in preparation that describe the range of behaviours, but there is no space to describe that here.

J. Hine (✉)
De Montfort University, Leicester, UK
e-mail: jhine@dmu.ac.uk

M. Ungar (ed.), *The Social Ecology of Resilience: A Handbook of Theory and Practice*,
DOI 10.1007/978-1-4614-0586-3_14, © Springer Science+Business Media, LLC 2012

England, and in particular, how this behaviour can be understood as resilience in particular contexts.

An Increase in Violence by Girls?

The last 15–20 years have seen growing and considerable attention from the media and policy-makers towards the behaviour of girls, particularly behaviour that is seen to be "unfeminine", such as being drunk in the streets and using violence. A "moral panic" (Cohen, 1972) has been generated in many countries about the apparent increase in such behaviour. A typical example in the United Kingdom (UK) is a BBC News Report entitled "Why are girls fighting like boys?" (Geoghegan, 2008), although the treatment of the issue is much more measured here than in some of the more populist newspapers such as the *Daily Mail* which has published headlines like "Ladette[2] Britain" (Slack, 2010). Articles such as these proffer a range of explanations for this behaviour, from feminism and equality, and the "masculinisation" of women and girls to the sale of cheap alcohol. However, all accept that the increased female presence in criminal statistics reflects a real increase in violent criminal activity by girls. This is disputed by much academic literature on the topic (Chesney-Lind, 2001). There has been a steady stream of academic interest in reviewing and discussing the issues, with a range of theories emerging about the extent to which the amount or nature of female violence has changed over time and the reasons for female violence, whether increasing or not.

Official statistics of England and Wales have demonstrated a rise in violent crimes committed by girls and young women over recent years, with a 48% increase recorded between 2004 and 2008 (Ministry of Justice, 2009). The media have reported and embellished this "rise" in violence, fuelling a growing concern that more girls are becoming more violent (Batchelor, Burman, & Brown, 2001; Slack, 2009). At the same time, research conducted within and outside the United Kingdom has highlighted the "commonplace" nature of violence in the lives of some girls, from low-level violence in "ordinary" communities (Burman, Brown, Tisdall, & Batchelor, 2000; Duncan, 2006), including the oft-ignored physical nature of female friendship groups (Brown, Burman, & Tisdall, 2001), to the routine use of more serious violence in some low-income, inner-city communities (Ness, 2004).

Academic challenges to this reported rise argue that a major contributor to any increase in statistics for violent offences by young women is changes in the management of violent behaviour, particularly in the policing of these acts. Violent offences that occur in the home (Acoca, 1999; Schaffner, 2007), school (Arnull & Eagle, 2009) and peer groups (Chesney-Lind & Irwin, 2008) that may not have been recorded in the past are now being prosecuted. This has been fuelled by the introduction of so called "zero tolerance" policies towards violent behaviour by many agencies, including police and schools. Adolescent girls and boys commit minor acts of violence at a similar rate (e.g. Armstrong, Hine, Hacking, & France, 2005) and these policies are applied equally to girls and boys, whereas in the past such incidents involving girls may have been dealt with more leniently.

A major shift in approaches to deal with young offenders in the United Kingdom saw the introduction of a new system of reprimands and final warnings for first offenders, aimed at intervening early in the offending behaviour of children and young people to prevent escalation. This policy drew more young offenders into the criminal justice system, both boys and girls, many of whom were being punished for childish behaviour that had no criminal intent (Hine, 2007). In the case of schools in the United States, high profile violent incidents and fear for the safety of pupils and teachers have prompted a rapid rise in such policies towards violence (Skiba & Peterson, 1999) contributing to a significant increase in the number of children suspended from school (Noguera, 2003). In the United Kingdom, policy-makers have responded to public fears over school safety

---

[2] The Oxford dictionary definition of "ladette" is "a young woman who behaves in a boisterously assertive or crude manner and engages in heavy drinking sessions" (http://oxforddictionaries.com/definition/ladette). This term is often used more informally to describe a girl or woman who demonstrates masculine traits or characteristics, or "laddish" behaviour.

by introducing measures that have led to an increase in the number of young people being excluded from mainstream schooling for violent behaviour (Osler & Starkey, 2005).

Serious violence by girls remains extremely rare (Burman et al., 2000; Miller & White, 2004; Ministry of Justice, 2009), and the reported increase in the number of girls committing violent offences must be placed in its social context. Girls' violence is typically perpetrated within or near the home and school (Steffensmeier, Schwartz, Zhong, & Ackerman, 2005) and girls are much more likely than boys to fight with a parent or sibling (Chesney-Lind, 2001). Acoca (1999) observes a trend of girls being increasingly drawn into the criminal justice system for less serious crime than their male counterparts. Her research shows that the majority of the "serious" crimes girls were charged with were non-serious assaults resulting from mutual combat situations with parents. Similarly, Mayer (1994) reported in his study of over 2,000 cases in Maryland that over half of the "assault" offences by girls were "family centred". The labelling of such incidents as violent offences by parents draws in the police and can lead to daughters being arrested and charged with an offence. Lederman and Brown (2000) go so far as to suggest that some mothers use detention as a "time out" from conflict with their daughters.

The Research Study

The narratives analysed in this chapter were collected as part of a larger study exploring young people's pathways in and out of crime.[3] Funded by the UK Economic and Social Research Council,[4] this research network conducted five research projects examining aspects of the influential risk paradigm[5] from the perspective of

[3] More details about the study can be found at http://www.pcrrd.group.shef.ac.uk and Boeck, Fleming, Hine, and Kemshall (2006).

[4] *Pathways Into and Out of Crime: Risk, Resilience and Diversity*, Grant No L330253001.

[5] The "risk paradigm" underpins much youth justice policy in England and Wales (see for example Farrington, 1996; Youth Justice Board, 2005).

young people, challenging traditional and narrow understandings of risk and resilience. This chapter draws on data collected from one of these studies which explored the impact of the risk factor of exclusion from school on offending behaviour. The study identified young people in three categories: excluded from school; having a statement of special educational need; or being a first time offender in contact with a youth offending team. One hundred and seven young people were interviewed for this study from four different parts of England during 2002–2003. Most were interviewed just once, with a sub-sample interviewed twice and a small sample identified as "case studies" who were interviewed several times. These youth also identified significant others to be interviewed. Twenty-seven of the study sample were girls, and it is their stories that we refer to in this chapter. Ten had experienced permanent exclusion from a school, six had been given a statement of special educational need and fifteen had contact with a youth offending team. Several girls fit into more than one category. The girls were aged between 11 and 18 with a mean age of 15 years. Eight belonged to minority ethnic groups.

In the results reported here, the experiences of girls were analysed independently of those of males in an attempt to challenge the normative naturalisation of male violence (Brown et al., 2001). Sociological theorisations of violent, aggressive and anti-social behaviour have been based almost entirely on male behaviour (Giordiano, Deines, & Cernkovich, 2006), and rarely is female violence described in the literature without comparison to male violence. This comparison underlines the perception that females who demonstrate violent and aggressive behaviour are unfeminine or unnatural (Burman et al., 2000; media headlines focusing on "ladettes" also stress this) and are emotional, irrational or "out of control" (Batchelor, 2005). Our work prioritises the young female voice asserting that much can be gained from investigating girls' experiences and perceptions of violence away from male-focussed understandings and frameworks. Such an approach raises questions about the patterns of behaviour available to young women to support resilience when they are in situations of risk and limited opportunity.

None of the interviews in the study specifically asked young people about the violence in their lives, and yet most raised it in some way. Every one of the 27 girls in the sample mentioned violence in their interviews, and of these only 4 did not mention engaging in physically violent acts themselves. Discussion of their experiences of being a witness, victim and/or perpetrator of violence arose from their answers to other areas of discussion such as family, school or their community, highlighting the social ecological context of their behaviours. Most of them talked about living in problematic neighbourhoods, with all but seven of the girls mentioning the prevalence of crime, anti-social behaviour and/or drugs during their interviews. The high proportion (85%) of these girls who did discuss being physically violent themselves strongly suggests its centrality in their lives, and its omission in the interviews of the remaining four girls does not necessarily signify a lack of use of violence in their lives. Four levels of violence were identified (Welford & Hine, in press): minor (4 girls); occasional reactive (14 girls); regular (7 girls); and serious (2 girls).

It's Not Criminal

The girls describe their behaviour in a number of different ways[6] but there was no acknowledgement that the violence they engaged in was serious or criminal. On the contrary, their narratives frequently trivialised the activity:

> It was something you can look back at now and laugh really (April[7]).

> We were messing about and then, the boy asked me to set him on fire, just messing about and that. And I didn't realise how flammable it were and then, when I did, it just went on fire, so I put him out quickly and took him home ... He got a few blisters and then they went and they didn't even scar (Anne).

> I just started messing around with friends and that but I'd get into trouble and then I had a couple of fights and then I used to throw stuff at the teacher and that and he used to catch me and that. I used to mess around and then, one time, I hit this boy

---

[6]See footnote 1.

[7]The names of all participants have been changed.

with a wooden ruler and I got caught by the headmaster. Nothing [happened to the boy]. He wasn't hurt (Sally).

Although the girls' descriptions trivialise the incidents, they were responded to as serious by adults. The incident where the boy was burnt led to a charge of grievous bodily harm for the girl involved (Anne), and the violence in school led to a permanent exclusion for Sally. In both of these incidents the girls talked about "messing around" with no real intent to harm and certainly no criminal intent, and yet the intervention by adults had serious repercussions for both of them.

A further indication of their view that their own violence is trivial was the response to a specific question about what they considered to be the most and least serious forms of crime. Despite their own violent behaviour, a number of girls believed that violence was the most serious crime, as it could result in physical injury and even death. In contrast, they identified thefts as less serious crimes, since they did not "hurt" people. Responses such as these disassociated their own violent behaviour from "serious" or criminal violence, suggesting that they did not consider themselves to be violent individuals. Answers to the questions elicited responses such as:

> Killing someone. Attacking people.
> [*So violent type crime. What about one that is not so serious?*]
> I don't know, taking money from your friend's house. No point in getting stressed over it is there? (Emily, who admitted violence towards peers and teachers in school and police involvement for criminal damage).

> Knifing someone ... Murder, and rape.
> [*And what would you put on the bottom, as something not as bad as the others?*]
> Robbing something from a shop. Because it's not hurting anyone (Alice, police involvement on numerous occasions for violence including the use of a weapon).

> Carrying something around with you, a deadly weapon.
> [*And what would you put at the bottom for being less serious, not as bad as the others?*]
> Fighting, but not intending to put in hospital (Barbara, violence at school and police involvement for criminal damage).

Barbara expresses her distinction between more and less serious crimes in a slightly different way:

both are violence, but they are distinguished by the intent to hurt someone. Similarly, despite admitting to a number of violent crimes, including using a knife, Alice still thought that this was among the most serious type of crime, with non-serious crimes being those that did not hurt others. She understands that violence and particularly knife crime is serious, but detaches this from her own experience, including describing an incident where she was hurt with a knife as, "It just felt like a scratch".

Anita presented a similar contradiction, highlighting the dangers of carrying a weapon, yet explaining her own such behaviour by underlining her lack of intent. When answering the question posed to her, she justifies and condemns carrying a weapon at the same time:

> I have carried a knife but not with intention to use it. That's what that one's about because this lass beat up me friend, I took it just to threaten her with it and then walk off.

> [*If you were to pick a crime that you thought of as being most serious?*]

> Carrying a knife because it's more dangerous. If I had have used it, I would have gone to court and been locked up in Youth Offending. Whereas, beating someone up, yeah it can hurt 'em and you can put them in hospital but it's not as serious as using a weapon (Anita).

This illustrates the difficulty of some girls have in conceptualising "serious violence" – here it involves a combination of the extent to which you could hurt someone and the associated punishment.

Their discussions also give an insight into the impact of environment on their understandings of criminal and acceptable behaviour, showing how their use of violence as a means of surviving in their community is an expression of resilience:

> [Y]ou get into a lot of trouble over and weapons and stuff. If someone hasn't done anything and someone goes and uses a weapon on them that's just, no I don't agree with weapons or car stealing or drugs – I don't agree with most of it … Maybe it's because you have to be like that when you're up our area, you have to be strong and mad – not mad as in psycho or something – but you have to stand up for yourself. I've never really stolen from anyone because the way I was brought up I was brought up not to steal – I need to fight back if someone hits me and if someone starts sounding

off my family (Janet, permanent school exclusion for violence towards a teacher).

Janet does not see her violence as criminal, justifying her behaviour as an appropriate response to provocation by others, as a "normal" way to be in her environment and coping well. Her own behaviour is detached from what she understands (and disagrees with) as criminal acts. Violence here is a legitimate, and in Janet's eyes, necessary form of protection.

Violence as Resilience?

There are numerous definitions of resilience and what it means in the context of young people's lives, all of which involve the notion of having a successful outcome in the face of adversity. To most observers, particularly adults, violent behaviour by girls is anything but a sign of resilience, usually being seen as an indicator of risk that must be addressed and stopped in order to secure their successful future. Although a range of risks in these girls' lives are acknowledged by their schools and other professionals who work with them, their violent behaviour is generally seen to add to their "problem-saturated identity" rather than being seen as "a healthy adaptation that permits them to survive in unhealthy circumstances" (Ungar, 2004, p. 6). Our research demonstrates that listening to the girls' descriptions of and motivations for their violent activity reveals a different understanding of their behaviour, one that we understand as resilience. Hauser, Allen, and Golden (2006) describe resilience as characterised by three elements: personal agency and a concern to overcome adversity; a self-reflective style; and a commitment to relationships. All of these are present in the girls' accounts of their behaviour. By considering the girls' behaviour within the social context of their lives, we see how violence might be viewed as resilience.

Most of the girls in the sample discussed difficulties in their lives – violence in the home, living in a poor neighbourhood, struggling at school, being bullied – but few related these experiences directly to their use of violence as a protective behaviour. Among the few that do make this link, Anita described how the difficulties she was having at home contributed to her violence at school:

> I've always been able to keep really calm but, in Year 9,[8] when this fight happened between me and Jane, she slapped me across my face and I'd just had that much pressure on me – my step dad, then my sister leaving, and my mum arguing with me all the time and my two little brothers playing up – it all just built up eventually and then she slapped me and I just flipped. I just couldn't stop (Anita).

Many of the girls described experiences of being a victim of violence themselves and several gave examples of resorting to violence in order to improve their situation. For instance, Janet discussed how she resorted to violence in order to take control of her school life from which she was disengaged as a result of being bullied:

> That's why I got kicked out, my temper, because I hit a teacher once and that's why I got kicked out because I couldn't put up with bullying … that's why I'm here because I got kicked out for hitting a teacher and I pushed the other teacher because she pushed me into the wall and I pushed her back … I got myself out because of how much bullying I had to put up with every single day of my life. I was refusing [to go to mainstream school] because I couldn't put up with the bullying, it made me so ill that I just couldn't go (Janet).

Whether her exclusion was a conscious decision or not, using violence at school led to a respite from the bullying that Janet experienced despite having a negative impact on her education. In her study of girls in further education college in London, Phillips (2003) found that being bullied at school can have damaging effects, particularly when missing school to avoid the bullying. Actively challenging bullying can however, stop the victimisation. One of the girls explained how she was bullied for a long time before reacting with physical violence:

> They [other kids] used to pick on me … I'd been from Year 6[9] in infants, to Year 9 in comp, constantly being bullied and I'd never stood up for myself before and this was the first time … I didn't

know I was going to do it, my arm just reached out, grabbed hold of her hair and I just smacked her … "My God, did I just do that, were that me?" I was walking up hill shaking, I think that were mainly just adrenalin that were going through me body at time, because anger … I know I were wrong for what I did but I was also glad I did it because it's let people know that I'm not messing, when I say stop and that's enough, I mean it. And not just carry on because I'm not going to do a lot about it (Anita).

Anita demonstrates how responding to bullying through the use of physical violence can have a positive effect on a young person's life: she feels that she has managed to promote a stronger identity and as a result, alters how people behave towards her, which in her opinion has reduced the bullying. Responding to victimisation in this way may be understood as a form of self-defence and a "normal" reaction to victimisation among young women. Jarman (2005), for example, in a study of girls aged 12–17 in mainstream school in Northern Ireland, found that 71% of respondents believed it was acceptable to use violence as a form of self-defence. For those who have to negotiate danger as part of their daily lives, violence and the search for respect is a form of risk management, helping to deter a future attack (Batchelor, 2007; Ness, 2004). This type of violence reduces these girls' chances of becoming a victim. As another of the girls suggests, a physical response to the threat of violence that they experience in their daily lives can help to prevent victimisation:

> I have to explain to my mum especially because, when I go out there, I have to beat up because if I don't do that I'm going to end up being beat up myself so I have to stand my ground … I don't go out there to pick fights but, if it comes in my way and I know that I'm seriously going to get hurt, I'm going to have to stand up for myself aren't I? There's lots of dangerous people out there because a lot of people go around with weapons and that. It's lucky for me that I'm a girl because not a lot of girls go round with knives and that but all the boys and that, they all go around with knives and everything (Kerry).

This type of violence is more proactive than the reactive form discussed by Anita and Janet, but has the same aim of preventing victimisation. Kerry also demonstrates her awareness of the differing perceptions of adults and young people in

---

[8] In the UK school system, Year 9 is normally young people aged 13–14.

[9] Year 6 is the final year of primary school, so young people in this year are aged 10–11.

stressing how her mother does not understand her adversity and the need to use violence to challenge this.

Criminalising Resilience: Adult Responses to Violence

"Violent girls" are not a homogenous group. They describe a variety of violent activity, both in type and motivation (Welford & Hine, in press). Only 2 of the 27 girls in the sample could be regarded as "seriously" violent, both having an extensive violent history and recurrent police involvement. Most of the girls were occasionally[10] violent. Their violence was overwhelmingly emotionally driven, often an immediate reaction for being victimised themselves, directed towards people known to them, and not pre-meditated. Violent victimisation was a common and sometimes serious experience for the girls in this group, either in the family, home or at school.

Nicola, for example, described how the police had been involved in family disputes on two occasions in her life. The first occasion was when she was younger and her step-mother called the police after Nicola kicked in the front door to her father's house trying to get to her belongings. The second occasion was very similar, but this time it was her mother who called the police:

> Yeah, that [getting arrested] was a day before I got taken into care. Mum had kicked me out and, because I was banging on the house because I wanted some stuff … I hadn't got anything, I just wanted some more clothes and deodorant and whatever else what you need to go and stay at a friend's or something, but she wouldn't give me it and I kicked the gate in at the back and they locked the doors and everything on me and then the police came round and they had to arrest me to take me away. Then I got arrested and taken to a cell and I was in the cell for about 6 or 7 hours and then my dad came and got me and the next day I went into foster care (Nicola).

The perceptions and reactions of adults clash with the understandings the girls themselves have

of their violence. This was particularly evident in one area of their lives – their use of violence to improve their lives. Their narratives reveal how adults respond to their violent behaviour, frequently imbuing it with an intent and purpose not anticipated by the girls themselves. Police are often brought in to deal with this behaviour (Welford & Hine, 2010), bringing longer-term negative consequences. Despite a lack of criminal intent and a belief that their violence was justified and often trivial, almost all of the girls in the sample had experienced some kind of official adult intervention for their violent behaviour. Most had been either excluded from school or dealt with by the criminal justice system for violence that was "one-off". The consequences were often severe, with the girls being forced to move schools, being placed at special behavioural treatment units, and acquiring police records. Girls who were not regularly or seriously violent were still sanctioned and criminalised for their behaviour, with potentially significant consequences for their future.

Adele highlights this disparity between how young people and adults view the adolescent world, and the damaging impact it can have on the developmental pathways available to young people:

> Well I was in school and this girl wanted to fight me and she was sending her friends up to me, blah-de-blah "she wants to fight you" and that and I sent the message back saying I'm not going to fight her in school because I'm going to get myself kicked out. So then she made an arrangement for doing it after … She tried to dowt fags in my face – she kept lighting up a fag and then tried to put it out [on me]. And then my cousin got mad and then I ended up hitting her. And then I come to school the next day and the teachers was waiting outside the gate to meet us, "go to the Head" or whatever and I said all right then, yes, I will. And I went there and he made us write down a statement what happened and other things and how it happened and her mum must have got the police involved and then I went down the police station and got arrested … At the time I thought I'll never get into trouble, I'm outside the school grounds but you do realise after (Adele).

Despite arranging the fight in what was considered a safe space, outside of school grounds, it still came to the attention of both families, the

---

[10]See footnote 1.

school and the police, leading to permanent exclusion from school and a formal police warning for Adele. At other points in the interview, Adele discussed being bullied in school, struggling with work but not wanting extra help and worrying that her exclusion from mainstream school would prevent her from "getting an education" and therefore a job. Exclusion and getting a police record, the likely results of girls' violence, may actually increase the young women's vulnerability and accentuate the need for future violence.

Furthermore, as a result of intervention, young people can then feel "labelled" as trouble-makers, a label which is difficult to shed and can lead to further problem behaviour. This is highlighted by one girl:

> I just did not like school and the way they did things that was like inappropriate … once you get into trouble in first year, they like target you, so, they think just because you got in trouble once you are going to do it all the time and then when they start pinpointing you it just makes you do it, so … I got a reputation (Caroline).

These girls were not from supportive and stable backgrounds, and may have had limited ways of dealing with the troubles they face. Escalation from verbal confrontation to physical violence is a frequent feature of their descriptions of conflict, particularly with peers; the girls may struggle to verbalise their frustration and resort to physical forms of aggression to assert themselves, concurring with Miller and White's (2004) finding that when girls in gangs had verbal altercations, they quickly escalated into physical conflict. Crick and Dodge (1994) suggest (albeit tentatively) that socially maladjusted children can respond to situations aggressively because they feel they have limited alternative solutions, and value aggressive behaviours more positively than pro-social alternatives. Even if more socially desirable alternatives are known by an aggressive young person, they may have difficulty in using that knowledge spontaneously (Camodeca, Goossens, Schuengel, & Meerum Terwogt, 2003).

Understanding the context in which these violent outbursts occur, from the words of the young people themselves, highlights the significance of contextual factors and seriously questions the appropriateness of the responses by authority figures in their lives. The young person is criminalised by an adult when perhaps protecting the child should be the first priority. Chesney-Lind and Irwin (2008) argue that the victimisation of young girls is masked by the increasingly public concern that they are becoming more violent, going so far as to suggest that "the well-documented social problems that haunt the lives of all girls can be neatly ducked, or even better blamed on the girls themselves" (p. 184).

Violence as Resilient Femininity

Violence can be important to some girls to make a statement to others about who they are (Ness, 2004). Messerschmidt (1997) calls this "bad girl femininity" to account for how girls can adopt traditionally masculine behaviours (such as interpersonal violence) within a specific type of femininity, rather than constructing a masculine identity. Alice, who discussed, at length, her experience of fighting, understood that in her world having a tough reputation was of great importance:

> I had a really good reputation in Newtown. There were these three girls; Joan was the third hardest in Newtown, Brenda – her best mate – was the second and Brenda's cousin was the hardest in Newtown centre. I beat up Joan, I beat up Brenda and I'm still waiting to find her cousin. So I've got respect down there (Alice).

In this type of environment, violence is not only a tool for survival, but also represents much more: it is a way to achieve success, to be respected by others and a way for girls to respect themselves, as well as protecting their emotional and physical selves. This situation highlights the place of violence in adolescent female development. If the context within which identity is being developed privileges violence then it has very real worth to girls. Fighting can bring "status and honour in a bleak and limiting environment" (Joe-Laidler & Hunt, 2001, p. 671). Where fighting is privileged, this can bring respect, praise and adulation (Ness, 2004). Ness found that for her group of inner-city girls, fighting was used to "make a statement about who they are" (p. 38). In this context, it was part of "being a girl" rather than contrary to it. In the United Kingdom, Batchelor et al. (2001) found that those girls who were violent "often spoke of fighting as an integral part of their sense of self" (p. 130).

Thus, far from being in opposition to adolescent femininity, violence can be an integral part of this stage of life for girls, providing both emotionally pleasurable and instrumental benefits. As one of the participants explained: "Everyone's like coming up to you – oh my God! I've seen your fight, that was good – and every time they was in trouble they would call you and stuff like that" (Thahmina).

Achieving status in terms of a violent reputation is enjoyed by some girls (Batchelor, 2007; Ness, 2004), with physical strength and dominance considered as desirable qualities (Phillips, 2003). The status this affords may ultimately be self-protective in their communities, but it can also bring popularity among peers in two distinct ways: admiration for a girl's violent achievements, and being valued as someone who can provide protection for others. When girls discuss the different identities available to them at school (being good and working/being bad) they express these identities as a choice without recognising the other areas of their lives that impact their behaviour.

> When I was getting in trouble I liked it, I didn't really want it to change. I just liked being bad … It's nasty really but like, in school, all the bad ones there's just loads of us and then you'd get the kids that wanted to be good and wanted to get on with their work and they was the ones that were scared of us and it felt good. Really like a bully really but, at the time, we thought we was good (Deana).

Once achieved, this "bad girl" identity has to be maintained by confronting threats to the image (Phillips, 2003). Girls who use fighting to defend and enhance their status cannot risk that reputation by walking away from fights (Brown & Tapan, 2008). Phillips (2003) describes a social hierarchy where physical strength and domination are regarded as desirable qualities, and can provide access to power, status and reputation. Some of the girls in our study demonstrated this, both by responding violently to threats to their

image, and by what has been termed "reluctant fighting" (Phillips) – engaging in fights so as not to let others "walk all over" them.

> I don't go out looking for trouble. If trouble comes to me then I have to deal with it, but I don't go out making trouble … Say if someone wants to frighten me or anything like that, I'd fight back. The police told me that, if anyone hits me again, I must stand there and get beaten up then go to the police. No, I'm not going to do that. If someone hits me I'm going to hit them back. Because, if you let people hit you, they're going to walk all over you (Thahmina).

Fighting back is considered a necessity in their environment. Anne discusses how not fighting back may result not only in being beaten up, but also being called "a wimp" among friends. For those girls who commit to their reputations as fighters, failing to maintain the "tough girl" identity can clearly have detrimental physical and emotional consequences. The search for respect through violence in the social world of these girls is, arguably, "a rational response to past and potential victimisation" (Batchelor, 2005, p. 370).

The girls in this study, despite demonstrating violent behaviours that are more traditionally associated with masculinity, did not build this into any type of "masculine" identity. All girls discussed stereotypically "feminine" interests such as shopping, hanging out with friends, boys, singing and dancing. Only one girl described how she was not very "girly girly" (Anita) and was into motorbikes and cars. Their intended careers were also traditionally feminine. The most common aspirations were health and beauty and childcare, with six girls discussing each of these. Other areas of work mentioned were social work, law, working with animals, secretarial, nursing, performing arts, fashion design, teaching and working in a hotel. One girl said she would likely be a housewife, as she was from a Traveller (Gipsy) community and that was the traditional path. These girls gave no indication that violent behaviour in any way compromised these goals. The only aspiration that incorporated any form of physicality was articulated by Sally who was considering joining the army.

One girl in the study seemed to exemplify this balance between violence and femininity. Alice was the most seriously violent girl in the sample. She listed her interests as "shopping, lads, ice skating and horse riding, swimming, football matches", suggesting that she manages to combine stereotypically feminine and masculine hobbies with little difficulty. As a result of the assault charge, she had to do community service, but was not happy with the proposed duty: "I might have to do gardening in an old people's home or something and I really don't want to because I'll break a nail and I've already snapped four" (Alice). She expressed her heterosexual femininity throughout the interviews, placing significant value on having a boyfriend:

> I was feeling a bit left out of the conversations because I know Ann's got Johnny, Rebecca's got Smithy, Lucy's got Paul and now there's me and Wayne and Jill's got Trev and Sarah's got Richy … Everyone had been saying like from first week, which were like three weeks ago, they've all been saying for three weeks now how good we look together. … He saw me and he said "are you alright Angel?" That's my new nickname, Wayne, he calls me Angel … I like that name … he's got lovely blue eyes and about 6'3" but like he's really lovely with me … (Alice).

Alice also highlights how boys can be the source of tension and fights between girls.

> The last time I did have a fight, I ended up getting stabbed … I knew who she were and I know why she did it. She accused me of shagging her boyfriend but then I turned round and told her that her boyfriend was a dog and I wouldn't touch him with a ten foot barge pole. I think she would have preferred for me to have said, yeah, I did shag him, but I didn't and he was ugly (Alice).

Research on girls who fight has highlighted the contradictory pattern that when girls engage in this "typically masculine" behaviour, boys are frequently the source of the conflict (see for example Brown, 2003). Although violent girls can be understood as empowered individuals, challenging the normalisation of the docile female body, fighting over boys may in fact "reproduce a patriarchal world view in which women are valued because of their affiliation to a male" (Adams, 1999, p. 130). Being "gender deviant" in this way may therefore simply reaffirm traditional gendered stereotypes. The girls' behaviour "ultimately serves the interests of a

sex/gender system that empowers boys and men" (Brown & Chesney-Lind, 2005, p. 85).

A further example of the way in which violence can be understood to fit with traditional views of femininity is the use of violence to demonstrate loyalty to and care for others. Five girls discussed how fights could be caused when someone close to them was criticised, such as "they were slagging off my family" (Janet), or:

> Sometimes [I hit them], I can't help it. If they talk about my family and things like that then I get in a bad mood and I don't like that. But if it's calling me names about me I don't really listen because I know it's not true (Mary).

Adams (1999) has suggested that this loyalty is merely an alternative method for performing femininity, validating what is traditionally viewed as a part of women's relationships (selflessness, loyalty and being caring).

For girls in a particular social context, adhering to feminine norms may require the use of violence as a tool for protection and resilience, whereas in a different context, where passivity is privileged, this would be less acceptable. Exactly how girls cement their adolescent feminine identity in such circumstances is unclear. What is clear is that the girls in this study used a range of techniques to reject a violent identity and retain a feminine identity despite engaging in violent behaviour. Female violence is mainly targeted at other girls and remains within systems of gendered power relations, and despite demonstrating resistance towards narrow feminine behavioural norms, existing relations between boys and girls may in fact be reinforced.

Conclusion

Listening to girls discuss their experiences of violence offers an insight into the factors that lead a girl to react violently to a particular situation at a particular time, and shows the importance of understanding the social and environmental context within which such behaviour takes place. We have seen how the uses, justifications and understandings of violence by young women are socially and culturally located in their lives and can play a central role for those who grow up in disadvantaged communities. Fighting is often a tool for survival in their difficult social context and can be seen as a form of self-empowerment (Adams, 1999) and an expression of agency when taking control of their lives (Batchelor, 2007). Given these patterns, we argue that these girls are demonstrating resilience as characterised by three elements: personal agency and a concern to overcome adversity; a self-reflective style; and a commitment to relationships (Hauser et al., 2006). Though these characteristics are manifested inappropriately according to those who hold authority over these girls' lives and who sanction the girls for their violence, the function of that violence as a protective factor cannot be denied in the narratives of the girls in our study.

Adult reaction does not consider the use of violence to be resilient behaviour in particular contexts of disadvantage. Rather, this behaviour is seen as a risk and predictor of future problem behaviour resulting in interventions that stigmatise and criminalise girls. The media-fuelled "panic" over a suspected rise in female violence has fed a public concern over "what to do" about the problem. This panic is likely not justified given that female violence is still relatively rare, dominantly low-level and between peers. However, female violence continues to be seen as "worse" than male violence as females are breaking gendered norms as well as criminal laws and this affects the way girls are dealt with by the criminal justice system.

The experiences of this sample of adolescent girls demonstrate a complex interplay between feminine norms and their understandings of violence in the discourses that frame their daily lives. Femininity is not a stable entity; it means different things to different people, and even to the same individual in different social situations. In discussing violence, these girls demonstrate both the ease and the difficulties adolescent girls face in challenging conventional feminine norms. They were independent, assertive and dominant in their use of violence to protect both themselves and others, with no apparent difficulty in combining these behaviours with being "a girl", as evident in the expression of conventionally female interests

(boys, dancing, shopping, friends) and careers (hairdressing, childcare). They were at once the same and yet different to other girls. In this regard, these girls appear to be creating an "acceptably deviant" understanding of their behaviour (Swart, 1991, p. 46). Our work lends support to the notion that for some girls, violence can be balanced with more traditionally feminine behaviours and traits, as a part of normative femininity (Messerschmidt, 1997; Ness, 2004). By adapting their adolescent female identities to accommodate stereotypically masculine violent behaviour, these girls are demonstrating resistance to the traditional (and restrictive) framework of normatively feminine behaviour – in this sense, demonstrating resilience.

References

Acoca, L. (1999). Investing in girls: A 21st century strategy. *Juvenile Justice, 6*(1), 3–13.

Adams, N. G. (1999). Fighting to be somebody: Resisting erasure and the discursive practices of female adolescent fighting. *Educational Studies, 30*(2), 115–139.

Armstrong, D. J., Hine, J., Hacking, S., & France, A. (2005). *Young people and crime: The On Track schools survey (Home Office research study, 278)*. London, UK: Home Office.

Arnull, E., & Eagle, S. (2009). *Girls and offending – Patterns, perceptions and interventions*. London, UK: Youth Justice Board.

Australian Institute of Criminology. (2007). *Australian crime facts & figures 2006*. Canberra, AU: Australian Institute of Criminology.

Batchelor, S. (2005). Prove me the bam!: Victimisation and agency in the lives of young women who commit violent offences. *Probation Journal, 52*(4), 358–375.

Batchelor, S. A. (2007). 'Getting mad wi' it': Risk-seeking by young women. In K. Hannah-Moffat & P. O'Malley (Eds.), *Gendered risks* (pp. 205–228). Abingdon, UK: Routledge-Cavendish.

Batchelor, S. (2009). Girls, gangs and violence: Assessing the evidence. *Probation Journal, 56*(4), 399–414.

Batchelor, S., Burman, M., & Brown, J. (2001). Discussing violence: Let's hear it from the girls. *Probation Journal, 48*(2), 125–134.

Boeck, T., Fleming, J., Hine, J., & Kemshall, H. (2006). Pathways into and out of crime for young people. *Childright, 228*, 18–21.

Brown, L. M. (2003). *Girlfighting: Betrayal and rejection among girls*. New York, NY: New York University Press.

Brown, J., Burman, M., & Tisdall, K. (2001). Just trying to be men? Violence and girls' social worlds. In P. Starkey & J. Lawrence (Eds.), *Child welfare and social action: The nineteenth and twentieth centuries.* Liverpool, UK: University of Liverpool Press.

Brown, L. M., & Chesney-Lind, M. (2005). Growing up mean: Covert aggression and the policing of girlhood. In G. Lloyd (Ed.), *Problem girls: Understanding and supporting troubled and troublesome girls and young women.* Abingdon, UK: Routledge Falmer.

Brown, L. M., & Tapan, M. B. (2008). Fighting like a girl fighting like a guy: Gender identity, ideology, and girls at early adolescence. *New Directions for Child and Adolescent Development, 120,* 47–59.

Burman, M., Brown, J., Tisdall, K., & Batchelor, S. (2000). A view from the girls: Exploring violence and violent behaviour. *ESRC Research Findings.* Retrieved from http://www1.rhbnc.ac.uk/sociopolitical-science/VRP/Findings/rfburman.PDF.

Camodeca, M., Goossens, F. A., Schuengel, C., & Meerum Terwogt, M. (2003). Links between social information processing in middle childhood and involvement in bullying. *Aggressive Behaviour, 29,* 116–127.

Chesney-Lind, M. (2001). Are girls closing the gender gap in violence? *Criminal Justice, 16*(1), 1–7.

Chesney-Lind, M. (2002). Criminalizing victimisation: The unintended consequences of pro-arrest policies for girls and women. *Criminology and Public Policy, 2,* 81–90.

Chesney-Lind, M., & Irwin, K. (2008). *Beyond bad girls: Gender, violence and hype.* New York, NY: Routledge.

Cohen, S. (1972). *Folk devils and moral panics.* Abingdon, UK: Routledge.

Crick, N. R., & Dodge, K. A. (1994). A review and reformulation of social information processing mechanisms in children's social adjustment. *Psychological Bulletin, 115*(1), 74–104.

Duncan, N. (2006). Girls' violence and aggression against other girls: Femininity and bullying in UK schools. In F. Leach & C. Mitchell (Eds.), *Combating gender violence in and around schools.* Stoke-on-Trent, UK: Trentham Books.

Farrington, D. (1996). *Understanding and preventing youth crime.* York, UK: Joseph Rowntree Foundation.

Geoghegan, T. (2008, May 5). Why are girls fighting like boys? *BBC News Magazine.* Retrieved from http://news.bbc.co.uk/1/hi/magazine/7380400.stm.

Giordiano, P. C., Deines, J. A., & Cernkovich, S. A. (2006). In and out of crime: A life course perspective on girls' delinquency. In K. Heimer & C. Kruttschnitt (Eds.), *Gender and crime: Patterns in victimization and offending.* New York, NY: New York University Press.

Hauser, S., Allen, J., & Golden, E. (2006). *Out of the woods: Tales of resilient teens.* Cambridge, MA: Harvard University Press.

Hine, J. (2007). Young people's perspectives on final warnings. *Web Journal of Current Legal Issues, 2007*(2). Retrieved from http://webjcli.ncl.ac.uk/2007/issue2/hine2.html.

Jarman, N. (2005). Teenage kicks: Young women and their involvement in violence and disorderly behaviour. *Child Care in Practice, 11*(3), 341–356.

Joe-Laidler, K., & Hunt, G. (2001). Accomplishing femininity among the girls in the gang. *The British Journal of Criminology, 41,* 656–678.

Kon, R., & AuCoi, K. (2008). *Female offenders in Canada (Statistics Canada – Catalogue no. 85-002-XIE, Vol. 28, no. 1).* Ottawa, ON: Canadian Centre for Justice Statistics.

Lederman, C. S., & Brown, E. N. (2000). Entangled in the shadows: Girls in the juvenile justice system. *Buffalo Law Review, 48,* 911–925.

Messerschmidt, J. W. (1997). *Crime as structured action: Gender, race, class, and crime in the making.* London, UK: Sage.

Miller, J., & White, N. A. (2004). Situational effects of gender inequality on girls' participation in violence. In C. Alder & A. Worrall (Eds.), *Girls' violence: Myths and realities.* Albany, NY: State University of New York Press.

Ministry of Justice. (2009, January). *Statistics on women and the criminal justice system.* Ministry of Justice.

Ness, C. D. (2004). Why girls fight: Female youth violence in the inner city. *The Annals of the American Academy of Political and Social Science, 595,* 32–48.

Noguera, P. A. (2003). Schools, prisons, and social implications of punishment: Rethinking disciplinary practices. *Theory into Practice, 42*(4), 341–350.

Osler, A., & Starkey, H. (2005). Violence in schools and representations of young people: A critique of government policies in France and England. *Oxford Review of Education, 31*(2), 195–215.

Phillips, C. (2003). Who's who in the pecking order? Aggression and 'normal violence' in the lives of girls and boys. *The British Journal of Criminology, 43,* 710–728.

Poe-Yamagata, E., & Butts, J. A. (1996). *Female offenders in the juvenile justice system: Statistics summary.* Pittsburgh, PA: National Center for Juvenile Justice.

Rutter, M. (2006). Implications of resilience concepts for scientific understanding. *The Annals of the New York Academy of Science, 1094,* 1–12.

Schaffner, L. (2007). Violence against girls provokes girls' violence: From private injury to public harm. *Violence Against Women, 13,* 1229–1248.

Skiba, R., & Peterson, R. (1999). The dark side of zero tolerance: Can punishment lead to safe schools? *Phi Delta Kappan.* Retrieved from http://www.cranepsych.com/Psych/Dark_Zero_Tolerance.pdf.

Slack, J. (2009, January 30). Scourge of the ladette thugs: Rising tide of violent crime committed by young women. *The Daily Mail.* Retrieved from http://www.dailymail.co.uk/news/article-1131719/Scourge-ladette-thugs-Rising-tide-violent-crime-committed-young-women.html.

Slack, J. (2010, January 29). Ladette Britain: Violence among women soars as record 250 are arrested every day. *Daily Mail Online.* Retrieved from http://www.dailymail.co.uk/news/article-1246802/Record-number-women-arrested-violent-crimes.html#ixzz14tFIHUFY.

Steffensmeier, D., Schwartz, J., Zhong, H., & Ackerman, J. (2005). An assessment of recent trends in girls' violence using diverse longitudinal sources: Is the gender gap closing? *Criminology, 43*(2), 355–405.

Swart, W. J. (1991). Female gang delinquency: A search for 'acceptably deviant behaviour'. *Mid-American Review of Sociology, 15*(1), 43–52.

Ungar, M. (2004). *Nurturing hidden resilience in troubled youth*. Toronto, ON: University of Toronto Press.

Welford, J., & Hine, J. (2010). Victim or offender: Girls and violence in the home. *Criminology Matters, 3*.

Welford, J., & Hine, J. (in press). *A typology of girls violence*.

Youth Justice Board. (2005). *Risk and protective factors*. London, UK: Youth Justice Board. Retrieved from http://www.yjb.gov.uk/Publications/Resources/Downloads/Risk%20Factors%20Summary%20fv.pdf.

Part IV

The Family

Facilitating Family Resilience: Relational Resources for Positive Youth Development in Conditions of Adversity

Froma Walsh

What is Resilience?

Resilience has become an increasingly valuable and timely concept in these challenging times. Resilience can be defined as the ability to withstand and rebound from stressful life challenges, strengthened and more resourceful. Not simply general strengths, or coping, resilience involves dynamic processes that foster positive adaptation in the context of significant adversity (Luthar, Cicchetti, & Becker, 2000).

The concept of resilience brings many varied images to mind. A Japanese colleague envisions a willow tree that bends in the storm, but does not break. A Korean colleague finds similarities to her culture's concept of *han*: suffering that is so deep, but not without hope (Yang & Choi, 2001). Such images capture the deeply rooted strengths in the human spirit that enable us to endure and overcome serious life challenges.

In Euro-American culture, there is a common misconception of resilience simply as: "Just bounce back!" In our popular media, "resilience" is in the daily news. A reporter hails the resilience of a football team for rebounding from a season of defeat to capture victory and glory. For women, there is an expensive face cream named *Resilience* for its purported ability to make aging skin spring

back to youthful elasticity and glow. Vulnerability, however, is part of the human condition, and with serious crises or persistent stresses we often can't simply bounce back or return to the old normal. Life may never be the same and we must construct a "new normal" on our journey forward. Thus, resilience involves struggling well, effectively working through and learning from adversity, and attempting to integrate the experience into our individual and shared lives as we move ahead.

Resilience has become an important concept in mental health theory and research over recent decades, as studies challenged the prevailing deterministic assumption that traumatic experiences and prolonged adversity, especially in childhood, are inevitably damaging. Many children who experienced multiple risk factors for dysfunction, such as parental mental illness, traumatic loss, or conditions of poverty, defied expectations and did remarkably well in life. Although many individuals were shattered by adversity, others overcame similar high-risk conditions, able to lead loving and productive lives and to raise their children well. Studies have found, for instance, that most abused children did not become abusive parents (Kaufman & Ziegler, 1987).

Individual Resilience in Multisystemic Perspective

To account for these differences, early studies focused on personal traits for resilience, or hardiness, assuming that innate strengths, or character

F. Walsh (✉)
Chicago Center for Family Health,
University of Chicago, Chicago, IL, USA
e-mail: fwalsh@uchicago.edu

M. Ungar (ed.), *The Social Ecology of Resilience: A Handbook of Theory and Practice*,
DOI 10.1007/978-1-4614-0586-3_15, © Springer Science+Business Media, LLC 2012

armor, made some children invulnerable to the damage of parental pathology. The work of Sir Michael Rutter (1987) led to recognition of the interaction between nature and nurture in the emergence of resilience. As research was extended to a wide range of adverse conditions impoverished circumstances, chronic medical illness, and catastrophic life events, trauma, and loss – it became clear that resilience involves an interplay of multiple risk and protective processes over time, involving individual, family, and larger sociocultural influences. Individual vulnerability or the impact of stressful conditions could be outweighed by positive mediating influences.

In a remarkable longitudinal study of resilience, Werner (Werner & Smith, 2001) followed the lives of nearly 700 multicultural children of plantation workers living in poverty on the Hawaiian island of Kauai. By age 18, about two-thirds of the at-risk children had done poorly as predicted, with early pregnancy, need for mental health services, or trouble in school or with the law. However, one-third of those at-risk had developed into competent, caring, and confident young adults, with the capacity "to work well, play well, love well, and expect well," commonly used indicators of resilience, as rated on a variety of measures. In later follow-ups through middle adulthood, almost all were still living successful lives. Of note, several who had been poorly functioning in adolescence turned their lives around in adulthood, most often crediting supportive relationships or religious involvement. These findings have important clinical implications, revealing the potential, despite troubled childhood or teen years, for later developing resilience across the life course.

Resilience is Nurtured in Relationships

Notably, the crucial influence of significant relationships stands out across many studies (Walsh, 1996). Individual resilience was encouraged by bonds with kin, intimate partners, and mentors, such as coaches and teachers, who supported their efforts, believed in their potential, and encouraged them to make the most of their lives. Vital kin and community connections enable children and adolescents at-risk to thrive (Ungar, 2004).In the field of mental health, however, the prevailing focus on parental dysfunction has blinded many to the family resources that might be tapped, even where a parent's functioning is seriously impaired. A family resilience approach to practice seeks out and builds "relational lifelines" for resilience in the broad kinship network.

A resilience-oriented systems approach to practice searches out relational resources in the kinship network, positive bonds that might contribute to a child's resilience – older brothers, sisters; aunts, uncles; grandparents, godparents, and informal kin, as well as community resources. Even in troubled families, there are islands of strength and resilience. Mental health practitioners identify and recruit members who can play an active role in the life of a troubled or at-risk child. From many qualitative studies, a number of relational components can be identified that build and sustain resilience. Most important are models of resilience (individuals who survived well despite adversity) and mentors who are invested in the youth's positive development. Practitioners can encourage the following relational processes:

- Convey conviction in a child's worth and potential
- Draw out and affirm strengths, abilities
- Inspire hopes and dreams
- Encourage a child's best efforts
- Stand by a child through difficulties
- See mistakes as opportunities for learning & growth
- Celebrate successes

The construction of a genogram (McGoldrick, Gerson, & Petry, 2008) is valuable in mapping all significant relationships within and beyond the household, including siblings, parents, and other caregivers, grandparents, aunts, uncles, cousins, godparents, and informal family members. Although genograms have traditionally been used mainly to note dysfunction and problematic patterns, conflicts, and cut offs, a resilience-oriented approach searches for islands of caring and competence. We hold the conviction that strengths and potential can be found in all families alongside vulnerabilities and limitations. We inquire about resourceful ways a family as a whole or individual family member dealt with past adversity and about models of resilience in the kin network that might be drawn on to inspire efforts to master current challenges. With recent or ongoing disruptive events, we rally the family to respond in ways that will foster resilience.

Family consultation sessions might be convened, inviting those who might be helpful, to explore how each can play a valuable part. Traditional approaches to clinical practice focus narrowly on an individual, such as the designated caregiver, or a legal guardian in kinship care, too often overloading that family member. In contrast, we approach the family as a team and assess how various members can each contribute to a successful team approach.

Family stories, too, can inspire resilience. Practitioners inquire about other adversities the family has faced, the strategies and resources they found useful, and the positive approaches by members in meeting their challenges. Stories of grandparents' "can do spirit" through economic hard times can be inspiring.

> I never met my own great grandmother Frimid (my namesake), but I was inspired by the many stories about her pluck and determination when she and her family forged a new life in the U.S, fleeing pograms against Jews in Hungary. While her husband found menial work, she ran a catering service, raising geese in the backyard for pate de fois gras. She also became involved in community service, helping other newly arriving immigrants to settle and adapt. The best story was told of her observation of peculiar local weather that reminded her of the season in Hungary when the onion crops had failed. With her husband's blessing (I assumed) she took their entire savings and invested them in the onion market. Sure enough, the crops failed and she made a fortune, with a story in the local news titled "Frimid, the Onion Queen." Such stories were wellsprings for my own resilience in imagining that I could forge a new and productive life beyond the impoverished conditions of my upbringing.

A family systems approach also seeks to build positive mutual influences. For instance, we explore how siblings can support each other, an older brother encouraging a younger one with homework and the younger one, in return, helping out the other with chores, and building a positive bond in so doing. Recognizing that parents, particularly single parents, are often under-resourced, therapists might facilitate shared childcare between a mother and her sister, who is also overburdened, giving each respite from chronic stresses. With the loss of a parent, or transfer to foster care, sibling bonds can be the most valued lifeline for children; it's crucial that they not be separated.

The Concept of Family Resilience

The concept of family resilience extends beyond seeing individual family members as potential resources for individual resilience. It focuses on risk and resilience in the family as a functional unit (Walsh, 2003, 2006). A basic premise in this systemic view is that serious crises and persistent adversity have an impact on the whole family. In turn, key family processes mediate the adaptation – or maladaptation – of all members *and* the family unit. The family response is crucial. Major stresses can derail the functioning of a family system, with ripple effects for all members and their relationships. Key processes in resilience (described below) enable the family system to rally in times of crisis, to buffer stress, reduce the risk of dysfunction, and support optimal adaptation.

The need to strengthen family resilience has never been more urgent, as families today are buffeted by stresses and uncertainties of economic, social, political, and environmental upheaval. When families suffer, their children suffer. When we can strengthen families' capacities for resilience, they are better able to nurture their children's resilience. The family resilience framework presented here aims to strengthen key family processes in dealing with adversity. This practice approach is based on a conviction that all families have the potential for adaptation, repair, and positive growth.

The concept of family resilience extends theory and research on family stress, coping, and adaptation (McCubbin et al. 1998a, b; Patterson, 2002).

It entails more than managing stressful conditions, shouldering a burden, or surviving an ordeal. It involves the potential for personal and relational transformation and growth that can be forged out of adversity. By tapping into key processes for resilience, families that have been struggling can emerge stronger and more resourceful in meeting future challenges. Members may develop new insights and abilities. A crisis can be a wake-up call, heightening attention to important matters. It can become an opportunity for reappraisal of life priorities and pursuits, stimulating greater investment in meaningful relationships. In studies of strong families, many report that through weathering a crisis together their relationships were enriched and became more loving than they might otherwise have been.

Practice Utility of a Family Resilience Framework

Resilience research offers a promising knowledge base for practice. My efforts over the past two decades have focused on the development of a family resilience framework for clinical intervention and prevention. This resilience-oriented approach builds on advances in the field of family therapy that focus on family strengths (Walsh, 2012). The therapeutic relationship is collaborative and empowering of client potential, with recognition that successful interventions depend more on tapping into family resources than on therapist techniques. Our language and discourse are strengths-oriented. Family assessment and intervention are redirected from how problems were caused to how they can be tackled, identifying and amplifying existing and potential competencies. Therapist and clients work together to find new possibilities in a problem-saturated situation and overcome impasses to change. This positive, future-oriented stance refocuses families from how they have failed to how they can succeed.

A family resilience approach shifts the prevalent view of troubled families as *damaged* and beyond repair to seeing them as *challenged* by life's adversities with potential to foster healing and growth in all members. Rather than rescuing so-called "survivors" from "dysfunctional families" this practice approach engages distressed families with respect and compassion for their struggles, affirms their reparative potential, and seeks to bring out their best qualities. Efforts to foster family resilience aim both to avert and reduce dysfunction and to enhance family functioning and individual well-being. Such efforts have the potential to benefit all family members as they strengthen relational bonds and the family unit. As families become more resourceful, risk and vulnerability are reduced and they are better able to meet future challenges. Thus, building family resilience is also a preventive measure for children and their families.

Putting Ecological and Developmental Perspectives into Practice

This family resilience framework combines ecological and developmental perspectives to understand and strengthen family functioning in relation to its broader socio-cultural context and multigenerational life cycle passage.

From a *bio-psycho-social systems orientation*, risk and resilience are viewed in light of multiple, recursive influences involving individuals, families, and larger social systems. Problems can result from an interaction of individual, family, or community vulnerability and stressful life experiences. Symptoms may be primarily biologically based, as in serious illness, or largely influenced by socio-cultural variables, such as barriers of poverty and discrimination that render many families and communities more at-risk. Family distress may result from unsuccessful attempts to cope with an overwhelming situation. Symptoms may be generated by a crisis event, such as traumatic loss in the family or by the wider impact of a large-scale disaster. The family, peer group, community resources, school or work settings, and other social systems can be seen as nested contexts for nurturing and reinforcing resilience. A multidimensional, holistic assessment includes varied contexts, seeking to identify common elements in a crisis situation and family responses, while also taking into account each family's unique perspectives, resources, and challenges (Falicov, 1995, 2007).

A developmental perspective is also essential to understand and foster family resilience. (1) Families navigate varied pathways in forging resilience with emerging challenges over time. (2) A pile-up of multiple stressors can overwhelm family resources. (3) The impact of a crisis may also vary in relation to its timing in individual and family life cycle passage. (4) Past experiences and stories of adversity and family response can generate catastrophic expectations or can serve as models for resilience in overcoming difficulties.

Varied pathways in resilience. Most major stressors are not simply a short-term single event, but rather, a complex set of changing conditions with a past history and a future course (Rutter, 1987). Family resilience involves varied adaptational pathways over time, from the approach to a threatening event on the horizon, through disruptive transitions, subsequent shockwaves in the immediate aftermath, and long-term reorganization. For instance, how a family approaches a parent's illness and death, facilitates emotional sharing and meaning making, effectively reorganizes and then fosters reinvestment in life pursuits will influence the immediate and long-term adaptation to loss for all members and their relationships (Rolland, 1994; Walsh & McGoldrick, 2004). Likewise, the experience of divorce proceeds from an escalation of predivorce tensions through disruption and reorganization of households and parent–child relationships; most will experience transitional upheaval again with remarriage and stepfamily integration (Hetherington & Kelly, 2002). Given such complexity, no single coping response is invariably most successful; different strategies may prove useful in meeting new challenges. Some approaches that are functional in the short term may rigidify and become dysfunctional over time. Practitioners work with families at various steps or transitions along their journey, offering compassion for their suffering and struggle, helping them to integrate their experience, and encouraging their best efforts in meeting their challenges.

Multistress conditions. Some families may do well with a short-term crisis but buckle under the strains of persistent or recurrent challenges, as with a chronic illness, prolonged unemployment, or a blighted and unsafe neighborhood. A pile-up of internal and external stressors can overwhelm the family, heightening vulnerability and risk for substance abuse or other subsequent problems.

Family life cycle perspective. Functioning and distress are assessed in the context of the multigenerational family system as it moves forward across the life cycle (McGoldrick, Carter, & Garcia Preto, 2011). A family resilience practice approach focuses on family adaptation around critical events, particularly unexpected, untimely, and traumatic events, such as the shooting death of a child. Resilience-oriented family therapy pays particular attention to the timing of symptoms in relation to family disruption. For instance, a son's drop in school grades may be precipitated by his father's job loss, increased drinking, and heightened parental conflict. Attention is given to stressful transitions, such as a parent's incarceration and a child's transfer to kinship care (Engstrom, 2012), requiring boundary shifts and redefinition of roles and relationships. It is important to attend to the extended kin network beyond the immediate household. For example, in one family with whom I worked, a teenager's binge drinking was triggered by the death of her grandmother who had been her mainstay through instability in her immediate family. In assessing the impact of stress events, it is essential to explore how the family handled them: their proactive stance, immediate response, and long-term "survival" strategies. Distress is heightened when current stressors reactivate painful memories and emotions from past experience, as in post-traumatic stress of war-related experiences. The convergence of developmental and multigenerational strains increases the risk for complications (McGoldrick et al., 2011).

Broad Range of Practice Applications

The very flexibility of the concept of family resilience complicates research efforts but lends itself to many practice applications (see Table 15.1). A family resilience framework can be applied usefully with a wide range of crisis situations and multistress conditions. Interventions utilize principles

Table 15.1 Practice guidelines to strengthen family resilience

Convey conviction in potential to overcome adversity through shared efforts

Use respectful language, framing to humanize and contextualize distress
  View as understandable, (normal response to abnormal or stressful conditions)
  Decrease shame, blame, pathologizing

Provide safe haven for sharing pain, fears, challenges
  Compassionate witness for suffering and struggle
  Build communication, empathy, mutual support of family members

Identify and affirm strengths, courage alongside vulnerabilities, constraints

Draw out potential for mastery, healing, and growth

Tap into kin, community, and spiritual resources to deal with challenges

View crisis also as opportunity for learning, change, and growth

Shift focus from problems to possibilities
  Gain mastery, healing, and transformation out of adversity
  Reorient future hopes and dreams

Integrate adversity – and resilience – into fabric of individual and relational life passage

and techniques common among many strength-based practice approaches, but attend more centrally to links between symptoms and significant family stressors, identifying and fortifying key processes in coping and adaptation. This approach also affirms the varied pathways that can be forged for resilience over time.

Therapists, as compassionate witnesses and facilitators, invite family members to share their experiences of adversity, often breaking down walls of silence or secrecy around painful or shameful events, to build mutual support and empathy. Respect for family strengths in the midst of suffering or struggle readily engages so-called "resistant" families, who are often reluctant to come for mental health services out of expectations (often based on prior experience) that they will be judged as disturbed or deficient and blamed for their problems. Instead, family members are viewed as intending to do their best for one another and struggling with overwhelming challenges. Therapeutic efforts mobilize family and community resources to master those challenges through collaborative efforts.

Clinical and community services can benefit from use of a family resilience meta-framework. A multisystemic assessment may be family-centered but include individual and/or group work with youth. Putting an ecological view into practice, interventions may involve coordination and collaboration with community agencies, religious communities, or workplace, school, healthcare, and other larger systems, depending on their relevance.

Over the past 20 years, faculty at the Chicago Center for Family Health, (co-directed by John Rolland and myself), have developed training, clinical practice, and community services grounded in this Family Resilience meta-framework. Programs have been designed in partnership with community-based organizations to address a range of challenges (Walsh, 2002, 2006, 2007), including:

- Serious illness, disability, and end-of-life challenges;
- Complicated bereavement;
- Recovery from traumatic loss and major disasters;
- Refugee trauma and migration challenges;
- Adaptation to divorce, single-parenting, and stepfamily reorganization;
- Family stresses and resources with job loss and transition;
- Family-school partnerships for the success of at-risk youth; and
- Challenges for gay, lesbian, and transgender individuals and their families (Herdt & Koff, 2000).

Resilience-based family interventions can be adapted to a variety of formats including periodic family consultations or more intensive family therapy. Psycho-educational multifamily groups emphasize the importance of social support and practical information, offering concrete guidelines for crisis management, problem-solving, and stress reduction as families navigate through stressful periods and face future challenges. Therapists may identify specific stresses the family is dealing with and then help them develop effective coping strategies, measuring success in small increments and maintaining family morale. Brief, cost-effective, psycho-educational "modules" timed for critical transitions or phases of a life challenge encourage families to digest manageable portions of a long-term adaptation process.

Key Processes in Family Resilience

The Family Resilience Framework was developed as a conceptual map for clinicians to identify and target key processes that can strengthen family capacities to rebound from crises and master persistent life challenges (Walsh, 2003). This framework is informed by social science and clinical research seeking to understand crucial variables contributing to resilience and well-functioning families. I have synthesized findings from numerous studies to identify key processes for resilience within three domains of family functioning: family belief systems, organization patterns, and communication processes (Table 15.2).

Family Belief Systems

Family belief systems powerfully influence members' perceptions and response to adversity. Shared constructions of reality, influenced by cultural and spiritual beliefs, emerge through family and social transactions; in turn, they organize family approaches to crisis situations and they can be fundamentally altered by such experiences. Adversity generates a crisis of meaning and potential disruption of integration. Resilience is fostered by shared beliefs that increase options for effective functioning, problem-solving, healing, and growth. Clinicians can facilitate family efforts to make meaning of their crisis situations, gain a hopeful, positive outlook, and tap transcendent or spiritual experiences.

Making Meaning of Adversity

Families strengthen their bonds and their resilience by viewing a crisis or prolonged adversity as a *shared* challenge. Professionals can foster this *relational view* of strength: in joining together, individuals strengthen their ability to overcome adversity.

Well-functioning families have an evolutionary sense of time and becoming – a continual process of growth, change, and losses across the life cycle and the generations. Clinicians can also help members to see disruptive transitions as milestones on their shared life passage. By *normalizing* and *contextualizing* distress, family members can enlarge their perspective and see their reactions and difficulties as understandable in light of their adverse situation and challenges. Interventions help to reduce blame, shame, and pathologizing by encouraging family members to view their problems as human dilemmas and their feelings and vulnerability as "normal" (i.e., common among families facing similar predicaments).

In grappling with adversity, families do best when helped to gain a *sense of coherence* (Antonovsky & Sourani, 1988), by recasting a crisis as a challenge that is comprehensible, manageable, and meaningful to tackle. It involves efforts to clarify the nature of problems and available resources. Family members attempt to make sense of how things have happened through *causal or explanatory attributions* and they look to their future course with hopes and fears. We can support their efforts to clarify explanations of their problems, to appraise their challenges and options ahead, and to plan active coping strategies.

Positive Outlook

Considerable research documents the strong psychological and physiological effects of a positive outlook in coping with stress, in recovering from crisis, and in overcoming barriers to success. *Hope* is as essential to the spirit as oxygen is to the lungs: It fuels energy and efforts to rise above adversity. Hope is a future-oriented leap of faith: no matter how bleak the present or immediate prospects, a better future can be envisioned. In problem-saturated conditions, it is essential to rekindle hope from despair, tap into potential resources, and encourage active striving and perseverance to surmount obstacles.

Well-functioning families tend to hold a more positive life. Seligman's (1990) concept of *learned optimism* has particular relevance for

Table 15.2 Key processes in family resilience

Belief systems
1. Make meaning of adversity
   View resilience as relationally-based – vs. "rugged individual"
   Normalize, contextualize adversity and distress
   Sense of coherence; view crisis as challenge: meaningful, comprehensible, manageable
   Causal/explanatory attributions: how could this happen? What can be done?
2. Positive outlook
   Hope, optimistic bias: confidence in overcoming odds
   En-*courage*-ment: affirm strengths and build on potential
   Seize opportunities: active initiative and perseverance (can-do spirit)
   Master the possible: accept what can't be changed
3. Transcendence and spirituality
   Larger values, purpose
   Spirituality: faith, healing rituals, congregational support
   Inspiration: envision new possibilities; creative expression; social action
   Transformation: learning, change, and growth from adversity

Structural/organizational patterns
4. Flexibility
   Adaptive change: rebound, reorganize to fit new challenges
   Stability through disruption: continuity, dependability
   Strong authoritative leadership: nurturance, protection, guidance
   Varied family forms: cooperative parenting/caregiving teams
5. Connectedness
   Mutual support, collaboration and commitment: team approach
   Respect individual needs, differences, and boundaries
   Seek reconnection, reconciliation of wounded relationships
6. Social and economic resources
   Mobilize kin, social and community networks: models and mentors
   Build financial security: balance work/family strains
   Institutional supports for families to thrive

Communication/problem solving
7. Clarity
   Clear, consistent messages (words and actions)
   Clarify ambiguous information: truth seeking/truth speaking
8. Open emotional expression
   Share range of feelings (joy and pain; hopes and fears)
   Mutual empathy: tolerance for differences
   Pleasurable interactions, respite; humor
9. Collaborative problem-solving
   Creative brainstorming; resourcefulness
   Shared decision-making: conflict management: negotiation, reciprocity
   Focus on goals: take concrete steps; build on success; learn from failure
   Proactive stance: preparedness: prevent problems; avert crises

fostering resilience. His earlier research on "learned helplessness" showed that with repeated experiences of futility and failure, individuals stop trying and become passive and pessimistic, generalizing the belief that bad things always happen to them and that nothing they can do will matter. Seligman then found that optimism could be learned, and helplessness and pessimism unlearned, through experiences of successful mastery, building confidence that one's efforts can make a difference. His research led to programs in schools for high-risk youth to build confidence and competence. He cautioned, however, that a positive mindset is not sufficient for success if life conditions are relentlessly harsh, with few opportunities to rise above them. As Aponte (1994) notes, many families who feel trapped in impoverished, blighted communities lose hope, suffering a deprivation of both "bread" and "spirit." This despair robs them of meaning, purpose, and a sense of future possibility. Thus, to rebuild and sustain a positive outlook, we need to foster successful experiences *and* a nurturing community context.

By affirming family strengths and potential in the midst of difficulties, we can help members to counter a sense of helplessness, failure, and blame while reinforcing pride, confidence, and a "can do" spirit. The therapist's encouragement bolsters courage to take initiative and persevere in efforts to master challenges. It helps families build confidence and competence through experiences of successful mastery, learning that their efforts can make a difference.

Initiative and perseverance – hallmarks of resilience – are fueled by unwavering shared confidence through an ordeal: "We'll never give up trying." This conviction bolsters efforts and makes family members active participants in a relentless search for solutions. By showing confidence that they will each do their best, families support members' best efforts and build competencies.

Mastering the art of the possible is a vital key for resilience, since some things cannot be changed. Clinicians can help families take stock of their situation – the challenges, constraints, resources, and aims – and then focus energies on making the best of their options. This requires coming to accept that which is beyond their control. We can help families who are immobilized, or trapped in a powerless victim position to direct their focus and efforts toward current and future possibilities: playing the hand that is dealt as well as possible. When immediate conditions are overwhelming, family members can be encouraged to take up tasks they can master. Although past events cannot be changed, they can be recast in a new light to foster greater comprehension, healing, and growth.

Transcendence and Spirituality

Transcendent beliefs and practices provide meaning and purpose beyond a family's immediate plight. Most families find strength, comfort, and guidance in adversity through connections with their cultural and religious traditions. Shared rituals and ceremonies facilitate passage through significant transitions and linkages with a larger community and common heritage (Imber-Black, Roberts, & Whiting, 2003).

Suffering, and any injustice or senselessness, are ultimately spiritual issues. As a large body of research documents, spiritual resources, through deep faith practices such as prayer and meditation and congregational affiliation, can be wellsprings for resilience, particularly for families struggling to surmount barriers of poverty and racism (Walsh, 2009). Many find spiritual nourishment outside formal religion, as through deep personal connection with nature, music, and the arts, or in community service or social action.

The paradox of resilience is that the worst of times can also bring out our best. A crisis can yield learning, transformation, and growth in unforeseen directions. It can be a wake-up call or epiphany, awakening family members to the importance of loved ones or jolting them to repair old wounds and reorder priorities for more meaningful relationships and life pursuits. Many emerge from shattering crises with a heightened moral compass and sense of purpose in their lives, gaining compassion for the plight of others. In Chicago, one father who had lost his son to gang violence found a healing pathway by leading a community effort to stop gun violence. It is most important to help families in problem-satu-

rated situations to envision a better future through their efforts and, where hopes and dreams have been shattered, to imagine new possibilities, seizing opportunities for invention, transformation, and growth.

Family Organizational Patterns

Contemporary families, with diverse structures, must organize in various ways to meet life challenges. Resilience is bolstered by flexible structure, connectedness (cohesion), and social and economic resources.

Flexibility

Flexibility, a core process in resilience, involves adaptive change. For instance, following parental disability, divorce, or separation, families must recalibrate relationships and reorganize patterns of interaction to fit new conditions. At the same time, families need to buffer and counterbalance disruptive changes, regaining stability and continuity. Children and other vulnerable family members especially need assurance of continuity, security, and predictability through turmoil. Daily routines and meaningful rituals can assist at such times.

Firm, yet flexible, authoritative leadership is most effective for family functioning and the well-being of children through stressful times. It is important for parents and other caretakers to provide nurturance, protection, and guidance, especially through periods of uncertainty. For instance, children's adaptation to divorce is facilitated by strong parental leadership and dependability as new single-parent household structures, visitation schedules, rules, and routines are set in place. With complex family structures, such as kinship care and stepfamilies, therapists can help them forge collaborative co-parenting and caregiving teamwork across households.

Connectedness

Connectedness, or cohesion, is essential for effective family functioning (Olson & Gorell, 2003). A crisis can shatter family cohesion, leaving members unable to rely on one another. Resilience is strengthened by mutual support, collaboration, and commitment to weather troubled times together. At the same time, individual coping differences, separateness, and boundaries need to be respected. When family members are separated, as with incarceration or migration, it is important to sustain vital connections through photos, letters, keepsakes, internet contact, and visits, as well as through cultural and spiritual roots. Family therapists can also facilitate reconnection and repair of wounded and estranged relationships. Intense pressures in troubled times can spark misunderstandings and cutoffs. Yet, a crisis, such as a life-threatening event, can also be seized as an opportunity for reconciliation.

Social and Economic Resources

Extended kin and social networks are vital lifelines in times of trouble, offering practical and emotional support. The significance of role models and mentors for the resilience of at-risk youth is well documented. Involvement in community groups and faith congregations also strengthens resilience. Families who are more isolated can be helped to access these potential resources.

Community-based coordinated efforts, involving local agencies and residents, are essential to meet such challenges as neighborhood crime or disaster recovery. Such multisystemic approaches facilitate both family and community resilience (Hernandez, 2002; Landau & Saul, 2004; Landau, 2007; Walsh, 2007). In one model program, multifamily groups and parent/teacher networks were organized in lower Manhattan neighborhoods directly affected by the 9/11 terrorist attacks, serving as a valuable resource for families to share their experiences, respond to concerns of their children, provide mutual support, and mobilize concerted action in recovery efforts.

Financial security is crucial for resilience. Job loss or a serious illness can drain a family's economic resources. Research clearly shows that financial strain is the most significant risk factor for children in single-parent families

(Anderson, 2012). Families may also need help navigating conflicting pressures of job and family responsibilities for two-earner and single-parent households.

Most importantly, the concept of family resilience should not be misused to blame families that are unable to rise above harsh conditions by simply labeling them as not resilient. Just as individuals need supportive relationships to thrive, families require social and institutional policies and practices that enable them to rebound and rebuild after major crises and to thrive in the face of prolonged hardships. It is not enough to help families overcome the odds against them; mental health professionals must also work to change the odds (Seccombe, 2002).

Communication/Problem-Solving Processes

Communication processes facilitate resilience by bringing clarity to crisis situations, encouraging open emotional expression, and fostering collaborative problem-solving. It must be kept in mind that cultural norms vary widely in regard to information sharing and emotional expression (Epstein, Ryan, Bishop, Miller, & Keitner, 2003).

Clarity

Clarity and congruence in words and deeds facilitate effective family functioning and the well-being of members. In times of crisis, communication and coordination can easily break down. Ambiguity fuels anxiety and blocks understanding and mastery. By helping families clarify and share crucial information about their situation and future expectations, mental health practitioners facilitate meaning-making and informed decision-making. Shared acknowledgment of the reality and circumstances of a crisis situation promotes adaptation, whereas secrecy, denial, and cover-up, especially in stigmatized cases such as suicide, can impede recovery (Walsh & McGoldrick, 2004).

Commonly, well-intentioned families avoid painful or threatening topics, wishing to protect children or frail elders from worry, or waiting until they are certain about a precarious situation, such as an unclear medical prognosis or parental separation/divorce. Anxieties about the unspeakable, however, can generate catastrophic fears and are often expressed in a child's somatic or behavioral problems. Parents can be helpful by keeping children informed as the situation develops and by openness to discussing questions or concerns. Parents may need guidance on age-appropriate ways of sharing information and can expect that as children mature, they may revisit issues to gain greater comprehension or bring up emerging concerns.

Emotional Expression

Open communication, supported by a climate of mutual trust, empathy, and tolerance for differences, enables family members to share a wide range of feelings that can be aroused by crisis events and chronic stress. Members may be out of sync over time; one may continue to be quite upset as others feel ready to move on. Parents may suppress their own emotions in order to keep functioning for the family; children may stifle their own feelings and needs so as not to burden parents. When emotions are intense or family members feel overwhelmed by a pile-up of stressors, conflict is more likely to spiral out of control. Respite from struggles is essential. Helping family members share small pleasures and moments of humor can refuel energies and lift spirits.

Collaborative Problem-Solving

Creative brainstorming and resourcefulness open new possibilities for overcoming adversity and for healing and growth after tragedy. Therapists can facilitate shared decision-making and conflict management through negotiation, with fairness and reciprocity over time. They can encourage a family's efforts to set clear, attainable goals and take concrete steps toward them. Therapists can help them build on small successes and use failures as learning experiences. When dreams have been shattered, mental health practitioners can encourage family members to survey the altered landscape and seize opportunities for growth in new directions.

To meet future challenges, therapists can help families shift from a crisis-reactive mode to a proactive stance. A resilience-oriented approach to practice focuses on the future, striving for the best while also preparing for the worst, anticipating future clouds on the horizon to prevent problems and avert crises. Encouraging families to devise a "Plan B" can enable them to rebound when unforeseen challenges arise.

Synergistic Influences of Key Processes in Resilience

These key processes in family resilience are mutually interactive and synergistic. For example, a relational view of resilience (belief system) fosters connectedness (organizational patterns) as well as open emotional sharing and collaborative problem solving (communication processes). A core belief that problems can be mastered both facilitates and is reinforced by successful problem-solving strategies. This family resilience framework provides a flexible map for practitioners to identify and target core processes in effective family functioning while also holding a contextual view and recognizing the viability of many varied pathways in resilience.

Conclusion

A family resilience framework offers several advantages. By definition, it focuses on strengths under stress, in response to crisis, and when facing prolonged adversity. With the growing diversity and complexity of contemporary family life, no single model of healthy functioning fits all families or their situations. Therapists help each family to find its own pathways through adversity, fitting interventions with the family's challenges, cultural orientation, life cycle passage, and personal strengths and resources. Beyond coping or problem-solving, resilience involves positive transformation and growth. Even experiences of severe trauma and very troubled relationships hold potential for healing and new possibilities across the life cycle and the generations.

A family resilience perspective holds a deep conviction in the potential of all families, even the most vulnerable, to gain strengths in mastering their challenges and provide relational resources for children to thrive. It involves a crucial shift in emphasis from family deficits to family challenges, with belief in the possibilities for recovery and growth out of adversity. By targeting interventions to strengthen key processes for resilience, families become more resourceful in dealing with crises, weathering persistent stresses, and meeting future challenges. This conceptual framework can be usefully integrated with many strengths-based practice models and applied with a range of crisis situations with respect for family and cultural diversity. This approach also builds relational resources in social and community networks and addresses the impact of larger social systems and socio-economic and cultural influences. Resilience-oriented services foster family empowerment as they bring forth shared hope, develop new and renewed competencies, and strengthen family bonds.

References

Anderson, C. M. (2012). The diversity, strengths, and challenges of single-parent households. In F. Walsh (Ed.), *Normal family processes: Growing diversity and complexity* (4th ed.). New York: Guilford Press.

Antonovsky, A., & Sourani, T. (1988). Family sense of coherence and family adaptation. *Journal of Marriage and the Family, 50*, 79–92.

Aponte, H. (1994). *Bread and spirit: Therapy with the new poor*. New York: Norton.

Engstrom, M. (2012). Family processes in kinship care. In F. Walsh (Ed.), *Normal family processes: Diversity and complexity* (4th ed.). New York: Guilford Press.

Epstein, N., Ryan, C., Bishop, D., Miller, I., & Keitner, G. (2003). The McMaster model: View of healthy family functioning. In F. Walsh (Ed.), *Normal family processes* (3rd ed., pp. 581–607). New York: Guilford Press.

Falicov, C. (1995). Training to think culturally: A multidimensional comparative framework. *Family Process, 34*, 373–388.

Falicov, C. J. (2007). Working with transnational immigrants: Expanding meanings of family, community and culture. *Family Process, 46*, 157–172.

Herdt, G., & Koff, B. (2000). *Something to tell you: The road families travel when a child is gay*. New York: Columbia University Press.

Hernandez, P. (2002). Resilience in families and communities: Latin American contributions from the psychology of liberation. *Journal of Counseling & Therapy for Couples and Families, 10*(3), 334–343.

Hetherington, E.M., & J. Kelly (2002) For Better or For Worse: Divorce Reconsidered. New York: Norton.

Imber-Black, E., Roberts, J., & Whiting, R. (Eds.). (2003). *Rituals in families and family therapy* (2nd ed.). New York: Norton.

Kaufman, J., & Ziegler, E. (1987). Do abused children become abusive parents? *American Journal of Orthopsychiatry, 57*, 186–192.

Landau, J. (2007). Enhancing resilience: Families and communities as agents for change. *Family Process, 46*(3), 351–365.

Landau, J., & Saul, J. (2004). Facilitating family and community resilience in response to major disasters. In F. Walsh & M. McGoldrick (Eds.), *Living beyond loss: Death in the family* (2nd ed., pp. 285–309). New York: Norton.

Luthar, S. S., Cicchetti, D., & Becker, B. (2000). The construct of resilience: A critical evaluation and guidelines for future work. *Child Development, 71*, 543–562.

McCubbin, H., Thompson, E. A., Thompson, E., & Fromer, J. (Eds.). (1998a). *Resiliency in ethnic minority families. Vol. 1. Native and immigrant families*. Thousand Oaks: Sage.

McCubbin, H., Thompson, E. A., Thompson, A. I., & Fromer, J. E. (Eds.). (1998b). *Stress, coping, and health in families: Sense of coherence and resiliency*. Thousand Oaks: Sage.

McGoldrick, M., Gerson, R., & Petry, S. (2008). *Genograms: Assessment and intervention* (3rd ed.), New York: Norton.

McGoldrick, M., Carter, B., & García-Preto. N. (2011). *The expanded family life cycle: Individual, family, and social perspectives* (4th ed.) Boston: Allyn and Bacon.

Olson, D. H., & Gorell, D. (2003). Circumplex model of marital and family systems. In F. Walsh (Ed.), *Normal family processes* (3rd ed., pp. 514–544). New York: Guilford.

Patterson, J. (2002). Integrating family resilience and family stress theory. *Journal of Marriage and the Family, 64*, 349–373.

Rolland, J. S. (1994). *Families, illness and disability: An integrative treatment model*. New York: Basic.

Rutter, M. (1987). Psychosocial resilience and protective mechanisms. *American Journal of Orthopsychiatry, 57*, 316–331.

Seccombe, K. (2002). "Beating the odds" versus "changing the odds": Poverty, resilience, and family policy. *Journal of Marriage & Family, 64*(2), 384–394.

Seligman, M. E. P. (1990). *Learned optimism*. New York: Random House.

Ungar, M. (2004). The importance of parents and other caregivers to the resilience of high-risk adolescents. *Family Process, 43*(1), 23–41.

Walsh, F. (1996). The concept of family resilience: Crisis and challenge. *Family Process, 35*, 261–281.

Walsh, F. (2002). A family resilience framework: Innovative practice applications. *Family Relations, 51*(2), 130–137.

Walsh, F. (2003). Family resilience: A framework for clinical practice. *Family Process, 42*(1), 1–18.

Walsh, F. (2006). *Strengthening family resilience* (2nd ed.). New York: Guilford Press.

Walsh, F. (2007). Traumatic loss and major disasters: Strengthening family and community resilience. *Family Process, 46*(2), 207–227.

Walsh, F. (Ed.). (2009). *Spiritual resources in family therapy* (2nd ed.). New York: Guilford Press.

Walsh, F. (2012). *Normal family processes: Diversity and complexity* (4th ed.). New York: Guilford Press.

Walsh, F., & McGoldrick, M. (Eds.). (2004). *Living beyond loss: Death in the family* (2nd ed.). New York: W. W. Norton.

Werner, E. E., & Smith, R. S. (2001). *Journeys from childhood to midlife: Risk, resilience, and recovery*. Ithaca: Cornell University Press.

Yang, O.-K., & Choi, M.-M. (2001). Korean's Han and resilience: Application to mental health social work. *Mental Health & Social Work, 11*(6), 7–29.

Contexts of Vulnerability and Resilience: Childhood Maltreatment, Cognitive Functioning and Close Relationships

Christine Wekerle, Randall Waechter, and Ronald Chung

Together the structural determinants and conditions of daily life constitute the social determinants of health and are responsible for a major part of health inequities between and within countries (Commission on the Social Determinants of Health, World Health Organization, 2008, p. 1).

> ...critical strategy is one which supports, augments and deepens the capacity of ...organizations and institutions to recognize the undertow of violence that is pulling down already vulnerable communities. Whether employing community organizing or cross dialogues, borrowing strategies from other movements or creating approaches anew, intensive focus is called for within neighborhoods.
> (Rosewater & Goodmark, 2007).

Child maltreatment creates a context for daily living that challenges victim health, in the short- and long-term. The concept of resilience is based upon the capacity of the individual to achieve positive and healthful outcomes despite stress and adversity (Ungar, 2007, 2008). For the victim growing up, a host of influences, both internal (self-functioning, mental health, experienced-based neural circuitry) and external (home, neighborhood, and school environment), interact and over time impact health outcomes (e.g., Cicchetti & Gunnar, 2008; Cicchetti & Toth, 1998; Luthar, 2006; Rutter, 2000; Sameroff & Chandler, 1975).

This chapter considers: (1) the concept of resilience within the context of vulnerability that is child maltreatment; (2) external resilience as predicated on relationship opportunities (e.g., adolescent romantic partnerships; caseworker as caring adult); and (3) internal resilience as based on neurocognitive functioning, including information processing and remediation of maltreatment-based neural circuitry that favors fear and anxiety (rather than positive emotions like calmness, optimism), response reactivity (rather than rational, reflective responding), and self-dysfunction (rather than self-regulation).

It is our position that resilience-related work in maltreatment reflects: (1) the natural repair tendencies, such as self-righting (Cicchetti & Rogosch, 2002, 2009); (2) self-protection that allows for day-to-day functioning for the developing youth (Yates, 2004); (3) cumulative resilience as at least as important as cumulative adversities (Rutter, 2000; Trickett & Putnam, 1998), and (4) resilience, like attachment, is a property of the individual, reflecting an interaction between internal resilience and external resilience (Cicchetti & Rogosch, 2009), such that over time adaptation to environments and situations yield no destruction to the self and others. Rutter (1987) proposed that changing the experience of and exposure to risk is important. For example, shifting the external environment to reduce traumatic reexperiencing symptoms (e.g., nightmares) may be accomplished by altering the

C. Wekerle (✉)
Department of Pediatrics, McMaster University
in Hamilton, Hamilton, ON, Canada
e-mail: wekerc@mcmaster.ca

M. Ungar (ed.), *The Social Ecology of Resilience: A Handbook of Theory and Practice*,
DOI 10.1007/978-1-4614-0586-3_16, © Springer Science+Business Media, LLC 2012

internal environment (i.e., understanding of and agency in personal safety), as well as the external environment (e.g., soothing practices at sleep time, provision of a safe night environment). As Rutter (2000) notes, perceptual elements and ongoing response to maltreatment recollections are part of the memory consolidation process towards a self-story that is coherent, reality-based positivity towards the self, and being generally healthful. This is consistent with defining resilience in terms of recovery or growth over time from dysfunction to functionality, rather than the absence of symptoms (Afifi & MacMillan, in press; Luthar, 2006) or as a class or category (e.g., McGloin & Widom, 2001). In this view, resilience reflects the process, whereby the external resources support internal resilience, and internal resources propel a youth to have a readiness for and "select into" positive external opportunities.

The Beginning of Resilience for Maltreatment Victims

The Adverse Childhood Experiences (ACE) Pyramid Model (http://www.cdc.gov/ace/index.htm) places development from conception to death, highlighting early death as the top risk outcome. The trajectory towards premature death is underscored as a preventable and unnecessary outcome of childhood adversities. At its base, then, the study of resilience among maltreated persons starts with ensuring the continuation of life. Childhood fatalities mainly capture the more vulnerable physical state of infants. In 2008, 1,740 children were identified as having died due to child abuse and neglect in the US, and this number has increased over the prior 5 years (U.S. Department of Health and Human Services, Administration for Children and Families, Administration on Children, Youth and Families, Children's Bureau, 2010). Later in development, maltreatment links with mid-childhood suicidal thinking (Cicchetti, Rogosch, Sturge-Apple, & Toth, 2009) and adolescent suicidality (Enns et al., 2006; Evans, Hawton, & Rodham, 2005; Rhodes et al., 2011). For example, one population study has placed the risk of suicide at 4–6 times higher with child welfare-involved youths,

as compared to the general youth population (Vinnerljung, Sundell, Lofholm, & Humlesjo, 2006). The first resilience challenge in maltreatment is making it through your physically vulnerable early years, and wanting to be in this world in the adolescent and adult years.

External Resilience: Close Relationships

Maltreatment-related trauma may represent unresolved loss, imparting challenges in utilizing attachment relationships confidently for consolation, support and stabilization (Bailey, Moran, & Pederson, 2007; Hankin, 2005; Wekerle & Wolfe, 1998). In maltreating families, interactions and interactants tend towards irregularity, unpredictability, and inconsistency, with sudden new entries and exits, and exposure to intimate partner violence (IPV) (Krug, Dahlberg, Mercy, Zwi, & Lozano, 2002; Wekerle & Wall, 2002). IPV, as observed relationship violence, may be especially damaging to relationships. For example, substantiation of maltreatment was found to be more prevalent when partner violence was present alongside primary caregiver vulnerabilities (e.g., Wekerle, Wall, Leung, & Trocmé, 2007). In a recent community survey where 10.3% of US children were maltreatment victims; among 14–17 year old youth, more than one-third had seen their parent(s) assaulted (Finkelhor, Turner, Ormrod, & Hamby, 2009). The Public Health Agency of Canada's national surveillance study, the Canadian Incidence Study of Reported Child Abuse and Neglect (PHAC, 2010; Trocmé et al., 2010), separates out exposure to IPV from other forms of emotional abuse. According to the 2008 CIS statistics, IPV exposure was the leading category of substantiated child maltreatment (34%) along with neglect (34%) and other forms of emotional abuse (9%) (Trocmé et al., 2010).

Maltreated youths may carry forward this relationship learning to other social contexts. Evidence supports this: in school, maltreated youths are more likely to experience social rejection (Bowers, McGinnis, Friman, & Ervin, 1999), bullying (Gilligan, 2000), and being bullied (e.g., Mohapatra et al., 2010). For youth whose maltreatment has been formally detected, close friendships with peers may have more challenge, due to system effects that include residential and school changes, as well as grouped care and placement breakdowns. Haynie, South, and Bose (2006) have examined the impact of mobility on the development of friendship networks among youth. Due to frequent school leaving and reentering, highly mobile youth are less likely to integrate with prosocial peer groups and more likely to socialize with peers who place little value on educational achievement and other social norms. Mobile youth occupied less central positions within their peer groups and had small networks of friends (South, Haynie, & Bose, 2007).

However, social support is identified as a key buffer to stress and a learning context for relational skills in the friendship and romantic domains (e.g., Nangle, Erdley, Newman, Mason, & Carpenter, 2003). In reviewing their work, Cicchetti and Rogosch (2009) suggest that self-reliance and interpersonal "reserve" may be part of resilience. But it can also be said that withdrawal from relating may be an unwanted consequence of maltreatment-related posttraumatic stress features, such as emotional numbing and dissociation, and may be part of nonrelationship coping, as with substance abuse (e.g., Wekerle, Leung, Goldstein, Thornton, & Tonmyr, 2009). It may be that to be highly adaptive, flexibility is required to match behavior to context (violent, nonviolent) in order to be resilient.

Adolescent Romantic Relationships

Adolescent romantic relationships are a transition point and a window for resilient processes (e.g., egalitarian, consent-based relating) and outcomes (e.g., nonviolent partnership; consensual not coercive sexual experiences) (e.g., Wekerle & Avgoustis, 2003). This is new relationship territory – with several firsts – first date, first intercourse, first committed relationship. A longitudinal study of maltreated children found that they could recover from early childhood insecure attachment and form "learned secure" attachments with romantic partners (Roisman,

Padron, Sroufe, & Egeland, 2002). In a study of heterosexual dating couples, albeit mainly a single religious affiliation, Galliher and Bentley (2010) found that among mid-adolescents, relationship satisfaction was related to the levels of conflict, sarcasm, and rejection sensitivity of both partners. Bouchey (2007) found that higher levels of romantic appeal and positive partner features were linked to better psychological adjustment. Maltreated youths who can achieve high relationship satisfaction may be demonstrating an external resilience.

For the maltreated youth, sex brings a host of challenges to self-care. There is some evidence for unique contribution of childhood sexual abuse to long-term reproductive and sexual health issues (Senn & Carey, 2010). A history of child maltreatment has been associated with high-risk sexual behaviors in both male and female adolescents, such as younger age at first consensual intercourse, unprotected sex, and multiple partners (Friedrich, 1993; Greenberg et al., 1999; Noll, Trickett, & Putnam, 2003; Randolph & Mosack, 2006; Senn, Carey, & Vanable, 2008; Trickett & Putnam, 1998; Wilsnack, Vogeltanz, Klassen, & Harris, 1997). In our own work with adolescents receiving child welfare services, 25% of males reported early intercourse (before age 13), but were no different than their Canadian age-counterparts in use of protection during sexual intercourse (Wekerle, Waechter, Leung, & Chen, 2009). Alternately, 12% of females reported that they never used protection during sexual intercourse, compared to 28% of their age-matched Canadian counterparts (Wekerle, Waechter, et al., 2009). This suggests a potential beneficial role of caseworker involvement, as there is sensitivity to pregnancy and disease prevention with their adolescent clients.

For maltreated youths, their family violence histories place them at risk for dating (Sears & Byers, 2010). In our work, youths who were child welfare system-involved and scored as mild-to-moderate intellectual disability reported more dating violence, particularly if having experienced emotional maltreatment and an avoidant attachment style (e.g., not wanting too much closeness) (Weiss, Waechter, Wekerle, & The MAP Research Team, 2011).

In understanding dating violence perpetration, for males, rejection sensitivity (Volz & Kerig, 2010), avoidant attachment style (Wekerle & Wolfe, 1998), avoidance/anger are predictive, potentially suggesting a male coping style of avoidance of close relationships, and a deflection to greater peer group investment (Ellis & Wolfe, 2008). Rejection sensitivity is suggested as related to female capitulation in a relationship (Galliher & Bentley, 2010), which is consistent with an ambivalence in relating (Wekerle & Wolfe, 1998). Romantic relationship functioning has a high skill/learning component (e.g., Florsheim, 2003; Silovsky, Niec, Bard, & Hecht, 2007). Maltreated youths, in particular males, appear to respond to co-educational group-based instruction, reporting less involvement in dating violence and greater condom use during intercourse as compared to females receiving relationship-focused education (Wolfe, Wekerle, Scott, & Pittman, 2003).

Community-Based Relationships

Resilience-promoting caring, including diverse and engaged social networks, are counterpoints to adversity. Nonparental adults who provide positive relationship features are associated with improved health, lowered risk, and higher job/school attainment among foster youth (Ahrens, DuBois, Richardson, Fan, & Lozano, 2008; Farruggia, Greenberger, Chen, & Heckhausen, 2006). Use of professional services, including child welfare, may function as a buffer to continued stress and impaired coping. Emerging evidence suggests that the longer the youth stays involved in foster care (and receiving child welfare services), the better the outcomes (Courtney, Dworsky, & Peters, 2009; Taussig, Clyman, & Landsverk, 2001). This is illustrated further by interviews with maltreated youth "aging out" of the child welfare system. Dunn, Culhane, and Taussig (2010) surveyed youth about their foster care experiences. Irrespective of maltreatment severity, group home youths reported that they would be better off with their family-of-origin, but foster care youth, girls, and emotionally and

sexually abused youth, reported their lives would have been worse staying with their family-of-origin. This may reflect, in part, the availability of safe, stable, nurturing professional relationships.

Research indicates that enhanced or therapeutic foster care is beneficial (e.g., see MacMillan et al., 2009; for a review). The Fostering Healthy Futures Preventive Initiative, (Taussig, Garrido, & Crawford, 2009) provides adult mentoring (social work graduate students) to preadolescents focused on risk prevention and health promotion (Taussig, Culhane, & Hettleman, 2007). Among youths who are have the government as corporate parents (i.e., biological parental rights have been terminated), a highly positive relationship with the foster mother is reported by the vast majority (Wekerle, Waechter, et al., 2009). Quality (re) parenting is a strongly protective when it provides structure, monitoring, limit-setting, and consistency (Luthar, 2006).

Cultural connection is an important feature as well. For example, about 32% of Aboriginal families self-referred to family healing services, where the focus is on validating and valuing relationships (Mi'kmaw Family & Children Services, 2009–2010). This stands in contrast to the typical pattern of child welfare referrals, most often by police and education staff and least often by self-referral (Tonmyr, Li, Williams, Scott, & Jack, 2010). The Aboriginal child welfare model would seem to value communal identity, a commitment to social reciprocity, and self-monitoring. The following example provides one culturally-based approach to connecting care-providers that emphasizes social inclusion and traditional rituals.

The ceremony included four grandmothers to represent the north, south, east and west directions to bear witness.... The family's hands were bound in white ribbon to represent the mother's umbilical cord. Traditional drumming played ... a Pipe ceremony was performed by an Elder of the community. After the family and grandmothers were seated in the inner circle a smudge was performed to cleanse every participant. The grandmothers wrapped the clan quilts around each member of the family to represent the unification of the family. Each family member was presented with an eagle feather to recognize their strength and commitment as a family. A traditional feast was held in honour... (Mi'kmaw Family & Children Services, 2009–2010, p. 22).

Finally, training foster parents to actively structure learning (e.g., scaffolding the interaction to maximize success experiences, promoting the child's learning about their learning) appears to promote resilient functioning (e.g., Dozier, Albus, Fisher, & Sepulveda, 2002). Since child maltreatment is a relational issue, one would predict that positive social connections act as an effective means of rewiring the stress response system and promoting resilience through prosocial behavior (Belsky, Jaffee, Sligo, Woodward, & Silva, 2005; Chan, 1994; Hashima & Amato, 1994; Rak & Patterson, 1996; Travis & Combs-Orme, 2007).

Internal Resilience: Neurocognitive Functioning

Resilience could be conceptualized as some set of brain-based factors that provide greater than normative resistance to the impact of adversity. The experience of childhood maltreatment could dampen this process in a variety of ways, such as focusing the learning environment towards threat-based pattern detection, and reducing the strength of the neural network supporting soothing. Harkening back to the experiential reality of maltreatment, the self-strivings and self-protection learning is thwarted by the high probability of ineffective personal agency (i.e., preventing, stopping, escaping the maltreatment event) within close relationships. However, with a consistent change in the experiential world of the child towards the positive (mastery experiences, therapeutic relationships, self-compassionate stance), a more balanced "steady state" of neural circuitry may ensue, reflecting a process of plasticity in adaptation to the new (nonviolent) environment. As Cicchetti and Cohen (2006) note, "it appears that the effects of maltreatment on brain microstructure and biochemistry may be either pathological or adaptive" (p. 14). This dynamic view recognizes that information in the brain is processed by distributed neuronal connections that are maintained, weakened, or strengthened based on experiential demands (Johnson, 1998). Recent work has considered changes to brain structure and chemistry, as well as

genetic vulnerabilities (for a review, see McCrory, De Brito, & Viding, 2010).

While this knowledge base is developing, very little work has been conducted in terms of neurocognitive processes considered to be most proximal to behavioral responses in maltreated youths. The attention, awareness, and memory of maltreatment-related perceptions, understandings and feelings are the proximal internal processes of resilience. The distal processes that may impact adaptation to nonhome environments reflect the more integrative information processing demands such as social cognition (i.e., self-knowledge, relationship conceptualizations; social scripts; understanding the less concrete cues typical of social interactions; decoding affective expressions).

One prominent viewpoint of maltreatment-related impairment is that poor health outcomes are driven by altered brain physiology associated with maltreatment experiences and underlie cognitive-emotional interactions (Perry, 2009). Lee and Hoaken (2007) have suggested that emotional processing must be considered in tandem with neurocognitive development to understand the relationship between child maltreatment and poor behavioral choices. A key theme in their proposal is the interface between maltreatment, stress/anxiety symptoms, cognitive functioning/information processing, and behavioral decision-making. The central tenet is that stress/anxiety undermines proximal information processing, and has a deleterious impact on long-term behavioral decision-making patterns. Anxiety drives the decision-making process in a bottom–up, reactive-oriented manner. Indeed, higher stress states are found with groups with greater likelihood of chronic maltreatment experiences, as seen with youths involved in child welfare (e.g., Wekerle, Waechter, et al., 2009) and juvenile justice (e.g., Kerig, Ward, Vanderzee, & Moeddel, 2009; Moretti, Obsuth, Odgers, & Reebye, 2006). Essentially, the stress response system is designed for *acute* stress. For maltreated persons, the initiation and termination of stress responding is out of balance, leading to situations where individuals are "over-reactive" to stress as a life/death or significant health threat (i.e., attaching a higher emotional significance to information than is needed) or "under-reactive" in habituating to stressful information and, therefore, not taking action to prevent, ameliorate, or effectively deal with stressors (Chrousos & Gold, 1992; Cicchetti & Rogosch, 2009; De Bellis, 2001; McCrory et al., 2010; Young, Abelson, & Cameron, 2005). However, over-practicing stress-driven bottom–up processing comes at the cost of the likelihood of using more effortful, goal-directed responding, known as top–down processing.

Bottom–Up Processing and Top–Down Processing

Bottom–up processing is driven by emotionality, signaling problems such as selective attention to negative affect information in the environment (Perry, 2009). The top–down information processing (i.e., reasoning-based processing) requires that there is conceptualization that guides the selection of the concrete moment-to-moment behavioral choices. There should be processing efficiency such that the needed sequences are over-learned, and can be updated with effortful thought. The reactive-type of processing should be used minimally in everyday situations, but maximally in crisis situations. When a child experiences fear and/or distress and activates this stress response in a prolonged or repetitive fashion, as with maltreatment, the neural networks involved in the response undergo a "use-dependent" alteration designed to be adaptive for coping with the fearful environment (Gordis, Granger, Susman, & Trickett, 2008; Perry, 2009; Susman, 2006). A dysregulated youth will have a difficult time participating in, and benefiting from, experiences that rely on top–down, goal-directed cognitive behaviors such as reading, decision-making, problem-solving, and skillful social interactions. These proximal behavioral and health-related decisions may then impact on longer-term socio-emotional outcomes such as attachment in close relationships, engagement in social networks, employer-employee relations, and parenting.

When maltreated persons encounter new situations (like dating), the concept for relating is limited. This would suggest that the interactant may be "caught up" and led through escalating coercive and aversive interactions until an explosive end, rather than skillfully detecting problem interactions and exiting these (e.g., Wekerle & Wolfe, 1998). Emotion-based processing may skew the outcomes towards further violence. For example, traumatic stress symptoms have been found to explain in part the relationship between childhood maltreatment and involvement in adolescent dating violence (e.g., Wekerle, Leung, et al., 2009). High felt stress (e.g., high engagement with or valuing of the actual and perceived stressor) makes disengagement (inhibition of a primed or initiated response) and change in strategy (flexibility) more challenging. Stop and flexibility cognitive processes are important components of resilient functioning (Davidson, 2000). These sophisticated thinking components are grouped under the term executive functioning. Executive functioning includes: (a) control of attention (where to direct attention and whether to sustain attention); (b) behavioral inhibition (putting a stop for unhealthful or maladaptive behaviors); (c) updating working memory representations (i.e., working memory capacity; ability to think up creative or novel solutions); and (d) shifting between cognitive tasks (e.g., multitasking).

At present, there is very little evidence to address the question of whether child maltreatment directly impacts the development of "top down" executive functions. From a resilience perspective, the impairment of executive functioning is a critical issue because it is viewed as foundational to the development of general IQ (Sternberg, 2008) that supports integrating information in the environment (Cicchetti & Rogosch, 1997; Heller, Larrieu, D'Imperio, & Boris, 1998; Herrenkohl, Sousa, Tajima, Herrenkohl, & Moylan, 2008; Luther & Zigler, 1992; Masten et al., 1999; Weiss et al., 2011). One study attempted to discriminate between types of maltreatment, finding that those children who were both neglected and physically abused showed larger deficits in problem solving, abstraction, and planning when compared to a control group (Nolin & Ethier, 2007). Another study found no relationship between maltreatment and measures of executive functioning in the verbal domain (verbal fluency, verbal processing speed) (Schenkel, Spauldinga, DiLilloa, & Silverstein, 2005), while other research showed an impairment in visual memory (e.g., remembering faces, or a complex drawing) (De Bellis, Hooper, Woodley, & Shenk, 2010). In the latter study, trends were noted for greater impulsive errors and poorer verbal memory linked to posttraumatic stress symptoms. Youths were mainly at average or above intelligence.

These sorts of studies are presently few and far between such that over-interpretation is a real risk. Applied to maltreatment, these sorts of challenges to recalling visual maltreatment cues (e.g., in reexperiencing PTSD symptoms) would make relationships very effortful since they rely much on verbal skills. Verbal mediation (e.g., self-talk) is one way to manage the impact of visual memory. This necessitates, though, an ease of access to word retrieval, a learning of the visual-verbal linkage, and the capacity to simultaneously work with an array of "information bits" (working memory) to coherently sequence information. While maltreatment experiences were not part of the study, Fikke, Melinder, and Landrø (2011) found that youths with high severity self-harm had poorer working memory than did youths with low-severity self-harm. Low severity youths would seem to be more susceptible to impulsivity, in that they made more errors in the stopping of a response that had started (inhibition). Their self-harm behaviors may be more impulsive and part of "trial-and-error" discovery. This sort of notion suggests that they may not have been highly driven by emotionality and bottom–up processing. In contrast, the high severity group had more depression, anxiety and anger than either the low-severity or control adolescents. These authors point to working memory impairment as a central issue for these youths in dampening the ability to distract from negative moods. Also, processing negative emotions may utilize limited immediate cognitive resources, at the expense of top–down or goal-directed cognitive

processing (Luo et al., 2010; Pourtois, Spinelli, Seeck, & Vuilleumier, 2010). In resilient functioning, emotionality would be more controllable. Compensatory strategies can be learned and, if part of the behavioral pattern, may impact the cognitive vulnerabilities. This would reflect self-organization – the reorganization of targeted brain systems to support adaptation in functioning when subjected to new constraints in the environment (Cicchetti & Curtis, 2006).

Resilience Implications for Practice with Maltreated Groups

Resilience promoting interventions are relative. If similar behavioral health outcomes and resilience can be achieved through structural changes in the child or youth's environment rather than targeting executive or intellectual functioning, this may prove to be equally effective at much less cost. Considering the interaction between internal and external processes, practical strategies directed towards establishing psychological, physical and relationship safety, as well as a balanced emotional life, may be the critical issues for maltreatment victims. Towards this end, psycho-pharmaceutical therapy and psychotherapy are part of the professional relationship development. There are less formal options also. For example, while we do not yet understand the mechanism, concrete, lifestyle actions (e.g., caring for pets, creative self-expression, music enjoyment) have been suggested as important for enhancing resilience (Luthar, 2006). Fun and interesting exercise classes have also been shown to reduce symptoms of anxiety and depression among individuals diagnosed with clinical disorders (Brosse, Sheets, Lett, & Blumenthal, 2002; Callahan, 2004) and prevent the onset of future symptom onset (Goodwin, 2003; Landers & Petruzello, 1994). Furthermore, the field of restorative neurology has for many years emphasized the positive impact of repetitive motor activity in cognitive recovery from stroke. This principle suggests that therapeutic massage, yoga, balancing exercises, and any other activity that provides patterned, repetitive neural input (i.e., calming) would diminish negative emotionality and promote balance across domains (Perry, 2009).

Under the subcategory of cultural factors, assisting individuals to explore their own spirituality, cultural/spiritual identification, and learn about and affiliate with a religious organization has been shown to reduce feelings of anxiety associated with medical illness (Koenig, Larson, & Larson, 2001).

From a community perspective, ensuring safety and security, providing a means for individuals to contribute via age-appropriate work, supportive social networks, and civic engagement would follow along these remediation, prevention and resilience lines.

Conclusion

This chapter has considered resilience as an interaction between internal processes, particularly neurocognitive functioning, and the potential implication of maltreatment on information processing and external processes, particularly close relationship resources. No maltreatment research, though, has directly tested the interaction between internal processes and external ones over time. There is an evidence base that the social learning domain outside the maltreating home is the chief context for resilience, once maltreatment has started. It remains an essential resilience intervention to provide maltreatment prevention to socially disadvantaged and at-risk parents, especially when first making the transition to parenthood (e.g., MacMillan et al., 2009).

Going forward, understanding the neurocognitive "symphony" among maltreated youths is a fundamental goal, and one that needs to take into account proximal distress. For youths, it is not clear whether it is the high level of negative emotionality (emotion load) or regulation issues (handling the emotions) or both that has the main impact on proximal cognitive functioning and more long-term neurocognitive style. Resilience research that combines the internal information-processing understanding with the external,

environmental resources experiences is clearly needed to better direct child welfare and community-based services for maltreated youth.

It should be noted that there are costs to not doing the necessary theoretical and intervention research. In 2007, it is estimated that there were 130,237 children who were abused or neglected for the first time in Australia. This figure could be as high as 490,000 children. Based on these numbers, the projected cost of child abuse and neglect over the lifetime of children who were first abused or neglected in 2007 was $13.7 billion, but could be as high as $38.7 billion (Taylor et al., 2008). It is a child welfare fact that many adolescents and young adults return to their family-of-origin from leaving the in-care home (e.g., Taussig et al., 2009). Adolescents are a special age group in need of extra support in their transition to adulthood – and – they still need adult care providers to help plan and achieve their life goals and dreams. To quote Bronfrenbrenner (1978), "If we can stand on our own two feet, it is because others have raised us up. If, as adults, we can lay claim to competence and compassion, it only means that other human beings have been willing and enabled to commit their competence and compassion to us – through infancy, childhood, and adolescence, right up to this very moment" (p. 767).

Acknowledgements First and foremost, we thank the hundreds of adolescents who have shared their experiences with us in research projects and who are only brave. We wish to acknowledge the Child Protection Service staffers who have partnered with us. "Our research" references refer to the Maltreatment and Adolescent Pathways (MAP) Project, a set of connected studies (for a free downloadable chapter, see Wekerle et al., 2011, available at the Child Welfare Research Portal, http://www.cecw-cepb.ca/publications/2212). Research support has been received by: the Canadian Institutes of Health Research, (CIIIR); CIHR Institute of Gender and Health (IGH); the Ontario Ministry of Child and Family Services; the Ontario Centre of Excellence in Child and Youth Mental Health; Health Canada; Public Health Agency of Canada. Aspects of work was supported by career grants to Dr. Wekerle mid-career award (CIHR IGH and the Ontario Women's Health Foundation) as well as the Public Health Agency of Canada for her Interchange Canada Assignment. The authors thank Dr. Michael Ungar for his leadership in resilience globally, and for on-going support on this chapter specifically.

References

Afifi, T. O., & MacMillan, H. L. (In Press). Resilience following child maltreatment: A review of protective factors. *Canadian Journal of Psychiatry*, 1–27.

Ahrens, K. R., DuBois, D. L., Richardson, L. P., Fan, M. Y., & Lozano, P. (2008). Youth in foster care with adult mentors during adolescence have improved adult outcomes. *Journal of Pediatrics, 121*(2), e246–e252.

Bailey, H. N., Moran, G., & Pederson, D. R. (2007). Childhood maltreatment, complex trauma symptoms, and unresolved attachment in an at-risk sample of adolescent mothers. *Journal of Attachment & Human Development, 9*(2), 139–161.

Belsky, J., Jaffee, S. R., Sligo, J., Woodward, L., & Silva, P. A. (2005). Intergenerational transmission of warm-sensitive-stimulating parenting: A prospective study of mothers and fathers of 3 year olds. *Child Development, 76*, 384–396.

Bouchey, H. A. (2007). Perceived romantic competence, importance of romantic domains, and psychosocial adjustment. *Journal of Clinical Child and Adolescent Psychology, 36*(4), 503–514.

Bowers, F. E., McGinnis, J. C., Friman, P. C., & Ervin, R. A. (1999). Merging research and practice: The example of positive peer reporting applied to social rejection. *Journal of Education and Treatment of Children, 22*(2), 218–226.

Bronfrenbrenner, U. (1978). Who needs parent education? *Teachers College Record, 79*, 767–787.

Brosse, A. L., Sheets, E. S., Lett, H. S., & Blumenthal, J. A. (2002). Exercise and the treatment of clinical depression in adults: Recent findings and future directions. *Sports Medicine, 32*, 741–760.

Callahan, P. (2004). Exercise: A neglected intervention in mental health care? *Journal of Psychiatric and Mental health Nursing, 11*, 476–483.

Chan, Y. (1994). Parenting stress and social support of mothers who physically abuse their children in Hong Kong. *Child Abuse & Neglect: The International Journal, 18*, 261–269.

Chrousos, G. P., & Gold, P. W. (1992). The concepts of stress and stress system disorders: Overview of physical and behavioral homeostasis. *Journal of the American Medical Association, 267*, 1244–1252.

Cicchetti, D., & Cohen, D. J. (2006). *Developmental psychopathology, Volume 3: Risk, disorder, and adaptation* (2nd ed.). Hoboken: Wiley.

Cicchetti, D., & Curtis, J. W. (2006). The developing brain and neural plasticity: Implications for normality, psychopathology, and resilience. In D. Cicchetti & D. J. Cohen (Eds.), *Developmental psychopathology, Volume 2: Developmental neuroscience* (2nd ed.). Hoboken: Wiley.

Cicchetti, D., & Gunnar, M. R. (2008). Integrating biological processes into the design and evaluation of preventive interventions. *Development and Psychopathology, 20*, 737–743.

Cicchetti, D., & Rogosch, F. A. (1997). The role of self-organization in the promotion of resilience in maltreated children. *Development and Psychopathology, 9*, 799–817.

Cicchetti, D., & Rogosch, F. A. (2002). A developmental psychopathology perspective on adolescence. *Journal of Consulting and Clinical Psychology, 70*(1), 6–20.

Cicchetti, D., & Rogosch, F. A. (2009). Adaptive coping under conditions of extreme stress: Multilevel influences on the determinants of resilience in maltreated children. In E. A. Skinner & M. J. Zimmer-Gembeck (Eds.), *Coping and the development of regulation. New Directions for Child and Adolescent Development* (pp. 47–59). San Francisco: Jossey-Bass.

Cicchetti, D., Rogosch, F. A., Sturge-Apple, M., & Toth, S. L. (2009). Interaction of child maltreatment and 5-htt polymorphisms: Suicidal ideation among children from low-SES backgrounds. *Journal of Pediatric Psychology, 37*(5), 536–546.

Cicchetti, D., & Toth, S. L. (1998). The development of depression in children and adolescents. *American Psychologist, 53*(2), 221–241.

Commission on the Social Determinants of Health. (2008). *Closing the gap in a generation: Health equity through action on the social determinants of health. Final Report of the Commission on Social Determinants of Health.* Geneva: World Health Organization.

Courtney, M. E., Dworsky, A., & Peters, C. M. (2009). *California's fostering connections to success act and the costs and benefits of extending foster care to 21.* Seattle: Partners for Our Children.

Davidson, R. J. (2000). Affective style, psychopathology, and resilience: Brain mechanisms and plasticity. *American Psychologist, 55*, 1196–1214.

De Bellis, M. D. (2001). Developmental traumatology: The psychobiological development of maltreated children and its implications for research, treatment, and policy. *Development and Psychopathology, 13*, 539–564.

De Bellis, M. D., Hooper, S. R., Woodley, D. P., & Shenk, C. E. (2010). Demographic, maltreatment, and neurobiological correlates of PTSD symptoms in children and adolescents. *Journal of Pediatric Psychology, 35*(5), 570–577.

Dunn, D. M., Culhane, S. E., & Taussig, H. N. (2010). Children's appraisals of their experiences in out-of-home care. *Children and Youth Services Review, 32*, 1324–1330.

Ellis, W. E., & Wolfe, D. A. (2008). Understanding the association between maltreatment history and adolescent alcohol use by examining individual and peer group conformity. *Journal of Youth and Adolescence, 37*, 359–372.

Enns, M. W., Cox, B. J., Afifi, T. O., De Graaf, R., Ten Have, M., & Sareen, J. (2006). Childhood adversities and risk for suicidal ideation and attempts: A longitudinal population-based study. *Psychological Medicine: Journal of Research in Psychiatry and the Allied Sciences, 36*(12), 1769–1778.

Evans, E., Hawton, K., & Rodham, K. (2005). Suicidal phenomena and abuse in adolescents: A review of epidemiological studies. *Child Abuse & Neglect: The International Journal, 29*(1), 45–58.

Farruggia, S. P., Greenberger, E., Chen, C., & Heckhausen, J. (2006). Perceived social environment and adolescents' well-being and adjustment: Comparing a foster care sample with a matched sample. *Journal of Youth and Adolescence, 35*(3), 349–358.

Fikke, L., Melinder, A., & Landrø, N. I. (2011). Executive functions are impaired in adolescents engaging in non-suicidal self harming. *Psychological Medicine, 41*, 601–611.

Finkelhor, D., Turner, H., Ormrod, R., & Hamby, S. L. (2009). Violence, abuse, and crime exposure in a national sample of children and youth. *Journal of Pediatrics, 124*(5), 1411–1423.

Florsheim, P. (2003). Adolescent romantic and sexual behavior: What we know and where we go from here. In P. Florsheim (Ed.), *Adolescent romantic relations and sexual behavior: Theory, research, and practical implications* (pp. 371–385). Mahwah: Lawrence Erlbaum Associates.

Friedrich, W. N. (1993). Sexual victimization and sexual behavior in children: A review of recent literature. *Child Abuse & Neglect: The International Journal, 17*(1), 59–66.

Galliher, R. V., & Bentley, C. G. (2010). Links between rejection sensitivity and adolescent romantic relationship functioning: The mediating role of problem-solving behaviors. *Journal of Aggression, Maltreatment & Trauma, 19*(6), 603–623.

Gilligan, R. (2000). The importance of listening to the child in foster care. In G. Kelly & R. Gilligan (Eds.), *Issues in foster care: Policy, practice and research.* London: Jessica Kingsley.

Goodwin, R. D. (2003). Association between physical activity and mental disorders among adults in the United States. *Preventive Medicine, 36*, 698–703.

Gordis, E. B., Granger, D. A., Susman, E. J., & Trickett, P. K. (2008). Salivary alpha amylase-cortisol asymmetry in maltreated youth. *Hormones and Behavior, 53*(1), 96–103.

Greenberg, J., Hennessy, M., Lifshay, J., Kahn-Krieger, S., Bartelli, D., Downer, A., et al. (1999). Childhood sexual abuse and its relationship to high-risk behavior in women volunteering for an HIV and STD prevention intervention. *Journal of AIDS and Behavior, 3*(2), 149–156.

Hankin, B. L. (2005). Childhood maltreatment and psychopathology: Prospective tests of attachment, cognitive vulnerability, and stress as mediating processes. *Journal of Cognitive Therapy and Research, 29*(6), 645–671.

Hashima, P., & Amato, P. (1994). Poverty, social support, and parental behavior. *Child Development, 65*, 394–403.

Haynie, D. L., South, S. J., & Bose, S. (2006). The company you keep: Adolescent mobility and peer behavior. *Sociological Inquiry, 76*(3), 397–426.

Heller, S., Larrieu, J., D'Imperio, R., & Boris, N. (1998). Research on resilience to child maltreatment: Empirical considerations. *Child Abuse & Neglect: The International Journal, 23*(4), 321–338.

Herrenkohl, T. I., Sousa, C., Tajima, E. A., Herrenkohl, R. C., & Moylan, C. A. (2008). Intersection of child abuse and children's exposure to domestic violence. *Trauma, Violence, & Abuse, 9*(2), 84–99.

Johnson, M. H. (1998). The neural basis of cognitive development. In D. Kuhn & R. Siegler (Eds.), *Handbook of child psychology: Cognition, perception, and language* (Vol. 2, pp. 1–49). New York: Wiley.

Kerig, P. K., Ward, R. M., Vanderzee, K. L., & Moeddel, M. A. (2009). Posttraumatic stress as a mediator of the relationship between trauma and mental health problems among juvenile delinquents. *Journal of Aggressive Behavior, 38*(9), 1214–1225.

Koenig, H. G., Larson, D. B., & Larson, S. S. (2001). Religion and coping with serious medical illness. *The Annals of Pharmacotherapy, 35*, 352–359.

Krug, E. G., Dahlberg, L. L., Mercy, J. A., Zwi, A. B., & Lozano, R. (2002). *World report on violence and health.* Geneva: World Health Organization.

Landers, D. M., & Petruzello, S. J. (1994). Physical activity, fitness, and anxiety. In C. Bouchard, R. J. Shephard, & T. Stephens (Eds.), *Physical activity, fitness, and health: International proceedings and consensus statement* (pp. 868–882). Champaign: Human Kinetics.

Lee, V., & Hoaken, P. N. S. (2007). Cognition, emotion, and neurobiological development: Mediating the relation between maltreatment and aggression. *Child Maltreatment, 12*, 281–298.

Luo, Q., Holroyd, T., Majestic, C., Cheng, X., Schechter, J., & Blair, R. J. (2010). Emotional automaticity is a matter of timing. *Journal of Neuroscience, 30*, 5825–5829.

Luthar, S. S. (2006). Resilience in development: A synthesis of research across five decades. In D. Cicchetti & D. J. Cohen (Eds.), *Developmental psychopathology, Volume 3: Risk, disorder, and adaptation* (2nd ed., pp. 739–795). Hoboken: Wiley.

Luther, S. S., & Zigler, E. (1992). Intelligence and social competence among high-risk adolescents. *Development and Psychopathology, 4*, 287–299.

MacMillan, H. L., Wathen, C. N., Barlow, J., Fergusson, D. M., Leventhal, J. M., & Taussig, H. N. (2009). Interventions to prevent child maltreatment and associated impairment. *Lancet, 373*(9659), 250–266.

Masten, A. S., Hubbard, J. J., Gest, S. D., Tellegen, A., Garmezy, N., & Ramirez, M. (1999). Competence in the context of adversity. Pathways to resilience and maladaptation from childhood to late adolescence. *Development and Psychopathology, 11*, 143–169.

McCrory, E., De Brito, S. A., & Viding, E. (2010). Research review: The neurobiology and genetics of maltreatment and adversity. *Journal of Child Psychology and Psychiatry, 51*(10), 1079–1095.

McGloin, J. M., & Widom, C. S. (2001). Resilience among abused and neglected children grown up. *Development and Psychopathology, 13*, 1021–1038.

Mi'kmaw Family & Children Services. (2009–2010). *Annual Report*.

Mohapatra, S., Irving, H., Paglia-Boak, A., Wekerle, C., Adlaf, E., & Rehm, J. (2010). History of family involvement with child protective services as a risk factor for bullying in Ontario schools. *Journal of Child and Adolescent Mental Health, 15*(3), 157–163.

Moretti, M. M., Obsuth, I., Odgers, C. L., & Reebye, P. (2006). Exposure to maternal vs. paternal partner violence, ptsd, and aggression in adolescent girls and boys. *Journal of Aggressive Behavior, 32*(4), 385–395.

Nangle, D. W., Erdley, C. A., Newman, J. E., Mason, C. A., & Carpenter, E. M. (2003). Popularity, friendship quantity, and friendship quality: Interactive influences on children's loneliness and depression. *Journal of Clinical Child and Adolescent Psychology., 32*(4), 546–555.

Nolin, P., & Ethier, L. (2007). Using neuropsychological profiles to classify neglected children with or without physical abuse. *Child Abuse & Neglect: The International Journal, 31*, 631–643.

Noll, J. G., Trickett, P. K., & Putnam, F. W. (2003). A prospective investigation of the impact of childhood sexual abuse on the development of sexuality. *Journal of Consulting and Clinical Psychology, 71*(3), 575–586.

Perry, B. D. (2009). Examining child maltreatment through a neurodevelopmental lens: Clinical applications of the neurosequential model of therapeutics. *Journal of Loss and Trauma, 14*, 240–255.

Pourtois, G., Spinelli, L., Seeck, M., & Vuilleumier, P. (2010). Temporal precedence of emotion over attention modulations in the lateral amygdala: Intracranial ERP evidence from a patient with temporal lobe epilepsy. *Cognitive, Affective, & Behavioral Neuroscience, 10*, 83–93.

Public Health Agency of Canada. (2010). *Canadian Incidence Study of Reported Child Abuse and Neglect: 2008 – major findings*. Ottawa: Public Health Agency of Canada.

Rak, C. F., & Patterson, L. E. (1996). Promoting resilience in at-risk children. *Journal of Counseling & Development, 74*, 368–373.

Rhodes, A., Boyle, M., Tonmyr, L., Wekerle, C., Goodman, D., Leslie, B., et al. (2011). Sex differences in childhood sexual abuse and suicide-related behaviors. *Suicide and Life-Threatening Behavior: The Official Journal of the American Association of Suicidology, 41*(3), 235–254.

Roisman, G. I., Padron, E., Sroufe, L. A., & Egeland, B. (2002). Earned-secure attachment status in retrospect and prospect. *Journal of Child Development, 73*(4), 1204–1219.

Rosewater, A., & Goodmark, L. (2007). *Steps Toward Safety: Improving Systemic and Community Responses for Families Experiencing Domestic Violence, Family Violence Prevention Fund*. Retrieved, from http://www.endabuse.org/userfiles/file/Children_and_Families/steps_toward_safety.pdf

Rutter, M. (1987). Psychosocial resilience and protective mechanisms. *American Journal of Orthopsychiatry, 57*(3), 316–331.

Rutter, M. (2000). Resilience reconsidered: Conceptual considerations, empirical findings and policy implications. In J. Shonkoff & S. Meisels (Eds.), *Handbook of early childhood intervention* (2nd ed., pp. 651–682). Cambridge: Cambridge University Press.

Sameroff, A., & Chandler, M. (1975). Transactional models in early social relations. *Human Development, 18*, 65–79.

Schenkel, L. S., Spauldinga, W. D., DiLilloa, D., & Silverstein, S. M. (2005). Histories of childhood maltreatment in schizophrenia: Relationships with premorbid functioning, symptomatology, and cognitive deficits. *Schizophrenia Research, 76*, 273–286.

Sears, H. A., & Byers, E. S. (2010). Adolescent girls' and boys' experiences of psychologically, physically, and sexually aggressive behaviors in their dating relationships: Co-occurrence and emotional reaction. *Journal of Aggression, Maltreatment & Trauma, 19*(5), 517–539.

Senn, T. E., & Carey, M. P. (2010). Child maltreatment and women's adult sexual risk behavior: Childhood sexual abuse as a unique risk factor. *Journal of Child Maltreatment, 15*(4), 324–335.

Silovsky, J. F., Niec, L., Bard, D., & Hecht, D. B. (2007). Treatment for preschool children with interpersonal sexual behavior problems: A pilot study. *Journal of Clinical Child and Adolescent Psychology, 36*(3), 378–391.

South, S. J., Haynie, D. L., & Bose, S. (2007). Student mobility and school dropout. *Social Science Research., 36*(1), 68–94.

Sternberg, R. J. (2008). Increasing fluid intelligence is possible after all. *Proceedings of the National Academy of Sciences of the United States of America, 105*(19), 6791–6792.

Susman, E. J. (2006). Psychobiology of persistent antisocial behavior: Stress, early vulnerabilities and the attenuation hypothesis. *Neuroscience & Biobehavioral. Reviews, 30*, 376–389.

Taussig, H. N., Clyman, R. B., & Landsverk, J. (2001). Children who return home from foster care: A 6-year prospective study of behavioral health outcomes in adolescence. *Journal of Pediatrics, 108*(1), e10.

Taussig, H. N., Culhane, S. E., & Hettleman, D. (2007). Fostering healthy futures: An innovative preventive intervention for preadolescent youth in out-of-home care. *Child Welfare: Journal of Policy, Practice, and Program, 86*(5), 113–131.

Taussig, H. N., Garrido, E. F., & Crawford, G. (2009). Use of a web-based data system to conduct a randomized controlled trial of an intervention for children placed in out-of-home care. *Social Work Research, 33*(1), 55–66.

Taylor, P., Moore, P., Pezzullo, L., Tucci, J., Goddard, C., & De Bortoli, L. (2008). *The cost of child abuse in Australia*. Melbourne: Australian Childhood Foundation and Child Abuse Prevention Research Australia.

Tonmyr, L., Li, Y., Williams, G., Scott, D., & Jack, S. M. (2010). Patterns of reporting by health care and non-health care professionals to child protection services in Canada. *Journal of the Canadian Paediatric Society, 15*(8), e25–e32.

Travis, W. J., & Combs-Orme, T. (2007). Resilient parenting: Overcoming poor parental bonding. *Social Work Research, 31*, 135–149.

Trickett, P. K., & Putnam, F. W. (1998). *Developmental consequences of child sexual abuse.* Washington: American Psychological Association.

Trocmé, N., Fallon, B., MacLaurin, B., Sinha, V., Black, T., Fast, E., et al. (2010). *Canadian Incidence Study of Reported Child Abuse and Neglect: Characteristics of maltreatment.* Ottawa: Public Health Agency of Canada.

Ungar, M. (2007). *Too safe for their own good.* Toronto: McClelland and Stewart. United States Department of Health and Human Services, Administration for Children and Families, Administration on Children, Youth and Families, Children's Bureau. (2010). *Child Maltreatment 2008.* Washington: U.S. Government Printing Office. Retrieved, from http://www.acf.hhs.gov/programs/cb/stats_research/index.htm#can.

Ungar, M. (2008). Resilience across cultures. *British Journal of Social Work, 38*(2), 218–235.

Vinnerljung, B., Sundell, K., Lofholm, C. A., & Humlesjo, E. (2006). Former stockholm child protection cases as young adults: Do outcomes differ between those that received services and those that did not? *Children and Youth Services Review, 28*(1), 59–77.

Volz, A. R., & Kerig, P. K. (2010). Relational dynamics associated with adolescent dating violence: The roles of rejection sensitivity and relational insecurity. *Journal of Aggression, Maltreatment, and Trauma, 19*, 587–602.

Weiss, J., Waechter, R., Wekerle, C., & The MAP Research Team. (2011). The impact of emotional abuse on psychological distress among child protective services-involved adolescents with borderline-to-mild intellectual disability. *Journal of Child and Adolescent Trauma, 4*(2), 142–159.

Wekerle, C., & Avgoustis, E. (2003). Child maltreatment, adolescent dating, and adolescent dating violence. In P. Florsheim (Ed.), *Adolescent romantic relations and sexual behavior: Theory, research and practical implications* (pp. 213–241). Hillsdale: Erlbaum.

Wekerle, C., Leung, E., Goldstein, A., Thornton, T., & Tonmyr, L. (2009). *Up against a wall: Coping with becoming a teen. (Substance use among adolescents in child welfare versus adolescents in the general population: A comparison of the Maltreatment and Adolescent Pathways [MAP] longitudinal study and the Ontario Student Drug Use Survey [OSDUS] datasets).* London: University of Western Ontario.

Wekerle, C., Leung, E., MacMillan, H. L., Boyle, M., Trocmé, N., & Waechter, R. (2009). The contribution of childhood emotional abuse to teen dating violence among child protective services-involved youth. *Child Abuse & Neglect: The International Journal, 33*, 45–58.

Wekerle, C., Waechter, R., Leung, E., & Chen, M. (2009). Chapter 6: Children and youth served by Ontario's Children's Aid Societies. In *Profile of Ontario's Children and Youth,* Ontario Ministry of Children & Youth Services Internal Policy Document.

Wekerle, C., & Wall, A.-M. (2002). *The violence and addiction equation: Theoretical and clinical issues in substance abuse and relationship violence.* New York: Brunner-Routledge.

Wekerle, C., Wall, A.-M., Leung, E., & Trocmé, N. (2007). Cumulative stress and substantiated maltreatment: The importance of caregiver vulnerability and adult partner violence. *Child Abuse & Neglect: The International Journal, 31*, 427–443.

Wekerle, C., & Wolfe, D. A. (1998). The role of child maltreatment and attachment style in adolescent relationship violence. *Journal of Development and Psychopathology, 10*, 571–586.

Wilsnack, S. C., Vogeltanz, N. D., Klassen, A. D., & Harris, T. R. (1997). Childhood sexual abuse and women's substance abuse: National survey findings. *Journal of Studies on Alcohol, 58*(3), 264–271.

Wolfe, D. A., Crooks, C., Jaffe, P., Chiodo, D., Hughes, R., Ellis, W., et al. (2009). A school-based program to prevent adolescent dating violence. *Archives of Pediatric and Adolescent Medicine, 163*(8), 692–699.

Wolfe, D. A., Wekerle, C., Scott, K., & Pittman, A. L. (2003). Dating violence prevention with at-risk youth: A controlled outcome evaluation. *Journal of Consulting and Clinical Psychology, 71*, 279–291.

Yates, T. M. (2004). The developmental psychopathology of self-injurious behavior: Compensatory regulation in posttraumatic adaptation. *Journal of Psychology Review, 24*(1), 35–74.

Young, E. A., Abelson, J., & Cameron, O. G. (2005). Interaction of brain noradrenergic system and the hypothalamic–pituitary–adrenal (HPA) axis in man. *Psychoneuroendocrinology, 30*, 807–814.

Averting Child Maltreatment: Individual, Economic, Social, and Community Resources that Promote Resilient Parenting

Kimberly DuMont, Susan Ehrhard-Dietzel, and Kristen Kirkland

Eighty percent of child abuse and neglect reports concern actions perpetrated by parents. The majority (70%) of these acts occur when children are between the ages of birth and age 7 (U.S. Department of Health and Human Services, 2010). The highest incidence rates of child maltreatment occur during infancy and the first few years of life when the mother and child are most isolated. During the preschool and early school years, the number of direct and indirect influences affecting parenting and the child's well-being grows exponentially. Experiences outside of the home become increasingly relevant for mother and child with the transitions to preschool and elementary school. Consequently, the nature of potential factors associated with a child's care and safety shifts from those related to the prenatal and birth experience to the quality of the child rearing and home and community environments. Thus, while the mother or partnering caregiver may remain consistent throughout the child's development, the kinds of support available to help her avoid engaging in child abuse and neglect change as the child develops. Understanding what factors compensate or counteract the adversities present has important implications for the healthy development of the mother, the child, and their relationship. Resilience theory provides a useful framework for understanding why some mothers at risk for abuse or neglect do not maltreat.

Resilience is often described as an individual achievement whereby a child, parent, or victim demonstrates successful behavior in spite of the adversity present in their lives (Luthar & Zelazo, 2003). The focus of this definition implicitly directs clinicians and researchers to explore qualities of the individual that may account for variations in his or her success, such as level of motivation or the presence of coping skills. Other factors within an individual's environment, however, may also help to strengthen individual resources (Ungar, 2006, 2011). These factors include the availability of and access to other nurturing caregivers, economic resources, and respite from daily stress.

While a wealth of information exists regarding potential risks for child abuse and neglect (Berger, 2004; Kotch, Browne, Dufort, & Winsor, 1999; Slack, Holl, McDaniel, Yoo, & Bolger, 2004), information regarding factors that promote resilient parenting is limited. Identifying what characteristics of individuals and resources in their environments support strategies that compensate for challenges to healthy parenting will enhance child rearing and inform the development and refinement of more effective and efficient prevention and intervention strategies.

As a first step toward demonstrating support for this process, we conducted a survey of the

K. DuMont (✉)
New York State's Office of Children
and Family Services, Bureau of Evaluation
and Research, Rensselaer, NY, USA
e-mail: Kimberly.DuMont@ocfs.state.ny.us

literature on parenting and child maltreatment to identify potential qualities or resources within the child, mother, social network, and community that may offset the adversities present in families' lives. Using longitudinal data from a sample of mothers who were determined while pregnant or shortly after the birth of their newborn to be at risk to maltreat, we then systematically assessed potential resources that may promote mother's resilience (e.g., not maltreating despite identified risks). Specifically, we tested the ability of select variables to explain the behavior of mothers who had no record of a child protective services (CPS) report between study initiation and the target child's seventh birthday as compared to a group of at-risk women who were confirmed subjects of child maltreatment. The goal was to identify factors in the lives of these women that are both amenable to change and make resilience more likely.

In this chapter, we briefly review the relevant literature. In doing so, we attend to two important questions: (1) Within an environment of identified risks to maltreat, do factors that promote resilience simply represent the other end of a risk continuum? or (2) Are there certain levels of resources required before they can effectively compensate for the demand characteristics of the environment to maltreat?

Characteristics of the Child

Maltreated children are victims and are not to be blamed for the abuse or neglect they experience. Nevertheless, certain characteristics of children have been linked to maltreatment. These characteristics include health issues and developmental and behavioral problems (Brown, Cohen, Johnson, & Salzinger, 1998; Scannapieco & Connell-Carrick, 2005; Zelenko, Lock, Kraemer, & Steiner, 2000). Although there is a general view that difficult child temperament or behavior may elicit neglectful and/or abusive parental behavior (Windham et al., 2004), temperament or behavior may also play a promotive role. For example, Kochanska, Friesenborg, Lange, and Martel (2004) found a positive effect for infants' expression of

joy and maternal responsive parenting. Similarly, in their comparison of mother–infant relationships with irritable and nonirritable infants, van den Boom and Hoeksma (1994) found that mothers of nonirritable infants were more interactive with and more responsive to their child. Thus, whether considering potential risk or promotive factors, existing evidence provides some support for the idea that children's physical and emotional status plays a contributing role to parenting and the perpetration or prevention of child maltreatment (Belsky, 1993).

Maternal Activities, Characteristics, and Resources

Breastfeeding. The child's immediate and long-term functioning and mothers' subsequent parenting may be influenced by the quality of the child's prenatal care, birth, and first few months of life. Traditionally, poor birth outcomes are framed as risks for poor future outcomes. For example, neonatal medical problems, low birth weight, and birth complications have been linked to maltreatment (McCormick, 1985; Zelenko et al., 2000). Conversely, quality prenatal care, a full-term delivery, a healthy birthweight, and being breastfed may help to establish quality caregiving during the initial months of the child's life and help to promote positive long-term outcomes.

The benefits of breast-feeding, both to the health of infants (Anderson, Johnstone, & Remley, 1999; Hanson, 1998) and to mothers, are, in particular, well known. Compared to mothers who bottle-feed, the breast-feeding experience may provide mothers with lower levels of stress (Mezzacappa & Katkin, 2002; Weisenfeld, Malatesta, Whitman, Grannose, & Vile, 1985), decreased negative mood (Else-Quest, Hyde, & Clark, 2003; Mezzacappa & Katkin, 2002), a stronger sense of knowing their child, and less anxiety in being able to assess and respond to the needs of the child (Virden, 1988). Breast-feeding may also facilitate the development of a positive mother–infant relationship (Lavelli & Poli, 1998; Wojnar, 2004), although results regarding the duration of these effects are mixed (Britton, Britton, & Gronwaldt, 2006; Else-Quest et al., 2003; Strathearn, Mamun, Najman, & O'Callaghan, 2009).

Explanations for the effects of breast-feeding on maternal emotion and on the maternal–infant relationship range from those pertaining to physical factors, including the role of hormones on mood, to preexisting psychological and sociological factors (see Jansen, de Weerth, & Riksen-Walraven, 2008; Mezzacappa & Katkin, 2002). Research also indicates that breast and bottle-feeding mothers differ with respect to age, employment, socio-economic status, and ethnicity (see Dennis, 2002 and Jansen et al., 2008 for a review), although further studies are needed to understand the mechanisms at play. Nevertheless, the research is suggestive of breast-feeding as a factor facilitative of nonabusive and nonneglectful parenting. Furthermore, Else-Quest et al. (2003) contend that breast-feeding may be particularly beneficial where other caregiving resources are lacking, such as socioeconomic resources and other risk factors for child maltreatment.

Emotional and physical well-being. Much research points to the influence of maternal emotional and physical well-being on child maltreatment. Most studies focus on risk factors, such as depression and physical illness, finding that mothers experiencing poor emotional and/or physical health are more likely to maltreat their children (Brown et al., 1998; Chaffin, Kelleher, & Hollenberg, 1996; Hildyard & Wolfe, 2007; Kotch et al., 1999; Wekerle, Wall, Leung, & Trocme, 2007). A few studies have revealed evidence supporting a conceptualization of positive well-being as a promotive factor. Turner, Lloyd, and Roszell (1999) found that persons who feel they have the capacity to influence the circumstance of their lives, those high in mastery (Pearlin & Schooler, 1978), were more likely to possess the skills and abilities needed to manage difficult circumstances, circumstances such as those faced by at-risk mothers. Thus, mastery may be a personal resource that assists at-risk mothers from engaging in abusive and/or neglectful parenting. It may also be a resource for positive parenting

behavior. Ardelt and Eccles (2001) suggest that parents who believe that their behavior will have a positive effect on their children are more likely to use parenting strategies that cultivate children's skills and interests. Furthermore, there is some empirical support for the role of mastery as a promotive factor in parenting. Jackson and Scheines (2005), for example, found a positive association between maternal level of mastery and quality of maternal parenting in the home environment. Ardelt and Eccles (2001) found mother's belief in her capacity to influence her circumstances to be a positive and significant predictor of cognitively stimulating and responsive parenting strategies.

Maternal sensitivity. Research concerning the etiology of child maltreatment typically points to qualities that are lacking among nonmaltreating mothers. For example, maltreating parents have been found to be characterized by low levels of parental involvement, warmth, and empathy (Brown et al., 1998; Connell-Carrick & Scannapieco, 2006; Kotch et al., 1999; Slack et al., 2004), to exhibit poor connections with their children (Connell-Carrick & Scannapieco, 2006; Scannapieco & Connell-Carrick, 2005), and to have difficulty appropriately labeling infants' emotions and recognizing infants' feelings of interest (Hildyard & Wolfe, 2007).

In contrast, in one of the few studies to isolate the presence of characteristics or resources that may promote healthy parenting practices, Egeland, Breitenbucher, and Rosenberg (1980) found that nonmaltreating mothers were more emotionally responsive and sensitive to their infants' cues and were better at timing the infant's feeding than maltreating mothers. Nonmaltreating mothers also had more appropriate attitudes towards the infant's aggression, indicating that mothers who do not maltreat may inherently be more empathic or more skilled in their approach to parenting. Similarly, a mother's understanding of appropriate attitudes and behaviors may be said to reflect the knowledge and skills she possesses that prevent her from maltreating her child/children (Bavolek & Keene, 1999). Thus, even within a high stress environment, personal qualities and/or parenting skills may assist mothers in averting abuse and neglect and being resilient to the risk to maltreat.

Socioeconomic Resources

Education. Research on child maltreatment generally assumes that maternal education is a risk factor. Although studies support this, finding an association between low maternal education level and child maltreatment (Brown et al., 1998; Kotch et al., 1999), theoretical explanations for this relationship are lacking. Education need not be assumed to be a risk factor. While lacking a high school diploma may put a parent at risk for maltreatment, a high level of education – one that exceeds the completion of high school – may offset other risks or subsequent adversities and help avoid abusive or neglectful parenting. One's level of education may speak to her knowledge of child development; her capacity to gather information and resources; and to perceive, integrate, and apply appropriate parenting behavior. Little research has explored level of educational attainment as a promotive factor, although the findings of Klebanov et al. (1994) are suggestive; they found a positive association between mother's level of education and maternal warmth.

Maternal Income and Employment. Much research indicates the significance of family income as a risk factor in child maltreatment (Berger, 2004), particularly for neglect (Brown et al., 1998; Chaffin et al., 1996; Kotch et al., 1999; Scannapieco & Connell-Carrick, 2005), and especially among single parents (Berger, 2005). Likewise, unemployment may be associated with neglect (Hildyard & Wolfe, 2007). Researchers have speculated that lower income and unemployment are associated with higher rates of welfare receipt, which in turn is associated with increased contact with the child welfare system (Lindsey, 1994) as a result of either heightened surveillance and detection or higher incidence of actual child maltreatment among poor or unemployed parents. In the current study, we propose that a mother's access to income and employment status be conceived of as resources. Income denotes the availability of finances that enables mothers to provide an environment where children are not neglected, to access resources for respite from childcare, and to flee an environment that is threatening (Berger, 2005). Similarly, employment provides mothers with access to positive social influences, while also reducing their opportunity to maltreat.

Social Resources and Supportive Networks

Social support is one of the few potential promotive factors to be addressed in the literature on child maltreatment. While some research grounds the measurement of social support in a strong theoretical framework (Hashima & Amato, 1994), other studies include a measure of social support either as a control variable or as a possible promotive factor, but with little explanation as to why social support might matter. Measurement is often broad, nonspecific, and inconsistent across studies. For example, Slack et al. (2004) define social support as the availability of material and emotional support (they do not specify from whom), whereas Chaffin et al. (1996) define it as the availability of a confidante, including friends, family, clergy, or any other informal source, with whom the respondent had discussed personal problems in the past year.

Measures of social support also often fail to make a distinction between sources of social support and types of social support. Support received from family may be different from that received from a partner or from friends, and tangible support may be different from emotional support (Crnic, Greenberg, Ragozin, Robinson, & Basham, 1983). The meaning and quality of social support is lost when it is measured broadly. Interestingly, not one of these studies found a significant effect for social support on child maltreatment. In the current study, we explicate and evaluate the role of three specific types of support: a supportive partner, informal support, and involvement with religious activities.

Supportive partner or spouse. Partners may help compensate for adverse circumstances by making an economic contribution, by caring for, teaching, and playing with the child, and by providing emotional support to the child's mother (Lamb & Tamis-Lemonda, 2004). Dubowitz, Black, Kerr, Starr, and Harrington (2000) examined the association between the involvement of father figures and child neglect among a sample of families at high risk for maltreatment, finding that neglect was less likely when the father was involved for a longer period of time, expressed more parenting effectiveness, and was involved in more household tasks. Dubowitz et al. (2000) suggest that the significance of the duration of father involvement may reflect the consistency of the relationship as well as a level of family stability. Along similar lines, Fagan and Palkovitz (2007) found that the more intimate the relationship between the father and the child's mother, the more involved the father was in childcare. Somewhat surprisingly, Dubowitz et al. (2000) did not find a significant effect for fathers' provision of economic support. They suggest that this finding may be explained by the fact that their sample involved mostly poor families where fathers' financial contributions may have been meager and inconsistent.

Informal sources of support. Partners, family members, and friends may be a resource, but the support and social integration they provide is only promotive if the values, norms, and activities they share serve to reduce the likelihood of child maltreatment. For example, in situations where others' advice constitutes negative parenting practices or is critical of the mother's parenting or other behavior, their "support" may exacerbate the often-cited risk factor of stress rather than diminish it. However, when these contributions reflect constructive parenting behavior, they can compensate for adversities and facilitate the avoidance of neglectful or harmful parenting (Chen & Kaplan, 2001; Cox et al., 1985).

In their study of the role of social support, Crnic et al. (1983) found a significant and positive effect of support from a partner on mothers'

parenting behaviors and their satisfaction with parenting. Coohey (1995) found that, compared with the partners of neglectful moms, nonneglectful moms' partners provided more companionship and more help with babysitting. Nonneglectful moms were also found to have more contact with their partners, to be married to or living with their partners, and to have at least one child with their partners. These findings are notable in that they point to the commitment and longevity of the mom–partner relationship, and speak to the findings of Dubowitz et al. (2000) regarding family stability, discussed earlier.

In addition to partner and family, friends may be a critical resource. For example, Crnic et al. (1983) found a significant effect of friendship support on mothers' satisfaction with parenting. Similarly, Manji, Maiter, and Palmer (2005) found friends to be a primary source of support, particularly emotional support but also tangible support provided in the form of help with transportation, childcare, and links to employment opportunities. Manji et al. (2005) identified a link between emotional support and childcare, noting that help with babysitting provided a respite for moms.

Religious Participation. Religious participation may help mothers navigate towards resilience by fostering a sense of belonging and togetherness. Unfortunately, research on the role of religious participation in child maltreatment is limited. However, in their study comparing neglectful mothers with nonneglectful mothers, Polansky, Gaudin, Ammons, and Davis (1985) found that 72% of nonneglectful mothers reported belonging to and attending a church more frequently, compared with 62% of neglectful mothers. Similarly, the literature from related fields documents that religiosity (how important religion is to someone) has some promotive influence on violence and adolescent mental health and behaviors (Baier & Wright, 2001; Ball, Armistead, & Austin, 2003; Benda & Toombs, 2000; Evans, Cullen, Dunaway, & Burton, 1995). Therefore, we included religion as a potential contributor to the quality of mother's mental health and parenting activities.

Community Resources

In contrast to the study of individual-level factors, which is more empirically than theoretically driven, the study of the influence of neighborhood level factors on child maltreatment is guided by consideration of how and why elements of the community setting may affect the likelihood of maltreatment. The contributing role of the environment to individual-level behavior was most notably explicated by Bronfrenbrenner (1974, 1977) and later Belsky (1980). They emphasized the importance of examining the larger context, viewing the behavior of individuals as nested within their surroundings, and conceptualizing contextual factors as resources encouraging the achievement of positive development. For example, in his application of Bronfrenbrenner's (1974) model to his study of neighborhood child maltreatment rates, Garbarino (1976) discussed the extent to which the immediate setting "nurtures" the parent–child interaction. In a similar vein, Coleman's (1988) well-known model of financial, human, and social capital is predicated on the identification of factors as resources. His notion of social capital in particular and the related concept of collective efficacy (see Sampson, Raudenbush, & Earls, 1997) have been used to explain the potential influence of neighborhood characteristics on child maltreatment.

Accordingly, Kohen, Leventhal, Dahinten, and McIntosh (2008) suggest that "the effects of social organization on parental behaviors such as maltreatment may result, in part, from the lack of community regulation of parenting behaviors" (p. 157). Residents who may not know and do not trust their neighbors, such as those living in areas with high rates of crime or residential mobility, may be wary of intervening in the supervision and control of children. Indeed, Sampson et al. (1997) argue that "one is unlikely to intervene in a neighborhood context in which the rules are unclear and people mistrust or fear one another" (p. 919). Residents may fear retaliation either by children and/or by the children's parents who may have different standards about what types of behavior call for reprimand and by whom (Korbin & Coulton, 1997).

Indeed, related research suggests that a mother's perception of her surroundings influences her parenting practices (Furstenberg, 1993; Jarrett, 1997). For example, Kriesberg (1970) found that mothers who perceived their neighborhoods to be dangerous and wrought with negative influences were more likely to use physical punishment as a parenting strategy, compared with mothers who described their neighborhoods more positively. Garbarino and Sherman (1980) found that mothers in a low, compared with a high, maltreatment neighborhood were more likely to have neighborhood children as playmates for their own children and were more likely to engage in neighborhood exchanges.

Along similar lines, Garbarino and Sherman (1980) also found a significant relationship between the neighborhood rating and the type of community services mothers use; mothers rating their neighborhoods as better places to raise their children reported greater use of recreational services (such as Boy Scouts) compared with treatment and rehabilitative services. In contrast, Korbin and Coulton (1997) found that, compared with low maltreatment neighborhoods, families in high maltreatment neighborhoods described their neighborhoods as fearful, distrustful, deteriorating, and lacking in services and supports. Parents' fears of their neighborhoods prevented them from using available resources, including playgrounds, which can be a source of interpersonal activity and support (Korbin & Coulton, 1997). This suggests that parents' perception of their neighborhood may influence their activities and the types of support services they utilize for assistance with childcare. However, the finding may also reflect differences in the perception of or actual availability of services.

In the remainder of this chapter we explore the influence of promotive factors in achieving resilience to child abuse and neglect among a sample of at-risk mothers, an indicator that has substantial implications for the child's development and long-term outcomes. We include in our analyses measures of each of the potential qualities or resources discussed in the literature: characteristics of the child, maternal characteristics, socioeconomic resources, social resources and supportive networks, and perceived neighborhood safety.

Methods

This study uses information available in a longitudinal dataset to explore whether the factors identified help to explain why a group of mothers assessed to be at risk for child abuse and neglect never engage in these behaviors. The longitudinal assessment of resilience combined with the analysis of varied and theoretically postulated supporting factors among a diverse group of mothers will help strengthen the body of knowledge regarding the promotion of resilience to maltreatment.

Evaluation Design

In 2000, the New York State Office of Children and Family Services' Bureau of Evaluation and Research, in partnership with the Center for Human Services Research at the University at Albany, initiated a randomized controlled trial in three counties to evaluate Healthy Families New York (HFNY), a home-visiting program designed to prevent child abuse and neglect. The program targets expectant parents and parents with an infant less than 3 months of age who have characteristics that place them at high risk for child abuse or neglect and who live in vulnerable communities marked by high rates of poverty, infant mortality, and teen pregnancy. Collaborating community agencies and individual HFNY programs identify and screen prospective families. Families who screen positive are referred to the HFNY program in their community, where they are systematically assessed by trained Family Assessment Workers for the presence of specific risk factors that place families at risk for child abuse or neglect using the Kempe Family Stress Checklist (Kempe, 1976). Families are eligible for the HFNY program if either parent scores at or above the established cutoff of 25 on the Kempe. Those who score below 25 on the checklist are ineligible to receive home-visiting services, but are provided with referrals to, and information on, other available community services. Recruitment for the study was conducted between March 2000 and August 2001 at three sites with long-standing HFNY programs. Women

eligible for HFNY at each site were randomly assigned to either an intervention group that was offered HFNY services or to a control group that was given information and referrals to other appropriate services.

Baseline interviews were conducted with 1,173 of the eligible women (intervention=579; control=594) in their homes. Follow-up interviews with study participants were conducted at the time of the child's birth (if applicable, $n=564$), and first ($n=1,060$) and second birthdays ($n=992$). A subset of respondents were assessed at age 3 ($n=522$). When the child was 7 years old, field staff completed 942 interviews with the original study participants. Study retention rates were high, with 90% of the women reinterviewed at Year 1, 85% reinterviewed at Year 2, and 80% at Year 7 ($n=942$) (see DuMont et al., 2008 for a complete description of the design for the randomized controlled trial).

Sample

For the present analysis, the sample was restricted to women in the control group who completed the baseline interview and gave birth to our target child ($n=591$). We chose to limit our analyses to women in the control group because the intervention group received services intended to reduce the likelihood of child abuse and neglect. It is likely that the receipt of such services influenced the relationships between the potential promotive factors and indicators of resilience for this group of women. The sample was further restricted to 524 women who had information available for all of the variables of interest. There were no significant differences in maternal risk factors or demographic characteristics between the 524 women who were included in the sample and the 67 women who were excluded due to missing data.

Procedures

Participating mothers and their children were typically assessed in their homes by a trained interviewer who was independent of the HFNY program and blind to group assignment. Interview data was collected using touch-screen laptop computers equipped with a Computer-Assisted Personal Interviewing (CAPI) system. Interviews generally took about 60–75 min to complete. If the mother was unable to complete the interview in a face-to-face setting or lived farther than a reasonable driving distance, interviews were conducted over the phone. At all waves of data collection, the research protocol was approved by the Institutional Review Board of the University of Albany.

Measures

Information for the current study come from data extracted from administrative databases describing experiences between the time of random assignment and target child's seventh birthday, and baseline and Year 1 interviews with study respondents.

Maternal risk factors. Maternal risk factors were assessed using the Kempe Family Stress Checklist (Kempe, 1976). This instrument taps a variety of life domains and is a widely used tool for predicting parents' future risk of maltreating their children. Previous studies have documented its association with abusive and neglectful parenting practices (Korfmacher, 2000).

Demographics. We included three relevant demographic characteristics from the baseline interview to describe mother's age, mother's race/ethnicity, and the target child's gender. Specifically, mother's age was represented by a dummy-coded variable indicating whether or not she was under 19 years of age at random assignment (1 = under 19; 0 = 19 or over). Two dummy-coded variables were used to represent mother's race/ethnicity: White, non-Hispanic, and Hispanic women vs. the reference group of African American, non-Hispanic women. We also included a variable representing the target child being female, with male being the reference group.

Promotive factors. We measured a series of promotive factors within the four distinct domains discussed earlier: child, parent, socioeconomic, social network, and community. Where possible,

we tried to isolate the highest functioning members of the sample within each domain to more fairly assess the potential of factors to promote resilience.

Child characteristics were reflected by a measure of having no identified disabilities within a year of birth, as indicated by items in the baseline, birth, and Year 1 interviews (as appropriate). This variable was dummy-coded, with 1 representing no identified disability and 0 representing an identified disability.

Maternal characteristics and resources were reflected by measures indicative of the five qualities discussed earlier: breastfeeding, emotional and physical well-being, maternal sensitivity, education, and maternal income and resources. In the Year 1 interview, mothers were asked whether and for how long they breastfed the target child. We used this information to create two dummy variables describing breastfeeding from 1 to 3 months, and breastfeeding for 4 months or more, with not breastfeeding as the reference group.

Three variables were used to represent mother's emotional and physical well-being. Two of these variables, emotional well-being and physical functioning, are subscales of the Rand SF-36-Item Health Survey (SF 36) (Hays, Sherbourne, & Mazel, 1993). The SF 36 is an indicator of health status and measures the effects of poor health on the ability to work, fulfill family responsibilities, engage in recreational and social activities, and perform activities of daily living. Higher scores reflect better functioning. A dummy variable for healthy emotional well-being was created by coding the top third of scores as 1 and the bottom two-thirds as 0. We also created a dummy variable to reflect no reported limitations in physical functioning. Those with a score of 100, reflecting no limitations, were coded 1, while those who scored below 100 were coded 0. The third variable within this domain is sense of control or mastery over life, which was measured using the Mastery of Psychological Coping Resources Scale (PSM) (Pearlin & Schooler, 1978). This instrument measures an individual's perceived capacity to influence the events and circumstance in one's life. Higher scores indicate better mastery. We used the total score for this instrument to create a variable reflecting positive mastery, with individuals who scored within the top third being coded as 1, and those in the lower two-thirds as 0.

We used two subscales from the Adult-Adolescent Parenting Inventory (AAPI) to represent maternal sensitivity (Bavolek & Keene, 1999). The AAPI measures attitudes regarding parenting and child-rearing. Individuals scoring in the sixth stanine or higher, which reflected positive parenting, were coded as 1 for both the appropriate expectations regarding child development and the empathic awareness of children's needs subscales. Individuals scoring below this cutoff were coded as 0.

Maternal education, income, and employment were measured with three variables: having greater than a high school education (1), mother being employed within the last 3 years (1), and having any income at random assignment (1). The absence of each characteristic served as the reference group.

Social resources and supportive networks were measured by variables reflecting a supportive partner, nondirective counseling, respite from childcare, and involvement with religious activities. Supportive partner refers to the presence of a spouse or partner and no domestic violence. Factor loadings of items from the Index of Socially Supportive Behaviors (ISSB) (Barrera, Sandler, & Ramsay, 1981) were used to create measures of nondirective counseling and access to respite care. Higher scores indicated greater support. Religious involvement was measured with a dummy coded variable where recent participation in religious activities was coded 1 and nonparticipation 0.

Community resources were represented by a variable describing the overall perceived safety of the neighborhood. This variable was created by reverse coding and averaging two items on a four-point scale: perception of the neighborhood as safe during the day and perception of neighborhood as safe at night. We then coded scores that were greater than or equal to 3.5 as 1, representing the safest neighborhoods, and scores below 3.5 as 0.

Resilience. Official reports of abuse and neglect were used to develop an indicator of resilience. Person-based searches of CONNECTIONS, the NYS Statewide Automated Child Welfare Information System, were conducted in order to determine whether mothers were ever the confirmed subject in an indicated NYS CPS investigation. This system tracks calls made to the NYS child abuse and neglect hotline from intake through investigation conclusion, and maintains the information in a searchable database. We abstracted data from these reports regarding the outcome of the investigation, the type or types of maltreatment involved, and the subjects and victims involved. For the purposes of the following analyses, resilience was defined as the mother not being the confirmed subject of a substantiated CPS report at any time between random assignment and the child's seventh birthday. Given the severity of risk faced by these women, the ability to refrain from abusing or neglecting a child for this sustained period of time is significant and serves as a proxy for healthier parenting practices.

Data Analysis

Descriptive statistics were conducted to examine the frequency with which categorical variables occurred and to obtain the mean values for interval variables. Bivariate correlations were examined between potential promotive factors to determine the strength of their relationships with each other. We used logistic regression models to analyze resilience to the initiation of child maltreatment post random assignment. Risk was assessed on the first step of the model to account for the variance explained by the levels of risk present in respondents' lives and to describe its limiting effects on opportunities for resilience. Demographic covariates were entered in the second step, and conceptually grouped potential promotive factors were entered on each subsequent step to assess their ability to compensate for the levels of risk present and increase the odds of being resilient.

Results

About one-third (35%) of the 524 mothers in the study sample were White, non-Hispanic; 17% were Hispanic, and 46% were African American, non-Hispanic. Similar to women deemed eligible for the HFNY program, women in the study sample were often young (29% under 19), first-time mothers (53%), and had not yet completed high school or received a GED (51%).

Risk to Maltreat

A necessary condition of resilience is the presence of some known adversity or challenge. We used the Kempe Family Stress Checklist (Kempe, 1976) to describe the risks present in families' lives as of random assignment. By virtue of their eligibility for the study, all women in the sample were at risk to maltreat and had considerable levels of adversity in their lives. Table 17.1 reveals some of the risks faced by the sample. More than half the mothers were victims of abuse or neglect as a child. Nearly a third of the mothers had records of mental illness or delinquent behavior,

Table 17.1 Kempe family stress checklist: maternal risk factors at random assignment ($n=524$)

	Rate or mean (SD) (%)
Kempe family stress checklist (% with severe rating)	
Beaten or deprived as child	57.6
Has criminal record, mental illness, or substance history	29.6
Suspected of abuse in the past	5.7
Low self-esteem, isolation or depression	38.7
Multiple stresses or crises	61.1
Violent temper outbursts	17.4
Rigid, unrealistic expectations of child	7.9
Harsh punishment of child	11.2
Child difficult and/or provocative or perceived to be by mother	1.2
Child unwanted or at risk for poor bonding	28.8
Kempe family stress checklist – average total	41.8 (13.5)

and many were prone to violent outbursts. Women frequently faced multiple stresses or crises in their lives, with a substantial number having low self-esteem and feeling isolated.

Extreme risk was defined as receiving a score of 40 or more on the Kempe assessment for child abuse and neglect. Fifty-eight percent of the women in this sample had a score of 40 or more. Scores lower than 40, while still indicating the presence of multiple and moderate levels of risk, were viewed as less adverse.

Potential Promotive Factors

Despite experiencing the risks above, a substantial number of families do not maltreat their children. What makes mothers "resilient" to perpetrating child maltreatment? Table 17.2 shows the domains and factors we identified through our review of the literature as having the potential to offset or compensate for risk. The items and scales summarized in Table 17.2 are primarily informed by the baseline interview. As shown, well over two-thirds of the women report having a supportive partner. About half the women report excellent physical health, and 82% report employment at some point within the past 3 years. Over a quarter report living in neighborhoods they perceive to be very safe. The data thus reveal the presence of resources that may serve to offset or buffer the influence of the multitude of risks faced by these women.

Next we examined whether the factors identified increased the odds that mothers would be resilient despite considerable risks to abuse or neglect their child. Prior to evaluating a multivariate model, we examined bivariate correlations among promotive factors. Correlations were generally low, with more than three-quarters of the variables having r values under 0.10. The strongest correlations were observed between the two types of social support: nondirective counseling and respite care ($r=0.56, p<0.001$), appropriate expectations and empathy ($r=0.48, p<0.001$), employment and income ($r=0.33, p<0.001$), education and employment ($r=0.24, p<0.001$), and education and income ($r=0.21,$

Table 17.2 Descriptive statistics for promotive factors ($n=524$)

Child characteristics (postbirth)	Rate or mean (sd)
Full-term with no identified disabilities within a year of the birth	89.7%
Maternal characteristics and resources	
Breastfeeding	
Breastfed for 1–3 months (assessed at Year 1)	15.6%
Breastfed for 4 months or more (assessed at Year 1)	16.8%
Emotional and physical well-being	
Emotional well-being (top third)	35.1%
No reported limitation of physical functioning	42.6%
Sense of control/mastery over life (top third)	36.8%
Maternal sensitivity (score in sixth stanine or higher)	
Appropriate expectations regarding child development	30.2%
Empathic awareness of children's needs	18.5%
Maternal income and employment	
Educational level exceeds high school	26.9%
Employment in past 3 years	81.9%
Any income at random assignment	32.6%
Social resources and supportive networks	
Supportive spouse/partner	70.6%
Non directive counseling	3.6 (0.9)
Access to respite care	2.6 (1.0)
Recent participation in religious activities	30.2%
Community resources	
Perception of neighborhood as very safe	26.3%

$p<0.001$). All other correlations were under 0.20. Thus, treating the proposed factors as individual predictors is appropriate, and concerns regarding multicollinearity were largely eliminated, except for the few cases noted above.

Promoting Resilience: Risks and Resources

More than three-fourths of the sample (79%) was considered resilient by the target child's seventh birthday. Table 17.3 shows the results of multivariate models that included risk and promotive factors as well as covariates to determine what qualities and circumstances of mothers' lives relate to resilience. The table displays nine models. The first model presents associations between adverse maternal risk factors and maternal resilience engaging in maltreatment. As expected, documented risk has the potential to jeopardize opportunities for resilience: Kempe scores 40 or higher significantly decrease the likelihood of being resilient by a factor of 0.22. As indicated by the r square in the bottom row of the table, exceptionally high levels of risk explain 11% of the variance.

The second model illustrates the relationship between the mother's demographic characteristics and maternal resilience. As a set, demographic characteristics increased the amount of variance explained by 2% ($p=0.18$). Being Hispanic was associated with increased odds of being resilient. Mothers who were Hispanic were 2.2 times more likely to be resilient than mothers who were African American, non-Hispanic. Across the first 7 years of the target child's life, the child's gender did not significantly affect the odds that mothers would refrain from maltreating.

The third through ninth models show the role played by the factors in each of the compensatory domains. Each domain was entered separately, allowing us to examine the effect of each new domain on the previously entered domains. The associations between the variables entered into the model and prevalence of child maltreatment did not change when characteristics of the child was entered (model 3). An additional 2% of the variance ($p<0.05$) was explained when the breastfeeding domain was entered in model 4. Breastfeeding for a relatively short period of time, from 1 to 3 months, did not significantly increase the odds of maternal resilience to maltreatment. However, the odds of being resilient were 3 times higher for mothers who sustained breastfeeding for 4 months or more. Mother's physical and emotional well-being and mastery were entered via model 5. Unexpectedly, these factors were not significantly associated with being resilient in a multivariate model, either as individual factors or a set. In addition, once healthy parenting attitudes and socioeconomic resources were added to the model, although still

Table 17.3 Effects of risk and promotive factors on substantiated reports of child abuse and neglect

Factor	Model 1 OR (95% CI)	Model 2 OR (95% CI)	Model 3 OR (95% CI)
Maternal risk factors			
Kemp score of 40 or higher	0.22 (0.13–0.38)***	0.24 (0.14–0.41)***	0.24 (0.14–0.42)***
Demographics			
Mother's age			
Under 19 years		1.04 (0.64–1.69)	1.02 (0.62–1.66)
Mother's race/ethnicity			
White, non-Hispanic		1.45 (0.88–2.39)	1.48 (0.89–2.43)
Hispanic		2.20 (1.08–4.49)*	2.28 (1.11–4.67)*
Target child's gender			
Female		1.15 (0.74–1.79)	1.16 (0.74–1.80)
Promotive factors			
No disabilities immediately identified			1.31 (0.66–2.60)
Breastfeeding			
1–3 months			
4 months or more			
Emotional well-being			
Excellent physical functioning			
Sense of control/mastery			
Appropriate expectations of child development			
Empathic awareness of children's needs			
Educational level exceeds high school			
Employment in past 3 years			
Any income at random assignment			
Supportive spouse/partner			
Non directive counseling			
Access to respite care			
Recent participation in religious activities			
Perception of neighborhood as very safe			
r-square[a]	0.11***	0.13***	0.13***
Factor	**Model 4 OR (95% CI)**	**Model 5 OR (95% CI)**	**Model 6 OR (95% CI)**
Maternal risk factors			
Kemp score of 40 or higher	0.26 (0.15–0.44)***	0.27 (0.16–0.47)***	0.28 (0.16–0.50)***
Demographics			
Mother's age			
Under 19 years	1.10 (0.67–1.80)	1.01 (0.67–1.81)	0.67 (0.39–1.18)
Mother's race/ethnicity			
White, non-Hispanic	1.44 (0.87–2.38)	1.44 (0.87–2.38)	1.19 (0.71–2.02)
Hispanic	2.15 (1.04–4.47)*	2.19 (1.05–4.57)*	2.15 (1.02–4.53)*
Target child's gender			
Female	1.15 (0.74–1.79)	1.16 (0.74–1.81)	1.13 (0.72–1.78)
Promotive factors			
No disabilities immediately identified	1.23 (0.62–2.46)	1.23 (0.61–2.45)	1.25 (0.62–2.53)
Breastfeeding			
1–3 months	1.14 (0.62–2.11)	1.13 (0.61–2.10)	1.09 (0.58–2.06)
4 months or more	3.02 (1.31–6.93)**	3.02 (1.31–6.93)**	2.78 (1.20–6.44)*

(continued)

Factor	Model 4 OR (95% CI)	Model 5 OR (95% CI)	Model 6 OR (95% CI)
Emotional well-being		1.14 (0.70–1.87)	1.16 (0.70–1.91)
Excellent physical functioning		0.99 (0.62–1.56)	1.12 (0.70–1.79)
Sense of control/mastery		1.16 (0.72–1.89)	1.04 (0.64–1.72)
Appropriate expectations of child development			1.69 (0.91–3.13)[+]
Empathic awareness of children's needs			3.14 (1.31–7.55)**
Educational level exceeds high school			
Employment in past 3 years			
Any income at random assignment			
Supportive spouse/partner			
Non directive counseling			
Access to respite care			
Recent participation in religious activities			
Perception of neighborhood as very safe			
r-square[a]	0.15***	0.15***	0.19***

Factor	Model 7 OR (95% CI)	Model 8 OR (95% CI)	Model 9 OR (95% CI)
Maternal risk factors			
Kemp score of 40 or higher	0.30 (0.17–0.54)***	0.31 (0.17–0.55)***	0.31 (0.17–0.55)***
Demographics			
Mother's age			
Under 19 years	0.97 (0.53–1.78)	0.87 (0.46–1.62)	0.88 (0.47–1.64)
Mother's race/ethnicity			
White, non-Hispanic	1.07 (0.62–1.85)	1.11 (0.63–1.96)	0.98 (0.54–1.76)
Hispanic	2.90 (1.32–6.35)*	3.03 (1.35–6.83)**	2.87 (1.27–6.47)**
Target child's gender			
Female	1.16 (0.73–1.85)	1.16 (0.72–1.86)	1.19 (0.74–1.91)
Promotive factors			
No disabilities immediately identified	1.02 (0.49–2.13)	0.93 (0.44–1.96)	0.93 (0.44–1.96)
Breastfeeding			
1–3 months	0.93 (0.48–1.80)	0.94 (0.48–1.82)	0.95 (0.49–1.85)
4 months or more	2.71 (1.15–6.36)**	3.10 (1.29–7.45)**	3.13 (1.30–7.52)**
Emotional well-being	1.17 (0.70–1.96)	1.11 (0.66–1.87)	1.10 (0.65–1.87)
Excellent physical functioning	1.20 (0.74–1.93)	1.25 (0.77–2.03)	1.29 (0.79–2.11)
Sense of control/mastery	0.87 (0.51–1.46)	0.87 (0.51–1.49)	0.88 (0.51–1.50)
Appropriate expectations of child development	1.56 (0.83–2.92)	1.67 (0.88–3.17)	1.63 (0.85–3.10)
Empathic awareness of children's needs	3.18 (1.30–7.81)**	3.16 (1.28–7.84)**	3.21 (1.30–7.97)**
Educational level exceeds high school	1.32 (0.70–2.48)	1.24 (0.64–2.38)	1.19 (0.62–2.30)
Employment in past 3 years	2.22 (1.20–4.11)**	2.17 (1.17–4.04)*	2.12 (1.34–3.96)*
Any income at random assignment	2.05 (1.13–3.72)*	2.12 (1.16–3.88)*	2.06 (1.12–3.78)*
Supportive spouse/partner		1.21 (0.72–2.02)	1.21 (0.72–2.02)
Non directive counseling		0.94 (0.67–1.31)	0.94 (0.67–1.32)
Access to respite care		1.37 (0.99–1.91)[+]	1.35 (0.97–1.89)[+]
Recent participation in religious activities		1.11 (0.61–1.91)	1.07 (0.62–1.89)
Perception of neighborhood as very safe			1.61 (0.86–3.05)
r-square[a]	0.24***	0.25***	0.26***

[+]$p<0.10$, *$p<0.05$, **$p<0.01$, ***$p<0.001$

[a]Nagelkerke pseudo r-square

nonsignificant, the direction of association between mastery and resilience changed, suggesting that a sense of control and mastery in and of itself is not necessarily promotive of resilience. Healthy parenting attitudes, entered in model 6, explained an additional 4% of the variance ($p<0.01$). Empathic awareness of the child's needs significantly increased the odds of the mother being resilient. Although only marginally significant, having appropriate expectations about child development also increased the odds of the mother being resilient. Given the moderately high correlation between the two parenting characteristics and the increase in variance explained for this set of variables, both appropriate expectations and empathic parenting attitudes may contribute to resilience.

The percentage of variance explained significantly increased (5%; $p<0.001$) when education, employment, and income were entered into the model; being employed at some point in the last 3 years and having income at random assignment both significantly increased the odds of the mother being resilient.

The addition of informal and familial supports increased the variance explained by only 1%. The odds of being resilient were 1.37 times higher for mothers who had access to respite care than for mothers who did not ($p<0.10$). Although mothers' perception of their neighborhood as safe contributed to an increase in the overall variance explained by the model (26%), the individual factor was not a significant predictor of resilience. Overall, the promotive factors explained 13% of the variance, a level equivalent to the amount of variance explained by heightened levels of risk combined with demographic factors. The relationship between the promotive factors and resilience generally behaved in the direction expected and highlight a few domains that may help to guide policy.

Discussion

The analyses suggest the importance of a diverse array of factors in the sustained and successful avoidance of child abuse and neglect among a sample of women at risk to maltreat. The explanatory power of promotive factors individually and collectively indicates that resilience does not simply represent the other end of a risk continuum but reflects the presence of considerable and accessible resources that compensate for a range of adversities. These resources include characteristics and activities of the mother, socioeconomic resources, and social resources available in the community in which she and her child live.

As discussed earlier, the literature suggests the promotive effect of several individual and socioeconomic factors in preventing child maltreatment, but is weak in providing theoretical explanations for such relations. Given the findings of the present study, it is especially important to address this gap.

Early conceptualizations of resilience emphasized that abilities within an individual, such as stamina, hardiness, and optimism, are needed to generate an adaptive response to an adverse condition, regardless of the stressor or outcome (Rutter, 2000; Smith, 1999; Ungar, 2011). Consistent with this individual-oriented interpretation, mothers' capacities alone would be viewed as producing resilient parenting, while contributions from other ecological systems would be viewed as minimal. In contrast, Coleman's (1988) model of human, financial, and social capital highlights the influence of social and community factors on behavior and provides a conceptual link between the characteristics of individuals and their environments (Furstenberg & Hughes, 1995). The model suggests that an individual's own capacities and resources, as well as those around her, help her navigate towards positive outcomes, understood here to be the achievement of nonneglectful and nonabusive parenting.

While individual-oriented interpretations of resilience and theories of capital overlap in their recognition of qualities within an individual that may help to avert a poor outcome, the two approaches diverge in the degree to which they attribute resilient outcomes to be the product of individual factors, and, by extension, evoke different implications for practice. With respect to individual-oriented interpretations of resilience, existing behaviors and thoughts within the individual provide the focal point for therapy or intervention, which strives to nurture and reinforce individual qualities. In comparison, interventions based on the capital model have multiple goals, including identifying or fostering sources of human capital, creating supportive social and community networks, and strengthening the connections between individual resources and compensating factors within the larger environment, such as opportunities for employment, education, or respite care. Given the potential for such a diverse set of personal, social, and environmental factors to compensate for the risk to maltreat, the capital model offers a unifying theoretical framework within which to interpret the chapter's results and offer recommendations for policy and practice.

According to Coleman (1988), human capital is "embodied in the skills and knowledge of an individual" (p. S100). It reflects the potential for a "cognitive environment" (Coleman, 1988, p. S109) that aids in the achievement of nonneglectful and nonabusive parenting. It may be reflected in the characteristics of the parent, such as her emotional and physical health, her attitudes and behaviors about parenting, her sensitivity to the needs of her children, and her capacity to gather and utilize information and resources. Results from the current study reaffirm the role of human capital in promoting resilience, including qualities of the mother such as empathic parenting attitudes and appropriate expectations. In addition, and consistent with results from a recent 15-year prospective study conducted in Australia (Strathearn et al., 2009), breastfeeding for 4 months or more emerged as a key compensatory factor, offsetting risks to maltreat, and improving the odds of resilience by about a factor of three. In contrast, breastfeeding for only a short duration did not contribute to resilience. Collectively, the findings underscore the need to identify exceptional qualities or activities to compensate for risks rather than considering behavior and capacities on a continuum, and the need to promote these factors. For example, while sustained breastfeeding may indicate a particular resolve or determination on the part of the mother, external support such as a lactation consultant or supportive work environment may help mothers more effectively negotiate this challenge and reach the same level of activity.

Financial capital "provides the physical resources that can aid achievement" (Coleman, 1988, p. S109). It is reflected principally by the economic resources of the parent, i.e., her employment and income. Notably, mother's employment may not only be an indicator of financial capital but social capital as well, as employment provides mothers with access to potentially positive influences. Results reported here suggest that, independently and as a set, access to financial capital and resources supporting the achievement of financial capital were associated with significantly higher odds of attaining resilience. Findings also imply that interventions that enhance expectant and new mothers' opportunities for employment and income, and policies that support their ability to sustain these resources, such as quality child care and paid leave, offer promising and enduring returns.

The third element of Coleman's theory is social capital, which encapsulates the relationships among people, institutions, and organizations. The embodiment of social capital depends on the existence of social relations as well as the characteristics of those relationships, particularly trust, and shared values, norms, and expectations (Coleman, 1988). As mentioned earlier, social capital may not be a promotive resource if shared norms reflect an acceptance of poor parenting. While Coleman's notion of social capital has been used to explain the influence of neighborhood characteristics on child maltreatment, we propose its application to the influence of social networks as well. In the current study, results regarding the role of social networks in the promotion of resilience were mixed. While access to respite care appears to play a marginally significant role in avoiding maltreatment, significant findings did not emerge for the other indicators of social support.

Studies addressing the influence of formal and informal sources of support for other outcomes point to their complexity. These studies suggest that in addition to looking at who is providing the support and the type of support being provided, as was done in the current study, it may also be necessary to explore the individual's ability to navigate access to and use of the support and the partner or community's ability to negotiate the provision of support (Barth, 1991; Ungar, 2011 forthcoming). Egeland et al. (1980) studied mothers experiencing high levels of stress who maltreated their child and mothers experiencing high levels of stress who did not maltreat their child. They found that the nonmaltreating mothers had more support and were better at seeking out support in times of need. They also found that compared with nonmaltreating mothers, maltreating mothers were more suspicious, defensive, and rigid, and had more difficulty trusting others. Egeland et al. suggest that these characteristics make it more difficult for these mothers to seek support from agencies, family, and friends, and to build and maintain relationships. As a result of the challenges nested within the person, communities may need to provide home-based or more comprehensive services to help mothers at risk capitalize on potentially promotive resources (Barth, 1991).

As with many studies, our ability to assess all potential promotive factors of resilience in this chapter was limited by the data available. For example, the current study did not explore the contributing role of parents' understanding of children's and their own competence and responsibility to resilience given a lack of data about mother's attributional style. However, the success of interventions that include cognitive and behavioral components for parents suggests that this maybe a fruitful avenue of research. For example, both Bugental et al. (2002) and Chaffin et al. (2004) found lower levels of harsh or physically abusive parenting among at-risk moms in an intervention group compared with those in a control group. These studies suggest that an understanding of parent–child attributions and an understanding of appropriate responses to children's aversive behavior may offset risks for abuse.

Most notably absent from the current study are census-derived indicators of neighborhood resources that would allow us to more appropriately assess how a neighborhood's socioeconomic composition fosters norms and supports that promote resilient parenting. While ratings of perceived neighborhood safety were used to approximate the presence of constructive standards and norms, additional research is needed to examine how measures of neighborhood social and economic resources affect the child-rearing environment and parenting behaviors.

A second important limitation of the current study was its restricted focus on only one aspect of resilient parenting: averting abusive or neglectful behavior for a sustained period of time, when the risk to maltreat is the greatest. As a reminder, approximately 70% of all child abuse and neglect reports occur for children from birth to age 7 years (U.S. Department of Health and Human Services, 2010). While this sustained aversion is an important ingredient, the construct of resilience implies more than just avoidance of a poor indicator. In future work, we will compare resilient mothers to nonresilient mothers to see if they engaged in healthier parenting practices and whether their children showed signs of being well-adjusted cognitively, emotionally, and behaviorally.

Recent developments in the practice of prevention of child maltreatment have resulted in a number of strength-based parenting models that have the potential to promote resilient parenting. These programs typically (i) focus on families who live within a context of disadvantage, (ii) target new or expectant parents, and (iii) initiate their efforts either prenatally or during the first few years of the child's life. The hope is that by bolstering a family's supports and resources during a time of heightened vulnerability, it will help to offset or moderate the consequences posed by the risks (Fraser, Kirby, & Smokowski, 2004; Wright & Masten, 2005). The current research provides evidence in support of the value of these efforts, and also offers guidance on how to refine existing models or develop more targeted services to better promote resilient and more adept parenting. These efforts will, in turn, likely benefit the safe development of children in families who face significant risk.

Acknowledgements This research was supported in part by an award from the Doris Duke Charitable Foundation (Grant # 2006102).

References

Anderson, J. W., Johnstone, B. M., & Remley, D. T. (1999). Breast-feeding and cognitive development: A meta-analysis. *American Journal of Clinical Nutrition, 70*, 525–535.

Ardelt, M., & Eccles, J. S. (2001). Effects of mothers' parental efficacy beliefs and promotive parenting strategies on inner-city youth. *Journal of Family Issues, 22*, 944–972.

Baier, C. J., & Wright, B. R. E. (2001). If you love me, keep my commandments: A meta-analysis of the effect of religion on crime. *Journal of Research in Crime and Delinquency, 38*, 3–21.

Ball, J., Armistead, L., & Austin, B. (2003). The relationship between religiosity and adjustment among African American, female, urban adolescents. *Journal of Adolescence, 26*, 431–446.

Barrera, M., Jr., Sandler, I. N., & Ramsay, T. B. (1981). Preliminary development of a scale of social support: Studies on college students. *American Journal of Community Psychology, 9*, 435–447.

Barth, R. P. (1991). An experimental evaluation of in-home child abuse prevention services. *Child Abuse & Neglect, 15*, 363–375.

Bavolek, S. J., & Keene, R. G. (1999). *Adult-adolescent parenting inventory (AAPI-2): Administration and development handbook*. Park City: Family Development Resources Inc.

Belsky, J. (1980). Child maltreatment: An ecological integration. *American Psychologist, 35*, 320–335.

Belsky, J. (1993). Etiology of child maltreatment: A developmental-ecological analysis. *Psychological Bulletin, 114*, 413–434.

Benda, B. B., & Toombs, N. J. (2000). Religiosity and violence – are they related after considering the strongest predictors? *Journal of Criminal Justice, 28*, 483–496.

Berger, L. M. (2004). Income, family structure, and child maltreatment risk. *Children and Youth Services Review, 26*, 725–748.

Berger, L. M. (2005). Income, family characteristics, and physical violence toward children. *Child Abuse & Neglect, 29*, 107–133.

Britton, J. R., Britton, H. L., & Gronwaldt, V. (2006). Breastfeeding, sensitivity, and attachment. *Pediatrics, 118*, 1436–1443.

Bronfrenbrenner, U. (1974). Developmental research, public policy, and the ecology of childhood. *Child Development, 45*, 1–5.

Bronfrenbrenner, U. (1977). Toward an experimental ecology of human development. *American Psychologist, 32*, 513–531.

Brown, J., Cohen, P., Johnson, J. G., & Salzinger, S. (1998). A longitudinal analysis of risk factors for child maltreatment: Findings of a 17-year prospective study of officially recorded and self-reported child abuse and neglect. *Child Abuse & Neglect, 22*, 1065–1078.

Bugental, D. B., Ellerson, P. C., Lin, E. K., Rainey, B., Kokotovic, A., & O'Hara, N. (2002). A cognitive approach to child abuse prevention. *Journal of Family Psychology, 16*, 243–258.

Chaffin, M., Kelleher, K., & Hollenberg, J. (1996). Onset of physical abuse and neglect: Psychiatric, substance abuse, and social risk factors from prospective community data. *Child Abuse & Neglect, 20*, 191–203.

Chaffin, M., Silovsky, J., Funderburk, B., Valle, L. A., Brestan, E. V., Balachova, T., et al. (2004). Parent–child interaction therapy with physically abusive parents: Efficacy for reducing future abuse reports. *Journal of Consulting and Clinical Psychology, 72*, 491–499.

Chen, Z., & Kaplan, H. B. (2001). Intergenerational transmission of constructive parenting. *Journal of Marriage and Family, 63*, 17–31.

Coleman, J. S. (1988). Social capital in the creation of human capital. *American Journal of Sociology, 94*, S95–S120.

Connell-Carrick, K., & Scannapieco, M. (2006). Ecological correlates of neglect in infants and toddlers. *Journal of Interpersonal Violence, 21*, 299–316.

Coohey, C. (1995). Neglectful mothers, their mothers, and partners: The significance of mutual aid. *Child Abuse & Neglect, 19*, 885–895.

Cox, M. J., Owen, M. T., Lewis, J. M., Riedel, C., Scalf-McIver, L., & Suster, A. (1985). Intergenerational influences on the parent-infant relationship in the transition to parenthood. *Journal of Family Issues, 6*, 543–564.

Crnic, K. A., Greenberg, M. T., Ragozin, A. S., Robinson, N. M., & Basham, R. B. (1983). Effects of stress and social support on mothers and premature and full-term infants. *Child Development, 54*, 209–217.

Dennis, C. (2002). Breastfeeding initiation and duration: A 1990–2000 literature review. *Journal of Obstetric, Gynecologic, & Neonatal Nursing, 31*, 12–32.

Dubowitz, H., Black, M. M., Kerr, M. A., Starr, R. H., Jr., & Harrington, D. (2000). Fathers and child neglect. *Archives of Pediatrics and Adolescent Medicine, 154*, 135–141.

DuMont, K. A., Mitchell-Herzfeld, C., Greene, R., Lee, E., Lowenfels, A., Rodriguez, M., et al. (2008). Healthy families New York randomized trial: Effects on early child abuse and neglect. *Child Abuse & Neglect, 32*, 295–315.

Egeland, B., Breitenbucher, M., & Rosenberg, D. (1980). Prospective study of the significance of life stress in the etiology of child abuse. *Journal of Consulting and Clinical Psychology, 48*, 195–205.

Else-Quest, N. M., Hyde, J. S., & Clark, R. (2003). Breastfeeding, bonding, and the mother-infant relationship. *Merrill-Palmer Quarterly, 49*, 495–517.

Evans, D. T., Cullen, F. T., Dunaway, R. G., & Burton, V. S. (1995). Religion and crime reexamined: The impact of religion, secular controls, and social ecology on adult criminality. *Criminology, 33*, 195–217.

Fagan, J., & Palkovitz, R. (2007). Unmarried, nonresident fathers' involvement with their infants: A risk and resilience perspective. *Journal of Family Psychology, 21*, 479–489.

Fraser, M. W., Kirby, L. D., & Smokowski, P. R. (2004). Risk and resilience in childhood. In M. W. Fraser (Ed.), *Risk and resilience in childhood* (pp. 13–66). Washington: NASW Press.

Furstenberg, F. F. (1993). How families manage risk and opportunity in dangerous neighborhoods. In W. J. Wilson (Ed.), *Sociology and the public agenda* (pp. 231–258). California: Sage Publications.

Furstenberg, F. F., & Hughes, M. E. (1995). Social capital and successful development among at-risk youth. *Journal of Marriage and Family, 57*, 580–592.

Garbarino, J. (1976). A preliminary study of some ecological correlates of child abuse: The impact of socioeconomic stress on mothers. *Child Development, 47*, 178–185.

Garbarino, J., & Sherman, D. (1980). High-risk neighborhoods and high-risk families: The human ecology of child maltreatment. *Child Development, 51*, 188–198.

Hanson, L. (1998). Breastfeeding provides passive and likely long-lasting active immunity. *Annals of Allergy, Asthma and Immunology, 81*, 523–537.

Hashima, P. Y., & Amato, P. R. (1994). Poverty, social support, and parental behavior. *Child Development, 65*, 394–403.

Hays, R. D., Sherbourne, C. D., & Mazel, R. M. (1993). The RAND 36-item health survey 1.0. *Health Economics, 2*, 217–227.

Hildyard, K., & Wolfe, D. (2007). Cognitive processes associated with child neglect. *Child Abuse & Neglect, 31*, 895–907.

Jackson, A. P., & Scheines, R. (2005). Single mothers' self-efficacy, parenting in the home environment, and children's development in a two-wave study. *Social Work Research, 29*, 7–20.

Jansen, J., de Weerth, C., & Riksen-Walraven, J. M. (2008). Breastfeeding and the mother-infant relationship-A review. *Developmental Review, 28*, 503–521.

Jarrett, R. L. (1997). Bringing families back in: Neighborhood effects on child development. In J. Brooks-Gunn, G. J. Duncan, & J. L. Aber (Eds.), *Neighborhood poverty* (Vol. II, pp. 48–64). New York: Russell Sage.

Kempe, H. (1976). *Child abuse and neglect: The family and the community*. Cambridge: Ballinger Publishing Company.

Klebanov, P. K., Brooks-Gunn, J., & Duncan, G. J. (1994). Does neighborhood and family poverty affect mothers' parenting, mental health, and social support? *Journal of Marriage and Family, 56*, 441–455.

Kochanska, G., Friesenborg, A. E., Lange, L. A., & Martel, M. M. (2004). Parents' personality and infants' temperament as contributors to their emerging relationship. *Journal of Personality and Social Psychology, 86*, 744–759.

Kohen, D. E., Leventhal, T., Dahinten, V. S., & McIntosh, C. N. (2008). Neighborhood disadvantage: Pathways of effects for young children. *Child Development, 79*, 156–169.

Korbin, J. E., & Coulton, C. J. (1997). Understanding the neighborhood context for children and families: Combining epidemiological and ethnographic approaches. In J. Brooks-Gunn, G. J. Duncan, & J. L. Aber (Eds.), *Neighborhood poverty* (Vol. II, pp. 65–79). New York: Russell Sage.

Korfmacher, J. (2000). The Kempe family stress inventory: A review. *Child Abuse & Neglect., 24*, 129–140.

Kotch, J. B., Browne, D. C., Dufort, V., & Winsor, J. (1999). Predicting child maltreatment in the first 4 years of life from characteristics assessed in the neonatal period. *Child Abuse & Neglect, 23*, 305–319.

Kriesberg, L. (1970). *Mothers in poverty: A study of fatherless families*. Illinois: Aldine.

Lamb, M. E., & Tamis-Lemonda, C. S. (2004). The role of the father: An introduction. In M. E. Lamb (Ed.), *The role of the father in child development* (4th ed., pp. 1–31). Hoboken: Wiley.

Lavelli, M., & Poli, M. (1998). Early mother-infant interaction during breast- and bottle-feeding. *Infant Behavior and Development, 21*, 667–684.

Lindsey, D. (1994). *The welfare of children*. New York: Oxford University Press.

Luthar, S. S., & Zelazo, L. B. (2003). Research on resilience: An integrative review. In S. S. Luthar (Ed.), *Resilience and vulnerability: Adaptation in the context of childhood adversities* (pp. 510–550). Cambridge: Cambridge University Press.

Manji, S., Maiter, S., & Palmer, S. (2005). Community and informal social support for recipients of child protective services. *Children and Youth Services Review, 27*, 291–308.

McCormick, M. C. (1985). The contribution of low birth weight to infant mortality and childhood morbidity. *New England Journal of Medicine, 312*, 82–90.

Mezzacappa, E. S., & Katkin, E. S. (2002). Breast-feeding is associated with reduced perceived stress and negative mood in mothers. *Health Psychology, 21*, 187–193.

Pearlin, L. I., & Schooler, C. (1978). The structure of coping. *Journal of Health and Social Behavior, 19*, 2–21.

Polansky, N. A., Gaudin, J. M., Ammons, P. W., & Davis, K. B. (1985). The psychology of the neglectful mother. *Child Abuse & Neglect, 9*, 265–275.

Rutter, M. (2000). Resilience reconsidered: Conceptual considerations, empirical findings, and policy implications. In J. P. Shonkoff & S. J. Meisels (Eds.), *Handbook of early childhood intervention* (2nd ed., pp. 651–682). New York: Cambridge University Press.

Sampson, R. J., Raudenbush, S. W., & Earls, F. (1997). Neighborhoods and violent crime: A multilevel study of collective efficacy. *Science, 277*, 918–924.

Scannapieco, M., & Connell-Carrick, K. (2005). Focus on the first years: Correlates of substantiation of child maltreatment for families with children 0 to 4. *Children and Youth Services Review, 27*, 1307–1323.

Slack, K., Holl, J. L., McDaniel, M., Yoo, J., & Bolger, K. (2004). Understanding the risks of child neglect:

An exploration of poverty and parenting characteristics. *Child Maltreatment, 9*, 395–408.

Smith, G. (1999). Resilience concepts and findings: Implications for family therapy. *Journal of Family Therapy, 21*, 154–158.

Strathearn, L., Mamun, A., Najman, J., & O'Callaghan, M. (2009). Does breastfeeding protect against substantiated child abuse and neglect? A 15-year cohort study. *Pediatrics, 123*, 483–493.

Turner, R. J., Lloyd, D. A., & Roszell, P. (1999). Personal resources and the social distribution of depression. *American Journal of Community Psychology, 27*, 643–672.

U.S. Department of Health and Human Services, Administration for Children and Families, Administration on Children, Youth and Families, Children's Bureau. (2010). Child Maltreatment 2008. Retrieved Jan 8, 2010, from http://www.acf.hhs.gov/programs/cb/stats_research/index.htm#ca.

Ungar, M. (2006). Pathways to resilience among children in child welfare, corrections, mental health and educational settings: Navigation and negotiation. *Child & Youth Care Forum, 34*(6), 423–444.

Ungar, M. (2011). The social ecology of resilience: Addressing contextual and cultural ambiguity of a nascent construct. *American Journal of Orthopsychiatry, 81*(1), 1–17.

van den Boom, D. C., & Hoeksma, J. B. (1994). The effect of infant irritability on mother-infant interaction: A growth-curve analysis. *Developmental Psychology, 30*, 581–590.

Virden, S. F. (1988). The relationship between infant feeding method and maternal role adjustment. *Journal of Nurse Midwifery, 33*, 31–35.

Weisenfeld, A., Malatesta, C., Whitman, P., Grannose, C., & Vile, R. (1985). Psychophysiological response of breast and bottle-feeding mothers to their infants' signals. *Psychophysiology, 22*, 79–86.

Wekerle, C., Wall, A., Leung, E., & Trocme, N. (2007). Cumulative stress and substantiated maltreatment: The importance of caregiver vulnerability and adult partner violence. *Child Abuse & Neglect, 31*, 427–443.

Windham, A. M., Rosenberg, L., Fuddy, L., McFarlane, E., Sia, C., & Duggan, A. K. (2004). Risk of mother-reported child abuse in the first 3 years of life. *Child Abuse & Neglect, 28*, 645–667.

Wojnar, D. (2004). Maternal perceptions of early breastfeeding experiences and breastfeeding outcomes at 6 weeks. *Clinical Effectiveness in Nursing, 8*, 93–100.

Wright, M. O., & Masten, A. S. (2005). Resilience processes in development: Fostering positive adaptation in the context of adversity. In S. Goldstein & R. B. Brooks (Eds.), *Handbook of resilience in children* (pp. 17–37). New York: Springer.

Zelenko, M., Lock, J., Kraemer, H. C., & Steiner, H. (2000). Perinatal complications and child abuse in a poverty sample. *Child Abuse & Neglect, 24*, 939–950.

Caring Relationships: How to Promote Resilience in Challenging Times

18

Gill Windle and Kate M. Bennett

This chapter examines the potential for resilience within the context of caring relationships, mainly from the perspective of the adult carer. They may be caring for children, spouses or parents with a range of complex problems, such as health or behavioural issues. We will examine the contexts of care provision, exploring what contributes to, or eases the challenge of care provision across the life course. In doing so, we will identify the factors that build resilience for the caregiver in the face of significant challenges.

Resilience Framework

To identify the factors that may promote or detract from resilience, it is important first to be clear about what exactly resilience is, and what we mean when we use the term. The complexities of defining what appears to be the relatively simple concept of resilience are widely recognised, especially within the behavioural sciences (e.g. Haskett, Nears, Ward, & McPherson, 2006; Kaplan, 1999; Luthar, Cicchetti, & Becker, 2000; Masten, 2007; Ungar, 2011). To inform the debate, an extensive review of over 270 resilience research articles, synthesised through the method

of concept analysis together with stakeholder validation, generated the following definition:

> Resilience is the process of negotiating, managing and adapting to significant sources of stress or trauma. Assets and resources within the individual, their life and environment facilitate this capacity for adaptation and 'bouncing back' in the face of adversity. Across the life course, the experience of resilience will vary (Windle, 2011).

In the context of caregiving, this definition identifies a number of factors that may increase the risk to the caregiver or act to enhance resilience (see Fig. 18.1). The key point is that the outcome of resilience is not super functioning or flourishing; rather it should reflect the maintenance of normal development or functioning (e.g. mental or physical health), or 'better than expected' development or functioning, given exposure to the adversity under question. This framework is used to inform the chapter and highlights how resilience operates across multiple levels, which interact with each other. These levels reflect the human ecology framework, also described as Ecological Systems Theory (Bronfenbrenner, 1994). Although mainly used for understanding child development, this theory has been receiving considerable attention in the gerontology literature and is cited in the resilience literature (e.g. Harney, 2007; Ungar, 2011) Reflecting this theory, the framework aims to understand people in the environments in which they live and to evaluate their interactions with these environments. People do not exist in isolation but interact with, and are influenced by, their physical, social and environmental contexts.

G. Windle (✉)
Dementia Services Development Centre,
Institute of Medical and Social Care Research,
Bangor University, Bangor, Wales, UK
e-mail: g.windle@bangor.ac.uk

M. Ungar (ed.), *The Social Ecology of Resilience: A Handbook of Theory and Practice*,
DOI 10.1007/978-1-4614-0586-3_18, © Springer Science+Business Media, LLC 2012

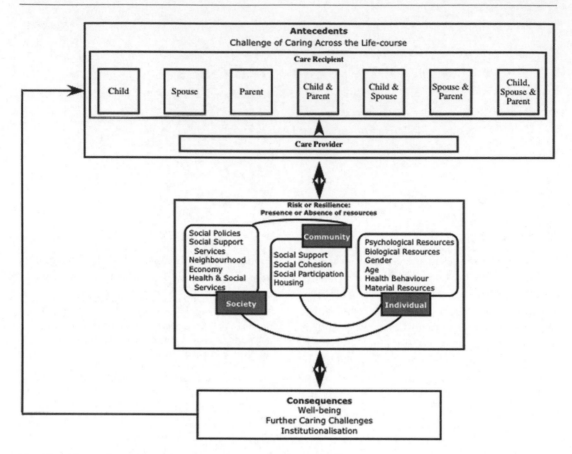

Fig. 18.1 The resilience framework in the context of caring relationships

Methods

For this chapter, we sought information from a number of sources. A previous review of resilience research using systematic principles (Windle, 2011) established a database of research abstracts (1989–2009). These were searched using keyword combinations resilience and carers or caregivers or care providers or social support. A further search was run in Social Sciences Cambridge Scientific Abstracts (ASSIA, Medline, PsycInfo), Web of Science and CINAHL to update those found previously. Statistics on caregiving were identified from population surveys. Broader information on the impact of caregiving was identified in relevant systematic reviews and national policy evaluations.

A Comment on the Evidence

When considering resilience in the context of caregiving, the majority of work in this area has focused on the carers of older adults (≥60 years old) and relatively little has focused on the carers of younger ages. As a result, this chapter focuses more often on caring for older adults, but it is clear that many of the factors that foster resilient caregiving for older adults are relevant to caring for younger adults, adolescents and children with complex needs. Likewise, caregiving occurs across the lifespan, and it is not uncommon for children and adolescents to provide significant care to a parent (Dearden & Becker, 2004).

Caring in the United Kingdom

The increasing rate of informal care given to older adults, in particular, has been driven by demographic changes both in the age structures and in family structures. The last decade of the twentieth century witnessed the effects of increased longevity and increases in the proportion over 60% of national populations. At the same time, fertility is declining. This demographic transition within societies has affected the shape of the family; the number within a single generation has become smaller but the number of living generations has increased. Economists often portray the demographic changes within the context of dependency ratios. The dependency ratio tells us how many young people (under 16 years of age) and older people (over 64 years of age) depend on people of working age (16–64 years). Although there is much debate about the reliability of dependency ratios, these ratios are expected to rise across Europe from 24 to 49% between 2000 and 2050 (Bond & Cabrero, 2007). There have also been considerable changes in household composition and family structure. In most European countries, a trend towards increasing numbers of people living alone and decreasing numbers of three generation or extended family households has been well documented (Tomassini, Glaser, Wolf, Broese van Groenou, & Grundy, 2004). This changing demographic profile can present considerable challenges to caregiving.

Many welfare systems have for some time pursued a policy of community care, which aims to enable people to live for as long as possible in their environment of choice, usually their own homes. In practice, a great deal of help is delivered through informal sources, mainly the family. A recent survey of carers in England found that 12% of people aged 16 years or over were caring for a sick, disabled or elderly person. This equates to 5 million carers in England (National Health Service [NHS] Information Service, 2010). Partners or spouses are most likely to deliver care to a member of the same household. Care provision to a member in a different household is most

likely to be for a parent (Department for Work and Pensions [DWP], 2008/2009). Thirty-five percent of carers in households were looking after or providing special help for a parent, 27% were caring for their spouse or partner and 14% were caring for their child. The remainder of the carers were looking after more distant relatives, friends or neighbours (NHS, 2010).

A recent survey found that 30% of carers were providing care for 35 h or more per week and 22% were providing care for 50 h or more per week (NHS Information Centre, 2010). Informal care of older people is particularly important because of the rising number of older people (aged 65 years and over), especially very old people (aged 85 years and over), in the population. Sixty percent of those receiving care are aged 60 years old and over (DWP, 2008/2009). Older adults have also been noted to provide the most care, with 20% of adults aged 65–74 years and 24% of those aged ≥75 years providing 50 or more hours of care per week (DWP, 2008/2009).

Responding to the effects of demographic changes and trends requires a range of initiatives designed to support carers in their caring role to help them maintain their own health and wellbeing. In the case of older care recipients, the spousal carers are often older adults themselves and also in poor health. Many other carers are of working age, raising issues concerned with the relationship between caring and paid work, whether the carers are caring for children, young adults, spouses in young and middle age, or parents and parents-in-law. The DWP survey notes that 41% of adult carers were also employed full time. Carers often do not wish to give up their jobs to take on caring responsibilities (Mooney & Statham, 2002). However, the reality for many is that there will be a reduction or cessation in paid employment, which has a serious impact on their financial situation (Department of Health, 1999). Yet, this essential but unpaid support for others makes a contribution worth £87 billion a year (Carers UK, 2008). Given that carers have been regarded as being amongst one of the most socially isolated groups in the United Kingdom (Department of Health, 1999), the potential detrimental effects of caregiving are substantial. This chapter expands on a number of these issues.

Caregiving Relationships

Informal care is the most important source of care for most older people living in the United Kingdom (Pickard, Wittenberg, Comas-Herrera, Davies, & Darton, 2000). For example, a large proportion of people with dementia continue to live in the community, with the majority of care being provided from unpaid sources such as a family member. Similarly, many physically frail adults also continue to live in the community supported by their families. Spouses are the first to provide care. However, when spousal caregivers are unable to continue to provide care or when they have died, adult children step in, and, therefore, they are the second most frequent source of informal help in old age (Qureshi & Walker, 1990). The benefits of this intergenerational support and solidarity not only concern the provision of care itself, but also contribute to more general quality of life in old age (Tesch-Romer, von Kondratowitz, & Motel-Klingebiel, 2001). It is also known that the importance of support from children increases with age (Tornstam, 1992).

Informal care is also an important resource for younger people and children with a range of needs including physical and mental health problems and intellectual disabilities. For example, parents and siblings provide much care for children, young people and, indeed, adults with intellectual disabilities (Grant & Whittell, 2000), which allow them to continue to live at home. Adults with mental health problems often have spouses and parents who provide care for them when they are living in the community and support for them when they are admitted to hospital (Enns, Reddon, & McDonald, 1999). Indeed, in some cases, it is the children of these people who are providing care, even in adolescence (Shifren, 2008; Shifren & Kachorek, 2003). A survey of 6,178 young carers in the United Kingdom found that their average age was 12 years, and the majority of people receiving care (51%) were

their mothers followed by siblings (31%), fathers (14%) and then grandparents (3%) (Dearden & Becker, 2004).

When thinking about caregiving, one often thinks about caregiving to only one individual, or perhaps to care recipients from the same generation (as with parents or offspring). However, increasingly caregiving may be to multiple persons across multiple generations. Adults in middle age are now termed the 'sandwich generation' (Grundy & Henretta, 2006). The more extreme form of this may be carers in families with a genetic condition such as Duchenne/Becker muscular dystrophy. Kenneson and Bobo (2010) found that some of their participants were caring for more than one person and sometimes across generations. Although they were not examining factors which contributed to resilience, they did find that those with high resilience had higher quality of life. The key question remains – how is resilience achieved under such challenging circumstances?

Caregiver Burden

One of the important benefits of informal care provision at home is that it prevents or delays a move into a formal care environment for the care recipient. This is an often cited critical factor for maintaining the well-being of the care recipient. An overwhelmingly common research finding is that when asked their preference, older people with varying degrees of dependency want to stay in their own homes (Poole, 2006). Residential or nursing care is an unpopular choice, viewed by many as the 'last resort' (Henwood & Waddington, 1998) or unable to meet key areas important for quality of life such as independence and control over decision-making (Burholt & Windle, 2007). However, the challenge of informal care provision can present as a considerable risk for negative psychosocial consequences to the carer, often associated with the chronic stress involved with caregiving (Sörensen, Pinquart, & Duberstein, 2002). Analysis of the 2001 census shows that carers who provide high levels of unpaid care for sick or disabled relatives and friends are more than twice as likely to suffer from poor health compared to people without caring responsibilities (Carers UK, 2004).

A considerable amount of research has examined the factors associated with the detrimental effects of providing care to older adults; Pinquart and Sörensen (2003) note that over 400 empirical studies examine the psychological effects of caregiving, which largely focuses on caregiver burden. Caregiver burden relates to the overall impact of the physical, psychological, social and financial demands of caregiving. Common psychological problems in dementia caregivers include depression, and emotional distress is common. Carers and those who live with someone with dementia are twice as likely as others to have significant psychological illness (Alzheimer's Disease International, 2009).

The majority of research which has examined resilience in the context of caregiving has focused on the care of older adults. However, research also indicates that poor mental health, chronic stress and poor physical health are found amongst people caring for younger adults and children with complex needs too (Tsai & Wang, 2009; Weiss, 1991; Williams, Donnelly, Holmlund, & Battaglia, 2008). Young carers providing high levels of care can experience friendship difficulties, limited time for social and leisure activities, limited time for school work and home work, which limits opportunities and can make transitions into adulthood more problematic (Dearden & Becker, 2004). Because of caring responsibilities, working age adult carers have less opportunity to earn and many are forced to live on benefits. They also face higher expenses associated with caring, such as higher heating, water and transportation costs (Carers UK, 2008).

Factors Which Contribute to Caregiver Burden

The type of impairment of the care recipient has been found to impact on the extent of caregiver burden. These include the level of physical and functional impairment in the activities of daily living, the amount and duration of care provision, the level of cognitive impairment and the level of behavioural problems. Pinquart and Sörensen produced two meta-analyses, one in 2003 focusing on caregiver burden and depression and the other in 2007 focusing on physical health. With respect to caregiver burden and depression, these were most strongly associated with the behavioural problems of the care recipient, followed by an inverse association of perceived uplifts (satisfaction with caregiving, enjoyable aspects of caregiving, increased closeness) of caregiving and the amount of care provision. They also found that spousal caregivers were more likely to suffer caregiver burden than adult children caregivers with respect to physical impairments and behavioural problems of the care recipient and being a caregiver over a longer duration. The authors suggest that adult children may be more likely than spouses to have alternative roles and social activities outside the home that could moderate the stresses associated with caregiving.

On the other hand, when Pinquart and Sörensen (2007) considered physical health, they found that being a spouse was associated with better health than being a non-spousal caregiver. This is somewhat surprising given the older ages of spouses compared with non-spouses, and one would expect associated poorer health amongst spousal caregivers since they are more likely to be older. However, this might be a selection effect, such that only those physically strong spouses undertake caring responsibilities. With respect to physical health, they also found that increased age, lower socio-economic status and lower levels of informal support were also associated with poorer physical health. The negative effects of caregiving on physical health are most likely to be found in psychologically distressed caregivers facing dementia-related stressors (Pinquart & Sörensen). Again, whilst Pinquart and Sörensen focused on older adults, challenging behaviour, physical impairments and length and duration of caregiving are also relevant factors for carers in general. Enns et al. (1999) found that resilience was lower when stressors such as pregnancy, job entry, and increased job loss, and resources in particular, communication and esteem and extended family support were lower. Williams et al. (2008) found that amongst carers of people with amyotrophic lateral sclerosis (ALS), physical and mental health was poorer if the carer lived with the care recipient. Unfortunately, the authors did not provide an explanation as to why this was the case.

Gaugler, Kane, and Newcomer (2007) operationalised resilience (or stress resistance) as low perceived caregiver burden and high care demands. In their large study of dementia caregivers, they found that caregiver instrumental activities of daily living (IADL), e.g. preparing meals, shopping, and doing routine house-work caregivers who lived with care recipients, and greater cognitive impairment of the care recipient were negatively associated with high resilience (i.e. higher levels of these factors had a detrimental impact on high levels of resilience). Also negatively associated with high resilience were ethnicity (Caucasian caregivers), greater caregiver education and income. The same study found that caregivers in the low resilience category at baseline were less likely than those in the high resilience category to experience a care recipient death, but more likely to have institutionalised the care recipient or left the study. Thus, it would seem that managing the caregiving role can pose considerable challenges to the balance and stability of informal relationships.

The age of the care recipient also highlights some differences in the potential for caregiver resilience. In Grant and Whittell's (2000) study of carers for people with intellectual disabilities across the lifespan, they found that carers with preschool age responsibilities were different from those with older children and adults. These carers had less self-belief in their ability to control environmental demands. They also had less confidence in their ability to cope, were less sure about their expertise as carers and were also less assertive with the care recipient than those carers caring for older children and adults. Carers of older adults were more resigned to their role and sought less information, and there was a danger that these carers might not seek support when they needed it.

Factors Which Reduce Caregiver Burden

Despite the negative effect of caregiving, other research indicates that even in the face of the challenge of considerable care demands, some carers are less likely to experience these effects. Longitudinal research indicates that caregivers of people with dementia often reported stability or even decreases over time on outcomes such as depression, role overload and role captivity (Gaugler, Davey, Pearlin, & Zarit, 2000). A number of factors have been found to reduce caregiver burden and thus create the potential for resilience.

Buchbinder, Longhofer, and McCue (2009) found that families with children where an adult member had cancer were able to be resilient when they were able to be creative with family traditions, habits and practices. For example, participants would celebrate chemotherapy milestones or ensure that they were always at home for their children's bedtimes. Zauszniewski, Bekhet, and Suresky (2009) found that women caregivers to family members with mental illness were more resilient and had less burden when they were able to employ positive cognitions, such as optimism about the future and considering oneself to be a worthwhile person. Similarly, Grant and Whittell (2000), in their study of carers across the lifespan of people with intellectual disabilities, found that those who were able to manage meanings (e.g. using cognitive coping, rationalising normative conflicts, and embracing paradoxes and experience control were better able to cope than those who did not).

A qualitative study of middle-aged caregivers identified a number of themes related to caregiver resilience. These included (1) experiencing the benefits of caregiving, including personal satisfaction and responsibility, fulfilment and more meaningful relationships, learning to be more tolerant and being able to keep your loved one with you; (2) managing stress through informal support, exercise such as taking a walk, participation in religious activities, hobbies and being able to take regular time out. Several caregivers had experience of caregiving since childhood and were able to rationalise their time spent caring by envisaging the same would be provided for them, should they need it (Ross, Holliman, & Dixon, 2003).

In a related context, it may be that a sense of obligation towards care provision of close family members makes a positive contribution to resilience (defined as maintaining psychological well-being, e.g. personal growth, despite functional decline). Obligation can be described as the way in which a person is expected to behave towards others. Greenfield (2009) reported that among adults aged 35–74 years, a measure of 'felt obligation' to help close others was protective over time against losses in a measure of personal growth. Thus, having and accepting a sense of obligation may enable the self to continue development and moderate the impact of negative outcomes. Obligation was also identified by Cohen, Colantonio, and Vernich (2002) as a positive factor identified by caregivers. They also found that caregiving was seen as providing companionship, it was fulfilling, enjoyable, and these positive factors were related to reduced caregiving burden. In related research, Gaugler et al. (2007) report that being a female care recipient, having provided care for a longer duration of time and spent more time providing care, having utilised greater formal and informal resources (in-home help services, overnight hospital services and extra help from friends and family), predicted high resilience at baseline, and higher resilience at baseline was associated with lower levels of institutionalisation during the 3 years of the study.

Individuals in stressful situations such as caregiving can benefit from social support networks as they can provide the resources to help them manage their situation. This is highlighted in Pinquart and Sörensen's (2007) meta-analysis. Furthermore, perceptions of the availability of support, and satisfaction with support, are considered to be more consistent predictors of caregiver well-being than the network size and the level of actual support given (Roth, Mittelman, &

Clay, 2005). This indicates that the quality of support is important. Shifren (2008) found that early caregiving experience (caregivers under 21 years of age) influenced later caregiver mental health and relationships with fathers but not mothers. A shorter caregiving experience and the older the age at commencement of caregiving, the more positive the relationship (warmth and care from the father).

There have also been studies of the importance of marital relationships and their impact on reducing (or increasing) caregiver burden and the fostering of resilient relationships. Hodgkinson et al. (2007) studied couples where a spouse or partner had cancer. They found that a high-quality marital relationship increased resilience, both for carer and care recipient. Munro and Edward (2008) noted the resilience of gay men who had cared for their partners who were dying from HIV/AIDS. Their participants had to cope not only with the illness of their partners, but also with the stigma associated with HIV/AIDS. The carer was prevented from accessing support services since the care recipient wanted to be cared for by their loved one to limit the shame and stigma they felt about their illness. They also pointed to the change in role from sexual partner to carer. These results suggest that the quality of the relationship between recipient and caregiver is an important one in facilitating resilience, but this has yet to be empirically tested more widely.

Both social exchange theory (Stoller, 1985) and equity theory (Rook, 1987) have been proposed as potential means of understanding dyadic relationships and their relationship to well-being and caregiver burden. Social exchange theory argues that individuals strive to maximise rewards and minimise costs, in this case in caregiving relationships. Individuals who receive more aid or support than they receive are described as over-benefitting, whilst those who receive less are under-benefitting. Those who over-benefit would evaluate their interactions more positively and have higher morale, and those who under benefit would experience the reverse. However, in some circumstances, over-benefitting can lead to negative outcomes also, when receiving assistance leads to a sense of dependence or a loss of independence. An extension to this theory is equity theory, which suggests that an imbalance between giving and receiving leads to dissatisfaction.

Wright and Aquilino (1998) tested these two theories in the context of female caregivers, and their care recipient husbands. They found that in terms of emotional exchanges, balanced or equitable relationships led to increased well-being. Tanji et al. (2008) looked at mutuality, that is, the reciprocity of sentiment in a relationship, and found that amongst couples where one partner has Parkinson's disease, greater mutuality decreased caregiver burden and led to lower levels of depression in both partners, but that this pattern was influenced by the severity of the disease.

Yet, others have focused on congruence in coping strategies within caregiving dyads. For example, Pakenham (1998) found that when problem-focused and division of labour coping styles were incongruent, there was less stress for both partners, but that the reverse was the case for emotional-focused coping. Bringing the focus back directly to resilience, Badr and colleagues have examined the importance of relationship maintenance and talk in promoting the well-being of couples where one is providing care to the other. They argue that these lead to resilient relationships and facilitate adjustment (Badr & Acitelli, 2005; Badr & Taylor, 2008).

There is some suggestion of ethnic variations in the social support of caregivers. A longitudinal study examined racial differences in changes in social support and psychosocial outcomes in dementia caregivers (Clay, Roth, Wadley & Haley, 2008). They found that white caregivers were more dissatisfied with their support networks than African-American caregivers, whilst African-American caregivers had fewer depressive symptoms and higher levels of life satisfaction, which was partially explained through their greater levels of satisfaction with social support. The same study also notes that over a 5-year period, caregivers of both races reported declines in the availability of people to provide informal support (Clay et al.). Picot (1995) also reported

that African-American caregivers were seen as more resilient, and that this was explained in part by higher religiosity but also by the use of accommodation rather than problem-focussed coping strategies.

One of the additional challenges to caregiving with respect to resilience is that in many cases the care recipient dies (Haley et al., 2008). Bennett (2010) found amongst older widowers that some of the resilient widowers who had been caring for their wives simply knew how to manage, and this facilitated their resilience both post-bereavement and in their subsequent lives as widowers. But social support, both formal and informal, was also valuable (Bennett). This relationship between bereavement and resilience is more likely with older adults but it is not confined to them. Caregivers may be caring for spouses with terminal cancer (Hodgkinson et al., 2007) or with progressive physical conditions such as ALS (Williams et al., 2008) or HIV/AIDS (Munro & Edward, 2008). It appears that a resilient caregiving experience may contribute to a resilient bereavement experience.

Can Social Policies and Services Facilitate the Resilience of Caregivers?

The previous section identifies the importance of a range of factors rooted within the individual and their immediate social environment that can potentially enhance resilience for the caregiver. Most of these factors are amenable to intervention through society level government action and subsequently could facilitate good outcomes. In an extensive appraisal of the literature, Ungar (2011) synthesises some of the key findings from resilience research together with theoretical debate to argue that the context plays a crucial role in facilitating resilience, and may, in fact, be where efforts should be first concentrated. Individual level resources for resilience may not be activated unless these environments facilitate the opportunities to negotiate, manage and adapt. Here, we explore the role of legislation, policy and services – the institutional environments with which the caregivers interact. The commitment by the UK government to supporting carers has been described as one of the most 'striking developments' in social policy (Moriarty & Webb, 2000). Within the United Kingdom, each of the devolved nations (Wales, Scotland and Northern Ireland) has developed strategies and legislation for supporting carers. Each introduced a range of initiatives designed to empower carers to take greater control of their lives and to promote a change of culture so that carers are fully acknowledged and respected. The 1995 Carers (Recognition and Services) Act entitled carers of any age, regularly providing considerable amounts of care to an assessment of their needs for statutory support and services. Subsequent legislation has reinforced the right to assessment. Key objectives in the Carers Strategy for Wales Action Plan (Welsh Assembly Government, 2007) state that carers:

• Are not disadvantaged because of their caring responsibilities
• Are listened to
• Maintain as normal a life as possible outside of their caring role, including access to employment, education and leisure opportunities

Although services for carers are not defined in legislation, organisations are encouraged to provide services that maintain carer health and wellbeing (Seddon et al., 2006). Set within the context of a resilience framework, the process leading to and the outcomes of resilience can be better understood.

A synthesis of qualitative and quantitative findings from a programme of carer-related research, including Carer Strategy Evaluation in England and Wales (Seddon et al., 2006) and more specific findings from evaluation of the Welsh Strategy (Seddon et al., 2009), provides some answers for understanding the potential importance of social policy and services in facilitating resilience. This research which sought to evaluate the core aims of the strategies notes a number of difficulties, but also positive findings.

An important factor in ensuring that carer needs are identified to provide support through an assessment. However, only 45% of carers in England and 41% in Wales had received a carer assessment. Although legislation entitles carers to

services, in many instances practitioners are reluctant to administer assessments, fearing that they will identify excessive needs, or because they perceive a lack of time to administer the assessment. In contrast, carers often had few expectations of assessment and presented modest service requests. The most likely service outcome of assessment in England was practical support, such as help with domestic activities and payments to purchase equipment (37%) whilst in Wales it was the provision of respite care (36%). The authors suggest that most carer assessment protocols are narrow in focus with an emphasis on practical aspects of caring, with far less attention paid to psychosocial and relational aspects. Only 3% of carers in England and 4% in Wales reported receiving any emotional support after their assessment. Forty-five percent of all carers in the evaluation of the Welsh strategy reported unmet needs for help. Fifty-six percent who had completed the assessment also reported needs that will still not being met. These tended to be for help such as flexible respite care and emotional help such as counselling support (Seddon et al., 2006).

However, new innovative support services were identified by practitioners as part of changes in care provision (Seddon et al., 2009). These included simple, 'low-level' support services such as help with ironing and gardening, or payments to cover the cost of driving lessons or a washing machine. A range of other services was also identified such as those that enabled carers to remain socially active, carer breaks and skills training to help the carer be better equipped in their caring role, and initiatives to maintain healthy living through flu immunisation and payments to meet the costs of gym membership (Seddon et al.). These practical supports were emphasised by carers as making a substantial difference to their daily lives and were highly valued. Despite the potential of this practical support, most of the carers interviewed had unmet needs for such services.

Thus, there is evidence that the correct assessment of needs and provision of appropriate, good quality services, especially those that facilitate the achievement of outcomes in relation to the key strategy objectives have the potential to increase resilience in carers. Findings from Pinquart and Sörensen's (2003) meta-analysis led the authors to suggest that interventions that reduce behaviour problems of the care recipient and increase caregiver skills in dealing with behavioural difficulties may reduce caregiver burden. Spousal caregivers may benefit most from services that reduce the objective level of stressors, such as respite care or adult day care.

Further evidence is provided by a review of the effectiveness and cost-effectiveness of support and services to informal carers of older people (Pickard, 2004). The review identified key studies relating to services for carers in England and Wales, existing reviews of services and wider international research. Services reviewed were day care (communal care, provided by paid or voluntary caregivers, in a setting outside the carer's home. Services are usually available for at least 4 h a day); in-home respite care (an alternative form of care at home, where a volunteer or professional may provide a sitter service, or undertake care tasks to enable the carer to take a break); institutional respite care (overnight care provided within residential or nursing homes, community hospitals or intermediate care facilities within the NHS); carer support groups (a mutual support and information sharing service that is directly provided to the carer. Venues and providers vary); social work and counselling (case work counselling, assessing need and implementing packages of care); and home help (a domiciliary service providing help with domestic tasks, self-care and social support).

Definitions of services for carers
Day care
In-home respite care
Institutional respite care
Carer support groups
Social work and counselling
Home help/care

In-home respite care was found to be popular with carers and care recipients; however, the availability of this service is limited and it is not universally available. Day care, home help/care, institutional respite care and social work/counselling services were found to be effective in

reducing the negative psychological effects of caring for carers. Day care was found to be often associated with very high levels of carer satisfaction and benefited carers with paid employment. Small amounts of day care (2 days or less), home help/care and institutional respite care were also found to delay the admission to institutional care of the care recipient, although an inverse effect was found for the latter when looking at groups of people described as having bad user–carer relationships or to be more reliant on others. For these, respite care shortened the length of time in the community. The review notes mixed results regarding the effects of respite care on the care recipient. Many are unwilling to use this type of service as they dislike the idea of going into an institution. The functioning of the recipient was found in some studies to deteriorate, but other studies reported no adverse effects.

Carer support groups were valued by those using them, but the review found no evidence for support groups as an effective intervention and no research had examined the cost-effectiveness of the groups. The same conclusion was drawn for in-home respite care. Day care, institutional respite care and social work/counselling were also found to be cost effective in reducing the negative psychological effects of caring for carers. Thus, services that are effective in supporting carers by supporting the people they care for, and supporting carers directly can improve their welfare and reduce the negative psychological consequences of caregiving.

Discussion

This chapter has examined the potential for resilience within the context of informal caregiving. It is clear that family caregivers are a vulnerable group; their capacities can be compromised by the physical, social, psychological and financial demands of caregiving. Given the current economic climate, where already limited services are likely to be reduced further and unemployment is rising, it is quite likely that the challenges posed by the need for informal care will increase.

It is important to see this challenge and the potential consequences from a lifespan perspective. Whilst most people experience caregiving from middle age onwards, children and adolescents are also the main providers of care in many families.

The limits caregiving imposes on the carer's social and leisure activities presents as a risk factor for all caregivers, although the impact is likely to have different effects. In later life, social networks are established, but the lack of opportunity to forge friendships can pose extra difficulties for young carers, and potentially render them isolated and lonely. In older people, the challenge is further enhanced because of many of the caregivers also having ill-health themselves. For young caregivers, limited time for school work and home work could minimise future employment opportunities.

The chapter has also highlighted the lack of research that has looked directly at resilience in the context of caregiving. Of the studies we identified, the majority focused on adults in mid and later life. Relatively, little work has focused on resilience in young people who take on caring responsibilities in adolescence. Not only do these early experiences focus the need for contexts that facilitate resilience at the time of caring, but also influence the capacity for future resilience (Shifren, 2008; Shifren & Kachorek, 2003).

Given the wide-ranging detrimental impact of caregiver burden, the identification of environments, strategies, services and therapies that have the potential to enhance resilience will be even more crucial for the future. From a society perspective, social policies and the services that they inspire have the potential to facilitate resilience in carers. Supportive environments for caregivers will help ensure that they can continue to face the challenge, function in their role as care providers and maintain their own well-being to the best of their abilities, given the circumstances. In other words, resilience can be achieved if facilitated.

This chapter has identified some of the services and interventions that could facilitate resilience within the caregiving context. Services can be effective in supporting carers directly by strengthening their personal psychological resources so they can find meaning in their role and effectively manage stress. Congruent with other resilience research (e.g. Luthar, 2006), we find that good quality social support and relationships are beneficial to caregiver resilience. Services can also be effective indirectly, by supporting the care recipient. However, far less research has investigated the potential for resilience by examining the carer and care recipient together, or explored the reciprocal aspects of their relationship. Where this has been examined, there is some indication that there may be some conflict between the carer and cared for (Pickard, 2004). Whilst the service might facilitate resilience for the caregiver, the same outcome might not be realised for the care recipient. More research is required to examine the most cost and therapeutically most effective ways to enhance the potential of resilience for both parties.

In conclusion, caregivers are a highly valuable resource to the family members they care for. They enable the care recipient to remain in their own homes, maintaining community cohesion. The care they provide is invaluable to society, and the economic savings to governments are substantial. Ensuring opportunities for developing the resilience of caregivers (and those that they care for) is essential if both are to continue to manage the complex challenges they face.

References

Alzheimer's Disease International. (2009). *World Alzheimer report*. Retrieved from http://www.alz.co.uk/research/worldreport/. May 2011.

Badr, H., & Acitelli, L. (2005). Dyadic adjustment in chronic illness: Does relationship talk matter? *Journal of Family Psychology, 19*, 465–469.

Badr, H., & Taylor, C. (2008). Effects of relationship maintenance on psychological distress and dyadic adjustment among couples coping with lung cancer. *Health Psychology, 27*(5), 616–627.

Bennett, K. M. (2010). How to achieve resilience as an older widower: Turning points or gradual change? *Ageing and Society, 30*(3), 369–382.

Bond, J., & Cabrero, G. R. (2007). Health and dependency in later life. In J. Bond, S. M. Peace, F. Dittman-Kohli, & G. Westerhof (Eds.), *Ageing in society: European perspectives on gerontology* (pp. 113–141). London: Sage.

Bronfenbrenner, U. (1994). Ecological models of human development. In T. Husen & T. N. Postlethwaite (Eds.), *International encyclopedia of education* (2nd ed., Vol. 3). Elsevier: New York.

Buchbinder, M., Longhofer, J., & McCue, K. (2009). Family routines and rituals when a parent has cancer. *Family Systems and Health, 27*(3), 213–227.

Burholt, V., & Windle, G. (2007). Retaining independence and autonomy: Older people's for specialised housing. *Research, Policy and Planning, 25*(1), 13–26.

Carers UK. (2004). *In poor health: The impact of caring on health*. London: Carers UK.

Carers UK. (2008). *Carers in crisis. A survey of carers finances in 2008*. London: Carers UK.

Clay, O. J., Roth, D. L., Wadley, V. G., & Haley, W. E. (2008). Changes in social support and their impact on psychosocial outcome over a 5-year period for African American and white dementia caregivers. *International Journal of Geriatric Psychiatry, 23*(8), 857–862.

Cohen, C. A., Colantonio, A., & Vernich, L. (2002). Positive aspects of caregiving: Rounding out the caregiver experience. *International Journal of Geriatric Psychiatry, 17*(2), 184–188.

Dearden, C., & Becker, S. (2004). *Young carers in the UK: The 2004 report*. London: Carers UK.

Department for Work and Pensions. (2008/2009). *The UK family resources survey*. Retrieved from http://research.dwp.gov.uk/asd/frs/2008_09/frs_2008_09_report.pdf July 1010.

Department of Health. (1999). *Caring about carers. A national strategy for carers*. England: Department of Health.

Enns, R. A., Reddon, J. R., & McDonald, L. (1999). Indications of resilience among family members of people admitted to a psychiatric facility. *Psychiatric Rehabilitation Journal, 23*(2), 127–136.

Gaugler, J. E., Davey, A., Pearlin, L. I., & Zarit, S. (2000). Modeling caregiver adaptation over time: The longitudinal impact of behavior problems. *Psychology and Aging, 15*, 437–450.

Gaugler, J. E., Kane, R. L., & Newcomer, R. (2007). Resilience and transitions from dementia caregiving. *The Journals of Gerontology: Series B: Psychological Sciences and Social Sciences, 62B*(1), 38–44.

Grant, G., & Whittell, B. (2000). Differentiated coping strategies in families with children or adults with intellectual disabilities: The relevance of gender, family composition and the life span. *Journal of Applied Research in Intellectual Disabilities, 13*(4), 256–275.

Greenfield, A. E. (2009). Felt obligation to help others as a protective factor against losses in psychological well-being following functional decline in middle and later life. *Journal of Gerontology: Psychological Sciences, 64B*(6), 723–732.

Grundy, E., & Henretta, J. C. (2006). Between elderly parents and adult children: A new look at the intergenerational care provided by the sandwich generation. *Ageing and Society, 26*(5), 707–722.

Haley, W. E., Bergman, E. J., Roth, D. L., McVie, T., Gaugler, J. E., & Mittelman, M. S. (2008). Long-term effects of bereavement and caregiver intervention on dementia caregiver depressive symptoms. *The Gerontologist, 48*(6), 732.

Harney, P. A. (2007). Resilience processes in context: Contributions and implications of Bronfenbrenner's person-process-context model. *Journal of Aggression, Maltreatment & Trauma, 14*(3), 73–87.

Haskett, M. E., Nears, K., Ward, C. S., & McPherson, A. V. (2006). Diversity in adjustment of maltreated children: Factors associated with resilient functioning. *Clinical Psychology Review, 26*(6), 796–812.

Henwood, M., & Waddington, E. (1998). *Expecting the worst? Views on the future of long term care. Help the aged report to the Royal Commission on long term care*. Leeds: Institute for Health.

Hodgkinson, K., Butow, P., Hunt, G. E., Wyse, R., Hobbs, K. M., & Wain, G. (2007). Life after cancer: Couples' and partners' psychological adjustment and supportive care needs. *Support Care Cancer, 15*(4), 405–415.

Kaplan, H. B. (1999). Toward an understanding of resilience: A critical review of definitions and models. In M. D. Glantz & J. Johnson (Eds.), *Resilience and development: Positive life adaptations* (pp. 17–83). New York: Plenum.

Kenneson, A., & Bobo, J. K. (2010). The effect of caregiving on women in families with Duchenne/Becker muscular dystrophy. *Health and Social Care in the Community, 18*(5), 520–528.

Luthar, S., Cicchetti, D., & Becker, B. (2000). The construct of resilience: A critical evaluation and guidelines for future work. *Child Development, 71*(3), 543–562.

Luthar, S. S. (2006). Resilience in development: A synthesis of research across five decades. In D. Cicchetti & D.J. Cohen (Eds.), *Developmental psychopathology: Vol, 3. Risk, disorder, and adaptation* (2nd ed., pp. 739–795). New York: Wiley.

Masten, A. (2007). Resilience in developing systems: Progress and promise as the fourth wave rises. *Development and Psychopathology, 19*, 921–930.

Mooney, A., & Statham, J. (2002). *The pivot generation. Informal care and work after 50*. Bristol: The Policy Press.

Moriarty, J., & Webb, S. (2000). *Part of their lives: Community care for older people with dementia*. Bristol: The Policy Press.

Munro, I., & Edward, K. L. (2008). The lived experience of gay men caring for others with HIV/AIDS: Resilient coping skills. *International Journal of Nursing Practice, 14*(2), 122–128.

NHS Information Centre. (2010). *Survey of carers in households in England 2009/10*. Retrieved from http://www.ic.nhs.uk/webfiles/publications/Social%20Care/carersurvey0910/Survey_of_Carers_in_Households_2009_10_England_Provisional_Results_post_publication.pdf July 2010.

Pakenham, K. (1998). Couple coping and adjustment to multiple sclerosis in care receiver-carer dyads. *Family Relations, 47*(3), 269–277.

Pickard, L. (2004). *The effectiveness and cost effectiveness of support and services to informal carers of older people. A review of the literature prepared for the audit commission*. Retrieved from http://www.audit-commission.gov.uk/SiteCollection

Documents/AuditCommissionReports/National Studies/LitReview02final.pdf August 2010.

Pickard, L., Wittenberg, R., Comas-Herrera, A., Davies, B., & Darton, R. (2000). Relying on informal care in the new century? Informal care for elderly people in England to 2031. *Ageing and Society, 20*, 745–772.

Picot, S. (1995). Rewards, costs, and coping of African American caregivers. *Nursing Research, 44*(3), 147–152.

Pinquart, M., & Sörensen, S. (2003). Associations of stressors and uplifts of caregiving with caregiver burden and depressive mood: A meta-analysis. *Journals of Gerontology Series B-Psychological Sciences & Social Sciences, 58*(2), 112–128.

Pinquart, M., & Sörensen, S. (2007). Correlates of physical health of informal caregivers: A meta-analysis. *Journals of Gerontology Series B-Psychological Sciences & Social Sciences, 62*(2), 126–137.

Poole, T. (2006). *Telecare and older people. Wanless social care review.* London: The King's Fund. Retrieved from http://www.kingsfund.org.uk/publications/the_kings_fund_publications/appendices_to.html August 2009.

Qureshi, H., & Walker, A. (1990). *The caring relationship: Elderly people and their families.* London: Macmillan.

Rook, K. S. (1987). Reciprocity of social exchange and social satisfaction among older women. *Journal of Personality and Social Psychology, 52*, 145–154.

Ross, L., Holliman, D., & Dixon, D. R. (2003). Resiliency in family caregivers: Implications for social work practice. *Journal of Gerontological Social Work, 40*(3), 81–96.

Roth, D. L., Mittelman, M. S., & Clay, O. J. (2005). Changes in social support as mediators of the impact of a psychosocial intervention for spouse caregivers of persons with Alzheimer's disease. *Psychology and Aging, 20*, 634–644.

Seddon, D., Robinson, C. A., Reeves, C., Tommis, Y., Woods, B., & Russell, I. (2006). In their own right: Translating the policy of carer assessment into practice. *British Journal of Social Work, 7*(8), 1335–1352.

Seddon, D., Robinson, C. A., Tommis, Y., Woods, B., Perry, J., & Russell, I. (2009). A study of the carers strategy (2000): Supporting carers in Wales. *British Journal of Social Work, 40*(5), 1470–1487.

Shifren, K. (2008). Early caregiving: Perceived parental relations and current social support. *Journal of Adult Development, 15*(3), 160–168.

Shifren, K., & Kachorek, L. V. (2003). Does early caregiving matter? The effects on young caregivers' adult mental health. *International Journal of Behavioral Development, 27*(4), 338–346.

Sörensen, S., Pinquart, M., & Duberstein, P. (2002). How effective are interventions with caregivers? An updated meta-analysis. *The Gerontologist, 42*(3), 356–372.

Stoller, E. P. (1985). Exchange patterns on the informal support networks of the elderly: The impact of reciprocity on morale. *Journal of Marriage and the Family, 47*, 335–342.

Tanji, H., et al. (2008). Mutuality of the marital relationship in Parkinson's disease. *Movement Disorders. 23*(13), 1843–1849.

Tesch-Romer, C., von Kondratowitz, H. J., & Motel-Klingebiel, A. (2001). Quality of life in the context of intergenerational solidarity: Ageing, intergenerational, care systems and quality of life. *Nova Rapport, 14*/01.

Tomassini, C., Glaser, K., Wolf, D., Broese van Groenou, M., & Grundy, E. (2004). Living arrangements among older people: An overview of trends in Europe and the USA. *Population Trends, 115*, 24–34.

Tornstam, L. (1992). Formal and informal support to the elderly in Sweden. In H. Kendig, A. Hashimoto, & L. C. Coppard (Eds.), *Family support for the elderly: The international experience* (pp. 138–146). Oxford: Oxford University Press.

Tsai, S. M., & Wang, H. H. (2009). The relationship between caregiver's strain and social support among mothers with intellectually disabled children. *Journal of Clinical Nursing, 18*(4), 539–548.

Ungar, M. (2011). The social ecology of resilience: Addressing contextual and cultural ambiguity of a nascent construct. *American Journal of Orthopsychiatry, 81*, 1–17.

Weiss, S. J. (1991). Personality adjustment and social support of parents who care for children with pervasive developmental disorders. *Archives of Psychiatric Nursing, 5*(1), 25–30.

Welsh Assembly Government. (2007). *Carers strategy for Wales action plan.* Cardiff: Welsh Assembly Government.

Williams, M. T., Donnelly, J. P., Holmlund, T., & Battaglia, M. (2008). ALS: Family caregiver needs and quality of life. *Amyotrophic Lateral Sclerosis, 9*(5), 279–286.

Windle, G. (2011). What is resilience? A review and concept analysis. *Reviews in Clinical Gerontology, 21*, 152–169.

Wright, D., & Aquilino, W. (1998). Influence of reciprocity of emotional support in marriage on elderly wives' marital satisfaction and caregiving experiences. *Family Relations, 47*,195–204.

Zauszniewski, J. A., Bekhet, A. K., & Suresky, M. J. (2009). Effects on resilience of women family caregivers of adults with serious mental illness: The role of positive cognitions. *Archives of Psychiatric Nursing, 23*(6), 412–422.

Young People, Their Families and Social Supports: Understanding Resilience with Complexity Theory

19

Jackie Sanders, Robyn Munford,
and Linda Liebenberg

Understanding how vulnerable youth can be supported to build capacity, to protect themselves from risks and to navigate a safe path to adulthood has been a focus of social workers, researchers and policy makers internationally for many decades. Resilience has been advanced as a conceptual framework for organising our understanding about how vulnerable youth can 'beat the odds' (Liebenberg & Ungar, 2009, p. 6) and develop their own capacities and competence (Sanders & Munford, 2008). Ungar (2011) traces in detail the development of resilience as a concept in youth studies and the insights it has given into how the construction of healthy identities and the achievement of positive outcomes are understood and negotiated by young people themselves.

This chapter considers the way complexity theory might contribute to an ecological understanding of resilience in youth. The chapter begins with a case profile of Ben, a young man who faced significant risk. His story provides an opportunity to consider the way in which thinking about complexity can help us to both understand resilience and explain why particular types of support make a positive difference. This case study is fundamentally ecological and interactional; it speaks to the multiple ways in which

Ben navigated and negotiated (Ungar, 2011) his way through his environment and the ways in which resources (e.g. service providers) in his environment responded to him. We then explore how three key ideas in complexity theory appear to speak directly to an ecological understanding of resilience and in so doing help make sense of what happened for Ben. Complexity theory is a useful conceptual framework that helps us think about the challenges youth in adversity face navigating a safe path to adulthood and in trying to conceptualise and then operationalise strategies that might assist them to do this well. We suggest ways in which key aspects of complexity theory can be applied to policies and practices in social work and provide a brief critique of complexity theory in relation to this.

Ben's Story

We met 16-year-old Ben at an alternative education programme that provided schooling for young people who had been expelled from school. Ben explained that things had started to go wrong for him at about the age of 8. He remembered really enjoying his first couple of years at school and believed that initially he had done well academically. At age of 8, he moved towns and had several changes in school over the next 3 years. Ben explained that 'naughty boys' targeted new arrivals at school as potential friends, while the 'good boys' stayed in their friendship groups. To build a peer group, he associated with children

J. Sanders (✉)
School of Health and Social Services,
Massey University, Palmerston North, New Zealand
e-mail: J.Sanders@massey.ac.nz

M. Ungar (ed.), *The Social Ecology of Resilience: A Handbook of Theory and Practice*,
DOI 10.1007/978-1-4614-0586-3_19, © Springer Science+Business Media, LLC 2012

who were already on the social and academic margins of the school. Over the following 2 years, he became known as one of the 'bad children', and his attempts to engage academically in class, by asking questions, were increasingly misinterpreted as challenging behaviour. Gradually, he fell behind his academically able peers.

The behaviours for which Ben consistently received attention (negative from school staff, positive from peers) were being disruptive in class and combative on the playground. Moving schools was his parents' response to the gradual deterioration in Ben's performance at school. Rather than creating the potential for positive change as his mother had hoped, each move of school saw Ben's involvement with 'bad' children being repeated and the amount of trouble in which he became involved increased. He started using drugs, fighting and engaging in other behaviours that reinforced the labels of 'bad boy' and 'academic failure'. Ben's mother worried about the steady deterioration in his academic performance and tried repeatedly talking with school staff. She enlisted the help of a counsellor who listened but was unable to help Ben to modify his disruptive behaviour at school or to catch up on lost learning. The choices Ben made during this time appear to be negative but from his perspective they were functional. Initially, the 'bad boys' provided Ben with a peer group when faced with integrating into a new school. His association with these young people masked the academic challenges he was facing as he gradually fell behind.

The move to high school at 13 confirmed for Ben what he had begun to realise; he was now too far behind in his education to catch up. Midway through his first year he was expelled for smoking marijuana and fighting. Sport had been one consistent part of his school life that he had enjoyed, but once he was expelled those opportunities were closed to him. Ben now had time on his hands and a circle of friends who were also out of school and getting into trouble. It was not long before he came to the attention of the local police. He was eventually arrested for stealing cars.

During his 18 months out of school, Ben continued on a downward spiral, but towards the end of this time his grandparents introduced him to the idea of an alternative education programme. Ben was receptive to this idea and he agreed to attend. Here, he met Richard, one of the staff, and a range of possibilities opened up for him. During the following year, Richard worked with Ben on his academic subjects, and by the year's end, Ben had caught up sufficiently to return to mainstream schooling. Richard encouraged Ben consistently, and when Ben found things difficult, Richard modelled positive solution-finding strategies which Ben could learn. He communicated an unfailing confidence in Ben's capacity to reduce his harmful behaviours (drug taking, offending) and to increase his academic knowledge. This confidence was critical to Ben's decision to continue attending school. Instead of focusing on what Ben was not doing, Richard focused on what the boy could do and used this as a base to build on. This reopening of educational opportunity was transformative for Ben. Ben spoke about important changes in how he saw his future:

Interviewer: So if I asked you here before you went to the alternative education programme… what do you hope for the future, what would you have said?

Ben: Probably would have said "get patched up" [become a gang member]

Interviewer: Okay, really. So if I say this to you now, here?

Ben: Now, I want to get a job, I am really hoping for a job, get a good job, something in engineering.

Exploring Resilience Through the Lens of Complexity Theory

Originating in the physical sciences, the terms chaos theory and complexity theory are often used interchangeably (Mason, 2009; Smith, 2005). Mason (2009) suggests that complexity theory grew out of chaos theory with its focus on the behaviour of volatile systems that never seemed to stabilise, but also never seemed to collapse – they sat at the edge of chaos (Langton, 1986) adapting and evolving to the changing demands of their environment (Lewin, 1999). Chaos, in this sense, is a neutral term: it is neither necessarily positive nor negative. It refers to systems at the midpoint between the totally random and the totally predictable (Plsek & Greenhalgh, 2001). Sometimes, complexity theory is referred to as complex adaptive systems theory highlighting the theory's focus on explaining the way that complex systems behave (Fenwick, 2010; Meek, 2008; Zimmerman & Hayday, 1999). Given the role of systems theory in the development of social work and other human service professions, complexity theory appears to have much to offer these disciplines with regard to their future development (Warren, Franklin, & Streeter, 1998).

In recent times, complexity theory has been utilised in the social sciences. For example, Bloch (2005), Campbell (in press) and Pryor and Bright (2007) examine its usefulness in understanding young people's career trajectories. Mason (2009) explored its potential to help build a sustainable approach to education globally. In the field of community development, practitioners and researchers have examined its relevance to understanding processes of community and family change under adverse circumstances (Handley et al., 2009). Butz (1992, 1997) has employed it to generate new understandings of conditions such as anxiety, stress, substance abuse, depression and neurosis. There is also a large body of literature in the general management, organisational development and change management fields, which has adapted complexity theory to explain human systems (Andriani, 2001; Fenwick, 2010; Litaker, Tomolo, Liberatore, Stange, & Aron, 2006; Meek, 2010; Mischen & Jackson, 2008; Smith, 2005; Trochim, & Cabrera, 2005; Zimmerman & Hayday, 1999; Zimmerman, Lindgberg, & Plsek, 1998). Of particular relevance to the current discussion is the work of LaBoucane-Benson (2005). She identified that the contribution complexity theory can make to an ecological understanding of resilience for First Nations peoples in Canada. She brought together resilience and complexity theory, indigenous science and human developmental theory to create meta-theoretical frameworks to guide research into family well-being. Her work emphasised interconnectedness, self-organisation, adaptation and emergence in First Nation's people's understandings of family resilience – all central concepts in complexity theory.

LaBoucane-Benson's works work shows the capacity of complexity theory to explain phenomena that appear to be more than the sum of their parts and has potential to add to the study of resilience. A central concern in the study of resilience is understanding better how to potentiate positive change in stressed and volatile situations that appear to be at one and the same time unstable and stable (Bloch, 2005). Complexity theory shifts attention 'from a concern with decontextualised and universalized essence to a concern with contextualised and contingent, complex wholes' (Mason, 2009, p. 119). It is fundamentally concerned with understanding how numerous and diverse parts interact together to create continually evolving systems where the parts and the whole need to be examined because the parts interact independently with each other and with components in external systems as well (Buckle Henning, 2010). Reductionism is avoided but at the same time analysis is able to focus intensely on small parts of systems and the ways in which these interact with each other (Fenwick, 2010; Meek, 2010; Plsek & Greenhalgh, 2001; Smith, 2005; Zimmerman & Hayday, 1999). The focus on multiple interactions within and between systems is relevant to the study of resilience where the concern is with understanding how individuals, social groups, political and economic systems and the services and supports they provide interact (Plsek & Greenhalgh, 2001; Smith, 2005) to create different opportunities and risks for young people.

The remainder of this chapter synthesises three aspects of complexity theory, the non-proportional relation between cause and effect, emergence, and entrainment, with an ecological understanding of resilience. It then considers implications of complexity theory as it is applied to the study of resilience. Finally, we provide a brief critique of complexity theory, and its application to human systems.

Non-Proportional Relation Between Cause and Effect

Proponents of complexity theory argue that small inputs can have disproportionately large effects (Hudson, 2000; Litaker et al., 2006; Meek, 2008; Munford, Sanders, & Maden, 2006; Plsek & Greenhalgh, 2001; Smith, 2005). Applied to the field of human services, it has been used, for example, to explain why risk assessment tools can fail to predict harm to children in child protection practice (Stevens & Cox, 2008; Stevens & Haslett, 2007). We are compelled therefore to focus on the way that whole systems and their many diverse constituent parts interact together over time to create the continually shifting ground on which individuals negotiate and navigate (Ungar, 2008) their way towards health and wellbeing. Thus, complexity theory holds exciting promise for the study of resilience in young people because of its ability to shed light on what often seem to be contradictory or paradoxical processes in young people's lives. For example, as detailed in the following, in Ben's case it was not until he became involved with the criminal justice system that serious attention was paid to what was required to keep him at school. Complexity theory can also help us understand the unintended outcomes from interventions. For instance, teen motherhood is often judged to be a negative outcome for both mother and child; however, it can also represent a significant turning point in a young woman's life and provide the leverage for services to engage effectively with her (Brodsky, 1996; Davies, McKinnon, & Rains, 2001; Geronimus, 2003). Paradox is a key concept in complexity theory. It is understood to be a positive, change generating characteristic of complex systems (Plsek & Greenhalgh, 2001; Smith, 2005; Zimmerman & Hayday, 1999; Zimmerman et al., 1998).

Youth research has drawn attention to paradoxes that hold positive, resilience-building potential. Ladner's (1971) work revealed the positive aspects of young women's sexual activity; according to the young women themselves, it was a part of their enactment of their growing maturity rather than simply the deviant or delinquent behaviour, it was typically portrayed as in popular discourse. In our own work (Sanders & Munford, 2008), we observed how girls at primary school used the 'good girl facade' to craft effective resistance strategies to the authority of the school when the expectation that they be 'good' became stifling.

Paradoxically, it was Ben's deteriorating situation that provided the impetus for his life to change. Had Ben been provided with relevant support from the teachers at school and, critically for Ben, had they taken the time to discover that his acting-out behaviour at school was his reaction to feeling marginalised, how different might Ben's pathway through mainstream school have been? Ben himself recognised that at many points, a relatively small change had the potential to make a major difference:

> Ben: If the teachers had just, if they had of talked, if they had of explained it at Intermediate [middle school]. If they had explained how to do all of the stuff that they had, if they had of explained it better. It was just too hard, it wasn't meaning nothing to me and if they had actually. Because I would put my hand up and they would say "Oh just do that and see how you get on". "But you are not telling me how to do it". And so then you just get naughty because there is nothing else to do and you can't join in lessons and stuff.

Small differences in the initial conditions may produce large variations in the long-term behaviour of complex systems (Smith, 2005). This non-proportional relationship between cause and effect reminds us to be cautious about thinking that there may be a single or limited number of factors that 'cause' resilience. Similarly, effective interventions seeking to moderate risk may vary in quantity and/or size. Risk and change need to be viewed from a range of different perspectives. Apparently marginal, trivial or inexplicable factors may be significant drivers of change, creators of growth and generators of resilience (Mason, 2009). For instance, in the complex and highly charged field of child protection, Stevens and Haslett (2007) argue that child protection policy and practice that is based on complexity theory would, among other things, widen its focus to consider all the systems within which risk of harm to children is nested rather than assuming a linear cause and effect approach and therefore focusing attention on the immediate environment. They argue that non-linear approaches to understanding how risk translates into harm increases the likelihood of averting or avoiding harm to children. Illustrative of this perspective is the work of Nguyen–Gillham, Giacaman, Naser and Boyce (2008) who used qualitative methods to explore resilience among Palestinian youth in the West Bank and identified that youth definitions of resilience had collective as well as individual components. They also noted a tension between the youths' desire for order and the impact of boredom on subsequent behaviour in their accounts of resilience. Likewise, Belliveau and Beare (2007) emphasise the relational dimensions of complexity theory, showing how complexity theory, as one part of an elaborate conceptual framework, enables theatre to contribute to positive youth development.

Handley et al. (2009) identified change effects rippling around their community following the engagement between city planners and a community centre over the refurbishment of a small playground. These effects ranged from positive individual change in the lives of parents, children and young people through to increased levels of participation by local residents in city planning processes and increased community involvement in neighbourhood celebrations. Apparently small actions on the part of practitioners, in this case, seizing the opportunity to support residents to become involved in a local planning process, can potentially create large ripple effects. These ripples can appear in widely disparate and unexpected places (Handley et al.).

The non-linearity resilience principle that Ungar (2011) describes has interesting parallels with the non-proportional relationship between cause and effect in complexity theory in that both recognise that changes are not necessarily directly proportional to the effort required to create them. In family work, for example, relatively mundane aspects of practice, such as assisting a parent to find childcare, have had significant but unpredicted positive effects (Munford et al., 2006). Moving schools can be a big event in a young

person's life but it is not an uncommon source of stress (Martin & Marsh, 2008); all young people ultimately move schools even if only upon graduation. However, as our case illustration shows, Ben's untimely move between schools brought with it access to children who were already located at the social margins. The initial approach by the 'naughty boys' to become friends with Ben was a relatively small event in itself. However, its ripple effects were substantial.

Emergence

Complex systems achieve order within what can appear to outside observers as chaos. This is called emergence or spontaneous self-organisation. Stevens and Haslett (2007) explain:

> The emergence of a system from a series of individual components depends on the properties of the individual components and the environment surrounding these. The key point to remember about emergence is that the emerging system strives for order. Also, the establishment of the new emergent system takes time. However, emergence itself cannot be controlled, predicted or managed (p. 131).

Interaction is an important component of complexity theory; understanding the ways in which parts engage with and shape each other helps with understanding the observable characteristics of whole systems at different points in time. As Stevens and Haslett (2007) note, earthquakes result from the interaction between a diverse range of components including the nature of the earth's crust, the movement of tectonic plates and the influence of forces at the earth's core. The interactions between the parts of this complex system generate unique combinations that dynamically shape the earth over time.

Thinking about interactional processes, we can see that Ben was not always an intentional actor directly shaping and controlling his journey through school. Neither did the locus of control reside wholly in his environment and the people around him. He acted and responded to the contextual cues he received from his different schools, interactions with his family and the organisations that came into his life. Equally, they acted and responded to him. It was not until Ben engaged with the alternative education programme where there was a focus on his particular individual and educational needs that things began to change for him. The environment (social and physical) finally provided resources in ways that were right for Ben. This allowed a new stability to emerge in Ben's life that held positive possibilities and which ended the blame and labelling he had been subject to at the mainstream schools he had attended.

Emergence is important to our thinking about resilience; complex systems are not completely random. Order is achieved. Furthermore, patterns emerge from the constant interaction between the various parts and change can be stimulated. These emergent patterns are not necessarily good or bad. They are the products of the endlessly variable interactions between the parts of the system. So it is with young people at the social margins; they marshal resources around themselves to create the best possible, or the most stable, circumstances achievable in their lives at any point in time. Factors that appear to be risk behaviour from the outside may in fact contribute to youth resilience.

Recently, we completed a study of girls who were the focus of much energy and concern in their local community because of their violent and disruptive behaviour (Munford & Sanders, 2007). While realising that marginality is a contested concept (Gordon, 2000), these young females could be described as occupying the social margins of their community in the sense that they no longer attended mainstream schools. Consequently, the usual opportunities to participate in extra-curricular activities that school involvement affords youth were closed to them. They were part of a larger group publicly defined in terms of their overt anti-social behaviour as difficult and delinquent. As such, public discourse situated them at the social margins of their community.

From the outside, it appeared that their lives were as chaotic as they were disruptive and destructive. It was relatively easy to see them as the sum of all the problems they presented – engaging in substance abuse, quite significant acts of violence, petty theft and vandalism, early sexual activity with its attendant risks, as well as

a lack of engagement with formal education. Indeed, the energy that was expended on these lively young females by the broader community was directed primarily at trying to stop or ameliorate the effects of these behaviours. While not dismissing the challenges presented by these behaviours, the research illustrated clearly that the young women could not be reduced simply to the sum total of these disturbing behaviours. Even when they were roaming at night, they would come home to care for younger siblings who were home alone. They also cared for each other, oftentimes providing the support and emotional stability for each other that was lacking in their own families. Despite curfews and other restrictions placed upon them, they would seek each other out to fulfil their needs for emotional intimacy. While appearing disruptive and often frightening to outside observers, the relationships between these girls were very important in their lives. They were part of a pattern of health-seeking behaviour in the same way that care for younger siblings represented the young women's capacity to give generously of themselves.

Understanding the way in which interactions with others, material resources and services contribute to the temporary stability of youth is critical to an effective theory of resilience (Buckle Henning, 2010). Approached through the lens of complexity theory, we can see young people who face significant risk as striving for balance and meaning rather than as dysfunctional, devious, destructive or beyond hope. Thinking ecologically, and drawing on the concepts of complexity theory, the processes associated with resilience help individuals access the resources that can be directed at finding equilibrium in multiple and constantly shifting fields in interaction with the available social and physical resources. This is the hidden resilience to which Ungar (2004) refers 'the functional but culturally non-normative substitute adaptations' (Ungar, 2011, p. 8) young people facing adversity make.

From the outside, Ben's academic journey and his developmental pathway appeared to be unstable and heading for catastrophe. It was relatively easy for those around him to dismiss him as 'another kid gone bad' and for the institutional attention to switch to those young people who demonstrated more promise. Ben, however, created stability and predictability in his school career by working hard at being challenging. He crafted an identity as a young person on the social margins of the school with a future in a gang thereby gaining some control over the responses of others. He maintained a sense of himself as competent when he was failing academically by doing well at being bad.

Entrainment

As can be seen from the preceding discussion, patterns do emerge and stability is achieved from time to time in complex systems (Hudson, 2000; Litaker et al., 2006; Plsek & Greenhalgh, 2001; Smith, 2005). Entrainment refers to the periodic crystallisation of these emergent patterns. Because they have become relatively stable for a period of time, these patterns then have the capacity to shape the way in which the system will evolve. Entrainment holds potential for social work. It also presents risks for young people as negative and destructive patterns can become entrained. The key task is to amplify positive instances of emergence and encourage their crystallisation (Emison, 2008). Seizing teachable moments in child protection work (Scott & O'Neil, 1996) is a good example of social work capitalising upon entrainment. In such cases, the worker observes moments of insight in a parent and uses these to support the development of further parental competence.

Thinking of the order that can be seen within dynamic complex systems, we can imagine Ben in interaction with his several schools striving for a zone of competence which he ultimately found by acting out. Although not in a way that was desirable, a balance had emerged where all agreed on who Ben was for the time being. Of course, this was not all Ben could potentially be, but initially it gave both Ben and the school a predictable set of operating principles. As he moved schools, and his label moved with him, the concept of entrainment helps explain how for young people like Ben these labels crystallise into a set

of working definitions that lend predictability to behaviour and then go on to structure future interactions. In this process, the chances that the young Ben would be able to find a positive way of functioning at school and elsewhere were reduced. In the end, it took focused work by Ben and the people around him (e.g. his teacher, his social worker, his mother and grandparents) to bring forward other possible definitions of him as an able and motivated student who had aspirations beyond becoming a 'patched' gang member. This was a joint project that drew not only on Ben's own capacities but also marshalled a range of resources around him. These resources were not solely focused on the negative aspects of who Ben had been, but took into account his past experiences as well as who he could become. Richard enabled Ben to do more than just 'get by' and assisted him to strengthen the webs of positive supports in his own environment (Backett-Milburn,Wilson,Bancroft,&Cunningham-Burley, 2008). Entrainment thus speaks to the principle of decentrality that Ungar (2011) notes in his ecological definition of resilience:

> By de-centering the child, we make it much clearer that, when growing up under adversity, the locus of change does not reside in either the child or the environment alone, but in the processes by which environments provide resources of use to the child. It is the complex interactive processes embedded in environments that contain levels of risk exceeding the norm (p. 5–6).

Implications for Policy and Practice

In this section, we consider how complexity theory could contribute to the development of policy and practice for youth facing significant adversity. We abstract four components from the preceding discussion and then briefly consider how these might be applied to the development of practice and policy aimed at enhancing resilience in young people.

1. Difficult to predict, not random

Complex systems are not completely random. Periodically, patterns do emerge. However, while stability is achieved, patterns never exactly repeat. Precision in prediction is not therefore possible (Emison, 2008). By working to understand how a system behaves and by becoming involved in the interactions within that system it is, though, possible to understand better the range of likely outcomes at different points in time, and also to identify optimal places to direct efforts for a positive impact.

2. Small inputs can create disproportionately large effects; conversely small problems may require large solutions

Because the relationship between cause and effect is not linear, efforts at creating change through policy and practice need to be carefully calibrated (Litaker et al., 2006; Smith, 2005). Those supporting young people need to remain attuned to the small inputs that hold possibilities for positive change at both the policy and practice levels.

3. Interactions shape the system

Relationships between all the people who are involved in young people's lives are critical (Buckle Henning, 2010; Plsek & Greenhalgh, 2001; Smith, 2005). The dynamic and fluid nature of complex systems requires that we think across traditional boundaries such as the boundary between statutory and non-statutory social work and also boundaries between practitioners, youth, their families and peer networks.

4. Entrainment has potential and also risk

Though complex systems periodically stabilise, it is not clear what precursor conditions give rise to entrainment. From both a practice and policy point of view, it is critical to learn to recognise and amplify situations that may be crystallising in positive directions to encourage further growth and development (Fenwick, 2010; Smith, 2005). Conversely, it is also important to recognise when crystallisation represents the solidifying of negative conditions around a young person and that effort is then put into resisting this.

Taken together, these four components suggest a different approach to the development of policy, including models for funding services, and also for the design of social services. Rather than being a cause of frustration because outcomes cannot

be predicted with precision, the dynamism of complex systems can be interpreted as holding significant potential for change. The importance of relationships and the interactions between agents in complex systems raises the possibility that locally driven solutions may be more effective than centrally driven responses. Policies that are less rather than more prescriptive and that allow programmes to adapt and respond to local conditions and to the changing circumstances of young people's daily realities are likely to be most effective.

A complexity-based approach to funding and policy requires a high level of ongoing interaction and openness between all parties (funders, policy makers, practitioners and clients). In creating an emergent set of relationships with service providers, funders and policy makers open themselves up to significant new sources of information that can be used to refine policy and shape funding decisions (Emison, 2008). Building open and trusting relationships between service providers, funders and policy makers is not a simple task, but there are some promising signs of the value that can be gained from this. In New Zealand, for instance, The SKIP[1] initiative is an innovative government funding programme that shows evidence of complexity theory (Zimmerman & Hayday, 1999). SKIP funds services to provide at-risk parents with information and strategies for working effectively with their children. SKIP adopted an open tender process where the government funder defined the issues it wanted to address (i.e., accessible and meaningful information and strategies for parents) and then invited local organisations to produce proposals that outlined how they would do this and then to collaborate in a process of determining how the government would know that the programmes were successful. It has resulted in a very diverse range of innovative programmes based in local communities across the country

---

[1] For information on the SKIP initiative, see http://www.familyservices.govt.nz/working-with-us/programmes-services/positive-parenting/skip-index.html. Accessed 21 Feb 2011.

that have been able to adapt, grow and develop over time. For example, one of the initiatives brings local parents together to share and learn from their own successful strategies for positively managing challenging behaviour in preschool children. Another works with children at middle school (aged 11 and 12 years) to identify strategies for managing community violence.

Social work practice typically has an intense focus on relationships, as these are the fundamental resources in interventions. A complexity approach calls for practice that works with young people in their whole context including their families, peers and communities and the wider systems that have an impact on their social relationships and networks as well. It suggests the need for practice that is fundamentally collaborative. Such practice will by definition cut across traditional boundaries such as the statutory services-non-governmental organisation interface and the practitioner-family interface. It would also help workers engage widely with the social networks and systems that become involved with young people such as education, mental health and justice. Supporting change for young people at significant risk requires practice that clearly understands the ways in which all agents in a system influence the nature of options available to young people and, importantly, that attends to the paradoxes in their world – the relationships and behaviours that are both good and bad, positive and negative. These paradoxical relationships and behaviours hold the most potential for change. Complexity theory raises the possibility that we may be able to have an impact on resilience-building by creating open and strong relationships across the multiple systems that shape young people's pathways as much as by working directly with young people themselves.

While ending comparatively well, Ben's story alerts us to the missed opportunities for an earlier, smaller intervention that might not have resulted in such a large number of challenges encountered in his young life and the resultant damage to himself and others. There were doubtless many opportunities during his early years when adults could have intervened with a small input and drawn Ben into activities that changed the direction his life was taking. Resilience-promoting activities can be diverse and call upon practitioners not only to take action, but also to carefully observe responses to see where the ripple effects go and how they establish themselves over time.

Critique

Complexity theory does not provide an answer to all the challenges we face in creating systems that work effectively to enhance resilience in young people at significant risk. In particular, alone, it does not address the issues of power that are an inherent part of human systems (Fenwick, 2010). While in principle supporters of complexity theory argue that there are endless possibilities for systems to transform, in human systems, individuals have differential power and thus different capacities to shape the way in which the system develops (Mischen & Jackson, 2008). In many ways, complexity theory is value free (Buckle Henning, 2010); it describes systems where the agents act and interact in more or less neutral ways. For this reason, Emison (2008) has argued for 'principled ongoing conscious learning behaviour' (p. 410). Others refer to the need for explicit articulation of a values framework when working with complexity theory (Zimmerman & Hayday, 1999; Zimmerman et al., 1998). To be useful to the development of social work practice, these issues need to be deliberately incorporated into any analysis and practice using complexity theory. In policy terms, complexity theory calls for approaches that are able to be less prescriptive and that encourage dialogue between policy personnel, practitioners and community members. It calls for policy makers who are willing to actively engage with the implementation of their policies in order that they understand how they may need to be adapted in light of local conditions. In service delivery terms, complexity theory requires practitioners who are able to take less prescriptive programmes, adapt them to local circumstances, and then be intentional about reporting how and why they made modifications or particular decisions in response to specific sets of circumstances.

Conclusion

The social and physical ecologies within which young people move and the kinds of relational processes that these ecologies contain create and constrain the possibilities for their growth and development. Complexity theory provides a conceptual framework that moves beyond linear ways of thinking about causes and effects (Bloch, 2005). While it will not produce the answers to all the questions we have about how to create optimal conditions for youth facing adversity, it does have potential to assist in the development of solutions. It works explicitly with the dynamic and variable ways in which individuals interact with others in their social ecologies, with both systems and individuals, and with the ways in which resources are available or not available at different times and in different combinations. In this way, it encourages us to look widely for a range of factors that may influence resilience.

References

Andriani, P. (2001). Diversity, knowledge and complexity theory: Some introductory issues. *International Journal of Innovation Management, 5*(2), 257–274.

Backett-Milburn, K., Wilson, S., Bancroft, A., & Cunningham-Burley, S. (2008). Challenging childhoods: Young people's accounts of "getting by" in families with substance use problems. *Childhood, 15*(4), 461–479.

Belliveau, G., & Beare, D. (2007). Theatre for positive youth development: A model for collaborative play-creating. *Applied Theatre Researcher, 7*. Retrieved from http://www.griffith.edu.au/__data/assets/pdf_file/0008/52892/04-beare-belliveau-final.pdf. Accessed 21 Feb 2011.

Bloch, D. (2005). Complexity, chaos and non-linear dynamics: A new perspective on career development theory. *Career Development Quarterly, 53*(3), 194–207.

Brodsky, A. E. (1996). Resilient single mothers in risky neighborhoods: Negative psychological sense of community. *Journal of Community Psychology, 24*(4), 347–363.

Buckle Henning, P. (2010). *Disequilibrium, development and resilience through adult life.* In Proceedings of the 54th annual meeting of the ISSS, Proceedings of the 54th meeting of the international society for the systems sciences. Wilfrid Laurier University, Waterloo.

Butz, M. (1992). Chaos: An omen of transcendence in the psychotherapy process. *Psychological Reports, 71*, 827–843.

Butz, M. (1997). *Chaos and complexity: Implications for psychological theory and practice.* Washington: Taylor & Francis.

Campbell, C. (forthcoming). *Exploring the career pathways of high school graduates in Canada: A grounded theory study.* Unpublished doctoral dissertation. Massey University, New Zealand.

Davies, L., McKinnon, M., & Rains, P. (2001). Creating a family: Perspectives from teen mothers. *Journal of Progressive Human Services, 12*(1), 83–100.

Emison, G. (2008). Complex adaptive systems and unconventional progress for the national air quality management system. *Public Administration Quarterly, 32*(3), 393–414.

Fenwick, T. (2010). Complexity theory, leadership and the traps of utopia. *Complicity: An International Journal of Complexity and Education, 7*(2), 90–96.

Geronimus, A. T. (2003). Damned if you do: Culture, identity, privilege, and teenage childbearing in the United States. *Social Science & Medicine, 57*(5), 881–893.

Gordon, T. (2000). Tears and laughter in the margins. *NORA: Journal of Women's Studies, 8*, 149–159.

Handley, K., Horn, S., Kaipuke, R., Maden, B., Maden, E., Stuckey, B., et al. (2009). *The Spinafex effect – A theory of change.* Wellington: The Families Commission.

Hudson, C. G. (2000). At the edge of chaos: A new paradigm for social work? *Journal of Social Work Education, 36*(2), 215–230.

LaBoucane-Benson, P. (2005). *A complex ecological framework of aboriginal family resilience.* Paper presented at 30th anniversary conference first nations – first thoughts. Centre of Canadian Studies, University of Edinburgh, Scotland. Retrieved from http://www.cst.ed.ac.uk/2005conference/papers/LaBoucane-Benson_paper.pdf. Accessed 21 Feb 2011.

Ladner, J. (1971). *Tomorrow's tomorrow: The black woman.* Garden City: Anchor Books.

Langton, C. (1986). Studying artificial life with cellular automata. *Physica D, 22*, 120–149.

Lewin, R. (1999). *Complexity: Life at the edge of chaos* (2nd ed.). Chicago: University of Chicago Press.

Liebenberg, L., & Ungar, M. (2009). Introduction: The challenges in researching resilience. In L. Liebenberg & M. Ungar (Eds.), *Researching resilience* (pp. 3–25). Toronto: University of Toronto Press.

Litaker, D., Tomolo, A., Liberatore, V., Stange, K., & Aron, D. (2006). Using complexity theory to build interventions that improve health care delivery in primary care. *Journal of General Internal Medicine, 21*, 30–34.

Martin, A. J., & Marsh, H. W. (2008). Academic buoyancy: Towards an understanding of students' everyday academic resilience. *Journal of School Psychology, 46*, 53–83.

Mason, M. (2009). Making educational development and change sustainable: Insights from complexity theory. *International Journal of Educational Development, 29*, 117–124.

Meek, J. (2008). Adaptive intermediate structures and local sustainability advances. *Pubic Administration Quarterly, Fall*, 415–432.

Meek, J. (2010). Complexity theory for public administration and policy. Editorial. *Emergence: Complexity and Organisation, 12*(1), 1–4.

Mischen, P., & Jackson, S. (2008). Connecting the dots: Applying complexity theory, knowledge management and social network analysis to policy implementation. *Public Administration Quarterly, Fall*, 315–338.

Munford, R., & Sanders, J. (2007). Drawing out strengths and building capacity in social work with troubled young women. *Child and Family Social Work, 13*, 2–11.

Munford, R., Sanders, J., & Maden, B. (2006). Small steps and giant leaps at Te Aroha Noa. *International Journal of Child and Family Welfare, 9*(1–2), 102–112.

Nguyen-Gillham, V., Giacaman, R., Naser, G., & Boyce, W. (2008). Normalising the abnormal: Palestinian youth and the contradictions of resilience in protracted conflict. *Health and Social Care in the Community, 16*(3), 291–298.

Plsek, P., & Greenhalgh, T. (2001). The challenge of complexity in health care. *British Medical Journal, 323*, 625–628.

Pryor, R. G. L., & Bright, J. E. H. (2007). Applying chaos theory to careers: Attraction and attractors. *Journal of Vocational Behavior, 71*(3), 375–400.

Sanders, J., & Munford, R. (2008). Conformity and resistance in self-management strategies of "good girls". *Childhood, 15*(4), 481–497.

Scott, D., & O'Neil, D. (1996). Beyond child rescue: Developing child-centred practice as St Lukes. Sydney: Allen and Unwin.

Smith, A. (2005). Complexity theory for organisational futures studies. *Foresight, 7*(3), 22–30.

Stevens, I., & Cox, P. (2008). Complexity theory: Developing new understandings of child protection in field settings and in residential child care. *British Journal of Social Work, 38*(7), 1320–1336.

Stevens, I., & Haslett, P. (2007). Applying complexity theory to risk in child protection practice. *Childhood, 14*(1), 128–144.

Trochim, W., & Cabrera, D. (2005). The complexity of concept mapping for policy analysis. *Emergence: Complexity and Organisation, 7*(1), 11–22.

Ungar, M. (2004). Nurturing hidden resilience in at-risk youth across cultures. *Journal of the Canadian Academy of Child and Adolescent Psychiatry, 15*(2), 53–58.

Ungar, M. (2008). Resilience across cultures. *British Journal of Social Work, 38*(2), 218–235.

Ungar, M. (2011). The social and physical ecology of resilience: Addressing contextual and cultural ambiguity of a nascent construct. *American Journal of Orthopsychiatry, 81*(1), 1–17.

Warren, K., Franklin, C., & Streeter, C. (1998). New directions in systems theory: Chaos and complexity. *Social Work, 3*(4), 357–373.

Zimmerman, B., & Hayday, B. (1999). A board's journey into complexity science: Lessons from (and for) staff and board members. *Group Decision and Negotiation, 8*, 281–303.

Zimmerman, B., Lindgberg, C., & Plsek, P. (1998). *Nine emerging and connected organisational leadership principles.* Retrieved from http://www.plexus institute.org/ideas/show_elibrary.cfm?id=151. Accessed 21 Feb 2011.

Local Resources and Distal Decisions: The Political Ecology of Resilience

20

Dorothy Bottrell and Derrick Armstrong

Introduction

This chapter analyses the resilience of young people as they negotiate processes of school exclusion, placement as students with emotional and behavioral difficulties (EBDs), and incorporation into the youth justice system. It has a particular focus on institutional processes and their policy derivations. The young people were interviewed for qualitative research on "Pathways Into and Out of Crime: Risk, Resilience and Diversity" funded by the Economic and Social Research Council (United Kingdom) (Armstrong, France, & Hine, 2006). Three overlapping groups comprise the cohort of 110. One group is first time or low level offenders in contact with youth offending teams (YOTs). They had received the final warning penalty, an option for first offenses (with reprimands or criminal charges the other options), which involves automatic referral to the YOT for assessment. Although it is not a formal prosecution, those on final warnings are generally required to participate in a program to address their offending behavior. Some young people within this group were referred to the YOT following penalties imposed by courts. The second group within the cohort had been permanently excluded from school; the third had been given a statement of special educational need specifying EBD.

D. Bottrell (✉)
Faculty of Education and Social Work, University of Sydney, Sydney, NSW, Australia
e-mail: dorothy.bottrell@sydney.edu.au

These young people have grown up in low-income families in some of the poorest communities in high crime areas in England and have experienced the disadvantages associated with trajectories of educational failure and offending. In analyzing their accounts, we adopt the broad definition of resilience as positive adaptation despite adversity (Garmezy & Rutter, 1983; Masten, 2001) and assume both the multifinality of adaptive outcomes (Luthar, Cicchetti, & Becker, 2000) and "multiple pathways to resilience" (Masten & Obradović, 2006, p. 22). Although we refer to resilient young people, the emphasis is not on individual traits as postulated in early theories of resilience but on individual agency (Rutter, 2006) and the social processes and opportunities (Rigsby, 1994) that enable and constrain it.

We foreground young people's perspectives and those of their families and professionals working with them, with emphasis on "the capacity of individuals' physical and social ecologies to provide… resources" (Ungar, 2008a, p. 22) and how these are significantly shaped by more distal decisions in policy, economic, social, and cultural systems. We will argue that recent policy in England (and in other "advanced economies" oriented toward neoliberalism) distinguishing resilient and nonresilient young people is the latest form of differentiating and regulating "problem youth." Based on the assumptions that behavioral problems are the cause of low achievement, and that these are problems of individuals and families, strategies for improving young people's coping and competence are aimed at the

M. Ungar (ed.), *The Social Ecology of Resilience: A Handbook of Theory and Practice*,
DOI 10.1007/978-1-4614-0586-3_20, © Springer Science+Business Media, LLC 2012

individual level with little attention to the broader social ecology.

Young people's "voices" are increasingly incorporated into policy processes, but it is often the perspectives of those deemed resilient according to policy definitions—successful, high achieving and entrepreneurial—who are invited to inform decisions and act as role models for their "hard to reach" peers (HM Treasury/Department for Children, Schools and Families [DCSF], 2007, p. 24). Perversely, this reinforces the very processes of social exclusion that the "inclusion" of young people's views ostensibly seeks to address. We argue that the collective story developed through thematic analysis of our interviews is important for identifying social and institutional processes that shape educational pathways, the distribution of adverse conditions, and availability of resources necessary for resilience.

Young people's perspectives reveal not only the shaping of local experiences by macro forces (Bronfenbrenner, 1977; Seccombe, 2002) but also how social policy is experienced and responded to individually and collectively. Elsewhere, we have detailed young people's accounts of their relations to crime and how they contrast with understandings common to youth justice policy and related practice (Bottrell, Armstrong, & France, 2010). That analysis details the young people's complex relations to crime as simultaneously that of witnesses, victims, and offenders. It indicates the significance of culture, consumption, and policy (policing and community infrastructure) in pathways to offending. This is in contrast to the discourse of policymakers and professionals in schools, YOTs, social services, and community agencies that is frequently limited to young people's deficits in self-regulation and anger management, antisocial tendencies, and/or poor parenting and character pathologies of both young people and their parents. Here, we build on that work in arguing that individual and collective experience is as much the outcome of effects of more distal systems (Bronfenbrenner, 1977). Policy decisions construct categories of "problem youth" and set guidelines for dealing with them. These include the parameters for school exclusion and how young people should

be placed and educated once excluded or assessed as having emotional or behavioral difficulties. Post-school employment opportunities are structured by the effects of economic policy in the context of global markets. The concentration of poverty and unemployment in "excluded" localities unequally distributes adversities. Similarly, the distribution of resources to communities to assist young people in and out of school is beyond the agency of young people and families. Obtaining sufficient resources is also often a challenge for schools and youth organizations aiming to foster young people's coping and competence.

The chapter begins by exploring different perspectives on resilience in the research literature and political context. In the first two sections, we problematize normative conceptual framings of resilience in research and policy. We argue that these incorrectly preclude our three groups from being judged resilient. In the following sections, we introduce the study and consider the young people's perspectives on official interventions and placements. Primarily, these occurred in pupil referral units (PRUs) for those excluded from school and special schools for those who are assessed as having emotional or behavioral difficulties. Some of the young people referred to YOTs are also in alternative educational placements. Some are involved in the youth justice system as a result of incidents at school. The accounts of interventions underline the significance of schools and PRUs as social ecologies of adversity and resilience constituted through relationships, authority and broader systemic priorities. The often problematic pathways to resilience recounted indicate how they are structured by the influences and requirements of multiple systems. Thus, a broad conceptualization of the social ecology of resilience and its political dimensions is necessary.

Perspectives on Resilience

Resilience is often understood in the literature in terms of such concepts as adversity, protective factors, adaptive responses, outcomes, and underlying mechanisms. However, these concepts are specified in different ways in empirical studies. For example, adversity may be defined in terms of extreme events like environmental disasters (Ratrin Hestyanti, 2006) or "everyday" stresses such as academic pressure (Martin & Marsh, 2008). Adversities may be of short or longer duration and of varied intensity, for example in conditions of war (McAdam-Crisp, 2006) or racial discrimination (LaFromboise, Hoyt, Oliver, & Whitbeck, 2006). Indicators of adaptive responses are broad (coping, competence, resourcefulness, etc.) or specific (internal locus of control, self-regulation, future orientation, etc.). Such indicators are sometimes identified as protective factors that enhance school attachment and achievement (Garmezy, 1993; Werner, 1989). Other studies argue that coping, competence, locus of control, and self-regulation are underlying mechanisms of resilience manifest in prosocial behavior and school success (Dishion & Connell, 2006; Masten, Herbers, Cutuli, & Lafavor, 2008). These mediating processes explain how individual agency is harnessed and enacted to deal with adversities (Rutter, 2006). Both processes and outcomes are generally accepted as necessary components of resilience. Common to the varied conceptualizations of resilience are developmental frameworks that provide normative reference points for judging positive or maladaptation. Relying on assumptions about society's norms and expectations of young people, common outcome measures of young people's resilience include academic performance, school attachment, and prosocial behavior and relationships.

However, defining resilience in terms of normative developmental outcomes may not adequately capture what risk, protection, and resilience mean in specific contexts. It may be argued that educational or youth justice interventions take place where there has been a failure of individuals or groups to positively adapt. We could expect to find an absence of important protective factors such as attachment to family, parental support and involvement in their child's education, low levels of family conflict, supportive extended family, and prosocial peers (Luthar, 2003). Dominant developmental and criminological explanations of school exclusion, emotional

and behavioral problems, and youth offending similarly emphasize inadequacies in parenting, family factors, and peer groups for young people's maladaptation and delinquent pathways (for example, Farrington, 2007). A fundamental assumption in both approaches is that there is nothing positively adaptive in offending or school-related problematic behavior, and that all these behaviors are not part of "normal development." Yet, these assumptions are challenged by empirical evidence that young people's problematic behavior and peer group "delinquency" may be health enhancing ways of coping in problematic environments (Ungar, 2004). Many self-report surveys indicate that minor law-breaking is common in adolescence at rates significantly higher than official estimates, while long-term analyses suggest that most young people grow out of crime (Bateman, 2004). School resistances may be reframed as resilience according to the young people's understandings of what is risky or threatening to their well-being (Bottrell, 2007, 2009). The "uncertainties in risk measurement" (Luthar et al., 2000, p. 549) are exacerbated by highly variable participant understandings of risk (France, 2000), and the potential mismatch with the interpretations of behavior by researchers (Gordon & Song, 1994). Moreover, young people may participate in "risky" cultural activities and nonetheless value education and hold aspirations for employment and "getting on" in the future. Such normative adaptations may become more visible behaviorally as opportunities become available. Thus, as Bronfenbrenner's (1986) theory of the chronosystem suggests and longitudinal and life course (Sampson & Laub, 2005; Werner, 1989) studies have shown, resilience may be evident at some points in time and not others (Rutter, 2006).

At the point of educational or youth justice intervention, it may be assumed that there has been a failure by the youth to positively adapt, but such interventions may also be among the adversities with which young people must cope. The analysis of how they cope suggests their resilience – including the achievement of the kinds of developmental tasks commonly associated with resilience. However, the timing, chains of events and decisions, and pathways to these attainments are inextricably linked to systemic policies and categories, the power of authoritative decision-making, and the opportunities that emerge for young people and their families. In context, coping is a necessity, but how well young people cope and whether they achieve developmental milestones is highly dependent on the resources available—the relational, material, emotional and practical supports available across the domains in which they participate. In this sense, resilience is understood ecologically, as determined by social processes that define coping as positive and provide resources that meet the young people's needs (Ungar, 2008b).

Moreover, within a broad understanding of social ecology, multiple mechanisms of resilience may be identified. While protective factors outside families such as positive school experience are recognized in the literature, the focus is often more on individual ability, skills attainment, connectedness, and both students' and parents' commitment to education or the school's success in nurturing these (Howard & Johnson, 2000; Masten et al., 2008; Sprott, Jenkins, & Doob, 2005). School and institutional cultural features and the impact of systemic processes on schools, such as resource allocations, national testing, and accountability regimes, are rarely analyzed as factors impacting on youth and as determinants of their resilience. Policies, regulations, and governance procedures are central influences on schools and community contexts in which young people's resilience is constructed. Institutional, systemic, and social processes may thus be understood as mediating mechanisms that intersect with personal agency for resilience.

The Political Ecology of Resilience

Recent social policy governing young people in England aims to ensure pathways to success (DCSF, 2009). Alongside mainstream education as the central route to higher education and employment, policies aim to regulate young people out of school. Increased school disciplinary powers, alternative provision for those excluded

from school, organized activities, youth justice, and community-based strategies tracking antisocial behavior aim to ensure that young people "stay on track" or "get back on track" (DCSF, 2008a, 2008b; Department for Education & Skills, 2005; HM Treasury/DCSF, 2007). Improving behavior and raising the educational achievement of disadvantaged young people are key strategies for "breaking the cycle of deprivation" (HM Treasury/DCSF, 2007, p. 9).

The political ecology of resilience is explicitly articulated in *Aiming High for Young People: A ten year strategy for positive activities* (HM Treasury/DCSF, 2007), which promotes the increase of youth participation in organized leisure activities, the building of resilience as manifested in school engagement, the avoidance of risky behaviors, and improved confidence and self-esteem among young people. Resilience is seen as important to managing risks and opportunities associated with transition to adulthood and specifically toward productive economic participation as employees, consumers, and active citizens. The concept of resilience as it was adopted emphasizes individual traits and skills, with three main factors identified for building resilience, namely academic achievement, positive parenting, and social and emotional skills. The latter is emphasized through education and out of school activities. Social and emotional skills are prioritized for disadvantaged young people and are expected to help them manage life's challenges, their own impulses, frustrations, and emotions; raise aspirations; and improve motivation. While the policy applies to all young people, the majority who are doing well are differentiated from a significant minority "who need further support to build their resilience against risk. For these young people, entrenched personal problems and social exclusion have meant that they have often been beyond the reach of the public services designed to help them" (p. 12). Their families with "the worst outcomes" (p. 63) are described as low achieving and lacking motivation to engage with services.

The responsibilization of the "hard to reach" is evident in provision for enforced participation and "nonnegotiable support" to young people and families deemed problematic. The principle of mutual obligation is invoked as the rationale for imposing parenting contracts and orders, intensive programs, which will clarify for recalcitrant youth that "disengagement is not an option" (p. 69). Similar sanctions feature in educational and youth justice policies. The policy discourse thus appears to shift from acknowledging adversities families contend with to problematizing *their* "adverse behavior." In policy, the latter is designated social harm as undue expenditure on them detracts from potentially better returns from investment in higher achieving and better behaving others. While such families are labeled inadequate, they are also expected to be more assertive and demand more of services. Agencies rendering deficient services will be similarly held accountable. In the case of schools, this will occur through more stringent school inspections and performance standards, national testing of students, flexible curriculum with more focus on the "basics" for students who fall behind, raising the school leaving age, and behavioral contracts for students and parents upon admission to school.

Other policy initiatives have intensified the regulation of young people and their families. Community- and school-based police initiatives that give power to principals to deal with behavior outside the school grounds, including on weekends where deemed appropriate, suggest new criminological pedagogies rather than support to schools to change organizational or cultural features. These changes fail to apply more democratic processes that may be conducive to fulfilling achievement and behavioral expectations (Armstrong, 2009). The "triple track" approach of prevention, enforcement, and required participation in support programs evident in school and leisure policies is largely a transfer of principles from youth justice and the Blair/Brown New Labor governments' promises to be tough on crime and its causes. Proactive policing of young people is a product of the "new punitiveness" (Goldson, 2002) embedded in populist law and order politics and legislative reform from the late 1990s. Despite declining youth offending rates youth justice has "hardened" through the introduction of reprimands, final warnings with

attached interventions, mandatory referral orders, and additional community based and parenting orders (Muncie, 2004).

Across education and youth justice and now out of school regulatory policies, deviation from the norm is increasingly met with punitive consequences. Although the policy agenda is "new," it represents continuities in the political and social construction and treatment of deviance. Separating out those who are deemed to be unable or unwilling to cope and achieve normatively characterizes the history of the management of young people with learning, behavioral, and emotional difficulties as well as young offenders. The social construction of educational failure and crime and their functionality for social order and cohesion (Armstrong, 2005, 2006) are "distal" notions eschewed in policy focused on individual deficits. Analysis of the social ecology of youth offending is generally limited to individual traits and problematic families and peer groups. Some criminologists have recognized the role of neighborhoods as potentially overpowering individual and family protective factors as young people spend more time in public places (Wikstrom & Löeber, 2000). However, other neighborhood features are more significant to young people in our research who rarely experience policing, closed circuit television, and neighborhood watch programs as contributing to their safety. Crime is part of the everyday activities they see in their neighborhoods, underlined by the regularity of police presence and the policing of young people whether or not they are doing anything illicit (Bottrell et al., 2010). Their experience confirms other evidence that young people in poor communities are targeted by official and informal policing (Crawford, 2009; Muncie, 2006; Sadler, 2008) based on locality crime rates and assumptions about the "types" of young people who live there. The young people epitomize their experiences of witnessing crime, victimization and being intercepted for offenses as "things happen," indicating the precariousness of protective features of neighborhoods.

The current differentiations of "types" or categories of young people in youth policies only make sense, however, in historical context as exemplars of vanishing welfare orientations and the entrenching of market regulation of public life. These shifts have caused "greater polarization between those who navigate with reasonable success routes from education into the labor market and those who stumble at the numerous obstacles which stand in the way in increasingly complex routes of transition" (Williamson, 2000, p. 167). The socially exclusionary effects of failed poverty reduction targets along with persistent gaps in educational and employment outcomes are reconfigured as the result of low achievement of young people and families.

Interventions are no longer framed in redistributive terms but in terms of supportive or coercive "inclusion" of the poor (Armstrong, 2003, 2005), through the principle of mutual obligation. This shift is most detrimental to "the disaffected, the disadvantaged and those with 'special needs' who may not contribute much to the economy…and who do not or cannot maximize their opportunities" (Thrupp & Tomlinson, 2005, p. 552) to accomplish the milestones that society expects. As dominant understandings of "the way things are" and could (or should) be, historically persistent patterns of disadvantage in education, employment, housing, health, and social opportunity associated with low socioeconomic status also constitute societal expectations. Limitations of the political and social "imaginary" further indicate limits to the capacities and political will of governments to shift the odds against people in disadvantaged circumstances. In ecological terms, as the intersection of local resources and distal decisions, resilience is essentially a creative process involving what young people make of circumstances not of their own making, but shaped by powerful others.

Introduction to the Study

Conducted over 3 years in four sites in England, the research focused on how young people, who have been officially defined as "problematic" by educational and youth justice processes, manage the risks they perceive in their lives and negotiate pathways that either accept or resist "deviant"

futures (Armstrong et al., 2006). It examines institutional contexts, interventions and how they impact on young people's lives. The cohort comprises three groups (those excluded from school, youth identified as having EBDs, and those involved with YOTs) recruited with the assistance of YOTs, local education authorities, PRUs, and special schools. Although the three groups are categorized according to their placements, there is considerable overlap in their experience. Over half the cohort of 110 experienced more than one type of intervention. Across the cohort, 68% ($n=75$) had been excluded from school, 56% ($n=60$) had official contact with the YOT, and 50% ($n=55$) had received statements of special educational needs.

Of the 110 participants, 81 were boys and 29 girls; 28 were of African-Caribbean or Asian descent. Around half were 14 or 15 years old, with a participant age range of 11–18. All the young people were interviewed between one and four times over the 3 years, and all completed a self-report offending questionnaire. First interviews focused on young people's understanding of the educational or youth justice intervention and investigated their experiences more holistically, of home, school, and the community. Second interviews with 46 participants focused on events and changes in the period of 6–12 months since the first interview. Additionally, thirteen young people were interviewed three or four times. All the young people interviewed more than once completed lifelines and ecomaps— diagrams that identify significant life events and relationships. For 22 of the young people, their accounts are complemented by interviews with professionals (teachers and community or YOT workers) and/or parents who self-selected for interview, with the young people's consent.

In the accounts that follow, articulation of young people's experience suggests that youth are other than hard to reach, hard to manage, hard to place, and hard to keep on track as recent policy discourses suggest. Young people's accounts speak back to assumptions in policy, elaborate key factors and processes identified in resilience research, and point to distal formative processes that structure circumstances and opportunities that could be changed to better support disadvantaged young people's resilience.

Young People's Experience of School Exclusion and Receiving EBD Statements

Exclusion features in young people's accounts of schooling as disruptive, stressful, isolating, and often demeaning. It adds to the adverse circumstances they face in socially excluded communities and poor families. It also represents new challenges they must negotiate. Feeling bad or angry is a common response to exclusions that mainly result from cumulative records of "disruptiveness" in class, fights with other students or hitting a teacher. Although the young people express responsibility for their actions and exclusion is accepted as a reasonable consequence for incidents like hitting or swearing at a teacher or bullying peers, the issue of unfairness is prominent regarding the context of precipitating events or inconsistent disciplinary measures. Being "egged on" by others in repeated disruptiveness is a common refrain. Walter (15) describes his "naughty" behavior in year 7 as an attempt to "fit in" by copying others "but worse," continuing it during lessons. Encouraged by classmates, he would create "a laugh for everyone" but was consequently always in trouble. Colin (15) was often sent out of class in similar circumstances: "it's not just you that's messing around, it's like everyone else does it with you... Colin do this... Colin throw this... when I'm with my friends then I just mess around and start making people laugh."

Young people see their behavior as part of group dynamics in the classroom or schoolyard and consider it unfair to be singled out. Fights in the schoolyard often start out of teachers' view and the teasing, bullying, insults to the individual or about their family or racist comments that instigate fights are rarely taken into account. Whoever comes off worst is assigned the label of victim. Similarly, Bruce (14) believes it is unfair to be singled out when he is excluded for raising his fist to a teacher he felt was picking on him. He explains the "flip out" as a build-up of frustration at being blamed for petty things like someone throwing a pen across the room and schoolyard fights. "I was just standing my rights because I got first years on me, third years and ninth years. I had... fights with them but then they were blaming me for being a bully but I weren't, even me mum could tell you that, so I couldn't find a solution to anything." The context of exclusion is thus more than individual failure to comply with behavioral norms. As teachers ultimately arbitrate disputes and rule transgressions, individual agency is activated within the constraints of authority and power relations. The complex dynamics of classrooms and schoolyards present many challenges for students' self-regulation.

Attempts by students to present their explanations are often futile because "they never listen to your side of the story" (Colin) or are taken as "backchat" adding to cumulative records and reputations of poor behavior. Charles' (16) claims that his history of "standing up to teachers" —when feeling disrespected—is significant to his exclusion. When suspended for swearing at a teacher, his vehement denial of having done so culminates in a tirade of abuse resulting in permanent exclusion. Knowing he has a temper, he says that some teachers provoke him and although he usually walks away he has at times punched a wall in anger rather than lash out at people. While other students were not excluded for physical aggression, Charles believes his verbal "not backing down" is seen as more threatening because he is bigger than his peers. In 4 years at the school, he never attacked another student or teacher but the risk of him doing so is given as a reason for exclusion. Similarly, Howard (15) is critical of teachers' prerogative to not listen to students: "We'd have to believe teachers from what they say but they don't take our side of the story." Frustrated at teachers not seeing his improved behavior in year 8 after many detentions in year 7 "for messing about in class," he feels he is a victim of his reputation: "then when I shut my mouth, and something happened, they just come straight back to me." In his final after-school detention, Howard goes to leave at the bell but the supervising teacher bars the door at the same time and is hit in the nose as Howard pulls it open.

... he just flipped on me... he put me hands behind me back - you know, like police do - and just
chucked me down on floor. And I told mum and
he come out and apologized and admitted him and
then, when we tried to get him done, he said he
didn't do it.

Sick of being blamed and not able to make a
fresh start Howard's response to the detention
incident is to self-exclude— "just left...I told
them I weren't going back." Although most
exclusions are school decisions, there are several
others in the study cohort like Howard who self-
exclude, believing that they have been treated
unfairly or disrespectfully or to avoid the official
processes when threatened with exclusion.

In these accounts, the school is experienced as
providing little support, and its distribution seems
arbitrary to many young people excluded from
school. In this context, defining resilience only in
terms of school engagement and achievement is
inadequate. There are arguably resilient features
in the young people's critiques of the exclusion
process. Indeed, self-exclusion could be regarded
as a resilient response to the adversity of schooling (Bottrell, 2007; Sanders & Munford, 2007).

Most of the young people receiving EBD statements cannot recall or explain the process and its
outcome. Walter is confused about whether he has
attention deficit disorder, how he may have
acquired it, nor why he has not been prescribed
medication as have most others he knows with
Attention Deficit Disorder or Attention Deficit
Hyperactivity Disorder. He sees medication as
potential control denied him: "if I had a disorder... I couldn't really do nothing about it."
Behavioral problems have largely defined his student identity. At the second interview, there is an
indication of how difficult this has been for Walter
over the long-term: "I don't know what it is...it's
like I'm someone else... [even] now I would join
in, I wouldn't even think about it...until after it's
happened and I'm getting in trouble... so I can't
really say, man, what I think it is... so all through
school I was classed as the bad kid." Categorization
is often a challenge to positive identity because of
how the youth are seen by others: "Some think it's
a bit whacky and some just think I'm a bit... gone
in the head" (Bruce). Walter is humiliated by having to catch the minibus which publicly signals

his "difference" as a special school student:
"Because when you go down the road everyone
stares at you... I have to hide my face."

Accounts of exclusion articulate the power of
teacher and systemic authority in dealing with
student behavior, depicted by Charles as indicative of class relations: "they're upper class and
you're pathetic, you ain't got a say, what they say
goes." The assumption that decisions made by
schools and the education authorities cannot be
challenged leaves most of the excluded young
people frustrated and unable to counter assigned
status: "at the end of the day, they just didn't want
to listen because to them I was just a problem
child" (Nicola, 14).

Experiences of "statementing" (the official
process of receiving EBD statements) are similar.
Bruce's mother requests assessment for learning
difficulties because he has trouble reading. When
the EBD statement is issued Bruce says his mother
"thought there's nowt [that is, nothing] we could
do so just [to] leave it as it is." He is ambivalent
about being placed in a special school as a consequence of statementing:

> In a good way, I've got me education back; in a
> bad way, some teachers just don't see you as nor-
> mal... They see you as somebody who's dumb
> and don't function properly... It's not really fair
> because really you're normal, you're just the same
> apart from you've got something wrong with
> you... a disadvantage and I just cope with it be-
> cause I know you can overcome something... Just
> try me best.

The Construction of Problem Behavior and Risk of Educational Failure

In young people's explanations of what happens
in classrooms, there is a common sequence that
reflects a chain reaction of events: difficulties
managing the work cause frustration with learning, which leads to messing around with peers or
losing tempers and challenging teachers, and this
ultimately results in being excluded on the basis
of behavior. Systemic policies for EBD assessment and exclusion that focus on behavior and
assume that problems are in the individual have

little impact on school and pedagogical practices. Young people's accounts indicate that they are more likely to be offered anger management programs in mainstream schools than additional literacy or learning resources. There appears in these case studies to be no room in policy for recognizing the social context of many "behavioral problems" including incidences of teachers bullying and assaulting young people. The procedural requirement of external assessment in part explains the failure of mainstream schools' to support students as resources are tied to expert views, which privilege the definition of the problem as the child's to fix rather than the school's.

For example, after her mother's repeated requests for testing in primary and early high school, Nicola is assessed in year 9 as "borderline dyslexic" and "about 2 years behind everyone else." She is told that "if I'd been basically past the borderline… then the school would have got money for, to give me help but because I didn't have that and I didn't have a price tag basically they just thought I was lazy and cheated and whatever else." Such funding arrangements with stringent accountabilities attached may encourage over-subscription to both EBD assessments and exclusion where unsuccessful. Placed in foster care, Alice commences at a new school with a trial period of several months but is excluded after only 8 days when she is caught smoking. Her account of the school's decision is that in light of its recent inspection, she does not meet requirements for boosting the school's reputation and "Ofsted" results (as monitored by the Office for Standards in Education): "they only wanted a perfect student and it's a bit obvious that I'm not." These complex requirements exert pressures on schools to exclude (Armstrong, 2003) and may have influenced the principal at Josh's (15) school who in 1 year excluded a large number of students. He was fined for unfairly excluding Josh and four other students. The dedication of teachers whose aim is for all students' success may be diminished to frustration, stress (Elias et al., 2006), and resigned to accept the inadequacy of the system:

> You know, at the end of the day you have to say "look we are a school, we are here to educate people, we're not here to restrain people and try and

> help them to behave themselves when they are being absolutely outrageous" so sometimes you just have to accept that there is no more you can do for that child and they just have to go somewhere else (Mainstream teacher).

Inadequate provision of effective learning support in part not only reflects the constraints on schools' access to resources but also reinforces reliance on external professionals without guarantee of any benefits to students and families. At his EBD assessment, Ian (14) told that his school will provide additional learning support, that the psychologist would review his progress, and that funding for this assistance is available. The only provision has been anger management classes. He feels he has not been appropriately supported and regards this as a factor in his exclusion— "how do they expect people to get better if they don't put [the supports] in?"

Referral protocols also leave few options for obtaining help other than through behavioral assessments, especially for low-income families that cannot afford services other than those controlled by the educational system. For some of the young people, exclusion, EBD statementing, or incorporation into the youth justice system are the most recent in a long line of ineffectual interventions. Early interventions initiated by primary schools in the form of referral to medical, psychological, and behavioral specialists have often failed to achieve a diagnosis or learning support. Support services to children and families provided through government initiatives are, in many of these cases, out of parents' reach, controlled by education authorities and often unavailable in their communities. Parents end up extremely critical of failed interventions and have low expectations of schools and the education system where once they closely allied themselves with them, hopeful for the benefits of professional expertise to make a difference in their children's education. Many students and parents, however, accept the EBD statement with relief because it provides some explanation for the difficulties they have faced. For Roger's (17) mother, the diagnosis of hyperactivity was a vindication of her concerns expressed over many years. The perception of expertise in this case points to its commanding place in the lives of "lay" people. Referring to

Roger's grandparents dismissing her concerns, Roger's mother says, "when somebody in a suit, a professional, told them, then it was okay." Referral to specialists may provide support to families but simultaneously underline the incapacity of their resources as the role of effectual agency is monopolized by expert others and opportunities for valuing parents in partnership approaches are not taken (Armstrong, 1995, 2003, 2006).

In a number of cases, schools rely on police intervention to deal with student transgressions. Some young people's only involvement with police is instigated by their school. Adele (16) is arrested when the school reports her for fighting after school outside the school grounds. Nigel (13) is taken to the station, fingerprinted, and given a 3-year reprimand for hitting a teacher. His version of events suggests the incident is not a criminal act. "I was in the playground and this boy hit me and I was trying to show this teacher how he hit me but obviously I hit a little bit too hard and he told the headmaster and I got chucked out… Me and my mum think it's because my brother goes to the same school and he was naughty through Year 7 and Year 8 and I think they chucked me out because they thought I was going to be like him." Frank (12) is also reprimanded and excluded for hitting a teacher when in year 6. He says he was told he is no longer trustworthy and offers this as an explanation for being placed in the special school. Jasper (13) goes to court and incurs a 9-month referral order and reparation community service for hitting a teacher. He says the teacher grabbed him by the shirt to stop him leaving and he hit his head against the wall. Then he just lashed out. These more punitive responses suggest systemic incapacities and what seems to be a fallback coercive position when educational interventions fail. In contrast, in special schools, there appears to be less resort to police, though physical restraint and being locked in "the quiet room" is commonly used to manage behavior. Such constraints are an ever-present threat that represents continuity in the history of coercive management of "the defective" through control and confinement (Armstrong, 2003).

Exclusion increases the risk of educational failure (Social Exclusion Unit, 1998). Despite official guidelines that those excluded from school would spend not more than 15 days out of school, in this cohort spending 6 months to 2 years out of school is common experience. For excluded students as well as students waiting for placement once they have been statemented, little support is available. Most of the young people participate in no educational activity during this time. A few receive weekly home tutoring but most spend their time watching television, helping with housework and childcare, tasks done for both immediate and extended family. Some obtain part-time jobs. Roger's mother is unsuccessful in requesting schoolwork for her son so uses the local library in an attempt to provide some home schooling during the period of exclusion. Walter's mother tutors him using books provided by a school liaison officer. Waiting for another mainstream high school to decide on his application, Howard says "they just kept leaving it and leaving it and not getting in contact with my mum so I just kept going fishing and fishing…" When he finally receives a reply, it is suggested that the referral unit would be more appropriate because he had missed so much school.

Exclusion also leaves young people at risk of further exclusionary processes. Being cut off from friends is a significant pressure and the dominant reason given by young people for their preference to stay in mainstream schools. The time out of school is described as boring, depressing and antisocial as routines and friendships are disrupted. Attempts to maintain contact with classmates may lead to incorporation into other regulatory systems. When Leonard (15) returns to school to visit friends during his exclusion, the school calls in the police who give him an informal warning. James' (15) school threatens the same action when he tries to visit friends. For some young people, it is time, boredom and finding other young people to "hang out with" that leads to criminalization. While waiting for a new placement post-exclusion, George (14) and his friends took to joyriding. At his first interview, he has a court date hanging over him that will determine whether he will spend summer "in a cell" or "playing football or going swimming or something." In areas with limited or no facilities or organized recreation, and where young people are highly policed, those out of school are more vulnerable to involvement in illicit recreations and to scrutiny by official and informal neighborhood policing (Bottrell et al., 2010). Overemphasis on individual factors for resilience may leave "invisible" the broader social and political ecology in which it is situated. The roles of policy and authority in the distribution of educational support are clear in these young people's accounts. Stepping back from the details of school practices and young people's experiences, we can see how macroecological systems (Bronfenbrenner, 1977) are not only influential but also directly produce consequential practices. These may constrain or enable young people's agency for resilience.

Experiences of Alternative Schooling and Reflection on Mainstream Schools

Educational categories are based on behavior and assessments that young people often resist. Their resistances to categorization are based in distinctions of fair and unfair discipline, teachers who do try to help, and those who are perceived to ignore students' educational needs and request for help, and claims for the right to respect. Glyn (12) rejects the "behavioral problem" category that places him in a special school maintaining that "racist comments" are the basis of his "temper problem." Although he feels that his temper is justified, he is obliged to control his anger to avoid restraint, a disciplinary measure that reinforces the responsibilization of racism as *his* problem. Even those who embrace the EBD assessment find ways to understand their situation as more than a deficit or individual failing. Ian describes himself as "just like any other person that had emotional behavior problems." These resistances to categorical identities along with making the most of resources available in families and alternative schools constitute an

expression of resilience. Now 7 months into a college hairdressing course that includes regular work in a salon, Adele (16) reflects on how she coped with the "very stressful" experience of exclusion, managing the time out of school and adapting to the PRU as "holding on to my courage and working and things," drawing on family and peer support and opportunities provided through alternative schooling. Having "been through a lot," Adele and her family are proud of her achievements.

The young people's accounts of mainstream schooling are not accounts of disengaged students; rather they elaborate processes of the education system disengaging them. Accounts of alternative schooling detail those processes through the contrasts made with mainstream experience. Despite enduring very negative schooling, long waits for new placements and, for some, incorporation into multiple regulatory systems (youth justice, social services, out of home placements), they maintain a desire to learn and to achieve credentials for employment. They also maintain openness to teachers and are responsive to those who are respectful, available to provide sufficient help with schoolwork, and convey emotional support. Teachers' attitudes and willingness to help are key factors for resilience and young people's success or failure when experiencing "second chances" or "fresh starts" in education.

The preference for alternatives to mainstream education is often explained as a benefit of smaller schools and smaller classes. Ivan's (12) teachers in his special school "don't get angry when they think that you've got a question wrong. They just turn around and help you." With this support, "you don't mess about as much" and "you don't get frustrated that everyone else is getting the attention." Many similar accounts of PRUs indicate that access to teachers is significant to minimizing frustration with schoolwork, and the kinds of behavior for which young people have had to rely upon as coping strategies, even if these same behaviors resulted in their exclusion. James differentiates teachers as "safe" ("cool") and "unsafe" according whether they are skilled in explaining what needs to be learned. For Josh

(15), the attention to literacy has meant "I could learn to read and then I was helping others after… and then I never stopped reading."

The connection between learning context and issues like bullying that are decoupled in official accounts of exclusion and statementing is made clear in young people's comparisons of mainstream and alternative schools. In contrast to "too many students and too much aggravation" (Bruce), more help with schoolwork, including one-to-one tutoring, enables more amicable peer relationships. When Josh has the opportunity to return to his former school, he opts to continue at the PRU because he believes that the high school is now worse in terms of bullying: "here you just get talked to and treated with respect." Donald (15) was excluded at both primary and high schools, then from a PRU moved to a special school. The most significant change came for him at the PRU because students helped each other with reading and class work rather than "slagging" each other: "if you need one-to-one, you shouldn't be ashamed to say…the lads in the school used to look at me like I'm a thicko…the [PRU] kids… say yeah, fair play kid for asking teacher for help." At the special school, his reading has continued to improve with individual assistance.

Teachers are described as more proactive in ensuring that students get along well together. They are quick to intervene in conflicts and teach strategies for cooperation. Ivan (11) describes teachers intervening before a verbal row escalates into a fight and a contract system for bullying that minimizes retaliations. Colin (16) (also in a special school) points out that "they say like the right things to do. They listen to your story and then like say things after what you could do." Darwin (12) describes peer support strategies of "stick[ing] up for the kid who is getting picked on" as also preventing a bullying student getting into trouble.

For many students, an aversion to shouting teachers is replaced by appreciation of teachers' communication styles. In the more personalized classroom, teachers' calmness and sense of humor are enabling factors in coping, learning, and achievement. Lewis (13) reports that calm teachers mean more settled students. Colin is happier because "teachers have a laugh with you… It's better than a normal school." He also finds that students who have the reputation of being difficult may "look mean but they're soft." Nicola suggests that people are "more relaxed about things and basically let you get on with your own but then they've got to have some set of rules." While alternative placements are officially for students that mainstream schools are unable to provide for, the young people's accounts suggest they actually provide fairly basic educational strategies for meeting students' needs that might reasonably be expected to be part of mainstream schools. With positive relationships and facilitated cooperation, abiding by rules is "easy." Young people say that in these alternative settings, they obtain the respect they desire. In tandem with attaining a sense of progress in their education, many are also proud of their achievements. Vince (16) was excluded for stealing a classmate's phone— "caught up with different people and they just asked me to do it and I was daft enough to do it as well" —but considers it has worked out positively as he is now at college studying General Certificate of Secondary Education (GCSE) subjects and receiving more individual tuition than he would at his former school. He has chosen subjects with the aim of going on to further study in forensic science or paramedics. Leonard (15) is "chuffed" about his record from the PRU, which provides evidence of his potential—that in the supportive environment he is focused, does his work, and is in no trouble. In contrast to the "foot thick" record in mainstream school that documented reasons for his exclusion, this new record counteracts negative interpretations of him as a person. He links these ideas to his employment goals. Given his past troubles at school, a good job will "just prove everyone wrong…a proper bully but look at him now!" Alongside the enablement of learning, cooperation, and achievement, young people are encouraged to think about their futures and articulate their aspirations for further education and employment.

For many of the older teenagers links to the Connexions interagency or local employment preparation schemes provide opportunities for them to demonstrate competence in work experience and to access support in the transition to vocational studies at college or into jobs. Connexions is a government funded set of partnerships comprising multiple agencies that provide integrated services. Through one site, 13–19-year-olds may access assistance for personal and career development (Bynner & Londra, 2004). Connexions advisors help Adele (16) negotiate the new environment of college and the hairdressing salon placement. Ironically, the behaviors she has learned for "getting on" at the PRU, combined with her initial shyness, are problematic in the new environment and she stops attending: "I was just getting my head down and not talking to no one and going on my breaks on my own." When Connexions staffs understand that she really does want to complete the placement, they facilitate her return and discuss with her ways to connect with the older experienced salon staff. "I started talking to a few people; it was easier…you just have to attend for a bit and then someone starts talking to you." In contrast with behavioral corrections, young people are provided opportunities to participate in mainstream pathways that are meaningful to them. These are accompanied by purposeful information, support, and learning.

For some students, their success in vocational learning strengthens trust in PRU staff and their confidence to seek help regarding issues like alcohol and other drug use. Bradley's (15) positive relationships with staff at school and the employment training center and optimism concerning his work future are significant to his asking for help to manage his marijuana use. The PRU also provides access to a gym, and Bradley works out regularly to regain his fitness.

Policies in mainstream schools that require exclusion for specific behaviors like drug use and verbal abuse are based on reasonable normative expectations:

> … if a child swears at you – that you go home – end of story. It's not acceptable and they're gone. You know, if a child is threatening to a member of staff they go home and that is just…. again, that is just

the school policy and I think that is a positive thing because the child needs to know that those actions are not acceptable…So that can be really frustrating but at the end of the day you just have to accept that I am not responsible for that kid at the end of the day, they are responsible for themselves and there's only so much I can do and then after that you either have to just go like that "OK, enough" otherwise you're going to break your heart, you know, you would, you'd just break your heart. So you have to just draw the line, just go "that's it" and let them go now – "I've got to" and that's that. And that's just again part of being a teacher I suppose (Mainstream teacher).

However, the different responses in alternative schools draw attention to the social construction and resolution of "their" problems that are feasible in the context of well-resourced environments that support and provide opportunities for young people and teachers alike.

Problematic Pathways to Resilience

Most of the young people are happier in alternative schools and the different pedagogical approaches forge a more protective and productive environment enabling achievement. However, some features of alternative schooling add to adversity for some students, and their success in terms of improved learning and behavior comes at a cost. Instances of bullying perpetuate the experience of mainstream schools for students like Daryl (12) whose request to move to another school to escape bullying led to statementing and placement in a special school. The scar up his side is the result of being thrown into a chair by another student. When he kicks in a door after being bullied, police are called and he is billed for damages. Despite initial difficulties, Jeremy (15) is elected student councilor by his peers (to represent the class in school development processes), successfully completes work experience, and plans to join his brother in the army. His history of struggles around behavior in mainstream school continues at the special school with many short-term exclusions early on for assaulting staff. He describes these episodes as an automatic response to physical restraint: "you just hit them back." Over time, Jeremy comes to understand restraints as necessary to calm and control his "hyped up" behavior. Similarly, Donald (15) considers restraint to be necessary control by others of behavior he feels unable to control. Though Jeremy and Donald fare better academically in special schools, restraint represents both reinforcement of emotional and behavioral deficits and a justified means to "good behavior." All three boys learn to cope with the challenges of their environment through enforced self-control. Normative outcomes (engagement and achievement at school) are attained, and the experience of special schooling may be regarded as significant to building resilience; however, the normalizing processes involved remain questionable on ethical and educational grounds, particularly regarding the empowerment of young people to be self-regulating.

School participation in "joined up services" is also experienced as surveillance and regulation. The cost of Adele's support in her transition to college and work is intensive accountability for her whereabouts with workers regularly checking that she is at work and punctual. Where young people are involved with YOTs, schools may actively enforce compliance with supervision orders or be asked to provide information about their behavior for court reports. Where this is positive, it benefits the young person but subjective views may be punitive. For example, a teacher in a special school regards a YOT request for information over the phone rather than in writing as problematic because the school staff had agreed the student should have a custodial sentence. They feel that their view is not going to be taken seriously.

Young people are expected and sometimes required to participate in behavioral change programs. Anger management counseling provided to support behavioral improvement is, however, described by young people as boring, irrelevant, and "rubbish." It seems ridiculous and unworkable to Donald that to avoid fights, as he is advised, he should stop and count to ten.

> If someone come up to me now and started whacking me, there's no counting to ten about it, I'll give him a slap back but if someone's around here saying, oh I want to fight you, I'll talk myself out of it first but, if someone hit me, I hit them back... If it's out on the street it's every man for himself, you have to fight, no way about it, you have to.

When young people fail to respond, they are vulnerable to more punitive consequences. Yet the methods suggested by some professionals indicate their failure to understand young people's experience and social context. In cases like Leonard's, the professionalism of those helping is questionable.

> ... this bloke handed me an elastic band and I go, what am I supposed to do with that? And he goes, well think. So I looked at the elastic band and I goes, ah-ha! And he goes, got it? And I goes, yeah, I'm supposed to flick people with it! And he goes, no put it on your wrist. So I put it on me wrist. And he said, pull it up as far as it can go, so I pulled it up, and he said let it go. So I let it go and it stung me wrist, it stung right there, and I went, that hurt! And he goes, good. Every time you feel yourself getting angry pull it up as high as you can and let go. I took off the elastic band and chucked it away and said, I ain't doing that, that hurts too much but, in the end, I stopped going. Because he kept asking me all these questions and I kept saying, I don't know, because I didn't know the answer. And he kept saying, well think, and I'm going I don't know the answer.

The most dominant concern of the young people in alternative schools is the more limited curriculum and credentials. They have no say in decisions about the number and level of subjects studied. These are judgments of staff as "work that suits the individual" (Head of unit, special school), though opportunities to complete sufficient GCSEs that would broaden subsequent options are what young people themselves see as best suiting them. Nigel (13) says his mother is aware of the limitations of the curriculum at the PRU and advises him to "to try harder at school so you can get back into a normal school... So that I can do my GCSEs and get good grades." This is good advice considering that PRU students are eight times less likely than mainstream peers to obtain five GCSEs and only 1% achieves them at the A–C grade level compared with nearly 46% in mainstream schools (DCSF, 2008a). Like many youth in the study, Emily (15) believes that her (special school) teachers see her as "thick" and incapable of passing the exams. Disappointed at not being entered for GCSEs, she stops attending school: "What's the point of me coming to school if I'm not allowed to do the exams?" Tom (14) is happy with his progress but being in the mainstream school "would be better…because you're getting a full education." He is not sure about what he will do after school— probably go to college, possibly to study mechanics with a mate or perhaps art. However, the perception of PRU education being inferior to mainstream, combined with awareness of challenges in the labor market— "Because it's hard to get jobs nowadays" —leave him wondering about how well he will fare when job-seeking. Despite initial expression of college aspirations, over time he is less confident about a career or even that he will get a job.

Opportunities for Resilience

Dynamic relations between adversity, adaptations, and outcomes and between resources, relationships, power, youthful creativity, and stoicism are key components of resilience in the context of these educational pathways. The processes enabling school success are clear yet for individuals much depends on how they are understood by teachers, other professionals, and education authorities. The barriers to reintegration into mainstream schools are identified by one special school teacher as fundamental features of the education system. According to Jack's teacher, "a lot of teachers in mainstream schools are crap at their job and cannot handle even mildly difficult kids…they just want to deal with nice children who sit down and they can deliver a dull lesson to them…I want him back in mainstream…It should be very realistic but the way the systems are set up, probably not as realistic as it should be – we're trying to change that." He and some of his colleagues advocate for change to the mainstream to meet the diversity of students' educational needs.

The interpersonal relationships experienced inside institutions structure young people's pathways through education, youth justice, and into post-school options. Yet, those relationships are in turn structured by policies, models of professional practice, the distribution of community resources, and unequal social opportunities. What happens next in any point in the ongoing negotiation of life pathways may strengthen or undermine resilience. While Roger (17) enjoys and receives more help at a special school, it comes only a few months before he will leave school. Reflecting on the convoluted pathway to where he is now and the uncertainty of post-school directions, he is aware of the significance of exclusion and alternative education in shaping who he is and who he will become: "It's had me thinking this last year, if I hadn't had done it, where would I be with me work, would I be clever?" Charles (17) is proud of GCSE results in English and higher Maths attained at PRU because despite being out of school for nearly 2 years, his results are better than those of his friends at mainstream schools. However, the knowledge of his own capability and sense of unrealized potential leave him "gutted." Lennie's (15) mother laments the failure of many attempts from the beginning of primary school to obtain literacy support for her son through educational authorities and social services. Referrals to a pediatrician and a psychiatrist, statementing toward the end of primary school, a year out of school and attendance at a special school have had little positive impact on the difficulties first identified in early childhood. Literacy support is ultimately obtained through youth justice. Three months into a college foundation course as part of an Intensive Supervision and Surveillance Program, and with work experience completed, Lennie is enjoying education for the first time. He expects that as his literacy improves, he will continue studies in a construction course. His recent achievements and hopeful plans are nonetheless under conditions that include regular reporting to the YOT, electronic tagging, prohibition of being in particular places, particular associations, and curfews. As "known to police" and regularly targeted, what happens next for Lennie is far from under his control. The "second-best" education is important to resilience building yet may not serve him and others well given the importance of educational credentials for employment the accompanying social opportunities.

Conclusion: Local Relations and Distal Decisions for Resilience

The young people's experiences are a complex mix of punishment and support in multiple placements that at different points facilitate or constrain their agency. Success in alternative schooling often comes with the requirement of meeting work and behavioral "targets," experiencing restraint procedures, labeling, losing contact with school friends, and reduced or no opportunity to sit for exams that would qualify them with the minimum secondary credentials for further study or higher entry level to the workforce. Young people are thus inducted into the ideology of mutual obligation that underpins policies affecting their lives and shaping their futures. For young people in particular policy categories, this means that in return for "good" behavior they acquire second-tier education and more limited social opportunities. There is thus a need for an alternative way of framing young people's experience of convoluted educational pathways. Instead of the intensified focus on "nonresilient" individuals improving their achievements, shifting the focus to (mainstream) school resilience may better support young people's success. This would require greater acknowledgment in policy of external impacts on schools in areas of social and economic disadvantage and the inequalities across the system of educational provision (Lupton & Thrupp, 2007). It would mean ensuring that schools can adapt to provide positive learning environments, engage young people, and provide additional learning support as needed. However, the positive adaptation of schools seems to have been overpowered by adverse conditions applied to them in the form of standards, national testing, and a host of other accountabilities that appear to be doing little toward fair and enriching education for the most disadvantaged (Reay, 2010).

Although young people may benefit from new policies that broaden options for alternative provision through partnerships with local agencies and "personalized" educational pathways, these initiatives may entrench a second-tier education diverting attention from the need for change in mainstream schools. Within these options, the roles of professionals, expertise and advocacy will be crucial to resilience building, or they may reinscribe young people as problematic. One special school principal sums up the prospects for three students with complex family circumstances and educational needs: "I don't think we can save any of those three girls." Unlike Jack's teachers who advocate for adaptations in the educational system, this principal personalizes the failure of individual students and their families even while recognizing the inadequacies of the multiple systems into which they are incorporated. All the students at the school are described as "in need of help… every single one and they can't possibly get it." Reflecting on exclusion processes a mainstream teacher comments "So it's not all success stories. But it's a balance you see, for every child that I've lost to whatever, I have another, do you see what I mean?" If professionals and systems accept that they are "not responsible for that kid at the end of the day, they are responsible for themselves" it is likely to perpetuate the social exclusion of young people that reaches back into the history of provision for those who find school difficult. Understanding how the allocation of responsibilities contributes to persistent social inequities may be significant for practitioners' contribution to fostering resilience.

The young people's accounts reveal the institutional shaping of their resilience in negotiating the complex requirements for accomplishing socially normative goals that they too hold as important. Despite the adversities in mainstream schooling, exclusion, statementing and multiple placements, and the precariousness of transitions from school, these young people do cope well. Their positive sense of themselves and their achievements are clearly facilitated by committed teachers in adequately resourced schools. However, constraints on young people's agency and the uncertainty of future opportunities suggest a dialectical resilience–problem matrix, strongly influenced by social, institutional, and policy constructions of behavior. What these accounts show is that near and distal decisions of those in authority, and aspects of institutional environments and social systems with which they interact, may support the resilience of some and thwart resilience in others. At any point within the young people's biographies, they may be judged resilient or nonresilient depending on definitions and dominant indicators selected from the evidence base for policy. Opening up those points to young people's own elaboration of circumstances suggests the inadequacy and injustice of policy that categorizes them only in terms of criteria that fix their identities beyond the context of continuing negotiation of adversity and opportunity.

References

Armstrong, D. (1995). *Power and partnership in education: Parents children and special educational needs.* London: Routledge.

Armstrong, D. (2003). *Experiences of special education: Re-evaluating policy and practice through life stories.* London: Routledge Falmer.

Armstrong, D. (2005). Re-inventing "inclusion": New Labour and the cultural politics of special education. *Oxford Review of Education, 31*, 135–152.

Armstrong, D. (2006). Becoming criminal. *International Journal of Inclusive Education, 10*, 265–278.

Armstrong, D. (2009). Educating youth: Assimilation and the democratic alternative. In J. Wood & J. Hine (Eds.), *Work with young people: Theory and policy for practice* (pp. 75–87). London: Sage.

Armstrong, D., France, A., & Hine, J. (2006). *Pathways into and out of crime. Final report.* London: ESRC.

Bateman, T. (2004). Youth crime and justice: Statistical "evidence," recent trends and responses. In B. Goldson & J. Muncie (Eds.), *Youth crime and justice* (pp. 67–77). London: Sage.

Bottrell, D. (2007). Resistance, resilience and social identities: Reframing "problem youth" and the problem of schooling. *Journal of Youth Studies, 10*, 597–616.

Bottrell, D. (2009). Understanding "marginal" perspectives: Toward a social theory of resilience. *Qualitative Social Work. Research & Practice, 8*, 321–339.

Bottrell, D., Armstrong, D., & France, A. (2010). Young people's relations to crime: Pathways across ecologies. *Youth Justice, 10*, 56–72.

Bronfenbrenner, U. (1977). Toward an experimental ecology of human development. *American Psychologist, 32*, 513–531.

Bronfenbrenner, U. (1986). Ecology of the family as a context for human development: Research perspectives. *Developmental Psychology, 22*, 723–742.

Bynner, J., & Londra, M. (2004). *The impact of government policy on social exclusion among young people. A review of the literature for the Social Exclusion Unit in the Breaking the Cycle series.* London: Social Exclusion Unit/HMSO.

Crawford, A. (2009). Criminalizing sociability through anti-social behaviour legislation: Dispersal powers, young people and the police. *Youth Justice, 9*, 5–26.

Department for Children, Schools and Families. (2008a). *Back on track. A strategy for modernizing alternative provision for young people.* Norwich: The Stationery Office, Cm 7410.

Department for Children, Schools and Families. (2008b). *Youth task force action plan 2008.* London: DCSF.

Department for Children, Schools and Families. (2009). *Your child, your schools, our future: Building a 21st century schools* system. Norwich: The Stationery Office, Cm 7588.

Department for Education and Skills. (2005). *Youth matters.* London: DfES.

Dishion, T., & Connell, A. (2006). Adolescents' resilience as a self-regulatory process: Promising themes for linking intervention with developmental science. *Annals of the New York Academy of Science, 1094*, 125–138.

Elias, M., Parker, S., & Rosenblatt, J. (2006). Building educational opportunity. In S. Goldstein, & R. Brooks (Eds.), *Handbook of resilience in children* (pp. 315–336). New York: Springer.

Farrington, D. (2007). Developmental criminology and risk-focused prevention. In M. Maguire, R. Morgan, & R. Reiner (Eds.), *The Oxford handbook of criminology* (4th ed., pp. 657–701). Oxford: Oxford University Press.

France, A. (2000). Towards a sociological understanding of youth and their risk-taking. *Journal of Youth Studies, 3*, 317–331.

Garmezy, N., & Rutter, M. (1983). *Stress, coping, and development in children.* New York: McGraw-Hill.

Garmezy, N. (1993). Children in poverty: Resilience despite risk. *Psychiatry, 56*, 127–136.

Goldson, B. (2002). New punitiveness: The politics of child incarceration. In J. Muncie, G. Hughes, & E. McLaughlin (Eds.), *Youth justice: Critical readings* (pp. 386–400). London: Sage.

Gordon, E., & Song, L. D. (1994). Variations in the experience of resilience. In M. Wang & E. Gordon (Eds.), *Educational resilience in inner-city America. Challenges and prospects* (pp. 27–43). New York: Routledge.

HM Treasury/Department for Children, Schools and Families. (2007). *Aiming high for young people: A ten year strategy for positive activities.* London: HMSO.

Howard, S., & Johnson, B. (2000). Resilient and non-resilient behaviours in adolescents. *Trends and Issues in Crime and Criminal Justice, 183*, 1–6.

LaFromboise, T., Hoyt, D., Oliver, L., & Whitbeck, L. (2006). Family, community, and school influences on resilience among American Indian adolescents in the upper Midwest. *Journal of Community Psychology, 34*, 193–209.

Lupton, R., & Thrupp, M. (2007). Taking local contexts more seriously. The challenge for educational research, policy and practice. In R. Teese, S. Lamb, & M. Duru-Bellat (Eds.), *International studies in educational inequality, theory and policy. Volume 3: Inequality: Educational theory and public policy* (pp. 109–127). Dordrecht: Springer.

Luthar, S. (Ed.). (2003). *Resilience and vulnerability.* Cambridge: Cambridge University Press.

Luthar, S., Cicchetti, D., & Becker, B. (2000). The construct of resilience: A critical evaluation and guidelines for future work. *Child Development, 71,* 543–562.

Martin, A. J., & Marsh, H. W. (2008). Academic buoyancy: Towards an understanding of students' everyday academic resilience. *Journal of School Psychology, 46,* 53–83.

Masten, A. (2001). Ordinary magic: Resilience processes in development. *American Psychologist, 56,* 227–238.

Masten, A., Herbers, J., Cutuli, J., & Lafavor, T. (2008). Promoting competence and resilience in the school context. *Professional School Counseling, 12,* 76–84.

Masten, A., & Obradović, J. (2006). Competence and resilience in development. *Annals of the New York Academy of Sciences, 1094,* 13–27.

McAdam-Crisp, J. (2006). Factors that can enhance and limit resilience for children of war. *Childhood, 13,* 459–477.

Muncie, J. (2004). Youth justice: Responsibilisation and rights. In J. Roche, S. Tucker, R. Thomson, & R. Flynn (Eds.), *Youth in society* (pp. 131–144). London: Sage.

Muncie, J. (2006). Governing young people: Coherence and contradiction in contemporary youth justice. *Critical Social Policy, 26,* 770–793.

Ratrin Hestyanti, Y. (2006). Children survivors of the 2004 tsunami in Aceh, Indonesia. A study of resiliency. *Annals of the New York Academy of Science, 1094,* 303–307.

Reay, D. (2010). Sociology, social class and education. In M. Apple, S. Ball, & L. Armando (Eds.), *Routledge international handbook of the sociology of education* (pp. 396–404). Oxon: Routledge.

Rigsby, L. (1994). The Americanization of resilience: Deconstructing research practice. In M. Wang & E. Gordon (Eds.), *Educational resilience in inner-city America. Challenges and prospects* (pp. 85–94). New York: Routledge.

Rutter, M. (2006). Implications of resilience concepts for scientific understanding. *Annals of the New York Academy of Science, 1094,* 1–12.

Sadler, J. (2008). Implementing the "youth anti-social behaviour" agenda: Policing the Ashton estate. *Youth Justice, 8,* 57–73.

Sampson, R. J., & Laub, J. (2005). A life-course view of the development of crime. *The Annals of the American Academy of Political and Social Science, 602,* 12–45.

Sanders, J., & Munford, R. (2007). Speaking from the margins – Implications for the education and practice of young women's experiences of marginalization. *Social Work Education, 26,* 185–199.

Seccombe, K. (2002). "Beating the odds" versus "changing the odds": Poverty, resilience and family policy. *Journal of Marriage and Family, 64,* 384–394.

Social Exclusion Unit (1998). Truancy and school exclusion. London: SEU/HMSO.

Sprott, J., Jenkins, J., & Doob, A. (2005). The importance of school. Protecting at-risk youth from early offending. *Youth Violence and Juvenile Justice, 3,* 59–77.

Thrupp, M., & Tomlinson, S. (2005). Introduction: Education policy, social justice and 'complex hope'. *British Educational Research Journal, 31,* 549–556.

Ungar, M. (2004). Nurturing hidden resilience in troubled youth. Toronto: University of Toronto Press.

Ungar, M. (2008a). Putting resilience theory into action: Five principles. In L. Liebenberg & M. Ungar (Eds.), *Resilience in action* (pp. 17–36). Toronto: University of Toronto Press.

Ungar, M. (2008b). Resilience across cultures. *British Journal of Social Work, 38,* 218–235.

Werner, E. (1989). High-risk children in young adulthood: A longitudinal study from birth to 32 years. *American Journal of Orthopsychiatry, 59,* 72–81.

Wikström, P., & Loeber, R. (2000). Do disadvantaged neighbourhoods cause well-adjusted children to become adolescent delinquents? A study of male juvenile serious offending, individual risk and protective factors, and neighborhood context. *Criminology, 38,* 1109–1142.

Williamson, H. (2000). Youth and policy: Contexts and consequences. Young men, transition and social exclusion. Aldershot: Ashgate.

Caring Teachers: Teacher–Youth Transactions to Promote Resilience

21

Linda C. Theron and Petra Engelbrecht

Some of the earliest resilience-related research emphasized the pivotal role of supportive adults (parental and nonparental) to youth resilience (Garmezy, 1985; Masten, Best, & Garmezy, 1990; Werner & Smith, 1982). As ecologically embedded resources, responsive adults are microsystemic strongholds toward which youth can navigate during the process of building resilience. These relationships provide a potential source of supportive bidirectional, developmental transactions (Sameroff, 2009). An adult presence, however, in itself is not sufficient to guarantee resilience: youth need to actively pursue resources that will enable them to cope well with adversity and adults need to reciprocate such youth actions in culturally sensitive ways (Ungar, Brown, Liebenberg, Cheung, & Levine, 2008; Ungar et al., 2007). As such, responsive adults are synonymous with protective resources that buffer risk and enable prosocial development, provided that youth and adults engage in reciprocal, resilience-promoting transactions.

Along with the tendency of societies to become increasingly urbanized and families more nuclear, youth's access to encouraging, caring adults has begun to diminish (Rhodes & Roffman, 2003). As more and more parents face increasing political, social, and economic challenges that impact positive parenting practices, and as extended family ties become attenuated (Evans, Matola, & Nyeko, 2008), youth are increasingly deprived of interaction with sympathetic, supportive adults. This holds true for the Majority World as well as industrialized nations (Evans et al.). One exception to this is teachers with whom youth spend a large proportion of their week.

In the main, resilience-focused literature has confirmed that schools are mesosystemic resources that are, or can be, instrumental to the process of resilience (Brooks, 2006; Dass-Brailsford, 2005; Ebersöhn, 2008; Greene & Conrad, 2002; Harvey, 2007; Hetherington & Elmore, 2003; Johnson & Lazarus, 2008; Masten, 2001; Masten & Reed, 2005; Rutter, 1979; Wyman, 2003). As part of this process, there has been acknowledgement of the role teachers play in promoting positive outcomes associated with resilience (Barbarin, Richter, & De Wet, 2000; Dass-Brailsford, 2005; Ebersöhn, 2008; Harvey, 2007; Johnson & Lazarus, 2008; Lewis, 2000; Rutter, 1984; Theron, 2007; Van Rensburg & Barnard, 2005; Werner & Smith, 1982), but the teacher as resilience-promoting resource is not emphasized in resilience-focused literature. This is an oversight, as the following chapter will show.

Drawing on existing literature suggesting that academic thriving and youth resilience are encouraged by teachers, and on empirical, qualitative evidence collected from 15 nonwhite South African adolescents between the ages of 14 and 20, we draw attention to teachers as active role-players that nurture young people's coping under adversity.

L.C. Theron (✉)
School of Educational Sciences, North-West University,
Vaal Triangle Campus, Vanderbijlpark, South Africa
e-mail: Linda.Theron@nwu.ac.za

M. Ungar (ed.), *The Social Ecology of Resilience: A Handbook of Theory and Practice*,
DOI 10.1007/978-1-4614-0586-3_21, © Springer Science+Business Media, LLC 2012

Although we focus on the teacher, we are mindful that the teacher is part of the collective of any ecology's protective resources (Howard, Dryden, & Johnson, 1999). As such we are not suggesting that teachers are sufficient in themselves to nurture and sustain youth resilience. We recognize instead that resilience is facilitated by dynamic, ecologically embedded transactions (Cyrulnik, 2009) of which teachers form only one part. Our discussion of teachers is motivated by their omnipresence in children's microsystems and almost daily routines, which positions them rather uniquely as a potential resilience-promoting resource. A better understanding of their role may allow researchers, academics involved in teacher preparation programs, and teachers themselves to advance their potential as facilitators of children's positive development.

Teachers as Caring Adults

Based on Beam, Chen, and Greenberger's (2002) survey with an ethnically representative sample of 11th Grade youth from the greater Los Angeles area (Beam et al.), Rhodes and Roffman (2003) conclude that teachers and coaches are the second most important adults in young people's lives after their parents. They also note that teachers are typically characterized by young people as supportive nonparental adults. More specifically, Beam et al.'s survey revealed that nonparental adults (including teachers) took on significant roles in young people's lives when they were nonjudgmental toward youth and when they offered tangible support (in the forms of advice or role-modeling, for example) (Beam et al., 2002).

Support from teachers is positively correlated with youths' adaptive academic and behavioral functioning at school and with the likelihood of school success: typically, youth who like and trust teachers, and who are liked and trusted by their teachers, are more motivated and better supported to engage at school, behave prosocially and succeed academically (Downey, 2008; Englund, Egeland, & Collins, 2008; Hamre & Pianta, 2001; Lynch & Cicchetti, 1997; Morrison & Allen, 2007). Even in adolescence, when youth

interact with multiple teachers and often report less positive relationships with teachers, teachers continue to be described as a stable protective resource (Hamre & Pianta, 2001). In fact, Lynch and Cicchetti (1997) suggest that supportive teacher–pupil relationships are even more crucial during the adolescent years, given the multiple challenges of this developmental phase.

In 1979, Rutter, Maughan, Mortimore, and Ouston studied the academic and behavioral outcomes of over 2,000 adolescents in 12 secondary schools in inner-city London (Rutter, 1983; Rutter et al., 1979). Their focus was on how schools, as social organizations, influence learning, behavior, and development. Rutter et al. (1979) note multiple factors (e.g., peer group stability, classroom management, administrative aspects, and ecological variables) that have the potential to influence adolescent behavior and academic progress. Teacher behaviors and attitudes are integral to classroom processes: when teachers adopted a disciplinary style of high praise and low punishment, their pupils were more inclined to achieve positive academic and behavioral outcomes. The same constructive results were attributed to teachers having positive expectations about pupil competence and pupil behavior, modeling positive social behavior, ensuring that pupils experienced classroom success most of the time, and to their provision of immediate and direct feedback (Rutter, 1983; Rutter et al., 1979).

As in Rutter et al.'s research with London youth, the importance of supportive teachers to academic engagement has also been demonstrated for immigrant youth (Green, Rhodes, Heitler Hirsch, Suárez-Orozco, & Camic, 2008). When teachers buffer the multiple emotional stressors fundamental to the school experience of immigrant youth, these youth engage better at school. Green et al.'s findings (2008) showed that Latin American youth who had recently immigrated to America were more likely to be motivated at school when they experienced a current connection to a supportive teacher. Because the study followed these youth for a period of 3 years, it was possible for the researchers to report that school engagement was variable over this period and positively correlated with an existing (as opposed to historical) positive teacher–student relationship.

A number of discourses in both Majority World and industrialized nations exhort teachers to care about more than youth's academic resilience and school engagement. There are specific imperatives for teachers to form caring bonds with young people in an attempt to meet young people's welfare, developmental and scholastic needs and to maximize youth prosocial development (Acker, 1995; Barber, 2002; Brooks, 2006; Goldstein, 2002; Morrow, 2007). In this sense, caring is not positioned as an affective construct, but as an intellectual and moral stance, or an "ethic of care" (Goldstein, 2002, p. 11). Within this understanding, a caring teacher is more than someone who is warm and friendly. Instead, a caring teacher acts decisively to meet the needs of a pupil in ways that would suit the pupil and her context best (Goldstein, 2002). To achieve this, Goldstein suggests that caring teachers enact Noddings' (1984) Theory of Care. This means that caring teachers engage actively and attentively with the pupil needing care and in so doing become "engrossed" (Goldstein, 2002, p. 14) in the pupil. Thereafter, caring teachers experience an obligation to prioritize the pupil's needs and respond to the pupil in ways that are contextually appropriate, regardless of the cost to the teacher (Goldstein, 2002).

This ethic of care is not without criticism, given its typically gendered application and relationship to perpetuating unquestioned politics and values (McCuaig, 2007). For example, in her reflections on how Health and Physical Education teachers in Australia are trained to be caring practitioners, McCuaig (2007) raises Foucaldian-like questions about pastoral pedagogy and how this may privilege specific religious and/or citizenship values and heighten teacher–student influence. Her reflections imply that deliberate acts of caring need to be grounded in teacher reflexivity (Pithouse, Mitchell, & Moletsane, 2009).

Nevertheless, in Majority World countries teachers' roles as caring adults often supersede their roles as teaching adults: research shows that in resource-poor and challenged contexts, teachers double as surrogate parents, counselors, social

workers, confidantes, and health promotion agents (Morrow, 2007; Theron, Geyer, Strydom, & Delport, 2008). In the case of South Africa, for example, the imperative to care is scripted by educational policy. The recent National Norms and Standards for Educators (Department of Education, 2000) expect teachers to fulfill different roles including being mediators of learning, interpreters, and designers of learning, as well as counselors and mentors (Nelson Mandela Trust, 2005). In practice, such care has extended to teachers' responsibilities for feeding, counseling, and comforting pupils who live challenging lives (Bhana, Morrell, Epstein, & Moletsane, 2006; Hoadley, 2007). The imperative to care is, in other words, a complex task that is made more difficult in resource-poor education and community contexts in developing countries.

Researchers have noted that caring teachers are associated with youth resilience (Benard, 1995; Werner & Smith, 1982; Zimmerman & Arunkumar, 1994). Werner and Smith's (2001) longitudinal study of high-risk youths born in 1955 and raised on the island of Kauai specifically identified "caring teachers" (p. 153) as crucial to at-risk youth's successful transition to adulthood. When youth reached age 40, caring teachers were still exerting a resilience-promoting influence on their ex-pupils' lives. Hetherington and Elmore's (2003) review of the resources that encourage youth to cope adaptively with parental divorce made mention of warm teachers that engaged in authoritative practices that included consistent discipline and communicating realistically high expectations about behavior and academic progress. Likewise, in a retrospective description of the variable trajectories of 16 Black South African teenagers from an impoverished context, Ramphele (2002) notes "the importance of caring teachers" (p. 96). She concludes that youth made better transitions to white, suburban schools and adapted well to nonfamiliar spaces when they were supported by caring teachers. Such caring included purposeful actions to defuse racial conflict and to encourage pupils to respect and empathize with one another. Two further South African studies reported that Black township youth described their teachers as instrumental to their resilience because these teachers actively motivated youth, role modeled positive behavior that youth could aspire to, and willingly functioned as counselors and/or mentors (Dass-Brailsford, 2005; Theron, 2007). Teacher capacity to listen to and advise young people, and the correlation of such caring with resilience, was also demonstrated in Van Rensburg and Barnard's (2005) study with sexually abused girls who demonstrated posttraumatic resilience. A final example of caring teachers encouraging resilience is found in Loots and Mnguni's (2008) study documenting how teachers provide pastoral care to AIDS orphans in an Eastern Cape metropole in South Africa. Their research identified that teachers encouraged orphan resilience when they demonstrated care that included listening actively when orphans related how their lives were difficult, showing orphans respect, and treating them warmly and empathically.

Thus, research to date suggests that teachers, as an ecologically embedded resource, are well situated to nurture resilience, particularly when they engage in supportive and caring acts. However, despite descriptions of teachers as caring adults, there is too little focus on, or explanation of, the processes or actions that inform their being resilience-promoting resources. With the exception of Beam et al.'s (2002) research and Werner and Smith's (2001) longitudinal findings, there is an absence of comment on whether the immediacy of supportive teacher actions is influential in youths' trajectories toward resilience. Furthermore, in most research except that by Dass-Brailsford (2005), teachers' ethnicity is not compared with pupils' or commented on. This then became the aim of our study: we sought to focus on the teacher as promoter of resilience and explore what mechanisms underpin teachers' potential to nurture youth resilience.

Research Design

To show how teachers contribute to resilience, we followed a phenomenological qualitative research design (Creswell, 2009). Specifically, we were interested in developing an understanding of how teachers nurture resilience by asking

resilient adolescents to comment retrospectively on how a teacher had contributed to their resilience (if at all). Our focus was rooted in the constructivist paradigm that emphasizes that reality is socially constructed: in order for us to understand how teachers encouraged youth toward resilience, we needed to engage with resilient youth and to invite them to share related experiences (Mertens, 2005).

Context

In order to fully appreciate the role of South African teachers as facilitators of processes associated with resilience, the complex education contexts within which they and their students function need to be taken into consideration. In 1994, the new democratic government inherited an education system with a host of problems. A fundamental issue was the embedded structural inequality in the education system based on race and insufficient and inadequate infrastructure facilities and support materials. The daunting task facing the new government was to restructure the entire education system and base it on human rights and equality. Impressive policy documents on all aspects of education were developed and implemented during the next 15 years but serious gaps still exist between policy goals and their implementation (OECD, 2008). Schools in poorer communities continue to be characterized by illiteracy and high rates of unemployment among parents, lack of resources (such as textbooks, libraries, audio-visual equipment, etc.), large classes and social problems (such as HIV&AIDS, violence, gang activity, etc.) that put youth at risk (Oswald, 2010). The impact of these factors on the motivation and morale of teachers is large. It has been reported that among the most important problems experienced by teachers are poor conditions of service including a lack of support from administrators, repeated introduction of new policies that dictate additional and/or unfamiliar teacher responsibilities, and consequent work overload (Nelson Mandela Trust, 2005; OECD, 2008).

Participants

The participants comprised 13 Black and 2 Colored[1] adolescents who had been exposed to a variety of stressors, including poverty; chronic family discord; parental pathology; orphanhood and/or loss of attachment figure; sexual, physical, and/or emotional abuse; academic failure; and depression. These youth came from similar backgrounds: their families (or caregivers) all resided in housing areas that were typically not well resourced and fringed on highly industrialized areas, and they all attended the same secondary, suburban school at the time of our study. There were five male and ten female participants, with ages ranging from 14 to 20.

The participants were identified by an Advisory Committee (AC). The AC consisted of three adults who had regular access to youth (i.e., language teacher, counselor, school principal) and who understood the concept of resilience. Their understanding was confirmed through discussion with a research assistant (RA), a Masters student who had conducted resilience-focused postgraduate research previously. The AC identified 17 young people who had coped adaptively with varied forms of adversity (as described above). Following this, the RA contacted the youth, explained the purpose and nature of the study, and ascertained whether the youth had in fact experienced a teacher as instrumental to their resilience. Fifteen youth had had such an experience and were subsequently recruited to participate. The RA emphasized what their participation would entail in terms of time, risks (e.g., thinking back about difficult times) and benefits, assured them of their rights (e.g., anonymity, freedom to withdraw at any time), and asked them to complete an informed consent form if they wished to volunteer as a participant.

---

[1] South Africa has four official race groups: Blacks, Coloureds, Indians and Whites. No White or Indian participants were included in our study because the Advisory Committee that guided recruitment did not identify any Indian or White youth to participate in this particular study.

Data Generation

The participants were asked to write brief narratives (Mertens, 2005) or descriptive accounts (one page in length) that illustrated how a teacher had been instrumental in enabling them to cope with a particularly difficult period or incident in their lives. The specific prompt read: "Please write a narrative (a number of paragraphs) about how this teacher(s) helped you to do well during a difficult time in your life. Please include what was difficult about this time, what the teacher did/said and what it was about this that helped you to do well, and how the teacher's(s') help made you feel." Participants were invited to write their narratives in any language. They all chose to write in English, possibly because they all attend an English medium high school. The narratives were completed during their own time and returned to the researchers 2 weeks later.

Participants were also asked to complete basic demographic questions relating to contact details, their race, current age, age when their teacher was supportive, and the race of the teacher.

Data Analysis

The first author and RA familiarized themselves with the data. Following multiple readings of the data, some of the participants were contacted to clarify parts of their narrative. Thereafter, the data were inductively coded by the first author and the RA, independently of one another (Patton, 2002), with a view to exploring how teachers nurture youth resilience. Codes emerging from the narratives of the participants were assigned to passages that allowed understanding of how teachers nurtured resilience. Once the researchers had reached consensus on the emerging codes, these were collaboratively grouped into themes. An effort was made to retain in vivo codes as theme names.

The researchers (both White female South Africans) were aware that their life experience and race positioned them differently from the adolescent, nonwhite participants (Mertens, 2009). Both had attended well-resourced schools that promoted academic and sporting achievement and were staffed by motivated teachers. In particular, the RA had experienced caring teachers who had buffered family trauma during her school years. The first author had 5 years experience of teaching characterized by experiences of transacting in health-affirming ways with emotionally needy pupils. The researchers therefore took care not to allow their personal histories to bias the analysis of the data. To this end, an independent party (a nonwhite postgraduate student with knowledge of resilience) was asked to audit the initial coding. The trustworthiness of the data was further heightened by asking a number of participants to confirm the researchers' interpretations of the data (Babbie & Mouton, 2007).

Findings

Before discussing the themes emerging from our data, it is important to note that in the majority of cases (14 out of 15), the race of the teacher and the student did not match. For example, Participant 1, a Black youth, was assisted by a White teacher; Participant 6, a Black youth, was assisted by an Indian teacher; Participant 15, a Black youth, was assisted by a Colored teacher. Although the majority of teachers mentioned by youth were female, there was also mention of male teachers who nurtured resilience.

The demographic data indicated that only five of the youth recalled a teacher's support toward resilience that had occurred within the past 6–12 months. The remaining participants referred to support that was more historical: four recalled support that had occurred a year ago, two reported support that took place 2 years prior, and four recalled support that had occurred between 3 and 6 years previously.

We clustered the themes emerging from the narrative data into two categories. The first related to teacher caring and included the themes of playing parent, being a mentor or teaching "many things," facilitating healing spaces or "room for anybody," advocating for youth or "coming to the rescue," and communicating positive regard or "I know someone believes in me." The second related to youth negotiations and included youth agency and youth reciprocity.

Teacher Caring

The first cluster of themes related to teacher actions. Their actions embodied deliberate caring (Goldstein, 2002) and are detailed in the five themes presented in the following section.

Playing Parent

Teachers nurtured resilience by accepting parental responsibility for vulnerable youth. In the words of Participant 5, a 20-year-old Black pupil, about his White teacher: "She would always encourage me … because she was now *playing a parent role* in my life which my family found it hard to play." In many instances, "playing parent" included the provisioning of basic needs such as clothing, food, and shelter. The following two excerpts illustrate the selfless, practical parenting of two different female, White teachers in the lives of two Black, male adolescents:

> When my mother passed away, life was very difficult for me, especially when it came to my school financial stability … I used to come to school hungry and I had no one to rely on because my family was also having difficulties at the time. The most difficulties I faced was when I came to school during some civvies days, because my friends used to look smart and had fancy things and it happened that Mrs.____ saw me and I told her my whole story and she opened her heart for me. She always supported me with money for some groceries at home and always tried her best to always make me look smart when I'm around other people (Participant 5, a 20 year old black male).
>
> During the middle of last year my father lost his job and my mother wasn't working. It was a first time for me, always getting home and finding both of my parents stressed and looking for work without any success. My mother drank a lot and did over-the-counter drugs and it was stressing me. My school marks also dropped dramatically, because I played provincial rugby and money was needed to pay for the tour. There was no one I could count on [financially] but myself - I didn't want to give my parents stress because their accounts were at a peak. A very special teacher noticed and asked me what was really going on in my life, but I hesitated to tell her. I was puzzled, stressed and my ego kicked in because I never want to be classified as poor.

Finally I told her. She told me that she will help me and I should not stress….but I didn't believe her. When we had to go play games, she gave me money for food or even made me food at home to eat (Participant 3, a 17 year old black male).

Other youth told stories of teachers paying for psychological services, organizing accommodation, providing daily bus or taxi fare so that youth could afford to come to school, paying for school trips out of their own pockets, and taking a personal interest in a youth's overall academic progress. At times, this involved teachers making use of their own networks and counting on community members to contribute financially or emotionally to the support of young people. For example, in addition to providing emotional comfort when his foster parents died leaving a then 9-year-old Colored participant destitute, he related that "My teacher sent someone around the school to collect money so that it can be contributed to my parents' funerals."

What these stories show is that when teachers "played parent" in practical and encouraging ways, they negotiated ways for youth to go on being typical young people: they made it possible for youth to go on playing sports, to dress fashionably, and to pursue an education. In short, teachers as parents ensured youth's continued belonging to the conventional mainstream when youth were struggling to negotiate continued belonging. In a very real sense, teachers as parents provided hope where none was expected.

Being a Mentor: Teaching "Many Things"

In the words of Participant 2, a 15-year-old Black male, teachers "Taught … many things." He was referring to teachers making themselves available to youth by spending time, talking to them, and mentoring them. Participant 2 continued: "She taught me to not always get your hopes up because we don't know what life has in store for us and that I should always be proud of who and where I'm from and never let people ruin my mood or day. The teacher helped me to gain my confidence since I had lost my confidence, and not take out my anger on innocent people who did nothing to me … and that you're the builder of your future."

Participant 7 (a 17-year-old Black female) was supported by her teacher (and a psychologist that the teacher took her to) to learn to cope adaptively with severe abuse. She noted similar lessons conveyed by her teacher: "She dedicated all her time and effort into seeing me better, saying that I should focus on where I'm headed and not on where I'm from. She told me that this was my time to grow for I would be a stronger person than I was then … and all of this is what brought me to where I am today. I am who I am because of my experiences, but I am healed, helped and moving on with life." In this instance (as in others), the lessons shared were embedded in the teacher's cultural and religious values. Participant 7 continued: "She went on to telling me more about learning to forgive and open my heart to God so he could help me. I learnt that letting go is the first step to moving on."

Thus, although the precise content of the wisdom teachers shared was eclectic, their "teachings" demonstrated two salient features: encouragement toward an internal locus of control and a forward-looking perspective (both of which are traditionally associated with resilience) (Anthony & Cohler, 1987; Luthar, 1991). In addition, much of this mentoring related to teachers sharing insights that they had learned through lived experience or through keen observation of life. For example, Participant 10, a 16-year-old Black female, said: "[My teacher] gave me advice … she told me stories she knew, and she also experienced." In a similar manner, Participant 7 (referred to earlier) conveyed that part of her teacher's caring including repeated reminders that trauma can be survived. The power of the reminder lay in the teacher speaking from experience: "She had once experienced such [an incident] in her life, a different situation… she spoke from experience and always reminded me that if she could do it, then I could get through it."

There were times, however, when teachers confronted their pupils and presented advice in less than collaborative ways. Participant 15, a 14-year-old Black female, noted that at first she had not wanted her teacher's counsel:

Mrs. __ realized my lack of concentration in class and my lack of marks, she confronted me about that. I tried lying saying that it's just a matter of win some, lose some. She told me that lying isn't going to help me with anything, but talking will. I got all aggressive about it, but she was all patient about it. She calmed me down and asked me what's my problem? I cried but ended up telling her the truth… And thanks to her, today I don't find that much trouble … and when I do I remember her words, I practise, practise and I always ask for help when needed.

The sequela of teachers sharing insights and advice with youth were positive, and included youth feeling "cheered" (Participant 3), "comforted" (Participant 4), "healed" (Participants 7 and 9), and "encouraged" (Participant 5). Participant 13 (a 15-year-old Black female) wrote: "This made me strong." Participant 10 (a 16-year-old Black female), echoing a similar theme, reported: "I felt my life was sprinkled with blessing."

Facilitating Healing Spaces: "Room for Anybody"

In many instances, youth reported that their teachers provided refuge. In some instances, this refuge was related to being unconditionally accepted by the teacher. For example, Participant 10, a Black 16-year-old female, related: "There was not even a friend I could talk to, but there was always a teacher who I knew could help. This teacher to me was the most open minded person, who had *room for* anybody, she was kind, loving, understanding, and respectful. I talked to her and told her everything in my mind and heart, she let me express myself and that to me made me feel so free."

Sometimes when youth were placed at risk by the absence of significant caregivers in their lives (e.g., when youth had lost their parents through death or divorce, or when parents were in jail, or chronically drunk) teachers provided comforting refuge and an adult to turn to. Participant 4, a 15-year-old Colored youth described his experience of how his teacher did this for him:

My foster parents were the closest to my heart and in 2003 something bad happened, which changed my life forever. My foster father passed away in August and a month later my foster mother passed away….

I was only 9 years old and it felt like my heart was totally broken and torn apart. I felt like I was left all alone in this world and there was no hope for me. But by the grace of God I was in Mrs. ____'s class. She is the teacher who comforted me and helped me in my time of need. She tried to make me feel better … Mrs. __ gave me hope, she was really a loving, kind and caring teacher.

In other instances, teachers encouraged simple reflective or projective activities that gave youth space in which to vent and heal. For example, Participant 14 (a 15-year-old female) shared a story about her teacher's encouragement to express her pain (in written and artistic ways): "I would have never been able to go through the pain if it was not for Mrs. ___. … She was concerned about me, so she started talking to me and tried to make me open up about my issues. She helped me by making me write about my issue and draw pictures so that I should not bottle things inside."

The participants emphasized the value of teachers creating healing spaces where any emotion (anger, sadness, despair, and anxiety were identified in the data) was acceptable. Participant 9, for example, noted that her teacher's acceptance of her visible emotion encouraged her to come to terms with the roots of her pain and to move on in resilient ways:

When I got to high school I would put on a fake smile and pretend I'm OK, but a teacher who didn't even teach me saw what was going on. She called me and talked to me, she saw how the abuse destroyed me mentally and emotionally. Every time I talked to her tears would flow and she would say "Don't worry, that's a process of healing". She showed me how powerful I am and how nothing can ever destruct who I really am. She taught me how to overcome this and how I have the ability to defeat anything in life. I still feel pain when I see males overpower females, but I no more blame myself. I now can smile freely without hiding any unhealed wounds.

In sum, the results of teachers "providing room" were salutary and encouraged youth to process and/or find closure to difficult periods in their lives. Participant 12, a 16-year-old Black female expressed this as: "Their approach to me … brought upon an experience which developed my being, which assisted me to find peace, release all the anger and the pain."

Advocating for Youth: "Coming to the Rescue"

In addition to the practical advocacy for youth discussed under the theme of "playing parent," teachers advocated for youth when they intervened directly or spoke on their behalf. Some of the youth commented that teachers' willingness to intervene on their behalves had encouraged them to rebound from difficult circumstances when parent–child interactions were complicated. In two instances, this related to teachers encouraging youth not to be bullied into parental approved expressions of sexuality, following parental outrage at discovering that youth were gay. In both instances, teachers mediated on behalf of these youths. In the instance of Participant 1, a 16-year-old Black male, teachers went so far as to organize accommodation for him when his parents evicted him when he refused to be coerced into being heterosexual: "My refusing led my mother (biological) to getting the police to throw me out …And then Mrs. __ and Miss __ with Mr. ___ and Mr. ___ came to my rescue. Knowing my story they organized for me to stay in the hostel, and now I'm good and happy and can't wait to celebrate my upcoming birthday."

There were also instances of teachers contacting divorcing parents and entreating them not to expect their children to take sides or to shelter their children from their fighting. After her friends encouraged Participant 8 (a 14 year old) to turn to a caring teacher for help, the teacher reciprocated and contacted the girl's divorcing parents to the great relief of the girl: "I couldn't handle it on my own … and so I went to her and told her my story and she made me realize that grown-ups do fight and I should know that it isn't my fault… and she asked for my parents numbers and she called them and talked to them, about what is going on and that I was not to hear or handle any more of it." Her teacher not only mediated on the girl's behalf, but she also normalized adult conflict and in so doing helped her understand her parents' actions.

In one instance, the teacher's "coming to the rescue" was literally life-saving. Participant 6, an 18-year-old Colored female, told a story of compounded risk, including a father who had spent time in jail, a prior hospitalization for attempted suicide and parental and sibling rejection when they realized that she had a lesbian relationship. Her teacher's efforts to support her toward living included gentleness (such as caring and comforting) and forcefulness (such as straight talking and impatience with despair), and left this girl with a sense that her life was changed for the better:

> Miss __ kept on comforting, telling me, "there is always someone worse off than you". If it wasn't for her, I would have probably been dead right now, because never have I felt so suicidal as I did with this tragic break up. No one has ever stopped me from killing myself so many times before. Just by a simple hug or a few comforting words, and even a harsh word or two, my life turned the opposite way.

Communicating Positive Regard: "Someone Believes in Me"

Some youth reported that it was their teachers' clearly communicated positive regard for them that nurtured their resilience. For example, Participant 8 (the Black 14-year-old female referred to above), related that her teachers provided her with positive feedback that helped her to move forward after her parents divorced: "So she said that I'm beautiful, intelligent and should never forget that … Both Ms __ and Mrs. __ made me feel like I was very special to them and this gave me hope and strength to move on and succeed."

When teachers communicated positive regard, it was often related to communicating about the young person's distinctive strengths: "When I was really down, she reminded me that I am unique and a very strong person" (Participant 9). Participant 9, a 15-year-old female whose parents were also divorcing, was enabled by her teacher's high regard of her: "She showed me how powerful I am and how nothing can ever destruct who I really am."

Such direct feedback allowed youth the opportunity to believe that there was someone who believed in them and this emboldened youth who were grappling with difficult lives. Participant 3, a 17-year-old male, illustrated this when he said "I've always done my best in everything I do because I know someone believes in me."

Youth Negotiations

The second cluster of themes related to youth actions that cofacilitated teachers being instrumental in youth resilience. Their actions are detailed under the themes of reciprocity and agency below.

Youth Reciprocity

None of the teacher actions described above would guarantee resilience if youth did not reciprocate teachers' efforts to engage them. In many instances, teachers played the role of provocateur and initiated the resilience process by navigating toward the youth at risk and negotiating (sometimes insistently) for an opportunity to collaborate with them to solve problems. Many of the participants made comments like "A very special teacher noticed and asked me what was really going on in my life" (Participant 3), "She confronted me" (Participant 15), "She was concerned about me, so she started talking to me" (Participant 14), and "A teacher who didn't even teach me saw what was going on. She called me and talked to me" (Participant 9). However, these teacher overtures would have amounted to little had youth not reciprocated by accepting the support teachers were offering. Youth reciprocity entailed acknowledging teachers' overtures, responding positively to them, and trusting teachers enough to open up and lay bare whatever adversity was making their lives difficult. The accounts of how teachers helped were littered with phrases like "I hesitated to tell her … Finally I told her" (Participant 3), "I cried but ended up telling her" (Participant 15), "She referred me to Mrs. ___ so I went to her and told her my story" (Participant 8), and "Then I talked to her and told her everything in my mind and heart" (Participant 10).

Sometimes reciprocity involved trusting a messenger sent by the teacher (mostly someone from the youth's peer group). In the case of Participant 11, a 16-year-old Black female who was left destitute when she was in grade 4, her trusting the teacher's messenger enabled the teacher to assist her: "For about two weeks I stayed at home, because I didn't have money to go to school. I had lost hope, all my dreams

crashed, being in grade 4 you'd think I didn't know anything but it hurt me real bad. … One day my homeroom teacher sent one of my classmates to ask why I wasn't coming to school. I then told her. The following day she (my classmate) came with 20 Rand [$3.00] which came from the teacher, saying I should come to school. From that day on she provided me with everything. She changed my whole life."

Youth Agency

Occasionally, youth initiated teacher actions when they navigated toward teachers and negotiated for assistance. Teachers, in turn, responded positively and actively engaged with youth to encourage resilience, but in these instances youth made teachers aware that they needed to play parent, or mediate, or provide a healing space. For example, Participant 6's account of her teacher's actions left no doubt that her teacher had reacted to a plea for support: "I ran to a teacher at my school, Miss __ for help. She did not know me that well … I explained the situation. Miss __ actually went to where my friend lived, and brought her to our school. Miss __ was with me all the way through it."

Youth agency appeared to be related to how they perceived a teacher. A positive perception encouraged youth to approach the teacher and ask for help. For example, this theme is present in Participant 7's account of why she had felt free enough to approach her teacher for assistance: "When I had thought no one cared about me, a brand new teacher came into the school. When I first laid eyes on her, I saw my door to happiness come closer and open slowly."

Lessons Learned from How Teachers Facilitate Resilience

When we review the findings emerging from written narratives of how teachers were instrumental to young people's navigation toward resilience, there are four salient points related to teachers as ecologically situated resources. First, it was clear that the processes and outcomes associated with resilience were facilitated by a social

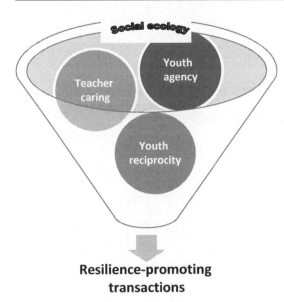

Resilience-promoting transactions

Fig. 21.1 Teacher–youth partnerships in the process of resilience

ecology that allowed youth access to competent, caring teachers on an almost daily basis. Interactions within this social ecology were characterized by teacher and youth reciprocity (see Fig. 21.1). Both teachers and youth were active in initiating protective processes and experiences and in responding to these. Youth and teachers were partners in the deliberate acts of caring that promoted youth resilience.

Secondly, when the focus is on the teacher-as-partner, it is clear that teacher nurturing of resilience includes being and doing, or purposive passive and active forms of engagement with youth (see Table 21.1). Passive engagement includes listening, being available, communicating unconditional positive regard, or providing a safe, accepting space. More often though, the measures taken by teachers to nurture youth resilience are active: among others, teachers overtly encourage youth to be future oriented, give advice, check on progress, affirm academic and personal competence, telephone and/or confront parents to mediate on youth's behalf, provide food, pay for trips, clothe youth, arrange accommodation, facilitate projection and/or expression of emotion, organize counseling, and confront youth. In essence, nurturing resilience implies

multifaceted doing. These activities resonate with previous understandings of teachers championing resilience by caring (Ramphele, 2002; Werner & Smith, 1982, 2001; Zimmerman & Arunkumar, 1994); treating youth well (Loots & Mnguni, 2008), being attentive, available, and respectful (Johnson & Lazarus, 2008; Loots & Mnguni, 2008; Van Rensburg & Barnard, 2005); and encouraging academic success and providing mentoring (Dass-Brailsford, 2005; Rutter et al., 1979; Theron, 2007).

The accounts of teachers as energetically and actively dedicated to nurturing youth resonate with understandings of teachers deliberately enacting an ethic of care (Goldstein, 2002). These teachers' being thoughtful, encouraging, attentive, and respectful, and doing for youth what parents and therapists ordinarily would do, reinforce understandings of teacher caring as being engrossed in young people and giving primacy to their needs and well-being. In other words, when teachers promote resilience, they deliberately perform acts of care and embody a caring way of being.

What also emerges from youths' accounts of teacher promotion of resilience is that teachers' passive and active acts of caring varied, depending on the young person in question and what risk the young person was facing. At times, teachers were gentle and comforting; at other times, they were confrontational and assertive. At times, teacher acts extended to securing safe living areas, and at other times, to providing emotionally safe spaces to vent or to grow. At times, teachers communicated positive regard; at others, they reprimanded. Thus, although teacher acts were always selfless and deliberate, they were also dynamic and illustrative of the belief that caring teachers "respond differentially to their students" (Noddings, in Goldstein, 2002, p. 27). Implicit in this dynamism is teacher sensitivity to the uniqueness of each pupil and a sense of teacher reflexivity (Pithouse et al., 2009). These teachers' capacity for varied, sensitive responses resonates with Ungar et al.'s (2007, 2008) assertion that resilience is encouraged by context-specific, culturally relevant adult–youth transactions.

Table 21.1 Actions implicit in teacher-youth resilience-promoting transactions[a]

Teacher-youth transactions to promote resilience

Teacher caring		Youth negotiation
Playing parent	Notice youth	Reciprocate
	Accept responsibility for youth	• Acknowledge teacher overture
	Encourage	
	Provide for basic needs (e.g., feed, clothe, transport, and arrange accommodation)	
	Network within ecology for youth	
	Be reliable	• Respond positively to teacher overture
	Give hope	
Being a mentor: teaching "many things"	Listen	• Trust teacher
	Talk/advise	
	Self-disclose	
	Be a role model	
	Egg on	
	Confront	
Facilitating healing spaces: "room for anybody"	Accept unconditionally	• Trust teacher's messenger
	Comfort	
	Tolerate display of emotion	
	Encourage expression of emotion	
Advocating for youth: "coming to the rescue"	Mediate	Invite teacher support
	Intervene	
	Arrange counseling	
	Educate	
	Confront parents	
Communicating positive regard: "someone believes in me"	Pay sincere compliment	
	Name distinctive strengths	
	Provide direct feedback	

[a]*Note*: Broken lines denote that actions are interactional

An important aspect of deliberate teacher caring that nurtured resilience was teachers taking the first step and initiating processes that contributed to resilience. Although there were instances where participants navigated toward teachers as protective resources, our participants mostly reported teachers as the initiators of the process (i.e., teachers navigated toward youth and negotiated for resources on their behalf or provided resources directly to them that nurtured these youths' capacity to cope in stressful environments). A second equally important part of the process of resilience was the youths' reciprocity to these teacher-initiated acts. As such the process of resilience was a relational one too. Nevertheless, teachers need to be aware that adults need to reach out to youth on their own initiative. This is even more important in school ecologies where students are disempowered within traditional teacher–pupil hierarchies, though some studies do report youth agency in such contexts (Dass-Brailsford, 2005; Howard et al., 1999; Van Rensburg & Barnard, 2005).

Third, the teachers referred to by our participants had access to ecologically diverse social and material resources and made good use of them. Their caring actions were complemented by local professionals (e.g., counselors and psychologists), school hostels, positive peers, school communities that were willing to contribute financially, and by school principals who provided their own active support to meet the needs of vulnerable young people. Teachers as an ecologically embedded resource are uniquely and relationally situated to encourage and nurture resilience, not only because this makes them accessible and available to youth, but also because this embeddedness affords teachers access to resources that augment and sustain resilience-promoting interventions.

Fourth, playing parent, being a mentor and teaching "many things," facilitating healing spaces or providing "room for anybody," advocating for youth and "coming to the rescue," and communicating positive regard, were not contingent on shared ethnicities, common skin color, or mutual mother tongue. As noted by Dass-Brailsford (2005), teachers' familiarity with youths' culture and communities negates the need for teachers and youth to share gender, race, or ethnicity to nurture positive outcomes. The influence of these caring actions on young people's resilient functioning seemed to persist: in the majority of cases, young people were recommended to the study as resilient even though the teacher acts that promoted their resilience occurred more than 12 months earlier. This durability of teacher influence resonates with the research of Werner and Smith (2001).

In summary, we acknowledge that we specifically probed for teacher contributions to youths' navigations toward resilience. Although our study was biased toward the teacher's role, participant responses illustrated unequivocally that their teachers make a positive difference to their lives. Our study did not explore what it was about the youth that might have encouraged teachers to make a positive difference, or whether the culture of these teachers promoted selflessness, or even whether these teachers were passing on caring because of personal experiences. Any or all of these factors might have played a role in why and how teachers transacted with youth. Nevertheless, regardless of whether teachers or youth initiated the transactions that encouraged their resilience, or why, the stories that youth wrote testified to deliberate, individual-appropriate and selfless teacher acts of caring that enabled young people to cope adaptively with a variety of challenging life events and circumstances. As such, teachers exemplified the potential role that can be played by a youth's social ecology in their positive development.

The Way Forward

Teachers need to be acknowledged, and developed, as caring adults who deliberately transact with youth to promote resilience within a social ecology that advances youth coping under adversity. Too few studies have given teachers recognition for their contributions to youth resilience, especially when teachers function in challenging pedagogical contexts such as those in South Africa (Oswald, 2010). More accounts of teachers as resilience-promoting adults need to be shared so that their examples, their deliberate transactions of differentiated caring, and their utilization of ecological resources to promote youth resilience, will encourage greater numbers of teachers toward similar commitment and actions. Simultaneously, these stories demonstrate that encouragement of youth toward resilience is reliant on ordinary ecological resources (Masten, 2001). In so doing, government, nongovernment organizations, and other stakeholders will recognize that ordinary ecological resources are within their power to provide. In contexts like South Africa where teachers are confronted by multiple challenges, the social ecologies in which schools are embedded need to make concerted efforts to support teachers who directly and indirectly help provide resilience-promoting resources.

Teacher preparation programs need to develop teachers to actively mediate for youth resilience. This implies making teachers aware that they are uniquely situated to promote and safeguard youth resilience, and that their influence may well be long-term (Werner & Smith, 2001). It also implies developing teacher attitudes of Rogerian unconditional positive regard (Rogers, 1959) and equipping teachers with relevant proficiencies, like listening and basic counseling skills. It certainly means that aspiring (and in-service) teachers need to understand that caring relates to deliberate, pupil-appropriate acts. In this regard, teachers would benefit from being made aware of the actions implicit to promoting resilience (see Table 21.1) and being encouraged to extend this inventory. Finally, teachers need to be encouraged to reflect on race and ethnicity to understand and appreciate the coping strategies available to youth in the contexts in which they live. It also means making teachers aware that youth need to feel they belong within the microsystem of the school for resilience-promoting processes to be meaningful. Finally, such preparation needs to sensitize teachers to power differentials as potential barriers to the resilience process and encourage educators to be the instigators of health-affirming processes.

Because teachers are ecologically situated, their preparation should emphasize referral networks, networking skills, and mapping of local resources (Kretzmann & Mc Knight, 1993). The latter is important as teachers should be guided toward understanding that resilience is embedded in a social ecology, rather than wholly dependent upon a teacher's actions or a youth's personal qualities alone.

Finally, to fully understand how, and why, teachers transact with youth to encourage their resilience, teachers' stories need to be explored too. Asking the teachers described as resilience-promoting by at-risk youth to reflect on their motivations for engaging in health-promoting ways, and to examine their actions, would encourage a fuller picture of teachers' caring roles in youth pathways to resilience.

Conclusion

In this chapter, we have argued that despite the challenges they are facing in the South African education system, teachers are uniquely situated within the social ecologies of youth and transact purposefully and meaningfully with them. Their position allows them to decisively reach out to youth living difficult lives, to reciprocate youths' navigations toward and negotiations for resilience-promoting resources, to harness protective resources within social ecologies, and to encourage multiple actors within the youth's social ecologies (in which schools are embedded) to commit to the promotion of youth resilience.

References

Acker, S. (1995). Carry on caring: The work of women teachers. *British Journal of Sociology of Education, 16*(1), 21–37.

Anthony, E. J., & Cohler, B. J. (1987). *The invulnerable child*. New York: Guilford Press.

Babbie, E., & Mouton, J. (2007). *The practice of social research*. Cape Town: Oxford University Press.

Barbarin, O. A., Richter, L., & De Wet, T. (2000). Exposure to violence, coping resources, and psychological adjustment of South African children. *American Journal of Orthopsychiatry, 71*(1), 16–25.

Barber, T. (2002). A special duty of care: Exploring the narration and experience of teacher caring. *British Journal of Sociology of Education, 23*(3), 383–395.

Beam, M. R., Chen, C., & Greenberger, E. (2002). The nature of adolescents' relationships with their "Very Important" nonparental adults. *American Journal of Community Psychology, 30*(2), 305–325.

Benard, B. (1995). *From risk to resiliency: What schools can do*. Retrieved 26 Aug 2010 from http://www.tanglewood.net/projects/teachertraining/Book_of_Readings/Benard.pdf.

Bhana, D., Morrell, R., Epstein, D., & Moletsane, R. (2006). The hidden work of caring: Teachers and the maturing AIDS epidemic in diverse secondary schools in Durban. *Journal of Education, 38*, 5–24.

Brooks, J. E. (2006). Strengthening resilience in children and youths: Maximizing opportunities through the schools. *Children and Schools, 28*(2), 69–76.

Creswell, J. W. (2009). *Research design. Qualitative, quantitative and mixed methods approaches*. Thousand Oaks: Sage.

Cyrulnik, B. (2009). *Resilience. How your inner strength can set you free from the past*. London: Penguin Books.

Dass-Brailsford, P. (2005). Exploring resiliency: Academic achievement among disadvantaged black youth in South Africa. *South African Journal of Psychology, 35*(3), 574–591.

Department of Education. (2000). *Norms and standards for educators*. Pretoria: Government Gazette No. 20844, February 4, 2000.

Downey, J. A. (2008). Recommendations for fostering educational resilience in the classroom. *Preventing School Failure, 53*(1), 56–64.

Ebersöhn, L. (2008). Children's resilience as assets for safe schools. *Journal of Psychology in Africa, 18*(1), 11–18.

Englund, M. M., Egeland, B., & Collins, W. A. (2008). Exceptions to high school dropout predictions in a low-income sample: Do adults make a difference. *Journal of Social Issues, 64*(1), 77–93.

Evans, J. L., Matola, C. E., & Nyeko, J. P. T. (2008). Parenting challenges for the changing African family. In M. Garcia, A. Pence, & J. L. Evans (Eds.), *Africa's future, Africa's challenge* (pp. 265–284). Washington: The World Bank.

Garmezy, N. (1985). Broadening research on developmental risk. In W. Frankenburg, R. Emde, & J. Sullivan (Eds.), *Early identification of children at risk: An international perspective* (pp. 289–303). New York: Plenum.

Goldstein, L. S. (2002). *Reclaiming caring in teaching and teacher education*. New York: Peter Lang.

Green, G., Rhodes, J., Heitler Hirsch, A., Suárez-Orozco, C., & Camic, P. M. (2008). Supportive adult relationships and the academic engagement of Latin American immigrant youth. *Journal of School Psychology, 46*, 393–412.

Greene, R. R., & Conrad, A. P. (2002). Basic assumptions and terms. In R. R. Greene (Ed.), *Resilience. An integrated approach to practice, policy and research* (pp. 29–62). Washington: NASW.

Hamre, B. K., & Pianta, R. C. (2001). Early teacher-child relationships and the trajectory of children's school outcomes through eighth grade. *Child Development, 72*, 625–638.

Harvey, V. S. (2007). Raising resiliency school wide. *Education Digest, 72*(7), 33–39.

Hetherington, E. M., & Elmore, A. M. (2003). Risk and resilience in children coping with their parents' divorce and remarriage. In S. S. Luthar (Ed.), *Resilience and vulnerability. Adaptation in the context of childhood adversities* (pp. 182–212). Cambridge: Cambridge University Press.

Hoadley, U. (2007). Boundaries of care: The role of the school in supporting vulnerable children in the context of HIV and AIDS. *African Journal of AIDS Research, 6*(3), 251–259.

Howard, S., Dryden, J., & Johnson, B. (1999). Childhood resilience: Review and critique of literature. *Oxford Review of Education, 25*(3), 307–324.

Johnson, B., & Lazarus, S. (2008). The role of schools in building the resilience of youth faced with adversity. *Journal of Psychology in Africa, 18*(1), 19–30.

Kretzmann, J. P., & Mc Knight, J. L. (1993). *Building communities from the inside out*. Chicago: ACTA Publications.

Lewis, J. (2000). The concept of resilience as an overarching aim and organizing principle for special education, and as a prerequisite for inclusive education. University of Manchester: *International Special Educational Congress Publications*. Retrieved 2 Aug 2011 from http://www.isec2000.org.uk/abstracts/papers_1/lewis_j_1.htm.

Loots, T., & Mnguni, M. (2008). Pastoral support competencies of teachers subsequent to memory box making. In L. Ebersöhn (Ed.), *From microscope to kaleidoscope. Reconsidering educational aspects related to children in the HIV&AIDS pandemic* (pp. 63–84). Rotterdam: Sense Publishers.

Luthar, S. S. (1991). Vulnerability and resilience: A study of high-risk adolescents. *Child Development, 62*(3), 600–616.

Lynch, M., & Cicchetti, D. (1997). Children's relationships with adults and peers: An examination of elementary and junior high school students. *Journal of School Psychology, 35*, 81–99.

Masten, A. (2001). Ordinary magic: Resilience processes in development. *American Psychologist, 56*(3), 227–238.

Masten, A. S., Best, K. M., & Garmezy, N. (1990). Resilience and development: Contributions from the study of children who overcome adversity. *Development and Psychopathology, 2*(4), 425–444.

Masten, A. S., & Reed, M. J. (2005). Resilience in development. In C. R. Snyder & S. J. Lopez (Eds.), *Handbook of positive psychology* (pp. 74–88). New York: Oxford University Press.

McCuaig, L. (2007). Sitting on the fishbowl rim with Foucault: A reflexive account of HPE teachers' caring. *Sport, Education and Society, 12*(3), 277–294.

Mertens, D. M. (2005). *Research and evaluation in education and psychology. Integrating diversity with quantitative, qualitative and mixed methods* (2nd ed.). London: Sage.

Mertens, D. M. (2009). *Transformative research and evaluation*. New York: Guilford press.

Morrison, G. M., & Allen, M. R. (2007). Promoting student resilience in school contexts. *Theory into Practice, 46*(2), 162–169.

Morrow, W. (2007). What is teachers' work? *Journal of Education, 41*, 3–20.

Nelson Mandela Trust. (2005). *Emerging voices: A report on education in South African rural communities*. Pretoria: HSRC Press.

Noddings, N. (1984). *Caring, a feminine approach to ethics and moral education*. Berkeley: University of California Press.

Organisation for Economic Co-operation and Development. (2008). *Reviews of national policies for education: South Africa*. Paris: OECD Publishing.

Oswald, M. M. (2010). *Teacher learning during the implementation of the Index for Inclusion in a primary school*. Unpublished PhD thesis, Stellenbosch University, Stellenbosch.

Patton, M. (2002). *Qualitative research and evaluation methods* (3rd ed.). Thousand Oaks: Sage.

Pithouse, K., Mitchell, C., & Moletsane, R. (2009). Introduction. In K. Pithouse, C. Mitchell, & R. Moletsane (Eds.), *Making connections: Self-study & social action* (pp. 1–9). New York: Peter Lang.

Ramphele, M. (2002). *Steering by the stars. Being young in South Africa*. Cape Town: Tafelberg.

Rhodes, J. E., & Roffman, J. G. (2003). Nonparental adults as asset builders in the lives of youth. In R. M. Lerner & P. L. Benson (Eds.), *Developmental assets and asset-building communities. Implications for research, policy and practice* (pp. 195–212). New York: Kluwer Academic.

Rogers, C. (1959). A theory of therapy, personality and interpersonal relationships as developed in the client-centered framework. In S. Koch (Ed.), *Psychology: A study of science* (Vol. 3, pp. 184–256). New York: McGraw-Hill.

Rutter, M. (1979). Protective factors in children's responses to stress and disadvantage. In M. W. Kent &

J. E. Rolf (Eds.), *Primary prevention of psychopathology: Social competence in children* (pp. 49–74). Hanover: New England Press.

Rutter, M. (1983). School effects on pupil progress: Research findings and policy implications. *Child Development, 54*, 1–29.

Rutter, M. (1984). Resilient children. Why some disadvantaged children overcome their environments, and how we can help. *Psychology Today, March*, 57–65.

Rutter, M., Maughan, B., Mortimore, P., & Ouston, J. (1979). *Fifteen thousand hours. Secondary schools and their effects on children*. Cambridge: Cambridge University Press.

Sameroff, A. (2009). The transactional model. In A. Sameroff (Ed.), *The transactional model of development. How children and contexts shape each other* (pp. 3–21). Washington: APA.

Theron, L. C. (2007). Uphenyo ngokwazi kwentsha yasemalokishini ukumelana nesimo esinzima: A South African study of resilience among township youth. *Child and Adolescent Psychiatric Clinics of North America, 16*(2), 357–375.

Theron, L. C., Geyer, S., Strydom, H., & Delport, C. S. L. (2008). The roots of REds: A rationale for the support of educators affected by the HIV and Aids pandemic. *Health SA Gesondheid, 13*(4), 77–88.

Ungar, M., Brown, M., Liebenberg, L., Cheung, M., & Levine, K. (2008). Distinguishing differences in pathways to resilience among Canadian youth. *Canadian Journal of Community Mental Health, 27*(1), 1–13.

Ungar, M., Brown, M., Liebenberg, L., Othman, R., Kwong, W. M., Armstrong, M., et al. (2007). Unique pathways to resilience across cultures. *Adolescence, 42*(166), 287–310.

Van Rensburg, E., & Barnard, C. (2005). Psychological resilience among sexually-molested girls in the late middle-childhood: A case study approach. *Child Abuse Research in South Africa, 6*(1), 1–12.

Werner, E. E., & Smith, R. S. (1982). *Vulnerable but invincible. A longitudinal study of resilient children and youth*. New York: McGraw-Hill.

Werner, E. E., & Smith, R. S. (2001). *Journeys from childhood to midlife. Risk, resilience and recovery*. London: Cornell University Press.

Wyman, P. A. (2003). Emerging perspectives on context specificity of children's adaptation and resilience. Evidence from a decade of research with urban children in adversity. In S. S. Luthar (Ed.), *Resilience and vulnerability: Adaptation in the context of childhood adversities* (pp. 293–317). Cambridge: Cambridge University Press.

Zimmerman, M. A., & Arunkumar, R. (1994). Resiliency research: Implications for schools and policy (social policy report). *Society for Research in Child Development, 8*(4), 1–17.1South Africa has four official race groups: Blacks, Coloreds, Indians, and Whites. No White or Indian participants were included in our study because the Advisory Committee that guided recruitment did not identify any Indian or White youth to participate.

Children with Disabilities and Supportive School Ecologies

22

Neerja Sharma and Rekha Sharma Sen

When one asks children whether they want to go to school, the answer is invariably a loud "yes," because school is a meaningful context that gives them a sense of well-being and identity (Beteille, 2005; Nsamenang, 2003). However, in India, schooling for children with disabilities is rare. In most societies children with disabilities are a silent minority. Their rights are only defended when public-spirited members of the civil society speak.

In this chapter we will discuss the construct of disability as understood in India, the construal of resilience as applicable to the child with disability, the nature of school education for these children, and the role of school experience as a context that facilitates resilience. We make the case for the inclusion of children with disabilities in general schools.

The chapter has two parts. The first introduces theoretical perspectives on disability, the construct of resilience in relation to disability, and the situation of schooling in India. In the second part, in an attempt to identify features of school ecologies that promote resilience, we have relied both on a review of existing research as well as on the data obtained from a qualitative study of children with disabilities in New Delhi.

N. Sharma (✉)
Department of Human Development and Childhood
Studies, Lady Irwin College, University of Delhi,
New Delhi, India
e-mail: neerja.lic@gmail.com

Changing Perspectives on Disability

One of the major paradigm shifts that has occurred in Western psychology is the realization that much of what happens to the individual is not primarily a consequence of the individual alone. The sociocultural matrix resonates with the individual to influence individual thought and action. Most recently, it has been this contextually sensitive understanding of person–environment interaction that has informed the field of psychology in Asia (Misra & Gergen, 1993; Sinha, 1997, 2002).This pattern reverses an earlier tendency within academic discourse to follow dominant Western paradigms, a consequence of years of immersion in the Anglo-Saxon tradition of learning, with its emphasis on objectivity, rationality, positivism, and the centrality of the individual (Misra, Srivastava, & Gupta, 1999).

In the context of disability studies, this realization of the situatedness of the individual in the environment has led to two interrelated shifts. The first is a change in the formulations about disability from the biomedical perspective (individual pathology) to a sociopolitical perspective (social pathology) culminating in the human rights approach to disability (Rioux, 2009). The second significant change is the World Health Organization's definition of disability. When based on the medical model, that definition was subsumed under the International Classification of Impairments, Disabilities and Handicaps, 1980 (ICIDH) and described disability in narrow terms of physical and intellectual functioning based on assumptions of impairment as debilitating. This view of disability has since altered. A different view of disability is articulated in the Convention on the Rights of Persons with Disabilities (2006), and has been adopted by the United Nations. The Convention does not confer any new rights on persons with disabilities but brings to center stage the responsibility of society to create conditions that enable persons with disabilities to exercise their choices as enshrined in the Universal Declaration of Human Rights, 1959.

Essentially, this repositioning of perspectives on disability is an indication of a shift from viewing individuals in terms of what they can or cannot do when compared to others of the same age, to emphasizing the impact of the environment on the ability of people to function effectively. Thus ecologically speaking, disability needs to be seen as the consequence of a nonaccommodating environment, not individual impairment alone. When the environment adapts itself in such a manner that the impairment of body structure or function does not affect the person's functioning (i.e., does not cause activity limitation) and does not cause problems to the individual in performing various roles and in involvement in life situations (i.e., does not cause participation limitation in familial and social life), the impairment does not disable the person. Thus the impairment, which occurs at the physiological level of the body, has to be seen with reference to the person concerned in terms of restrictions it places on him or her carrying out activities, and at the level of the society in terms of the difficulties it creates for the person to be successfully integrated. Disability does not result from the mere fact of presence of impairment in the person – it results as a consequence of interaction between the features of a person's body and features of the society (environment) in which the person lives. Therefore, when the environment is supportive and barrier-free, the person is not limited or restricted in performing functions and the impairment does not lead to disability. The experience of disability is determined by the supports (both resources and strategies) available to individuals in their environments

(Hardman, Drew, & Egan, 2008). Disability, from a human rights perspective, is assessed in terms of the opportunity provided by the environment to facilitate a person's full and equal participation as a citizen.

Articulation of this perspective in national and international documents has not necessarily meant a concomitant social transformation in the understanding of the construct. Change in social structures and perception is a much slower process. Broadly speaking, the dominant approach to disability even today is to equate disability with the presence of personal impairment. Almost universally, it is associated with antecedents of adversity (Grotberg, 1995). This is true in the Indian context as well.

The Child in India

Across all social class and subcultural groups, the newborn in India is regarded as being "fresh from God" and "is generally treated as God's gift to the family" (Anandalakshmy, 2010, p. 27). However, there are certain conditions attached to the unconditional acceptance of children. The desire for male children overrides the preference for the female child in most parts of the country. Biological children are preferred over adopted children, although informal adoptions within the extended family are not uncommon. And finally, a healthy, "fully formed" child is preferred to a child without "defects."

In this context, a child who is either born with a disability or who develops a disability after birth, be it physical or intellectual, is seen as developmentally flawed and socially inconvenient (Ghai, 2005; Joshi, 2006). From the very beginning, there are chances that the child will be neglected. While the mother may not withhold care deliberately, her position as the one who is seen as responsible for producing a child with a disability places her under pressure from her immediate and extended family to not invest emotionally or economically in the child. A self-perpetuating process of expectations and outcomes justifies the assumption that the child may not live very long. However, research (Angirish, 2010; Vaidya, 2008) shows that most mothers report being very attached to their child with a disability despite the hostile attitude of the people around them, and that they struggle to provide care to their children, sometimes with the support of other members of their families.

Given the social disadvantage facing children with disabilities in India, it is not surprising that when we examine educational paths for these children, their outcomes are dismal. According to the National Centre for Promotion of Employment for Disabled People (2005), there are 70 million persons with disability in India, of which approximately 28 million are children and youth. Only 2% of these children receive any form of education. Thus, when we discuss the issue of schooling for children with special needs, we are conscious that we are talking about a very small percentage of the children who should be eligible for this service.

The image of the child with disability in India is multidimensional. At the social level, cross-cultural literature on disability suggests that there is significant diversity in the construal of meaning and causes of disability among India's many social and cultural groups (Dalal & Pande, 1999). The perception of who is "disabled" or "who has disability" is mediated by the social context and the value system of children's caregivers and those in the child's wider community, not necessarily by the nature and degree of the child's impairment. It is possible to come across exemplary care of a child with a disability in a poor home and harsh treatment in an affluent one. A child with a mild form of disability may face exclusion in his or her context, while another with a severe form of disability, such as blindness, may experience no discrimination whatsoever. The reasons for such variability in response to disability lie in the social, cultural, religious, economic, and demographic heterogeneity of Indian society, which is also marked by a network of culturally sanctioned hierarchies. There is tacit acceptance of superiority of the male over the female, of older persons over younger ones, of some caste groups over others, and of the "normal" child over the one with a disability.

Resilience in the Context of Schooling for Children with Disabilities

There is enormous diversity in the usage of the construct of resilience; it is employed variously as a quality, a trait, a process, or an outcome (Glantz & Sloboda, 1999). When seen as a trait, resilience can be viewed as the basic capacity nascent in all individuals that emerges in the face of adversity (Sharma & Sharma, 1999). When understood in this way, Masten (1994) distinguishes between "resiliency" which invokes individual traits and "resilience" which is process-oriented. Alternatively, an ecological understanding of resilience situates it as a process that is determined by "the nature of the child's social and physical ecology first, interactional processes between the environment and the individual child second, and the child-specific propensities toward positive development third" (Ungar, 2011). The process approach to understand resilience enables us to answer the questions "Do all children who have a disability face greater adversity?" and "Are they more vulnerable than those who do not have a disability?" Invoking the ecological perspective to understand resilience, we hypothesize that the presence of a disabling condition creates a situation of high-risk in itself. However, we also hypothesize that disability only becomes a serious disadvantage to the extent that the child's environment fails to provide adequate support.

For the purpose of this chapter we subscribe to (Ungar 2008; 2011) definition of resilience which states:

> In the context of exposure to significant adversity, resilience is both the capacity of individuals to *navigate* their way to the psychological, social, cultural, and physical resources that sustain their well-being, and their capacity individually and collectively to *negotiate* for these resources to be provided and experienced in culturally meaningful ways.

While the above definition seems to invoke the trait model for understanding resilience by focusing on the individual's ability to navigate and negotiate, a closer scrutiny reveals that the definition equally locates resilience within the child's culture and context as a process facilitated by a proactive environment. Though navigation implies personal agency and motivation to access resources, it also suggests that resources must be made available and accessible by those in power to those who are marginalised (Ungar, 2005). Negotiation refers to the meaning ascribed by individuals to the resources that are accessible to them (Ungar, 2007). When navigation is thwarted, or the resources provided lack relevance and meaning, the environment could be said to be lacking in resilience-promoting features. In the context of children with disabilities, research shows that it is not only the individual's latent capacities that contribute to developmental success, but also the capacity of the environment to create conditions for fuller self-expression that makes resilience more likely (Deb & Arora, 2008; Landesman-Dwyer, 1981). Such an understanding of resilience is consonant with the changing approach to disability discussed earlier which ascribes the origin of difficulties experienced by the person to systemic barriers and a non-accommodating environment rather than to individual deficits (Rioux, 2009). Under conditions of risk and disadvantage, a child's social and physical ecology (including the child's school) is likely to account for more variance in developmental outcomes than personal factors.

Research in India and elsewhere demonstrates that school can play a mitigating and empowering role in the lives of children with special needs (Chhuakling, 2010; Connors & Stalker, 2003; Vyas, 2008). Interestingly, it is not the nature and severity of the disability that influences the quality of the school experience. Factors such as early intervention, parent–school relationship, and everyday social–emotional experiences of the child while in school result in more or less risk and resilience. Therefore, our focus here is on the microsystem (Bronfenbrenner 1979a) of the school that nurtures resilience. Our intention is to uncover processes that potentiate positive developmental outcomes in keeping with the belief that social and ecological processes frame the context for emerging developmental features. While an understanding of such processes may emerge from context-specific research and point toward the need

for greater understanding of context in children's development (Vygotsky, 1978), the processes themselves can be generic. Each may be applicable, albeit in a somewhat modified form, to other contexts than the one from which it emerged.

For example, there is research evidence that staying in school is an asset when it is a culturally relevant prosocial behavior (Benson, 2003; Donnon & Hammond, 2007). One of the ways in which the school can promote resilience is by providing children the experience of normalization, a concept associated with the expression of social justice. Normalization reflects a belief that people are entitled to live as normally as possible in their own community. In the context of education, this principle suggests that all children with disabilities should have the opportunity to attend school in the same way that would be expected of children without disabilities (Foreman, 1996). The routine of going to school has a normalizing effect not only for the child, but also for the child's family. In India, where most children with disabilities stay at home while their siblings and other children attend school, the fact that the child with a disability begins to go to school can dramatically shift the experience of the child at home. The taken-for-granted activities associated with attending school such as getting up at a fixed time, dressing, traveling on public transport, being away from one's parents for a few hours, and returning home and doing school-related work with the help of parents and siblings, combine to create a more normal identity construction for the child with a disability. In this way, the act of attending school promotes a sense of well-being for the entire family (Angirish, 2010; Vaidya, 2008).

This change is not surprising. In a comparison research study between Australian and Indian families with children with disabilities on correlates of parental empowerment (Dempsey, Foreman, Sharma, Khanna, & Arora, 2001), it was reported that Indian parents who could make use of school services for their children considered themselves fortunate, although only 28% of the 100 families studied received once a month contact from their child's school. This rate is significantly less than that found among the 105 Australian families who reported regular contact with their child's school. The researchers concluded that parental perception of satisfaction from educational programs for their children reflected satisfaction with what is culturally normative. They observed that in India, "services for people with disability are not available to all those who need them" (Dempsey et al., p. 126)

For children with disabilities who develop and display resilience in the face of individual and social adversity the microsystem interactions with family, peers, and teachers are promotive of well-being. Studies by Grover (2003) and Vyas (2008) of school-going adolescents with physical disabilities in India demonstrate that most of those who expressed a positive view of life reported being liked both at home and by their teachers. These dual constructions of the self as well-regarded appear to reflect the cumulative advantage of resilience-promoting processes.

Being in a suitably structured classroom provides children an environment that activates a range of potential learning behaviors linked not only with the acquisition of academic concepts, but also with social and emotional competence. When children who have disabilities meet and play with peers, it triggers the learning of advanced social skills such as negotiating and problem solving (Vyas, 2008). In a study that documented mentoring by school adolescents of younger students with disabilities in an inclusive high school, Sinha and Sharma (2010) found that benefits of the mentoring process included reports by teachers of more acceptance of the children and the instilling of confidence in them by the mentors. Both were important outcomes above and beyond the intended goal of delivering academic support. These secondary outcomes, however, proved critical to motivate younger students to become more engaged as learners.

Schooling for Children with Disabilities in India

India is a diverse country with a population of over 1 billion in 2010. There are 220 million children between the ages of 6 and 14. Of these, 8 million do not go to school for different reasons (Census 2011, 2010). While the Constitution of India gave all children the right to free education,

it had not become mandatory until The Right to Free and Compulsory Education Act was passed in August 2009, which legislated this right for children between 6 and 14 years of age. It is noteworthy that the law provides for equal opportunity for children with special needs to enjoy the same right to education as their nondisabled peers (Sibal, 2010). In addition to this recent Act, there are other constitutional provisions, laws, and policies in place that provide for the education of children with disabilities in India. These include:

(a) The Persons with Disabilities (equal opportunities, protection of rights, and full participation) Act, 1995, has special provisions for children with disabilities. It ensures that every child with a disability has access to free education in an appropriate and inclusive environment until she or he attains the age of 18 years (Ministry of Law, Justice & Company Affairs, 1996).

(b) The National Trust for Welfare of Persons with Autism, Cerebral Palsy, Mental Retardation, and Multiple Disabilities Act, 1999, legislates appropriate responses for those who require higher levels of support and long-term care. It enables them to live as independently as possible within, or close to, the community to which they belong (Ministry of Law, Justice & Company Affairs, 1999).

(c) The National Policy for Persons with Disabilities, 2006, emphasizes that all children with disabilities will receive education beginning with preschool and continuing until they have graduated secondary school and are able to attend postsecondary or vocational training (Indira Gandhi National Open University, 2009).

(d) The Right to Education Act, 2009, provides that every child with disability shall have the right to pursue free and compulsory elementary education. It promotes the principle of inclusive education and appropriate training of all teachers (Sibal, 2010).

While the federal government in India has taken proactive measures to enable access to schooling, social perceptions, and weak bureaucratic interest to engage children with disabilities in school have left many children and their families without access to education or the means to pursue legal challenges to secure their rights. The education of children with disabilities continues to be neglected.

At this point, it is pertinent to briefly present the meaning of the two main formats in which education is being provided to children with disability in India: special education and inclusive education. Special education refers to an individualized system of education based on the child's abilities, interests, and needs, and designed to help him or her achieve optimal self-sufficiency and success in learning. It involves sequencing the learning tasks from simple to complex, being cognizant of the child's readiness to learn and the arrangement of learning environment so that it promotes learning. Thus, it is specially designed instruction that meets the unique needs of the child with a disability. Typically, special education is provided in schools which are meant exclusively for children with disabilities, often with a particular disability, though some schools may cater to more than one disability. Special education invariably segregates children with disabilities from their nondisabled peers (Hardman et al., 2008).

For more than two decades, across the world, there has been a movement toward inclusive education which aims to provide education to disabled children in regular schools and regular classrooms together with nondisabled children, right from the beginning of the child's schooling. The onus here is on the regular education system to develop its capabilities to meet the educational needs of children with disabilities (Jha, 2002).

While both forms of education have their defenders, what is important is that every child has access to a learning environment. In India, with the implementation of the Right to Education Act, 2009, most children are finding themselves in inclusive settings. However, schools can take a long time to adopt the principles of inclusive education. If a child experiences support in a special education program and it provides positive developmental outcomes, special education could be the best practices for some children (Chhuakling, 2010; Sharma, 2010).

Four Children

Four profiles of children with disabilities, two rural and two urban, are provided to give a sense of the adversity these children experience, especially with respect to schooling. The profiles also serve to highlight the type of educational provisions in India for children with disabilities in different geographic settings. Significantly, according to the 2001 India census, over 72% of the population lives in rural and tribal areas.

Rural Children

Case #1: Meenu (2.5 years old). Meenu belongs to a tribal village of Andhra Pradesh, a state in the south-eastern part of India. She has congenital problems and multiple disabilities, although no clinical diagnosis is available. She can barely stand and speaks inarticulately, but is an alert and lively child. She is the middle child among three sisters. Her parents are agricultural laborers and very poor. When Meenu's parents go to work her maternal grandfather takes care of her with a great deal of visible love and affection. There are no facilities for children with disabilities in her village (adapted from Education Resource Unit, 2003).

A child like Meenu may eventually attend the nearby school in her village, but the school is unlikely to have any facilities for children with special needs. Consequently, the school and Meenu will find it difficult to mutually adjust to each other. It is expected that she will soon dropout and stay at home. The family will socialize her in housekeeping skills as much as possible and try to marry her off by the time she is 14 if a groom can be found. If not married, she will remain with her family of origin as long as she lives. For many children like Meenu who have severe disabilities, physical, social, and attitudinal barriers prevent them from engaging in school.

Case #2: Ahmed (8 years old). Ahmed has a hearing impairment. He lives in a north Indian village with his parents and four siblings He uses gestures and body language to communicate. He started going to a regular public school when he was 6. There is no provision of services for children with disabilities anywhere near his village. His grade one teacher, who is not trained in inclusive education methods, allowed him to be in her class with his peers, but believed that he would not learn very much. After 2 years, Ahmed was moved to grade three since the education policy states that no child should be held back until at least grade five. Ahmed can neither read nor write at his grade level though socially he copes well. He has friends and is good at running errands for his teachers.

Children like Ahmed remain part of the school system until formal examinations result in them being screened out. At that point most leave school permanently. Their disability is seldom so severe as to hamper their social adjustment in school. They cope by creating a space for themselves in the school largely on their own. The teachers are tolerant of their presence since they are not required to adapt themselves or their methods of instruction to these children's special needs.

Urban Children

Case #3: Sakshi (13 years old). Sakshi was part of a study of the relationship between gender and orthopedic disability in New Delhi (Grover, 2003). Sakshi was polio affected, but independent in mobility with the use of calipers. She lived in a low SES urban residential area with her parents and five siblings. Despite frugal resources, Sakshi's parents sent her to a government primary school, and later to an NGO-run inclusive school that caters to children with orthopedic disability. When interviewed, Sakshi was in grade five. She said she liked her school because "my teachers love me a lot, they encourage me to be independent and self-reliant" (translated from Hindi) (Grover, p. 45).

Children such as Sakshi are likely to complete their education if they receive both family and school supports. While there are many factors responsible for a favorable prognosis with regard to educational attainment, one of the most important is the fact that Sakshi's disability is orthopedic and does not interfere with her being able to follow a regular school curriculum in an inclusive classroom.

Case #4: John (5 years old). John has autism. He is part of a middle-income family living in New Delhi. Both his parents go to work. He is enrolled in an inclusive preschool program supervised by

higher education faculty at the University of Delhi (Sharma, 2004). He benefited from an early intervention program conducted by a student trainee that helped John develop social skills. At the end of a 3-month intervention, John had shown improvement in his social behavior which included making eye-contact, being responsive to interaction in group settings, and demonstrating pretend play.

John is one of those few children with disabilities in selected urban areas who have access to early childhood centers that support their development and education within a rights-based framework. Clearly, Meenu and Ahmed are at-risk of not deriving substantial benefits from long-term engagement with schooling, while both Sakshi and John have opportunities to develop along a more normal childhood trajectory because of the facilitative social ecologies that are provided to them. Unfortunately, for the majority of Indian children, the right to receive appropriate education within regular schools is a distant promise in spite of legislation that emphasizes inclusion. Instead, the onus remains on children themselves to adapt to the demands of regular schooling if education is to be accessed. Only rarely, there is evidence of the education system adapting itself to the needs of students with disabilities. Thus, while both paradigms of integration and inclusion are discussed in the disabilities literature, in actual practice whenever children with disabilities find placement in regular schools in India, integration rather than inclusion is practiced. As a consequence, only high functioning children make it to the mainstream schools. They are the only ones with enough personal resources to adapt to the demands placed on them for classroom integration.

By and large, children with disabilities who study full time in general classes with their peers are those who have mobility skills, are able to communicate with functional speech, cope with the academic syllabus with minor pedagogical and infrastructure modifications, and can accomplish most of the tasks assigned to their able-bodied peers. Thus, the admission policy in many schools, while claiming to be inclusive, is actually being selectively inclusive. For many of the school personnel, the term inclusion is equated with the mere presence of a child with disability in the regular class, with no adaptations in infrastructure, curriculum, or pedagogical practices.

In a study of inclusive education practices in Delhi, one of the administrators in the school stated, "There are no adaptations required. The child sits in the regular class and we ensure that he should not be pointed out in the class or made to feel special" (Lamba & Malaviya, 2010, p. 99). A large predictor of the adjustment by children in such school environments is their capacity for perseverance and the supports provided by their families.

Supportive School Ecologies

To further explore, the themes discussed in the four case vignettes we interviewed seven mothers of children 4–11 years old with disabilities (including autism, cerebral palsy, intellectual impairment, ADHD, and learning challenges), one special educator, and a school principal. Together, they reflected on their experiences of eight schools and a special education center. Three of these educational settings were actively practicing inclusion (schools A, B, and C – A being a preschool), three were general schools with no proactive policy of inclusion (schools D, E, and preschool F), and two were special schools for children with disabilities (G and H). Some parents had experience of more than one type of school. We base our analysis of these individual narratives on the work of Bernheimer and Weisner (2007) who explain, "Families' stories offer a window into the way in which families make sense of their worlds" (p. 198).

Guiding our work with these families, following were the assumptions:

- The emotionally interdependent dyad of the parent and the child leaves each highly vulnerable to the emotional state of the other. Resilience in the child may mirror and be nurtured by the feelings of well-being and satisfaction experienced by the parent.
- With reference to young children, a good source of resilience, or at least potential resilience, may be the feelings of well-being experienced

by the parent with respect to the child's school. Features of school as a supportive ecological niche can be inferred from reports by the parent of her or his child's experience of the educational system.

Through content analysis of qualitative interviews, we identified overarching ideological and philosophical concepts that contribute to the well-being and coping capacity of children with disabilities and their families. The emphasis was not on identifying specific school-based transactions (results more likely from an ethnography of children's schools), but instead the discovery of positive ideological stances that we hypothesized would translate into helpful practices at the level of the school – such as appropriate teaching strategies in the classroom, empathetic interactions among peers and adults in school, and the creation of facilitative physical environments.

Theme A: Openness and Transparency

For the group of five mothers whose children were now attending School A, the most comforting aspect of the preschool was the willingness of the system to lay itself bare to scrutiny by the parents. As one mother put it, "They let us be at the Centre and we can see what our child is doing. They give us a room to sit. They are not scared of us watching them." Another added, "Teachers do not lie about the child – if he has eaten only three mouthfuls they tell us so. In other schools they throw away the child's uneaten food to avoid answering the parents' questions."

Each of these parents had oppressive experiences in other schools which the children had attended prior to enrolling at School A. One mother with such an experience said:

> In other schools parents are told to leave the child at the gate and go; we are not allowed to see the class … I would try to peep in through one small window … I would find [my child] sitting idle most of the time.

According to this mother, her child did not acquire any competencies in the 1 year that she was with that school and yet the school insisted that the child continue with them.

We interpret the willingness of School A to be open and flexible as indicative of the confidence of the school that it is implementing developmentally appropriate practices and of its receptivity to suggestions from parents and others. As one mother explained, "The teachers are flexible and open to suggestions – they changed her therapy timing so that my daughter could get a full two hours in the school." It is this ability of the school to reassure parents and promote a positive attitude toward their child's education that appears to enhance the parent's sense of well-being. This in turn may indirectly influence the child's capacity to cope with school stressors and access resources necessary to physical and psychosocial development.

Theme B: Permeable Home–School Boundaries: Empowering Parents and Children

It is well known that the school and the home need to work together to support children's development (Hayes, 1994; Seligman, 1979). Both need to be accepting the child's disability in order to promote the child's well-being (Vaidya, 2008). Strong home–school links can be a key protective process for a child at-risk due to disability, not the least because of the sense of empowerment this generates for the parents.

At School A, the boundaries between the home and the school are permeable, which are evident from the following parent and teacher reports:

- When parents want to share their feelings, they find empathetic listeners in teachers who spend time with the parents listening to what they have to say, often even beyond the school hours. When it seems to the teachers that the parents have not accepted the child as he or she is or are in a state of denial about the child's disability, the teachers counsel the parents, though they may not always be successful in convincing them that the child has special needs.
- The mothers have formed themselves into a formal parent group on the school premises.

This is a mutually rewarding relationship – the school benefits by the group's inputs, as the mothers assist the teachers in making teaching–learning materials, and the mothers provide emotional support to one another. As one mother explained: "We really look forward to meeting each other at the Centre. It keeps our sanity intact …. We miss each other so much the day we can't come."

- The parents are free to question the practices in the school and the teachers respond to their concerns and doubts. "Here we tell the parents questioning is your right," said the educator interviewed.
- By respecting the experience and situation of the parents and the child, the teachers help to empower them. An educator said: "Most parents who come here have been treated badly by other schools. In other schools the parents are blamed for the child's behaviour whereas here they are accepted with open arms."

Contrast these experiences with those of a mother who had earlier been sending her child (with cerebral palsy) to another preschool (School F). It is a regular preschool, and at the time of admission the mother was assured that it had the resources (including a counselor) to cater to her child's needs. A year later, she discovered that neither had her child learned anything nor did the school have a special educator to work with the child.

Theme C: No Compromise on Inclusion

School A is inclusive in the broadest meaning of the term. It is one of the few preschools that admit children without assessing their level of functioning. The school assumes it will adapt to the needs of each child. Even the schools that actively practice inclusion take in only high functioning children. As an example, the principal of School B, one of the forerunners to actively initiate inclusion in her school, explained, "We admit only those children who can function in an integrated environment – we reserve the right to refuse. We are not a special school. We do not admit children who urinate in the class, are socially and physically harmful and are too disabled."

Not surprising, mothers with children attending School A worried at the thought of them graduating from the preschool and attending formal schooling. As one mother lamented, "It is doubtful if my child will get admission. I will have to keep him at home or put him in a special school which I do not want."

Theme D: Sensitivity to Children's Individual Needs

This resilience-promoting feature of school A is best described by quoting two examples of insensitive behavior displayed by schools C and F where parents had enrolled their children prior to transferring them to school A. Also a preschool, school F, was preparing for its Annual Day celebrations. The teacher asked the parent to send the child's costume to be worn for the show so that she could help the child change into it. The child, however, returned home with the unworn costume neatly folded in her bag. The mother, visibly hurt, said: "My child was made to sit the whole day and she did not participate."

In another instance, a child enrolled in the special section of a regular school, school C, returned home still wearing clothes that she had defecated in. The teacher and the helpers had not bothered to clean her. When the mother took up this matter with the principal, she was told, "Am I supposed to be cleaning her up?"

In both these cases the schools' insensitivity toward the children was seen by the parents as evidence of a lack of concern for children with special needs.

Theme E: Nurturing Cognition in a Social Context

In the mothers' opinion, the single most important reason why their children were showing marked positive changes in all areas of development after enrolling in school A was that learning at the school took place in group settings that included nondisabled children. While individualized teaching through one-on-one interaction is an important teaching strategy in special education as a means to enhance the child's cognitive abilities, the mothers felt that focusing exclusively on cognitive functioning that lacked efforts to improve affect and social interaction, coupled with uninspiring physical surroundings, would not lead to positive developmental outcomes. Mothers who had the experience of sending their children to school G, a special education facility for children with disabilities, described the mechanical nature of the child's learning environment:

> [My] child is given a slotted time of 30 minutes. The teachers carry out the assigned task in a routinized manner without developing rapport with the child. The learning area is divided into cubicles with not much space to move about which adds to the feeling that the child is just another client instead of being an individual.

In contrast, school A provides an inclusive environment. While the child receives one-on-one learning time, much of the day is spent in the company of peers as the teacher attends to the whole group of which the child is a part. One mother observed, "This is a big advantage. The teacher behaves with my child as she does with all the other children … she speaks in the same way … she behaves normally … my child has begun to understand." Another mother of a child diagnosed as hyperactive said, "Earlier I could not sit when Arun was around … now he can participate in school activities for three hours."

These findings do not necessarily show preference for inclusion. There may be quality special education schools that are resilience-promoting and capable of meeting different needs of the children. However, the inclusive nature of school A was appreciated by the mothers whose children attended it. Two features in particular stand out:

- The company of typically growing peers provides the child with a disability stimulation of the kind that cannot be provided in a special school.
- The routinization that may tend to creep into the special school program is the overcome in an inclusive school simply because of the variety of activities that are carried out as part of the regular school curriculum.

Theme F: Generating a Sense of Belongingness and Social Identity

The principal of school B (a school that actively practices inclusion) explained that the most important resilience-promoting feature of an inclusive environment was that inclusion serves to bring the child with disability into a larger social network with other children and fosters a sense of belonging. According to her, "This leads to the development of a sense of social identity which nurtures children's feelings of self-importance and self-esteem." Specific features of the school, she administers, that help to generate a sense of belonging, as enunciated by her, are as follows:

1. The school uniform and the school bag that give the child the physical sense of being the same as others.
2. Within the larger social group, positive personal attention to children which strengthens their self-esteem. This, she explained, was provided in a variety of ways:
   • Each class had two student council members and they took special note of the needs of children with disabilities in each classroom.
   • Each child was attached to a student of class XI or XII, who conducted mentoring under the Community Service Program for senior students. The objective of mentoring, apart from academic support, was to provide the child with a disability opportunities for social interaction with competent and caring seniors. Often the mentoring took place over and above the stipulated hours as both the mentor and the mentee found the relationship mutually satisfying.
   • There was a conscious attempt to identify talent in each child and to give the children opportunities to participate in cocurricular activities at the school.
   • Children were given awards publicly for their achievements at the school's Annual Day.
3. The resource center Saath-Saath (a Hindi expression meaning "being together") in school B was "their haven." Every week, each child was given some time to be at the Centre. Unlike similar spaces in most schools, it was not a room to be avoided, but a fun place to be in. It is aesthetically well-equipped with attractive furniture, books, toys, art material, and computers, where the special educators and mentors work with the children individually.
4. While the teachers were not specially trained to work with children with disabilities, they were sensitized to the needs of the children. Classrooms selected for placement of the children had teachers who were more experienced educators, well-versed with the school's programs, flexible, creative, gentle, and patient with children. Parents reported that their children liked being with them.

Theme G: Accepting and Accommodating the Unexpected

Two male children with disabilities included in the sample were enrolled in schools D and E which did not actively practice inclusion. At the time the children entered their nursery classes, there had been no indication of a disability. Later, by primary class, one child was diagnosed with dyslexia and the other child as a "slow learner." Each child's disability became apparent as he progressed. While neither of the two schools had a policy of inclusion, there was a marked difference in how the administration and the teachers responded once the fact of the child's disability became apparent. In school E the child's learning difficulties started to become apparent from class three. The school responded by accepting the fact that the child was having difficulties in scholastic work due to a learning disability and implemented measures to help the child. The teachers and the counselor advised the mother to get the child assessed for formal diagnosis. In the mother's words:

> The school is supportive … they have been telling me that I should take the child for tests but I could not as my husband would not agree. They tell me that there are children like him in class 10 and 12 who are doing well and so will my child and that I should not worry.

The mother felt that the teachers and the school had adapted to the child's needs by adopting supportive measures that adapted the school environment. These adaptations included ignoring spelling mistakes; testing the child in a group setting and explaining to the mother the purpose and results of the assessment; giving extra time in examinations; letting the child sit in the front row; and letting the child sit next to an academically brighter child.

The mother whose child was attending school D and was in class six had a very different experience with the school and reported feeling harassed. The school seemed not to have noticed that her child had difficulty in comprehension and were equally unwilling to accept the mother's assessment that her child needed special accommodations:

> They see that the child is performing at an average level in the class and therefore do not believe that he has a problem. What they do not understand is that the child is performing at this level after his special educator outside the school and I have put in so many hours each day. We simplify the content and then help him to learn that by focusing on key concepts and words.

Whenever the mother tried to have a discussion with the teachers, she was told, "You are the problem and not the child – let your child be."

The lessons emerging from these interviews suggest that: (1) resilience engendering practices of schools cannot be limited to their effect on the child alone – their impact is mediated by the meaning they have for parents and educators; (2) sensitivity to individual differences and transparency in school practices, and attempts to empower parents, help to develop positive self-regard and well-being, both in the child and the parent; and (3) appropriate pedagogical practices can reduce the impact of adversity that comes with disability and promote opportunities for enhanced learning.

Schools and Inclusion

With inclusive education having been accepted as the guiding principle in the education of children with disabilities in India, the stakeholders – students, teachers, administrators, parents, and the community – will be looking for local models to orient the process. There are several in different part of the country. For example, Joshi (2010) attempted to enable a special school in a rural area of Rajasthan make a transition to become an inclusive school. A critical analysis of the exercise she recounted led us to surmise that it involved the following processes:

1. *Collaboratively conceptualizing and internalizing the meaning of inclusion*: The most critical step in the transition is that of conceptualizing inclusion in a manner that is internalized, owned, and can be worked toward. To this end, Joshi initiated the process of transition by inviting the various stakeholders – all those who are expected to bring about the change – in the school to collaboratively construct an understanding to the question, "What is inclusion?" by drawing upon multiple meanings. This enabled the stakeholders to own the vision and the process of inclusion, work toward it and strive toward the goal even in the face of adversity. The stakeholders were about 30 participants including the NGO management, teachers, resource persons, support staff, and field workers. All were involved in bringing about inclusion in their various roles within the school.

   Such an approach to understand inclusion is in contrast to the standard approach wherein the experts seek to educate lay participants about a predetermined conception of inclusion, treating the stakeholders as passive recipients in the process. The participants then simply voice the outcomes that are essentially those preferred by the experts. Ownership of the process is minimal and so is the sense of loss when inclusion does not happen.

2. *Visioning the change*: Joshi's next step was to create a common vision of the direction in which the organization wanted to move. This was done through a visioning workshop involving a range of activity sessions in which the stakeholders participated, followed by reflections on the key points raised through these activities. Some of the key questions which formed the basis for generating activity

sessions and learning experiences in the visioning workshop were the following:

- What is education like today?
- What are children's experiences in the classroom and outside?
- How is diversity among learners desirable and actually helpful?
- How can children with different abilities and backgrounds study together?
- What are the changes needed for this to happen?
- What will these changes lead to?
- What do children with disabilities need in a learning situation?
- What are the likely difficulties?
- What would the new school be like?
- What steps are needed to get such a school to work?

The visioning was not a dreaming exercise. Rather, it involved an understanding that the vision informed the changes needed, an analysis of the difficulties that must be overcome, and the steps required for change. From this reflective process, participants were able to move on to the planning and implementation of specific program elements, letting go of many long-held notions of what their school should look like.

3. *Emotional commitment to the vision*: According to Joshi, the strength of such an approach was that through the democratic visioning process a vision that was intellectually understood became one which was emotionally owned. The unexpected enthusiasm, involvement, and self-exploration which the participant visioning process generated led to a deep emotional commitment to realize what had been experienced. This was in contrast to the cognitively oriented approach of getting people to change practices because the argument advanced by an outsider change agent is academically sound.

Conclusion

As in the case of most psychological constructs, the concept of resilience and the conditions for its manifestation have both a universal and an indigenous tenor. Creating the conditions for children with disabilities to thrive in India involves many of the same challenges posed to children in other countries, as well as challenges unique to the Indian educational context. Meaningful research acknowledges both the etic perspective of the researchers and the emic perspectives of research participants as equally valid. We believe that resilience requires a culturally relevant construction of its meaning which emphasizes its nurturance through interobjectivity (understandings that are shared within and between cultures about social reality) (Moghaddam, 2003). Equally, intersubjectivity (Valsiner, 1994, 2003) is needed to understand the meaning and nurturance of resilience in an individual child's life. The locally specific articulations may find resonance with the specific experiences of a group of people in a culturally diverse context to a far greater extent than the objective formulations assumed to have cross-cultural relevance.

Specifically, our research finds that the resilience-promoting features of schools are those values, actions, and behaviors that are expected in a socially just and humane society. The vision of a rights-based society embodies resilience-promoting features. The protective and promotive features of supportive school ecologies reflect this position. Schools that create the conditions that potentiate children's positive growth and development (Ungar, 2011) appear to:

- Take the onus for reducing the impact of risk faced by the child with disability by changing their own structures and processes to meaningfully adapt to each child's needs.
- Foster self-esteem in the child with a disability through interactions within the school such that each child is enabled to deal with life's challenges and accept outcomes without unduly attributing failure to him or herself.
- Focus on the long-term empowerment of the parent–child dyad rather than the management of routines and crisis on a daily basis.
- Generate in the child and the family a sense of belonging and social identity.
- Be proactive in providing opportunities for positive growth at critical developmental turning points in children's lives, thereby reducing negative chain reactions that follow risk exposure.

Though supported by research, there persists great difficulty putting the values of socially just education for children with disability into practice in India. While hardly anyone would disagree with the features of supportive schools that have been identified in this chapter, barriers to their implementation continue to disadvantage the learning opportunities, and the resilience, of these children. Greater self reflection on the part of educators and system administrators appears to be needed if the goals of legislation are to be realized and resilience-promoting contexts created that can nurture and sustain the positive development of all children.

References

Anandalakshmy, S. (2010). *Through the lens of culture: Centuries of childhood and education in India* [Monograph]. Chennai, India: Bala Mandir Research Foundation.

Angirish, S. (2010). *Mothers of children with disability.* Unpublished master's thesis, University of Delhi, New Delhi, India.

Benson, P. L. (2003). Developmental assets and asset-building community: Conceptual and empirical foundations. In R. M. Lerner & P. L. Benson (Eds.), *Developmental assets and asset-building communities: Implications for research, policy and practice* (pp. 19–46). New York, NY: Kluwer Academic/Plenum.

Bernheimer, L. P., & Weisner, T. S. (2007). "Let me just tell you what I do all day…": The family story at the center of intervention research and practice. *Infants and Young Children, 20*(3), 192–201.

Beteille, A. (2005). The school as an institution. In R. Kumar, A. Sethi, & S. Sikka (Eds.), *School, society, nation: Popular essays in education* (pp. 166–178). New Delhi, India: Orient Longman.

Bronfenfrenner, U. (1979a). *The ecology of human development: Experiments by nature and design.* Cambridge, MA: Harvard University Press.

Census 2011. (2010, April 2). Gov't. begins mother of all headcounts. *Hindustan Times*, p. 1.

Chhuakling, Z. A. (2010). *School experiences of children with disability in Mizoram.* Unpublished master's thesis, University of Delhi, New Delhi, India.

Connors, C., & Stalker, K. (2003). *The views and experiences of disabled children and their siblings.* London, UK: Jessica Kingsley.

Convention on the Rights of Persons with Disabilities. (2006). Downloaded June 14, 2010. from http://www.un.org/esa/socdev/convention.html.

Dalal, A. K., & Pande, N. (1999). Cultural beliefs and family care of the children with disability. *Psychology and Developing Societies, 11*(1), 55–75.

Deb, A., & Arora, M. (2008). Resilience in children and adolescents. *Psychological Studies, 53*(2), 114–121.

Dempsey, I., Foreman, P., Sharma, N., Khanna, D., & Arora, P. (2001). Correlates of parental empowerment in families with a member with a disability in Australia and India. *Developmental Disabilities Bulletin, 29*(2), 113–131.

Donnon, T., & Hammond, W. (2007). Understanding the relationships between resiliency and bullying in adolescence: An assessment of youth resiliency from five urban junior high schools. *Child and Adolescent Psychiatric Clinics of North America, 16*(2), 449–472.

Educational Resource Unit (ERU). (2003). *Snakes and ladders: Factors that facilitate or impede successful primary school completion.* Unpublished report of the The World Bank, New Delhi, India.

Foreman, P. (1996). Disability, integration and inclusion: Introductory concepts. In P. Foreman (Ed.), *Integration & inclusion in action* (pp. 1–26). Sydney, NSW: Harcourt Brace.

Ghai, A. (2005). Inclusive education: A myth or reality. In R. Kumar, A. Sethi, & S. Sikka (Eds.), *School, society, nation: Popular essays in education* (pp. 244–262). New Delhi, India: Orient Longman.

Glantz, M. D., & Sloboda, Z. (1999). Analysis and reconceptualization of resilience. In M. D. Glantz & J. L. Johnson (Eds.), *Resilience and development: Positive life adaptations* (pp. 109–128). New York, NY: Kluwer Academic/Plenum.

Grotberg, E. (1995). *A guide to promoting resilience in children: Strengthening the human spirit* (Early childhood development: Practice and reflections (Occasional Paper No. 8)). The Hague, The Netherlands: Bernard van Leer Foundation.

Grover, R. (2003). *Role of gender: Perceptions of adolescents with orthopedic disability and their caregivers.* Unpublished master's thesis, University of Delhi, New Delhi, India.

Hardman, M. L., Drew, C. J., & Egan, M. W. (2008). *Human exceptionality: School, community and family* (9th ed.). Boston, MA: Houghton, Mifflin Company.

Hayes, A. (1994). Families and disabilities. In A. Ashman & J. Elkins (Eds.), *Educating children with special needs* (pp. 37–69). Sydney, NSW: Prentice Hall.

Indira Gandhi National Open University. (2009). Statutory provisions, concessions and barrier-free environment for persons with disabilities: Cerebral palsy. Block 4 of *Certificate in early childhood special education enabling inclusion.* New Delhi, India: Author.

Jha, M. M. (2002). *School without walls: Inclusive education for all.* Oxford, UK: Heinemann.

Joshi, P. (2006). Negotiating identity: Voices of children with disabilities in regular schools. *Contemporary Education Dialogue, 3*(2), 175–195.

Joshi, P. (2010). Developing a vision for inclusive education: A case study. In N. Sharma (Ed.), *The social ecology of disability* (Technical series 3, Lady Irwin College, pp. 77–85). New Delhi, India: Academic Excellence.

Lamba, R., & Malaviya, R. (2010). Inclusive education in schools of Delhi. In N. Sharma (Ed.), *The social ecology of disability* (Technical series 3, Lady Irwin College, pp. 86–108). New Delhi, India: Academic Excellence.

Landesman-Dwyer, S. (1981). Living in the community. *American Journal of Mental Deficiency, 86,* 223–234.

Masten, A. S. (1994). Resilience in individual development: Successful adaptation despite risk and adversity. In M. Wang & E. Gordon (Eds.), *Risk and resilience in inner city America: Challenges and prospects* (pp. 3–25). Hillsdale, NJ: Erlbaum.

Ministry of Law, Justice and Company Affairs. (1996). *The persons with disabilities (equal opportunities, protection of rights and full participation) act 1995.* New Delhi, India: Government of India.

Ministry of Law, Justice and Company Affairs. (1999). *The national trust for welfare of persons with autism, cerebral palsy, mental retardation and multiple disabilities act 1999.* New Delhi, India: Government of India.

Misra, G., & Gergen, K. J. (1993). On the place of culture in psychological science. *International Journal of Psychology, 28,* 225–243.

Misra, G., Srivastava, A. K., & Gupta, S. (1999). The cultural construction of childhood in India: Some observations. *Indian Psychological Abstracts and Reviews, 6*(2), 191–218.

Moghaddam, F. M. (2003). Interobjectivity and culture. *Culture and Psychology, 9*(3), 221–232.

National Centre for Promotion of Employment for Disabled People. (2005). *The journey towards promotion of inclusive education in India.* New Delhi, India: Author.

Nsamenang, A. B. (2003). Conceptualizing human development and education in Sub-Sahara Africa at the interface of indigenous and exogenous influences. In T. S. Saraswathi (Ed.), *Cross-cultural perspectives in human development* (pp. 213–235). New Delhi, India: Sage.

Rioux, M. H. (2009). Disability: The place of judgement in a world of fact. In R. Addlakha, S. Blume, P. Devlieger, O. Nagase, & M. Winance (Eds.), *Disability and society: A reader* (pp. 86–102). New Delhi, India: Orient Blackswan.

Seligman, M. (1979). *Strategies for helping parents of exceptional children.* New York, NY: Free Press.

Sharma, N. (2004). Linking higher education with ECCE and education of children with disabilities: A case study. In K. Chanana (Ed.), *Transforming links between higher and basic education* (pp. 137–148). New Delhi, India: Sage.

Sharma, N. (2010). Education for children with disability: Reflections on 'best practices' to assimilate children in the mainstream. In N. Sharma (Ed.), *The social ecology of disability* (Technical series 3, Lady Irwin College, pp. 125–149). New Delhi, India: Academic Excellence.

Sharma, N., & Sharma, B. (1999). Children in difficult circumstances: Familial correlates of advantage while at risk. In T. S. Saraswathi (Ed.), *Culture, socialization and human development* (pp. 398–418). New Delhi, India: Sage.

Sibal, K. (2010, April 1). Joining hands in the interest of children. *The Hindu,* p.10.

Sinha, D. (1997). Indigenizing psychology. In J. W. Berry, Y. H. Poortinga, & J. Pandey (Eds.), *Handbook of cross-cultural psychology, volume 1: Theory and method* (2nd ed., pp. 131–169). New Delhi, India: Sage.

Sinha, J. B. P. (2002). Towards indigenization of psychology in India. In G. Misra & A. K. Mohanty (Eds.), *Perspectives in indigenous psychology* (pp. 450–456). New Delhi, India: Concept.

Sinha, P., & Sharma, N. (2010). Significance of inclusive education for non-disabled adolescents. In N. Sharma (Ed.), *The social ecology of disability* (Technical series 3, Lady Irwin College, pp. 109–124). New Delhi, India: Academic Excellence.

Ungar, M. (2005). Introduction: Resilience across cultures and contexts. In M. Ungar (Ed.), *Handbook for working with children and youth: Pathways to resilience across cultures and contexts* (pp. xv–xxxix). Thousand Oaks, CA: Sage.

Ungar, M. (2007). Contextual and cultural aspects of resilience in child welfare settings. In I. Brown, F. Chaze, D. Fuchs, J. Lafrance, S. McKay, & S. Thomas-Prokop (Eds.), *Putting a human face on child welfare* (pp. 1–24). Toronto, ON: Centre of Excellence for Child Welfare.

Ungar, M. (2008). Resilience across cultures. *British Journal of Social Work, 38,* 218–235.

Ungar, M. (2011). The social ecology of resilience. Addressing contextual and cultural ambiguity of a nascent construct. *American Journal of Orthopsychiatry, 81,*1–17.

Vaidya, S. (2008). *A sociological study of families of autistic children in Delhi.* Unpublished doctoral dissertation, Jawaharlal Nehru University, New Delhi, India.

Valsiner, J. (1994). Co-construction: What is (and what is not) in a name? *Annals of Theoretical Psychology, 10,* 343–363.

Valsiner, J. (2003). Editorial introduction: Beyond intersubjectivity. *Culture and Psychology, 9*(3), 187–192.

Vyas, N. (2008). *Negotiating resilience: An exploratory study of adolescents with physical disability.* Unpublished master's thesis, University of Delhi, New Delhi, India.

Vygotsky, L. S. (1978). *Mind in society: The development of higher mental processes.* Cambridge, MA: Harvard University Press.

Resilience in Schools and Curriculum Design

23

Nan Henderson

Resiliency studies offer evidence of what educators have long suspected and hoped: more than any other institution except the family, schools can and do provide environments and protective conditions that are crucial for fostering resiliency in today's children and youth (Henderson & Milstein, 1996, 2003). Several fields related to resiliency affirm the power of educators and schools in fostering resiliency in all children, and show that the factors that promote resiliency can be readily available in schools. They also connect fostering resiliency to academic success, increased school safety, and student social and emotional well-being for students who are experiencing extreme stress as well as students simply experiencing the typical challenges in today's high stress world (Benard, 2004; Blum, McNeely, & Rinehart, 2002; Perkins, 2006).

How Does a Child Become More Resilient?

Benard (2007) states that resiliency is an inherent part of the human organism, not just descriptive of a few "super kids" but an inborn capacity for human self-righting that exists in all. She notes that effectively facilitating the self-righting process

requires an increased focus on the promotion of protective factors that enhance student resiliency, rather than a more meticulous focus on student "risk factors." Protective factors buffer, ameliorate, and mitigate the impact of risk and stress and also propel children and youth to healthy self development.

Schools are by nature filled with protective factors; however, schools as organizations and educators and other caring adults within the schools often unknowingly impart protective factors without specific knowledge of the processes that produce them. For schools to become more effective as resiliency-building institutions, all "stakeholders" in the school community need a better understanding of protective factors as a crucial component of student overcoming and student academic and life success.

Students overcome adversity in two ways. First, they draw upon their own internal strengths, which include sociability (building relationships); involvement in service to others; utilization of life skills, including a sense of humor, self-motivation, and distancing from unhealthy situations; maintaining an inner locus of control; having a positive view of one's personal future; feelings of self-worth and self-confidence; perseverance; creativity; and spirituality (Benard, 2004; Benson, 1997; Higgins, 1994; Werner & Smith, 1992; Wolin & Wolin, 1993). Second, involvement in environments that provide environmental protective factors fosters student resiliency (Benard, 2004; Henderson & Milstein, 1996, 2003). Educators are agents of protective

N. Henderson (✉)
Resiliency In Action, Paso Robles, CA, USA
e-mail: nhenderson@resiliency.com

M. Ungar (ed.), *The Social Ecology of Resilience: A Handbook of Theory and Practice*,
DOI 10.1007/978-1-4614-0586-3_23, © Springer Science+Business Media, LLC 2012

297

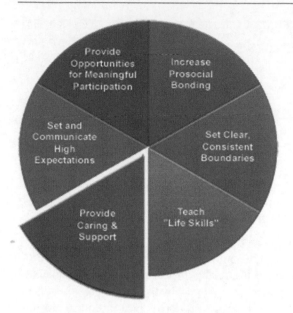

Fig. 23.1 The resiliency wheel: environmental protective factors that foster resiliency

factors in two ways: First, they can see the individual strengths in each student, and engage in interactions and processes to help these strengths grow (recognizing, as Wolin and Wolin, 1993, note, that even two or three individual strengths become life lines of resiliency). Second, they can create learning activities, classrooms, and entire school communities that are rich in environmental protective factors. It is these environments which are the focus of this volume. These environmental protective factors are diagrammed in a model called the Resiliency Wheel (see Fig. 23.1; Henderson & Milstein, 1996).

In the seminal study of risk and protective factors by Werner and Smith (1992), which continues to follow a group of 700 children born in 1955, children with several risk factors at birth (including being born to teen parents, into poverty, to a mother addicted to alcohol or another drug, into a family with a history of violence, to parents diagnosed with mental illness, and/or without prenatal care) demonstrated increased resiliency as the cohort matured, showing life outcomes increasingly similar to their peers in the study who were not assessed as high risk at birth. By the time the "high risk" group reached

age 32, only one in six were still struggling. Werner and Smith (1992) drew this conclusion about the power of protective factors:

> Our findings and those by other American and European investigators with a life-span perspective suggest that these buffers make a more profound impact on the life course of children who grow up under adverse conditions than do specific risk factors and stressful life events. They appear to transcend ethnic, social class, geographical, and historical boundaries. Most of all they offer us a more optimistic outlook than the perspective that can be gleaned from the literature on the negative consequences of perinatal trauma, caregiving deficits, and chronic poverty. They provide us with a corrective lens—an awareness of the self-righting tendencies that move children toward normal adult development under all but the most persistent adverse circumstances (p. 202).

Werner (1996, 2003) reinforces the power of educators as agents of protective factors: "Teachers and school were among the most frequently encountered protective factors for children in the Kauai Longitudinal Study who overcame the multiple odds of poverty, perinatal stress, parental psychopathology, and family dysfunctions" (p. viii). She adds:

> But it's not the trappings of the school—the building, the bricks, the resource rooms [that make the difference]. It seems to be the model of adults that [students] find in the schools. That comes right back to you, whether you are a teacher, or a counselor, or a school nurse, or whatever. One of the wonderful things we see now in adulthood is that these children really remember one or two teachers who made the difference. And they mourn those teachers when they die…some of those teachers more than they do their own family members. Because what went out of their life was a person who looked beyond outward experience, their behavior, their unkempt—oftentimes—appearance and saw the [student's] promise (1999, 2007, p. 20).

Resiliency, School Climate, and Academic Success

The importance of creating protective-factor rich schools is validated by recent research on the power of school climate to improve academic success, especially for struggling students in U.S. urban schools (Perkins, 2006). This research, the most comprehensive published to date on the importance of school climate, focused on the impact of school climate in 108 urban schools from 15 school districts across the U.S. More than 30,000 students from 110 self-identified ethnicities or national origins were included in this research, sponsored by the Council of Urban Boards of Education (CUBE) and the National School Boards Association (NSBA).

Key components of a positive school climate are synonymous with the environmental protective factors diagrammed in the Resiliency Wheel. These include the following:

• Feelings of safety among staff and students.
• Supportive relationships within the school.
• Engagement and empowerment of students as valued members and resources in the school community.
• Clear rules and boundaries that are understood by all students and staff.
• High expectations for academic achievement and appropriate behavior.
• Trust, respect, and an ethos of caring (Elfstrom et al., 2006; Perkins, 2006).

The CUBE study found that an improvement in these key elements of school climate led to higher student achievement, higher morale among students and teachers, more reflective practice among teachers, fewer student dropouts, reduced violence, better community relations, and increased institutional pride (Bryant & Kelley, 2006). Whether termed key components of school climate, or key environmental protective factors, it is clear students do better, academically, socially, and emotionally when surrounded by these factors. Such evidence led to Perkins' (2006) recommendations that schools should assess these elements in their annual evaluations, and purposely work to improve one or more of these key areas based on their findings.

Other recent studies confirm the importance of these environmental characteristics as protective factors in schools. The National Longitudinal Study of Adolescent Health (ADD Health) is the most comprehensive study of American youth ever undertaken. Commissioned by Congress, and funded by 22 federal agencies and foundations, this study involved in-school surveys of more than 90,000 American adolescents in grades 7–12.

In addition, several thousand of these students were selected for more in-depth research that involved in-home interviews between 1994 and 2008. Results show: "When middle and high school students feel cared for by people at their school and when they feel like they are part of school, they are less likely to engage in unhealthy behaviors. When they feel connected to school they also report higher levels of emotional well-being" (Blum et al., 2002, p. 5).

Resiliency research is challenging the "at-risk orientation" prevalent in schools in recent decades: "By the mid-1990s, findings were reported describing the stigma of labeling young people as having something wrong with them before they had demonstrated failure. The implementation of the model itself had become a way of labeling young people as being at risk for a multitude of negative outcomes with or without just cause" (Brown, D'Emidio-Caston, & Benard, 2001, pp. 6–7). This resulted in many schools that a majority of students were identified as at-risk (Baizerman & Compton, 1992). Blue-Swadener and Lubeck (1995) pose the question of whether "the term 'at risk' is ever justified or serves children and families" (p. xi).

With longitudinal studies such as the one by Werner and Smith showing the innate, self-righting capacity inherent in each person, the idea of boxing students into labels that often hinder that process is now being seriously questioned. Some educators questioned the "at-risk" label approach even before research findings questioned it and have realized they were using recommendations from resiliency research in their teaching practice before knowing such research existed (Henderson & Milstein, 1996, 2003; Werner, 1996, 2003).

Turn Around Teachers

With the evidence that it is one-to-one personal relationships that are the most powerful resiliency builders in schools, Benard (2000) coined the term "turn around teacher." One reason teachers may hold so much power to influence resiliency is that "resiliency research points out over and over that the transformation…exits not in programmatic approaches per se but at the deeper level of relationships, beliefs, and expectations" (Benard). Teachers are in prime roles for creating these resiliency relationships, often spending more "quality time" with children each day than parents or other family members. Teachers can more consciously use the enormous power they have to build "bounce-back kids" by following these research-based suggestions for "turnaround teachers" (adapted from Henderson, 2008):

Turnaround teachers:

1. Provide caring and connection:
   • Convey the message they are "there" for a child or youth
   • Communicate unconditional caring about the child or youth
   • Meet the basic survival needs of students and their families
   • Communicate caring availability, unconditional positive regard
   • Regularly offer simple kindnesses such as a greeting or smile
   • Convey the messages "you matter" and "it does not matter what you have done in the past"
   • Do not take students' behavior personally
   • Show compassion, seeing students' pain and suffering beneath negative behaviors.
2. Build competence through resiliency beliefs, high expectations, and social/emotional learning:
   • Communicate a fundamental belief in students' innate competence and self-righting capacities
   • Challenge students to achieve beyond what students believe they can do
   • Recognize existing strengths and competencies and mirror these to students
   • Use these strengths in intervening to ameliorate challenges and problems
   • Teach "metacognition" – how thoughts and feelings influence behaviors
   • Teach that internalized environmental messages (thoughts) about not being good enough, smart enough, rich enough, etc. can be overcome
   • Facilitate students learning other life skills such as anger management, assertiveness, communication skills, goal setting, and conflict resolution.
3. Let children and youth contribute and participate:
   • Allow students to participate very actively in all that happens in school
   • Encourage students' involvement in creating and maintaining classroom rules and school policies
   • Asking for students' ideas and using their creativity in dealing with any classroom or school problem
   • Create a physically and psychologically safe and structured environment for student participation
   • Make learning more reflective and experiential (such as in service learning, cooperative learning, and project-based learning)
   • Involve students in curriculum planning and evaluation strategies
   • Utilize students in the governing of the classroom and school (Benard, 2000; Higgins, 1994; Thomsen, 2002; Werner, 1999, 2007).

Creating a greater understanding of the enormous power they have as agents of student resiliency is a motivating force for educators to focus on becoming more effective as "turn around teachers." Furthermore, according to Benard (2000), the term applies to any adult who interacts with a child in school, who becomes a "turn around mentor" with the same impact as a "turn around teacher."

Curricular, Structural, and Programmatic Strategies

Although resiliency research repeatedly confirms relationships between a student and a teacher (even if unbeknownst to the teacher) to be among the most important protective factors in a student's life, it also suggests the importance of curricular and programmatic strategies (Benard, 2004; Werner, 1996, 2003). Given the importance of such relationships, the onus is on schools to ensure that every student has a caring and supportive relationship with at least one adult at his or her school.

Caring and Support

Caring and support is promoted in schools when educators find ways for students to experience support similar to a "healthy extended family" (Werner & Smith, 1992): people work together, play together, and help one another. Providing this crucial environmental protective factor also necessitates intervention services (e.g., in the form of student assistance programs), and approaches to discipline that keep students connected. Student-run conflict mediation programs, peacemaking circles, and peer courts are examples of this type of discipline.

One powerful way to make students feel more cared for is to engage them in many small group instructional and support activities, which allow for personalization and the "extended family" experience. These approaches include cooperative learning, adventure-based learning, and service learning – all of which are inherently resiliency-building opportunities. They offer not only caring and support but also other environmental protective factors as well, especially opportunities for meaningful participation, prosocial bonding, and life skills training.

High Expectations

"Turn around teachers" are strength-based teachers, who mirror strengths back to students, and see students' strengths as more powerful than problems. They refuse to engage in boxing students into self-defeating categories that do not convey the fullness of a student's potential. Organizationally, schools can be most effective in providing this protective function by eliminating tracking, the "labeling and segregating practice that hangs on in schools despite two decades of scientific studies documenting its negative effects" (Benard, 2004, p. 75). James, Jurich, and Estes (2001) found that schools that are closing the achievement gap refuse to "dumb down" or limit opportunities for lower-achieving students.

A high expectations approach to learning that transcends the narrow definition of student success now prevalent in this era of "high stakes testing" is Gardner's (1983) work on Multiple Intelligences. Gardner initially identified seven primary brain-based ways that students learn (Thomsen, 2002). Later he added an eighth intelligence (Gardner, 2000). According to Gardner, the eight forms of intelligence are verbal-linguistic, logical-mathematical, bodily-kinesthetic, musical, interpersonal, intrapersonal, spatial, and naturalist. Most schools emphasize just the first two, contributing to the difficulty students experience developing other intelligences at school. Thomsen (2002) explains:

> Kids can be smart in many ways. The educational system may recognize that fact, but the knowledge is not always put into action. In most cases, teachers are trained to teach without truly perfecting ways to use the eight intelligences to help students learn. Assessments that they use, both standardized and teacher created, mostly rely on linguistic and verbal or mathematical intelligence…It is important not to give up on students who are having trouble reading and writing (p. 69).

A recognition that students can "be smart" in multiple ways puts the protective factor of high expectations for student success into practice. The message, "Together we will find the way that *you* learn best," can be communicated through one-to-one conversations, and through a process of student assessment and teaching approaches that honor students' potential for success. Other strategies to convey this same message include learning that includes the arts, music, nature and ecological hands-on experiences, movement activities, and service learning projects. In addition,

> As part of recognizing each student's unique strengths, high expectation education capitalizes on students' life experiences and cultural contexts. Not only do students find their experiences and cultures embedded in rather than 'decorating' the curriculum, but their teachers understand that how children learn is influenced by the basic organization of their culture….the expectations communicated to students whose home language is not English should [also] validate students' home language (Benard, 2004, p. 78).

Opportunities for Meaningful Participation

Many of the recommendations for schools to become "high expectation schools" also entail schools providing opportunities for meaningful participation. Providing meaningful participation for students means seeing them as resources rather than problems, and collaborators in the school community rather than simply recipients of service. Small group processes, all types of service projects, and adopting a school wide attitude of giving students "voice and choice" in their daily experience at school are all ways of providing the protective factor of meaningful participation.

Providing this protective factor also means asking students in as many ways as possible for their ideas about school, their learning process, and how to solve the school's problems. This can be done even in elementary schools where students of all ages exhibit a wisdom that most often goes unrecognized unless adults in the school prioritize asking for student input. One way to do this is to ask students to identify three or four issues or challenges they experience in their classroom or school and then brainstorm all that is "right" about their school. Next, children can be asked, "How can we as a school use what is strong here to intervene with these challenges?" When asked to train and consult in public schools labeled "persistently dangerous" in New York City, I refused to do so if student input was not a key part of the process. Children as young as eight were acutely aware of the problems in their schools, expressed empathy and concern for their teachers, and pleaded with their principals to become part of the solutions to the violence in their schools.

In Albuquerque, New Mexico, students are routinely trained and used as conflict mediators in elementary school, and are the first to be called if there is a conflict on the school campus. Two students per school period put on conflict mediation vests and are the first on the scene in playground or other school skirmishes. An unexpected outcome of this program has been students taking this process home, teaching it to their families, as well as mediating neighborhood conflicts (Henderson & Milstein, 1996, 2003).

Thomsen (2002) notes that a "transformation…occurs when students are offered the opportunity to do something that is…useful. Children and adolescents almost always jump at the chance…to contribute in some way" (p. 58). She goes on to offer many practical suggestions for doing this in schools including brainstorming with students jobs and responsibilities they can perform that contribute to the smooth running of the classroom, or that contribute to the strengthening of the environmental protective factors in schools.

Prosocial Bonding

Children and youth who bond to positive people, engage in prosocial activities, and are involved in supportive schools and other organizations, experience protection against the negative behaviors and activities that pull on all students, even in elementary school (Hawkins, Smith, & Catalano, 2004). Therefore, most of the above suggestions for creating protective factor-rich schools are also useful in facilitating prosocial bonding. Students who have a caring connection with at least one supportive, strengths-oriented adult in school will be more bonded to school. Prioritizing family connection to school is a way to further bond students, and involving the family in student learning furthers student bonding to the process of learning (Benson, 1997).

Blum et al. (2002), in their analysis of the Attention Deficit Disorder research, conclude that bonding to school is increased by good classroom management, smaller school size, the absence of overly harsh or punitive discipline, greater student participation in extracurricular activities, and students' positive friendships at school with varied social groups. Since extracurricular activities can provide all six environmental protective factors named in the Resiliency Wheel, they are obviously important in bonding students to school. Many students candidly admit they come to school primarily for the social connections they experience there and for extracurricular activities. In 2006, the American Academy of Pediatrics (AAP) issued a warning about the repercussions of reduced child play time, including recess at school. The report concluded that the research is clear that play and physical movement are absolutely necessary for optimum brain development and learning: "Play is integral to the academic environment…it has been shown to help children adjust to the school setting and even to enhance children's learning readiness, learning behaviors, and problem-solving skills" (p. 4).

The AAP termed "play and unscheduled free time" protective factors crucial for healthy child development, stating that these factors "increase resiliency for children and youth" (p. 16). Though coming to school for recess has typically been dismissed as irrelevant to learning, this research suggests that students' desire to play may in fact be motivated by an innate need for play's contribution to healthy brain development.

Similar conclusions have been drawn about arts education and related activities (including the visual arts, music, drama, and dance) to academic success. The Arts Education Partnership (AEP), a coalition of more than 100 education, arts, philanthropic and government organizations, funded by a cooperative grant from the U.S. Department of Education and the National Endowment for the Arts, recently reviewed 62 "outstanding arts education studies." The AEP published its conclusions in 2002 showing that student involvement in the arts positively impacts six aspects of education, including basic reading and writing skills and comprehension, mathematics (through music instruction), fundamental cognitive skills, motivation to learn, social behavior, and the overall "school environment." In commenting on the AEP findings, Caterrall (2002) noted that the impact of the arts is especially potent for "economically disadvantaged children" and added, "Notions that the arts are frivolous add-ons to a serious curriculum couldn't be farther from the truth."

Clear and Consistent Boundaries

When students are asked which of the six environmental conditions diagrammed in the Resiliency Wheel they would like strengthened,

the most frequent answer is "clear and consistent boundaries." Clear and consistent boundaries provide children and youth with feelings of safety, as well as an external limit that assists them in learning to set internal limits. The best way to set and maintain clear, consistent boundaries is to spend time at the beginning of the school year in a classroom discussion about the rules of behavior that are the class's shared "agreements to live by." Younger students will need more adult coaching and input; older students can brainstorm the entire list, including consequences. Benard (2004) notes: "Unfair and inequitable discipline policies and procedures are continually cited by students in focus groups as a major area for school improvement…classrooms and schools that set behavioral expectations without student input reflect…a lack of belief in children's capacities" (p. 79).

Allowing student involvement in setting and maintaining clear and consistent boundaries in their schools is one way of incorporating several aspects of building student resiliency. Boundary setting helps provide caring and support, high expectations (that students are capable), opportunities for meaningful participation, a route to prosocial bonding to school, and skills training in brainstorming, listening, building consensus, and appropriate conflict resolution.

Life-Skills Training

Life skills range from teaching kindergarteners to stand in line, take a turn, and share to teaching high school students how to apply for a job, select an appropriate college, and effective communication skills. Arguably, all students need to learn cooperation skills, emotional management skills, conflict resolutions skills, assertiveness skills, goal-setting skills, refusal skills, and study skills. This is only a partial list. Each educator assesses what each student needs in life skills training and plans accordingly.

"The process through which we learn to recognize and manage emotions, care about others, make good decisions, behave…responsibly, develop positive relationships, and avoid negative behaviors" (Zins, Weissberg, Wang, &

Walberg, 2004, p. 3) is known as Social and Emotional Learning (SEL). SEL research and related strategies offer one systematic approach to life skills training. Such training helps create a positive school climate. A 2006 article by Torres in the American Association of School Administrators publication, *The School Administrator*, connects SEL, school climate, and academic success. It concludes:

> [That] a strong relationship that exists between social-emotional development and academic achievement cannot be denied. Caring relationships between adults and children in schools foster a desire to learn and a connection to school. When students' barriers to learning are removed, students do better, learn more, and are more engaged... Social and emotional learning programs improve students' behaviors and academic learning. They do not focus on behavior at the expense of academics. The reverse is true. If we ignore students' social-emotional learning, we shortchange students' academic performance (p. 1).

Torres bases his conclusions on a comprehensive research-based discussion of the power of social-emotional learning by Zins et al. They document decades of research on the positive impact of social-emotional learning in schools, and conclude the research findings on the powerful positive impact of SEL are "so solid that they emboldened us to introduce a new term, 'social, emotional, and academic learning or SEAL'" (Zins et al., 2004, p. 19). The "essential characteristics of the effective" social-emotional learning programs recommended include the following:

- Careful planning, based on theory and research
- Teaching SEL skills that are relevant to "daily life" (such as recognizing and managing emotions, respecting others, positive goal-setting, making responsible decisions, and "handling interpersonal relationships effectively")
- Addressing affective and social dimensions of learning by actively building positive attachment to school, strengthening relationships in school, providing opportunities for meaningful participation in school, using "diverse, engaging teaching methods," nurturing safety and belonging in school, and emphasizing respect for diversity

- Linking to academic outcomes through integrating with professional development on academic success, and coordinating with student support efforts (health, nutrition, service learning, physical education, counseling, nursing, etc.)
- Addressing key implementation factors, such as policies, staff development, supervision, adequate resources, and evaluation issues
- Involving family and community partnerships
- Including continuous improvement, outcome evaluation, and dissemination components (Zins et al., 2004).

Conclusion

These programmatic and curricular approaches demonstrate the powerful opportunities schools have to create protective-factor rich environments. Numerous formal studies as well as countless anecdotal reports confirm this power and suggest the strategies that schools can incorporate to become more effective resiliency-building institutions. In so doing, they will also increase student academic success, reduce school violence, and assist the healthy social and emotional development of students (Henderson, 2007, p. 153). Tonya Benally, for example, as a student in an alternative school in Gallup, New Mexico, explained that "school is the only family" she had, and she credited her school with healing her substance abuse issues and depression that had resulted in three suicide attempts. She said, "The only time I felt good about myself was when I went to school. Ms. Hill, our librarian was always nice, smiling, giving us compliments...The library felt like home because she was always there... And [all the teachers] told us, 'We are a family.' We heard that from the principal all the time. That's why I went to school every day. Because people there respected me and talked to me. I don't get that...at home" (Henderson, 2000, pp. 77–78).

The best scenario for students to achieve resiliency is when schools and families work together to cooperatively strengthen protective factors in students' lives. When families hear what is "right" about their children, especially students who are experiencing challenges at school or at home, they are often more willing to become collaborators with the school. A strengths-approach is a useful way to increase family involvement. Yet, even without the optimum family support, the resiliency research is rich with reports of the power of the "turn around" teachers and mentors students find at school and the protective-factor rich environments there that influence their lives.

References

American Academy of Pediatrics. (2006). *The importance of play in promoting healthy child development and maintaining strong parent-child bonds.* Elk Grove Village: American Academy of Pediatrics.

Arts Education Partnership. (2002). *Critical links: Learning in the arts and student and academic social development.* Washington: Arts Education Partnership. Retrieved 8 Feb 2011 from http://aep-arts.org/files/publications/CriticalLinks.pdf.

Baizerman, M., & Compton, D. (1992). From respondent and informant to consultant and participant: The evolution of a state agency policy evaluation. In A. M. Madison (Ed.), *Minority issues in program evaluation* (New directions in program evaluation, Vol. 53, pp. 5–16). San Francisco: Jossey-Bass.

Benard, B. (2000). How to be a turnaround teacher/mentor. Retrieved 8 Feb 2011 from http://www.resiliency.com.

Benard, B. (2004). *Resiliency: What we have learned.* San Francisco: WestEd.

Benard, B. (2007). The foundations of the resiliency paradigm. In N. Henderson (Ed.), *Resiliency in action: Practical ideas for overcoming risks and building strengths in youth, families, and communities* (pp. 3–7). Ojai: Resiliency In Action, Inc.

Benson, P. L. (1997). *All kids are our kids: What communities must do to raise caring and responsible children and adolescents.* San Francisco: Jossey-Bass.

Blue-Swadener, B., & Lubeck, S. (1995). *Children and families "at promise": Deconstructing the discourse of risk.* Albany: State University of New York Press.

Blum, R. W., McNeely, C. A., & Rinehart, P. M. (2002). *Improving the odds: The untapped power of schools to improve the health of teens.* Minneapolis: Center for Adolescent Health and Development, University of Minnesota.

Brown, J. H., D'Emidio-Caston, M., & Benard, B. (2001). *Resilience education.* Thousand Oaks: Corwin Press.

Bryant, A. L., & Kelley, K. (2006). Preface. In B. K. Perkins (Ed.), *Where we learn: The CUBE survey of urban school climate* (p. 11). Alexandria: National Schools Boards Association.

Caterrall, J. (2002). *Critical links: Learning in the arts and student social and academic development (book summary).* Balatimore: New Horizons for Learning.

Retrieved 8 Feb 2011 from http://home.avvanta.com/~building/strategies/arts/catterall.htm.

Elfstrom, J., Vanderzee, K., Cuellar, R., Sink, H., & Volz, A. (2006). *The case for programs that address school climate.* Oxford, OH: Miami University Department of Psychology Center for School-Based Mental Health Programs. Retrieved 8 Feb 2011 from http://www.unitsmuohio.edu/csbmhp/network/network-pubs.html.

Gardner, H. (1983). *Frames of mind: The theory of multiple intelligences.* New York: Basic Books.

Gardner, H. (2000). *Intelligence reframed: Multiple intelligences for the 21st century.* New York: Basic Books.

Hawkins, J. D., Smith, B. H., & Catalano, R. F. (2004). Social development and social and emotional learning. In J. E. Zins, R. P. Weissberg, M. C. Wang, & H. J. Walberg (Eds.), *Building academic success on social and emotional learning: What does the research say?* (pp. 135–150). New York: Teachers College Press.

Henderson, N. (2000). Tonya Benally: "School is the only family I have". In N. Henderson (Ed.), *Schoolwide approaches for fostering resiliency* (pp. 77–79). Ojai: Resiliency In Action, Inc.

Henderson, N. (2007). Questions and activities for teaching about resiliency. In N. Henderson (Ed.), *Resiliency in action: Practical ideas for overcoming risks and building strengths in youth, families, and communities* (p. 153). Ojai: Resiliency In Action, Inc.

Henderson, N. (2008). Checklist for "turnaround teachers." In Pennsylvania Department of Education. *Promoting student success through resiliency* (on-line course). Harrisburg: Pennsylvania Department of Education.

Henderson, N., & Milstein, M. M. (1996). *Resiliency in schools: Making it happen for students and educators.* Thousand Oaks: Corwin Press.

Henderson, N., & Milstein, M. M. (2003). *Resiliency in schools: Making it happen for students and educators.* Thousand Oaks: Corwin Press.

Higgins, G. (1994). *Resilient adults: Overcoming a cruel past.* San Francisco: Jossey-Bass.

James, D. W., Jurich, S., & Estes, S. (2001). *Raising minority academic achievement: A compendium of education programs and practices.* Washington: American Youth Policy Forum.

Perkins, B. K. (2006). *Where we learn: The CUBE survey of urban school climate.* Alexandria: National School Boards Association.

Thomsen, K. (2002). *Building resilient students: Integrating resiliency into what you already know and do.* Thousand Oaks: Corwin Press.

Torres, J. (2006). Building academic success on social and emotional learning. In *The school administrator, April, 2006.* Arlington: American Association of School Administrators. Retrieved 8 Feb 2011 from http://www.aaa.org/School Administrator Article.aspx?id=9602 & terms=Building+Academic+Success+on+social+and+Emotional+learning.

Werner, E. (1996). Foreword. In N. Henderson & M. M. Milstein (Eds.), *Resiliency in schools: Making it happen for students and educators* (pp. Vii–ix). Thousand Oaks: Corwin Press.

Werner, E. (1999). How children become resilient: Observations and cautions. In N. Henderson (Ed.), *Resiliency in action: Practical ideas for overcoming risks and building strengths in youth, families, and communities* (pp. 15–23). Ojai: Resiliency In Action, Inc.

Werner, E. (2003). Foreword. In N. Henderson & M. M. Milstein (Eds.), *Resiliency in schools: Making it happen for students and educators* (pp. vii–ix). Thousand Oaks: Corwin Press.

Werner, E. (2007). How children become resilient: Observations and cautions. In N. Henderson (Ed.), *Resiliency in action: Practical ideas for overcoming risks and building strengths in youth, families, and communities* (pp. 15–23). Ojai: Resiliency In Action, Inc.

Werner, E., & Smith, R. (1992). *Overcoming the odds: High risk children from birth to adulthood*. New York: Cornell University Press.

Wolin, S., & Wolin, S. (1993). *The resilient self: How survivors of troubled families rise above adversity*. New York: Villard.

Zins, J. E., Weissberg, R. P., Wang, M. C., & Walberg, H. J. (Eds.). (2004). *Building academic success on social and emotional learning: What does the research say?* New York: Teachers College Press.

Part VI

The Community

How Prior Social Ecologies Shape Family Resilience Amongst Refugees in U.S. Resettlement

Stevan M. Weine, Elise Levin, Leonce Hakizimana, and Gonwo Dahnweih

Background

The mental health professions borrowed the term resilience from engineering where it refers to, "the capacity of a material or system to return to equilibrium after a displacement" (Norris, Stevens, Pfefferbaum, Wyche, & Pfefferbaum, 2008, p. 127). They have applied resilience at individual, family, and community, levels. For example, Norris reviewed community resilience and defined it as, "a process linking a set of adaptive capacities to a positive trajectory of functioning and adaptation after a disturbance" (2008, p. 130). Ungar studied resilience in youth in 11 countries and concluded that resilience is: "the capacity of individuals to navigate their way to the psychological, social, cultural, and physical resources that sustain their well-being, and their capacity individually and collectively to negotiate for these resources to be provided and experienced in culturally meaningful ways" (Ungar, 2008, p. 225).

Walsh developed a family therapy theoretical model of family resilience for family therapy that focused on three domains of family life that are described as follows: (1) family belief systems: shared beliefs that make meaning out of a crisis, positive outlook, transcendence, and spirituality; (2) family organization: flexibility, connectedness, social and economic resources; and (3) communication processes: clarity, open emotional expression, collaborative problem solving (Walsh, 2003). Based upon this model, Walsh described the helpful roles played by family therapists, programs, and policies in enhancing family resilience, including in situations of war and disasters.

Several researchers have approached family resilience using the, "double ABCX model of family crisis" (Caldwell & Boyd, 2009; Focht-Birkerts & Beardslee, 2000; Greeff & Holtzkamp, 2007). This model focuses on coping as an interplay of the type and quantity of the stressors, resources available to the family, and the family perception of the stressors. In a study of farming families impacted by drought, Caldwell and Boyd (2009) identified multiple coping strategies, including problem-focused coping, optimism, and reliance on social capital. Focht-Birkerts and Beardslee (2000) investigated children of parents with depression from an object relations perspective and found that resilience was dependent upon a family's ability to tolerate elaborate negative affect.

A number of small and mostly cross-sectional quantitative studies have identified possible protective resources, such as family and social support (Beiser, Devins, Dion, Hyman, & Lin, 1997; Beiser, Turner, & Ganesan, 1989; Hsu, Davies, & Hansen, 2004), parental well-being and lower caregiver distress (Melville & Lykes, 1992),

S.M. Weine (✉)
College of Medicine, University of Illinois at Chicago, Chicago, IL, USA
e-mail: smweine@psych.uic.edu

M. Ungar (ed.), *The Social Ecology of Resilience: A Handbook of Theory and Practice*,
DOI 10.1007/978-1-4614-0586-3_24, © Springer Science+Business Media, LLC 2012

connection to the larger community and the culture of origin (Birman, Trickett, & Vinokurov, 2002; Servan-Schreiber, Lin, & Birmaher, 1998). Researchers have identified various properties of families as components of resilience, including: family strengths (commitment, cohesion, adaptability, spirituality, family time, intrafamilial support, and coherence); economic resources; parental education; cultural heritage and religious and spiritual beliefs; shared values; affectionate rituals; shared family traditions; support system accessible to the family; participation in church activities; accommodation; and instilling positive self-esteem in children (Howard, 1996).

Several studies of refugees, migrants, and survivors of political violence have considered the phenomenon of resilience and identified additional contingencies and complexities related to social and economic adversity (Bennett, Rigby, & Boshoff, 1997; Betancourt & Khan, 2008; Eggerman & Panter-Brick, 2010; Rousseau, Rufagari, Bagilishya, & Measham, 2004; Ungar, 2008, 2011). For example, Rousseau et al. (2004) conducted a longitudinal study with 12 refugee families from the Congo, and found that the strategies for dealing with ambiguous loss of family members were protective. Betancourt & Khan (2008) reviewed the literature on the mental health of children affected by armed conflict and found several factors related to resilient mental health outcomes, including attachment relationships, caregiver health, resources and connection in the family, and social support in peer and extended networks. Eggerman and Panter-Brick (2010) conducted interviews with children in Afghanistan and found that resilience was based on shared cultural values, but that in the face of violent conflict, ineffective governance, and economic impediments, cultural values can also give rise to "entrapment," or the sense of having nowhere to go. In a study of migrants in South Africa, Bennett, Rigby, & Boshoff (1997) found that the degree of control that a family reported having over the family crises and their relocation were important to their psychological adaptation. Ungar discussed the case of an adolescent African refugee in Canada, outlining an approach to resilience as a "social ecological construct" that focuses on the individual's interaction with culture and context, including

the family (Ungar, 2008, 2011). According to Ungar, "resilience is dependent on a family's ability to both access available resources that sustain individual and collective well-being, as well as participate effectively in the social discourse that defines which resources are culturally and contextually meaningful" (2010, p. 421). Family resilience has also been linked with community resilience, for example through "social hope" (Walsh, 2007) wherein the families' expectation of access to resources is needed to facilitate family members' dreams of social mobility.

Prior work has taught that immigrant families will create a new family life in their new location that contains elements from premigration family life, shaped by social and cultural influence from their home country, and elements from their new life. For example, Kibria (1993) studied Vietnamese families and linked cooperative kin-based economic practices with the cultural ideology of family collectivism. Other work has documented hybrid or creolization models of cultural change among immigrant families (e.g., Foner, 1997).

The enthusiasm for facilitating family resilience has not been matched by very extensive critical thinking or inquiry into family resilience as a social ecological construct. Bottrell (2009) has written about resilience as a social theory and suggested that interventions focused on resilience need to take into account cultural practices, social inequities, social processes, and the differentiated societal and ideological expectation of young people. This includes a specific focus on "resistance as resilience," which is described in terms of, "young people's resilient critiques of inadequate resources of support for education and opposition to stereotypes and stigmatizing" (Bottrell, 2009, p. 336). A social ecological approach is especially called for in migrants and refugees. These families find themselves in situations of social and economic adversity, where there are likely gaps between what the family encourages its members to hope for and what is likely attainable. These families also present social and cultural differences, which may lead to misunderstandings by program leaders and policymakers.

This chapter addresses the following questions based on an ethnographic study of refugee families from two African countries: (1) How has the family resilience of African refugee families been shaped by their living experiences in prior settings (prewar in their home country; internment in the refugee camp)? (2) What are the new, continued, or modified forms of family resilience in African refugee families in U.S. refugee resettlement? (3) How can policy, program, and research initiatives be developed that fit better with the social ecological construct of family resilience among African refugees?

Liberian and Burundian Refugees

Nearly ten thousand Burundian refugees from Tanzanian refugee camps were resettled in the U.S. beginning in 2007. The 1972 Burundians are mostly Hutu and fled a violent campaign from the Tutsi controlled government (Center for Applied Linguistics, 2007). Living in exile in Tanzania for more than three decades, they experienced ongoing political and criminal violence, sexual assault, poverty, unemployment, dependency, an absence of freedom of movement, family break-up, and poor education for their children.

Similarly, from 1989 until 2003, Liberia suffered a series of conflicts among armed groups. An estimated 150,000 people were killed in the fighting and hundreds of thousands were forced to flee to neighboring nations or overseas (Voice of America, 2009). Over 71,000 Liberian refugees lived in refugee camps in Ghana, Cote d'Ivoire, and other neighboring countries. Between 1992 and 2004, the U.S. resettled approximately 23,500 Liberian refugees who fled the civil war in Liberia. Like Burundians, these refugee families experienced separations as well as economic, social, and cultural pressures in resettlement (Franz & Ives, 2008).

Family Ecodevelopmental Framework for the Investigation

To frame this investigation of family resilience, we applied family ecodevelopmental theory, which envisions children and youth in the context of family systems and community networks

interacting with educational, health, mental health, and social service systems (Szapocznik & Coatsworth, 1999). We also drew upon resilience theory (Fergus & Zimmerman, 2005; Rutter, 1987; Walsh, 2003), trauma theories (Bracken, 2002; Friedman & Jaranson, 1994; Silove, 1999), and migration theories (Falicov, 2003; Portes & Rumbaut, 2001). Based upon these theories, we devised a conceptual framework to guide this research which posited the following: (1) war, migration, and resettlement exposes refugees to family and ecological risks factors; (2) protective factors also exist in refugees' family and social environments; and (3) these protective factors mitigate the family and ecological risks for negative individual behavioral (e.g., poor educational functioning) and mental health (e.g., depression and alcoholism) consequences. Thus we conceptualized family resilience from a multi-level, cross-cultural, and positive development perspective, which we believe is needed to understand the individual, familial, community, educational, and developmental factors that are involved. Protective factors included as family and ecological characteristics that stop, delay, or diminish negative individual behavioral and mental health consequences for youth or adult family members. Protective factors can include within-family resources (e.g., parenting style, parental monitoring and supervision, and family communication), family connections with others (e.g., family outreach, family advocacy), and community protective factors (e.g., helpful support from church, voluntary agencies, or other families). By employing this framework, we acknowledged that refugee families experience not only trauma exposure but also "ecological transitions" (Betancourt & Khan, 2008; Bronfenbrenner, 1979), which impact family life in multiple realms.

Methods

We conducted a 3-year, multisite, longitudinal ethnographic study of Burundian and Liberian refugees resettled in metropolitan Chicago, Illinois and Boston, Massachusetts. Study subjects were 73 at-risk refugee adolescents, their families, and service providers, interviewed within the first 3 years following resettlement. At-risk was defined as refugee youth with one or more of several specific factors that have been empirically associated with mental illness or behavioral problems in published studies of migrant youth (Hernandez, 2004). These are (1) a one parent family; (2) poverty, as indicated by monthly family income below U.S. Census poverty threshold (U.S. Bureau of the Census, 1992); (3) living in a linguistically isolated household (i.e., no one in house over age 14 speaks English very well, U.S. Census, 2003); (4) a mother or father with less than a high school education; and (5) a parent who has sought or received mental health treatment (either counseling or medications). All participants gave written informed consent as approved by the institutional review boards of the University of Illinois at Chicago and Harvard University.

Data collection consisted of minimally-structured interviews and shadowing observations of individual study participants, and focused field observations carried out with each family in homes, communities, and service organizations. A minimally-structured interview is a discussion with the participant that begun with a small number of introductory questions. The conversation proceeded in whatever direction allowing the participant to speak most meaningfully to the research questions from his/her personal experience. Shadowing field observations involved the ethnographer accompanying the family or its members on his/her normal daily routine in a variety of sites (these included home, school, church, community, and services). Shadowing observations allowed the ethnographers to directly witness the interactions between protective resources, risks, culture, and service sectors over time.

The interviewers were Burundian, Liberian, and American fieldworkers trained and supervised by the principal investigator and coinvestigator (Dr. Norma Ware of Harvard University). Data were collected and analyzed based upon established approaches to ethnography and qualitative analysis (Corbin & Strauss, 2008; LeCompte & Schensul, 1999; Miles & Huberman, 1994). The initial study questions were refined

through an iterative process of data collection and analysis that followed standardized qualitative methods utilizing a grounded theory approach (Corbin & Strauss, 2008) to data analysis until a model emerged. Through an iterative process, and discussion among project staff, a grounded theory model of family resilience in social ecological context was developed.

Results

Domains of Family Resilience in Social Ecological Context

This section describes a grounded theory model of family resilience in resettlement (See Table 24.1). Overall, family resilience in resettlement has been shaped significantly by the refugee families' prior living places and associated social ecologies, including in their home countries prewar and internment in refugee camps. The large majority of the family resilience processes seen in resettlement represent modifications of previously existing resilience processes, such as finding or building new churches, finding or creating a living place that is reminiscent of a refugee camp, and sharing parenting responsibilities with other parents in the new settings. Several new family resilience processes emerged such as learning to be more active parents, moving to other cities to find lower rents, and allowing greater adolescent autonomy. The sections that follow provide additional details on these family resilience processes in social ecological context.

Home Country (Prewar)

This section describes the domains of family resilience while living in their home countries prior to the recent wars and forced migration.

Belief Systems and Social Systems

Relaxed Christianity. The majority of the Burundians and Liberians were raised in Christian families and identified themselves as believers and regular churchgoers who tried to teach their religion to their children. Most Liberians attended

Table 24.1 Domains of family resilience in social ecological context

Family resilience domains	Resilience processes fostered by home country prewar	Resilience processes fostered by refugee camp	Resilience processes fostered by resettlement
Belief systems	Relaxed Christianity	Hanging on to faith in God	Finding or creating new churches (C/M)
	Patriarchal family order	Exposure to pentacostals	Pursuing opportunity in the new life through education (C/M)
	Children should remain dependent until marriage	God will bring you to the U.S.	Daughters and wives become more independent (N)
	Children support their parents into old age	Expectations for better life in the U.S.	Marriages adapt to changes in gender roles (N)
	Showing respect and deference for elders	Children go free in the camp	
Organizational patterns	Family centered subsistence economy	Developing close relationships with nonextended family	Finding a living place like a refugee camp (C/M)
	Large extended family in close proximity	Family financial dependency on UN, NGOs, and relatives in America	Building financial security through both parents working hard (C/M)
	Parenting responsibilities shared	Black market and criminal means of gaining resources	Reuniting with family (C/M)
	Fosterage for a better tomorrow	Parents form networks with other families in camp to advocate and protect themselves	Sharing parenting responsibilities with other families (C/M)
			Finding and supporting community leaders (C/M)
			Learning to be more active parents (N)
			Church congregants, agency workers, and volunteers become like new family (N)
			Family learns to become independent of agencies (N)
			Moving for lower rent (N)
			Sending money to family in Africa (N)
Communication processes	Eating meals together	More family togetherness	African church becomes venue for emotional expression about war and refugee hardships (straight talk) (C/M)
	Family storytelling	Storytelling less focused on family	Family decision making regarding moving (N)
	Home devotion	Telling them what we have to keep our family together	Parents talk with their children and teachers re children's education (N)
	Parents trust the teachers and the school		

(C/M) – continuation and modification of existing family resilience process
(N) – new family resilience process

churches of Protestant denominations, though a few attended Pentecostal churches or Roman Catholic churches. Most Burundians considered themselves Roman Catholics. However, prior to the war, Christian spirituality and religion were not as highly emphasized as it was during and after the conflict.

Patriarchal family order. Liberian and Burundian families had a patriarchal social organization. In most families, men were the primary breadwinners and decision-makers. Women had primary responsibility for household chores and childcare, as well as sharing responsibility for agricultural work and earning some income. Divorce was rare, especially in rural areas. In some Liberian households, men had two or more wives. In Burundi, some men had two or three wives residing in separate households. Upon marriage, daughters moved to their husbands' family compounds and sons remained with their parents bringing wives to the compound when they married.

Children should remain dependent until marriage. Children were economically and socially subservient to their family and father's authority until marriage, when they gained some autonomy. Rituals marked the transition to adulthood, yet there was no single point when a young adult transitioned to maturity. Rather, a sequence of stages occurred from childhood, and expectations of adult behavior were taught from an early age. For example, in Liberia, the Poro society for boys and the Sande society for girls taught leadership, housekeeping, hunting, fishing, dancing, and other adult tasks during ritual initiation rites, and conducted genital circumcision and excision rituals.

Children support their parents into old age. Children began supporting their parents immediately after completing their education or in late adolescence if they were not in school. This support was expected to continue until the parents' death. Having children attend school incurred heavy costs, including school fees and losing the child's farm labor. Making this sacrifice, parents sometimes selected a child they thought was more likely to succeed, believing that having an educated child ensured a solid means of support in their old age. Responsibility for the care of aging parents fell mainly on the wives of their sons, who typically lived close to the parents. However, if a daughter lived nearby, she may have been the main caregiver, and elderly parents could go to live with a daughter. As one woman said, "At my age, I want her to find a rich man so they can take care of me." Another said, "My grandma had only three children and so longed for a large number of grandchildren, boys especially." For this reason, not having children was considered disastrous.

Showing respect and deference for elders. Showing respect for adults was essential to demonstrate having been properly raised. Children were taught never to interrupt an adult, to gaze downwards when adults spoke, and to follow orders without question in the presence of other adults, especially nonfamily. If another adult reported a child's bad behavior to the child's parent, the parent would punish the child, usually using corporal punishment. Self-discipline was a central principle of adult life, and garnered respect from others for oneself and one's family. Elders were thought to be those closest to joining the ancestors upon death, and the ancestors in turn, were understood to intervene in daily life. All adults, elders especially must be respected with reverence, therefore.

Organizational Patterns

Family centered subsistence economy. Liberian and Burundian families depended mainly on subsistence farming. Even children contributed by working in the fields or selling in the market. Each household was an economic unit that was interdependent with other local households. Subsistence farming was inherently fraught with worry and few families had ample food to last the whole year from farming alone. In the larger towns, salaried workers and merchants also contributed income to their households.

Large extended family in proximity. Social life was structured around large kin groups based largely on place of residence, and life was built around elaborate networks of relationships, offering reciprocal support of various kinds. Households typically were composed of a husband, his wife or wives (in Liberia) who may live in the same or adjacent houses and all of their children, including married sons and their wives and children. Married sons and their wives lived in added homes next to their parents' homes until parents moved in with them when incapable of independent living. Nearby, the man's siblings, other kin, and possibly, his wives' kin also lived. Other people, more distantly related, or neighbors related through marriage or not related, became entwined in daily life and some were as close as kin.

Parenting responsibilities shared. Parenting responsibilities were shared across extended families and broadly defined kin groups, villages, or neighborhoods. One parent said, "A child belongs to the community, not just the family." In multi-generational households composed of several or more adults, childrearing was spread across adult members of the household and some older children as well. Local languages did not distinguish between cousins and siblings, or between father and his brothers or mother and her sisters. Father's other wives might be referred to as "small mothers," "big mothers," "stepmothers," or just "mothers." This extended network allowed families considerable flexibility in parenting in contexts of hardship, where average life expectancy was short, and many children lost parents before they were grown.

Fosterage for a better tomorrow. Lending one's child to be raised by another family, usually for a temporary period, was common. This practice was seen as beneficial in raising children, who were thought to be less likely to be spoiled while living away from their biological parents as they grew up. For example, in Burundi it was common for the first child to stay with his parents, and the second child to be sent to his grandparents remaining with them until he completed elementary school. Subsequent children would remain with parents or be sent to other family members. A childless couple was seen as an opportunity for this type of fosterage, solving both the problem

of an empty household (with no one to do the chores) and parents overburdened with the responsibilities of child rearing. Fosterage also fulfilled the crucial need for a child, since bareness meant disgrace and the lack of future security. The fostered child developed a relationship which bound him or her to the foster couple in an obligatory manner, in some cases, ensuring them security in old age.

Communication Processes

Eating meals together. Household members ate meals together divided by gender and age. Older men ate in one group, typically from one large tray, whereas adolescent boys, women, and children each from their own group's tray or pot. Only the most important messages were conveyed during meals. In Liberia, boys ate with men while girls ate with women and children were taught to not speak while eating as it was disrespectful. Storytelling, relaxed conversation, and gossip took place after the evening meal.

Family storytelling. In the evening, men told stories, men and women conversed, children had a chance to talk, and parents played with the children and applied discipline. For example, a parent while teaching her children to toss away fingernail clippings included a story, telling them that bad people could poison them through the nails found strewn on the floor, causing the children to die. Or, when instructing children to get water for drinking, the parent would warn them that in case God comes to the house, they should have water ready. In the prewar context, where the spirit world was an important part of daily life and formed part of the social ecology, storytelling evoked bad spirits to motivate children. Similarly, in Burundi, there was a two-step process of disciplinary action. A child who came late from school would be punished by his mother verbally and possibly physically as well. Then after dinner his mother would use the incident as an example for the other children, telling them how to behave. "We tell our children what is right. We teach them from our experiences, and when you make a mistake, that mistake will follow you. When you are big, it will come back and wrestle you. So we tell about the society in which we live, and we tell them that the competition is hard. We tell them to study enough, and more than other children."

Home devotion. In some Christian homes, Christian devotions were held daily for 30 minutes to an hour. During this time, individual and family concerns were shared in the form of "prayer requests," and gratitude was expressed in the form of "praise items." For example one might say, "We prayed yesterday for Junior to pass his final exam and now we praise the Lord because he passed." Everyone rejoiced and praised God. If Junior did not pass, it was due to his lack of effort or some other interference. Junior would be told to study harder and have more faith in God. Devotion was important because the family focused on positive thoughts and outcomes; members reflected together on their hope in God and the expectation that they would be good citizens on earth. Through the devotion the family believed that they were teaching the children Christian values, and they left the devotion singing, energized, believing that God was with them.

Parents trust the teachers and the school. Parents' involvement in schooling was not encouraged or wanted by teachers or administrators, following the traditions and rules of colonial education. Parents rarely entered the school buildings. Help with homework was accepted from educated parents, but rarely done. Parents trusted teachers with their children and might ask teachers to help with discipline at home. Some children stayed away from school for fear of punishment by teachers who carried whips with them, always ready to use corporal punishment, even outside of the schools. The parents respected teachers for their educational and social status, and deferred to the teachers.

Refugee Camp

This section traces the changes that occurred in the domains of family resilience after the families fled their homes and settled in refugee camps.

Belief Systems

Hanging on to faith in God. Many refugees' faith in God increased by large measure in the refugee camps as a way of coping with feelings of vulnerability, hopelessness, and loss of their normal sense of protection. One said, "I got to know the church in the refugee camp." Having lost their homes and material possessions, and feeling let down by their government, families organized long devotions every morning. One Liberian said, "With my family around me, everyone talked about God. And I saw a lot that God did for me in my refugee life when I lived in the Ivory Coast all alone with my kids, moving then to Guinea, in the miracle God performed in my life." The practice of devotions increased in refugee camps, as more families practiced them more frequently and for longer times.

Exposure to pentecostals. In prewar Burundi, most refugees were Roman Catholics, but became Protestants in the camps. Liberians came from many denominations, and in camps, most became involved in Pentecostal churches. Typically, Liberians felt that the Pentecostal church addressed their forms of spiritualism, including witchcraft. The Pentecostal church was considered by many to be syncretistic in practice, teaching that a person could bewitch another and that the spirit could be cast away, ideas that resonated with African forms of the spirit world. The church also taught members how to obtain specific changes in their lives through reading Scripture.

Expectations for better life in the U.S. For adult refugees, the camp was, as one said, "the worst experience of my life." In camps, families were subject to illness, lack of adequate medical care, politically motivated attacks, rape, criminal attacks, poverty, and hunger. Preachers would tell them, "God is going to bring your kids to America to have a better future." Rumors spread during orientation sessions prior to resettlement led many to believe that if they went to the U.S., they would be eligible for 5 years' financial support there, in the "caring hands of Christians." One said, "We were told we won't have to work for at least 5 years. We were told that cars, clothes, and houses full of foods and other needs will be waiting for us. It was not the case."

Children go free in the camp. A positive part of camp life was the freedom children had to run free, play, and mix socially with other children. Children under the age of 13 were required by their parents to be home at dusk, but older children could stay out later. Houses were arranged close together, and there was plenty of open space. Camp school was not as strict as back home and there was very little or no homework. Children had minimal chores at home and there were few organized activities so they could run free after school.

Organizational Patterns

Developing close relationships with nonextended family. In the chaos of war and relocation to refugee camps, ties to large kin groups were loosened or broken. Extended families were replaced by relationships with strangers. However, extended family or larger kin groups helped the refugees adapt in camps and in resettlement, as people were able to trust one another and share responsibilities.

Family financial dependency on UN, NGOs, and relatives in America. Few Liberian or Burundian refugee families were able to bring their belongings from home, and all depended on United Nations and NGOs for their material needs. Refugees who had relatives in the U.S. and other countries might receive money and items from them while in camps. Some Burundian families spent 30 years or longer in camps, and many children were born and raised there, not knowing how to financially support themselves, and having no memories of families who were economically self-supporting.

Black market and criminal means of gaining resources. Many refugees resorted to trading food received from the U.N. for other items outside the camp. Liberians in the Ivory Coast traded in counterfeit money, sometimes traveling as far as North Africa for this illegal activity, and those who were caught went to prison. In the hardship of the refugee life, some women and girls became sex workers.

Parents form networks with other families in camp to advocate and protect themselves. In camps, Liberian and Burundian refugees formed financial associations. Similar to associations they had at home, they pooled resources so that when a member needed funds for a family event such as a christening, she could draw on the group's reserves. They established women's and men's groups where issues such as keeping families together and camp security were discussed.

Communication Processes

More family togetherness. In camps, refugees had few responsibilities and little to occupy their time, and there was ample time for family time and socializing with friends. People cooked, ate, did chores, played games, talked, and read together. Family devotions were an integral part of communication strategies, focusing on faith in God, belief for the future, and hope. One man said, "It is said that 'the family that prays together stays together,' and it worked for my and many other families."

Storytelling less focused on family. In camps, there was less storytelling than before the war. The tents were small and there was little privacy or space for gathering. Children played all day and at night and did not take time to listen to stories. The recent experiences of war and life in the refugee camp were too painful for the parents to include in stories, and they preferred not to reflect or dwell on their circumstances. Rather than reinforcing children's awareness of their surroundings, as stories were meant to do, parents avoided talking about the war and the struggles of their daily lives.

Telling them what we have to do to keep our family together. Parents reported having told authorities that the people they were living with were their family, because they wanted to be able to stay with their newly formed camp families, having lost track of many of their own kin from home. Normally, in African cultures that practice fosterage of children, all those children and adults who live together in a household are considered a part of the "family," and it would be unconscionable to abandon another person's child. An older Liberian woman brought her grandson to the U.S. as her "child," who years later, moved in with his biological parents after their arrival in the U.S. However, this practice was distinct from cases of overt fraud whereby places for resettlement were bought and sold.

U.S. Refugee Resettlement

This section describes changes in the domains of family resilience after the refugees entered U.S. refugee resettlement. In this section, C/M indicates the continuation and modification of an already existing family resilience practice or protective process, and N indicates a newly emerged family resilience practice.

Belief Systems

Finding or creating new churches (C/M). Refugee families selected new churches based on proximity, the welcoming extended to the family, and the resources made available (food, clothing, money, and contacts for work). Initial contacts were made directly by the churches, sometimes through other African members, or by resettlement agencies. Some preferred larger congregations because they had resources. Others tried to find the same denomination they had attended in their home country or camp. Help came from volunteers who provided friendship, cultural instruction, introduction to other families, and sometimes, partial rent for the family to live in a better neighborhood. Churches provided youth activities and Sunday school for the children. Some families tried more than one church and were flexible about the type of church. Some refugee communities established their own congregations, with the help of a host church. "With the help of a Nigerian church, we were able to start our own church. We don't pay rent. We use this space from 10:00 am to 1:00 pm. We were blessed to find this place," explained a Burundian pastor. These new churches, housed in American church facilities, became Burundian or Liberian churches, where people worshipped in the same manner they had in their home country, with a Liberian or Burundian pastor and leaders.

Pursuing opportunities in the new life through education (N). Upon arriving in America and having children placed in schools, parents found that schooling was mandatory (unlike their home countries or refugee camps) and viewed this as a central element of the new opportunity in America, in the belief that schooling would lead to a better life. They also discovered new expectations of parents to be involved in children's schooling, by attending events, communicating with teachers, and supervising homework.

Daughters and wives become more independent (N). Resettlement presented women with new work and educational opportunities, even though few were educated or had employable skills. Some women reported having more ability to make independent decisions in finding jobs or deciding where the family would live. Some women spoke about their understanding of the American system, where they were not required to obey their husbands, about which several husbands complained. Daughters still in school became independent in their social lives, going out with friends, and planning their own lives as young, single women. Some daughters who had graduated from high school moved away from home and had jobs or attended training programs. Some women chose to leave their husbands, and at least one had her husband arrested for domestic abuse.

Marriages adapt to changes in gender roles (N). In contrast to the prewar situation, gender roles in American cities were by necessity more equal, because all adults had to work in order to pay the household bills and child rearing in resettlement was expected to be shared by fathers and mothers, creating new kinds of pressure in marriages. Most marriages where both partners accepted their new roles have remained intact; women who were willing to get jobs and training, and husbands who accepted and supported their wives' working, and who were involved day-to-day with children and household appear to have a smoother transition.

Organizational Patterns

Finding a living place like a refugee camp (C/M). To our initial surprise, some refugees expressed the desire to reproduce living spaces that were reminiscent of life in the camp. Having lived in the U.S. for years, some still missed aspects of camp life: the freedom of movement for their children, friendships with people living nearby, having a garden for food; reciprocal help with child care, shared religious holidays, communication with and visits with relatives, or the time and resources to spend time with their families. While people were happy to forget the negative associations with camps (poverty, cramped living quarters, lack of adequate food, the violent crime, the lack of personal freedom), a particularly fond memory was having friendly neighbors, something the families were more likely to find in the U.S. if they were living close to their country people. A family that had first settled in Chicago who then moved to the southern United States, described finding this friendliness in their new home as, "Old-fashioned country way of living."

Building financial security by both parents working hard (C/M). Parents understood that their financial dreams would be realized through hard work. Most of the refugee parents were dedicated to finding jobs to earn money and become financially independent, and most who were able to work did find employment. In two parent households, this meant that both parents worked, taking available jobs, including maintenance and janitorial work, working in hospitals and nursing homes, as cooks or nurses' assistants. Some adults had two or three jobs, and some attended school while working. Those that could not find jobs were distressed at remaining dependent upon the resettlement agencies and the government, and many of those who had jobs looked for better jobs or improved life situations. In some cases, such as where a parent had a disability, or difficulty keeping a job, chronic illness, or did not speak English, employment was more difficult to find.

Reuniting with family (C/M). Refugee families reported a strong desire to be reunited with other family members who remained in Africa or who resettled elsewhere in the U.S. or other countries. One parent said, "We were promised that if we put them on the lists, the family would join us in the U.S. As it looks, this hope will not be fulfilled. The entire family is losing hope of life because of this. Everyday life in the U.S. brings sorrow and we regret being here. We are refugees and maybe we were better where we were." Another stated, "We are safe here but we are not very happy because of the children that we left behind." Many parents spent time almost every day trying to advocate for

family members applying for refugee status and communicate with family still "at home."

Sharing parenting responsibilities with other families (C/M). Now separated from family by large distances, refugees found that they had to rely on other families to help care for children so that the parents could work or attend school or job training. For many families, finding appropriate childcare was a major challenge. Where families were resettled in proximity, they shared child care – baby sitting, transporting children to school and other activities, providing after school care – and through this communal child care, created social networks that maintained cultural bonds among the parents and children. In one community, Liberian refugee families lived in proximity and made conscious efforts to remain connected by sharing childcare and other responsibilities as well as holidays and other events. Even at a distance, relationships forged in the camps provided support in parenting. One refugee mother in the U.S. sent the most difficult of her children to live with an older couple she had met in a refugee camp in Sierra Leone. She referred to them as her uncle and aunt, and forged with them what became a relationship of African fosterage in resettlement, eventually moving the rest of her family to live with them in another state.

Finding and supporting community leaders (C/M). Refugee families knew when first resettled that they would need community elders and leaders to guide and protect them in the new settlements and they deliberately established those roles. The persons most trusted outside their families were pastors and priests. Burundian families elected an *umushingantahe*, or a "man of justice," someone they could trust and count on to address problems and disputes. Liberian families looked to older men and women who had been community and or church leaders in the past, and to younger persons who had shown promise of leadership.

Learning to be more active parents (N). Some families learned to be more regularly and intensively involved with monitoring, supervising, talking with, and supporting their children.

Becoming more active parents required being more involved and aware of what was going on daily in school, talking to their children, and to teachers at the school. A few families set meeting times or talked over dinner about each child's day and the challenges she/he was facing. These changes were supported in several ways. Schools invited parents to events and meetings. Some American friends and hosts have helped the parents, going to the school along with, or on behalf of the parent, and teaching them the ropes. For example, the mother of a 17-year-old boy attended her son's gymnastics competitions, even driving him to and from the gym, after her American sponsor had worked with her on this issue.

Church congregants, agency workers, and volunteers become like new family (N). Liberian and Burundian families learned to look for help from others. Where help had previously come from family or refugee camp staff and structures, during resettlement, establishing a positive relationship with volunteers led to at least short-term financial, instrumental, and emotional support. New "relatives" and friends were made through agencies or churches. In addition, many volunteers included their own family members in the relationships with refugee families, visiting the families, providing transportation, clothing, and recreation. One Burundian said, "Members of the church replaced my relatives I left back in refugee camp. Actually, they did more than that, they were sent by God to take care of me. My family receives financial and spiritual help from them. They gave us clothes, paid rent for us, helped us with shopping, etc. We were blessed to have them in our lives."

Family learns to become independent of agencies (N). Within the first 2 years in the U.S. most of the refugee families severed their formal relationship with the resettlement agencies. In most cases, this transition occurred as adults found work and families adjusted to their situations. As part of this adjustment adults and children found resources they could go to for information or various kinds of support, including churches, government agencies, and other individuals. For some this transition was difficult, because many refugees felt disappointed or frustrated by the agencies and by the U.S. government that arranged for their resettlement. Many had specific complaints over the discrepancy between what was told to them in refugee camps and the realities of resettlement. Yet for others, leaving behind the resettlement agency represented an important step toward independence.

Moving for lower rent (N). Some Burundians found jobs, but many did not. High rent in large cities made it difficult to make ends meet, even for those who were employed. A solution for some families was to move out of the city to a smaller town, or to a rural or suburban area nearby or further away from their initial resettlement place. One Burundian said: "In Chicago, we were paying $1,100 for a two bedroom apartment. Our new house has four bedrooms and we only pay $800. We have a big back and front yard. Our children have enough space to play with their friends and we don't have to worry about strangers being around." Most Liberian families became gainfully employed but still found moving a solution to financial worries, having learned about lower rents from other families in their community. The lower rents enabled them to send money to their families in Africa, a priority for them.

Sending money to family in Africa (N). An important value held by Africans was to send money to their family members in Africa. Those who could not send money felt they were not fulfilling their most basic obligation, and believed that their relatives back home considered them heartless and or perhaps Americanized. In fact, almost all the refugees sent money every month. "Western Union money transfers are the single most vibrant economy upholding Liberia since the war." Some families, especially the Liberians, planned to return to Liberia after their children were educated and settled, and thus the money they send home was also an investment in their own future. Some had already purchased land in Liberia, and with the help of their relatives there, were building houses there while still living in the U.S. Many held onto hopes of retiring to those homes at some time.

Communication Processes

African church becomes venue for emotional expression about war and refugee hardships (C/M). In addition to having an African type of worship experience, churches were vital locations for talk, support, sharing of information, and recreation. For example, at Wednesday night prayer meetings, families sharing with others their challenges through formal discussion, would be asked, "What can we pray for, for you, and your family?" Liberians spoke of experiences they had during the war that they could not tell other people, about miracles witnessed, or warlords and fighters getting power from demonic forces. Some refugees recalled encounters with ancestors or spirits during the war, believing that Americans would not accept or understand their stories. Some refugees had scars from the war or from ritual scarification that they believed protected them from bullets. The war and its memories were discussed in the safety of the African churches, among others who had similar experiences.

Family decision-making regarding moving (N). For years the refugee families felt a lack of control about where they went, from their first host country to refugee camp to the place of resettlement. Once in the U.S. some families viewed moving elsewhere within the U.S. as a way to regain a sense of control over their own lives, in deciding for themselves where and when to go, where to live, and how. Creating their own space became an important goal. For some of the families who moved to smaller cities, having lower rent and more money to spend on comforts, or to send home to Burundi or Liberia, enhanced the feeling of control over one's life. For some others, reasons for moving were shorter commutes to work, a safer or better environment for struggling or unfocused children, or just to get a new start, having learned about the American system. A mother who moved to Missouri reported that a small town with no buses was better for her drug-using son who had dropped out of school.

Parents talk with their children and teachers about children's education (N). Although talking with teachers was difficult for many African parents, some adjusted to the new system, checking in regularly with teachers and going to school for conferences and meetings. Language was a major barrier, so parents who had proficient English had an advantage. In some cases, the school staff made the first contact encouraging the parent to ask questions or raise concerns. Talking with children about homework and school was a new form of communication that many parents learned to engage in at home.

Discussion

Nowadays resilience is reported to be everywhere. Resilience perspectives serve as a corrective for the mental health field's historic preoccupation with psychopathology and behavioral risks. As a rhetorical device, resilience has become a favored term of programs and policymakers, shifting attention toward prevention and public health perspectives. One concern is whether the claims being made about resilience are adequately supported by scientific evidence, especially evidence specific to the context. Another concern is that our understanding of resilience remains too simplistic, and should consider not only how resilience is different from pathology or risks, but also how resilience itself is textured and dynamic, emerging in response to new social ecological contexts. This study addressed both of these concerns, using ethnographic evidence to investigate the changes in resilience across time and place in refugee families from two countries.

The findings indicate that family resilience is more than a static property, checklist of protective factors, fixed positive outcome, or lack of negative outcomes. Family resilience is a dynamic property which is shaped by social, economic, cultural, and historical contexts. For African refugee families in U.S. refugee resettlement, family resilience has been shaped by the refugee families' prior living places, including pre-war in their home country and internment in refugee camps. These former living places tended to foster family resilience, which revolved around large kinship networks, family subsistence economies, family rituals and physical proximity, and long standing cultural practice. On the contrary,

U.S. resettlement called upon very different properties of resilience, such as emphasis on nuclear family parenting, adolescent autonomy, and financial independence.

The large majority of the family resilience processes seen during resettlement represent modifications of previously existing resilience processes, such as finding or building new churches, finding or creating a living place that is reminiscent of a refugee camp, and developing ways to share parenting responsibilities with other parents in the new settings. Several new family resilience processes were identified as well, such as learning to be more active parents, moving to other cities to find lower rents, and allowing greater adolescent autonomy. We expect that the process of modified or emergent family resilience will continue beyond initial resettlement, and will be part of their longer-term adjustment and development.

Programs and policymakers in resettlement want refugee families to exhibit the specific types of resilient processes that would facilitate their adjustment in the new setting. The findings of this study suggest that for most refugee families, this is an unrealistic expectation, given that they have learned to be resilient in former settings with radically different social ecologies. Instead of comparing these families to an idealized refugee family, perhaps we should start by comparing them with themselves, by asking: (1) What types of existing family resilience processes can what types of families modify on their own? (2) What types of existing family resilience processes in what types of families are modifiable through intervention (of what types)? (3) What types of existing family resilient processes in what types of families cannot be modified through intervention? and (4) What types of new emergent family resilient processes in what types of families can be generated through interventions (of what types)? These same questions could also inform future studies. Rigorously designed intervention studies, using community collaboration, large sample sizes, mixed-methods with focused ethnography, and longitudinal design are needed (Weine, 2011).

Using these questions as starting points, program administrators and policymakers could respond through developing resilience-based initiatives that fit better with the social ecological context of family resilience of refugee families, either through modifying existing elements or building new elements of family resilience. New initiatives are needed to help families adapt, involving: gender roles, family finances, secondary migration, and parenting. Modification of existing elements should involve faith community and cooperating with other families. These are all topics that would be appropriate to include in parent support and education initiatives, though not all at once and for the same groups. In conclusion, program leaders and policymakers should respond by developing resilience-based initiatives that better facilitate the modification of existing family resilience processes or the emergence of new processes.

Acknowledgments This research was supported by NIMH 5R01MH076118.

References

Beiser, M., Devins, G., Dion, R., Hyman, I., & Lin, E. (1997). *Immigration, acculturation and health*. Report to the National Health Research and Development Program (NHRDP), Project No. 6606-6414-NPHS, Ottawa, Canada.

Beiser, M., Turner, R. J., & Ganesan, S. (1989). Catastrophic stress and factors affecting its consequences among Southeast Asian refugees. *Social Science and Medicine, 28*(3), 183–195.

Bennett, H., Rigby, C., & Boshoff, A. (1997). The relationship between tenure, stress and coping strategies of South African immigrants to New Zealand. *South African Journal of Psychology, 27*(3), 160–165.

Betancourt, T. S., & Khan, K. T. (2008). The mental health of children affected by armed conflict: Protective processes and pathways to resilience. *International Review of Psychiatry, 20*(3), 317–328.

Birman, D., Trickett, E. J., & Vinokurov, A. (2002). Acculturation and adaptation of Soviet Jewish refugee adolescents: Predictors of adjustment across life domains. *American Journal of Community Psychology, 30*, 585–607.

Bottrell, D. (2009). Understanding "marginal" perspectives: Towards a social theory of resilience. *Qualitative Social Work, 8*, 321–339.

Bracken, P. (2002). *Trauma: culture, meaning, and philosophy*. London and Philadelphia: Whurr.

Bronfenbrenner, U. (1979). *The ecology of human development: Experiments by nature and design*. Cambridge: Harvard University Press.

Caldwell, K., & Boyd, C. P. (2009). Coping and resilience in farming families affected by drought. *Rural Remote Health, 9*(2), 1088.

Center for Applied Linguistics. (2007). *The 1972 Burundians.* COC Center Refugee Backgrounder, No. 2. Retrieved Aug 8, 2011 from http://www.cal.org/CO/pdffiles/backgrounder_burundians.pdf.

Corbin, J., & Strauss, A. (2008). *Basics of qualitative research: Techniques and procedures for developing grounded theory.* Thousand Oaks: Sage Publications.

Eggerman, M., & Panter-Brick, C. (2010). Suffering, hope, and entrapment: Resilience and cultural values in Afghanistan. *Social Science and Medicine, 71*(1), 71–83.

Falicov, C. J. (2003). Immigrant family process. In F. Walsh (Ed.), *Normal family processes* (3rd ed.). New York: Guilford Press.

Fergus, S., & Zimmerman, M. (2005). Adolescent resilience: A framework for understanding healthy development in the face of risk. *American Journal of Public Health, 6*, 399–419.

Focht-Birkerts, L., & Beardslee, W. R. (2000). A child's experience of parental depression: Encouraging relational resilience in families with affective illness. *Family Process, 39*(4), 417–434.

Foner, N. (1997). The immigrant family: Cultural legacies and cultural changes. *International Migration Review, 31*, 891–904.

Franz, B. & Ives, N. (2008). Wading through muddy water: challenges to Liberian refugee family restoration in resettlement. Paper presented at the annual meeting of the International Studies Association, San Francisco, California.

Friedman, M. J., & Jaranson, J. (1994). The applicability of the post-traumatic stress disorder concept to refugees . In: A. M. Marsella, T. Bornemann, S. Ekblad, & J. Orley (Eds.), *Amidst Peril and Pain* (pp. 207–227). Washington D.C.: American Psychological Association.

Greeff, A. P., & Holtzkamp, J. (2007). The prevalence of resilience in migrant families. *Fam Community Health, 30*(3), 189–200. PubMed PMID: 17563481.

Hernandez, D. (2004). Demographic change and the life characteristics of immigrant families. In *The Future of Children: Children of Immigrant Families, 14*(2), 17–48.

Howard, D. E. (1996). Searching for resilience among African-American youth exposed to community violence: Theoretical issues. *Journal of Adolescent Health, 18*(4), 254–262.

Hsu, E., Davies, C. A., & Hansen, D. J. (2004). Understanding mental health needs of Southeast Asian refugees: Historical, cultural, and contextual challenges. *Clinical Psychology Review, 24*(2), 193–213.

Kibria, N. (1993). *Family tightrope: The changing lives of Vietnamese Americans.* Princeton: Princeton University Press.

LeCompte, M., & Schensul, J. (1999). *Designing and Conducting Ethnographic Research.* Walnut Creek, CA: Altamira Press.

Melville, M. B., & Lykes, M. B. (1992). Guatemalan Indian children and the sociocultural effects of government-sponsored terrorism. *Social Science & Medicine, 34*(5), 533–548.

Miles, M. B., & Huberman, A. M. (1994). Qualitative data analysis. California: Sage Publications.

Norris, F. H., Stevens, S. P., Pfefferbaum, B., Wyche, K. F., & Pfefferbaum, R. L. (2008). Community resilience as a metaphor, theory, set of capacities, and strategy for disaster readiness. *American Journal of Community Psychology, 41*(1–2), 127–150.

Portes, A., & Rumbaut, R. (2001). *Legacies: The story of the second generation.* Berkeley: University of California Press.

Rousseau, C. C., Rufagari, M. C., Bagilishya, D., & Measham, T. (2004). Remaking family life: Strategies for re-establishing continuity among Congolese refugees during the family reunification process. *Social Science and Medicine, 59*(5), 1095–1108.

Rutter, M. (1987). Psychosocial resilience and protective mechanisms. *American Journal of Orthopsychiatry, 57*, 316–331.

Servan-Schreiber, D., Lin, B. L., & Birmaher, B. (1998). Prevalence of posttraumatic stress disorder and major depressive disorder in Tibetan refugee children. *Journal of the American Academy of Child and Adolescent Psychiatry, 37*, 874–879.

Silove, D. (1999). The psychological effects of torture, mass human rights violations, and refugee trauma: toward an integrated conceptual framework. *Journal of Nervous and Mental Disease, 187*(4), 200.

Szapocznik, J., & Coatsworth, J. D. (1999). An ecodevelopmental framework for organizing the influences on drug abuse: A developmental model of risk and protection. In M. Glantz & C. Hartel (Eds.), *Drug abuse: Origins & interventions.* Washington: American Psychological Association.

U.S. Bureau of the Census. (1992). Selected Social and Economic Characteristics for the Asian Population: 1990. Washington, D.C.

U.S. Census Bureau. (2003). Migration of natives and the foreign born: 1995 to 2000 (Census 2000 Special Reports). Washington, DC: Perry, M. J. & Schachter, J. P.

Ungar, M. (2008). Resilience across cultures. *British Journal of Social Work, 38*, 218–235.

Ungar, M. (2010). Families as navigators and negotiators: Facilitating culturally and contextually specific expressions of resilience. *Family Process, 49*(3), 421–435.

Ungar, M. (2011). *Counseling in challenging contexts: Working with individuals and families across clinical and community settings.* Belmont: Brooks/Cole.

Voice of America. (2009). Obama order aids Liberian refugees. Retrieved Nov 12, 2009 from http://www.voanews.com/uspolicy/2009-03-27-voa2.cfm.

Walsh, F. (2003). Family resilience: A framework for clinical practice. *Family Process, 42*(1), 1–18.

Walsh, F. (2007). Traumatic loss and major disasters: strengthening family and community resilience. *Family Process, 46*, 207–227.

Weine, S. M. (2011). Developing preventive mental health interventions for refugee families in resettlement. *Family Process, 50*(3).

Young People, Sexual Orientation, and Resilience

Rebecca Harvey

Introduction

Gay, lesbian, bisexual, transgender, and questioning (glbtq) youth[1] are a vulnerable, marginalized group at elevated risk of suicidality, homelessness, school drop out, addiction, harassment, and violence (Espilage, Aragon, & Schuster, 2009; Kosciw, Greytak, & Diaz, 2009; Thompson, Safyer, & Polio, 2001). In this chapter, I argue that therapeutic efforts to support and protect queer youth from these negative outcomes are made more effective through a constructionist understanding of resilience. In this conception, resilience is not a trait that resides solely within a queer youth but rather is a dynamic that exists between that individual and their various social milieus. In other words, as Ungar (2004) suggests, resilience is: "…the outcome from the negotiations between individuals and their environments for the resources to define themselves

as healthy amidst conditions collectively viewed as adverse" (p.342). These negotiations should be understood as co-creations in which all involved affect one another and bear some responsibility. Co-creating a healthy identity is especially problematic for marginalized youth since definitions of "normal" and "healthy" are subjective and context dependant (Kaplan, 1999; Martineau, 1999; Ungar, 2004), and queer youth must frequently negotiate with those who are openly hostile to their existence (Savin-Williams, 2005; Stone Fish & Harvey, 2005).

A constructionist viewpoint is a useful tool through which to examine ways co-creation might nurture or interrupt the development of resilience. Additionally, constructionist thinking reveals that it makes little sense to attempt to develop queer youths' resilience in isolation. Rather, all parts of the social ecology must be seen to have something at stake. Ungar (2004) argues that social context determines how resilient behavior is created and defined, and in fact whether it is even recognized as such. To view resilience relationally as a co-creation promotes reflexivity (Munford & Sanders, 2007; White, Fook, & Gardner, 2006) in clinical practice and invites practitioners to examine their unique role in establishing protective factors that nurture resilience. From this perspective, we are afforded a more nuanced view of the lives of queer youth including (1) the unique risk factors they face, (2) their often overlooked hidden resilience strategies (Ungar, 2007), (3) ways to work

[1]This chapter is based on a paper presented at the American Family Therapy Academy's annual conference in June 2010. Throughout I cite case examples from my experience as a queer family therapist and supervisor. To protect anonymity, I use amalgamations of youth I have worked with. In addition, I use the umbrella term "queer" interchangeably with glbtq to refer to gay, lesbian, bisexual, transgender, and questioning individuals.

R. Harvey (✉)
Seton Hill University
e-mail: Harvey@setonhill.edu

M. Ungar (ed.), *The Social Ecology of Resilience: A Handbook of Theory and Practice,*
DOI 10.1007/978-1-4614-0586-3_25, © Springer Science+Business Media, LLC 2012

with hidden resilience clinically, and (4) the ecological factors that can optimize their development, including the development of a glbtq affirmative stance (Ritter & Terndrup, 2002). In what follows I explore these four key aspects in an effort to understand the particular experiences of growing up queer and how to effectively promote resilience in glbtq individuals.

The driving philosophy throughout this chapter is that cultural blind spots get in the way of best efforts to help children grow up queer. This is still a very controversial notion, that one should help a child fully embrace and develop their queer identity. A constructionist viewpoint is one way to shift our focus off the youth and on to the culture and caretakers. Bottrell (2009) argues that marginalized youth often experience "over attention to maladaptive behavior" (p.476) by adults trying to intervene on their behalf. It makes sense to be worried about and for queer youth, but it is a disservice to be overly organized around this worry. This only serves to further marginalize queer youth, and ignores growing evidence that despite real vulnerability and risk queer youth often thrive (Savin-Williams, 2005).

Unique Stressors

Heteronormativity

Queer youth face social stressors similar to any marginalized group. Yet they also face additional stressors specific to their glbtq identities (Savin-Williams, 2001). Like all adolescents, queer youth wrestle with how to develop healthy sexuality and gender identity. However, queer youth face the added difficulty of a culture that presumes only two essential sexes, male and female, and two naturally corresponding genders, masculine and feminine. This culture further assumes that heterosexuality is normal, natural, and therefore superior (Warner, 1991). In order to develop a healthy sense of self, queer youth must negotiate with environments that almost universally define their queer identity as pathological. The practical consequences of heteronormativity on queer youth run the gamut from simple passive denial that they exist to active oppression and repression.

Decreasing Age/Increasing Complexity and Fluidity

Complicating such issues of heteronormativity, this generation of queer youth increasingly discloses their sexual minority identity to families and communities at younger ages (Boxer, Cook, & Herdt, 1991; Floyd and Bakeman, 2006; Cianciotti & Cahill, 2003; Diamond, 2008; Dube, 2000; Sanders & Kroll, 2000; Savin-Williams, 2005). "What once was a more internal, individual process of sexual identity development, has become more overtly a family systems process, begun oftentimes while youth are still living at home" (Stone Fish & Harvey, 2011). Moreover, gender and sexual identities of queer youth are increasingly complicated and fluid (Diamond, 2008; Dube, 2000; Sanders & Kroll, 2000; Savin-Williams, 2005; Stone Fish & Harvey, 2011). Such complexities do not translate well to the larger surrounding heteronormative culture and in fact are viewed as a direct threat to heteronormative standards by many in their communities.

Frankly, this generation of youth explores territory most of us never knew existed. Their insights are fascinating, compelling, disconcerting, and often alienating to many around them. Their lives and gender conceptions openly challenge heteronormative societal structures of gender roles, romantic relationships, marriage, and family. They are less interested in anatomy defining them or in society labeling their sexuality. Instead many glbtq youth push on the boundaries of gender, exchanging the relative safety of labels like man, woman, gay, straight, masculine, feminine, for something less resolved. They fight for the freedom of spaces in between these labels. In their world many genders are possible. Words such as male, female, heterosexual, gay, lesbian, or bisexual seem like anachronisms that increasingly belong to a previous age. These queer youth may simultaneously have a 5 o' clock shadow and a French manicure. Some sport buzz cuts and tank tops while going braless. Some boys may look like girls, while being attracted to boys that look like women. Other girls may look like boys who fall in love with women who are femme, or butch, or both, or neither. They may be transgender youth who often pass as conventionally gendered until they do not. They may be masculine young men attracted to masculinity in others, or feminine women attracted to feminine men, or women, or both, or neither.

So, clearly glbtq youth provoke and unnerve many around them, but they also simultaneously are vulnerable and in need of support. Kelly (2003) argues that all youth create anxiety for adults who care about them through ideas or behaviors that the adults do not understand or approve of. This leads to disrupted relationships characterized by power struggles and mistrust. This dynamic can happen in any context, but is especially prevalent in the lives of queer youth whose identities undermine basic social constructions of gender and sexuality. In so doing they often alienate the very people they most need protection and nurturing from. As a consequence queer youth too often experience profound systemic interruptions of protective factors.

Increased Polarization and Fragmentation

The extreme cultural polarization that currently exists around queer issues is an additional unique stressor for glbtq youth. The divisive nature of these issues, which makes deeply personal issues public and political, often leads to fragmentation and disconnection between queer youth and their various social ecologies, and has the potential to further interrupt the development of resilience. Yet, despite these current difficulties, there lies the real potential to recruit family and social groups into a more positive, resilience-fostering dynamic with the queer youths in their lives. I have seen this potential realized in my professional practice. For example, in the mid-nineties, when I was involved in developing support groups for queer youth, we were careful to plan meetings so that the youth could attend without having to ask parents for permission, rides, or support. Clearly, there was and is good reason to protect queer youth given the level of parental hostility often reported. Yet, in retrospect, we paid no attention at the time to the needs of parents and the importance of family.

As the support group progressed, some parents began to show up early to drop off or pick up their children. At first we were tense and awkward. We did not trust one another. They seemed to want something that I could not quite place. However, it slowly dawned on me that this was a missed opportunity. I was so focused on protecting youth that I did not imagine families as partners in resilience. I began to arrive earlier, hang out later, and open myself to the parents. Some were warm and funny, others were scared or sometimes rude and hostile. Some were worried sick with questions of whether their child would be okay, and would they be safe? Others wanted to know if they were to blame for their child being queer; or if I was. Many wanted to be supportive of their child but had no idea how. Most had never met openly gay adults, so interacting with well-functioning, out adults proved a very successful intervention. It provided them with an alternate vision to their overwhelmingly negative stereotypes of glbtq people.

As the parents spoke with each other and group facilitators they relaxed and were less easily rattled. They talked more openly. They seemed better able to recognize that their child was the same person they had always been despite recent revelations about gender identity or sexual orientation. Their child was still creative and interesting, or still stubborn and willful, still intense, still grandma's favorite. Some were better able to manage their anxiety and started to envision a less scary future for their child. This allowed them to discuss sexuality more openly with their child rather than obsessively force the issue in an attempt to calm their own anxiety. In short, they were better able to parent.

Throughout this experience, I remembered how fragmented I often felt as a queer teen. I simply did not know how to be queer and my mother's daughter at the same time. These two essential aspects of myself were seemingly incongruous; they did not make sense together, yet neither could they exist in isolation. I realized that the support group parents faced a similar dilemma. They struggled to integrate what seemed to be contradictory truths. Could they have a queer child and still think of themselves as sound parents? Were they to blame for their child's sexuality? What did having a queer child mean about the parents they thought they were? What did it mean for them and their identity as a woman, a man, a Christian, a Jew? What did it mean for their relationship not just with their child but with their homophobic father, or their fundamentalist sibling, or the gay cousin who was cut off from the family for 20 years?

My experience in the support group was a powerful watershed moment that broadened my understanding of what it means to be supportive of queer youth. In order to improve their resilience, the surrounding environments inhabited by youth must also be considered, included, and supported. Families of queer youth, particularly those that are struggling or hostile, need help coming to terms with their child's sexual identity. Schools also need to be engaged, even when they are maddeningly bureaucratic or dangerously politicized. Finally, whole communities should be welcomed into the discussions rather than just those members of the communities already sympathetic to glbtq youth. This ecological view recognizes the potential for family, community, church, and school to be something other than indifferent or antagonistic. It opens up the possibility that any of these spheres might also be beneficial, protective, supportive, or transformative.

Systemic Disruption of Resilience

In summary, there are unique stressors faced by queer youth that cause widespread systematic disruption of resilience. Most marginalized groups inherently face adversity, while queer youth face unique stressors directly related to their sexual minority status. These stressors negatively affect youth in exactly those milieus that might otherwise protect them. School systems are often conflicted about how or whether to support and protect queer youth. Peer groups, typically already preoccupied by their collective burgeoning sexuality, are hyper-interested in discussing, gossiping, and hypothesizing about who may be gay, straight, overly-effeminate, too masculine, and everything in between. Religious communities are more often condemning or

silent than openly supportive of queer youth. Surrounding family and cultural expectations typically presume heterosexuality at best, and are openly hostile and rejecting of queer identities at worst. Even those who care about queer youth and want to be supportive find few precedents to help them know how to achieve this (Russell, 2010; Stone Fish & Harvey, 2011). As a result of this complicated cultural stew predicated on heteronormativity, queer youth and their particular struggles are often invisible or minimized. If they draw attention to their unique identities they may receive much needed support, but they also run the real risk of becoming targets. Queer youth must run the gauntlet in all milieus they inhabit. They are vulnerable and risk rejection or denial at every turn; from peer groups, school communities, religious communities, and even in their own homes (Russell, 2010; Savin-Williams, 2005). The widespread nature of these vulnerabilities multiplies the potential disruption of resilient factors.

Hidden Resilience

Queer youth are likely members of several communities simultaneously, each with conflicting views about health and growth. The youth's family may be unaware of their burgeoning identity issues while the best friend, often the first person a youth confides in, knows about this struggle but is an outsider to the family context. The youth may be part of a church or other religious community, as well as a gay/straight alliance populated with agnostics and atheists. The local community where they grew up may be their literal home, but they may also inhabit an online community, perhaps an internet chat site where they feel their queer identity is understood and affirmed. In this polarized context, youth are often left to their own devices to figure out how to bridge the divides between their different communities and within their own mind and bodies. Given the enormous pressure to fit into inflexible gender and sexual categories, it stands to reason that glbtq youth might seek unconventional ways, what Ungar (2007) calls hidden resilience, to protect them and promote their own growth. These strategies, typically viewed as problematic by families, schools, religious groups, and others, may in fact be valid self-driven attempts to succeed and grow in unsupportive cultures and contexts. These types of coping strategies have a clear down side for queer youth. The unconventional behaviors and attitudes often confuse, discomfort, unnerve, and anger those used to operating within a more conventional, heteronormative worldview. The unfortunate result is that queer youth are often punished or ostracized for exactly those behaviors that help them successfully process, integrate, and celebrate their minority identity. However, Ungar (2007) points out that hidden resilience has an upside: "Such plurality provides many avenues to resilience. Viewed through the binocular lenses of culture and context, even socially unpopular behavior by a child or the family that resists intervention or places the child more in harm's way may, in fact, be the child and family's hidden pathway to resilience" (Ungar, p.4). As the adults in their lives, we must become more skilled at understanding motives and discerning benefits of these unconventional behaviors. By doing so we can more effectively see the variety of ways glbtq youth might arrive at resilience and therefore more effectively nurture them as they do so.

As a therapist and supervisor I interact with glbtq youth who developed hidden resilience strategies to negotiate worlds for which they are not well-suited or fully accepted. Some of these hidden resiliencies may be short-lived experiments that the youth will outgrow; others may become core aspects of their subsequent lives and personalities. In either case, it is important for clinicians to learn how to recognize, affirm, and work with these hidden resiliencies.

Examples of Hidden Resilience

Flamboyance

One such youth, Michaelangelo, is a 15-year-old Caucasian referred to treatment for his constant fighting at school. School personnel report that he makes a spectacle of himself with his effeminate behavior and dress. Most provocatively, he aggressively pursues young men at his school. He blows them air kisses and loudly asks them out on dates, which often provokes physical altercations. Michaelangelo's flamboyance is problematic in that it makes those around him annoyed and uncomfortable. School officials consistently encourage him to tone it down.

Michaelangelo reports that he cannot remember a time in his life when he was not physically abused, verbally harassed, or made fun of for not being suitably masculine. Such relentless cruelty could easily cause timidity, sullenness, or withdrawal and indeed for awhile as a middle school student Michaelangelo was treated for depression and hospitalized following a suicide attempt. Yet, Michaelangelo now describes himself with enthusiasm and wit as "fabulously queer." Over the difficult preceding years, he learned to wield his sexual identity both as a banner of pride as well as a weapon. What emerged from those lonely, troubled years is a young man who has learned to embrace the very things he has been ridiculed and marginalized for being.

Once flamboyance is understood in the context of years of bullying, aggression, and isolation, it begins to make more sense. To survive, Michaelangelo had to develop an inner sense of his unique worth that is no longer reliant on the approval of those proximate to him. His flamboyance loudly broadcasts his self-acceptance despite what others think. He no longer feels powerless or victimized because now he accepts who he is: fabulously queer. This flamboyance also serves to protect him from further rejection. He can be sure that those close to him love him for the queer youth he actually is since he is no longer hiding or voiceless.

Gender Rigidity

Jaye is a 13-year-old male-to-female transgendered African–American youth. She is stunningly beautiful and focused on keeping it that way. She fixates on maintaining her flawless skin and perfect feminine shape in order to catch the "perfect man". Jaye is also very smart and has undeniable charisma, although she is often critical of women she interacts with, condescendingly offering them "advice" about their hair, clothes, or make up. Jaye's adherence to rigid ideas about femininity confuses her therapist at first. Her fixation on appearance seems particularly trivial given the current realities of Jaye's home life. She is homeless. Her mother is incarcerated following years battling a drug addiction. Most recently, Jaye lived with her younger brothers and sister at her maternal grandmother's until it was discovered that Jaye was sexually involved with a neighborhood boy. At that point, Jaye was beaten and harassed repeatedly. She began spending less time at home and more in the streets. She also began prostituting herself and eventually left home permanently.

Jaye's therapist encourages her to get her GED [high school leaving certificate], or perhaps a part time job. Jaye is concerned that a job might be too physical. She does not want to hurt her hands or scar her face. Her greatest fear is that manual labor will build muscles and masculinize her appearance. At one point during therapy she announces "I just want to make my man breakfast in the morning, greet him at the door at night when he comes home, rub his neck and get his slippers." The young therapist I supervise freezes up. She stares blankly and asks to take a break. Dumbfounded, she proffers, "He is more feminine than I am." This is the third time that session the therapist uses "he" rather than Jaye's preferred feminine pronoun. "I don't understand her," she continues, "I don't know what to do when he … I mean she says things like that. She is not being realistic." I empathize with the young therapist's concern but I also know it is more complicated.

Jaye's domestic visions for her future are vivid, captivating, detailed, and policed by strict gender rules. The therapist and I begin to explore the hidden resilience in these rules. I sense they are not frivolous to Jaye at all but central to her survival. Seen from the perspective of the context around her, this stance begins to make more sense. Jaye has consistently been unwanted and unprotected. There was little room in her life to nurture any identity, much less a complicated

transgendered one. Given the strict gender choices afforded to her, she was clear she was not a male which made proving herself a female extremely important. Clear rules and strict procedures make this complicated task more attainable. Jaye has been teaching herself what it means to be female and equally important how to be a woman in a relationship with a man. The lessons she has taught herself are heavily influenced by her own experience. The gender rigidity is comforting because it is familiar culturally and because it validates her femininity and endorses her as female. "If all women are this way and I act this way, then I am a real woman."

Moreover, as she perfects her beauty she feels more worthy of the love, protection, and comfort that she is dreaming she will receive in return. She believes if she follows gender rules, if she takes care of her physical beauty, and if she learns to selflessly focus on her man, than she will finally get what she most wants which is to be loved and protected. The lessons she has learned are certainly imperfect and incomplete but they have helped her establish a hard fought identity in the face of enormous odds. She is learning piece by piece about the woman she is. And though much remains untested she is forging an increasingly solid sense of herself.

Passing

Another teenage client, Nicole, recently came out to her mother as a lesbian. In response her mother has decided to ignore this as just a passing phase. Nicole identifies as a woman but can pass for a young man and she uses this to her advantage every chance she gets. Dressed in button down shirts and baggy jeans with a cap slung backwards over her short hair, she strolls hand-in-hand through the mall with her girlfriend Marla or kisses her on a park bench. Most people smile as they walk by assuming the girls are actually a young, heterosexual couple. Nicole enjoys fooling people who assume she is a heterosexual young man. Her behavior infuriates her parents who see her open affections as an affront to "normal" teenage behavior. They are distressed that she is unapologetically in love with another young woman and are especially frustrated that the very next day Nicole can style her hair, wear a skirt, and be their perfectly beautiful daughter. It seems to them that Nicole is lying about who she is and putting herself in danger. Stone Fish and Harvey (2011) write "Disclosure represents a major opportunity for queer youth to be meaningfully seen and accurately known by their families. It also means they are able to invest less emotional and psychological energy in concealing their sexual identity" (p.[note to editor: article is about to be published]). For Nicole, her androgyny is a ticket to freedom. She can love whoever she wants, wherever she wants, and even receive tacit social approval from those who do not know her true gender. To her this public openness is exhilarating and a hopeful prelude to a future society she idealistically believes can happen. It feels good to be comfortable in her own skin, so she learns to care less and less about those disturbed by her differentness.

Working Clinically with Hidden Resilience

It is helpful for clinicians to stay alert for strategies of hidden resilience when working with glbtq youth. Although it may initially seem counterintuitive, these resiliencies are typically connected to recurring problematic interactions in these youths' daily lives. Problematic behavior or situations often indicate contextual stressors caused by constrained choices for marginalized youth. They have been forced to do more with less, or to fit a square peg in a round hole, so have developed alternate ways to get through their day: "This is not to deny the negative and destructive effects of some of the behaviors and actions of these young people. Rather it is to argue for recognition that the lives lived by excluded young people have positive, health-enhancing characteristics and that successful attempts at change need to build upon the social bonds and integrative characteristics that coexist with the harmful and troubling behaviors (Munford & Sanders, 2007, p.3)."

In Jaye's case, her rigid gender categories are problematic because they imprison her in a narrow set of rules about whom she has to be in order to be loved and accepted as a real woman. In Michaelangelo's case, his flamboyance is problematic because he routinely alienates people around him. Nicole's desire to pass gets her in trouble because those around her feel she is lying about who she is. This leaves them confused and feeling fooled, which further alienates them from her.

Munford and Sanders (2007) argue that the resourcefulness of marginalized young people is often overlooked by professionals in lieu of focusing only on negative aspects of their coping behaviors. Once identified and understood contextually, clinicians can focus treatment to capitalize on hidden resilience and mitigate over-attention to maladaptive behaviors. This process also invites queer youth be an active participant in the ongoing discourse about their lives. Jaye, for example, was used to being mislabeled as male. As a result, she tenaciously focused on gender stereotypes to actively redefine how people saw and interacted with her. She was less interested in discussing her troubles as a "homeless youth" than as a "homeless young woman." The therapist began to understand that Jaye had been developing her female identity with little positive input or nurturing from role models. Therapy was shifted to focus on this. The therapist stopped confusing gender pronouns, realizing how important this was. Instead of focusing on Jaye's maladaptive behavior, we developed ideas to utilize her tenacity and energy to focus on gender. The therapist and Jaye identified some safe women in her life, develop questions she is interested in, and then assign her the task of interviewing them. "What is the hardest thing about being a woman?" "What is it like to love a man?" "What did you learn about clothes and make up?" In this way, the therapist could participate with Jaye while she was in the process of forging her unique feminine identity.

I supported the therapist to see Jaye as incomplete, her identity still a work in process. She is careful not to get caught wanting Jaye to be so ahead of where she actually is that she misses nurturing the young woman Jaye is in the moment.

From this access point, the therapist is also more effectively able to share concerns or ask questions designed to nurture, support, and challenge all at once.

In another example, Michaelangelo is utilizing flamboyance as a way of refusing to succumb to the majority sense of who he should be and how he should act. Michaelangelo has learned through years of necessity to get by without others' approval. Repeated attempts to pressure him through punishment or disapproval to be different than what he is will have limited effect. Despite all his bravado and pride, there is still a young man struggling to be a part of a community. Why else would he relish the disapproval of his peers and teachers so much? Working with key school personnel we deemphasized the use of punishment except when absolutely necessary and emphasized instead the integration of Michaelangelo as a full and productive member of the community. We worked with Michaelangelo to explore how his preferred sense of himself as unique and gifted might be utilized to benefit other younger youth who are bullied and harassed. Michaelangelo's bravery in the face of pressure is a major strength. We utilize this by creating opportunities for him to share his story so that parts of the community might come to understand his flamboyance differently. Likewise, as a less marginalized member of the community he might not feel the need to use his sexuality so aggressively.

In summary, when working with glbtq youth resilience can be improved when clinicians mindfully look for hidden strategies of resilience, shift the focus of intervention so that it deemphasizes maladaptive behavior and focus instead on mobilization of the strengths queer youth possess.

Toward an Ecological and Affirming Stance of glbtq Identity

To help glbtq youth combat pervasive unique stressors, it is most effective to use an ecological stance that (1) affirms rather than pathologizes glbtq identities (Ritter & Terndrup, 2002), (2) recognizes heternormativity, and (3) addresses adult anxiety.

An affirmative perspective of queer people is an evolving stance in our culture and in clinical work. It increasingly moves beyond tolerance or even openness about homosexuality toward recognition of the *necessity* of glbtq people and their perspectives (Sedgwick, 1993). As noted at the outset, it is still quite controversial to intentionally assist a young person grow up with a healthy and well integrated queer identity. Yet this is surely an idea whose time has come. To affirm queer youth, we must see them as individuals with unique gifts and perspectives, not despite, but because of their gender and sexual identities (Stone Fish & Harvey, 2005): "Affirmative therapy for sexual minorities is an evolving practice which is being learned as we go by those of us practicing, teaching and writing about it. To do it well one must question basic assumptions and one's own dearly held beliefs about gender, sexuality, masculinity, femininity and essentialist notions about identity, desire, sex and romance. No small task" (Stone Fish & Harvey, 2011, p. [note to editor, article to be published shortly]). An affirmative ecological stance is challenging because it requires self-examination and a willingness to let our perspectives be altered through our work with queer youth.

Adult Anxiety and the Gifts of Queerness

The anxiety many adults feel around youth (Kelly, 2003) disrupts relationships with queer youth and negatively impacts our ability to see their strengths and accept their gifts. Perel (2007) argues that to resolve intimate/sexual dilemmas most adults have disavowed pieces of their sexual or emotional selves that are vital for vibrant, long-term sexual connections. She argues this is done to avoid the scary, uncertain spaces like those in between male and female, heterosexual and homosexual, and masculine and feminine. What is known and safe is embraced over what is unknown and threatening. The anxiety that blocks adult eroticism also prevents us from nurturing queer youth who are sometimes further along in understanding the fluidity of sex and gender than are the adults in their lives. It is likely that queer youth provoke anxiety in adults around them because their lives require that we either disapprove of their choices or acknowledge what we relinquished as we forged identities as men, women, heterosexual, queer, mother, husband, wife. Driven by these anxieties, adults are arguably less able to recognize hidden resilience or take an affirming stance. To mitigate and manage our anxiety, we are more likely to pay attention to what is maladaptive about the youth we interact with. If we can stay open, queer youth might teach adults new tools to navigate the erotic potentials Perel argues are so vital to life-long sexual and emotional connections. Accepting these gifts from glbtq youth is an effective intervention technique that has the potential to build resilience in the queer youth, in ourselves, and in the communities we share. To do so, adults must become more aware of our disavowed parts. We must be willing to follow the lead of queer youth who have already begun to explore these deep, rich, and treacherous waters of identity.

Wrestling with Heteronormativity

At a recent conference for clinicians, a well-known and respected therapist discussed a young couple she currently worked with. During the course of her talk, she repeatedly made reference to "the woman in the couple…" and "the man in the couple…" Such statements powerfully, though subtly and probably unintentionally, codified heteronormativity for everyone in the room. She assumed that there is always one woman and one man in a couple. Therefore "couple" remains the property of heterosexuals, and furthers essentialist notions about acceptable gender and gender roles.

But then again, who among us has not made the mistake of assuming heterosexuality? Certainly in my own practice I too have unfortunately assumed heterosexuality for youth simply because they did not give me reason to think otherwise. This is an important point; that heteronormativity is still pervasive enough to routinely stymie the needs of queer youth. Their experience is often ignored or unanticipated, even among adults who are otherwise supportive of glbtq youth. This has serious consequences for queer youth who face being invisible and without support, or risking visibility in order to seek the support they need.

Although some would argue that such attention to gendered language is overly politically correct, such language reveals our shortsightedness and exposes the lack of space in our theories and our minds to accept and nurture diversity. Sedgwick (1993) writes "There are many people in the worlds we inhabit … who have a strong interest in the dignified treatment of any gay people who may happen to already exist. But the number of persons or institutions by whom the existence of gay people is treated as a precious desideratum, a needed condition of life, is small" (p.23). A heightened awareness around these issues is not only beneficial for glbtq people. Being open to understanding queer experience allows all of us to revisit and reintegrate more complicated notions of ourselves and our society.

Conclusion: Fighting Fragmentation

As noted earlier, the current cultural polarization around sexuality means that the various social contexts in a youth's life are often quite isolated from and antagonistic toward one another. These environments might nurture and sustain one part of a sexual minority youth's experience while remaining hostile and undermining of another. These divergent and varied social contexts have the potential to be hostile, or to be necessary and vital partners in fostering resilience. This relational balkanization makes me wonder where glbtq youth might go to find safe, civil, engaged, open conversations between these disparate and precious pieces of themselves. How do they learn to be in dialogue around these differences? As adults and caretakers we must participate with them. We must and fully engage in these difficult and crucial dialogues without falling victim to the polarization and cynicism that easily derails progress.

Queer youth are a richly diverse group (Savin-Williams, 2001) and while they face some similar stressors they do so in widely divergent family, community, school, and religious contexts. What unites these disparate youth? They are complicated and evolving and do not have it all neatly figured out. Instead they create themselves as they go, defining and redefining their gender and sexual identities through the clothes they wear, their hair, their attitude, their ever changing desires, their mistakes, and their questions. They wrestle, with the meaning of life while simultaneously wondering which bathroom to use in the mall and how to handle the reactions of those they encounter there. They need help to anticipate and handle all these variables. They are fearful and fearless at the same time; angry and defensive, but still they yearn for validation and hope to make us proud. They want respect, but they also need mentoring as they learn how to be themselves in a world that often misunderstands them.

Recent literature affirms the importance of supportive ecological surroundings for glbtq youth, and confirms the potentially protective qualities these environments can offer (Russell, 2010). Resilience is a relational process where the capacity of an individual to overcome the challenges of their stigmatized identity meets with the capacity and the bravery of those around them to nurture them while they do it, even if these negotiations are sometimes clumsy or unresolved. In short, the creation of resilience is the creation of hope. It can not be left to youths, or their families, or to school districts alone. Fostering hope is not the responsibility of individual youth but rather of whole communities (Weingarten, 2000). It is our communal responsibility, and something that benefits all of us. We must move forward together.

References

Bottrell, D. (2009). Dealing with disadvantage: Resilience and the social capital of young people's networks. *Youth & Society, 40*(4), 476–501.

Boxer, A. M., Cook, J. A., & Herdt, G. (1991). Double jeopardy: Identity transitions and parent-child relations. In K. Pillemer & K. McCartney (Eds.), *Parent-child relations throughout life* (pp. 59–92). Hillsdale: Erlbaum.

Cianciotti, J., & Cahill, S. (2003). *Education Policy: Issues Affecting Lesbian, Gay, Bisexual, and Transgender Youth.* Retrieved 18 August 2011, from http://www.thetaskforce.org/reports_and_research/education_policy: The National Gay and Lesbian Taskforce Policy Institute.

Diamond, L. M. (2008). Female bisexuality from adolescence to adulthood: Results from a 10-year longitudinal study. *Developmental Psychology, 44*, 5–14.

Dube, E. M. (2000). The role of sexual behavior in the identification process of gay and bisexual males. *Journal of Sex Research, 37*, 123–132.

Espilage, D. L., Aragon, S. B., & Schuster, M. A. (2009). Homophobic teasing, psychological outcomes, and sexual orientation among high school students: What influence do parents and schools have? *School Psychology Review, 37*(2), 202–216.

Floyd, F. J., & Bakeman, R. (2006). Coming out across the life course: Implications of age and historical context. *Archives of Sexual Behavior, 35*(3), 287–296.

Kelly, P. (2003). Growing up as risky business? Risks, surveillance and the institutionalized mistrust of youth. *Journal of Youth Studies, 6*(2), 165–180.

Kosciw, J. G., Greytak, E. A., & Diaz, E. M. (2009). Who, what, where, when, and why: Demographic and ecological factors contributing to hostile school climate for lesbian, gay, bisexual, and transgender youth. *Journal of Youth and Adolescence, 38*(7), 976–988.

Munford, R., & Sanders, J. (2007). Drawing out strengths and building capacity in social work with troubled young women. *Child and Family Social Work, 13*, 2–11.

Perel, E. (2007). *Mating in captivity.* New York: Harper Collins.

Ritter, K., & Terndrup, A. (2002). *Handbook of affirmative psychotherapy with lesbians and gay men.* New York: Guilford Press.

Russell, S. T. (2010). Contradictions and complexities in the lives of lesbian, gay, bisexual, and transgender youth. *The Prevention Researcher, 17*(4), 3–6.

Sanders, G. L., & Kroll, I. T. (2000). Generating stories of resilience: Helping gay and lesbian youth and their families. *Journal of Marital and Family Therapy, 26*, 433–442.

Savin-Williams, R. C. (2001). *Mom, dad, I'm gay.* Washington: American Psychological Association.

Savin-Williams, R. C. (2005). *The new gay teenager.* Cambridge: Harvard University Press.

Sedgwick, E. K. (1993). How to bring your kids up gay. In M. Warner (Ed.), *Fear of a queer planet: Queer politics and social theory* (pp. 69–81). Minneapolis: University of Minneapolis Press.

Stone Fish, L., & Harvey, R. G. (2005). *Nurturing Queer Youth: Family therapy transformed.* New York: Norton.

Stone Fish, L., & Harvey, R. G. (2011). In J. J. Bigner & J. L. Wetchler (Eds.), *Handbook of LGBT-affirmative couple and family therapy.* New York: Routledge.

Thompson, S. J., Safyer, A. W., & Polio, D. E. (2001). Differences and predictors of family reunification among subgroups of runaway youths using shelter services. *Social Work Research, 25*(3), 163–172.

Ungar, M. (2004). A constructionist discourse on resilience: Multiple contexts, multiple realities among at-risk children and youth. *Youth and Society, 35*(3), 341–365.

Ungar, M. (2007). *Playing at being bad: The hidden resilience of troubled teens*. Toronto: McClelland and Stewart.

Warner, M. (1991). Introduction: Fear of a queer planet. *Social Text, 9*(4), 3–17.

Weingarten, K. (2000). Witnessing, wonder, and hope. *Family Process, 39*(4), 389–402.

White, S., Fook, J., & Gardner, F. (Eds.). (2006). *Critical reflection in health and social care*. Maidenhead: Open University Press.

Community Resilience: Fostering Recovery, Sustainability, and Growth

26

Kate Murray and Alex Zautra

There are many ways that resilience is revealed in the lives of people and their communities. Examples of resilience are abundant, with the topic permeating our daily conversations and serving as a source of inspiration for perseverance in challenging times. A focus on resilience is only a part of a larger movement in the social sciences emphasizing the role of strengths and social processes in promoting well-being and quality of life among diverse populations. Although a rich literature on stress and pathology provide important information about peoples' experiences, acknowledging both the positive and the negative is essential to fully understanding and appreciating our day-to-day lives (Zautra, 2003).

Definitions of resilience, too, are numerous with questions over how best to define the term. Definitions are important as they serve as a basis for understanding and to provide a framework for interventions and research. Many scholars acknowledge the basis of the term resilience in the physical sciences. At its root, *resilire*, resilience refers to the ability of a material to rebound or recoil; to bend when strained and return to its original form (Barnhart, 1988). However, scholarly and colloquial use of the term frequently includes additional conceptualizations of resilience, which expand beyond this initial definition. Norris and

colleagues argue, "Its metaphorical origins notwithstanding, human resilience, we believe, must now be studied on its own terms without undue concern with how those meanings correspond to known physical properties or laws" (Norris, Stevens, Pfefferbaum, Wyche, & Pfefferbaum, 2008; p. 128).

In this chapter, we use this broader conceptualization of resilience to define the term as an adaptive response to adversity through the three processes of recovery, sustainability, and growth. Each process captures unique aspects of resilience that are evident in peoples' experiences, as well as in the literature focusing on resilience. First and foremost is *recovery*, which has been the predominant definition and focus of the resilience literature. In response to a significant stressor, people frequently experience affective distress, accompanied by physiological markers, and at times, greater social discord as they attempt to rally resources to meet the challenge. Recovery suggests that people are able to make the necessary psychophysiological and social adjustments and return to their pre-stress level of functioning; successfully alleviating any disturbances in homeostasis that resulted from the stressor. Line 1a in Fig. 26.1 provides a visual representation of recovery.

To understand the meaning of the two other forms of resilience, we need to broaden our conceptual framework for what constitutes well-being. Ryff and Singer (1998) offer a particularly useful distinction between two fundamental aspects of well-being: the hedonic, which concerns the degree of affective adjustment; and, the

K. Murray (✉)
San Diego State University-University
of California, San Diego Cancer Center Comprehensive
Partnership, CA, USA
e-mail: kmurray@projects.sdsu.edu

M. Ungar (ed.), *The Social Ecology of Resilience: A Handbook of Theory and Practice*,
DOI 10.1007/978-1-4614-0586-3_26, © Springer Science+Business Media, LLC 2012

Resilience trajectories of recovery, sustainability, and growth

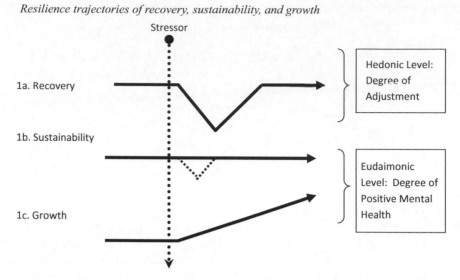

Fig. 26.1 Resilience trajectories of recovery, sustainability, and growth

eudaimonic, which is concerned with success in attaining positive mental health through mastery, self-acceptance, positive social relations, purpose in life, and growth. The challenges that need to be met in response to adversity for sustainability and growth are those that reflect eudaimonic dimensions of well-being. Many people are able to *sustain* their sense of purpose, and their engagement in valued social relationships in the face of adversity. They are able to persevere and continue forward with little to no signs of the impact of the stressor. This "ordinary magic" attests to the common experience of sustainability and the ability of many to thrive despite adversity (Bonanno, 2004; Masten, 2001). As illustrated by line 1b in Fig. 26.1, people may experience a slight dip in functioning or continue moving forward with personal goals and purposes that give their lives meaning with little or no impact on their overall health and well-being. This may also entail people sustaining positive affect, the positive pole of hedonic aspects of well-being, even when negative affects arise in the context of adversity.

Third, resilience also refers to *growth*, which includes the additional gains and advancement following adversity through new learning and attainment of a stronger sense of self. It may even

contribute to a new direction in life that gives life meaning. This aspect of resilience is also related to the concepts of posttraumatic growth (Tedeschi, Park, & Calhoun, 1998) and Adversity-Activated Development (Papadopoulos, 2007). In reference to the experiences of people who have faced persecution, Papadopoulos (2007) shows that not only do people frequently survive horrific conditions largely intact, but also that they may also be strengthened by their experiences in challenging times. He states, "This means, that, paradoxically, despite their negative nature, devastating experiences (regardless of the degree of their harshness and destructive impact) may also help people reshuffle their lives and imbue them with new meaning" (p. 305). Line 1c in Fig. 26.1 is a visual representation of the notion that people can grow and evolve following a stressor in ways that enhance their overall well-being such as gaining new skills, enhancing self-esteem, or providing a new perspective.

One point often overlooked in the examination of features of resilient responding is that people and communities can be successful in one aspect of resilience without succeeding in another. It is possible to recover from adverse circumstances without learning from the experience. It is also possible to grow from traumatic events, yet still struggle with recovery. This is evident among soldiers returning from combat with a greater sense of purpose in their lives, but still suffering from posttraumatic stress disorders (PTSDs) (King, King, Keane, & Adams, 1998).

A second important point to note is the challenge of defining a resilient outcome. A perceived healthy and resilient outcome to one person or culture may not carry over to other people and cultures. For example, someone asserting his or her needs in an interpersonal conflict may bring a sense of relief, self-contentment, and be viewed as resilient in some cultures, but could be very undermining to social processes, be a source of shame, and viewed negatively in other cultures (Ungar, 2010). This is a noted challenge in resilience research that is beyond the scope of this chapter. Instead, we focus on examining community and social processes associated with resilience.

Individuals are resilient within a larger social context, which can include their history of success in navigating challenges with or without help from others, the quality of their current social ties, and the responsiveness of the communities where they live. Community and other contextual factors can have a profound impact on individual health and behaviors (Sallis, Owen, & Fisher, 2008) and the importance of safe, healthy environments and social supports has been touted as important for children and adults alike. For example, community infrastructures such as the inundation of fast-food and processed food options alongside a reduction in access to fresh produce will naturally influence individual food options, nutrition, and health (Davis, Cook, & Cohen, 2005). People live within contexts which unquestionably influence their options and decisions in both positive and negative ways.

Community resilience is important in its own right and the three aspects of resilience (recovery, sustainability, and growth) apply equally to communities as they do to individuals. Although there are similarities between individual and community resilience processes, there are also differences. For example, communities can be characterized by the degree of age, gender, or ethnic diversity in social networks, with more diverse networks thought to have an advantage in mounting an effective response to a community-wide threat (Elmqvist et al., 2003; Norris et al., 2008). A person with a social network that is highly homogeneous, however, may not be at any disadvantage. Social structures and processes within the community can influence individual illness and well-being through the availability and provision of resources. Community variables, such as availability of green space, organized and efficient public programs and infrastucture, and safe community gathering places all influence people's daily experiences and opportunities (Zautra, Hall, & Murray, 2008). Although this information can be assigned to an individual person for research purposes, they inherently occur at a community level and may affect individuals even if they are not directly exposed (Okvat & Zautra, 2011).

Community resilience has an important role to play in helping researchers and practitioners to foster health and well-being. By intervening on a systemic level, not only can we improve the quality of our families and communities but also we can simultaneously influence individual resilience. This belief in using both individual and community-based interventions cuts to the heart of fields like public health. Public health has a long-standing history of emphasizing the need for simultaneous and multifaceted approaches to promote human health. While critiquing more recent shifts away from population-focused research in Public Health Epidemiology, Pearce (1996) notes "Thus, any meaningful analysis of the causes of disease [and health] in populations must integrate the individual-biologic and population levels of analysis without collapsing one into the other or denying the existence of either" (pp. 680–681).

Table 26.1 identifies some illustrative examples for both individual and collective resilience following adverse events across the three primary dimensions of resilience. The individual- and community-level examples in Table 26.1 highlight concerns at each level of analysis as well as potential targets for intervention.

These targets may not all change in the same direction following a shift in policy or the introduction of a new program. The best innovations

Table 26.1 Public policy targets for resilience

	Individual resilience	Collective resilience
Recovery from:	Chronic pain, bereavement, job loss, economic hardship	Inequities in safety-nets, disincentives for proper diet, nutrition, and exercise
Sustainability of:	Agency, choice, creativity, self-efficacy, vitality	Participative democracy, collaboration, shared identity
Growth in:	Meaning in life, wisdom, maturity, sense of purpose	Common purpose, empowerment, collective wisdom, leadership

are those that build collective resilience across domains when benefitting individuals and groups. Worse programs are those applied without concern for their effects at different levels and with different types of resilience. A program may be devised that speeds recovery from some stressor like experiencing a traumatic event, but provides no window for learning from the experience and no gain in collective wisdom about how people may help one another in times of community crises. For example, after PTSD was classified as a psychiatric disorder, therapeutic programs were developed and tested to treat individuals cases (Foa, Keane, & Friedman, 2000). More recently, emotional resilience programs have been developed to prevent PTSD in individual soldiers, but without concern for the resilience of the military community confronted with challenges of war and its social consequences (France-Presse, 2009). What is needed is a social resilience program to complement clinical approaches with methods to address collective resilience (Cacioppo, Reis, & Zautra, 2011). For both individual and community resilience, we must balance current and future needs across a range of domains to develop the best course of action.

Community resilience also requires us to think about how to examine this larger scope and how to define the term community itself (Norris et al., 2008). Communities are dynamic and ever-changing social worlds that include communities of geography and those formed based on mutual interests (Zautra et al., 2008). Communities are complex and vibrant and require us to be thoughtful in our selection of measures, assessments, and interventions to enhance quality of life. To capture this complexity, we need to examine communities using a bidimensional model which examines resilience processes over time.

Individual and community research have strong traditions in risk-based models, examining ways in which people and communities may be vulnerable to trauma or environmental disasters. However, examination of the positive aspects of individual and community life is equally important, with a proliferation of discussion on strengths, assets, and resources to complement prior risk-based research. When applying a bidimensional model to community resilience, the absence of a community stressor, such as neighborhood crime, does not mean that the neighborhood has high levels of social cohesion and civic engagement. It is important to assess each dimension independently to reveal a more complete picture of resilience processes and community life (Zautra, Hall, & Murray, 2010).

Lastly, community resilience is a process and must be examined longitudinally, not through single, cross-sectional assessments. Just as each of us is shaped by past experiences and hopes for what is yet to come, communities also face new challenges and shape policies based on previous successes and downfalls as well as goals for the future (Hughes, 2004; McKinlay, 2000). Only by examining both the past and forward movement in a community we can understand its current dynamics. More longitudinal examinations of community resilience are needed to better understand the ever-changing dynamics of community life.

The Role of Community in Cross-Cultural Resilience

Over and above individual resilience, community resilience may play a more prominent role in how people in other cultures respond to adversity and be a more salient point for intervention.

Summerfield (1996) highlights the cultural differences in the importance and applicability of individual resilience concepts. He states:

> Non-western peoples have different notions of the self in relation to others and the maintenance of harmonious relations within a family and community is generally given more significance than an individual's own thoughts, emotions and aspirations. The cultural emphasis is on dependency and interdependency rather than the autonomy and individualisation on which many western ideas about mental injury are predicated. (p. 6)

He and others argue that healing happens only through social processes (e.g., Bracken, 2002). Fundamental differences in perceptions and conceptualizations across cultures are paramount in developing further resilience research with diverse populations. However, social science research and theories have largely developed through efforts with Western and white populations, despite the fact this represents a small minority of the world's population (Arnett, 2008). As a result, we do not fully understand the processes of resilience among non-western cultures and there is a need for additional research and theory development in regard to the similarities and differences of resilience processes across cultures (Ungar, 2008).

In the trauma literature, many underscore the limitations and potential iatrogenic effects of applying Western, individual-based models to other cultures (Bracken, 2002; Summerfield, 1996). In particular, PTSD is defined by an internal disruption of thoughts and behaviors *within* a person following a trauma. While this is the gold-standard diagnosis with prescribed individual-based treatments in Western countries, Joan Giller, a UK-based physician, asserts that the PTSD-framework and related individual treatments may not be appropriate when working with diverse cultures and communities. She states:

> The great danger in projects such as ours is that we actually leave people in a more vulnerable position than before, by leading them to believe that their ways of coping are somehow inferior to Western ones; that we have a knowledge about the effects of trauma on the individual and its treatment which supersedes their own knowledge of the ways in which healing is brought about…This demands a respect for local priorities, which should extend respect for local forms of healing if some kind of 'treatment' is required. (Giller, 1998, p. 144)

These concerns underscore the challenge of cross-cultural resilience research and the fundamental importance of acknowledging and understanding the culturally similar and dissimilar responses to stress and adversity. Therefore, even the most well-established of Western theories and treatments may be too culturally narrow and unable to clearly capture or support healing and recovery within more collectivistic cultures.

Working with resettled refugee communities in Australia, Westoby (2008) highlights the critical role of social processes and community-development in rebuilding the fractured and lost social relationships and structures.

> Within post-war and humanitarian context this social process involved supporting refugees in rebuilding their physical (homes, schools), economic (jobs, livelihoods), social (relationships, networks), and moral worlds (justice, rights). In doing this and doing it collectively, people are able to recover from the suffering of war-related violence and disruption. People rebuild their lives, they mourn and grieve together, work, socialize and struggle together – their recovery is intimately connected to these social processes. (pp. 486–7)

Each of these authors is underscoring that individual resilience does not occur in a vacuum. They assert that individual models are not sufficient and at times can be harmful. Even within Western theories, people's lives are always influenced by the people around them, their cultural values and beliefs (developed and honed through socialization processes), and the environments in which they live. Therefore, social and systemic interventions provide an important added tool for enhancing recovery among both individuals and communities.

Community Resilience in Resettlement

Building upon these arguments, we use the experience of a forcibly displaced community as an exemplar for illustrating these themes of community resilience in cross-cultural research. More specifically, we examine the experiences of the

Sudanese community in Australia to illustrate aspects of community resilience based on semi-structured qualitative interviews conducted with ten Sudanese adults (five males, five females; mean age=36.5 years) who had been in Australia a mean 5.2 years (SD=2.7) when the data was collected in 2007. Greater detail on this research and its methodology is presented elsewhere (Murray, 2010). Our focus here is on key themes from those analyses that provide examples of the resilience processes within the Sudanese community.

Recovery

Resettlement in Australia represents a significant disruption of the social fabric of Sudanese life. Many of the participants spoke of social losses as a primary stressor from which they were forced to recover. As Rihab[1] said, "The bad thing for me is community. I really miss my old community because, like I have a value in my community back in Sudan, in the place where I have been born…I have a value over there." For Peter, "Leaving my brothers, my sisters; that was a big thing. It was very hard, it was very hard for me to do it, to just leave everything." Although many view resettlement as a fortunate opportunity [less than 1% of all refugees are resettled in a country such as the U.S., Canada, or Australia (UNHCR, 2003)], it also represents a far departure from one's known experiences and people. Deng said,

> When I found out that I was coming to Australia we couldn't live in the camp, we became really desperate and we knew that when I get to Australia that life would change and before I arrive there I working in my mind, I was asking myself will I really see again the people I am living by? Then there's family friends that I left in the camp, that's what came in my mind and I was thinking how will I see them again?

These social losses are manifest throughout these interviews and elsewhere in the literature (e.g., Miller, 1999) and represent a primary stressor for the newly resettled communities.

---

[1]Pseudonyms are used and identifying information has been changed to ensure the confidentiality of the participants in the study.

The recovery process, in turn, focuses on rebuilding social relations and supports in their new home country. Wal stated "In life, actually, we need each other…Even the nations, they need each other. If the nations need each other, then what about [me]? What about [you]? So everybody, in lifetime, somewhere are stuck, we need [a] helping hand." People receive not only support but also encouragement from those social relations. As John said, "I have support from friends, who say, "Oh, you've got potential." Support I've got from friends, I've got from families. Yeah, and encouragement from people that I've met…that makes me, you know, feel good that I'm on the track and I'm doing well. So I'm proud and happy about it!"

Rebuilding a social network and community is a gradual process. Peter said meeting a few people at his church led to him interacting with more and more people. After meeting a few people at church, he said, "From there, it just, everything just ran smoothly because I started knowing people, so I know young people; meeting together, going out together, have a social life, all of that. Everything come a bit easier and easier." Mary agreed,

> What can we do? But what we do to balance our life, to give our life some change, help those people who are suffering in a refugee camp, and be together sometime as a community, sharing life, forget about the difficulty, and thinking about the future.

At the time of data collection, each of the individuals interviewed had established employment, many had attained educational degrees, and most reported they had developed social networks in Australia. The Sudanese community had established a center which served as a community gathering place and had elected leaders for both the Sudanese community and for an African Council, which addressed the needs of the African community as a whole. As African migration was relatively new to the region where the research took place (the largest numbers resettled between 2002 and 2007; Commonwealth of Australia, 2007), the Sudanese and African communities were active in their efforts to establish new social networks, a sense of collective identity in

Australia, and advocating on behalf of the needs of their communities. Through their collective efforts, the community had obtained additional positions to provide community liaison efforts with the local schools and police forces and was proactive in advocating for programs that addressed the unique needs of the Sudanese community. There were many volunteers working diligently to assist community members in completing paperwork and collecting funds to support applications to bring other family members to Australia. These accomplishments attest to the collective resilience in the Sudanese community in facilitating recovery.

Sustainability

However, the community continued to face challenges in sustaining their community recovery efforts, including continued poverty and unrest in Sudan, experiences of discrimination in daily life (e.g., workplace discrimination), and negative socio-political commentary in Australia that targeted the Sudanese community in 2007. Around the time of the announcement of a federal election, the Sudanese resettlement program was halted with political figures identifying the lack of integration of the Sudanese community as the primary reason for the policy change. This public announcement challenged the community's sense of identity and perceived acceptance in Australia.

John stated "You know, we expected to come and find a better life, good hospitality. Especially that, they did that; when I came I was welcome and very happy. But now I think they are going in a different direction." He also discussed the ways in which the negative public statements about the Sudanese community affected his own and others' attitudes toward remaining in Australia indefinitely and his sense of belonging. He said, "So I'm a bit afraid about living in Australia in the future because this thing will grow and grow and grow and grow and Australia will become racist society towards us." He added, "So if there's peace in my country, I will go back instead of adding problem."

There was a community counter-response to the negative public commentary, including Australian-African gatherings in solidarity and a formal press conference held by the African Council. Collectively, the African community and their Australian compatriots who stood in opposition to the remarks and policy changes mounted a public defense to assert the strengths of the Sudanese community and underscore the damage done by negative public comments about the community. There were letters written, petitions signed, and public statements made that were possible because of the well-established connections the community had made with local officials, organizations, and fellow Australians. At a community-level, the opportunity to respond to such accusations was possible in a way that individually could not have been achieved. Through collective action, the community was able to draw together to sustain its sense of agency, self-respect, and to maintain their hopes for their futures in Australia. While the statement was not retracted by the public official nor an apology issued, many organizations and Australian leaders openly condemned the statements and gathered in support of the Sudanese community.

Growth

Lastly, the opportunities and desire for collective community growth were readily apparent. This is a common theme with migrants more generally, who frequently enter their new countries with high hopes and strong desires for a better life (Portes & Rumbaut, 1996). Most of the participants highlighted their gratitude for the educational opportunities in Australia and their hopes to build a better tomorrow. Rihab stated:

> I'm happy to be in Australia. I came holding my dreams, improving myself and also working very hard to get good money and to have good life in Australia, and also to guarantee that I send money back to my parents, and my sisters to help my mom and my dad.

Jacob said, "we [my wife and I] are content with what we have and we are looking forward that our kids will achieve something better." He went on to say,

> But, uh say in 10, 15 years to come, I am really hoping that my children will one day be here, giving out the most they can in order to participate in the development of this country...what I am expecting is that these kids of today are successful with their lives so that tomorrow they can be participants in the development of their own country. And that they would also be able to talk about their country of origin that they come from and make their brothers and sisters here understand and help them maybe bringing up other countries in the third world, from where we came. Because without doing so, I believe this flow will be continuing, the flow of refugees and the flow of people escaping poverty and all this from their countries and going to another country.

These desires for a better future are not about personal gain, but about collective opportunities to advance the community and to address ongoing struggles in Sudan. Through collective action, these participants are underscoring the common resilience theme that through struggle and hardship people still find the will to move beyond adversity.

Conclusion

A community resilience framework provides an important way of understanding human adaptation that is useful in guiding research, intervention, and advocacy. The study of resilience is best undertaken in dynamic settings where challenges and even threats to well-being are present and responses to those stressors are examined over time. Both quantitative and qualitative approaches are needed to capture the complexity of human experience within a rich mosaic of community life. The study of resilient adaptations is inherently multilevel, from the study of genes (Lemery-Chalfant, 2010) and psychobiological mechanisms (Feder, Nestler, Westphal, & Charney, 2010), to the successful adaptations of whole nations. We have focused in this article on collective resilience, to draw attention to the value of extending our understanding of resilience from individuals to communities. Policies and programs that support community and social healing processes can be powerful and cost-effective tools for enhancing the lives of many.

In particular, among cultures and groups with more collectivistic beliefs and attitudes a focus on collective resilience may be most important.

Resilience thinking also requires adopting a more comprehensive conception of well-being, one that encourages a discourse of sustainability and advancement of individual and collective strengths, not only the capacity for recovery to baseline levels of adjustment. Attention to the components of resilience (recovery, sustainability, and growth) offers specificity and breadth for those who have found purpose in working to enhance the capacity of their communities to cope over time with adversity. The tools of inquiry, both methods and concepts, are also tools for advocacy. The resilience inquiry draws attention to the assets and capabilities of people and their communities in ways that inspire and motivate people to take action for the public good.

When examining the experiences of the Sudanese community in Brisbane, Australia, we see these three processes as they relate to adaptation in the context of refugee resettlement. Through an emphasis on community, policies and interventions can foster adaptation in culturally salient and effective ways. The reconstruction of social ties and community capacities are a necessity for all communities facing forced displacement and diaspora. By acknowledging and fostering communities,' natural and adaptive ways of coping, resettlement programs and policies can enhance their effectiveness in promoting the processes of recovery, sustainability, and growth.

Acknowledgments Many thanks to all of the members of the Sudanese community who contributed, both directly and indirectly, to this work. The first author was supported by the Australian-American Fulbright Commission and National Cancer Institute Grants #U54 CA132384 and #U54 CA132379. The second author was supported in part by the National Institute on Aging Grant R01 AG 026006 (Alex Zautra, PI) in the preparation of this work.

References

Arnett, J. J. (2008). The neglected 95%: Why American psychology needs to become less American. *American Psychologist, 63*, 602–614.

Barnhart, R. K. (1988). *The Barnhart dictionary of etymology*. Bronx: H. W. Wilson.

Bonanno, G. A. (2004). Loss, trauma, and human resilience: Have we underestimated the human capacity to thrive after extremely aversive events? *American Psychologist, 59*, 20–28.

Bracken, P. J. (2002). *Trauma: Culture, meaning & philosophy*. London: Whurr Publishers Ltd.

Cacioppo, J. T., Reis, H. T., & Zautra, A. J. (2011). Social resilience: The value of social fitness with an application to the military. *American Psychologist., 66*(1), 43–51.

Commonwealth of Australia. (2007). *Sudanese community profile*. Canberra: Commonwealth of Australia.

Davis, R., Cook, D., & Cohen, L. (2005). A community resilience approach to reducing ethnic and racial disparities. *American Journal of Public Health, 95*, 2168–2173.

Elmqvist, T., Folke, C., Nyström, M., Peterson, G., Bengtsson, J., Walker, B., et al. (2003). Response diversity, ecosystem change, and resilience. *Frontiers in Ecology and the Environment, 1*, 488–494.

Feder, A., Nestler, E. J., Westphal, M., & Charney, D. S. (2010). Psychobiological mechanisms of resilience to stress. In J. W. Reich, A. J. Zautra, & J. S. Hall (Eds.), *Handbook of adult resilience* (pp. 35–54). New York: Guilford Press.

Foa, E. B., Keane, T. M., & Friedman, M. J. (2000). *Effective treatments for PTSD: Practice guidelines from the International Society for Traumatic Stress Studies*. New York: Guilford Press.

France-Presse, A. (2009). *Army wants GIs emotionally 'resilient.' Military.com*. Retrieved, August 20, 2009, from http://www.military.com/news/article/army-wants-gis-emotionally-resilient.html.

Giller, J. (1998). Caring for 'victims of torture' in Uganda: Some personal reflections. In P. J. Bracken & C. Petty (Eds.), *Rethinking the trauma of war* (pp. 128–145). New York: Free Association Books.

Hughes, R. (2004). *Resilience: Health in a new key*. Phoenix: St Luke's Health Initiatives.

King, L. A., King, D. W., Keane, T. M., & Adams, G. A. (1998). Resilience-recovery factors in post-traumatic stress disorder among female and male Vietnam veterans: Hardiness, postwar social support, and additional stressful life events. *Journal of Personality and Social Psychology, 74*, 420–434.

Lemery-Chalfant, K. (2010). Genes and environments: How they work together to promote resilience. In J. W. Reich, A. J. Zautra, & J. S. Hall (Eds.), *Handbook of adult resilience* (pp. 55–78). New York: Guilford Press.

Masten, A. S. (2001). Ordinary magic: Resilience processes in development. *American Psychologist, 56*, 227–238.

McKinlay, J. B. (2000). To boldly go. *American Journal of Public Health, 90*, 25–32.

Miller, K. E. (1999). Rethinking a familiar model: Psychotherapy and mental health of refugees. *Journal of Contemporary Psychotherapy, 29*, 283–304.

Murray, K. E. (2010). Sudanese perspectives on resettlement in Australia. *Journal of the Pacific Rim Psychology, 4*, 30–43.

Norris, F. H., Stevens, S. P., Pfefferbaum, B., Wyche, K. F., & Pfefferbaum, R. L. (2008). Community resilience as a metaphor, theory, set of capacities, and strategy for disaster readiness. *American Journal of Community Psychology, 41*, 127–150.

Okvat, H. A., & Zautra, A. J. (2011). Potential consequences of community gardening on emotional well-being in a post-disaster context. In K. Tidball & M. Krasny (Eds.), *Greening in the red zone*. New York: Springer.

Papadopoulos, R. K. (2007). Refugees, trauma and adversity-activated development. *European Journal of Psychotherapy and Counselling, 9*, 301–312.

Pearce, N. (1996). Traditional epidemiology, modern epidemiology, and public health. *American Journal of Public Health, 86*, 678–683.

Portes, A., & Rumbaut, R. G. (1996). *Immigrant America: A portrait*. Berkeley: University of California Press.

Ryff, C. D., & Singer, B. (1998). The contours of positive human health. *Psychological Inquiry, 9*, 1–28.

Sallis, J. F., Owen, N., & Fisher, E. B. (2008). Ecological models of health behavior. In K. Glanz, B. K. Rimer, & K. Viswanath (Eds.), *Health behavior and health education: Theory, research, and practice* (pp. 465–486). San Francisco: Jossey-Bass.

Summerfield, D. (1996). The impact of war and atrocity on civilian populations: Basic principles for NGO interventions and a critique of psychosocial trauma projects. *Relief and Rehabilitation Network (Network Paper 14)*. London: Overseas Development Institute.

Tedeschi, R. G., Park, C., & Calhoun, L. G. (Eds.). (1998). *Post-traumatic growth: Theory and research in the aftermath of crisis*. Mahwah: Erlbaum.

Ungar, M. (2008). Resilience across cultures. *British Journal of Social Work, 38*, 218–235.

Ungar, M. (2010). Cultural dimensions of resilience among adults. In J. W. Reich, A. J. Zautra, & J. S. Hall (Eds.), *Handbook of adult resilience* (pp. 404–423). New York: Guilford Press.

United Nations High Commissioner for Refugees. (2003). *Framework for durable solutions for refugees and persons of concern*. Geneva: United Nations High Commissioner for Refugees.

Westoby, P. (2008). Developing a community-development approach through engaging resettling Southern Sudanese refugees within Australia. *Community Development Journal, 43*, 483–495.

Zautra, A. J. (2003). *Emotions, stress, and health*. New York: Oxford University Press.

Zautra, A., Hall, J. S., & Murray, K. E. (2008). Community development and community resilience: An integrative approach. *Community Development: Journal of the Community Development Society, 39*, 1–18.

Zautra, A. J., Hall, J. S., & Murray, K. E. (2010). Resilience: A new definition of health for people and communities. In J. R. Reich, A. J. Zautra, & J. S. Hall (Eds.), *Handbook of adult resilience* (pp. 3–30). New York: Guilford Press.

The Social Ecology of Resilience in War-Affected Youth: A Longitudinal Study from Sierra Leone

Theresa S. Betancourt

Introduction

Children and youth in crisis and in humanitarian settings are at the top of the global mental health agenda, not only due to their immediate needs but also because of the long-term implications for societies and nations as they grow into adulthood. Overall, mental disorders are the second largest contributor to the global burden of disease among youth and adults aged 14–55 years and are projected to be the highest contributor of disability adjusted life years (DALYS) by 2030 (Mathers & Loncar, 2006; World Health Organization, 2008). Most funding and programming for mental health interventions related to complex humanitarian emergencies (CHEs) are relegated to short-term humanitarian responses in the immediate crisis period; however, much greater needs persist over the long term. It is estimated that the level of untreated mental disorders among adults in low- and middle-income countries may be as high as 78% (Kohn, Saxena, Levav, & Saraceno, 2004). This figure is likely to be even higher for children and adolescents, and is most striking in war-affected countries in the global south (Jacob et al., 2007).

T.S. Betancourt
Department of Global Health and Population
at the Harvard School of Public Health (HSPH),
François-Xavier Bagnoud Center for Health
and Human Rights, Boston, MA, USA
e-mail: Theresa_Betancourt@harvard.edu

Eleven years of civil war in Sierra Leone devastated the nation's infrastructure and economy. Human Rights Watch estimates that over 50,000 people of the country's nearly six million citizens were killed during the decade of war. The majority of youth in Sierra Leone – both combatants and civilians – have been exposed to high levels of violence (Human Rights Watch, 2005). In Sierra Leone, children and youth were widely used in various capacities from performing domestic chores and other military support roles to committing acts of violence (McKay & Mazurana, 2004; UNICEF, 2001, 2007). Many were sexually abused and the forced use of alcohol and drugs was common. The long-term psychosocial adjustment and social reintegration of these Children Associated with Armed Forces or Armed Groups (CAAFAG) is of great concern. In the postconflict environment, risk for poor health and adverse developmental outcomes among all war-affected youth is compounded by low rates of school completion and limited opportunities for economic self-sufficiency (Bayer, Klasen, & Adam, 2007; Betancourt et al., 2008; Derluyn, Broekaert, Schuyten, & De Temmerman, 2004).

Despite increased discussion of the psychological consequences plaguing former child soldiers and other war-affected youth (Barenbaum, Ruchkin, & Schwab-Stone, 2004; Bolton et al., 2007; Lustig et al., 2004), there is very limited information on their long-term prospects. The present study aimed to address this gap in information by seeking to understand processes associated with resilience.

Methods

In 2002, collaboration between the Harvard
School of Public Health and the International
Rescue Committee (IRC) led to the launch of a
longitudinal study of war-affected youth in Sierra
Leone. The study was designed to identify risk
and protective factors in psychosocial adjustment
and social reintegration. The research was
informed by an ecological approach to child
health and well-being, which examines the interaction of influences at the individual, familial,
peer, community, and cultural/collective level
(Betancourt & Khan, 2008; Bronfenbrenner,
1979). The study was also shaped by contemporary theory and research related to resilience in
the mental health and development of children
and families in adversity (Garmezy, Masten, &
Tellegen, 1984; Luthar, Cicchetti, & Becker,
2000; Luthar & Goldstein, 2004).

Survey interviews were conducted at 3 time
points, in 2002, 2004, and 2008. The referred
portion of the sample were a cohort of children
($N=259$) who had been involved with the
Revolutionary United Front (RUF), the main
rebel group in the civil conflict, and had later
been referred to the IRC's Disarmament,
Demobilization, and Reintegration (DDR) program in Sierra Leone's Kono District. This sample was drawn from a master list of all youth
($N=309$) that were served by the IRC's Interim
Care Center (ICC), which supported reintegration of former child soldiers across five of Sierra
Leone's 14 districts during the most active period
of demobilization (June 2001 to February 2002).
Registries of youth served by this ICC were
reviewed to identify 10–17 year-olds (at the time
of release from rebel groups) for whom current
contact information was available. The study
design also included a comparison group of community children identified by random door-to-
door sampling, and in 2004, an additional cohort
of former child soldiers who were not served by
ICCs was added.

All participants were interviewed by trained
Sierra Leonean research assistants, in Krio, the
local language. Questionnaires contained a mix of
standard measures and locally derived measures,
developed in close consultation with local staff
and community members. Our study team collected basic demographics along with information
on family configuration, age, and length of
involvement with armed groups, and war-related
experiences. In addition, all interviews used a
scale of psychosocial adjustment developed and
validated for use among former child soldiers in
Sierra Leone by researchers at the Oxford Refugee
Studies Program (MacMullin & Loughry, 2004).
The measure contained a mix of both adaptive
behaviors/attitudes, such as confidence and prosocial behaviors, as well as measures of anxiety,
depression, and hostility. In emphasizing an
ecological model and the nature of the enabling
environment for child well-being, the questionnaires also included questions about relationships
upon return, family socio-economic status, community acceptance, social support, and access to
educational and skills training opportunities. The
2004 and 2008 follow-up surveys repeated these
baseline measures and added other items to examine additional community processes such as collective efficacy (nonformal social control and
social cohesion), stigma/discrimination, and other
variables of relevance to young adulthood including high-risk behavior, civic participation, and
experiences of postconflict daily hardships such
as housing and food insecurity, as well as family
conflict and parent–child relationships.

Quantitative Findings

This research has led to several publications
about how war-related and postconflict experiences affect the long-term mental health and
psychosocial adjustment of war-affected youth
(Betancourt, Agnew-Blais, Gilman, Williams, &
Ellis, 2010; Betancourt et al., 2008; Betancourt,
Borisova, et al., 2010; Betancourt, Brennan,
Rubin-Smith, Fitzmaurice, & Gilman, 2010;
Betancourt & Ettien, 2010; Betancourt, Zaeh,
Ettien, & Khan, In press). Overall, our study
underscores how the long-term mental health
of former child soldiers is shaped by both
war experiences and postconflict factors. For

instance, lower levels of prosocial behavior (such as helpfulness towards others) were associated with having killed or injured others during wartime. Young people who reported having been raped exhibited heightened anxiety and hostility after the war (Betancourt, Borisova, et al., 2010). Worsening anxiety and depression over time were also closely related both to younger age of being involved in fighting forces and to social and economic hardships in the postconflict environment (Betancourt, Brennan, et al., 2010). However, looking at the role of stigma (including discrimination and lower levels of community and family acceptance), we found that it served as a partial mediator between war-related experiences and postconflict psychosocial adjustment. In addition, we observed that stigma associated with being a child soldier explained a significant proportion of the variance in levels of hostility that the cohort of youth reported over time (Betancourt, Agnew-Blais, et al., 2010). Greater stigma was also associated with less prosocial behavior.

The most exciting aspects of the research findings are those related to protective processes that have the potential to be leveraged by policies and programs. For instance, increases in prosocial behavior were associated with remaining in school and increases in community acceptance over time. In addition, higher levels of family acceptance were associated with lower levels of hostility over time, and improvements in community acceptance were associated with positive adaptive attitudes and behaviors (Betancourt, Brennan, et al., 2010). In fact, community acceptance – both initially and over time – had a beneficial effect on all outcomes studied.

The findings of this first longitudinal study of male and female former child soldiers indicate that psychosocial adjustment and community reintegration of war-affected youth are complex processes involving a range of factors across time and ecological levels. However, postconflict factors that play a role in determining long-term outcomes are of particular interest to researchers, practitioners, and policy makers, since many postconflict factors can be modified while war experiences cannot. In order to better understand these dynamics,

vignettes or individual case studies present a unique opportunity to understand how these factors play out in a young person's developmental trajectory.

Qualitative Data

To complement the quantitative data, beginning in 2004, we also included a series of in-depth qualitative interviews with adolescents and their caregivers, and focus group interviews with young people, caregivers, and community members in heavily war-affected communities in the Kono, Kenema, Bo, Mkeni, Pujehun, and Moyamba districts of Sierra Leone. Interviews were conducted with 31 CAAFAG; for 12 of these, we were able to conduct a matching caregiver interview. In 2004, 10 focus groups were conducted with youth and 17 with caregivers and community members in Kono, Kenema, Bombali, and Bo districts. In 2008–2009, we were able to conduct repeat in-depth interviews with 21 youth and 13 caregivers, as well as 17 focus groups with war-affected youth.

According to many participants, the effects of the war on young people still linger and are seen as linked to problem behaviors such as drug and alcohol problems as well as sexual risk taking:

> Some are still on drugs and their attitudes are different … their actions and the way they interact are aggressive …. A majority of drug addicts now were with the fighters [at the time of the war].
> (CAAFAG male in focus group, Kenema)

> It is the women who are affected the most …. There are some of our peers who go into the streets and sleep with men just so they can survive.
> (CAAFAG female in focus group, Makeni)

Caregivers complained of volatile behaviors and problems with interpersonal relationships:

> Those that were with those people (rebels) in the bush were obedient but the problem they had was that they were highly temperamental. No one makes fun of them. No one laughs at them. At the slightest offence they broke into fights.
> (Caregiver, Kenema)

> I always got complaints from the school. At one time the teacher even threatened to expel him from the school if he didn't change his attitude.
> (Caregiver, Kenema)

Community influences on healthy integration were pervasive and unmistakable. In fact, many returning child soldiers faced stigma, "provoking" suspicion upon return home (Betancourt, Agnew-Blais, et al., 2010). As both caregivers and youth explained:

> With the return of those children, people were disgruntled about them because according to the popular opinion these children have destroyed our lives, houses and property. Therefore these ex-child combatants were called different names. There was total rejection of them, some people even disowned their own children.
>
> (Caregiver, Makeni)

> Throughout this country in the aftermath of the war as long as you have been with the rebels there are those who would never have a clean heart for you. Some would think that you probably killed their father or mother or that you might have been the one who burnt their house down. So there will always be this lingering suspicion of you. And you have to be very careful in anything you do.
>
> (CAAFAG male, Kono)

With time and committed guidance and support from caregivers, many of these former child soldiers demonstrated improved adjustment and community relations. In fact, many of the youth in our sample held very ambitious dreams for themselves and their futures. Despite limited opportunities, most youth expressed a desire to study and earn a living. As one 12-year-old female explained:

> I only feel better when I am studying … studying is a source of encouragement. I know that if I am educated I will be successful and people will appreciate me.
>
> (CAAFAG female, Kenema)

However, it was most common that youth would describe a situation of financial constraints and difficulty in affording school fees. For many young people, this could mean dropping out of studies or a pattern of stopping and starting one's education, even well into their late teens:

> When I was promoted to Form One, my parents couldn't pay our school fees any longer for my brother and I.
>
> (CAAFAG male, Bo)

For youth in this environment, their personal agency was certainly one way forward. One male adolescent who started a car wash business with a friend described how they proactively pursued support for their initiative:

> After school I had no tasks to occupy me, so I decided not to be idle so my ideas would not run to other things that would be bad things … we saw … this Fullah man working there. So we called and told him that "Father, we want you to help us. We are students and our families are not here. But we don't want to return from school and be idle and go cussing and doing bad things in the street. So we want you to engage us so we would learn and we would be able to buy small things like books and pens." So he allowed us. So that is how we are here now.
>
> (CAAFAG male, Kono)

Personal agency was also an important factor in helping a young person to better withstand community stigma. Of the personal qualities and capabilities that were important, skills in emotional regulation and prosocial attitudes were especially critical:

> Even though you are called a rebel if your attitude is good they won't hold anything against you. They would want to make friends with you.
>
> (CAAFAG female)

Also important was family support and guidance about how to interact with others in the community. For youth who had such supports, they could be a critical source of problem solving and anticipating how to handle community "provoking."

> When my child returned, I advised him not to think of doing anything evil and that he should try by all means to live peacefully with others. Since he came he has caused no problems. Although people were afraid of him and called him funny names he never did anything to retaliate. Now he plays peacefully with other children.
>
> (Caregiver, Bo)

In some cases, with the right support, some of the former child soldiers were faring even better than their non-CAAFAG peers:

> I just continued to counsel and talk to him. Now he has started reforming. Now when someone bothers him he complains to me. Some of his peers in his school are even more often in trouble than he is lately.
>
> (Caregiver, Kenema)

These findings suggest that psychosocial adjustment and community reintegration for former child soldiers involve a diverse set of factors including individual competencies as well as the availability of family and community resources and supports at all levels of a youth's social ecology. These resources constitute a continuum from more or less enabling environments depending on the degree to which they are oriented towards supporting vulnerable youth and helping them overcome hardship. Our qualitative data indicate that even young people who experienced extreme trauma could reintegrate well if their social ecology was enabling – meaning that they had strong family and community support (Betancourt & Ettien, 2010). We also found that youth who had an accumulation of war-related risk factors and lacked strong, effective support were on a much riskier developmental path characterized by social isolation and high-risk behavior such as substance abuse and, in some cases, engagement in high-risk or abusive relationships in order to secure basic needs.

These dynamics are best illustrated through in-depth analyses of a few select cases. The following vignettes arise from the key informant interviews conducted in 2004 and 2008 (Betancourt & Ettien, 2010). Two cases are presented here. Both have been exposed to significant war-related risk including young age of involvement with an armed group, prolonged family separation, exposure to extreme violence, and community stigma. However, these two cases differ in the degree to which an enabling environment and support system was able to advocate for and meet the youth's needs.

Sahr: Poor Emotional Regulation and Community Stigma

When interviewed in 2008, Sahr was 17 years old and living near Kono in the diamond mining district of Sierra Leone. He was abducted at age seven while with his grandmother and uncle in the bush and spent 4 years with the RUF. Sahr was initially used for domestic chores; in fact, that is why he was captured: "The rebel then came and told my grandmother that he has a wife in the jungle that had just delivered a child and she needed a little child to be with her to help her

with little things in taking care of the baby, and as such he is taking me with him." He describes that he was so small when first taken by the rebels that they had to carry him to move quickly through the bush: "So [the rebels] used to carry me on their backs as at that time that I could not walk properly on my own." With time, however, he matured and was driven into more violent activities including involvement in fighting and even the killing and injury of others. He was forced to eat food laced with gunpowder, which was thought to have stimulant properties.[1] He witnessed massacres, bombings, amputations, and violent deaths and was often assigned to spy and gather information for his captors.

After the war, Sahr was released to an ICC and then spent 2 years in the care of a foster mother. Eventually, Sahr was reunited with his mother, grandmother, and uncle. Interviews with his mother underscore the deep love and forgiveness that the mother and grandmother felt for the young boy. As his mother explained: "He came back to us because he loved us" and they tried to respond in kind. However, his uncle, who was the head of household considered him to be a "troublesome" boy. As such, the most powerful force in the family - the uncle - was not invested in defending or supporting Sahr. The family overall was struggling after the war. The mother herself suffered from mental health problems, likely depression, which was highly impairing. Upon return home, Sahr had difficulties reintegrating within the community. Community members called him names and beat him in an attempt to "correct" behavior and attitudes that they saw as undesirable. As his mother explained: "They [community members] used to disturb him; beat him saying they were reforming him …. The townspeople would come and beat him. There was a time when everybody gathered around him, wanting to beat him up. They said they wanted him to change, I don't know which change they wanted. I had to come and fight them off for the

---

[1] Smokeless gunpowder was used in this part of Africa as a psychological ploy. Users were told that it brings on aggression.

sake of my son. I didn't see any sense in beating a child in the name of correcting him."

When community tensions were high, Sahr fought back, once pulling a knife on community members in an act of self-defense. For Sahr, this community aggression only deepened his sense of social isolation. He became known for stealing and was often blamed for any theft in the area, even if he had not been involved. Sahr eventually dropped out of school and remained unemployed. His mother says he was an agreeable boy before being abducted, but now has difficult relationships with others. At the time of her 2008 interview, his mother did not know of his whereabouts.

The interesting aspect of Sahr's story is that he had deep love from his mother and grandmother, but was not supported by the most powerful figure in his family. This fact coupled with painful and aggressive community rejection served to drive Sahr into deeper isolation and antisocial behavior which fed a cycle of social rejection and dramatically influenced his psychosocial development.

Amina: Individual Will and a Mother's Guiding Force

Amina was abducted from her Temeni tribe village at age 10 by the RUF. Her captors threatened to kill her family if she did not go with them. She spent two and a half years fearing she would be raped or killed. Though she was never sexually assaulted, she was forcedly drugged by injection, ingestion, and the rubbing of the substances into open wounds. She was also frequently beaten, and the abuse left her with a permanent leg deformity and limp. Amina was forced to carry supplies and do domestic chores. She witnessed raids, amputations, stabbings, killings, bombings, and massacres. She also reports having wounded or killed two people during her time with the rebels. She explains: "I was afraid because they killed people in front of me and they gave me a gun during battles. They used us as human shield[s] so we stand in front with our guns, but I never shot or killed somebody."

After going through the IRCs DDR program, Amina returned to her mother and grandmother in a small village in the Moyamba District. Her mother described the process of being reunited: "A lady who used to visit me when I was in town brought her to me because I was kind to her back then. This lady was also captured by the fighting forces so when they took over the country during the AFRC (Armed Forces Revolutionary Council) period the rebels were asked to go to Freetown (to surrender the child combatants) so this lady met my sister and told her." Her mother explained: "I later collected her in Freetown and brought her back here.... We were so happy when we heard the news. When I actually saw that God brought back my children it made me so happy. Agencies provided us with food that made me very happy." In 2004 at age 16, Amina reported feeling jumpy and experiencing sleepless nights, though she did not feel helpless and had dedicated herself to her schoolwork.

Amina, like Sahr, faced community stigma upon returning home. When she first returned to her village after the war, Amina reported that she was often stubborn and had no respect for elders. Some children called her "rebel" when she first returned. However, with help from her mother, a teacher, Amina stayed focused on school and eventually built positive relationships with the community. Amina's mother was able to use school as a motivation to modify Amina's attitude. She said, "It was because they encouraged me and told me that I'll go to school again that is why I changed … I was disrespectful to my teachers. My mother used to go to school to talk to the teacher and explain my situation."

According to her mother, most people in the community now do not even know Amina was with the RUF. Amina provided several examples of how her mother helped facilitate her reintegration, explaining: "my mother threatened that she will tell the chief if anyone provokes me." Amina's community is not perfect. In fact, neither mother nor daughter has full trust in the community, and for good reason: "The Chairman, Clerk and Treasurer that were appointed to spearhead the affairs of the child ex-combatants in this town … have not been honest. When we received supply of rice they sold it and made another request. The rice was brought and they sold it again, but this time we did not see the money." Nonetheless, the family has been able to remain united and make progress towards shared goals.

By age 23 at the time of her 2008 interview, Amina was living with her aunt in another town, so she could receive better schooling. She had given birth to a daughter who was 3 years old at the time of interview, and was also caring for her mother. Amina is no longer with the child's father, who had been physically abusive to her. However, she reported that he loves the child and does not cause problems. Amina is still in school and not planning to have another child until she is finished. She often thinks of what happened to her during her time with the RUF and has suffered "toment"[2] and a strong sense of insecurity since her return. Nevertheless, she has always felt loved and supported by her mother. Amina says she has been able to forgive, but that the people who committed so much violence should be punished further and that their wrongs have not yet been put right. This feeling, however, does not interfere with her working towards her own personal goals. She is not supported by any outside agency, but manages nonetheless. As she explained: "I don't have any serious problems yet that cannot be solved." Although her economic status is worrisome at times, she knows that people are invested in her well-being. She said: "my mother is going through a lot of strains to educate me." Amina also maintains a forward-thinking perspective on her life: "I want to be educated and become a respectable person in society and make my mother proud of me."

Summary

Our data show that there are multiple influences on psychosocial adjustment and social reintegration for child soldiers. Certainly, individual-level war experiences, coping skills, and competencies

matter, but outcomes are also strongly shaped by family, community, and even larger macro-level factors such as the availability of education programs for youth who have missed many years of schooling due to war. Such enabling environments have a critical role to play in supporting the healthy adjustment of war-affected youth. Overall, the disappearance of many youth-focused NGOs and government initiatives aimed at increasing opportunities and support indicates the degree to which the national and international community has not effectively prioritized these pathways to healthy development, nor made them sustainable to address the long-lasting effects of conflict on young people.

Future Directions: Using An Ecological and Developmental Approach to Support Healthy Life Trajectories in War-Affected Youth

In future work aimed at nurturing the resilience of demobilized child soldiers and their community peers, it is clear that intervention efforts must support community-level monitoring of risk, help build social supports, and make available protective resources to troubled youth. Such efforts would support earlier investments made to family and community reintegration in postconflict environments. Additionally, interventions should target war-affected youth broadly rather than force a narrow and potentially stigmatizing focus solely on select label-driven groups such as "former child soldiers" or "survivors of gender based violence." Community-based interventions focused on encouraging healthy coping resources like communication with family and caretakers, friendships and the development of social networks are critical to assisting *all* war-affected youth. For many CAAFAG, the return to their communities and families went a long way towards giving them the basic foundations for success. However, for certain subgroups, particularly those whose families have limited capacity to support their children's ongoing success, additional enabling supports may be required. This may entail reinvigorating efforts at the community

---

[2]Toment is an anxiety-like syndrome that has aspects of guilt, withdrawal, and sometimes fearfulness.

level to discuss and address the risks posed by exclusion.

In addition, a more robust effort is needed to ensure that youth-focused services reach beyond the capital district to the rural provinces where poverty is endemic. Unfortunately, the funding streams, technical assistance, and human resources required to assist youth and families during the initial humanitarian emergency and DDR period have not translated into sustainable opportunities and systems of care for vulnerable children, youth, and families in places like Sierra Leone.

Although significant efforts were made in Sierra Leone to provide assistance to CAAFAG in the immediate postconflict period, very few social services or mental health services for war-affected youth and families of any kind remain today. Furthermore, for many youth, initial support for educational goals has not been sustained. However, our data indicate that there is an alarming concentration of particularly toxic risk factors among a portion of CAAFAG, and that a number of the family and community placements made immediately after the war have fallen apart, as is well illustrated by Sahr's story. Failure to invest in broad-based systems which have the capacity to ensure long-term monitoring, assessment and follow-up with high-risk youth who continue to struggle (for many reasons) threatens to undermine the investments made in returning young people home.

Successful grassroots intervention models do exist. One example is the group that handled our risk-of-harm referrals in Kono, the Community Association for Psychosocial Services (CAPS). CAPS is a local organization trained by the Center for Victims of Torture (CVT), a torture treatment center based in the US. Local stakeholders organized by CAPS have filled a service gap when CVT withdrew from Kono District. CAPS staff have been trained to provide counseling to survivors of torture and war trauma using adapted CVT models. These models were first implemented immediately after the war in refugee camps in Guinea (Gupta & Zimmer, 2008; Stepakoff et al., 2006) and have given the staff a long-term understanding of the experiences of war-affected youth. CAPS also has good relationships with Sierra Leone's Ministry of Social Welfare and Gender, which is a supportive partner in this work. The challenge in Sierra Leone now is how to evaluate such promising programs and how to bring them to scale in order to widely serve populations in need. Such approaches to identifying, evaluating, and scaling up interventions within existing national and local health structures and future policy designs merit inclusion in the development agendas for many postconflict countries.

Of equally important consideration is the need for investments in supportive and enabling communities. We see from the cases of Sahr and Amina that both war-affected youth had loving caregivers who would go to their defense. In the case of Amina, her mother was able to be effective, despite extreme corruption in the community, given her strong links to other supportive people. In the case of Sahr, however, the deep love of his mother and grandmother were not enough to overcome the resentment of his uncle and the negative reactions of the community. These negative interactions were likely deepened by Sahr's inability to regulate his emotions and his own antisocial behavior.

Ultimately, our data point to the potential for building on the capacity of existing social institutions like the family, and the need to adopt culturally appropriate and contextually specific models of psychosocial support and mental health care that can be integrated across several sectors serving youth. These include health, education, and economic initiatives. In a case such as Sahr's, community-level interventions addressing stigma might be coupled with individually focused interventions to build a young person's skills in emotional regulation.

It is important to consider the findings presented here in light of the current situation of social and mental health services for war-affected youth in Sierra Leone. At present, policymakers in Sierra Leone and the international community are focused on economic development and stability for the country. There has also been recent progress in the country with regard to the establishment of a National Mental Health Policy which has focused attention on community-based services and youth issues. However, real challenges remain. For instance, the budget for the Sierra Leone Ministry of Social Welfare has dropped from nearly $800,000 USD in 2009 to less than $500,000 USD in 2010. Without the right investments, a failure to address the consequences of the war specifically on Sierra Leone's sizable younger generation threatens the development of human capital and the investments being made in education and youth employment schemes. These young people, despite all that they have endured, demonstrate a great deal of capacity to thrive if given the right rehabilitative supports and opportunities to improve their lives.

References

Barenbaum, J., Ruchkin, V., & Schwab-Stone, M. (2004). The psychological aspects of children exposed to war: Practice and policy initiatives. *Journal of Child Psychology and Psychiatry, 45*(1), 41–62.

Bayer, C. P., Klasen, F., & Adam, H. (2007). Association of trauma and PTSD symptoms with openness to reconciliation and feelings of revenge among former Ugandan and Congolese child soldiers. *Journal of the American Medical Association, 298*(5), 555–559.

Betancourt, T. S., Agnew-Blais, J., Gilman, S. E., Williams, D. R., & Ellis, B. H. (2010). Past horrors, present struggles: The role of stigma in the association between war experiences and psychosocial adjustment among former child soldiers in Sierra Leone. *Social Science & Medicine, 70*(1), 17–26.

Betancourt, T. S., Borisova, I. I., Brennan, R. B., Williams, T. P., Whitfield, T. H., de la Soudiere, M., et al. (2010). Sierra Leone's former child soldiers: A follow-up study of psychosocial adjustment and community reintegration. *Child Development, 81*(4), 1077–1095.

Betancourt, T. S., Brennan, R. T., Rubin-Smith, J., Fitzmaurice, G. M., & Gilman, S. E. (2010). Sierra Leone's former child soldiers: A longitudinal study of risk, protective factors, and mental health. *Journal of the American Academy of Child and Adolescent Psychiatry, 49*(6), 606–615.

Betancourt, T. S., & Ettien, A. (2010). *Transitional Justice and Youth Formerly Associated with Armed Forces and Groups in Sierra Leone: Acceptance, Marginalization and Psychosocial Adjustment Innocenti Working Paper* (Vol. 2010–2017). Florence: UNICEF Innocenti Research Centre.

Betancourt, T. S., & Khan, K. T. (2008). The mental health of children affected by armed conflict: Protective processes and pathways to resilience. *International Review of Psychiatry, 20*(3), 317–328.

Betancourt, T. S., Simmons, S., Borisova, I., Brewer, S. E., Iweala, U., & de la Soudiere, M. (2008). High hopes, grim reality: Reintegration and the education of former child soldiers in Sierra Leone. *Comparative Education Review, 52*(4), 565–587. doi: 10.1086/591298r.

Betancourt, T. S., Zaeh, S. E., Ettien, A., & Khan, L. N. (In press). Psychosocial adjustment and mental health services in post-conflict Sierra Leone: Experiences of CAAFAG and war-affected youth, families and service providers. In S. Parmentier, J. Sarkin, & E. Weitekamp (Eds.), *New Series on Transitional Justice*. Antwerp: Intersentia.

Bolton, P., Bass, J., Betancourt, T. S., Speelman, L., Onyango, G., Clougherty, K. F., et al. (2007). Interventions for depression symptoms among adolescent survivors of war and displacement in northern Uganda: A randomized controlled trial. *Journal of the American Medical Association, 298*(5), 519–527.

Bronfenbrenner, U. (1979). *The ecology of human development: Experiments by nature and design.* Cambridge: Harvard University Press.

Derluyn, I., Broekaert, E., Schuyten, G., & De Temmerman, E. (2004). Post-traumatic stress in former Ugandan child soldiers. *Lancet, 363*(9412), 861–863.

Garmezy, N., Masten, A. S., & Tellegen, A. (1984). The study of stress and competence in children: A building block for developmental psychopathology [Article]. *Child Development, 55*(1), 97. doi: 10.1111/1467-8624. ep7405463

Gupta, L., & Zimmer, C. (2008). Psychosocial intervention for war-affected children in Sierra Leone. *The British Journal of Psychiatry, 192*(3), 212–216.

Human Rights Watch. (2005). *Youth poverty and blood: The lethal legacy of West Africa's regional warriors*. New York: Human Rights Watch.

Jacob, K. S., Sharan, P., Mirza, I., Garrido-Cumbrera, I. M., Seedat, S., Mari, J. J., et al. (2007). Mental health systems in countries: Where are we now? *Lancet, 370*, 1061–1077.

Kohn, R., Saxena, S., Levav, I., & Saraceno, B. (2004). The treatment gap in mental health care [Article]. *Bulletin of the World Health Organization, 82*(11), 858–866.

Lustig, S. L., Kia-Keating, M., Knight, W. G., Geltman, P., Ellis, H., Kinzie, J. D., et al. (2004). Review of child and adolescent refugee mental health. *Journal of the American Academy of Child and Adolescent Psychiatry, 43*(1), 24–36.

Luthar, S., Cicchetti, D., & Becker, B. (2000). The construct of resilience: A critical evaluation and guidelines for future work. *Child Development, 71*(3), 543–562.

Luthar, S. S., & Goldstein, A. (2004). Children's exposure to community violence: Implications for understanding risk and resilience. *Journal of Clinical Child and Adolescent Psychology, 33*(3), 499–505.

MacMullin, C., & Loughry, M. (2004). Investigating psychosocial adjustment of former child soldiers in Sierra Leone and Uganda. *Journal of Refugee Studies, 17*(4), 460–472.

Mathers, C. D., & Loncar, D. (2006). Projections of global mortality and burden of disease from 2002 to 2030. *PLoS Medicine, 3*(11), 2011–2030.

McKay, S., & Mazurana, D. (2004). *Where are the girls? Girls in fighting forces in Northern Uganda, Sierra Leone, and Mozambique: Their lives during and after war Curr Opin Psychiatry*. Montreal: International Center for Human Rights and Democratic Development.

Stepakoff, S., Hubbard, J., Katoh, M., Falk, E., Mikulu, J. B., Nkhoma, P., et al. (2006). Trauma healing in refugee camps in Guinea: A psychosocial program for Liberian and Sierra Leonean survivors of torture and war. *The American Psychologist, 61*(8), 921–932.

UNICEF. (2001). *The state of the world's children 2001*. New York: United Nations.

UNICEF. (2007). *The Paris principles: Principles and guidelines on children associated with armed forces or armed conflict*. Paris: UNICEF.

World Health Organization. (2008). *The global burden of disease: 2004 Update*. Geneva: WHO Press.

Travelling Through Social Support and Youth Civic Action on a Journey Towards Resilience

Pat Dolan

In recent years, resilient youth, or those who can bounce back and do better than expected, has received consistent attention from policymakers, practitioners and the academic community (Gilligan, 2009; Rutter, Giller, & Hagel, 1998; Ungar, 2008). This strength-based perspective, rather than a problem-centred approach, has also been implicit in relation to the new sociology of childhood, which highlights the value and capacity of young people as civic actors. The potential of youth as societal leaders has also focused on resilience as a key factor particularly, given that we rear children and youth not just to the benefit of families but as contributors to society. For example, adapting Maslow's hierarchy of needs from the 1970s, Van Linden and Fertman (1998) highlight three Ss, safety, survival and self-esteem, as important factors for enabling young people to demonstrate hardiness. Like others (see Rutter et al., 1998), they discuss the need to view resilience as occurring in the face of severe adversity rather than just coping with daily hassles and stress. However, we can also be hopeful in terms of viewing the capacity of youth to adjust and reconfigure. This flexibility, which can be deemed one of the benefits of being young, is typified by Van Linden and Fertman as "a time during which people develop their individuality and are interested in trying new things and learning new skills" (p. 36).

While many of these assumptions are based on how young people cope under adversity, how "in practice" youth can be enabled to do better needs greater attention. Specifically, the role, power and process of using social support networks as positive allies for youth experiencing adversity have not been given due attention (Pinkerton & Dolan, 2007). This being the case, this chapter will first explore the core connection between resilience and social support including their interplay at individual, family and wider ecological levels. Similarly, the influence and benefits of youth civic engagement and action to enable both better social support enlistment and robust resilience are considered. Importantly, the contexts of daily life as well as incidents of crises are highlighted as factors influencing this relationship. Finally, these three concepts of social support, youth civic action and resilience are brought together into a tentative conceptual framework, with three short vignettes presented to illustrate its application to policy and practice.

Connecting Resilience to Social Support

Whereas much has been written on the importance of social support and social networks as proven buffers to stress (Cutrona, 2000), less attention has been paid to the wider context of social networks and how they are related to building the resilience

P. Dolan (✉)
School of Political Science and Sociology,
National University of Ireland, Aras Moyola,
Galway, Ireland
e-mail: pat.dolan@nuigalway.ie

M. Ungar (ed.), *The Social Ecology of Resilience: A Handbook of Theory and Practice*,
DOI 10.1007/978-1-4614-0586-3_28, © Springer Science+Business Media, LLC 2012

of youth, their families and communities. While more generally, much is known about the role of kin as a source of social support (Tracy & Whittaker, 1990) and as a protective factor, the more distinct supportive role of young people's schools and community settings is less well researched (Dryfoos, Quinn, & Barkin, 2005). It could be argued that many helping professionals often assume that by ensuring a youth has multiple sources of support, and that better mental health and associated coping capacity will ensue. However, social support has more discrete and nuanced aspects that influence well-being (Cobb, 1976), and these should influence interventions from professionals. Key coping issues for young people and their families relate to their access to emotional and instrumental assistance, usable advice and the dependability of the help offered to them. These social network factors are essential to resilience building in youth and go deeper than just identifying who can help.

Although there are contexts where optimal support can be best accessed from professionals, overall, most youth access the help they need from informal sources. Often described as natural helpers (Cotterell, 1996), these informal supporters are "unpaid" and typically comprise parents, siblings, other family members and close friendships (Dolan, 2010). Nevertheless, despite the fact that such help is available outside office hours, is a naturally occurring form of sustenance, and is generally the lowest cost of intervention, this key function of informal support tends to be overlooked by frontline professionals, policymakers and service designers alike. Most importantly, this connection between natural help and reciprocity within networks, when operative, has solid benefits for youth. This includes minimising a young person's sense of being stigmatised. In addition, on the basis of "returning a favour" by reciprocating support received, it lessens his or her sense of feeling beholden to others. Increased interest in utilising such informal support has been highlighted in the literature as having particular value (Cutrona, 2000; Ghate & Hazel, 2002).

Two further specific concepts in social support theory have emerged which are of particular importance for building resilience in youth. First, hidden support that relates to assistance which a young person receives but remains unaware of its donation has been seen to be very effective. Second, convoyed help from the social networks of others enables a young person to access help from new contacts (Levitt, 2005). Both of these social support factors are now explored briefly in the context of resilience building.

While hidden support is help which one does not realise one is receiving, or is provided in a very low key way, it must be delivered so that the recipient feels little impingement on his or her actions. Bolger and Amarel (2007) show that when one receives support through a straightforward transaction of help from another person, whereas the recipient may appreciate the support, he or she will often feel worse after the event. This can result in a young person or his or her family harbouring feelings of now owing something to others or with feelings of inadequacy at not being able to reciprocate support once it has been received.

Where the exact same type and level of help is provided in a hidden way, for example via a third more neutral party, or provided anonymously, the positive effects for the recipient include a heightened sense of self-esteem and increased self-efficacy (Bolger & Amarel, 2007). In terms of using social support as a tool to build protective factors for individual youth, families and communities, this is particularly important. It highlights that for youth in need, their journey of recovery or capacity to bounce back or just cope can be enhanced by discrete acts of social support.

In addition to the potential of hidden help, accessing social support through sources outside of a young person's immediate network has been highlighted as having particular potential for practice and programme interventions (Levitt, 2005). Mary Levitt has developed this concept of support being convoyed for a person with a weak network by channelling help through one reliable alliance. This can act as an antidote for youth who have poor or toxic social network ties with few supporters including family and friends. Thus, by accessing help from the positive supporters of another person's network, a youth can derive benefits and he or she cannot access alone. As with bridging social capital (Putnam, 2000), convoyed support may occur where a young person can both "get by and get ahead" by identifying one responsive person in his or her otherwise poor network who opens up a range of new network contacts and opportunities. For example, through using the contacts of a friend, a youth seeking a job accesses employment. Furthermore, while most appreciative of the introduction to this work contact, the youth may be unaware of the additional hidden help by this friend, which enabled such a successful outcome.

This process of utilising hidden and convoyed help is in opposition to the early image of social support, which sought to create an ideal network by encouraging people to change their relationships (Tracy & Whittaker, 1990). The approach is also gaining interest among frontline practitioners including social workers. For instance, both Youth Mentoring and Family Group Conferencing are programmes that use social support network interventions and have been developed and well-tested over recent decades (Connolly, 2004; Tierney, Grossman, & Resch, 1995).

Limitations of Social Support

As well as emphasising its strengths, it is important to highlight the limitations of social support in the lives of young people (Cotterell, 1996). Not all help is positive and networks can often contain dangers such as unfair criticism from the donor, or lack of reciprocity, which has a negative impact on a young person, particularly so when he or she is feeling vulnerable (Whittaker, 2009). Similarly, a recent negative incident in a relationship with a parent or friend can impair any accurate assessment by the young person of the amount of support he or she has on offer (Ungar, 2004). Therefore, when those who are close fall out even briefly, the negative impact on the supply of support for a young person can endure (Dolan, 2008). Such events or confrontations are often overlooked or not fully accounted for by professionals in considering the bank of supporters available to a young person. The support that

a youth perceives to be available can sometimes be "wishful thinking" on his or her part rather than an accurate account of the actual help available. Cotterell (1996) indicates that youth often over-report the range of sources, level and quality of support on offer.

Young people can also overuse their supply of help. Where social support is over used, negative or ineffective, it can lead to youth having poorer coping capacity and reinforce their sense of helplessness and hopelessness. It can also have the effect of diminishing a young person's sense of self-compassion, happiness, optimism positive effect, wisdom and personal initiative (Neff, Rude, & Kirkpatrick, 2007).

Support in Everyday Living and in Crises

Although Tracy and Whittaker (1990) describe social support as "direct acts of assistance between human beings" (p.23), the timing and context in which help is offered is of equal importance. While supporting individual youth in the face of imminent stress tends to be the focus for professionals, help in everyday living contexts does not get the same attention (Dolan, 2010). For example, when a youth loses a parent through sudden death, the initial well-meaning onslaught of emotional support from professionals and non-professionals alike can be a cause of additional stress and impair the youth's capacity to grieve. This flood of support can wane quickly and go from too many people offering help to the bereaved youth, to no one providing comfort at all.

The difference between crisis and everyday social support has been further highlighted by Hawkins and Maurer (2010). They studied how families coped during and after Hurricane Katrina in New Orleans and found that youth and their families utilised differing forms of social support during the immediate crisis of the flood compared to help they accessed later as part of their recovery. They also found that locally sourced social supports were a key factor in the capacity of youth to be resilient and retain hopefulness. In sum, to bridge the gap between working with individual youth and working with communities, there is a need not just to see both social support networks and resilience as concepts that come into play in a crisis, but to view both as having important usage in the context of everyday life when stress is high.

Civic Engagement to Enlist Social Support and Enable Resilience

The concept of social civic engagement that engages youth in altruistic acts in their family and/or wider community holds potential for young people to develop heightened resilience (Dolan, 2010). Youth civic action provides the potential for the enablement of resilience, thought this aspect of resilience has received little attention (Flanagan & Nakesha, 2001). Youth civic engagement is described in terms of leadership and defined by Van Linden and Fertman (1998) as "individuals who think for themselves, communicate their thoughts and feelings to others, and help others understand and act on their own beliefs" (p. 17).

However, civic engagement and civic action can be thought of as different concepts. Civic engagement relates to the process of enabling civic interaction to commence or recommence, while civic action is the ongoing process of achieving civic good. Civic engagement and actions by youth are often portrayed in political terminology, including procedures for youth agency, their right to participate in society and methods for advocating for social justice. However, social altruism, including youth who volunteer in their community, tends not to be seen as an equal part of the civic engagement menu (Dolan, 2010). Although political civic engagement may be perceived as fulfilling rights, and social civic engagement as meeting need, both forms are in effect intertwined for youth in terms of the daily contexts in which they live. For example, youth who volunteer to assist vulnerable older people in their neighbourhood do so on the premise that elders have a right to be supported.

The civic engagement of youth in society is often seen as investment in young people on the basis that their positive contribution to society now will pay dividends for them and the rest of society in the future. However, this may be a very limited point of view. The new sociology of childhood (and adolescence) suggests that we should value the contributions that youth make while they are still young and that like all others in the human race, they have ongoing capital that can bring benefit to civic society. This highlights the fact that while youth are still young, just like all other citizens, they can contribute to the common good.

Conversely, when young people are viewed as a cost to civic society, for example through anti-social behaviour, their negative conduct tends to be more quickly noticed. This portrays youth as mad, bad or sad rather than in a positive light, which is strength based (Hoghughi, 1999; Saleeby, 1996). Put more bluntly, it is argued here that even for young people who have significant problems, they can contribute to civic good. Their positive actions, apart from benefiting others, can be a way they help themselves as well. Thus, through participation in civic action, a positive connection between what a youth needs and their deeds can be created. For example, many youth who live in fragile states or countries in conflict function in a context of violence as a method for survival. However, UN programmes (UNICEF, 2007) focus successfully on deterring youth from soldiering by engaging them in humane and peaceful civic activities. Bartone (2006) has shown that in a conflict state, there are six key stressors, which can impair any person, young or old:

1. Isolation
2. Ambiguity
3. Powerlessness
4. Boredom
5. Danger
6. Workload

These stressors, however, can be counteracted to enable resilience via more positive participation in society. For youth living in fragile states, civic activity has strong meaning and can activate protective factors. Known benefits of youth civic programmes include building a young person's sense of belonging, mastery, independence and generosity (Hill, McGuire, Parker, & Sage, 2009).

Mastery, Generosity, Belonging and Independence

For youth in need of support, specific benefits accrue from their social and/or political civic engagement. First, through new social network relationships resulting from community civic action, friendships emerge that can become future sources of help and support, which assist coping. To date, however, much of the focus on youth civic engagement has focused on individual leadership by young people and only in the context of general youth populations (Van Linden & Fertman, 1998). Civic action by children and youth from vulnerable populations such as those with a disability needs to be further explored. For example, Chaskin, Brown, Venkatesh, and Vidal (2001) highlight the potential of community capacity building through combined civic action by youth across generations. They suggest that this can have the multiple benefits of enabling resilience for the community as a whole as well as for its individual constituents. This implies the need for a wider view of the four well-established benefits of youth civic action, namely mastery, belonging, generosity and independence, all aspects of resilience and all important factors when considering service design.

Mastery

For any individual, mastery relates to having command (or the perception of it) of some subject or activity, and is usually associated with an acquired skill and knowledge, which induces positive self-perception (Neff et al., 2007). Self-confidence and self-efficacy are key factors in the process of establishing ongoing resilience (Rutter et al., 1998) in youth. Conversely, poor self-esteem can accelerate on-going risk factors that impair development and adjustment. Thus, seen as an acquisition, mastery enables youth to be in a position to offer advice on how to do something or provide practical skills to others. This donation in turn can lead to enhanced social networks for those young people who donate their skills

and, reciprocally, to a greater supply of support from others if and when required.

Mastery can also bring with it the benefit of having a positive incremental effect on the individual in terms of building capacity to become more resilient. In part, this is achieved by helping others over time, as when a youth participates in a team sport or passes on a skill to a younger sibling (Klau, 2006). However, mastery can also result in the development of negative talents, as is often the case when youth develop criminal capital through incarceration (Youth Justice Board UK, 2005).

Belonging

It has been argued by Flanagan and Nakesha (2001) that one of the main benefits of civic engagement for any individual regardless of age is that it brings an accompanying sense of belonging and enhanced community membership. Through positive civic activities, youth can develop a sense of being part of a team, or having a purpose. This occurs regardless of whether the actions are related to political or social causes. Research by Chae et al. (2007) for the World Bank and UNICEF found strong benefits for youth from their positive engagement in local communities in post-conflict situations. Under these conditions, young people can when mentored become community actors demonstrating positive and strong leadership. Chae et al. found that by being civic actors, young people develop "a sense of affiliation and commitment to their community" (p. 3). Importantly, just as the concepts of social support and resilience should not be viewed individualistically, the development of a sense of belonging to community should be seen as a wider but equally important outcome of youth civic action.

Generosity

Another strong connector for individual youth positive civic interactions and social support accrues through the development of generosity.

The potential of youth civic engagement to enhance a youth's sense of altruism or capacity to "do good rather than harm" has been identified in the youth leadership literature (Van Linden & Fertman, 1998). However, it is often the lack of opportunity rather than lack of interest that impairs such provision of generosity through youth social civic action. This shortage of opportunity was highlighted as far back as the 1960s by youth programmes such as the Winthrop Project in the United Kingdom, which sought to redress this fact by targeting the development of altruism in youth as an antidote to anti-social behaviours (Dolan, 2010).

Secondly, the development of altruism in young people is often seen as only having value into the future. Youth are members of society and already contribute very positively in their own right to everyday life (Catalano, Hawkins, Berglund, Pollard, & Arthur, 2002). This view is further reinforced by Article 12 of the United Nations Convention on the Rights of the Child (UNCRC, 1990), which establishes positive "participation" by children and youth as a human right. So given that altruism in young people is or should be more than an aspiration, it is suggested here that opportunities that enable their civic action, particularly among vulnerable young people, can have added and immediate benefits (UNESCO).

Independence

During adolescence, independence from kin and community is seen as key normative milestones in the maturation process (Coleman & Hendry, 2009; Feldman & Elliot, 1993). Such autonomy is typified by increased contact with and usage of friendships, more engagement in school and extra-curricular activity, less dependency on parents (although increasingly this does not apply to financial dependence among youth in a first world) and by living away from home. While for many young people and their parents, this process is sequential and not particularly stressful, for some youth it can be tumultuous, particularly where there are other underlying difficulties in their family relationships or school-related problems.

Fertman and Long (1990) indicate that as a side product of his/her civic action including the attainment of new social networks ties unconnected to home, a young person can develop the requisite skills, which can assist independent living and coping. Neff et al. (2007) also suggest that the development of appropriate opportunities for independence can assist young people enhance their capacity for "self-compassion" even where there exists adversity in the young person's life. This suggests that civic engagement actions by youth can smooth the pathway towards independence.

Towards a Connecting Construct

It is proposed here that where youth want to be positively civically engaged and active on issues and projects, either political or social, that interest and motivate them, they will require their communities to provide them with opportunities to experience engagement. When such opportunities are provided, youth will respond, though not always with the support of adults and informal community sources. Over time, the benefits to young people include their capacity for mastery and accomplishment, generosity through altruism, a growth in capacity to be independent and their increased sense of belonging.

Furthermore, such civic action is likely to enable their having better social support, which in turn has a known connection to better well-being and mental health. Such social support is most powerful where it is perceived as hidden or discrete, and where natural networks are opened up to facilitate access to convoyed help. These conditions for enhancing social support can be made available as a product of civic action. Accomplishment through leadership by young people also supports their capacity to be resilient to stress by enhancing existing or enabling protective factors. Civic activity is associated with improving a young person's sense of self-efficacy by focusing away from problems of self towards the needs of others.

Apart from personal benefits to youth, this action can ultimately lead to gains for their family, school and wider community, as they demonstrate their capacity to be civic actors in these contexts.

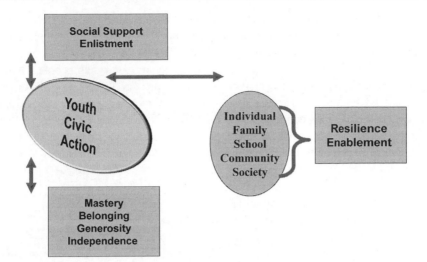

Fig. 28.1 Interconnecting youth civic action and resilience

Over time, this can lead to better democracies in terms of both human and economic social capital by building young citizens who are creative, confident and caring. This interconnected conduit from youth civic action to resilience is illustrated in Fig. 28.1.

Contexts for Youth

To demonstrate the potential of this tentative conceptual model, three scenarios involving youth are now described. These are considered from the perspective of individual youth, school and wider community contexts to highlight the importance of resilience as an ecological and contextual concept, and for similar aspects of both social support and civic engagement and action.

Context 1: Young Carers

It could be argued that young carers (youth who care for family members, often their parent(s) and/or a family member with a disability) are "hidden" in that they provide help in private homesteads and receive little attention. For example, research in Ireland (Fives & Kennan, 2010) highlights a lack of acknowledgement of the contributions and personal sacrifice of young carers to their families, communities and civic

society. Apart from the considerable personal cost to the young person in terms of educational and social opportunity loss, their civic action is generally not recognised. For youth who act as carers in the home, if they were displaying the same altruism in the community as part of a formal programme, they would be recognised as youth leaders.

The nature of the support they provide as carers is both tangible and emotional and operates at the individual and familial levels. It can be easily seen that while there is a risk of their being overburdened as carers, the main benefit for them as youth is their ongoing capacity to cope and to be or become generous and retain a strong sense of belonging. This process in part assists youth by keeping the focus from their own problems. As donors of help, young carers obviously benefit their immediate family, but they also provide hidden support to extended family and the wider civic state who would otherwise have to provide the service offered by the young carer.

Context 2: Peer Mentors

School mentors offer support by providing youth with regular advice and emotional support (Rhodes & Lowe, 2008). Although somewhat more limited in its success than community-based mentoring, school-based programmes have been found to have benefits for both the mentor and mentee (Hamilton & Hamilton, 1992). In practical terms, having a peer mentor helps to reduce the risk of school bullying and can help youth gain mastery through common interests.

Where effective peer school mentoring programmes also have a positive influence is in the help, they make accessible for the mentee through the mentor's network. For example, although a young person might have few friends, getting to know and accessing the friends of the school mentor, the young person has new opportunities to prosper. Through mastery and convoyed support, mentees can also gain a better sense of belonging in their school environment which can assist learning. Importantly, where both the mentor and mentee live near the school, there can be a positive and informal spillover effect where help from the mentor continues to positively influence the life of the mentee in the community setting.

Context 3: Youth Leaders

Youth leadership and citizenship programmes provide a range of opportunities for young people to serve their community. Typically, youth leadership programmes focus on the potential of young people to serve as individual leaders while citizenship programmes are concerned more with groups of youth working together offering tangible assistance on social or environmental issues. Such citizenship projects can be quite diverse, ranging from local community cleanup expeditions to the provision of regular hot meals to vulnerable older people living in the locality. In both leadership and citizenship contexts, the benefits to youth themselves as a result of their civic action are multiple, and include the creation of new social ties with peers and those whom they serve.

Importantly, such programmes, which are typically task focused, also produce a by-product of enabling support exchange between young people. Where available, such support can occur either as part of everyday living or as emergency help in the context of a sudden crisis. Citizenship programmes also enable youth to increase their sense of altruism as part of their personal development.

As citizenship takes place outside of the environs of home and school, it can contribute to the process of independence and personal growth among youth. Finally, for young people who do not particularly prosper in school or have difficulty at home, community citizenship provides them with a new and different site to demonstrate a capacity to be successful as a civic actor. It is this change in personal view which can also contribute to their resilience.

Conclusion

This chapter has explored the connection between the social support landscapes of youth, their capacity to be or become resilient and youth civic engagement and action. These concepts have been presented as a connected triad of factors, which play a positive role in the lives of youth generally and in particular for those who experience adversity. It has been shown that support through reciprocal helping can assist in creating supportive relationships and the capacity to be and stay resilient during the process of adolescence. The role of civic engagement as a source of mastery, belonging, independence and altruism has been highlighted in these contexts. Importantly, the positive potential of civic action for coping in everyday living as well as its transferability from individual youth to their family, school, community and society has been outlined.

Finally, rather than stating that social support through youth civic action is a panacea, which will guarantee resilience, it is suggested here that this represents untapped promise, which needs further testing. To fulfil this potential for youth, more knowledge needs to be generated on how the relationship between the three concepts connect and when and where they work best.

References

Bartone, P. T. (2006). Resilience under military operational stress: Can leaders influence hardiness? *Military Psychology, 18*(Suppl), S131–S148.

Bolger, N., & Amarel, D. (2007). Effects of social support visibililty on adjustment to stress: Experimental evidence.

Journal of Personality and Social Psychology, 92(3), 458–475.

Catalano, R. F., Hawkins, J. D., Berglund, M. L., Pollard, J. A., & Arthur, M. W. (2002). Prevention science and positive youth development: Competitive or cooperative frameworks. *Journal of Adolescent Health, 31*(6 Suppl), 230–239.

Chae, S., Taylor, R., Douglas, A., Stroud, S., Hutter, K., McDowell, C., et al. (2007). *Service as a strategy: A visionary strategy for post-conflict recovery*. USA: World Bank.

Chaskin, R. J., Brown, P., Venkatesh, S., & Vidal, A. (2001). *Building community capacity*. New York: Aldine de Gruyter.

Cobb, S. (1976). Presidential Address-1976. Social support as a moderator of life stress. *Psychosomatic Medicine, 38*, 300–314.

Coleman, J. C., & Hendry, L. B. (2009). *The nature of adolescence* (3rd ed.). New York: Routledge.

Connolly, M. (2004). *Child & family welfare: Statutory responses to children at risk*. Christchurch: Te Awatea Press.

Cotterell, J. (1996). *Social networks and social influences in adolescence*. London: Routledge.

Cutrona, C. E. (2000). Social support principles for strengthening families: Messages from the USA. In J. Canavan, P. Dolan, & J. Pinkerton (Eds.), *Family support: Direction from diversity* (pp. 103–122). London: Jessica Kingsley Publishers.

Dolan, P. (2008). Social support, social justice and social capital: A tentative theoretical triad for community development. *Journal of the Community Development Society, 39*(1), 112–119.

Dolan, P. (2010). Youth civic engagement and support: Promoting well-being with the assistance of a UNESCO Agenda. In C. McAuley & W. Rose (Eds.), *Child well-being: Understanding children's lives* (pp. 111–125). London: Jessica Kingsley Publishers.

Dryfoos, J. G., Quinn, J., & Barkin, C. (2005). *Community schools in action: Lessons from a decade of practice*. Oxford: Oxford University Press.

Feldman, G. R., & Elliot, S. S. (1993). Capturing the adolescent experience. In G. R. Feldman & S. S. Elliot (Eds.), *At the threshold: The developing adolescent* (pp. 1–15). Cambridge: Harvard University Press.

Fertman, C. I., & Long, J. A. (1990). All students are leaders. *School Counsellor, 37*(5), 391–396.

Fives, A., & Kennan, D. (2010). *Study of young carers in the Irish population*. Research report commissioned by the Office of the Minister for Children and Youth Affairs, Republic of Ireland, Government of Ireland Publications, Stationery Office Dublin.

Flanagan, C., & Nakesha, F. (2001). Youth civic development: Implications of research for social policy and programs. *Social Policy Report, 15*(1), 3–14.

Ghate, D., & Hazel, N. (2002). *Parenting in poor environments: Stress, support and coping*. London: Jessica Kingsley Publishers.

Gilligan, R. (2009). *Promoting resilience: A resource guide on working with children in the care system*

(2nd ed.). London: British Association for Adoption and Fostering.

Hamilton, S. F., & Hamilton, M. A. (1992). Mentoring programs: Promise and paradox. *Phi Delta Kappan, 73*, 546–550.

Hawkins, R. L., & Maurer, K. (2010). Bridging, bonding and linking: How social capital operated in New Orleans following Hurricane Katrina. *British Journal of Social Work, 40*(6), 1777–1793.

Hill, L., McGuire, J., Parker, L., & Sage, R. (2009). *4-H healthy living literature review and recommendations for program planning and evaluation*. USA: National 4-H Council.

Hoghughi, M. (1999). Troubled and troublesome: Perspectives on adolescent hurt. In B. Tizard & V. Verma (Eds.), *Vulnerability and resilience in human development: A Festchrift for Ann and Alan Clarke* (pp. 217–232). London: Jessica Kingsley Publishers.

Klau, M. (2006). Exploring youth leadership in theory and practice. *New Directions for Youth Development, 109*, 57–87.

Levitt, M. J. (2005). Social relations in childhood and adolescence: The Convoy model perspective. *Human Development, 48*, 28–47.

Neff, K. D., Rude, S., & Kirkpatrick, K. L. (2007). An examination of self-compassion in relation to positive psychological functioning and personality traits. *Journal of Research in Personality, 41*, 908–916.

Pinkerton, J., & Dolan, P. (2007). Family support, social capital, resilience and adolescent coping. *Child & Family Social Work, 12*, 219–228.

Putnam, R. D. (2000). *Bowling alone: The collapse and revival of American community*. New York: Simon & Schuster.

Rhodes, J., & Lowe, S. R. (2008). Youth mentoring and resilience: Implications for practice. *Child Care in Practice. Special Issue: Building resilience in children, families and communities, 14*(1), 9–17.

Rutter, M., Giller, H., & Hagel, A. (1998). *Antisocial behaviour by young people*. Cambridge: Cambridge University Press.

Saleeby, D. (1996). The strengths perspective in social work practice: Extensions and cautions. *Social Work, 41*(3), 296–305.

Tierney, J., Grossman, J., & Resch, N. (1995). *Making a difference: An impact study of Big Brothers Big Sisters of America*. Philadelphia: Public Private Ventures.

Tracy, E., & Whittaker, J. (1990). The social network map: Assessing social support in clinical practice. *Families in Society, 71*(8), 461–470.

UNESCO. *United Nations Education Science and Cultural Organisation, Global Strategy on Youth 2009–2013*.

Ungar, M. (2004). The importance of parents and other caregivers to the resilience of high-risk adolescents. *Family Process, 43*(1), 23–41.

Ungar, M. (2008). Resilience across cultures. *British Journal of Social Work, 38*(2), 218–235.

UNICEF. (2007). *Child poverty in perspective: An overview of child well-being in rich countries*. Florence: Innocenti Research Centre Report Card 7.

United Nations. (1990). *United Nations Convention on the Rights of the Child*. New York: UN Publications.

Van Linden, J. A., & Fertman, C. I. (1998). *Youth leadership: A guide to understanding leadership development in adolescents*. San Francisco: Jossey-Bass Publishers.

Whittaker, J. K. (2009). Evidence-based intervention and services for high-risk youth: A North American perspective on the challenges of integration for policy, practice and research. *Child & Family Social Work, 14*(2), 166–177.

Youth Justice Board for England and Wales. (2005). *A summary of risk and protective factors associated with youth crime, and effective interventions to prevent it*. London: Youth Justice Board for England and Wales.

Part VII

Culture

Understanding Culture, Resilience, and Mental Health: The Production of Hope

Catherine Panter-Brick and Mark Eggerman

Resilience research is increasingly attentive to social contexts and developmental processes, beyond the study of individual attributes shaping better-than-expected health outcomes in the face of adversity. This attention to "social ecology" (see Ungar, 2011b) and to contextual variation across social space and temporal specificity introduces noteworthy complexity in the conceptualization, measurement, and promotion of resilience. Assessing social ecologies presents a particularly challenging task for researchers and policymakers who work across cultures, especially for those who work in conflict and humanitarian settings with children and families affected by violence, displacement, poverty, and insecurity. In this chapter, we offer a specific example of mixed-methods, longitudinal research from work conducted in Afghanistan, to chart a journey between broad conceptual frameworks and practical field-work applications. We show how a transdisciplinary framework integrating quantitative and qualitative methodologies helps to better contextualize adversity, trauma, violence, and resilience in the context of everyday lives. It also helps to evaluate how and why culture matters for resilience, and identify the social and cultural milestones that prove to be significant "turning points" for health and well-being. In this chapter, we examine the intersection of structural resilience

and psychosocial resilience in terms of how the fabric of a society impacts individual mental health trajectories.

Social Ecology, Turning Points, and Resource Provision

Social resilience research aims to develop a robust theoretical framework and a relevant body of empirical evidence pertaining to health in the face of adversity. This is because the "central mission" of resilience research is to use scholarship to derive "critical ingredients" for effective interventions to maximize life chances and healthy development (Luthar & Brown, 2007). Our understanding of resilience has certainly become more sophisticated. A decade ago, in the child development literature, resilience was conceptualized as a "dynamic process encompassing positive adaptation within the context of significant adversity" (Luthar, Ciccheti, & Becker, 2000). In 2000, a major theoretical breakthrough thus consisted in conceptualizing the construct of resilience as an interactional process between individuals and their environments, rather than as the mere presence or absence of fixed individual-level attributes. Given significant adversity such as poverty and social marginalization, resilience was to be measured as different *socio-ecological levels* of a child's interactions with family, community, and society – a focus on material and social interactions in multi-layered contexts. This demanded attention to the variation observed in

C. Panter-Brick (✉)
Department of Anthropology and Jackson Institute for Global Affairs, Yale University, New Haven, CT 06511, USA
e-mail: catherine.panter-brick@yale.edu

M. Ungar (ed.), *The Social Ecology of Resilience: A Handbook of Theory and Practice*,
DOI 10.1007/978-1-4614-0586-3_29, © Springer Science+Business Media, LLC 2012

developmental processes, through trajectories of time as well as boundaries of space. It also focused attention on the sets of resources that shape variation in social and developmental pathways, toward enhanced or compromised health outcomes. This understanding of resilience captured a more sophisticated understanding of child health and development as processes of adaptation, accommodation, recovery, and resistance to adversity (Layne, Waren, Watson, & Shalev, 2007).

Understanding social ecology and measuring developmental processes is, however, easier said than done. To-date, in 2011, the challenge for social resilience research is to identify the kinds of relational processes that really matter, at what given points in an individual's development, in what context and culture, impacting what particular features of positive outcome (Ungar, 2011a). To phrase this a little differently, we have to grasp salient *tipping or turning points* – where, how, and when to focus policy and intervention efforts in effective and sustainable ways to change aspects of material, social, and emotional ecologies that impact health. This area of investigation is where the research agenda will meet the policy agenda, and where consolidation of theoretical and empirical knowledge is still to be made. For instance, Ungar (2011a) has convincingly argued that the discourse of resilience is now positioned *"as one of process and resource provision."* Rather than focus on individual attributes (based on an understanding of how individuals succeed despite the odds stacked against them), an ecological understanding of resilience will focus attention on the social and material contexts that shape individual trajectories (based on evidence of how supportive environments help individuals navigate and negotiate their way to resources that sustain well-being). As a first step, resilience research needs to examine why and how people respond differently to adversity.

As argued by Rutter (2011), research on resilience is not a matter of relabeling the existing body of work on risk and protective factors, or existing notions of competence and coping – this would simply trivialize research of public health importance. A starting point of resilience research is to recognize the "huge heterogeneity in the response to all manner of environmental hazards, physical, and psychological," leading to a systematic investigation of the specifics of different responses and a broader range of causal processes – this includes turning point effects (such as schooling, marriage, or employment), which provide opportunities to "knife off a disadvantaged past" (Rutter, 2011, p. XX). Thus a key emphasis of resilience research is to contextualize developmental and social trajectories, identifying what critical changes need to be made in the social, educational, and material environments to turn individual trajectories toward more favorable health outcomes. Contexts and resource provision are of central importance to turning points fostering trajectories of resilience.

Measuring and Evaluating Resilience Across Contexts

Measuring resilience, namely how we operationalize rather than conceptualize this construct is also a challenge. Luthar and Brown (2007) have rightly emphasized that resilience research requires integrated levels of inquiry, namely a transdisciplinary perspective on the ontological, biological, and social dimensions of health and well-being. To ground such a necessary, ambitious, and comprehensive analytical effort, they offer a "hard core" tenet of resilience theory, a central postulate that boils down the simple point that "relationships lie at the 'roots' of resilience" (p. 947). To validate this tenet across different contexts would mean testing the proposition that the "major antecedents or predictors of resilience" arc largely similar across time and place, such that "when everyday relationships reflect abuse, rancor, and insecurity this profoundly threatens resilience" while conversely relationships based on love, comfort, and security foster resilience and recovery in ways that can be measured both biologically and behaviorally. This requires "multi-level analyses of youth competence, and careful understanding of their experiences in the context of family." It also requires attention to "relationships-based interventions" (p. 947) as the most promising turning points to modify risk factors and strengthen protective factors, tipping individual trajectories toward better outcomes.

Few examples of transdisciplinary research on resilience exist in non-Western settings. One emerging body of work is found in the field of mental health and psychosocial support in humanitarian settings. This field bridges research and humanitarian work in transcultural psychiatry, social work, and social and economic family and community-building. In particular, the Inter-Agency Standing Committee guidelines on mental health and psychosocial support in humanitarian settings (IASC, 2007) represent a concerted effort to put together a package of care to systematically address a range of needs for vulnerable individuals and families as well as build upon the specific strengths of affected communities. This has led Jordans et al. (2010), among others, to propose a model of a multilayered psychosocial care system, components of which have been tested in war-affected low-and middle-income countries with promising results (Tol, Komproe, Susanty, Jordans, Macy, & De Jong, 2008). Such a package consists in a multi-layered provision for providing mental health and psychosocial support, to address both the clinical needs of individuals and the broader needs of community revitalization. This care package works across health, education, social welfare, and economic sectors – it comprehensively addresses the social ecology of mental health and is likely to have sustainable impact where integrated into existing community and government systems (Weiss, Saraceno, Saxena, & Van Ommeren, 2003).

Research on mental health in humanitarian settings is still, however, dominated by a paradigm narrowly focused on individual responses to trauma; consequently, our understanding of a social ecology of resilience is only, as Ungar (2011a) argues, nascent. Over the last decade, to quote Layne et al. (2007), the fields of developmental psychopathology and traumatic stress research have been replete with basic studies investigating a "shopping list" (p. 508) of risk and protective factors, with little understanding of the intervening variables that mediate or moderate pathways of influence. Consequently,

"the knowledge base of interventionists is invariably limited to a comparatively static list of variables that discriminate between 'resilient' and 'nonresilient' groups" (p. 501). This type of evidence leads to largely vacuous recommendations, limited to interventions at comparatively superficial levels, based on known attributes such as "be resourceful," "have a sense of mastery and self-efficacy," or "talk to a friend" (p. 508). The real challenge is to conduct more theoretically-informed and meaningful research on the "*how*, *why*, and *when* the mechanisms and processes that underlie positive adaptation in stressful contexts operate." Specifically, trajectories of resilience are different from those of resistance to stressors: resilient individuals are responsive to adverse events but "flex back" to full recovery, as measured by indicators of mental health and social functioning, whereas individuals displaying resistance to stressors show little perturbation of functioning. This is a more sophisticated understanding, based on prospective rather than cross-sectional data, of the heterogeneity of mental health trajectories in response to adverse exposures.

A Social Ecology of Resilience in Conflict Settings

The most commonly used theoretical framework to organize risk and protective factors impacting child health and development is one that draws on the early work on Bronfenbrenner: his 1979 model posited nested levels of influence, ranging from individual (ontogenic) domains to micro-level (family, peer, school), meso/exo-level (neighborhood), and macro-level (society and culture) domains (Bronfenbrenner, 1979). Recent systematic reviews of the literature have used this conceptual framework to bridge major gaps between scientific evidence and policy-making pertaining to war-affected children (Tol, Jordans, Kohrt, Betancourt, & Komproe, in press) and forcibly-displaced children (Reed, Fazel, Jones, Panter-Brick, & Stein, 2011). One example of an ecological resilience framework summarizing risk and protective factors for children affected

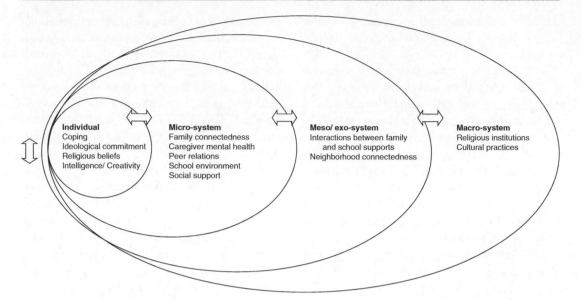

Fig. 29.1 A social ecological framework for resilience for children in conflict settings, from Tol et al. (in press). *Arrows* indicate interactive processes across systems. The societal and cultural blueprint of resilience at macro-level is less well understood than resources at individual, family, and neighborhood levels

by political violence is shown in Fig. 29.1. All literature reviews in this field have noted "the relative paucity of research that explores predictor variables beyond the individual domain and the relative neglect of other variables in tracing causal associations, including potential mediators and moderators identifiable in longitudinal work" (Reed et al., 2011).

Appraisal of mediators and moderators is critically important for resilience research. The former are the active ingredients in causal pathways, such as direct exposure to violence leading to mental health psychopathology. The latter are variables that modify the strength or direction of pathways, such as gender, parental well-being, or social support. Quantitatively, to demonstrate their impact requires longitudinal rather than cross-sectional data, and sophisticated multi-level and latent growth modeling rather than simple regression analyses. This has been rarely attempted in conflict-settings, although a good example of this is found in Hobfoll et al.'s work modeling resilience as the "conservation of resources" in the face of adversity (Hobfoll & Lilly, 1993; Hobfoll et al., 2009). One powerful way to test

the impact of potential mediators and moderators on mental health trajectories is to implement a treatment study targeting those active ingredients thought to promote resilience. To our knowledge, only one intervention study has tested the mediators and moderators of a school-based psychosocial intervention for children affected by political violence, using a cluster randomized controlled trial in Indonesia (Tol et al., 2010). In that study, ecological resilience was operationalized through measures of hope, coping, and social support, measures intended to capture strengths and capabilities that could potentially mediate associations with posttraumatic stress and social functioning. The class-based psychosocial intervention showed mixed results: there were just three groups (girls, children from smaller households, and children receiving support from adults outside the household) who did show postintervention improvement in outcomes. This would caution against simplistic expectations that an intervention aimed to increase strengths (e.g., social support) will always decrease mental health difficulties and unilaterally benefit all participants. The "why" and the "how" questions still loom large in resilience research, regarding the heterogeneity of responses to psychosocial treatment or "relationships-based" intervention.

To inform prevention and intervention efforts and reach a global consensus on key psychosocial action in the wake of disaster and mass violence, Hobfoll et al. (2007) have identified five empirically-supported principles, akin to the active ingredients mentioned above, for effective intervention. These include the following: promoting a sense of safety, calming, a sense of self- and community-efficacy, connectedness, and hope. The five key principles therefore focus attention on the kinds of *resource provision* that promote or maintain a sense of agency and sense of coherence. Yet few studies have been able to demonstrate, with any depth, how these five constructs are articulated in the everyday life of people affected by war or disasters. The challenge here is to integrate a social sciences evaluation of resources such as "hope," with epidemiological evidence that heterogeneous resource distribution impacts prospective changes in health outcomes.

Such work advances the field of global mental health away from "basic" toward more "sophisticated" studies of the pathways of resilience. Currently, quantitative analyses show a good grasp of individual-level variables and a fair understanding of social interaction variables that matter for resilience, measuring for example coping, social support, and social capital. Most, however, have not demonstrated a nuanced understanding of societal-level variables. This is hardly surprising, given the relative ease of measurement of proximate, individual-level risk factors, and the relative difficulty of measuring distal, macro-level variables such as culture and religion in quantitative research. Much of the literature invokes the importance of environment and culture in the singular, in ways that encompass all cultural, social, economic, and political facets of everyday life – brushing aside all heterogeneity of structural data into a fixed single datum. Thus we still know little of what Bronfenbrenner called the "societal blueprint" for a particular culture, with reference to the macro-system, or structure overarching the micro-, meso-, and exo-systems that influence human development. As Tol et al. (in press) pointed out in their review (p. 19), this societal blueprint is often conflated with a *cultural* blueprint that examines the cultural practices that shape risk and resilience. There is little appreciation of complexity at this level: in brief, "culture is perhaps the most neglected topic in the study of risk and resilience" (Feldman & Masalha, 2007, p. 2).

We do know that contexts potentiate the development of resilience, and that context is culturally, historically, and temporally embedded: the benchmarks of child development, social functioning, and everyday social practices are negotiable across cultures (Ungar, 2011a). Specifically, youth have their own constructions of resilience that differs across cultural contexts (Ungar, 2008). These rest upon social transactions and negotiated cultural consensus, which opens the way to culture being measured in quantitative ways as the governing logic in everyday social transactions (Dressler, 2005), with social stressors having a noteworthy impact on physiological manifestations of stress (Dressler, Balieiro, Ribeiro, & Dos Santos, 2007; Panter-Brick, Eggerman, Mojadidi, & McDade, 2008). The point is that culture and religion matter for resilience, but these are variables captured in social interactions rather than fixed attributes. When, why, and how culture and society matter for resilience are questions that remain difficult to answer: studies to-date are either predominantly epidemiological, or strictly ethnographic, finding it difficult to integrate a critical understanding of the societal blueprints of resilience with analyses of individual trajectories of health.

In summary, the above body of work highlights resource provision and social relationships as salient in the conceptualization, measurement, and promotion of resilient trajectories – but more sophisticated analyses of resilience are needed to better understand the macro-level, structural, and societal blueprints governing how people access resources to mitigate adverse circumstances. In the remainder of this chapter, we provide one example of child mental health research in Afghanistan, a longitudinal study designed to understand adversity, risk, and resilience in the wake of war and displacement. Integrating the field of epidemiology, transcultural psychiatry, and biocultural anthropology, this work sought to answer the following research questions: what does resilience mean in the contemporary Afghan context? What are drivers of psychosocial well-being and mental health in this setting? And from a social ecological framework of resilience, what turning points are scripted in this culture and what are the critical targets for intervention?

Adversity in Afghanistan

Afghan lives are nested in environments of social adversity and structural violence – their country has been afflicted by over three decades of armed conflict. Many young Afghans are growing up in environments marked by violence and deep-seated poverty – living and breathing a noxious combination of military conflict, economic stressors, gender discrimination, ethnic divisions, and widening social inequalities. Although it is unhelpful to portray the whole of Afghanistan as a war zone and its general population as deeply traumatized, it is true to state that violent conflict and population displacement has permeated the fabric of society and disrupted access to health care, steady employment, and formal education. For many outsiders, Afghanistan encapsulates the ongoing brutality of war, the misery of poverty, and the basic violation of many human rights. It is a country well-known for showing very poor, albeit improving, health, education, and socio-economic indicators (Oxfam, 2006) (Trani, Bakhshi, Noor, Lopez, & Mashkoor, 2010). In this context, "risks" to health are multiple, and multifaceted, as well as socially produced and perpetuated. Afghanistan serves as a case in point to exemplify some of the central precepts in the field of global health, namely that poor health is the product of human action or inaction, and that health differentials across populations are demonstrably unnecessary, avoidable, and unjust (Panter-Brick & Fuentes, 2010).

Afghan families, however, have demonstrated a striking fortitude in coping with political, social, and economic stressors that range from simply irksome everyday difficulties to traumatic life events. Where human-made and natural crises have been chronic, and state governance has had little clarity of purpose, the family has proven the only stable institution available to help provide a strong network for social support and economic advancement (Dupree, 2004). Families are the primary resource for structuring individual and collective life – and for structuring all instrumental aspects of the material and social ecologies relevant to child development, health, education, and social or economic advancement. In terms of fortitude in the face of long-term adversity, the people of Afghanistan could be held up as a prime example of collective resilience, an everyday resilience embedded in the social contexts of family and community networks.

How do these general points play out in the lives of actual people? From a research standpoint, what kind of evidence do we look for when characterizing or uncovering resilience? And from a policy or intervention standpoint, what kind of risks need to be addressed, and what kind of material, social, and cultural environments may be strengthened to promote health and well-being?

Interdisciplinary Research on Mental Health

We examined these issues in the context of conducting a large-scale survey on mental health and analyses of adversity and resilience. An interdisciplinary project was designed to weave together insights from the standpoint of biomedical and social sciences research, to document mental health, resilience, stress, suffering, and functioning from the perspectives of young people and their adult caregivers. At all stages of the research, social sciences analyses and epidemiological surveys informed one another. For example, we used extensive focus groups, expert panel reviews, and survey pilots to assess the face validity and construct reliability of mental health instruments and measures of psychosocial stressors, resources, and life events, following recommended procedures for cross-cultural work (van Ommeren, 2003). We used psychometric instruments recommended as brief and reliable measures of mental health in cross-cultural, low-income, or war-affected settings, and for adults, were able to corroborate a WHO-recommended internationally-used questionnaire with a culturally-specific questionnaire developed for Afghans in Kabul (Panter-Brick, Eggerman, Gonzalez, & Safdar, 2009). Preparation for this work took the better part of 2 years. In addition, we conducted a smaller-scale study in Kabul to evaluate whether self-reports of distress and frustration left biological signatures "under the skin," implementing a survey to map exposure to psychosocial stressors with levels of blood pressure and immune responses (Panter-Brick et al., 2008). For this study of the biocultural underpinnings of stress, we conducted focus groups with young adults and asked them to free-list their life goals and most irksome psychosocial stressors. We then implemented, with a random stressors and physiological biomarkers.

After all this preparation work, in 2006 we conducted the first systematic child mental health survey in Afghanistan, providing solid evidence regarding the range of mental health problems for young people in contemporary Afghanistan (Panter-Brick et al., 2009). We interviewed 1,011 children (age 11–16 years), as well as 1,011 caregivers, and 358 teachers, to assess the child's mental health and social functioning in the family and school environments, as well as the mental health of the primary caregiver. The qualitative work consisted of panel reviews to assess the face validity of measures and chosen instruments, as well as extensive face-to-face interviews with all participants to understand life stressors, trauma, and professed solutions (Eggerman & Panter-Brick, 2010b). We also conducted careful fieldwork evaluations to appraise local understandings of our work (Eggerman & Panter-Brick, 2010a). One year later, we undertook a follow-up study with 264 families in the Kabul area – logistic challenges and security conditions meant that we did not conduct the follow-up in other areas (Panter-Brick, Goodman, Tol, & Eggerman, 2011). The work was funded with an academic research grant from the Wellcome Trust, an independent sponsor. It was conducted with permission from the Ministry of Education in Afghanistan, in partnership with ALTAI, an independent Kabul-based research agency, and academics with expertise in child and adolescent psychiatry and social work from a number of western and local institutions.

The large-scale mental health survey was based in schools, which provided the best point of contact to draw a community-level sample, to access both male and female youth, and their male and female caregivers, and to provide a safe context for in-depth research activities. The security situation proved very volatile; during 2004, a local NGO withdrew support for the project because the vehicle transporting the female interviewers had returned after dark; during 2006, our project office was sprayed by gunfire during riots in Kabul; during 2007, suicide bombings in Kabul had become a significant threat. Working with schools made it possible for the field-team (three male and three female Dari/Pahstu interviewers, one translator, and a bilingual project manager) to take time, build trust, and obtain multiple measures of mental health and social functioning from a wide range of informants in order to assess a broad picture of Afghan lives according to age, generation, socioeconomic group, ethnicity, and rural–urban location. This was why schools were the best location to facilitate a complex protocol and face-to-face interviews with boy and girl students and male and female caregivers. Working in other locations, such as mosques or homes, was simply not possible if we wanted interview privacy. We were not able to access children who were kept out-of-school, because their families were too conservative, or too poor even to access state-provided education. Nationally, 64% of children 7–14 year-old (48% girls, 77% boys) were enrolled in school in 2004–2005 (Bakhshi & Trani, 2006).

To achieve a random sample of participants, we conducted a two-stage cluster sampling design. We selected three research areas, the central and northern municipalities of Kabul, Bamyan, and Mazar-e-Sharif, in which to work, as a deteriorating security situation did not make it possible to work in southern areas of the country. We listed all government-run schools in these municipalities, and randomly selected 10% of schools in each area, totalling just 25 schools for the target age-range, with probability sampling proportional to the size of the school and equivalence of boy/girl schools, to achieve representation across gender and geographical areas. We targeted older age groups (11–16 year olds), who because of curtailed education under the Taliban, might still be at primary rather than secondary school. We established class lists, and randomly sampled 40 students per school, the equivalent of 5% of students in the relevant class-grades. Students then contacted their principal caregiver (the adult primarily responsible for their everyday care), and asked them to come for an interview at the school. Participants engaged well in the research: children told us that this was the first time someone had ever asked them about their problems and difficulties; teachers told us this was the first time they had been asked to reflect on how children's psychological health might hamper their educational performance; our survey provided the first-ever opportunity for some women, from conservative families, secluded at home, to visit their children's school. In this way, we were able to survey a large, representative sample of Afghans, working with youth old enough to recount their own experiences, and with their adult caregivers.

Baseline Mental Health, Trauma, and Everyday Violence

Our baseline survey showed that one in five (22%) school-children in Afghanistan suffer from mental health problems in the clinical range (a probable psychiatric disorder, depression, or posttraumatic stress symptomology), with girls two-and-a-half times more likely to have disorders than boys (Panter-Brick et al., 2009). As measured by the Strength and Difficulties Questionnaire, which triangulates child, parent, and teacher ratings of the child's mental health difficulties and their actual impact on everyday functioning, this was twice the rate expected for children of this age-range (11–16 years). Children who had suffered five or more traumatic events were two-and-a-half times more likely to have ratings indicative of a psychiatric disorder, as well as three times more likely to report symp-

toms of posttraumatic stress, than those who had experienced four or less events. Caregiver mental health was correlated to the well-being of the children under their care: there was a 10% increase in the likelihood of child psychiatric disorder for each and every symptom of psychological distress reported by caregivers. Moreover, children living in Kabul were more likely to have a psychiatric disorder and symptoms of posttraumatic stress than those living in Bamyan or Mazar-e-Sharif.

Those findings signal that poor mental health is a significant issue for the next generation in Afghanistan. However, they also signal that a majority of children managed to function quite well according to ratings given by local respondents, both children and adults in the community, despite cumulative exposure to adversity entailing a toxic combination of sheer poverty, ongoing violence, family deaths, illness, debts, overcrowding, and forced displacement. One could conclude that 1 in 5 Afghan school-children were at risk of a probable mental health disorder, but that 4 in 5 children proved fairly resilient. We gathered strong evidence regarding risk factors for child mental health: gender, trauma exposure, caregiver well-being, and geographical area. Yet a firm understanding of resilience did not emerge from the epidemiological data based on associations with individual, family, and area-level variables; to achieve this, more in-depth qualitative analyses were needed.

One of the striking findings of this survey pertained to the nature of trauma, namely the broad range of violent and distressing experiences reported by youth. Trauma was not confined to acts of war, but reflected an ongoing exposure to social and economic stressors that manifested themselves in brutality or violence close to home. Thus children identified trauma events related to accidents, domestic beatings, violence in the neighborhood, and painful medical treatments, not just war-related injury, loss of relatives, and forced displacement. Thus it was not just war-related violence that created trauma in the lives of children, but violence at the level of family and community life, generated by the pressure of daily social and economic stressors

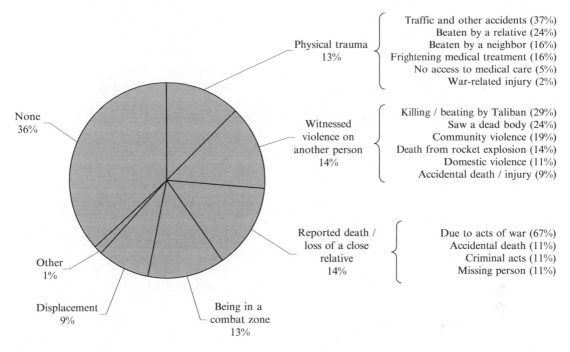

Fig. 29.2 Types of traumatic experiences reported by a random sample of 1,011 Afghan school-children (after Panter-Brick et al., 2009)

and uncertainties. Our data suggested that, in Afghan children's lives, "everyday violence" matters just as much as "militarized violence" in the recollection of traumatic experiences.

We reached this largely unexpected conclusion by integrating results from quantitative and qualitative methodologies (Fig. 29.2). We assessed exposure to traumatic events in a standard way, implementing a Traumatic Events Checklist, adapted from the Harvard Trauma Questionnaire and the Trauma Event Checklist used with Gaza adolescents, in order to systematically assess trauma events relevant to the lives of children in the Afghan context. We followed this standard Checklist with open-ended questions, asking respondents to contextualize specific trauma events, identify which lifetime event has been the most distressing, and articulate, in their own words, reasons why. The survey data ($n=1,011$ respondents) showed that 63.5% of children reported at least one traumatic event, while just 8.4% were exposed to five or more events in their lifetime (by contrast, 96% of adult caregivers reported exposure to at least one trauma).

Thus, Afghan children were remarkably good at discriminating traumatic from merely stressful life events. Most families were also very good at shielding children from traumatic experiences. The thematic categorization of trauma, based on the most distressing lifetime experience, showed that traumatic experiences were not solely contingent on war and displacement: they included trauma caused by individual accidents, family violence, and brutalities in the neighborhood.

The Social, Developmental, and Cultural Contexts of Individual Experiences

The thematic analyses of interview data provided a very large source of data on the social ecology of suffering and adversity (Eggerman & Panter-Brick, 2010b). The following two vignettes provide an example of the importance of contextual, subjective, and social experiences in the recollection of traumatic experiences. These are two examples of young people who described trauma events falling across a range of family, community, and military violence, but who prioritized a single event over all others in terms of psychosocial significance.

The first example is the narrative of a 16 year-old girl, who saw the beheaded body of her grandfather, "killed in a rocket attack in Kabul during the Taliban." Her father was also killed in a rocket attack. She described her close relatives as having been "martyred" (Dari: *shaheed*) as a result of the war – although they might have been civilian casualties, who were not directly engaged in combat. However, she identified as the most distressing event in her lifetime an operation to remove a lump in her right breast, for which she had been taken on a long bus journey to Pakistan 4 months earlier, to be operated upon by unfamiliar male surgeons. This happened just at the end of the school year: the operation prevented her from taking her final-year school exams. She would have to repeat the school year – particularly frustrating, given her ambition to go on to university and become a medical doctor, and also difficult to negotiate given social pressures to marry. Her drive to complete schooling was shaped by a sense of duty toward her parents, and her wish to improve her family's financial prospects; her 25-year-old brother was unemployed, living at home and addicted to opium. Her severe psychological distress was consistent with posttraumatic stress disorder.

It was Kleinman (2006) who asked the question "What really matters to ordinary people, in normal and extraordinary times, when living a life amidst uncertainty and danger?" He examined, through narratives, the moral dimension of heart-wrenching experiences, and posed the ultimate question of what "*should* really matter" (p. 231) as we "unearth the huge varieties of cultural meanings" when recounting subjective and social experiences. This girl was clearly wrought by an acute sense of failure and injustice. Her grief, with respect to the deaths of her father and her grandfather, could be articulated in terms of a socially-sanctioned ideology of martyrdom. However, she could make no sense of a lost year of schooling, given the anxiety and fear of being taken out of school before she could get a prized school-leaving certificate, as she attains marriageable age. In her words, she had lost "all I had ever worked for." What mattered, in this experience, was the wider impact of the operation: she had a physical, emotional, and social scar, due to a break in the scaffolding of her life – a rupture of meaning and moral order.

The second narrative is that of a 14 year-old boy in Kabul – born in 1992, the year the heavy fighting between Mujaheddin factions over control of the capital began. He had experienced ten different frightening, violent and/or distressing events over his lifetime. Seven of his close relatives had been killed in the wars, going back to the Communist period, and one of his brothers had been missing for the last 16 years. His mother had twice attempted suicide – and had suffered a miscarriage following a severe beating by his father. In addition, the boy had been knifed in the leg in a neighborhood fight, and had also had a run-in with the police, who had beaten him and jailed him for a day. Despite all these events, the boy identified his most distressing lifetime experience as a severe beating by his father 6 months earlier. He now wished "to escape from the house," and become a journalist. He was in love with a girl, his cousin, but knew this love would anger his parents if they ever found out. He expressed a desire to leave Afghanistan – to be in a place "where boys and girls can be together" – and he bluntly described the crux of his misfortune as "having been born in such a desolate, God-forsaken country." The boy was severely depressed, his emotional problems clearly rooted in fraught family life and macro-level social and cultural stressors.

Prospective Evidence on Mental Health Trajectories

Thus Afghans suffer ongoing forms of violence that are not necessarily confined to war: an exposure to *everyday and structural violence*, to contrast with exposure to militarized violence. This is a novel contribution to our understanding of child

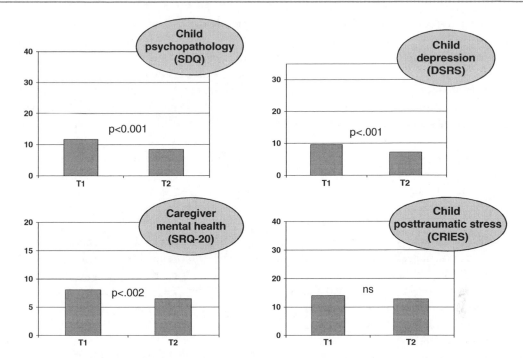

Fig. 29.3 Changes in mental health from baseline (T1) to follow-up (T2), for 234 school-children and 234 caregivers in Kabul (after Panter-Brick et al., 2011). Data are mean scores for (**a**) children: Strength and Difficulties Questionnaire (SDQ) total difficulties scores, rated by the caregiver or by the child; Depression Self-Rating Scale (DSRS); and Child Revised Impact of Events Scale (CRIES); and for (**b**) caregiver: Self-Report Questionnaire (SRQ-20). *P* values shown for one-year changes (two-tailed *t*-tests, corrected for clustering by school)

mental health in conflict zones: everyday suffering in the family and community context matters just as much as exposure to war-related violence. The weight of the evidence, here and elsewhere in the literature (Miller & Rasmussen, 2010), is that ongoing, everyday stressors – factors other than war-related violence, although linked to the social and economic upheaval of war – account for much of the psychological distress and mental health problems experienced by children. This means that we cannot focus attention on the most visible forms of violence, but need to understand how military, structural, and domestic violence are intertwined.

This insight into the everyday lives and experiences of civilian Afghan populations was then tested, quantitatively, with a follow-up survey, 1 year after baseline. Because of some formidable logistic and security problems, however, we undertook this second survey in Kabul only, and not in Bamyan and Mazar-e-Sharif. In Kabul, we could only trace 64% of children at school (other students had left school, and due to the absence of records regarding home addresses, all but 234 families were lost to follow-up); there was no evidence of attrition bias with respect to sample demographic, socioeconomic, or mental health characteristics (Panter-Brick et al., 2011). The same field team of interviewers implemented psychometric and trauma questionnaires with children and adult caregivers. In addition, we featured questionnaires specifically designed to tap past-year stressful life events and protective factors, to broaden the study beyond a focus on traumatic experiences.

We were surprised by the data: over a period of a year, child and adult mental health outcomes had improved for the cohort under study, for all measures except posttraumatic stress symptoms (Fig. 29.3). This improvement in mental health trajectories occurred in the absence of a dedicated mental health intervention, or even better political and economic security. In this follow-up, 234 families had managed to keep their children in their current school; among these, over the intervening-year, 45 moved home, 16 were threatened with eviction, 51 lost a wage-earner, and 178 incurred a substantial debt. Thus some families were able to anchor their adolescent children in school, despite incurring substantial debt, being afflicted by illness, being anxious about the surrounding violence, and confronting economic and cultural dictates to have adolescent boys earn money and adolescent girls to get married. In this context of poverty and insecurity, keeping children in school was an important indicator of fortitude in the face of material and social adversity. We concluded that: "In Afghanistan, the ability of families to maintain psychosocial and material resources, and particularly to remain geographically stable, economically robust, and socially supportive enough to keep near-adolescent boys and girls in school for yet another year, may capture an important facet of resilience" (Panter-Brick, et al., 2011, p. 360). Adults and children alike were focusing on school as the gateway to socioeconomic advancement, to alleviate economic stressors and to maintain family unity. In this sense, the follow-up sample consisted of families able to anchor their children in school, a significant expression of hope and resilience in a high-risk environment.

Strikingly, we found that violence inside the family was a critical predictor of prospective mental health, even in the context of exposure to extraordinary levels of collective violence. The quality of past-year family relationships was a key predictor of psychiatric mental health difficulties and depression: domestic violence, traumatic beatings, and family conflict predicted worse outcomes, while family "harmony and unity" (Dari: *ittifaq and wahdat*) – local terms meaning a sense of family connectedness – predicted better outcomes. Socioeconomic status and exposure to militarized violence had no impact on data variation. This is noteworthy, given that participants knew of suicide bombings that had resulted in the deaths of children on a school-trip, had witnessed suicide bomb attacks at bus stops/police stations, or seen the aftermath of such attacks. We concluded that proximate family environments were more salient than collective violence for their prospective impact on mental health outcomes measuring psychiatric and depressive burden. This was not the case for posttraumatic stress symptomology, which did not abate over the intervening year, and for which lifetime trauma exposure trumped all other risk and protective factors. This suggests distinct pathways of risk and resilience: different types of childhood adversities impact different sorts of trajectories for mental health and social functioning. The result is a complex picture that nonetheless points to the quality of family relationships being central to developmental resilience, as evidenced by better-than-expected prospective mental health outcomes.

Psychosocial and Structural Resilience

Afghan families articulated quite clearly the material, social, and political threats to mental health, as well as the psychosocial and structural dimensions of resilience. An everyday struggle for life was first and foremost expressed in terms of its material dimensions: as one father succinctly stated, "Lack of work is the root of all a man's miseries." For men, access to work was the root of personal dignity, and lack of work was the root of social misery. For women, lack of money meant that families had to crowd together in very small residential spaces, or live under tents in communal courtyards, which generated huge stressors, especially given cultural dictates on female seclusion; one woman flatly stated that she would rather go hungry than live without having her own home, meaning that she would not have to co-reside with her husband's extended family. Both adults and children spoke of a "broken economy" (Dari: *iqtisad kharab*), as the central driver of pain, violence, and misery. Thus, youth explained the occurrence of domestic violence in terms of the frustrations and strains engendered by material poverty. One 16-year old girl expressed this as follows: "My father's salary is not enough for us, he has *takleef asabi* [affliction of the nerves] and he beats us…. If he finds a decent job then maybe he will calm down." This statement is emblematic of narratives expressing economic drivers as the nexus of social suffering, with suffering engendering family-level violence and cascading from one generation to another.

The core reasons for psychosocial suffering were thus structural, regarding overwhelming economic impediments to physical, social, and emotional wellbeing. Another example shows how social aspirations and expectations are crushed by harsh material realities, leading in extreme cases, to attempted suicide. An 18-year old boy stated: "I'm the eldest son in my family. We've got six people in our home, and I am the only one working….. Because we have economic problems, my father forced me to quit school. So I swallowed rat poison after that, and I was in hospital for a week. They pumped my stomach out and I couldn't eat for nine days" (Eggerman & Panter-Brick, 2010b, p. 80). The statement shows how critical is the hope associated with access to education, perceived as the gateway to success.

The counterpoint to this discourse of suffering was a discourse of fortitude and resilience. Our thematic analyses of interviews with 1,011 children and 1,011 adults showed that families bring up their children to espouse six fundamental cultural values: religious faith, family unity and harmony, the obligation of service to family and community, perseverance or effort, good morals, and social respectability or honor (Eggerman & Panter-Brick, 2010b). These cultural values provided the bedrock of hope and resilience that gave order and promise to life. Resilience was most clearly expressed in this short statement by a 28-year old mother: "Life feeds on hope." Another expressed this sentiment as follows: "The only way to make life better is to be hopeful… If a person has hope, then he or she can work and acquire knowledge to make their life better" (Eggerman & Panter-Brick, 2010b, p. 76). Simply put, Afghans put their faith in the belief that hard work and effort can help them make life better. Their sense of hope is directed toward accessing the resources that will create social and economic opportunities for their family. Thus social hope is the bedrock of resilience.

Indeed, one of the most surprising aspects of this research was the expressions of hope in the midst of everyday suffering. For children, the height of their personal and social ambitions was well demonstrated in the drawings which students produced for this study. As part of rapport-building, before implementing the survey, we asked students to draw themselves in the present and in the future. Most students drew themselves in rags and tears in the present, and as excellent doctors, remarkable engineers, and dedicated teachers in the future. We reproduce here two drawings that clearly encapsulated hardship in the present, hope for the future, and demonstrate that while Afghan children may live in poverty, they do not show a poverty of aspiration.

The drawings of a 14-year-old girl, who attended a school catering to vulnerable social groups (street-children and war widows), provide a striking example of this hopeful orientation toward the future. She was the only breadwinner in her household, living from rag-picking and finding scrap plastics, before and after school, for resale in a junkyard. Her severely depressed mother stated that her greatest worry in life was to see her daughter grow up – because when puberty happened, she would not be able to send her into the streets to work. The girl drew herself in the present, and at a table with a microphone in the future, saying that she would be the first female newscaster at radio Kabul (Fig. 29.4). Such high hopes and aspirations, engendered by access to education, might well have been raised here to the point of illusion. Far more elaborate were the drawings of a 14-year-old boy, who attended an art class at his school (Fig. 29.5). He drew his great hardship in the present day: he worked, outside school hours, because his father was disabled and his three brothers were "martyred" in the war. In the future, his ambitions to be a doctor were a world away from his present circumstances, but he could picture his car, briefcase, and doctor's office in striking detail.

a

b

Fig. 29.4 Drawings by a 14-year old girl, portraying herself (**a**) in the present, and (**b**) in the future; she stated: "I want to be a painter, newscaster and actress"

Fig. 29.5 Drawings by a 14-year old boy, portraying himself (**a**) in the present, and (**b**) in the future; he writes: "I want to be an excellent doctor in the future." Reproduced from Eggerman and Panter-Brick (2010b, p. 79), with permission

Beyond Superficial Views of Culture: Social Entrapment

Despite the protective effect of cultural values that emphasized faith, effort, and family unity, young people also found themselves oppressed by cultural dictates governing their choices and life trajectories. This "entrapment" of cultural values, on the one hand, fostered resilience to everyday adversity, and on the other hand, it caused people to feel they were falling short of material and social expectations.

Afghan respondents described unfavorable consequences for how people live their lives according to their cultural values. Culture may be essential to forming one's social identity, sense of order, and hope for the future – but people suffered great psychological distress when they found themselves unable to conform to the high standards of "what makes an honorable Afghan." Adherence to Afghan cultural values could thus bring about intense hardships. Failure or frustration in attaining social and cultural milestones was articulated in local idioms of stress, anxiety, and depression, or conflicts that are debilitating and life threatening. In our published work, we drew on the notion of "social suffering" and "social hope" as crucial for understanding the complexities of living in a world where cultural values are necessary for survival, yet also lead to forms of oppression: we described culture as the anchor of resilience, but also as an anvil of pain (Eggerman & Panter-Brick, 2010b).

Understanding suffering on a social scale includes the consideration of structural factors that impact peoples' sense of well-being and material lives. In not fulfilling their cultural obligations, such as arranging a good marriage or securing a good job to achieve social and material status, young Afghan men and women become entrapped within a series of cultural standards that they are not always able to live up to. Afghan youth strove to bring themselves out of poverty, to work hard and obtain a good education, but simultaneously they had to provide service to their family, and leave school to obey cultural directives for girls to marry and boys to provide

financial support. They become entrapped within the system of cultural values that define their lives while struggling to cope with political violence, insecurity, and the structural violence engendered by everyday social stressors. Thus owning one's own home and holding down employment is a salient milestone in the context of forced displacement and a broken economy; getting married, begetting children, and providing service to one's family is another, given the importance of family as a social institution; accessing formal education, after the forced curtailment in the Taliban regime, is yet another precious goal, necessary to achieve economic and social standing in the Afghan context. Education, employment, timing of marriage, home ownership, these were the salient turning points to achieve the societal blueprint of social prominence, respectability and honor (Dari: 'izzat). For Afghans, these are the economic, social, and moral goals that underpin honor and self-respect.

Such life goals are not intrinsically different from the standard American set of "goods" and milestones that comprise the normative life course of youth in the US, the core elements of a "good enough" life (Worthman, in press). But in Afghanistan, there are huge impediments to achieving the outward manifestations of an "honorable life," given economic, social, legal, and political barriers to accessing resources and deep-seated gender and ethnic inequalities structuring resource provision. Furthermore, living an honorable or good enough life is a family matter rather than a personal objective: families are at once the most important sources of social support, and the most important sources of social pressure, in the pursuit of culturally-relevant milestones.

The Policy Aspects of Resilience

Many forms of violence and suffering arise from structural barriers and social entrapment. If young Afghans are to become more resilient to the challenges they face, we argue that a better understanding of social aspirations and resource provision is needed, both to alleviate suffering and to foster hope-building. How young people in Afghanistan cultivate resilience could be greatly assisted by listening to their accounts of their experiences.

Fostering psychosocial resilience would advance quicker with policies that address the structural determinants of risk and resilience. Afghans tell us of suffering engendered by ongoing political violence, frustration with the lack of economic momentum, a dearth of service infrastructure, poor governance, and fraught relationships played out at the family and community level. In the Afghan context, a culturally-relevant mental health intervention would be a structural intervention to strengthen families and sever the insidious linkages between political insecurity, economic instability, domestic crowding, and domestic violence that threaten well-being. These efforts would provide structural, social, and economic resources to families who struggle with everyday stressors. To accomplish this requires efforts to revitalize the economy to give dignity to men; providing better housing and reducing overcrowding which would make families feel more secure and alleviate considerable stressors for women; in schools, increasing the quality of education would help children thrive in an environment they greatly value, and in particular, paying teachers a decent wage which would mean they would not be compelled to hold down two jobs. Such interventions, focused on resource provision, would enhance a sense of safety, a sense of coherence, a sense of moral order, a sense of hope, and a sense of family connectedness – all of which are essential elements of intervention efforts (Hobfoll et al., 2007) and principles at the heart of mental health and psychosocial resilience. Specialized psychotherapy is needed for individuals with trauma-related problems such as posttraumatic stress disorder, while resource provision is needed to strengthen and revitalize communities, providing psychosocial support to individuals and families whose major problems are not solely the consequence of trauma (IASC, 2007). As emphasized by the recent WHO Commission for the determinants of health in conflict areas (WHO, 2008), what is important to advance global and local health-related agendas

is concerted action to address the structural causes that debilitate well-being.

Finally, our work leads us to emphasize an important ethical issue inherent in intervention efforts to "build hope" in humanitarian areas. In Afghanistan, a program of massive refugee repatriation promised hope to returnees, but largely disappointed their expectations (Turton & Marsden, 2002). A massive "Back to School" campaign was launched in 2001, after the fall of the Taliban regime, to provide hope for children and their families in the form of state-sponsored free education (Oxfam, 2006). As critiqued by Hage (2003), "searching for hope" brings disillusionment in societies where there is a shrinking configuration of social opportunities, widening inequalities, poor distribution of capital, and inequitable state policies. Our data show that hope for the future is central to resilience, but that access to school has raised aspirations to the point of certain disillusionment, as families anchor their children to school despite significant socioeconomic impediments, to achieve the promise of a school-leaving certificate, a good job, and socioeconomic advancement. Paying close attention to resource provision and social processes is important: social policies and intervention programs that build up hope and raise expectations must not promise more than they can deliver.

Conclusions

One great challenge for resilience research is to ensure that theory, methods, and interventions are sound in terms of their global reach and local relevance. In this chapter, we examined both the psychosocial and the structural dimensions of resilience. For general mental health what matters most is family connectedness, as measured by the local concept of family unity. For a sense of coherence pertaining to cultural and social trajectories, what matters most for resilience is the expression of social hope. Understanding the social and cultural milestones that matter for people in a specific cultural context helps us to understand the macro-level context of human development, and the specific milestones associated with risk and resilience.

The social ecology of resilience is best understood in terms of trajectory, a sense of meaning-making that orders the world and gives coherence to the past, present, and the future. In conflict zones, researchers are tempted to conceptualize and measure resilience as merely the absence of mental health problems despite exposure to significant trauma (Almedon, Evelyn, & Adam, 2010; Almedom & Glandon, 2007). This is a significant shortcoming, focusing as it does on the past as it affects the immediate present – a perspective that is peculiar to western, trauma-focused psychiatry. By contrast, an emic view of resilience in Afghan societal and cultural contexts is best captured by the expression of "life feeds on hope" (Eggerman & Panter-Brick, 2010b). This places the focus of attention squarely on the future, rather than the past, as it impacts psychosocial well-being in the here and now.

References

Almedom, A. M., Evelyn, A. B., & Adam, G. M. (2010). Identifying the resilience factor: An emerging counter narrative to the traditional discourse of "vulnerability" on "social suffering". In H. Bradbey & G. H. Hundt (Eds.), *Global perspectives on war, gender and health: The sociology and anthropology of suffering* (pp. 127–145). England: Ashgate.

Almedom, A. M., & Glandon, D. (2007). Resilience is not the absence of PTSD any more than health is the absence of disease. *Journal of Loss & Trauma, 12*(2), 127–143.

Bakhshi, P., & Trani, J. (2006). *Towards inclusion and equality in education? From assumptions to facts. National disability survey in Afghanistan 2005*. Lyon: Handicap International.

Bronfenbrenner, U. (1979). *The ecology of human development: Experiments by nature and design*. Cambridge: Harvard University Press.

Dressler, W. (2005). What's cultural about biocultural research? *Ethos, 33*(1), 20–45.

Dressler, W., Balieiro, M., Ribeiro, R., & Dos Santos, J. (2007). Cultural consonance and psychological distress: Examining the associations in multiple cultural domains. *Culture, Medicine and Psychiatry, 31*, 195–224.

Dupree, N. H. (2004). The family during crisis in Afghanistan. *Journal of Comparative Family Studies, 35*, 311–331.

Eggerman, M., & Panter-Brick, C. (2010a). Fieldwork as research process and community engagement. In J. McClancy & A. Fuentes (Eds.), *Fieldwork: Examining its practice* (pp. 137–155). Oxford: Berghahn.

Eggerman, M., & Panter-Brick, C. (2010b). Suffering, hope, and entrapment: Resilience and cultural values in Afghanistan. *Social Science & Medicine, 71*, 71–83.

Feldman, R., & Masalha, S. (2007). The role of culture in moderating the links between early ecological risk and young children's adaptation. *Development and Psychopathology, 19*, 1–21.

Hage, G. (2003). *Against paranoid nationalism: Searching for hope in a shrinking society*. London: Pluto Press.

Hobfoll, S., Watson, P., Bell, C., Byrant, R., Brymer, M., Friedman, M., et al. (2007). Five essential elements of immediate and mid-term mass trauma intervention: Empirical evidence. *Psychiatry, 70*(4), 283–315.

Hobfoll, S. E., & Lilly, R. S. (1993). Resource conversation as a strategy for community psychology. *Journal of Community Psychology, 21*, 128–148.

Hobfoll, S. E., Palmieri, P. A., Johnson, R. J., Canetti-Nisim, D., Hall, B. J., & Galea, S. (2009). Trajectories of resilience, resistance, and distress during ongoing terrorism: The case of Jews and Arabs in Israel. *Journal of Consulting Clinical Psychology, 77*(1), 138–148.

Inter-Agency Standing Committee. (2007). *Guidelines on mental health and psychosocial support in emergency settings*. Geneva: Inter-Agency Standing Committee.

Jordans, M., Tol, W., Komproe, I., Susanty, D., Vallipuram, A., Ntamatumba, P., et al. (2010). Development of a multi-layered psychosocial care system for children in areas of political violence. *International Journal of Mental Health Systems, 4*(15), 1–12.

Kleinman, A. (2006). *What really matters: Living a moral life amidst uncertainty and danger*. Oxford: Oxford University Press.

Layne, C., Waren, J., Watson, P., & Shalev, A. (2007). Risk, vulnerability. resistance, and resilience: Towards an integrative conceptualization of posttraumatic adaptation. In M. Friedman, T. Keane, & P. Resick (Eds.), *Handbook of PTSD* (pp. 497–520). London: Guilford Press.

Luthar, S., Cicchetti, D., & Becker, B. (2000). The construct of resilience: A critical evaluation and guidelines for future work. *Child Development, 71*(3), 543–562.

Luthar, S. S., & Brown, P. J. (2007). Maximizing resilience through diverse levels of inquiry: Prevailing paradigms, possibilities, and priorities for the future. *Development and Psychopathology, 19*, 931–955.

Miller, K. E., & Rasmussen, A. (2010). War exposure, daily stressors, and mental health in conflict and post-conflict settings: Bridging the divide between trauma-focused and psychosocial frameworks. *Social Science & Medicine, 70*(1), 7–16.

Oxfam. (2006). *Free, quality education for every Afghan child*. Oxford: Oxfam International. Retrieved 1 August 2011, from www.unicef.org.

Panter-Brick, C., Eggerman, M., Mojadidi, A., & McDade, T. (2008). Social stressors, mental health, and physiological stress in an urban elite of young Afghans in Kabul. *American Journal of Human Biology, 20*, 327–641.

Panter-Brick, C., Eggerman, M., Gonzalez, V., & Saftar, S. (2009). Violence, suffering, and mental health in Afghanistan: A school-based survey. *The Lancet, 374*, 807–886.

Panter-Brick, C., & Fuentes, A. (2010). Health, risk, and adversity. In C. Panter-Brick & A. Fuentes (Eds.), *Health, risk, and adversity*. New York: Berghahn Books.

Panter-Brick, C., Goodman, A., Tol, W., & Eggerman, M. (2011). Mental health and childhood adversities: A longitudinal study in Kabul, Afghanistan. *Journal of the American Academy of Child & Adolescent Psychiatry, 50*(4), 349–363.

Reed, R., Fazel, M., Jones, L., Panter-Brick, C., & Stein, A. (2011). The mental health of refugee and internally displaced children. Part I: A systematic review of risk and protective factors in low and middle-income countries. *The Lancet.* Published online August 10, 2011.

Rutter, M. (2011). Resilience: Causal pathways and social ecology. In M. Ungar (Ed.), *The social ecology of resilience: A Handbook of Theory and Practice*. New York: Springer.

Tol, W., Jordans, M., Kohrt, B., Betancourt, T., & Komproe, I. (in press). Promoting mental health and psychological wellbeing in children affected by political violence: Current evidence for an ecological resilience approach. In C. Fernando & M. Ferrari (Eds.), *Children and war: A handbook for promoting resilience*. New York: Springer.

Tol, W. A., Komproe, I. H., Jordans, M. J., Gross, A. L., Susanty, D., Macy, R. D., et al. (2010). Mediators and moderators of a psychosocial intervention for children affected by political violence. *Journal of Consulting and Clinical Psychology, 78*(6), 818–828.

Tol, W. A., Komproe, I. H., Susanty, D., Jordans, M., Macy, R., & De Jong, J. (2008). School-based mental health intervention for children affected by political violence in Indonesia: A randomized cluster trial. *Journal of the American Medical Association, 300*, 655–662.

Trani, J.-F., Bakhshi, P., Noor, A. A., Lopez, D., & Mashkoor, A. (2010). Poverty, vulnerability, and provision of healthcare in Afghanistan. *Social Science & Medicine, 70*(11), 1745–1755.

Turton, D., & Marsden, P. (2002). Taking refugees for a ride? The politics of refugee return to Afghanistan. In Afghanistan Research and Evaluation Unit (AREU), *Issue paper series*. Kabul, Afghanistan.

Ungar, M. (2008). Resilience across cultures. *British Journal of Social Work, 38*, 218–235.

Ungar, M. (2011a). The social ecology of resilience: Addressing contextual and cultural ambiguity of a nascent construct. *American Journal of Orthopsychiatry, 81*, 1–17.

Ungar, M. (2011b). Introduction. In M. Ungar (Ed.), *The social ecology of resilience: Culture, context, resources and meaning*. New York: Springer.

van Ommeren, M. (2003). Validity issues in transcultural epidemiology. *British Journal of Psychiatry, 182*, 376–378.

Weiss, M., Saraceno, B., Saxena, S., & Van Ommeren, M. (2003). Mental health in the aftermath of disasters: Consensus and controversy. *Journal of Nervous and Mental Disease, 191*(9), 611–615.

World Health Organization (WHO) (2008). *Social determinants of health in countries in conflict: A perspective from the Eastern Mediterranean region*. Cairo, Egypt: World Health Organization Regional Office for the Eastern Mediterranean.

Worthman, C. M. (in press). Inside/out and outside/in global developmental theory, policy, and youth. *Ethos*.

Case Study: Promoting Community Resilience with Local Values – Greenland's Paamiut Asasara

30

Peter Berliner, Line Natascha Larsen, and Elena de Casas Soberón

This chapter will show – and discuss – the promotion of community resilience in Paamiut in Kalaallit Nunaat (Greenland). The community mobilization program Paamiut Asasara was launched as a response to a history of a high rate of crime, violence, suicide, drug abuse, and child neglect. Climate change adds a new challenge to these social problems, as people's living conditions change rapidly. The goal of the program is to strengthen community resilience, well-being and revitalization of the culture through locally formulated values and resources, shared activities, social networks, and options for creativity. After 2 years, the program has been shown to have contributed to a 45% decrease in domestic violence and a 30% decrease in other kinds of violence, a changed discourse of parenting, more sharing of emotions and concerns, and a revitalized cultural life in the community.

We will focus on the participants' description of the changes that have happened since the program was launched, showing how a community-based intervention can not only address social problems but also build a community's resilience to cope with future adversity. The population in Paamiut is mainly Inuit who speak Kalaallissut. The program helped them, through a multi-family community approach, to address the particular kind of silence they have experienced in the face of adversities and the cycle of violence to which that silence has contributed.

In the following section we discuss the background of the community and the resources and risk factors present in Paamiut as they are detailed in the narratives of the program's participants.

Background

The population of Paamiut faces a process of depopulation, increasing unemployment and – especially before the program started – a number of social problems including a high rate of violence, domestic violence, child neglect, substance abuse, and lack of social support. The town is very dependent on the fishery and when the activities at the fish factory decrease because of reduced supplies of fish, shrimps, or crabs, the unemployment rate increases immediately. The changing climate, especially the temperature of the sea, had an immense impact on the fish and shellfish stocks. As well, the demand for crab and shrimp is vulnerable to changes in the global purchasing power during economic downturns.

Paamiut Asasara comprises a series of locally defined initiatives aimed at improving the quality of life for all residents in the community, including the more vulnerable groups. It is an example of community-based psychosocial programming (Bolton & Tang, 2002; Bragin, 2005) but also includes cultural and economic activities as well as a theory of collective learning. Combined, these components contribute to a broader understanding of resilience

P. Berliner (✉)
Department of Education, University of Aarhus, Copenhagen, NV, Denmark
e-mail: Peer@dpu.dk

M. Ungar (ed.), *The Social Ecology of Resilience: A Handbook of Theory and Practice*, DOI 10.1007/978-1-4614-0586-3_30, © Springer Science+Business Media, LLC 2012

as transformation. The ethical dimensions of the program and of the research on the program make it clear that both aspects should contribute to the well-being of community members and promote social and civil rights. This has meant that every activity of the program must be implemented in a way that ensures equal opportunities for participation in the design and the implementation of activities. Overall, the goal of *Paamiut Asasara* is to revitalize the cultural life and the economy of Paamiut while enhancing well-being, especially for families with children.

Building Capacities for Resilience in the Context of Community Change

When designing the *Paamiut Asasara* program, the idea surfaced among the groups of young people, mothers and fathers of the community as an emergent source of cooperation confronting changes together. As a result, it became clear that the success of the program was dependent on the active participation of as many members of the community as possible. During debates in the community hall, it became clear that it was not possible to return to a previous state in the history of the community, but it was possible to develop a community that revitalizes values of mutual respect in a new way. This perspective opened up a new understanding of the community as a group of people who together can address the challenges it faced. This change in perspective led to the embrace of an emergent community concept, underlined by the participation of the administrative unit of Paamiut as a municipality in 2008 and its subsequent inclusion in the larger municipality of Sermersooq. This inclusion made it very obvious that flexible social organization was required to better cope with the community's challenges. To some extent this change of understanding was already preceded by the growing awareness of the need for locally based initiatives to solve social problems. This process of community reflection leading to program interventions started shortly after 2000 when the community faced a high number of suicides among young people. During

the following years *Paamiut Asasara* was created by the mayor as an organizational structure for collective capacity building.

The process of program development helped to promote a change in attitude from surviving as a community to building capacities for resilience in a context of perpetual change. Individual resilience came to be understood as being dependent on social support, especially in times of adversity. This was in contrast to a culture of silence that had previously been the norm, with many people not getting the social support they needed. As the rate of deaths related to suicides, accidents, and illness is high, there is a need for sharing one's experience of these tragedies with others if the community is to become a group of survivors instead of individuals with personal challenges.

The program is based on the idea that a community can become more supportive and more capable of adapting to changes (i.e., it can become more resilient). Zautra, Stuart Hall, and Murray (2010) present a definition of community resilience "as an outcome of successful adaptation to adversity. Characteristics of the person and situation may identify resilient processes, but only if they lead to healthier outcomes following stressful circumstances" (p. 4). They argue that to study resilience is to try to understand how people and communities achieve and sustain health and well-being in the face of adversity. The definition suggests that resilience includes two processes: recovery and sustainability. At the individual level resilience involves both healing and sustained capacities that make it possible for the individual to maintain a sense of engagement in life that contributes to well-being.

The individual's capacity for building resilience may include active coping, flexibility, self-efficacy, sense of purpose, engagement in life at work, at home and at play, emotional regulation, and physical regulation (Zautra et al., 2010). Many of these elements of individual resilience were evident in the program outcomes achieved through Paamiut Asasara. To achieve these goals, however, individuals need social support: "Resilient children need resilient families and communities" (Ungar, 2008, p. 221). Emphasizing this balance between individual coping and the capacity of social structures to provide supports to individuals, Ungar (2010) offers the following definition of resilience: "In the context of exposure to significant adversity, whether psychological, environmental, or both, resilience is both the capacity of individuals to navigate their way to health-sustaining resources, including opportunities to experience feelings of well-being, and a condition of the individual's family, community and culture to provide these health resources and experiences in culturally meaningful ways" (p. 405). Resilience, according to Ungar, includes processes of navigation and negotiation. Navigation is the exercise of personal power directed toward the acquisition of resources. Negotiation is the process whereby people are able to access health-sustaining resources and have the power to define one's self and one's coping strategies as successful. Community resilience, therefore, builds on individual resilience.

Magis (2010) defines community resilience as the community's ability to respond to change and lists eight dimensions: (1) community resources; (2) development of community resources; (3) engagement of community resources; (4) active agents; (5) collective action; (6) strategic action; (7) equity; and (8) impact. Community resilience is the result of a learning process. This learning process is in itself part of the sustained resilience a community experiences to change when confronted with adversity: "Resilient communities, hence, learn to cope with, adapt to and shape change" (p. 412). A resilient community takes action to increase the capacities of its members and institutions to respond to, and influence the course of change. Zautra et al. (2010) support the idea of the resilient community as a learning community by saying that: "A working hypothesis that guides current research on community resilience is that communities, like people, can be taught to be resilient" (p. 13). They add that the learning process to a great extent must build on existing relationships and institutions, and that "sustainable resilience capacities are built over time, require a focus (often a refocus) on strengths not weaknesses, and rest on improved self-organization, self-control (mastery), and social connection" (p. 13).

Norris, Stevens, Pfefferbaum, Wyche, and Pfefferbaum (2008) propose a related model of community resilience which they describe as a set of networked adaptive capacities. The concept of community capacity is used to describe all matters related to communities and community development, whereas the concept of community resilience focuses on a community's capacity with regard to change in the presence of adversity. The model proposed by Norris et al. has four components: economic development; information and communication; social capital; and community competence. It shows that community resilience is complex and is comprised of a number of supportive factors.

Through the activities of Paamiut Asasara, the citizens of Paamiut started to view community resilience as a necessary context for individual resilience. The program was based on traditional community values but these values were transformed into a new framework of understanding as they were put into practice in the changing social context. It became apparent that the population of Paamiut was facing a situation that could develop into a persistently dysfunctional community unless action was taken (Norris et al., 2008). As a response to threats to the social cohesion of the community, Paamiut Asasara was designed with five specific goals: the first two were to decrease the crime rate by 50% and to eliminate child neglect completely. The process of intervention was understood as a form of community healing. As such, it became clear that it had to involve children and youth as well as parents, other adults, professionals and local leaders in a change process with a clear focus on increasing access to social resources and building the capacity of individuals and institutions in the community. This process of changing the context involved finding a better fit between the citizens of Paamiut and their institutions (e.g., the social welfare system, the educational system, the healthcare system and the legal system). This, then, was the third program goal. As a means to achieve this goal, community members emphasized the need for decision-making processes and practices within the institutions to become more transparent. It was believed this would make them more efficient at providing their services to the public, while also ensuring that the public became more committed to supporting the institutions.

As the school plays a particularly important role in providing resources for the well-being and safety of children, as well as for educating them for participation in the information society, a fourth goal was to strengthen the capacity and academic outcomes of the local school.

The fifth goal was to develop work opportunities, in particular employment opportunities that were not directly related to the fishing industry. It was felt that these would increase the social resilience of the entire community as it would be less dependent on just one economic resource.

The Paamiut Asasara Program

A framework for the program was chosen that emphasized contextual factors that included cultural, social, and institutional aspects of the community. The cultural context included a formulation of values pertaining to the community and to values cherished by individuals. The social context was understood as the interactions between people, especially those related to meeting their needs for social support at the individual and family levels. The institutional level covered specific institutions such as law enforcement, social welfare, education, the healthcare system, and the public administration overarching all the institutions. Principles of the program included a high degree of citizen involvement in, and responsibility for, the activities which resulted in less emphasis on the role of institutional responses to risk and capacity building and more emphasis on what people themselves could do collectively. As the program has been quite successful in terms of citizen involvement, it remains unclear just how important institutions are to a process of community resilience building such as Paamiut Asasara.

The program took place in the community through shared activities. One type of activity was to provide options for building social support networks for specific groups such as young mothers and parents, as well as for people suffering from prolonged grief and survivors of sexual abuse. These groups were mobilized through workshops with a focus on resources and capacity building. In this way the program challenged the idea of globally vulnerable individuals or families and replaced it with a balanced view of vulnerabilities and resources as changing over time as contexts make resources more or less available. The activities were seen as collective learning processes in the groups based on the sharing of individual life stories and narratives in the group. The groups of young mothers started out with eating breakfast together, followed by relaxation exercises and mindful focusing on the fetus, then gradually developed into sharing of concerns and ways of coping and building sustainable mutual support while supporting each other in daily life between the sessions. Some of these groups developed into sustained support networks and loosely structured civic society organizations.

Cultural activities are another type of activity which are part of the program. They include concerts, sporting events, theater, community dinners, and community meetings. One of these activities is the summer university with a curriculum of fishing and hunting skills and a staff of seasoned and highly skilled hunters as professors. Ten to twelve families spend 10 days together hunting and fishing in the wide fiords and the mountains surrounding Paamiut. Through this, the social network is strengthened and the families spend time together as a family and as part of a larger community.

Sporting activities contribute to social inclusion as these activities are open to everyone and the local coaches emphasize team spirit. When a football team of teenage boys won the National Championship for their age group, most people in Paamiut went to the harbor to welcome them home when they returned on the ferryboat. Paamiut Asasara has revitalized sport activities in the town and has added more options for young people, adults, and elderly people to participate in these activities.

The program also supports music and theater activities for citizens of Paamiut. In a theater activity for young people, 14 youth wrote and performed a monolog on their lives in Paamiut and how it was to grow up during a time of prevalent alcohol abuse, sexual abuse, and violence. Almost everyone in Paamiut came to attend the performance and in that way the young people managed to start a shared reflection process in the town. Later another group of teenagers participated in a photo workshop and made a series of photos and texts which were then projected on a wall in the town and later in Nuuk, the capital of Greenland. These activities were initiated as a study in 2009 showed that the young people wanted to become more active as citizens and influence the future of their community.

Concerts and community dinners, where people bring food and eat together outside in the summer evenings, are seen by the citizens as a means for strengthening social bonds and nurturing a sense of belonging. In interviews to assess the impact of the program, they reported that being together in this way without fear of violence or abuse of alcohol conveys a feeling of togetherness and social responsibility for them as residents of the town.

Finally, the program supports the development of small businesses and helps generate ideas for creating new jobs.

The majority of people in Paamiut attended one or more of these activities. More than 200 people participated in community dinners; 400–500 attended the concerts and more that 600 participated in the "clean-up the town" days twice a year. At least 120 individuals (out of a population of 1,600) are continuously engaged in participating in workshops or in sustaining the social networks emerging from these workshops. Paamiut Asasara has grown into a significant force for community mobilization, promoting the active participation of local residents.

Promoting Resilience Through a Collective Learning Process

The activities of Paamiut Asasara include cultural events, sports events, and social support groups. Among the many group activities are self-help groups, family competency trainings, groups for mothers with infants, theater groups, art classes addressing social issues, groups for young people, and rehabilitation groups. These groups were established based on the needs of the citizens in close cooperation with the health and social service sectors. Individual and focus-group interviews with a large number of citizens who participated in these activities, as well as quantitative data received from government sources, were used to evaluate the effectiveness of the program.

Fifty-nine initial interviews were conducted to identify the needs of residents. A study of values was also conducted on a randomly chosen sample of 72 citizens. At the start of the project a baseline was set through interviews with 23 key professionals from social security, health, the police, and the educational system, with young people in the educational system (8), with participants in the summer-university (45), and with participants in the supportive group for young mothers (15). The interviews with the professionals have been replicated annually through the first 3 years of the program and will be continued during the coming years. At the onset of the program a local research council was established to guide and direct the research. In-depth reflections with the staff at the community family center – 32 sessions of 2 or more hours – and participation in counseling sessions (40 sessions) with individuals, families and couples in the center made it possible to make detailed description of the types of challenges which made people seek support at the center and of the methods which were developed and applied to give this support. In the second year of the program, a study – including a survey, focus group interviews, and individual interviews – with a sample of 62 young people was conducted (Wattar, Fanous, & Berliner, 2010). The same year, four life story interviews were conducted to give an understanding of life in Paamiut as it is reflected in the lived experience of its residents (Berliner & Glendoes, 2010). Data on crime rates, domestic violence, unemployment, forced removal of children from families, and general health have been collected from public sources annually. Eight parents were interviewed annually to study how they see the development of their community and the program. These interviews are part of the annual evaluation of the program.

Most of the citations in the following sections are taken from the interviews with the parents in the eight families interviewed in March 2009 and April 2010. Each interview lasted 1–1.5 h and focused on resources in the family and in the community. The interviewees included young couples without children, young couples with children, middle-aged parents with adult children, and single mothers. A few of the quotes are taken from five focus groups with participants in the groups for young mothers or in the parenting capacity-building group. The focus group interviews were transcribed and then analyzed in a dialog between the researchers and the participants in sessions specifically designed for that process. The focus groups had from 8 to 16 participants. One quotation is from an interview with a professional.

In the following section, we present the qualitative data gathered under themes relevant to the program goals. As the research process was collaborative, the analysis reflects the points of view of community members and the research team who together investigated participants' experiences of change and transformation in their individual, family, and community lives.

Theme 1: Breaking the Culture of Silence

At a community meeting in 2008 with more than 100 participants in attendance, a working group was formed to focus on the need for social support. They concluded that the population could be broken into three groups: people with a long family history in Paamiut; people from the now abandoned settlements in proximity to Paamiut; and people from other parts of Greenland, especially people who came to the town almost 4 decades earlier when mining activity in Qullissat stopped and the work force unwillingly migrated. The working group explained that there has been a certain level of separation between the groups and that people in the two last groups in

some cases felt that they were looked down upon. A middle-aged man explained during one meeting:

> I have been very quiet and I have been very lonely in this town. We moved to here and thus we were new in town. We came from the North of the country, from the old mining town that was closed down in 1972 and we were forced to move here to Paamiut as we had no other options. It was very hard to be a new kid in town here as I did not know anybody and the local kids were very tough with me. They threw stones and sticks at me. One day somebody even threw a rake at me. Then I myself started to defend me and to hit the others. And in the gym I learned how to do judo and self-defense. I did that for 4 or 5 years. I believe that the local people here behaved in that way because they hate people from out of town, especially those who move to here. I felt that on my own body. But it is much better today.

The social exclusion that results from differentiation between groups has been labeled by the community as a form of bullying and was common among both adults and children in school. Differences in socio-economic status and social roles further marginalize different groups within the population of Paamiut. These same points were made during support groups by young mothers who said that it could be difficult to share worries as others in the community might laugh and see one as a weak person with problems. In interviews with participants in the parenting capacity-building groups, researchers were told:

> In this town a lot of people – children as well as grownups – seem to hide behind a mask. They feel that they have nobody to talk to and that they are all alone with their problems – and that they are the only ones with problems. It's like the air in this town is quite stuffy. You dare not to say that you have problems. You fear that all the worst will happen if you speak openly about problems. When I had a job I tried to speak with my colleagues at work. Twice I tried to speak about problems, but they said that we could talk later. And we never did. I don't know why.(…) When you think about yourself and who you are, then you want to protect yourself by hiding that from the others. You feel that they should not know who you are. And that they should not talk to others about you. My problems are mine and they are nobody else's business (Middle-aged father).
>
> It takes a lot of courage to open up. It may be because people are afraid of being disappointed and then they start to think "what if"- and "what

if" – and so on. This "what if" – way of thinking – it can be very dangerous. "What if the others think this or that about me?" "What if this or that person doesn't like me"? "What if"? All that fuzz about "what if"? Then you better stop talking to anyone or you get completely passive. It's like avoiding the risk. Then you become very withdrawn from others and isolate yourself (Mother in her mid-twenties).

The process of hiding problems is explained by the citizens of Paamiut as more complex than just keeping silent. To talk about problems and risks may result in making one's self seem incapable of coping with life's problems. Furthermore, one's problems are then seen as a kind of social stigma, keeping the bearer in her or his social position. Typically, disclosure of a need for social support has not produced a sense of shared reflection and mutuality:

> People are very afraid of talking about problems. If you have a problem and you talk about it – it may be ok, because they may think that you are one of those people that do not cope well. But if you ask if somebody else has a problem, then they suddenly shut up and get silent. That is how it is (Father in his early twenties).
>
> This town, it's a small community, where people know about each other, but one can say that there are too many people waiting – waiting for being together and talking together (Woman in her twenties).

It was in this context of a culture of silence that the program was implemented. It was acknowledged by focus group participants during the program design phase that it is difficult to change one's way of living, especially to stop drinking alcohol, because others then may mock you for being pretentious and self-righteous. One of the fathers in the parent capacity-building group explained that:

> There is too many who run after you and tell you that they know who you are. If you get better and get a job then people will talk about you and say: what happened now, what is this about? We are very good at keeping each other down and as saying: don't think that you are better than us. Or people say: we've helped you so much when you were down, so please tell us why you behave like this now when you feel good. Why are you not behaving like us anymore? Before, when I drank, they had no comments, but now as I stopped drinking, they have a lot of negative comments about why I have changed and why I'm not as I used to

be. It is as if I don't fit into the picture anymore. It is about that they prefer that you know your place and stay there (Middle aged father).

A young man in his early twenties had the same experience and called for more respect and mutual responsibility in the town:

> In this town we lack respect and social responsibility. Even the kids show no respect to others. It was not like that in the past. There is a lot of belittling and, let's say, libel here. That's how it is. It's like if people just are waiting for you to do a mistake, then, immediately, they attack you. That's the problem here in this town – if a family is doing well or achieve something, then somebody will come from the outside and start trying to destroy the good they have. It is because people are envious. When it goes well for somebody else – then people start to think: "But what about me?"

Likewise, a middle-aged father explained:

> The problem is that you cannot be together with other people when you are having a lot of problems and you are feeling low down and miserable. Then you will be envious of anyone who comes there and is happy.

Though a different age and gender than the last two speakers, a young woman spoke of similar experiences, specifically noting that stopping rumors from circulating around the community was a significant challenge:

> There are many rumours in this town. It has been like that for a very long time, many years. Rumours mean that a person does not herself talk about how she feels about things, but that others without any reason instead start to tell stories about her and hurt her through that. Rumours just go on and on and little by little they develop into a completely different story and a completely different person. This way of talking about others is called the Kamik-post – as it is brought about by walking from house to house, retelling the rumour about others when they are not present. Then the rumours will live on and go around even though they may not be true. In that way people create stories about others. The people who spread the rumours and bully others are people who do not look at themselves – people who are jealous, who lie, and who hurt other people. That's why a lot of people are so afraid of doing something wrong. They are afraid that others will start to speak badly about them.

Thus, aspects of social control are used to prevent individuals from speaking to others about their worries. The need to be accepted makes people keep silent. However, as program results showed, when these challenges are addressed, the collective capacity to change them increases. Specifically, the program helped to formulate a vision of an inclusive community where people could share worries without being excluded and where people could change their behavior without being bullied by others.

Theme 2: A Sense of Belonging

The program has opened spaces for people to be together. Program activities have provided forums to start talking more openly about concerns.

> If one does not feel that you are related to others, you will feel very alone with your problems and then you may easily start to drink a lot of alcohol. When people are together and relate to each other then you have a feeling of being close to them and to work on something shared. All are invited. Anyone can join in. Everyone has something to say and something to contribute. If you don't have that kind of togetherness, it is so difficult to live, it's like the sun sets and everything becomes dark. The feeling of being together is huge and overwhelming. Through our activities here I got that feeling, it's a feeling of that it was us – we started it and we are the ones who lived it together. I feel that I gave something and I got a lot back. It's like the space around me has grown bigger, you know, metaphorically speaking. I have gained a wider perspective (Young mother in her mid twenties).

The greater the sense of belonging that people experienced, the more they challenged the culture-of-silence-when-having-problems. A father in one of the families that participated in the family capacity-building workshops explained how the families created activities that strengthened a sense of belonging to a group of families:

> We began to arrange social gatherings, celebrations, and journeys into the mountains and the fiords. We have always enjoyed that – both with the family and with friends. It is important to be together. In the beginning we didn't talk much, but we just enjoyed having fun together. When you want to have fun and enjoy being together, it's not the right time to think a lot about problems. You push the problems away and avoid them in that moment. Problems can ruin the joy as they make you feel sad and then it becomes difficult for you to be with other people. The joy in itself lessens the problems as it takes away the bad mood. So when

you are full of joy, everything else is less important as you have made space for something else than the problems.

In the sharing of activities, a good mood resulted and temporarily alleviated problems. In this sense, these activities provided an alternative way to avoid negative thoughts and feelings rather than remaining silent.

Similarly, another father explained how his family's participation in the fishing and hunting academy arranged by Paamiut Asasara opened opportunities for more social interaction with other families:

> Now we are really good at arranging journeys into the fiords with the other families. We put tents up, we play hide and seek with the kids and we go fishing. When it's the season for that we sometimes hunt caribous together. It's good for the family and for being together. The kids like being in the nature instead of sitting on their behind and bore themselves to death in town. It is necessary that they have good experiences with their family and with kids from other families. When we do that we feel very good. We laugh a lot and tell stories. Now we have more cohesion in the family and with other families. And after that we can talk about how we feel inside, in the body. The children also tell us more now. We care a lot for our children.

A third father said:

> It has been important to me to realize that we are not the only family with problems. My wife always said to me that we were the only family with a lot of problems. Now I have l listened to the stories of the other families and now I clearly see that we are not alone with our problems. That helps a lot because then you can share your problems and reflect on them with the others.

Though it is difficult to show that the program had a direct impact on domestic violence, the community did experience a 45% drop in family-based violence over the first 2 year period that the program operated. Five removed children were also returned to their families by child welfare services. One father suggested that programming and the reduction in family violence may be directly related:

> Now I have become much more calm and quiet at home and I stopped shouting at the children. I always try to get eye contact with them now and I play with them. I can see that my wife is much calmer now and that she feels much safer at home now. We have many children and in between there is a lot of commotion and stress, but we see that the

children have noticed that we parents don't fight that much now. We stopped drinking alcohol. I'm calmer now. I realize that I have done much harm to my wife and children when I yelled at them and beat them and was violent. I will have to learn to live with that past, but the present and the future will be ok if I just continue to talk with my wife and we keep supporting each other (A middle aged father).

Theme 3: Action

Many of the participants in the Paamiut Asasara activities emphasized the importance of collective social activities as action-oriented strategies to make the community a healthier place to live:

It is good to do something together, some physical activities – it is much better that just talking. When it is just talk, talk, talk of course, you'll get good ideas about the future and how we can impact on that. How we can form it. But if it's talk and talk and nothing else, it may lead to nowhere. When you actually do something and you do an activity together – then something really happens. It has more vitality. (….) Paamiut is just about to blossom. Before, it was as if the sun had settled and it was all dark. People were waiting for something to happen. Everybody was on her or his own. The drinking is less now. Before, it was rather chaotic here. Now it's more calm and relaxed. I think that we have realized that it is up to us to make the difference – we will have to do something to make a change in this town. We are not so many but we know each other. People realize that we are the ones who have to take action and to make the difference – so that people wake up – it is our responsibility. What can we do to do that? That's the feeling you get. It's like it's now we have do to something, to take action. It's now! (….) The initiative is ours. We have to say: Come on, we must do this. Let's start a group now, let's do some activities, let's take on the task. It's like saying: Come on, folks, come and join us, let us know your ideas, what do you think, and what expectations do you have? It is crucial to sustain what's happening. We must not stop now where things are getting much better (Mother in her mid thirties).

Through member participation a transformation in the social and cultural life in the community resulted:

We have managed to make the town a safer place to live. Let me put it this way: When you feel safer, then you'll start to have more openness between people. Then the possibilities become manifold. (….) The town is coming back to life. We have

concerts, debates, workshops. The town is alive again. We have more fun, safety, and a sense of togetherness among us. And more and more citizens want to be part of it. Before that the town was almost at a halt (Mother in her forties).

Resilience in Paamiut

Summarizing the impact of Paamiut Asasara on the community and its capacity to meet the needs of its members, one mother from the parenting capacity building group told the researchers:

We have become better citizens in the community, as we take part in – how to say that – the good and healthy way of thinking instead of the evil way of thinking. To be a good citizen is to know more about each other without pointing fingers and saying: you are such and such. That we are together face to face and that we have an understanding for each other. It means that we participate jointly. We have made a difference in the family, we have strengthened the family and we have opened a reflection on options for families, on how to be parents, and how to bring up children in a good way. We have found ways of listening to the opinions of other people and know more about them. We have learned to support each other in a way that is not blurred – that means that you support and help a family that struggles with problems instead of just turning your back to it. You reinforce its values. We have learned how to lift each other up. For instance, if I have a good experience with how to bring up my children – then I can share it with the others. Now we have more bonding, belonging, a good atmosphere, and more joy in being a citizen.

Program participants described the positive outcomes of the program as learning, social support (more bonding and linking with others for support), talking more openly about challenges, more hope for the future, and collective action. These outcomes underscore a change in attitudes and behavior across the entire community, not just individually or in specific families. There is now a sense that people have permission to talk about their problems and an acknowledgement of the stress related to community integration.

This greater tolerance for self-disclosure is having an effect on the rates of alcohol abuse. Participants explained that an individual's obedience to the social demand of being always in a good mood has been replaced through the Paamiut Asasara activities with a more balanced view of human emotions. Worries can now be shared without risking social stigma.

The oppressive silence that participants described were deeply entrenched in the culture of Greenland and resulted from negative rumors created because of envy and a lack of self-esteem on the part of those talking badly about others. Hansen (1995) describes how *kayak dizziness,* a culture-bound mental disorder, is understood by Inuit as the result of envy. The kayaker experiences an intense fear at sea. The cultural explanation was that he is attacked by a *tupilak*, a murderous monster sent out to kill him by a person full of envy and evil. This means that the mental disorder is not *in* the kayaker, but in another person in the village: *In popular Greenland cosmology, it is the envious person who is ill. The "illness" is called "ilisiinneq." Kayak dizziness is an expression of social tension. The person suffering from kayak dizziness has unintentionally created an environment for jealousy to thrive.* In a similar vein, a professional who is also a local citizen of Paamiut said in an interview:

> The reason for mocking and even bullying each other is envy. Envy of those that are doing well, but it also makes people behave in a very tough way towards the ones who are seen as weak. But it has changed, it is less now.

The program aimed to change the circumstances in which envy could be experienced by opening a space where resources and worries could be shared without creating fear and isolation. Thus, community resilience in this context is built through an ongoing process of strengthening social support and the sense of belonging that community members feel between each other.

Conceptualizations of community resilience discussed earlier are very relevant to understanding the process of creating community resilience in Paamiut. Community programming sought to influence: (1) equity of resource distribution – in this case, social capital; (2) received and perceived social support; (3) the availability of cultural capital (and changes to cultural capital to break patterns of silence); and (4) community action. The nature of the relationships between community members is critical to the adaptive

capacity of communities and the achievement of these goals (Adger, 2003; Paton, Millar, & Johnston, 2001). Communities have characteristics that make them vulnerable to specific changes. But, as results from an evaluation of Paamiut Asarara show, communities may also have the resources and adaptive capacities which enable challenges to be overcome (Fenton, Kelly, Vella, & Innes, 2007). Resilience involves transformation through learning, innovation, renewal, and re-organization (Folke, 2006). In this regard, community resilience is commonly understood as a process of transition and as a response to change and adversity. In the face of change, community members develop new knowledge, attitudes and skills, which are useful for coping flexibly with the challenges emerging over time.

In Paamiut, the learning process in the workshop for young mothers and in the workshops for parents has fuelled a very large change in the understanding of how values of silence and of being in a festive mood should be expressed. This learning process makes it clear that the community has a profound capacity for change (i.e., of engagement in transformation in the current situation of rapid external and internal changes). Particularly important to Greenland are the changes taking place in traditional values and the benefits to the community when maladaptive coping strategies are replaced with more collective, mutually supportive ways of interacting. In this sense, resilience has resulted from transformation of patterns of coping already present in the community. Thus, community resilience can in this context be understood as a capacity for transformation in an adaptive way. Maguire and Cartwright (2008), arguing a similar point, explain that the transformation view of resilience is particularly useful for understanding how a community can respond positively to change.

Community resilience in Paamiut has been built through an ongoing process of strengthening social support, developing a sense of belonging for everyone, and encouraging people to become more actively engaged with one another. Shared locally defined values of social responsibility and mutual trust and respect are the focal points for Paamiut Asasara which has contributed to greater community resilience as a whole. Creating more supportive links between the individual, the family, and the community is a means of sustaining these results.

Acknowledgment We are grateful to Heidi Jeremiassen and Soeren Lyberth, both members of the Board of Paamiut Asasara, for inputs and comments on the text. The article is built on data collected through various methods by the authors. Most of the cited excerpts are from a series of interviews with couples and focus groups conducted in March 2009 and April 2010 by Line Natascha Larsen. The analysis was conducted with inputs from all the authors. The research was made possible through a grant from Bikuben Fonden.

References

Adger, W. N. (2003). Social capital, collective action and adaptation to climate change. *Economic Geography, 79*(4), 387–404.

Berliner, P., & Glendoes, M. (2010). *"It's like getting rid of a heavy load": Changes in structural violence in Paamiut.* Manuscript submitted for publication.

Bolton, P., & Tang, A. M. (2002). An alternative approach to cross-cultural function assessment. *Social Psychiatry and Psychiatric Epidemiology, 37*, 537–543.

Bragin, M. (2005). The community participatory evaluation tool for psychosocial program: A guide to implementation. *Intervention: International Journal of Mental Health, Psychosocial Work and Counselling in Areas of Armed Conflict.* Retrieved Nov 1, 2010, from http://www.interventionjournal.com/downloads/31pdf/03_24%20Bragin%20.pdf.

Fenton, M., Kelly, G., Vella, K., & Innes, J. (2007). Climate change and the Great Barrier Reef: Industries and communities. In J. E. Johnson & P. A. Marshall (Eds.), *Climate change and the great barrier reef: A vulnerability assessment.* Australia: Great Barrier Reef Marine Park Authority and Australian Greenhouse Office.

Folke, C. (2006). Resilience: The emergence of a perspective for social-ecological systems analyses. *Global Environmental Change, 16*, 253–267.

Hansen, K. G. (1995). Kayak dizziness: Historical reflections about a Greenlandic predicament. *Folk, 37*, 51–74.

Magis, K. (2010). Community resilience: An indicator of social sustainability. *Society & Natural Resources, 23*(5), 401–416.

Maguire, B., & Cartwright, S. (2008). *Assessing a community's capacity to manage change: A resilience approach to social assessment.* Canberra: Bureau of Rural Sciences.

Norris, F. H., Stevens, S. P., Pfefferbaum, B., Wyche, K. F., & Pfefferbaum, R. (2008). Community resilience as a metaphor, theory, set of capacities and strategy for disaster readiness. *American Journal of Community Psychology, 41*, 127–150.

Paton, D., Millar, M., & Johnston, D. (2001). Community resilience to volcanic hazard consequences. *Natural Hazards, 24*(2), 157–169.

Ungar, M. (2008). Research note. Resilience across cultures. *British Journal of Social Work, 38*, 218–235.

Ungar, M. (2010). Cultural Dimensions of Resilience among Adults. In J. W. Reich, A. J. Zautra, & J. Stuart Hall (Eds.), *Handbook of adult resilience* (pp. 404–423). New York: Guilford Press.

Wattar, L., Fanous, S., & Berliner, P. (2010). *Challenges of youth participation in participatory action research – Methodological considerations of the Paamiut Youth Voice research project.* Manuscript submitted for publication.

Zautra, A. J., Stuart Hall, J., & Murray, K. E. (2010). Resilience. A new definition of health for people and communities. In J. W. Reich, A. J. Zautra, & J. Stuart Hall (Eds.), *Handbook of adult resilience* (pp. 3–29). New York: Guilford Press.

Toward an Ecology of Stories: Indigenous Perspectives on Resilience

Laurence J. Kirmayer, Stéphane Dandeneau,
Elizabeth Marshall, Morgan Kahentonni Phillips,
and Karla Jessen Williamson

Introduction

The concept of resilience recognizes the fact that many individuals and communities do well despite enduring severe hardships, trauma and deprivation (Luthar, Sawyer, & Brown, 2006; Masten, 2007). A focus on resilience shifts attention from vulnerability and pathology toward the analysis of resources, strengths and positive outcomes. This shift has been very welcome among Indigenous communities that have suffered from high levels of mental health problems in recent decades. However, the models of resilience that have emerged in recent years are based largely on studies with the children of parents with severe mental health problems or with inner city youth facing poverty, violence, discrimination and other forms of social adversity (Garmezy, 1993; Rutter, 1985). While certainly relevant to the experience of Indigenous populations, we believe these models require systematic rethinking to address the unique cultures, histories, social and geographical settings of Indigenous peoples as well as their definitions of health, wellness and well-being (Burack, Blidner, Flores, & Fitch, 2007; Fleming & Ledogar, 2008; Holton, Brass, & Kirmayer, 2009).

L.J. Kirmayer (✉)
Culture and Mental Health Research Unit,
Institute of Community and Family Psychiatry,
Montreal, QC, Canada
e-mail: laurence.kirmayer@mcgill.ca

In this chapter, we present some observations from an ongoing study of concepts of resilience in Aboriginal communities in Canada. The central aims of this project are to understand resilience in Indigenous terms and to identify the social–contextual factors that may foster resilience at crucial life transitions. In addition to helping to build comprehensive theories of resilience, understanding culture and context can contribute to more effective clinical and public health interventions (Gone & Kirmayer, 2010).

Models and Metaphors of Resilience

Studying resilience does not mean simply looking at the converse of risk factors – as seen in some of the psychiatric literature (e.g., Charney, 2004) – but invites us to consider unique dimensions of development and adaptation that may contribute to human flourishing (Keyes, 2007).

The metaphor of resilience is based on observations of physical materials and refers to the ability of a material to return to its original state after being stressed or deformed. This physical model of resilience does not capture the nature of human biological or psychological adaptation and development across the lifespan. For biological systems facing stressors, resilience generally does not involve a simple return to a previous state but dynamic processes of adaptation, involving changes in self-regulation, injury and repair, as well as growth and transformation in response to new challenges and demands.

M. Ungar (ed.), *The Social Ecology of Resilience: A Handbook of Theory and Practice*,
DOI 10.1007/978-1-4614-0586-3_31, © Springer Science+Business Media, LLC 2012

In psychology, resilience tends to be approached as a feature of individuals associated with personality traits or characteristics including general hardiness, cognitive flexibility, problem-solving ability, intelligence, sense of humor, and social skills (Iarocci, Root, & Burack, 2008). Although resilience can be understood as the result of individual characteristics, it also has systemic, collective and communal dimensions (Kirmayer, Sedhev, Whitley, Dandeneau, & Isaac, 2009). At the systemic level, resilience may reside in the durability, flexibility and responsiveness of the relationships that constitute extended families or wider social networks (Ungar, 2004; Walsh, 2006). The individualistic models that dominate psychology, therefore, need to be enlarged to take into account the dynamic systems that may confer resilience on individuals, communities and whole peoples. Indigenous concepts can provide ways to approach a more dynamic, systemic, ecological view of resilience.

The stressors faced by Indigenous communities are similar to those faced by others in situations of social adversity (Marmot, 2007). In Canada, as in other settler societies, Indigenous peoples suffer from poor physical and mental health compared to the general population (Adelson, 2005; Gracey & King, 2009; King, Smith, & Gracey, 2009; Reading, 2009). But there are also social determinants of health specific to Indigenous populations. These include: the impact of colonization, which resulted in organized efforts to displace, exclude or destroy Indigenous communities; the effects of residential schools and other methods devised to suppress or extinguish Indigenous cultures through forced assimilation, which separated children from their families and communities, resulting in injuries of attachment and confused models of parenting; ongoing experiences of racism and discrimination associated with the negative stereotypes of Aboriginal people in mass media[1]; and the importance for Indigenous identity of the human relationship to the land,

animals and environment (Alfred, 2009; Carson, Dunbar, Chenhall, & Bailie, 2007; de Leeuw, Greenwood, & Cameron, 2010; Reading & Wien, 2009; Richmond, 2009; Wilson & Rosenberg, 2002). Of course, all of these factors are related and interact in ways that reflect political and economic processes of colonization, marginalization and oppression that have resulted in particular patterns of structural inequality.

Each of these specific social determinants of health points to potential sources or strategies for resilience. Some of these strategies draw from traditional knowledge, values and practices of Indigenous peoples, but they also reflect ongoing responses to new challenges posed by evolving economic systems and political arrangements, with emerging global movements of Indigenous peoples making common cause through the language of human rights and the medium of electronic networking (Niezen, 2009; Richmond, Ross, & Egeland, 2007; Stout & Kipling, 2003; Whitbeck, Chen, Hoyt, & Adams, 2004).

The Roots of Resilience Project

Roots of Resilience is an interdisciplinary research collaboration that is exploring the factors that promote resilience in mental health among Indigenous peoples across the lifespan. We approach resilience as the outcome of dynamic processes of social and psychological adaptation and transformation that can be found at the level of individuals, families, communities or larger social systems and is manifested as positive outcomes in the face of historical and current adversity.

The diverse historical, social, psychological and physical contexts of Indigenous communities have resulted in different individual and communal patterns of exposure and experiences of stress. This variation provides a valuable opportunity to identify the social roots of resilience through case studies and systematic comparison. In particular, we are interested in how personal, family and community level processes interact with larger social structural barriers or constraints to enable some individuals and communities to do well while others languish.

---

[1]The recent documentary film *Reel Injuns* provides an instructive history of these prevalent stereotypes.

One multisite project within the larger research program, *Stories of Resilience*, focuses on local Indigenous understandings of resilience as expressed through life narratives. The study follows the principles of community-based participatory research (Fletcher, 2003; Macauley et al., 1999; Potvin, Cargo, McComber, Delormier, & Macaulay, 2003). Research in each participating community is conducted in partnership with a local steering committee and a community-based Indigenous researcher (Canadian Institutes of Health Research, 2007). In each community, the project follows a sequence with initial interviews with key informants and then focus groups stratified by age (youth, adults and elders) to explore local understandings of adversity, definitions of good outcomes or "doing well," as well as the specific individual and contextual factors that participants believe may contribute to "doing well despite adversity." This is followed by intensive interviews with individuals identified as resilient by a community advisory committee. A detailed manual for adapting the research protocol to specific community interests and conducting the focus groups and semi-structured interviews is available online from the project website (www.mcgill.ca/resilience/resources).

A major focus of our research has been on the ways that stories of individual and collective identity and transformation may contribute to resilience at personal and collective levels. The idea that resilience might reside in the ways that individuals make use of stories follows from the very large literature on the narrative basis of the self (Bruner, 1990, 2002; Kirby, 1991; McAdams, 1991; Sarbin, 1986). Every day explanations of choices, actions and outcomes draw from culturally rooted narrative templates that organize what counts as a good explanation (Tilly, 2006). Autobiographical accounts, in which individuals narrate part of their own history, typically invoke core cultural values as well as culture-specific construals of personal and historical time (Adelson, 2000; Herbert & McCannell, 1997; Norton, 1989; Roberts & Holmes, 1999). In addition to their own biography, people can make sense of their predicaments, map possibilities for adaptation, and articulate a positive vision for the future by drawing on collective history, myths and sacred teachings. At the same time, these collective narratives reinforce a shared identity and so contribute to the vitality and continuity of a community or a people (Chamberlin, 2003; King, 2003).

Narrative resilience, therefore, also has a communal or collective dimension, maintained by the circulation of stories invested with cultural power and authority, which individuals and groups use to articulate and assert their identity, affirm shared values and attitudes toward challenges, and generate creative strategies to address new predicaments. Research methodologies that focus on narrative are particularly welcome in Indigenous communities, where story telling has played a central role in the transmission of culture and is widely respected as a source of knowledge, wisdom and affirmation of identity (Denham, 2008; Dion Buffalo, 1990; Episkenew, 2009; Hodge, Pasqua, Marquez, & Geishirt-Cantrell, 2002; King, 2003).

For Indigenous peoples, attention to collective stories seems doubly apt, both because of the value of story in the transmission of oral tradition and also because it speaks directly to the ruptures and losses that occurred with the systematic suppression and dismantling of Indigenous cultures. Lear (2006) has described how the disruption of Indigenous ways of life created a radical disjunction in the possibilities for self-narration, which in turn led to a profound sense of despair. Loss of continuity in a collective narrative may lead individuals to falter as well. Continuing the narrative arc of individual stories beyond this cultural rupture requires a strong vision or imaginative engagement with refashioning the world. The individual can be supported in this task by collective stories that are recovered, revisioned and retold.

A focus on narratives also can help capture some of the wide individual variation in strategies of resilience seen within a community. Forms of resilience may vary by the individual's age, gender, education and life history and change over time with developmental transformations. At the same time, collective narratives can point toward some of the culturally distinctive strategies of resilience that reflect the specific histories, environments, worldviews and ways of life of Indigenous communities. Our work in Mi'kmaq, Mohawk, Métis and Inuit communities indicates commonalities across different groups and individuals as well as distinctive ideas about resilience relevant to mental health promotion and intervention.

Mi'kmaq Resilience: The Spirit of the Treaties

The Mi'kmaq are Indigenous people of Atlantic Canada and currently number about 40,000, with communities from eastern Quebec to Cape Breton Island and Newfoundland. British colonization of eastern Canada resulted in a process of displacement, marginalization, usurpation of lands and decimation of the population (Reid, 1995). Despite the devastating impact of colonization, residential schools and forced assimilation, the Mi'kmaq in many communities have continued to flourish, speaking their language, practicing traditions in daily life, and striving to protect their Treaty rights through the courts. The Mi'kmaq language is a rich repository of knowledge about local ecosystems important for subsistence activities. It also has a vocabulary that conveys Indigenous concepts of conflict resolution and spirituality (Hornborg, 2008). Through collaboration and cooperation based on traditional values, Mi'kmaq have responded to the challenges of colonization and maintained their sense of cohesiveness as a people for centuries.

From a contemporary Mi'kmaq perspective, one source of resilience lies in the treaties with the British Crown, negotiated from the late seventeenth century until the signing of the Watertown Treaty of 1776 (Marshall & Kirmayer, 2009). Although intended by the British colonizers as instruments to contain and, ultimately displace the Indigenous population, the Mi'kmaq recognized these treaties as agreements to share their knowledge of the land with the Europeans. As expressed in the language of these treaties, Mi'kmaq believed that a true human being was one who could live in peace and friendship. According to oral tradition,

at the signing of the 1752 Treaty, the Mi'kmaq chief told the representative of the Crown: "I never truly believed you to be human."[2] In signing the Treaty, Mi'kmaq recognized the colonizers as vulnerable human beings, and brought them under the protection of the Treaty, to show the newcomers the path of peaceful co-existence. On this interpretation, the Treaty affirmed a system of beliefs and values that went far beyond any of the material benefits, rights or responsibilities that it established.

This broader spiritual meaning of the treaties is central to contemporary self-understandings of Mi'kmaq not as a people dispossessed of their lands but as equal partners and active agents in political arrangements with Canada and other nations. At an individual level, this is strikingly illustrated by the actions of a group of Mi'kmaq construction workers who, on learning of the destruction of the World Trade Center on September 11, 2001, decided they must travel to Manhattan to assist in rescue efforts because they had to honor the spirit of their treaties, which stated: "Indians shall use their best endeavors to save the lives and goods of any people shipwrecked on the coast..." (Treaty of 1752, Article 7) (Marshall & Kirmayer, 2009). This sense of moral agency and power drawn from the treaties stands in marked contrast to the usual view of the disempowering and humiliating relationship of colonizer and colonized.

This contemporary story – though it belongs to the few who experienced it – reflects a larger narrative strategy present throughout Mi'kmaq tradition, of stories that re-balance, re-harmonize and re-establish a fundamental symmetry of exchange or reciprocity. The traditional stories of the culture hero/trickster figure Kluskap tell of encounters with Christ before European colonization in

---

[2]The spiritual meaning of the Treaties we discuss here is part of oral tradition. One of the reasons the sacred Treaty teachings were shared as oral traditions was to ensure that the story was told from the heart so that the truth was told. There is no other method of sharing the true spirit of Treaty except by sharing the spirit from one person to the next, face to face.

which each figure tries to outdo the other with demonstrations of power:

> [Christ] took Gluscap to the ocean, and told him to close his eyes. Then Christ moved close to the shore an island which lay far out to sea. When Gluscap opened his eyes, he saw it. Christ asked him if he could do as much as that. Then Gluscap told Christ to close his eyes a while. When Christ opened his eyes, he found that Gluscap had moved it back to its place again (Speck, 1915, pp. 60–61).

Although Kluskap stories are no longer told frequently in Mi'kmaq communities (Reid, 2005), the essential strategy of equalizing power by constructing a narrative that includes the other within a system of egalitarian exchange persists in modern stories as well as in efforts to establish mechanisms of restorative justice within the communities.

The spirit of peace, friendship and reciprocity that Mi'kmaq have found in the language of the treaties is also expressed in traditional notions of conflict resolution and forgiveness associated with "apisiktuaqn" – one of the most powerful words in the Mi'kmaq language (Barsh & Marshall, 1998). The closest English translation of *apisiktuaqn* is "forgiveness" or "reconciliation." Apisiktuaqn refers to a sacred process that was reserved for situations when peace and friendship were disrupted, and the ties that bond the individual to family, community and the Creator were challenged.

For example, when there was a dispute within a family, community or nation, the parties involved were assembled in a circle around a ceremonial fire by the *Kinup* – the ritual leader or Elder who was trusted to lead prayer and ceremony. Everyone in the community who might have been affected by the offense, whether directly or indirectly, would participate in the gathering, which began with prayer to invoke the spirit of the Creator as the community sought the second spirit, called Wise Council, to restore the good health of the spirit of community. The offended person sat with his family on one side of the circle, while the offender and his family sat on the opposite side. The ritual began with a process of recognition or acknowledgment. The Kinup or Elder then led a discussion to clarify the sequence of events and to help everyone to reach agreement on the circumstances that led to the offense. The next phase was restitution, which involved a discussion regarding what action would be most appropriate to compensate for the offense. The offender was expected to carry out this act as restitution, humbly serving the family and community.

The process of reconciliation was enacted by the offender crossing the circle to stand before the offended person, and then dropping to one knee to kiss the cheek of the offended. The offender then stood up and said, "I'm sorry for having offended you, would you please forgive me [*Apisiktuwi*]?" Once having returned to their place in the circle the offended person would repeat the same process of reconciliation, requesting apisiktuaqn from the offender before returning to his own side of the circle.

The Kinup or Elder would then rise to recount the whole process for everyone to hear, beginning with the circumstances surrounding the offense. The process of reconciliation itself was described and the Kinup asked the crowd assembled if they had anything else to question or to add. Once these speakers were heard, the Kinup would describe how everything had been restored to harmony and the incident or offense was not to be discussed again in the future. The Kinup then led prayers to complete the restoration of peace and harmony before everyone left the circle.

This traditional process for resolving conflict and re-establishing harmony is now rarely seen as a formal ceremony. Today, apisiktuaqn is usually practiced only privately between individuals. In the Mi'kmaq communities of Eskasoni and Unama'ki on Cape Breton Island, apisiktuaqn is still sometimes practiced to resolve conflicts for a person who is dying or, when someone has passed on. The Elder will recite a prayer of apisiktuaqn on behalf of this person, in which peace between the person and all living things is sought. However, the spirit of reconciliation evident in this formal ceremony of forgiveness and reconciliation is an important source of resilience among contemporary Mi'kmaq and has informed efforts to develop alternative forms of sentencing and restorative justice (Clairmont & McMillan, 2001).

Mohawk Resilience: Resistance and Revitalization

Our team has also worked with partners in Kahnawake, one of eight communities located in Quebec, Ontario and New York State that make up the Kanien'kehá:ka (Mohawk/People of the Flint) nation. The Mohawk are one of the six nations of the Iroquois Confederacy or Haudenosaunee (People of the Longhouse). Originally, over 50,000 acres in extent, Kahnawake's land has been gradually diminished through land cessions, including those associated with the construction of the St. Lawrence Seaway, various bridges, railways, highways and hydroelectric power lines (Phillips, 2000). Today, Kahnawake has a land base of 12,000 acres, with a population of 7,556 on reserve (approximately 1,300 households) and 2,224 off reserve.[3] The Mohawk Council of Kahnawake (band council) employs approximately 250 people on a full-time basis.

The community has faced many stressors including the collective losses associated with the destruction of the riverfront during the creation of the St. Lawrence Seaway, the constriction of its land base, and the challenges posed by changing legal definitions of community membership. However, the Oka Crisis in 1990, sparked by efforts to oppose the appropriation of sacred land to expand the city of Oka's municipal golf course into the sister community of Kanehsatake, is widely recognized as a crucial turning point for the Kanien'kehá:ka (York, 1991). The crisis led to a renewed sense of political agency and engagement, with a reawakening of nationalism and pride in Mohawk language and culture (Alfred, 2005).

Our interviews indicated that the community members see the Oka Crisis as a catalyst for social change that laid the groundwork for the integration of traditional healing programs in local health and social services organizations

(Phillips, 2010) and that reignited a drive to ensure that opportunities are available for all community members to learn Mohawk language and culture. The Kanien'kehá:ka Onkwawén:na Raotitióhkwa Cultural Center holds a community mandate to develop, implement and deliver language and cultural education programs designed to safeguard the sustainability of language and culture for the benefit of present and future generations. Since 2002 over 90 adults from Kahnawake have graduated from a Mohawk language immersion program that incorporates traditional cultural knowledge in its curriculum (see http://www.korkahnawake.org/).

The Oka Crisis also increased awareness of historic injustices in the larger society, giving impetus to a sequence of political responses at the federal level, including the establishment of the Royal Commission on Aboriginal Peoples, the Aboriginal Healing Foundation, the official apology by the federal government for the residential school system, and most recently, the Truth and Reconciliation Commission (Brant Castellano, Archibald & DeGagné, 2008).

The Indian Act and subsequent Canadian government policies suppressed traditional government, prohibiting the use of the Kanien'kéha language and cultural practices and placing political authority in the hands of the federal Minister and the Department of Indian Affairs. In recent years, the community has responded to these challenges by working to revitalize language and culture, and re-assert control over local health services, education, economic development and community services while strengthening links to sister communities throughout the Iroquois Confederacy.

Prior to contact with European colonizers, the Haudenosaunee were bound together through a powerful democratic covenant, the Great Law of Peace (Kaianere'kó:wa) with a worldview that connected humans with nature in the spirit realm. The orally transmitted Creation Story taught how humans came to live on Mother Earth – the name given to the planet because it was first inhabited by Sky Woman who fell from the skyworld (spirit world) and was gently placed on the back of a giant sea turtle by sea fowl. The Creator gave direct instructions for beautifying the earth and

---

[3]Source: Indian and Northern Affairs Canada; Population Statistics Report; Indian Registration System for 2009; and the Mohawk Council of Kahnawake.

making it more pleasing for human habitation, and enjoined humans to see to it that Mother Earth is taken care of for the next seven generations (a generation that will never be seen by the present generation) (Blanchard, 1980). The extended time perspective symbolized by "seven generations" suggests the forward-thinking outlook common among the Iroquois (Wieman, 2008).

Re-establishing a connection to cultural foundations is part of contemporary Mohawk healing practices. For the Haudenosaunee, cultural congruence begins with the Creation Story, which underlies a worldview, collective identity and mode of existence (Phillips, 2010). The Creation Story conveys core cultural values and outlines a moral system, worldview and identity. Throughout our research, youth, young adults, adults and elders identified sources of strength within the Creation Story that resonated with their own experiences of overcoming adversity. As one of our participants put it:

> To me, every single time I read it [the Creation Story], because I don't speak the language so I read it. And every single time I read it, I get something else out of it...for me, the Creation Story, it made me resilient...the story that resonates with me more than anything else is the whole Creation Story... Sky Woman is that catalyst that made the change [for me].

Precontact with Europeans, men and women had comparable authority in Haudenosaunee society. Although the Indian Act and Euro-Canadian ways have greatly influenced daily community life and diminished the power and influence that women hold among the Haudenosaunee, the community still views the women of Kahnawake as being especially strong willed. Women are seen as the caretakers of the land and clans, teachers of the children, and wives who "keep our husbands on the straight and narrow, teach our boys to be men, and teach our young girls to be women," in the words of one woman interviewed for our study. Women hold the majority of executive directors' positions in the community's nine public service organizations. Within the traditional Longhouse system, women hold positions as clan mothers who are responsible for selecting traditional chiefs who

represent each of the six nations of the Iroquois Confederacy.[4] Sky Woman has provided strength and empowerment during times of adversity to many women of Kahnawake. There is wide recognition in the community that women who empower other women, such as through mentoring, can be a source of strength for overcoming future challenges.

According to oral tradition, at a dark time in Haudenosaunee history when culture, ceremonies and peaceful ways of life were almost lost, a man known as the Peacemaker brought together the Haudenosaunee, formed a confederacy and, along with others, created a constitution known as The Great Law of Peace (Porter, 2008). An important protocol that was renewed and that has been practiced since that time by the Haudenosaunee is called the Ohénton Karihwaté́khwen Thanks giving Address, or "what we say before we do anything important" (Porter, 2008, p. 8). This prayer is designed to give thanks and acknowledgment to all creations and sets the tone for an event, or the day. One participant explained that her source of resilience is obtained from reciting the Thanksgiving Address on a daily basis.

Clearly, culture and language provide resources for resilience not only for the individual but also for the whole community, the Mohawk Nation and the Haudenosaunee. Responding to historical challenges has resulted in tenacity, dignity, resourcefulness and hope. It also directs community efforts to strengthen connections to a proud heritage and the rebuilding of communal institutions based on the values and principles found within the Creation Story and the Kaianera'kó:wa (The Great Law of Peace).

---

[4]Within the Haudenosaunee Six Nations Iroquois Confederacy (Mohawk, Oneida, Onondaga, Cayuga, Seneca and Tuscarora), there are 50 traditional male chiefs. Each chief works in conjunction with a clan mother and clan family. A clan mother can depose a chief if she feels that he is not fulfilling his duties and responsibilities to the collective and to the constitution of the Great Law of Peace.

Métis Resilience: Self-Reliance, *Débrouillardise* and Relational Resilience

Métis trace their ancestry to unions between First Nations and European colonial ancestors (Peterson & Brown, 1993). Of the over 300,000 people in Canada who self-identify as Métis, the majority live in urban settings or peri-urban communities (Statistics Canada, 2008). Unlike many of the First Nations who were placed in geographically localized reserves with the imposition of the Indian Act, Métis communities, however, are spread across a wide geographical area. This political and geographic reality is reflected in distinctive strategies and a language of resilience that values autonomy and self-reliance.

Historically, Métis have faced discrimination because of both their Indigenous origins and their mixed heritage, which presents a threat to other groups' definitions of the boundaries of "native" identity. The Métis people were forged from the interaction of two or more ancestries, a process termed "métissage" (Peterson & Brown, 1993; Russell, 2003; Sawchuk, 2001; St-Onge, 2006). The resultant identity is not a patchwork but an integrated whole that is distinct from its constituent parts. Métis identity goes beyond merely having a mixed heritage – which many other Canadians can also claim – and integrates Indigenous and explorer worldviews into a culturally meaningful whole that has persisted despite social pressures for assimilation. However, because the sources of Métis identity vary across the country, the Métis are themselves a culturally diverse nation.

Cultural values that link Métis across diverse communities include the emphasis on self-reliance, autonomy and independence (Peters & Rosenberg, 1991). This emphasis on independence has fostered a strong work ethic, enabling Métis to adapt to many of the challenges they have faced. The value of self-reliance is associated with being *débrouillard* (a Michif/French word that roughly corresponds to "resourceful"), a "Jack of all trades," with the skills to provide whatever is needed for oneself and one's family (Vermette & Ferland, 2006). Most importantly, it

also refers to perseverance and the ability to carry on in the face of challenges or setbacks. In discussions, people often refer to a resilient person with the Michif term "un capable," referring to someone able to harness their resourcefulness to support family and community. To be *débrouillard* and *un capable* means that one draws from all available physical, ecological and psychological resources in order to "get the job done" (Edge & McCallum, 2006).

Focus group discussions with Franco-Métis[5] elders, adults and youth from Manitoba, carried out as part of our collaborative research, have indicated that changing social, political and economic circumstances faced by each generation resulted in different social ecological challenges. Faced with different sociopolitical contexts, each generation has adopted somewhat different strategies. However, there are important continuities in the fundamental resources on which Franco-Métis people have relied. Common sources of strength noted across all generations were people's relationship with *others*, with their *language*, with their *culture* and with their *homeland*. The greatest challenges were those events that threatened or undermined people's relationships and connections to their social ecological surroundings. There was a clear sense that the Métis, as a nation, cannot survive without positive relationships among the people, a strong connection to culture and language, and to the land. These fundamental sources of strength, which have been challenged in different ways during each generation, were seen as contributing to the individual, collective and cultural resilience needed to face and overcome each generation's social and ecological challenges.

Notwithstanding the shared value of autonomy and independence, the Franco-Métis continue to be engaged in a process of what might be called "relational resilience" – that is, an effortful maintenance of the relationship of individuals or the group with sources of strength in order to face and

---

[5]Franco-Métis refers to French-speaking Métis, in this case specifically to members of communities in southeastern and western Manitoba.

overcome adversity. Here, relational resilience refers to the process of responding to adversity in ways that promote the maintenance and/or rebuilding of eroded relationships and connections with sources of strength.

Each generation has reacted to socio-environmental challenges in ways that have aimed to protect their connections to the Métis as a people, as well as to language, culture and the land. For example, many elders shared stories of facing harsh discrimination and oppression from mainstream society and government in the early 1900s. As a result, many chose to hide their Franco-Métis identity in order to avoid derogatory treatment and overt discrimination from the dominant society. People adopted an identity-protection strategy in which the Franco-Métis identity essentially went "underground" to avoid constant pejorative attacks. The Franco-Métis knew who the other Franco-Métis were – and their connection to language, culture and identity was maintained through frequent family gatherings and house parties. For today's generation of Franco-Métis, who no longer face the same degree of discrimination, a common challenge is maintaining and making sense of their identity in an increasingly globalized society with high levels of intermarriage. Relationship with grandmothers and grandfathers, who are Franco-Métis knowledge holders, is recognized as an essential way to maintain and reinforce Métis identity. Through inter-generational discussions, shared narratives transmit the fundamental value placed on relationships as key sources of personal, cultural and socio-ecological strength. For Métis today, being *débrouillard* is more a matter of finding ways of reconnecting with Métis culture than of being able to remain steadfast in the face of social discrimination.

Inuit Resilience: Drawing Strength from Language and the Land

Living in the demanding environment of the arctic for over a thousand years, the Inuit have long been emblematic of human resilience and re-sourcefulness (Brody, 1987). Prior to the arrival of Europeans, Inuit lived in small bands or extended family groups of perhaps 25–30 people following annual patterns of migration for hunting and fishing. Each group was self-sufficient, and every individual owed his or her life to the family, the camp group or community, and the good will of the animals, spirits of the land (Jessen Williamson, 2000). Links with the land and the animals sustained human life and well-being and were central to the Inuit concept of the person (Kirmayer, Fletcher, & Watt, 2008).

Over the last 150 years, however, Inuit life has been radically transformed from its traditional nomadic pattern through interactions with the traders, missionaries and colonial powers that laid claim to the vast regions of the Inuit homelands (Berger, 1977). Foreign ideas of social organization and structure have been introduced and imposed, bringing together families and groups who had relatively limited contact in the past to live in communities with hundreds of people (Jessen Williamson, 2011). This process of sedentarization has required rapid adaptation to new modes of subsistence and, equally, to new political and bureaucratic institutions.

Inuit enjoy high levels of fluency in their language, Inuktitut. With more than 35,000 speakers, Inuktitut is currently the most robust Indigenous language in Canada. The regional government conducts its sessions in Inuktitut and official documents are published in Inuktitut syllabics. Although the numbers of those who read the syllabic script easily may be declining (Hot, 2009), there are active publishing programs making Inuktitut materials tailored to youth and others available through books, magazines and on the Internet (Adamson, Daborn, Houston, & Tootoo, 2009; see www.inuitmyths.com and www.inuitq.com).

Inuktitut is replete with culture-specific notions related to ecology, subsistence activity and a distinctive worldview. The concept of resilience resonates strongly with the concept of *niriunniq*, an Inuktitut word that can be glossed as "hope" in the face of adversity. For many, niriunniq is an elusive experience but its potency as a life-sustaining power is never questioned. Traditionally, Inuit understood the world as shaped by environmental and spiritual forces that are beyond any person's control. Expressions like "ajurnarmat" ("cannot be helped") or "isumamminik" ("on its own will") reflect the Inuit recognition of human limitations. For Inuit health and well-being depend not only on the body but on the physical and social environment as well as cosmological forces. In some ways, the Inuit concept of person can be described as both eco-centric and cosmocentric (Kirmayer et al., 2008; Williamson & Kirmayer, 2010). In contrast to the "anthropocentric" view intrinsic to Western individualism, which puts individual human agency at the center of the world, in Inuit thought the person is only one active agent in a world shaped by powerful forces with their own often unpredictable aims and activities. Given that the world does not conform to human wishes, Inuit seek health through finding balance among the powerful forces that surround the person.

In interviews on traditional concepts of resilience conducted by Korhonen in Nunavut, Inuit elders emphasized the importance of spirituality, interconnectedness with others and knowledge of culture and traditional practices as key protective mechanisms (Ajunnginiq Centre, 2006; Korhonen, 2007). Key cultural practices surround the production and consumption of "country foods" (i.e., raw meat and fish), which are obtained by hunting and fishing and shared with others in the community. Consumption of country foods is closely associated with feelings of health and well-being (Kirmayer et al., 2008).

Inuit notions of personhood view human beings as deeply embedded in connections to the land and environment (Kirmayer, 2007). Thinking about the person as fundamentally connected to the environment transcends the European opposition between nature and culture (Tanner, 2004). The human predicament is one of working with powerful forces that operate both within and outside the person. In this animistic perspective, the whole world is alive with intelligent forces (Harvey, 2006). Approached with respect, the natural environment provides not only sustenance but also opportunities for emotion regulation, guidance and healing (McCormick, 2008). Inuit mythology and folktales are full of stories of

humans and animals interacting and changing places in ways that teach respect for the power of the environment (van Deusen, 2009).

For Inuit today, resilience is no longer essentially about adaptation to the demands of the arctic environment, as it reflects the ability of individual and communities to adapt to a complex social environment created by the incongruent and often conflicting policies and institutions introduced by "southern" governments, whether in Ottawa or in the regional governments that have restored a measure of autonomy while embedding the Inuit still further within larger geopolitical systems. Increasingly, the need for resilience is driven by global economic and climatological phenomena that are dramatically changing the arctic environment (Warren, Berner, & Curtis, 2005). Inuit have responded to these challenges by developing their own research to support political advocacy and legal challenges that can raise awareness of the profound consequences of global warming for their communities and spur action to protect the environment (Ebi & Semenza, 2008; Brody, 2000).

Toward a Political Ecology of Stories

The power of stories has its roots in our evolutionary biology, supporting human adaptation by amplifying our capacities for social cognition, communal cooperation and creative imagination (Boyd, 2009). Stories have come to serve more complex social functions over time both within and between communities. There are political and ecological dynamics in the circulation and impact of stories. Politically, stories function both rhetorically and legally to stake claims and persuade others to look at the world in specific ways (Bruner, 2002). Ecologically, stories function to constitute a social landscape, configuring identities and the imagined world within which we live (Bringhurst, 2008). Stories give individuals rhetorical tools to position themselves within local worlds and fashion their own biographies.

For Indigenous peoples, these functions of stories are shaped by oral traditions, with epistemologies that value first-hand, lived experience over written texts, and sacred stories transmitted in ceremonial contexts. Though the precise terms and categories vary across cultures, Indigenous peoples recognize two broad types of story: myths and histories (Bringhurst, 2008; Nabokov, 2002). By invoking and retelling myths, individuals and communities locate their experience within a larger moral universe. In recounting histories, individuals braid their own lives into the stories of family and community that give their identity collective meaning and resonance (Dion, 2009).

A provocative body of work within psychology approaches resilience from an ecological perspective, viewing individual and community resilience as shaped by interactions in local social and environmental systems (Kelly, 2006). This is entirely consonant with Indigenous perspectives, save that the natural environment is understood not as something external to or in opposition to human interests but as itself constitutive of human nature. But stories that were once told only within families and communities now operate in a much larger arena. This requires rethinking the potential contributions of stories of resilience in terms of broader political processes (Niezen, 2009).

Local cultures and communities are embedded in larger national, transnational and global or planetary systems that influence individual's experience, as well as the dynamics of family, and community. Through mass media and economic forces, macro-social economic and political processes reach down to the individual to reshape their daily life, presenting with new challenges, opportunities and constraints. But the new forms of networking made possible by the Internet and electronic media also allow individuals and remote communities to advance their interests in larger popular and political arenas. In these ways, Indigenous cultures and communities may come to play an increasingly active role in the global exchange of cultures and ideas.

Conclusion

Indigenous concepts of resilience are grounded in cultural values that have persisted despite profound changes in the nature of community life. Culturally

distinctive aspects of resilience identified by the participants in our studies in Aboriginal communities include ways of configuring individual and collective identity in relation to traditional creation stories, collective history, the renewal of Aboriginal languages and the honoring of deeply felt connections to family and to the land. Table 31.1 summarizes some of the distinctive sources of resilience in Aboriginal communities, along with methods of promotion and potential measures for use in future research.

The ongoing renewal of identity and community among Aboriginal peoples in Canada involves revisioning collective history in ways that valorize Indigenous traditions. This critical history recognizes the scale and scope of the challenges faced by Indigenous people and sees their persistence despite great odds as clear evidence of individual and collective resilience (Sioui, 1992). Re-examining the historical record from an Indigenous point of view underscores the ethical values that lay behind the original negotiations and treaties with the European colonizers. Indeed, the philosopher and social critic John Ralston Saul has outlined the crucial contributions of Indigenous thought to the original political framing of Canada as a new nation (Saul, 2008). He argues that the language of fairness and equity that is characteristic of Canadian political rhetoric and identity stems directly from our collective Aboriginal heritage (Saul, 2008).

Another source of individual and collective resilience comes from ongoing efforts to preserve and transmit language, culture, and spiritual wisdom to the next generation as resources for self-fashioning, communal solidarity and well-being. Every Aboriginal language has unique vocabulary associated with specific environments and a way of life (Harrison, 2007). The recuperation and transmission of language and culture strengthens a sense of collective identity and directly counteracts the cultural discontinuity and dispossession that resulted from the efforts of governmental and religious institutions to extinguish Aboriginal identity (LaDuke, 2005).

In addition to the sources of resilience that result from affirming their unique cultures, identities and communities, many Indigenous peoples

Table 31.1 Sources of Aboriginal community resilience[a]

Dimensions	Strategies for promotion	Indicators
Family and community connectedness	Parenting programs Early childhood programs Recreational and leisure activities Supporting voluntary community associations Religious congregations	Level of support from relatives Intergenerational communication Positive parenting and family communication Strengths-based interactions in families
Oral tradition and storytelling	Sharing of history and tradition through storytelling activities at family, ceremonial and informal events Story telling on local radio and at communal events	Knowledge of traditional stories Community sharing of stories
Connection to the land	Maintaining access to traditional lands and subsistence activities Hunter support programs	Participation in land-based activities Consumption of country food
Healing traditions	Recognizing healers and associated traditions Integrating healing practices in primary health care and other settings	Number of healers or others with healing knowledge Frequency of healing activities Number of people participating
Spirituality and ceremony	Honoring traditional forms of spirituality Powwows and other ceremonial activities	Number of elders or others with ceremonial knowledge Frequency of ceremonies Number of people participating
Collective knowledge and identity	Culture camps Language programs	Number of different types and frequency of activities to learn, honor or celebrate collective knowledge and identity
Cultural continuity	Developing local government Adapting traditional forms of social organization to meet new challenges	Local control of fire, police, education, social services and other organizations Cultural heritage centers
Political activism	Recognizing indigenous rights Programs to develop youth leadership	Participation in land claims, self-government, involvement of community in challenges to development

[a]Based in part on Kirmayer et al. (2010), p. 89)

are strengthening individual and collective agency through political activism. Active engagement in land claims or other forms of political action, including the recognition of Indigenous rights, can bring material benefits but it also reinforces collective identity, efficacy and self-esteem (Chandler & Lalonde, 2008). Collective efficacy, in turn, may strengthen individual efficacy and help individuals feel more capable of taking action to address their own needs (Tiessen, Taylor, & Kirmayer, 2010).

Aboriginal perspectives remind us that much of what seems to promote resilience originates outside the individual. While work on resilience within psychology and psychiatry has emphasized individual traits or skills, resilience can also be a feature of whole communities. To the extent that communities exist in an ecological balance with their surrounding environment, they require a moral economy regulated by ideas about co-existence. For Indigenous peoples, these images of co-existence have been conveyed through traditional and contemporary stories that are built around culturally informed notions of personhood that link the individual to family and community (both past and present), to the land and, often, to a spiritual world of ancestors and other-than-human persons that demand respect (Nadasdy, 2005).

Ethnographic research suggests that culturally based narratives provide cognitive and rhetorical resources for resilience in Aboriginal communities. Narratives of historical continuity speak directly to the ruptures that have occurred because colonization and the institutional suppression of Indigenous cultures. Traditional stories of origin and creation along with the adventures of culture heroes and trickster figures encode ideas about the right relationship of individuals to others and to the environment as well as moral and esthetic ideas about balance, harmony, peace and friendship. These ways of narrating identity can contribute to resilience through emotion regulation, problem solving, social positioning and communal solidarity. Of course, resilience is not simply a matter of processes internal to individuals or communities. The ways that Aboriginal peoples are portrayed in mass media and popular culture as well as in the discourse of the bureaucratic and technocratic institutions of government impact powerfully on their well-being (de Leeuw et al., 2010). Stories of Aboriginal history and identity circulate both within and beyond the community, reconfiguring representations of Aboriginal peoples in the larger society in ways that can foster resilience through recognition, respect and reconciliation (Warry, 2007). These stories also provide ways to think about the social and political changes that must occur to reduce health disparities and ensure well-being not only for Indigenous peoples but for all who share this planet.

Acknowledgment This work was supported by a grant from the Canadian Institutes of Health Research, Institute for Aboriginal Peoples Health, "Roots of Resilience: Transformations of Identity and Community in Indigenous Mental Health" (CIHR-77837), L.J. Kirmayer, Principal Investigator. Portions of the chapter are adapted from Kirmayer, Dandeneau, Marshall, Phillips, and Jessen Williamson (2011).

References

Adamson, A., Daborn, G., Houston, J., & Tootoo, V. (2009). Inuit cyberspace: The struggle for access for Inuit Qaujimajatuqangit. *Journal of Canadian Studies, 43*(2), 220–249.

Adelson, N. (2000). Re-imagining aboriginality: An indigenous peoples' response to social suffering. *Transcultural Psychiatry, 37*(1), 11–34.

Adelson, N. (2005). The embodiment of inequity: Health disparities in Aboriginal. Canada. *Canadian Journal of Public Health, 96*(Suppl 2), S45–S61.

Ajunnginiq Centre. (2006). Suicide prevention: Inuit traditional practices that encouraged resilience and coping. Ottawa: Ajunnginiq Centre, National Aboriginal Health Organization.

Alfred, G. T. (2009). Colonialism and state dependency. *Journal of Aboriginal Health, 5*(2), 42–60.

Alfred, T. (2005). *Wasáse: Indigenous pathways of action and freedom*. Peterborough: Broadview.

Barsh, R. L., & Marshall, J. B. (1998). Mi'kmaw (Micmaq) constitutional law. In B. E. Johansen (Ed.), *The encyclopedia of Native American legal tradition* (pp. 192–209). Westport: Greenwood Press.

Berger, T. R. (1977). *Northern frontier, northern homeland: The report of the Mackenzie Valley pipeline inquiry*. Ottawa: Minister of Supply and Services.

Blanchard, D. (1980). *Seven generations: A history of Kanienkehaka*. Montreal: Church Baines.

Boyd, B. (2009). *On the origin of stories: Evolution, cognition and fiction*. Cambridge: Harvard University Press.

Brant Castellano, M., Archibald, L., & DeGagné, M. (Eds.). (2008). *From truth to reconciliation: Transforming the legacy of residential schools.* Ottawa: Aboriginal Healing Foundation.

Bringhurst, R. (2008). *The tree of meaning: Language, mind and ecology.* Berkeley: Counterpoint.

Brody, H. (1987). *Living arctic: Hunters of the Canadian North.* Vancouver: Douglas & McIntyre.

Brody, H. (2010). *The other side of Eden: Hunters, farmers and the shaping of the world.* Vancouver: Douglas & McIntyre.

Bruner, J. (1990). *Acts of meaning.* Cambridge: Harvard University Press.

Bruner, J. (2002). *Making stories: Law, literature, life.* New York: Farrar, Straus and Giroux.

Burack, J., Blidner, A., Flores, H., & Fitch, T. (2007). Constructions and deconstructions of risk, resilience and wellbeing: A model for understanding the development of Aboriginal adolescents. *Australasian Psychiatry, 15*(Suppl 1), S18–S23.

Canadian Institutes of Health Research. (2007). *Guidelines for health research involving Aboriginal people.* Ottawa: Canadian Institutes of Health Research.

Carson, B., Dunbar, T., Chenhall, R. D., & Bailie, R. S. (Eds.). (2007). *Social determinants of indigenous health.* Crows Nest: Allen & Unwin.

Chamberlin, J. E. (2003). *If this is your land, where are your stories? Finding common ground.* Toronto: A. A. Knopf.

Chandler, M. J., & Lalonde, C. E. (2008). Cultural continuity as a moderator of suicide risk among Canada's First Nations. In L. J. Kirmayer & G. Valaskakis (Eds.), *Healing traditions: The mental health of Aboriginal peoples in Canada* (pp. 221–248). Vancouver: University of British Columbia Press.

Charney, D. S. (2004). Psychobiological mechanisms of resilience and vulnerability: Implications for successful adaptation to extreme stress. *American Journal of Psychiatry, 161*(2), 195–216.

Clairmont, D., & McMillan, J. (2001). *Directions in Mi'kmaq justice: An evaluation of the Mi'kmaq Justice Institute and its aftermath.* Halifax: The Tripartite Forum on Native Justice.

de Leeuw, S., Greenwood, M., & Cameron, E. (2010). Deviant constructions: How governments preserve colonial narratives of addictions and poor mental health to intervene into the lives of Indigenous children and families in Canada. *International Journal of Mental Health and Addiction, 8,* 282–295.

Denham, A. R. (2008). Rethinking historical trauma: Narratives of resilience. *Transcultural Psychiatry, 45*(3), 391–414.

Dion, S. D. (2009). *Braiding histories: Learning from Aboriginal peoples' experiences and perspectives.* Vancouver: University of British Columbia Press.

Dion Buffalo, Y. R. (1990). Seeds of thought, arrows of change: Native storytelling as metaphor. In T. A. Laidlaw, C. Malmo, et al. (Eds.), *Healing voices: Feminist approaches to therapy with women.* San Francisco: Jossey-Bass.

Ebi, K. L., & Semenza, J. C. (2008). Community-based adaptation to the health impacts of climate change. *American Journal of Preventive Medicine, 35*(5), 501–507.

Edge, L., & McCallum, T. (2006). Métis identity: Sharing traditional knowledge and healing practices at Métis Elders' gatherings. *Pimatisiwin: A Journal of Aboriginal and Indigenous Community Health, 4*(2), 83–115.

Episkenew, J. (2009). *Taking back our spirits: Indigenous literature, public policy, and healing.* Winnipeg: University of Manitoba Press.

Fleming, J. E., & Ledogar, R. (2008). Resilience, an evolving concept: A review of literature relevant to Aboriginal research. *Pimatisiwin: A Journal of Aboriginal and Indigenous Community Health, 6*(2), 7–23.

Fletcher, C. (2003). Community-based participatory research relationships with Aboriginal communities in Canada: An overview of context and process. *Pimatziwin, 1*(1), 27–61.

Garmezy, N. (1993). Children in poverty: Resilience despite risk. *Psychiatry, 56*(1), 127–136.

Gone, J. P., & Kirmayer, L. J. (2010). On the wisdom of considering culture and context in psychopathology. In T. Millon, R. F. Krueger, & E. Simonsen (Eds.), *Contemporary directions in psychopathology: Scientific foundations of the DSM-V and ICD-11* (pp. 72–96). New York: Guilford.

Gracey, M., & King, M. (2009). Indigenous health part 1: Determinants and disease patterns. *Lancet, 374*(9683), 65–75.

Harrison, K. D. (2007). *When languages die: The extinction of the world's languages and the erosion of human knowledge.* New York: Oxford University Press.

Harvey, G. H. (2006). *Animism: Respecting the living world.* New York: Columbia University Press.

Herbert, E., & McCannell, K. (1997). Talking back: Six First Nations women's stories on recovery from childhood sexual abuse and additions. *Canadian Journal of Community Mental Health, 16*(2), 51–68.

Hodge, F. S., Pasqua, A., Marquez, C. A., & Geishirt-Cantrell, B. (2002). Utilizing traditional storytelling to promote wellness in American Indian communities. *Journal of Transcultural Nursing, 13*(1), 6–11.

Holton, T. L., Brass, G. M., & Kirmayer, L. J. (2009). The discourses of resilience, "enculturation" and identity in Aboriginal mental health research. In T. Teo, P. Stenner, A. Rutherford, E. Park, & C. Baerveldt (Eds.), *Varieties of theoretical psychology: International philosophical and practical concerns* (pp. 194–204). Concord: Captus.

Hornborg, A.-C. (2008). *Mi'kmaq landscapes: From animism to sacred ecology.* Burlington: Ashgate.

Hot, A. (2009). Language rights and language choices: The potential of Inukitut literacy. *Journal of Canadian Studies, 43*(2), 181–197.

Iarocci, G., Root, R., & Burack, J. A. (2008). Social competence and mental health among Aboriginal youth: An integrative developmental perspective. In L. J.

Kirmayer & G. Valaskakis (Eds.), *Healing traditions: The mental health of Aboriginal peoples in Canada* (pp. 80–106). Vancouver: University of British Columbia Press.

Jessen Williamson, K. (2000). Celestial and social families of the Inuit. In R. Laliberte, P. Settee, J. B. Waldram, R. Innes, B. Macdougall, L. McBain, & F. L. Barron (Eds.), *Expressions in Canadian native studies* (pp. 125–144). Saskatoon: University of Saskatchewan Extension Press.

Jessen Williamson, K. (2011). *Inherit my heaven: Kalaalliit gender relations.* Nuuk: Inussuk.

Kelly, J. G. (2006). *Becoming ecological: An expedition into community psychology.* New York: Oxford University Press.

Keyes, C. L. (2007). Promoting and protecting mental health as flourishing: A complementary strategy for improving national mental health. *American Psychologist, 62*(2), 95–108.

King, M., Smith, A., & Gracey, M. (2009). Indigenous health part 2: The underlying causes of the health gap. *Lancet, 374*(9683), 76–85.

King, T. (2003). *The truth about stories: A native narrative.* Toronto: House of Anansi Press.

Kirby, A. P. (1991). *Narrative and the self.* Bloomington: Indiana University Press.

Kirmayer, L. J. (2007). Psychotherapy and the cultural concept of the person. *Transcultural Psychiatry, 44*(2), 232–257.

Kirmayer, L. J., Dandeneau, S., Marshall, E., Phillips, M. L., & Jessen Williamson, K. (2011). Rethinking resilience from indigenous perspectives. *Canadian Journal of Psychiatry, 56*(2), 84–91.

Kirmayer, L. J., Fletcher, C., & Watt, R. (2008). Locating the ecocentric self: Inuit concepts of mental health and illness. In L. J. Kirmayer & G. Valaskakis (Eds.), *Healing traditions: The mental health of Aboriginal peoples in Canada* (pp. 289–314). Vancouver: University of British Columbia Press.

Kirmayer, L. J., Sedhev, M., Whitley, R., Dandeneau, S., & Isaac, C. (2009). Community resilience: Models, metaphors and measures. *Journal of Aboriginal Health, 7*(1), 62–117.

Kirmayer, L. J., Whitley, R., & Fauras, V. (2010). Community team approaches to mental health services and wellness promotion. Ottawa: Health Canada, First Nations and Inuit Health Branch.

Korhonen, M. (2007). Resilience: Overcoming challenges and moving on positively [Tittatuuniq : aniguatittiniq pijariatujunik amma sivumuagiarniq naggaittukkut]. Ottawa: Ajunnginiq Centre, National Aboriginal Health Organization.

LaDuke, W. (2005). *Recovering the sacred: The power of naming and claiming.* Toronto: Between the Lines.

Lear, J. (2006). *Radical hope: Ethics in the face of cultural devastation.* Cambridge: Harvard University Press.

Luthar, S. S., Sawyer, J. A., & Brown, P. J. (2006). Conceptual issues in studies of resilience: Past, present, and future research. *Annals of the New York Academy of Sciences, 1094,* 105–115.

Macauley, A. C., Commanda, L. E., Gibson, N., McCabe, M. L., Robbins, C. M., & Twohig, P. L. (1999). Participatory research maximises community and lay involvement. *British Medical Journal, 319,* 774–778.

Marmot, M. (2007). Achieving health equity: From root causes to fair outcomes. *Lancet, 370*(9593), 1153–1163.

Marshall, E., & Kirmayer, L. J. (2009). *Becoming human: The Three Crosses and Mi'kmaq understandings of resilience.* Montreal: Culture and Mental Health Research Unit, Institute of Community and Family Psychiatry.

Masten, A. S. (2007). Resilience in developing systems: Progress and promise as the fourth wave rises. *Developmental Psychopathology, 19*(3), 921–930.

McAdams, D. P. (1991). Self and story. In A. J. Stewart, J. M. Healy Jr., D. Ozer, & R. Hogan (Eds.), *Perspectives in personality* (Vol. 3B, pp. 133–159). London: Jessica Kingsley Publishers.

McCormick, R. (2008). Aboriginal approaches to counselling. In L. J. Kirmayer & G. Valaskakis (Eds.), *Healing traditions: The mental health of Aboriginal peoples in Canada* (pp. 337–355). Vancouver: University of British Columbia Press.

Nabokov, P. (2002). *A forest of time: American Indian ways of history.* New York: Cambridge University Press.

Nadasdy, P. (2005). Transcending the debate over the ecologically noble Indian: Indigenous peoples and environmentalism. *Ethnohistory, 52*(2), 291–331.

Niezen, R. (2009). *The rediscovered self: Indigenous identity and cultural justice.* Montreal: McGill-Queen's Press.

Norton, C. S. (1989). *Life metaphors: Stories of ordinary survival.* Carbondale: Southern Illinois University Press.

Peters, E., & Rosenberg, M. (1991). The Ontario Metis: Some aspects of a Metis identity. *Canadian Ethnic Studies, 23*(1), 71.

Peterson, J., & Brown, J. S. H. (Eds.). (1993). *The new peoples: Being and becoming Metis in North America.* Winnipeg: University of Manitoba Press.

Phillips, M. (2010). *Understanding resilience through revitalizing traditional ways of healing in a Kanien'kehá:ka community.* MA thesis, Concordia University, Montreal.

Phillips, S. K. (2000). *The Kahnawake Mohawks and the St. Lawrence Seaway.* MA Thesis, McGill University, Montreal.

Porter, T. S. (2008). *And grandma said: Iroquois teachings as passed down through the oral tradition.* Philadelphia: Xlibris Corporation.

Potvin, L., Cargo, M., McComber, A. M., Delormier, T., & Macaulay, A. C. (2003). Implementing participatory intervention and research in communities: Lessons from the Kahnawake schools diabetes prevention project in Canada. *Social Science & Medicine, 56,* 1295–1305.

Reading, C. L., & Wien, F. (2009). *Health inequalities and social determinants of Aboriginal peoples' health.*

Victoria: National Collaborating Centre for Aboriginal Health.

Reading, J. (2009). *The crisis of chronic disease among Aboriginal peoples: A challenge for public health, population health and social policy.* Victoria: Centre for Aboriginal Health Research.

Reid, J. (1995). *Myth, symbol and colonial encounter: British and Mi'kmaq in Acadia, 1700–1867.* Ottawa: University of Ottawa Press.

Reid, J. I. M. (2005). Angels of light: A Mi'kmaq myth in a new arché. *Canadian Journal of Native Studies, 25*(2), 463–475.

Richmond, C. A. (2009). The social determinants of Inuit health: A focus on social support in the Canadian Arctic. *International Journal of Circumpolar Health, 68*(5), 471–487.

Richmond, C. A., Ross, N. A., & Egeland, G. M. (2007). Social support and thriving health: A new approach to understanding the health of indigenous Canadians. *American Journal of Public Health, 97*(10), 1827–1833.

Roberts, G., & Holmes, J. (Eds.). (1999). *Healing stories: Narrative in psychiatry and psychotherapy.* Oxford: Oxford University Press.

Russell, F. (2003). *The Canadian crucible: Manitoba's role in Canada's great divide.* Winnipeg: Heartland Associates.

Rutter, M. (1985). Resilience in the face of adversity: Protective factors and resistance to psychiatric disorder. *British Journal of Psychiatry, 147*, 598–611.

Sarbin, T. R. (Ed.). (1986). *Narrative psychology: The storied nature of human conduct.* New York: Praeger.

Saul, J. R. (2008). *A fair country: Telling truths about Canada.* Toronto: Viking Canada.

Sawchuk, J. (2001). Negotiating and identity: Metis political organizations, the Canadian government and competing concepts of aboriginality. *American Indian Quarterly, 25*(1), 73–92.

Sioui, G. E. (1992). *For an Amerindian autohistory: An essay on the foundations of a social ethic.* Montreal: McGill-Queen's University Press.

Speck, F. G. (1915). Some Micmac tales from Cape Breton Island. *Journal of American Folklore, 28*, 59–69.

Statistics Canada. (2008). *Aboriginal peoples in Canada in 2006: Inuit, Métis and First Nations, 2006 census.* Ottawa: Ministry of Industry.

St-Onge, N. (2006). Uncertain margins: Métis and Saulteaux identities in St-Paul-des-Saulteaux, Red River 1821–1870. *Manitoba History, 53*, 2–10.

Stout, M. D., & Kipling, G. (2003). *Aboriginal people, resilience and the residential school legacy.* Ottawa: Aboriginal Healing Foundation.

Tanner, A. (2004). The cosmology of nature, cultural divergence, and the metaphysics of community healing. In C. J. S. Poirier & E. Schwimmer (Eds.), *Figured worlds: Ontological obstacles in intercultural relations* (pp. 189–222). Toronto: University of Toronto Press.

Tiessen, M., Taylor, D. M., & Kirmayer, L. J. (2010). A key individual-to-community link: The impact of perceived collective control on Aboriginal youth well-being. *Pimatisiwin: A Journal of Indigenous and Aboriginal Community Health, 7*(2), 241–267.

Tilly, C. (2006). *Why?* Princeton: Princeton University Press.

Ungar, M. (2004). The importance of parents and other caregivers to the resilience of high-risk adolescents. *Family Process, 43*(1), 23–41.

Van Deusen, K. (2009). *Kiviuq: An I hero and his Siberian cousin.* Montreal: McGill-Queen's University Press.

Vermette, A., & Ferland, M. (2006). *Au temps de la Prairie.* Winnipeg: Éditions du Blé.

Walsh, F. (2006). *Strengthening family resilience* (2nd ed.). New York: The Guilford Press.

Warren, J. A., Berner, J. E., & Curtis, T. (2005). Climate change and human health: Infrastructure impacts to small remote communities in the north. *International Journal of Circumpolar Health, 64*(5), 487–497.

Warry, W. (2007). *Ending denial: Understanding Aboriginal issues.* Toronto: Broadview Press.

Whitbeck, L. B., Chen, X., Hoyt, D. R., & Adams, G. W. (2004). Discrimination, historical loss and enculturation: Culturally specific risk and resiliency factors for alcohol abuse among American Indians. *Journal of Studies of Alcohol, 65*(4), 409–418.

Wieman, C. (2008). Six Nations Mental Health Services: A model of care for Aboriginal communities. In L. J. Kirmayer & G. Valaskakis (Eds.), *Healing traditions: The mental health of Aboriginal peoples in Canada* (pp. 401–418). Vancouver: University of British Columbia Press.

Williamson, K. J., & Kirmayer, L. J. (2010). Inuit ways of knowing: Cosmocentrism and the role of teasing in childrearing. In C. Worthman, P. Plotsky, D. S. Schechter, & C. Cummings (Eds.), *Formative experiences: The interaction of caregiving, culture, and developmental psychobiology* (pp. 299–307). New York: Cambridge University Press.

Wilson, K., & Rosenberg, M. W. (2002). Exploring the determinants of health for First Nations peoples in Canada: Can existing frameworks accommodate traditional activities? *Social Science and Medicine, 55*(11), 2017–2031.

York, G., & Pindera, L. (1991). *People of the Pines.* Toronto: Little, Brown & Company (Canada) Ltd.

Macro, Meso, and Micro-perspectives of Resilience During and After Exposure to War

Orit Nuttman-Shwartz

The contemporary world is characterized by ongoing terror, wars, and ethnic conflicts that primarily harm civilian populations. Terror is defined as a violent act that targets innocent citizens at random in an attempt to create an atmosphere of fear. Terrorist attacks occur at unexpected times and places, and in supposedly safe environments such as coffee shops, shopping malls, and public transportation (Primoratz, 2002/2003).

There is a broad consensus that exposure to terror and war has a negative effect on the emotional health of adults (Bleich, Gelkopf, & Solomon, 2003) as well as on children and youth (Pat-Horenczyk, Schiff, & Dopplet, 2005; Sagy & Braun-Lewensohn, 2009). As such, situations of trauma and stress are related to a host of physical, social, and emotional problems that can intensify developmental conflicts (Macksoud, Dyregrov, & Raundalen, 1993). One of the most prevalent consequences of exposure to war is posttraumatic stress disorder (PTSD) (American Psychiatric Association, 1994; Laufer & Solomon, 2006; Lavi & Solomon, 2005), the effects of which are even more accentuated in situations of ongoing and recurrent exposure to terror. In those situations, there is a need to deal not only with the physical and emotional damage in the immediate aftermath of the attack, but also to deal with the long-term

stress evoked by a threat that is constantly looming (Kline & Mone, 2003). Terr (1991) indicated that such exposure has far-reaching implications for emotional adjustment, and even for the personality of youth who experience it. Nonetheless, the rates of mental health symptoms resulting from exposure range from 5 to 11% of the total population. Therefore, one of the main questions that arise is what is the nature of resilience in the face of terror attacks in general and when there is an ongoing threat of terror in particular.

Coping and Resilience

According to stress theory, personal and social resources enable people to cope with the aftermath of traumatic events (Ben-Sira, 1991; Lazarus & Folkman, 1984). According to Conservation of Resources Theory (Hobfoll, Dunahoo, & Monnier, 1995), the impact of a traumatic event is exacerbated when the event includes loss of personal and social resources. In those cases, coping strategies include instrumental action, problem solving, support seeking, distraction, escape, opposition, and social withdrawal (Skinner & Zimmer-Gembeck, 2007). However, it is still unclear what constitutes a good way of coping, especially in situations of ongoing threat. For example, studies that have examined patterns of coping with ongoing threat suggest that social action tends to exacerbate anxiety, whereas a certain positive detachment might be a better way to cope (Gelkopf, Solomon, Berger, & Bleich, 2008).

O. Nuttman-Shwartz (✉)
Chairperson, The Israeli National Council
for Social Work and the Dean, School of Social Work,
Sapir College, Israel
e-mail: orits@sapir.ac.il

M. Ungar (ed.), *The Social Ecology of Resilience: A Handbook of Theory and Practice*,
DOI 10.1007/978-1-4614-0586-3_32, © Springer Science+Business Media, LLC 2012

Herman (1992) indicated that the victim's social environment can affect the consequences of exposure to a traumatic event. For example, a supportive response from the environment can mitigate the negative consequences of such exposure, whereas a hostile or negative response from the environment can exacerbate the damage and intensify posttraumatic responses. A study conducted in the United States after the bombing of the federal building in Oklahoma in 1995 revealed that when people received low levels of social support, they were at higher risk for developing pathological symptoms (Tucker, Pfefferbaum, Nixon, & Dickson, 2000). Similar findings were revealed in studies conducted among residents of New York after the September 11th attacks (Galea et al., 2002, 2003; Silver, Holman, McIntosh, Poulin, & Gil-Rivas, 2002). In addition, studies that examined adjustment to ongoing terror among Israelis revealed a negative correlation between social support and posttraumatic symptoms (Bleich et al., 2003; Bleich, Gelkopf, Melamed, & Solomon, 2006).

It is important to take personal, social, and environmental resources into account. All of these resources can explain and predict the different responses that people will have to traumatic events (Breckenridge & James, 2010), as well as their ability to cope afterwards (Nuttman-Shwartz, Dekel, & Toval Machiach, 2010). In this regard, recent research on the effects of traumatic events has revealed that the environment and community in general, and the individual's sense of belonging in particular, may protect the individual from the negative consequences of adversity (Masten, 2001; Norris, Stevens, Pfefferbaum, Wyche, & Pfefferbaum, 2008), and can have a positive effect on coping.

Sense of belonging refers to the perception of one's self as part of a collective group (Newbrough & Chavis, 1986) such as the neighborhood, community, or nation. Sense of belonging is characterized by mutual concern, connection, community loyalty, and trust that one's personal needs will be fulfilled through commitment to the group as a whole (Chavis, Hogge, McMillan, & Wandersman, 1986), as well as through the individual's desire to remain in the community (nation, community, place of living, organization

etc.), and the desire to encourage others to join it (Itzhaky, 1995). These manifestations may represent emotional attachment to the land itself, and commitment to the place as evidenced by the desire to continue living there.

According to Fisher, Sonn, and Bishop (2002), people who experience a strong sense of community receive multiple benefits. They are better adjusted, they have goals that reach beyond their own limited aspirations, and they enjoy higher levels of social support and social connectedness. A strong sense of belonging acts as a buffer against external threats, provides a place in which individuals are free to express their identities, and helps individuals deal with changes and difficulties in society at large.

Research findings have revealed that different types of sense of belonging can facilitate coping with stress and traumatic events. Specifically, sense of belonging to the community and to the country or nation can moderate pathological responses (Billig, Kohn, & Levav, 2006; Dekel & Tuval-Mashiach, 2010; Kovatz, Kutz, Rubin, Dekel, & Shenkman, 2006). Schools and colleges have also become communities and support systems for their students, which provide not only education, but also serve as a framework for social, cultural, and interpersonal activities. In that connection, a study conducted by Kia-Keating and Heidi-Ellis (2007) among young refugees revealed that a higher sense of belonging to the school was associated with lower levels of depression and higher levels of self-efficacy, regardless of the level of past exposure to adversity. In addition, Henrich and Shahar (2008) found that school served as a protective resource for middle school students in Israel who experienced Qassam rocket attacks, and that the school had protective effects which helped prevent depression at a time of traumatic stress.

The view that systems in the environment explain the individual's ability to cope with traumatic events is also expressed in the definitions of resilience proposed by Ungar (2008). According to Ungar, resilience is defined as:

> The capacity of individuals to navigate their way to resources that sustain well-being; the capacity of individuals' physical and social ecologies to provide those resources; and the capacity of individuals, their

families and communities to negotiate culturally meaningful ways for resources to be shared. (p. 225)

Ungar's definition highlights the importance of considering the broad system of the individual, community, and state as factors that explain the ability to cope with exposure to traumatic events, and as factors that are consistent with contemporary definitions of war as well as with how the relationships between a society and its citizens are understood. According to these perspectives, security is not just a military or political issue, but is also affected by the individual's sense of security and by the sense of personal, social, and national resilience. As such, security is manifested in the citizen's willingness to live with the ongoing threat of war and terror, and the citizen's ability to maintain a routine life and even develop a quality of life despite exposure to nonnormative stressors (Nuttman-Shwartz, 2008).

In this chapter, we will discuss research related to two levels of an ecological system based on Bronfenbrenner's (1979) ecological systems approach: the macrosystem, as reflected in the nation; and mesosystem, as reflected in the protective social contexts of the community and the school or college. In light of this approach, the following section will begin with a description of the context in which the present study was conducted.

The Macrosystem: Israeli Society

The State of Israel was born as a national home for the Jewish people, and has engaged in continuous battles and struggles since its establishment. This history has contributed to a strong sense of identity among Israelis but also threatens Israel's image as a strong and heroic country. Despite these threats, there are several social mechanisms that protect Israel from fragmentation. Paradoxically, Volkan (1997) argued that the ongoing conflict has helped Israelis continue to propagate social myths such as "glorifying fallen soldiers, Zionism, settlement of the land, and ideological thinking," and has strengthened the social matrix that promotes social solidarity, strengthens the sense of belonging to the country,

justifies governmental social policy, targets an outside enemy, and protects society from external threats (Nuttman-Shwartz & Weinberg, 2008). All of these factors together have helped Israeli society withstand these difficulties, and have even led to high levels of life satisfaction (Bleich et al., 2003).

The Mesosystem: Development Towns, Kibbutzim, and Communities in the Western Negev Region

The Western Negev is on Israel's western border with the Palestinian authority. During the last decade, the Western Negev has been the target of Qassam rocket attacks, which steadily increased until the Israel Defense Forces engaged in a operation in early 2009. Since then, the number of the missile attacks has decreased dramatically. However, from time to time missiles are still fired and continue to threaten the residents of that area.

Qassam rockets are relatively unsophisticated weapons, with low accuracy and low deadliness. At the same time, the frequent firings at all hours of the day and night have generated considerable uncertainty and anxiety in the lives of the residents of the stricken area, and have led to a heightened state of physical and emotional alertness. However, because the interval between the time the missile is fired and the time it lands is very short, there is little opportunity for self-protection. People abruptly stop what they are doing, run for shelter in inadequately protected areas, and wait for impact. Occasionally, Qassam rockets have penetrated into people's homes. Although most of the damage has been caused to property, several persons including children have been killed in direct Qassam hits.

The Western Negev consists of two different types of localities. One type of locality is development towns, as exemplified by Sderot. Like the other 28 development towns in Israel, Sderot was established in the 1950s, a few years after Israel's declaration of independence, in an attempt to absorb the massive influx of immigrants who arrived in the country during that period, and with the aim of populating the peripheral areas of the country.

Despite the efforts of the government, most of these towns have not managed to build a strong and diverse economic base. Hence, over the years they have become pockets of deprivation and poverty (Yiftachel, 2000). Like most of these towns, Sderot is characterized by high unemployment and a low level of education among its residents. Moreover, there is a pervasive sense of deprivation among people living in Sderot, who feel that they are being neglected by their government and ignored by wealthier, more fortunate populations that live elsewhere in the country.

The other type of locality in the Western Negev region is rural localities, which include kibbutzim. Kibbutzim are unique Israeli communities, which were originally established to farm and protect the land, and were inspired by ideals of economic and social equality, mutual help and responsibility. Until the 1980s, kibbutzim were centers of the Israeli elite, and their members served in an extraordinarily high proportion of senior military and government posts. Since then, the economic situation of most of the kibbutzim has deteriorated, and their prestige has declined considerably. As a result, most have undergone processes of privatization which has resulted in economic inequality and a loosening of social bonds. Nonetheless, kibbutzim are still characterized as relatively tight-knit communities, and their members retain the original elements of communal ideology and pride. Moreover, even on less affluent kibbutzim, the quality of life is relatively high, with lots of greenery, good schools, cultural activities, and very low crime rates.

Earlier studies have revealed that kibbutz residents fare better emotionally under stressful conditions than do residents of other communities (Benyamini et al., 2004). This was attributed to the kibbutz ideology and communal lifestyle, which provide a measure of protection against stress.

Although the comparison is somewhat difficult to make because of the different levels of exposure to rocket attacks in the respective locations, it is also important to attempt to examine the impact of the Qassam attacks on different types of social systems with varying levels of community resources. Specifically, the study discussed in this chapter focused on residents of Sderot, members of kibbutzim in the Western Negev region, and students at a college in the Western Negev.

Method

The data are based on two studies conducted among residents of the region. The first study was conducted in 2005 among 134 residents of the Western Negev region: 67 lived on two kibbutzim (rural localities), and 67 lived in the development town of Sderot. Participants were matched by gender and age. The participants ranged in age from 18 to 76 years ($M=44.89$, SD$=13.34$). More than half (55%) were born in Israel; 60% were married; 26% were single, and 14% divorced or widowed. Fifty four percent of the participants reported below-average income, 25% reported above-average income, and 21% indicated that their income is about average. However, significant differences were found between the participants from the two groups of localities ($\chi^2=12.53$, df$=4$, $p<0.05$). Thirty percent of the kibbutz residents reported that they had not been directly exposed to rocket attacks, compared to only 14% of participants living in Sderot. Conversely, 12% of the residents of Sderot reported that a rocket had fallen on or very close to their home, whereas no kibbutz residents reported such an experience. The differences in education levels and direct exposure were taken into account in our analyses.

The second study was conducted in 2007. The sample consisted of 500 students at a community college in the area. The students were from three main localities: Sderot ($n=69$), rural settlements adjacent to the border of the Gaza Strip ($n=73$), and localities outside of the confrontation zone ($n=358$). Significant differences between groups were found in levels of personal exposure to rocket attacks: ($X^2=24.53$ df$=2$ $p<0.01$). Ninety four percent of the students from Sderot ($n=65$) had been directly exposed to an attack, compared with 88% of those from rural settlements ($n=64$), and 70% of the students from other areas ($n=245$). No significant differences were found among the three groups in any of the sociodemographic variables – age, gender, religiosity, year of study, family status, exposure to other traumatic events, and self-reported economic and occupational status. Most of the participants in the overall sample were women (71%, $n=331$), and they ranged from 19 to 33 years of age ($M=25$, $SD=2$); the majority of participants were born in Israel (79%, $n=373$), and 17% ($n=80$) were born in the Commonwealth of Independent States; most were never married (89%, $n=420$); 70% ($n=330$) were in their first year of college, and 30% ($n=142$) were in their second or third year.

Measures

The measures consisted of several questionnaires, which examined the following variables: socio-demographic characteristics, exposure to rocket attacks, distress, ways of coping, and scores on three Sense of Belonging scales.

Socio-demographic characteristics. The questionnaire contained data on gender, age, family status, education, and economic status.

Exposure to Qassam rocket attacks. Exposure to Qassam rocket attacks was assessed by one question, in which participants were asked to indicate whether they had ever been exposed to the rockets (no/yes).

PTSD. This variable was measured by the PTSD Inventory (Solomon et al., 1993), a self-report scale consisting of 17 statements that correspond to the 17 core PTSD symptoms listed in the *Diagnostic and Statistical Manual of Mental Disorders, Fourth Edition* (American Psychiatric Association, 1994). Participants were asked to indicate whether they had the symptom described in each statement, on a scale ranging from 1 (*not at all*) to 4 (*very often*). Participants were identified as having PTSD if they endorsed at least one intrusive symptom (Criterion A), three avoidant symptoms (Criterion B), and two hyperarousal symptoms (Criterion C). In addition, distress was calculated as the mean number of symptoms endorsed by the participants. The scale has been found to have high convergent validity compared with diagnoses

based on structured clinical interviews (Solomon et al., 1993). In the current study, the Cronbach's alpha for the 17 items was 0.91.

Sense of belonging. This variable was measured by three scales. The first scale was developed by Itzhaky (1995), and consisted of 12 items, which tapped the participants' sense of belonging to Israel (e.g., I feel part of the country), as well as their commitment to the country (e.g., I won't leave the country even if the security situation deteriorates). For each item, participants were asked to indicate their agreement on a scale from 1 (*not at all*) to 4 (*very much*). The Cronbach's alpha in the current study is 0.87. The second scale was developed for the second study, and consisted of three items which measured the participants' sense of belonging to the college: "I feel part of the college," "I like to study at the college," and "I recommend that others study at the college." Participants were asked to indicate the extent to which they agree with each statement, on a scale ranging from 1 (*not at all*) to 4 (*very much*). One overall score for sense of belonging was derived by calculating the mean of the responses to the three items for each participant. The Cronbach's alpha in the current study was 0.90. The third scale was the Neighborhood Cohesion Scale (Buckner, 1988) – a six-item self-report measure which assessed the participants' sense of belonging to the community (e.g., "I feel connected to my neighborhood," and "the neighbors in our community are nicer than in other places"). Participants rated their agreement with the statements on a four-point Likert scale ranging from 1 (*strongly disagree*) to 4 (*strongly agree*). The higher the scores, the stronger the participants' sense of belonging to the community. The original scale has good psychometric properties. Cronbach's alpha for the current study was 0.83.

Ways of coping. This variable was assessed through a modified version of the COPE questionnaire (Carver, 1997), which was used by Bleich et al. (2003) to examine how the Israeli population copes with terror. Participants were asked to indicate how often they used each coping strategy, on a five-point scale ranging from

0 (*not at all*) to 4 (*a great deal*). Factor analysis with Varimax rotation for the items revealed three distinct factors: support-seeking activities; use of alcohol and medications; and acceptance of the situation. The Cronbach's alpha reliability of the questionnaire used in the current study was 0.71.

Results

Group Comparison

In both studies, the residents of Sderot reported more PTS symptoms than did the residents of rural localities, although the levels of PTS were still relatively low. The first ANOVA for PTS revealed a significant effect for place of residence: $F(1,121)=7.69$, $p<0.01$. In the second study, the students from Sderot reported the highest levels of distress. Interestingly, however, the levels of distress among students from localities surrounding the Gaza Strip were similar to those found among students living outside of the area that was exposed to rocket attacks: 26% of the students from Sderot were classified as having PTSD, compared with 12.5% in the first study. In contrast, 6% of the students from localities surrounding the Gaza Strip had PTSD in the second study, compared with 4.5% in the first study; and 6% of the students living elsewhere were found to have PTSD in the second study.

Sense of Belonging

As mentioned, in the first study we measured the participants' sense of belonging to their community and the country. The findings showed that the participants' sense of belonging to their community and the country were also high (over 3 on a scale of 1–4) in both groups. For example, a high percentage of the participants living in Sderot indicated that their relationships with the residents of the area are important to them, and that they can ask their neighbors for help when they have a problem. In contrast, the kibbutz residents emphasized the sense of belonging to the country more than the sense of belonging to their community.

Most of the kibbutz residents indicated that they "are proud to belong to the country" (91%), that they "feel part of the country" (94%), and that "they don't want to leave the country" (80%). About 74% "would recommend that their children stay in Israel," and about 80% felt that their "social relationships in Israel are very important."

In the second study, we investigated the participants' sense of belonging to the college. The findings showed that the sense of belonging to the college was highest among students from the localities surrounding the Gaza Strip, and was significantly higher than among the students living outside of the area exposed to attacks.

Sense of Belonging as a Protective Factor

Sense of belonging to the community. No correlation was found between sense of belonging to the locality and the intensity of stress symptoms ($p>0.05$).

Sense of belonging to the country. In the first study, regressions were conducted, with PTS as dependent variable. All of the variables together explained 54.8% of the variance in posttraumatic stress symptoms: $F(11, 121)=12.15$, $p<0.001$. The variables that entered in the second step explained an additional 21.6% of the variance in PTS symptoms, where sense of belonging to the country mostly contributed to the explaining of that variance. That is, higher levels of sense of belonging were associated with fewer posttraumatic stress symptoms. The variables entered in the third step explained an additional 10.1% of the explained variance in PTSD, and several interactions contributed significantly to explaining that variance. To understand the interaction between place of residence and sense belonging, the *b* coefficients for sense of belonging as a predictor of posttraumatic stress symptoms were calculated separately for the residents of Sderot and the residents of kibbutzim. The calculations showed a significant negative *b* coefficient for sense of belonging and posttraumatic stress symptoms among the kibbutz residents ($b=-1.60$), and a low positive *b* coefficient ($b=0.15$) among the Sderot residents.

In other words, the association between sense of belonging to the country and posttraumatic stress was different for residents of the two types of localities. More specifically, among the residents of kibbutzim, a higher sense of belonging to the country was associated with fewer posttraumatic stress symptoms. To understand the interaction between sense of belonging and appraisal of threat, we calculated the b coefficients for predictors of posttraumatic stress symptoms separately for participants with a high and low sense of belonging to the country. The findings showed that among those with high sense of belonging, the correlation between appraisal of threat and posttraumatic stress was low and positive ($b=0.84$), whereas the correlation among participants with a low sense of belonging to the country was higher ($b=2.56$). This finding indicates that sense of belonging moderates the relationship between appraisal of threat and posttraumatic stress. The b coefficients, which were calculated separately for participants with a high and low sense of belonging to the country, showed that the correlation between appraisal of challenge and posttraumatic stress symptoms among participants with a high sense of belonging to the country was positive ($b=0.88$), whereas the correlation among participants with a low sense of belonging to the country was negative (-0.50). This indicates that the sense of belonging to the community had a moderating effect on the association between appraisal of challenge and posttraumatic stress symptoms.

Sense of belonging to the college. Hierarchical regressions were conducted to identify the contribution of the various study variables to distress. The combined set of variables explained 46.6% of the variance in PTSD: $F(13, 433)=30.08, p<0.001$. In the first step, economic status, place of residence, and level of exposure to attacks contributed significantly to the variance: low economic status, living in Sderot, and exposure to Qassam attacks were associated with a high level of posttraumatic stress symptoms. In the second step, all of the variables were found to contribute significantly to posttraumatic stress symptoms: the higher the participants' sense of belonging to the college and the more they used accommodation as a way of coping with the situation, the lower their levels of posttraumatic stress, whereas high levels of alcohol consumption, support seeking, and disengagement were associated with high levels of posttraumatic stress.

The second significant interaction was between the coping pattern of accommodation and sense of belonging to the college. The regression revealed that the association between accommodation and posttraumatic stress depended on the student's level of belonging. Among students with a high level of belonging to the college, the association between accommodation and posttraumatic stress was lower than among those with a low level of belonging ($b=-0.05$ and $b=-0.14$, respectively). This suggests that the coping pattern of accommodation may help students compensate for the lack of a strong sense of belonging to the college community.

Discussion

The findings of the two studies reveal that despite their exposure to ongoing threat, the participants' sense of belonging to the country, the locality, and the college remained high. In contrast to the results of previous research conducted in the region before the onset of the ongoing threat (Yiftachel, 2000), no significant differences were found between the residents of kibbutzim and the residents of Sderot with regard to sense of belonging. A possible explanation for this finding is that the situation of ongoing threat causes residents of the area to change their attitudes and focus more on equality, similarity, and creating a sense of cohesiveness with the understanding that everyone in the region is vulnerable, irrespective of ethnic origin and economic status. Therefore, the sense of mutuality and shared destiny increases. Moreover, several studies conducted among children and adolescents at times of war indicate that the sense of cohesion might also derive from the need to encourage mutual assistance and stay in a familiar environment in order to cope effectively with the threat (Laor et al., 2006).

Attachment to a place is a source of protection and satisfaction. According to Bowlby (1973), attachment to a place, like attachment to a person, can be conceptualized as a series of emotions and behaviors that modulate distance from the object of attachment and enable the individual to maintain contact with that object. As such, individuals need to live in a satisfactory environment that is characterized by strong, well-developed relationships, and in which they develop a sense of belonging (Fullilove, 1996). However, various theorists have argued that in situations of danger, and especially when communities face a common enemy, they tend to establish a heightened sense of cohesion (Volkan, 1997). In those situations, the community, neighbors, and friends play a protective family role, which can improve relationships and strengthen affiliation with the community (Hobfoll, Canetti-Nisim, & Robert, 2006). When a security threat exists, some residents and their family members prefer to stay away from the danger zone. In those cases, the community also plays a familial role and can compensate for the absence of family members. Consistent with this argument, studies conducted in the Gaza area prior to the evacuation of settlements and the enforcement of the Disengagement Plan Law in 2005 have revealed that the local community played a significant role in providing support (Dekel & Tuval-Mashiach, 2010). Other studies have highlighted the importance of the environmental system in promoting personal resilience and enhancing the ability of the residents in that area to withstand the threat (Norris et al., 2008; Ungar, 2008). Consistent with those findings, even though no significant correlation was found between sense of belonging and distress, the levels of belonging reported by the participants were much higher than expected. This might indicate that the sense of belonging not only moderated their posttraumatic symptoms, but also enhanced their ability to cope despite high levels of distress.

A similar finding, and one which is surprising, relates to the participants' sense of belonging to the country. Contrary to the negative feelings that Israeli border populations commonly express (e.g., "we are forgotten" and "we are the distant periphery"), the participants in this study expressed positive feelings toward the country. Moreover, the residents who reported higher levels of identification and belonging to the country also had lower levels of posttraumatic stress symptoms. The feeling of living in a good place is a source of resilience and strength, whether it derives from the reality of not having anywhere else to go, or whether it reflects an ideological attachment to the land. These feelings not only reflect the resilience of communities, but also provided an incentive for the members of those communities to make a concerted effort to cope with the existential threat. The participants' decision to stay in the region might indicate the presence of defenses that promoted optimism and posttraumatic growth, and that enhanced the residents' resilience and stamina. Otherwise, they would have reasonably decided to leave the vulnerable kibbutz and the insecure country. Moreover, they would have faced the difficult task of discussing the significance of their choice to live in the face of a constant existential threat. This finding points to social and cultural dimensions that are a source of strength that enable people to cope with stressful situations. Studies have found that on the one hand, endorsement of a social ideology and ethos can promote resilience in the face of security threats. On the other hand, they help to justify continuing to live in the shadow of an ongoing security threat resulting from political conflict (Gretz, 1995; Schermer, 2003).

In this regional cultural context, it is possible that a sense of belonging facilitates acceptance of "the price of being Israeli," and reflects agreement with the ideology and mission of the country as a whole. This can lead to a strong sense of belonging to the locality of residence, as reflected in the findings of the first study, and to a strong sense of belonging to a college that is under fire, as reflected in the findings of the second study.

Before concluding, several limitations of the studies need to be mentioned. The studies were conducted at different points in time, and it was evident that many of the participants coped successfully with the ongoing traumatic reality even though levels of distress increased with prolonged exposure to trauma. However, the research populations in the two studies were not identical, and the studies did not continue to examine the same participants over an extended period of time. Notwithstanding this limitation, the findings add new insights into the contribution of social systems to facilitating resilience in situations of threat and terror. Whereas previous studies focused mainly on short-term exposure to situations of terror and war (Shacham & Lahad, 2004), the present study focused on an ongoing traumatic reality, and examined social dimensions of national security such as sense of belonging to the country, sense of belonging to the locality, and sense of belonging to the college. Those dimensions reflect consensus and social solidarity, which are considered to be components of psychosocial and political resilience. This is particularly important in environments such as those examined by the two studies presented here, where any return to routine life is accompanied by the constant fear that an attack will happen again soon. In those situations, there is not only a need to repair physical and emotional damage in the aftermath of the conflict, but also the need to cope with a perpetual state of stress in the face of a threat that is still looming.

Moreover, there is a dearth of research on adjustment and on the ability of individuals to lead a routine life in a situation of ongoing threat. In particular, there is a lack of longitudinal research that examines the same population at various points in time and in different situations of exposure to trauma. Further, there is a lack of research focusing specifically on resilience and on emotional and behavioral responses to trauma, and on the factors that can enhance coping and resilience while moderating distress. In light of ecological perspectives on resilience, there is a need for further research that will enhance understanding of the ways in which different communal resources, including a sense of belonging to one's community, country and school, influence and mediate human responses to trauma and stress.

References

American Psychiatric Association. (1994). *Diagnostic and statistical manual of mental disorders* (4th ed.). Washington: American Psychiatric Association.

Ben-Sira, Z. (1991). *Regression, stress and readjustment aging: A structured, biopsychosocial perspective on coping and professional support.* New York: Praeger.

Benyamini, Y., Fuchs, Z., Shapira, Z., Novikoy, I., Walter-Ginzburg, A., & Modan, B. (2004). The effect of a communal lifestyle on depressive symptoms in late life. *Journal of Aging and Health, 16*, 151–174.

Billig, M., Kohn, R., & Levav, I. (2006). Anticipatory stress in the population facing forced removal from the Gaza Strip. *Journal of Nervous & Mental Disease, 194*, 195–200.

Bleich, A., Gelkopf, M., Mclamed, Y., & Solomon, Z. (2006). Mental health and resiliency following 44 months of terrorism: A survey of an Israeli national representative sample. *BMC Medicine, 4*(21), 1–11. doi: 10.1186/1741-7015-4-21.

Bleich, A., Gelkopf, M., & Solomon, Z. (2003). Exposure to terrorism, stress-related mental health symptoms, and coping behaviors among a nationally representative sample in Israel. *Journal of the American Medical Association, 290*, 612–620.

Bowlby, J. (1973). *Attachment and loss: Vol. 2. Separation: Anxiety and anger.* New York: Basic Books.

Breckenridge, J., & James, K. (2010). Educating social work students in multifaceted interventions for trauma. *Social Work Education, 29*, 259–275.

Bronfenbrenner, U. (1979). *The ecology of human development: Experiment by nature and design.* Cambridge: Harvard University Press.

Buckner, J. C. (1988). The development of an instrument to measure neighborhood cohesion. *American Journal of Community Psychology, 16*, 771–791.

Carver, S. C. (1997). You want to measure coping but your protocol's too long: Consider the brief COPE. *International Journal of Behavioral Medicine, 4*, 92–100.

Chavis, D. M., Hogge, J. H., McMillan, D. W., & Wandersman, A. (1986). Sense of community through Brunswik's lens: A first look. *Journal of Community Psychology, 14*, 24–40.

Dekel, R., & Tuval-Mashiach, R. (2010). Multiple losses of social resources following collective trauma: The case of the forced relocation from Gush Katif. *Psychological Trauma: Theory, Research, Practice, and Policy.* doi: 10.1037/a0019912.

Fisher, A. T., Sonn, C. C., & Bishop, B. J. (2002). *Psychological sense of community: Research, applications, and implications.* New York: Kluwer.

Fullilove, M. T. (1996). Psychiatric implications of displacement: Contributions from the psychology of place. *American Journal of Psychiatry, 153*, 1516–1523.

Galea, S., Ahern, J., Resnick, H., Kilpatrick, D., Bucuvalas, M., Gold, J., et al. (2002). Psychological sequelae of the September 11 terrorist attacks in New York City. *New England Journal of Medicine, 346*, 982–987.

Galea, S., Vlahov, D., Resnick, H., Ahern, J., Susser, E., Gold, J., et al. (2003). Trends of probable post-traumatic stress disorder in New York City after the September 11 terrorist attacks. *American Journal of Epidemiology, 158*, 514–524.

Gelkopf, M., Solomon, Z., Berger, R., & Bleich, A. (2008). The mental health impact of terrorism in Israel: A repeat cross-sectional study of Arabs and Jews. *Acta Psychiatric Scandinavica, 117*, 369–380.

Gretz, N. (1995). *Captive of a dream: National myths in Israeli culture.* Tel Aviv: Am Oved (in Hebrew).

Henrich, C. C., & Shahar, G. (2008). Social support buffers the effects of terrorism on adolescent depression:

Findings from Sderot, Israel. *Journal of the American Academy of Child and Adolescent Psychiatry, 47,* 1073–1076.

Herman, L. J. (1992). *Trauma and recovery.* New York: Basic Books.

Hobfoll, S., Canetti-Nisim, D., & Robert, J. (2006). Exposure to terrorism, stress-related mental health symptoms, and defensive coping among Jews and Arabs in Israel. *Journal of Consulting and Clinical Psychology, 74,* 207–218.

Hobfoll, S., Dunahoo, J., & Monnier, J. (1995). Conservation of resources and traumatic stress. In J. R. Freedy & S. E. Hobfoll (Eds.), *Traumatic stress from theory to practice* (pp. 29–47). New York: Plenum Press.

Itzhaky, H. (1995). Can social work intervention increase organizational effectiveness? *International Social Work, 38,* 277–287.

Kia-Keating, M., & Heidi-Ellis, B. (2007). Belonging and connection to school in resettlement: Youth refugees, school belonging and psychosocial adjustment. *Clinical Child Psychology and Psychiatry, 12,* 29–43.

Kline, P. M., & Mone, E. (2003). Coping with war: Three strategies employed by adolescent citizens of Sierra Leone. *Child and Adolescent Social Work Journal, 20,* 321–333.

Kovatz, S., Kutz, I., Rubin, G., Dekel, R., & Shenkman, L. (2006). Comparing the distress of American and Israeli medical students studying in Israel during a period of terror. *Medical Education, 40,* 389–393.

Laor, N., Wolmer, L., Alon, M., Siev, J., Samuel, E., & Toren, P. (2006). Risk and protective factors mediating psychological symptoms and ideological commitment of adolescents facing continuous terrorism. *Journal of Nervous and Mental Disease, 194,* 275–278.

Laufer, A., & Solomon, Z. (2006). Posttraumatic symptoms and posttraumatic growth among Israeli youth exposed to terror incidents. *Journal of Social and Clinical Psychology, 25,* 429–447.

Lavi, T., & Solomon, Z. (2005). Palestinian youth of the Intifada: PTSD and future orientation. *Journal of the American Academy of Child and Adolescent Psychiatry, 44,* 1176–1184.

Lazarus, R. S., & Folkman, S. (1984). *Stress, appraisal, and coping.* New York: Springer.

Macksoud, M., Dyregrov, A., & Raundalen, M. (1993). In J. P. Wilson & B. Raphael (Eds.), *International handbook of traumatic stress syndromes.* New York: Plenum.

Masten, A. (2001). Ordinary magic: Resilience processes in development. *American Psychologist, 56,* 227–238.

Newbrough, J. R., & Chavis, D. M. (1986). Psychology sense of community. *Journal of Community Psychology, 14,* 3–5.

Norris, F. H., Stevens, S. P., Pfefferbaum, B., Wyche, K. F., & Pfefferbaum, R. L. (2008). Community resilience as a metaphor, theory, set of capacities, and strategy for disaster readiness. *American Journal of Community Psychology, 41,* 127–150.

Nuttman-Shwartz, O. (2008). Life is our desire. *Hade'a Harovahat (Common Knowledge).* Bulletin of the Israel Council on Social Work, 10–13 (Hebrew).

Nuttman-Shwartz, O., Dekel, R., & Toval Machiach, R. (2010). Post-traumatic stress and growth following forced relocation. *British Journal of Social Work.* doi: 10.1093/bjsw/bcq124

Nuttman-Shwartz, O., & Weinberg, H. (2008). Organizations in traumatized societies: The Israeli case. *Organizational and Social Dynamics, 8,* 138–153.

Pat-Horenczyk, R., Schiff, M., & Dopplet, O. (2005). Maintaining routine despite ongoing ongoing exposure to terrorism: A healthy strategy for adolescents? *Journal of Adolescent Health, 39,* 199–205.

Primoratz, I. (2002/2003) *State terrorism and counterterrorism.* Centre for Applied philosophy and public ethics. Australian National University.

Sagy, S., & Braun-Lewensohn, O. (2009). Adolescents under rocket fire: When are coping resources significant in reducing emotional distress? *Global Health Promotion, 16,* 5–15.

Schermer, V. L. (2003). Terror and groups: Updating psychoanalytic group psychology for a new era. *Psychotherapy and Psychoanalysis, 20,* 199–222.

Shacham, M., & Lahad, M. (2004). Stress reactions and coping resources mobilized by children under shelling and evacuation. *The Australasian Journal of Disaster and Trauma Studies.* Retrieved December 8, 2006, from http://www.massey.ac.nz/~trauma/issues/2004-2/shacham.html.

Silver, R. C., Holman, E. A., McIntosh, D. N., Poulin, M., & Gil-Rivas, V. (2002). Nationwide longitudinal study of psychological responses to September 11'. *Journal of the American Medical Association, 288,* 1235–1244.

Skinner, E. A., & Zimmer-Gembeck, M. J. (2007). The development of coping. *Annual Review of Psychology, 58,* 119–144.

Solomon, Z., Benbenishty, R., Neria, Y., Abramowitz, M., Ginzburg, K., & Ohry, A. (1993). Assessment of PTSD: Validation of the revised PTSD Inventory. *Israel Journal of Psychiatry and Related Sciences, 30,* 110–115.

Terr, L. C. (1991). Childhood traumas: An outline and overview. *American Journal of Psychiatry, 148,* 10–20.

Tucker, P., Pfefferbaum, B., Nixon, S. J., & Dickson, W. (2000). Predictors of post-traumatic stress symptoms in Oklahoma City: Exposure, social support, peri-traumatic responses. *The Journal of Behavioral Health Services and Research, 27,* 406–416.

Ungar, M. (2008). Resilience across cultures. *British Journal of Social Work, 38*(2), 218–235.

Volkan, V. D. (1997). *Bloodlines from ethnic pride to ethnic terrorism.* New York: Farrar, Straus & Giroux.

Yiftachel, O. (2000). Social control, urban planning and ethno-class relations: Mizrahi Jews in Israel's 'development towns'. *International Journal of Urban and Regional Research, 24,* 418–438.

Predictors of Resilient Psychosocial Functioning in Western Australian Aboriginal Young People Exposed to High Family-Level Risk

33

Katrina D. Hopkins, Catherine L. Taylor,
Heather D'Antoine, and Stephen R. Zubrick

A sizeable multidisciplinary literature shows children and adolescents exposed to high levels and multiple combinations of economic impoverishment, family violence, and neglectful or harsh parenting are placed at heightened risk for a range of adverse developmental outcomes including antisocial behaviors, anxiety and depression, and posttraumatic stress disorder (Bolger & Patterson, 2003; Evans, Gonnella, Marcynyszyn, Gentile, & Salpekar, 2005; Lansford et al., 2002; Margolin & Vickerman, 2007; Owens & Shaw, 2003; Yexley, Borowsky, & Ireland, 2002; and for a review: Gapen et al., 2011; Holt, Buckley, & Whelan, 2008; Margolin & Gordis, 2000). High risk has been variously defined in the resilience research from single, acute exposures to multiple and chronic risks. One often observed characteristic of high risk circumstances is the propensity of risks to cluster or covary with low socioeconomic status (Adler & Rehkopf, 2008; Greenberg, 2006; Jaffee, Caspi, Moffitt, Polo-Tomás, & Taylor, 2007; McLoyd, 1998). For example, where high-risk exposure may include "multiple familial

disadvantages; impaired parenting; a neglectful and abusive home environment; marital conflict; family instability; family violence; and high exposure to adverse family life events" (Fergusson & Horwood, 2003, p.130).

The study of resilient adolescent development when the family environment is characterized by stress and violence offers important insights into processes that protect and support emotional and behavioral development of young people. The aim of the study discussed in this chapter was, therefore, to investigate factors associated with resilient emotional or behavioral functioning of young people in the context of high family-level risks using a model of resources and contexts of child development (Bronfenbrenner & Evans, 2000; Zubrick, Silburn, & Prior, 2005). To do this we drew upon a rare sample of young people exposed to exceptionally challenging circumstance by using data from the Western Australian Aboriginal Child Health Survey (WAACHS) (Zubrick et al., 2005).

In this chapter, we first provide a background to the social ecology of Western Australian Aboriginal children and young people data from the WAACHS, a large-scale representative survey of Aboriginal children aged 0–17 and their families. We then introduce key concepts used in the current study and define resilient emotional or behavioral functioning as the principal adaptive outcome of interest.

K.D. Hopkins (✉)
Population Sciences Division, Telethon Institute
for Child Health Research, Centre for Child Health
Research, University of Western Australia, Crawley,
WA, Australia
e-mail: khopkins@ichr.uwa.edu.au

M. Ungar (ed.), *The Social Ecology of Resilience: A Handbook of Theory and Practice*,
DOI 10.1007/978-1-4614-0586-3_33, © Springer Science+Business Media, LLC 2012

425

Background: Risk and the Australian Aboriginal Circumstance

Australian Aboriginal young people are members of one of the oldest living cultures dating back at least 40,000 years (Hudjashov et al., 2007) and have highly structured and complex traditions with hundreds of distinct languages. Many Aboriginal people maintain deep spiritual connections to and responsibilities for ancestral land. Although there is great diversity within the Aboriginal population, the history of dispossession and colonization is shared by all Aboriginal people. The transgenerational consequences of colonization are revealed in the many inquiries and royal commissions (e.g., Australian Royal Commission into Aboriginal Deaths in Custody, 1991; Human Rights and Equal Opportunity Commission, 1997) into the disadvantaged circumstances of Aboriginal people today. In the mid-1970s, a national inquiry into poverty noted key issues affecting the social conditions of Aboriginal people. Prominent among these were the "breakdown of the family, the devastation of Aboriginal male roles, displacement from opportunities to maintain a self-determined economic base, and the entrenchment of Aboriginal disempowerment" (Riley, 1997, p.12). The distal influence of these historical acts and policies is reflected in the contemporary socioeconomic inequalities between the Aboriginal and mainstream Australian population across key socio-demographic indicators of human development (Steering Committee for the Review of Government Services Provision, 2009). For example, the impact of forced separation of Aboriginal children from their natural families has been demonstrated to have a transgenerational impact on emotional or behavioral difficulties (De Maio et al., 2005).

The many valuable cross-cultural and indigenous studies of resilient functioning create opportunities for understanding the universal and context-specific nature of human adaptation to a spectrum of developmental adversities (e.g., Ungar, 2005, 2008, 2010). However, studies of resilience in Australian Aboriginal populations are exceedingly rare. Moreover, until the advent of the WAACHS (Zubrick et al., 2005) none had specifically featured Australian Aboriginal children within their families and within their communities. The results of this survey provided one of the first comprehensive descriptions of adversity and its relationship to the Australian Aboriginal circumstance.

The broad risk profile of the Australian Aboriginal population is disconcerting. The WAACHS data revealed that the primary carers of Aboriginal children experienced on average 3.9 life stress events in the previous 12 months prior to the survey (Zubrick et al., 2005). This is compared to an average of 1.2 life stress events reported by non-Aboriginal primary carers over the same period. Fully 20% of Aboriginal children and young people lived in households where primary carers reported 7–14 life stress events. Comparatively, Aboriginal children and young people experience more than 5 times the number of life stress events as their non-Aboriginal counterparts (Zubrick et al.). The findings further showed that exposure to 7–14 life stress events was associated with increased risk of clinically significant emotional and behavioral difficulties in 4–17 year olds.

The number of life stress events and community problems also co-occur, with primary carers who reported being bothered by more than 11 community problems also being more than 4 times as likely to experience 7–14 life stress events (Silburn et al., 2006). Life stress events such as financial strain, unemployment, poor health, and family violence, undermine the resources families have to engage with and parent their children, and comprise a profile of factors often associated with socioeconomic disadvantage (Bryant & Willis, 2008; Zubrick, Silburn, & Prior, 2005). The extent to which these risks accumulate and impact on Aboriginal families is well-documented and can be illustrated by hospitalization rates of Aboriginal women due to family violence assaults at some 30 times the rate of other Australian women (Anderson & Wild, 2007; Cripps, 2010; Cripps & McGlade, 2008; Homel, Lincoln, & Herd, 1999; Jamieson, Harrison, & Berry, 2008; Stanley, Kovacs, Tomison, & Cripps, 2002; Steering Committee for the Review of Government Services Provision, 2009).

In all, relative to non-Aboriginal families, many Aboriginal families and their children are exposed to multiple and cumulative socioeconomic risks that decrease the resources available to parents and communities to provide care and nurturance for their children, which in turn decreases the chances of young people's positive development (Zubrick et al., 2005). Where social and economic disadvantage is shown to systematically and disproportionately affect a specific population, it becomes critically important to not only address the causes of this disadvantage, but also to enhance our understanding of the protective factors exerting an influence in the most developmentally challenging environments.

Quantifying Risks to the Emotional or Behavioral Functioning of Aboriginal Young People

In previous research, we compared the predictive efficiency of three groups of measures in their differential influence on two domains of functioning – connection to education or employment, and social or emotional well-being (Hopkins, Taylor, & Zubrick, under review). The three groups of measures were (a) a measure of cumulative risk, (b) three composite measures of risk types (family discord, family physical health, and community risks), and (c) a set of single socio-demographic risk measures. We identified a distinct group of single risks in the family domain to be associated with lower likelihood of emotional or behavioral functioning. These were harsh parenting, low nurturing parenting, family violence, and living in unemployed sole parent households. Together, these five single risks decreased the likelihood of positive emotional or behavioral functioning.

In this current study, we investigate the processes of resilient emotional or behavioral functioning using these five identified single risks to define high risk exposure. First, we define resilient emotional or behavioral functioning as young people at low risk of emotional or behavioral difficulties despite exposure to high-level family-risk. We then ask what are the factors in these resilient young people's lives that serve to promote coping and adaptation despite their high-risk exposure?

Methods

The measurement framework for the WAACHS was guided by an ecological model of child development (Bronfenbrenner & Evans, 2000; Bronfenbrenner & Morris, 2006). This model views child development as an interplay between the child and the proximal (i.e., maternal and family) and distal (i.e., community and societal) resources that influence development.

Sample and Procedure

Data for this study are drawn from the 2000–2002 WAACHS, a population representative survey of the health, psychosocial and educational characteristics of 5,289, or 1 in 6, Aboriginal children aged 0–17 years, their families and communities. The WAACHS used an area-based clustered multi-stage sample design, with in-scope families selected by whether there was an Aboriginal or Torres Strait Islander child aged 0–17 years living in the household. A response rate of 84% of eligible families was obtained. Face-to-face surveys were conducted with the primary carer, who was the most knowledgeable about the survey children. The majority of primary carers were also birth mother of the child (80%). Further methodological detail is contained elsewhere (Zubrick et al., 2004).[1] Findings of the original survey are summarized in a series of reports commissioned for public policy application (Silburn et al., 2006; Zubrick et al., 2004, 2005, 2006).

The WAACHS collected data on 12–17 year olds from their primary carers and from young people themselves. Of eligible youth, 73% completed a Youth Self Report. Relative to those young people participating, nonparticipants were more likely to be at high risk of clinically significant emotional or behavioral difficulties, living in census areas classified in the lowest socioeconomic

---

[1]All survey instruments and reports may be freely downloaded online at http://www.ichr.uwa.edu.au/kulunga.

level of disadvantage, and to have had some contact with the police or justice system (Zubrick et al., 2005). For this current study, a sub-group of 12–17 year olds at high family risk and with complete data available ($N=2,390$) were identified from the WAACHS sample. The WAACHS survey design permits estimation of the responses expected from the total WA population of Aboriginal carers and young people. We report 95% confidence intervals (CIs) as a measure of the reliability of estimates derived from weighted sample data.

Measures

Dependent Variable: Resilient Emotional or Behavioral Functioning

Young people in this study were classified as having resilient emotional or behavioral function if they were at low risk of emotional or behavioral difficulties *and* if they were exposed to contexts of high family risk (see Table 33.1). Classification proceeded as follows.

Emotional or Behavioral Difficulties

Goodman's Strengths and Difficulties Questionnaire (SDQ, Goodman, Ford, Simmons, Gatward, & Meltzer, 2000) was used as the principal measure of social and emotional well-being (Zubrick et al., 2005). Extensive pilot-testing and modeling of the SDQ subscales was undertaken for the WAACHS to confirm its reliability and validity for use with a diverse population of Aboriginal families and the 20 item total score produced a scale reliability of 0.93 (De Maio et al., 2005). The SDQ was scored according to published

criteria with scores classifying the *risk* of "low" (score 0–15), "moderate" (score 16–19) or "high" (score 19–40) clinically significant emotional or behavioral difficulties. In this current study, we used responses from the Youth Self Report form of the SDQ and combine categories of borderline and high risk creating a binary measure of "low risk" (scores 0–15) or "high risk" (scores 16–40). This enabled identification of those young people clearly at low risk of emotional or behavioral difficulties as distinct from those estimated to be at borderline risk or high risk. The range of scores for the 12–17 year old sample was 0–27, with the majority of young people (69%) at low risk.

Family-level Risk

This is a binary variable derived by summing responses to the following five items derived from young people's responses to the Youth Self Report (Zubrick et al., 2005). Scores of family-level risk exposure ranged from 0 to 5, with binary categories defined as "low family risk" (0–1 risk exposures), and "high family risk" (2–5 risk exposures). Only 14% of Aboriginal young people were not exposed to any of the above risks, while 38.4% had one exposure. The remainder of this sample was classified as "high family risk" exposed. The five risk items significantly associated with emotional or behavioral functioning in Aboriginal young people, and used in this measure, were as follows:

1. *Low-nurturing parenting*. Responses to four items using a 4-point scale of 1 (never) to 4 (very often) were combined into *nurturing parenting*: "Your parents smile at you," "Your

Table 33.1 Quantifying emotionally or behaviorally resilient Western Australian Aboriginal young people, 12–17 years, $N=5,760$ (95% CI 5420, 6100)

	Emotional or behavioral functioning	
	Low risk of emotional or behavioral difficulties	High risk of emotional or behavioral difficulties
Low risk exposed (0–1 risk events)	Expected Good 42.1% (37.5, 46.5) 2,420 (2,140, 2,740)	Vulnerable 10.3% (7.8, 3.2) 590 (450, 760)
High risk exposed (2–5 risk events)	Resilient 27.0% (23.1, 31.0) 1,550 (1,320, 1,810)	Less resilient 20.7% (17.5, 24.3) 1,190 (1,000, 1,410)

parents praise you for the good things you do," "Your parents seem proud of the things you do," and "Your parents give you lots of help when something is worrying you."

2. *Harsh parenting.* Responses to two items using a 4-point scale of 1 (never) to 4 (very often) were combined into the harsh parenting measure: "Your parents hit you or threaten to do so" and "Your parents threaten punishment more than they use it."

3. *Exposure to family violence.* A binary measure of exposure to family violence was derived from youth self reports where 1 = "exposed to family violence" and 2 = "not exposed to family violence." "Exposed to family violence" was derived from three questions from the YSR indicating young people's definition of family violence included physical pushing, shoving, fighting or hitting; that they had been exposed to in such situations; or that they reported their parents had hit or threatened to hit them.

4. *Primary Carer Employment status.* Primary carer employment status was coded in three categories: 1 = Employed; 2 = Unemployed; 3 = Not in the labor force. "Unemployed" primary carer status was an identified risk factor for positive emotional or behavioral functioning.

5. *Family Household Care Arrangement.* The structure of the family was assessed relative to the arrangements that were made within each household to care for the survey child. This variable allowed for considerable capture of the multitude of arrangements that households used to care for children. In this study, we used a four level variable where 1 = Both original parents, 2 = Sole parent; 3 = Two parent step/blended family; and 4 = Other (aunties/uncles, grandparents), which describes the care arrangements as they apply to each child or young person in the family. Status of "Sole parent" status was identified as a risk factor for positive emotional or behavioral functioning.

Predictor Variables

Commensurate with the ecological model predictor variables are grouped by domain of influence: young person, primary carer, family, and community. These variables have been associated with positive emotional or behavioral functioning in 12–17 years olds (Zubrick et al., 2005) or are strongly implicated in the resilience literature as protective factors for young people in the context of high risk families (Luthar, 2003).

Young Person

Characteristics of the young person included their sex and age group (1 = "12–13 years"; 2 = "14–15 years"; 3 = "16–17 years").

Primary Carer

Educational Status

This variable describes the primary carer's highest level of educational attainment. Education was recorded in five categories: 1 = "Did not attend school," 2 = "1–9 years of education," 3 = "10 years of education," 4 = "11–12 years of education," 5 = "13+ years of education."

Family

Parental encouragement

This was measured using three items of youth responses to how much support and encouragement they received from their parents for (1) having good marks at school; (2) attending school regularly; and (3) finishing Year 12. Responses on these three items used a 5-point scale from 1 (none) to 5 (very much).

Alcohol Causes Problems at Home

Young people reported whether alcohol causes problems in their household as a binary response where 1 = "No" and 2 = "Yes."

Parental Drug Use

Young people reported whether either of their parents use drugs on a three category item where 1 = "No," 2 = "Yes" and 99 = "Don't know."

Forced Separation

Australia has a history of forced separation of Aboriginal children from their natural families by churches, government, or welfare authorities. Primary and secondary carers were asked whether they or either of their parents had been forcibly removed from their natural families by "a mission, the government, or welfare" (No/Yes). Youth with carers responding "not known/not applicable" were excluded from this analysis.

Household Occupancy

The WAACHS constructed an index of house-hold occupancy based on primary carer reports of number of bedrooms and whether the number of people usually sleeping in the home exceeded the number of bedrooms by four or more (Zubrick et al., 2005). This index was used to create a binary Household occupancy variable where 1 = "Low household occupancy" and 2 = "High household occupancy."

Community

Socioeconomic Index for Areas (SEIFA)

This is a measure of geographic socioeconomic disadvantage, in which the Australian Bureau of Statistics (ABS) calculates from Census data an index of relative socio-economic disadvantage for each census CD in Australia (Australian Bureau of Statistics, 2006). Lower values indicate greater relative disadvantage. For this current study, the SEIFA categories are 1 = Bottom 5%, 2 = 5–10%, 3 = 10–25%, 4 = 25–50%, 5 = In the top 50% (or above the median).

Level of Relative Isolation (LORI)

A measure of geographic remoteness or accessibility, the LORI – was designed for the WAACHS based on an extension of the Accessibility/ Remoteness Index of Australia (ARIA) (Department of Health and Aged Care, 2001). Levels of relative isolation categories are 1 = None, 2 = Low 3 = Moderate, 4 = High, 5 = Extreme. The category of "None" represents highly urban settings (e.g., the capital city of Perth) while levels of Low and Moderate are associated with increasingly rural settings. Levels of High and Extreme geographic isolation represent the most isolated locations in the State.

Culture and Language

Two items measured in the WAACHS are used as indicators of young people's connection to Aboriginal culture and language. Young people responded to a question asking "How much do you know about Aboriginal culture?" on a 5-point scale where 1 = "None/not much at all" to 5 = "very much." Young people were also asked whether they understand or speak an Aboriginal language and this was measured by a single item with three response options where 1 = "No," 2 = "Yes, a few words," and 3 = "Yes, a conversation."

Prosocial Friendship

Prosocial friendship is a three category derived variable where 1 = "No special friend or close mate," 2 = "Low-prosocial special friend," and 3 = "High-prosocial special friend." This variable was derived from two questions which asked first whether young people had a "special friend or a really close mate" (where 1 = "No" and 2 = "Yes"); second, for young people with a special friend or close mate, a further eight items indicated the extent of their friend's prosocial activities. These items included: "takes an active part in school/ community sports, clubs or activities," "uses drugs other than alcohol" (reverse coded), "gets drunk" (reverse coded), "likes to spend lots of time with his/her own family," "gets into fights" (reverse coded), "goes to church," "gets into trouble with police" (reverse coded), and "supports and encourages you." Responses were recorded as 1 = "No," 2 = "Yes." These scores were summed and a binary variable created around a mean score split, with scores 9–14 = Low Prosocial Friend, and scores 15+ = High Prosocial Friend.

Participation in Organized Sport

This item is thought to reflect resources in the community that provide opportunities for young people to participate in organized sport. The item asks young people whether they had taken part in any organized sports over the past 12 months, excluding school physical education classes, with 1 = "No" and 2 = "Yes."

Has Done Exercise Requiring Strong Exertion Recently

This item asked young people whether over the past 7 days they had exercised or played sport or games that made them sweat or breath hard (e.g., basketball, netball, football, riding a bike, running), with responses 1 = "No" and 2 = "Yes."

Racism

A single item asking young people whether, in the past 6 months, people had ever treated them badly or refused to serve them because of their Aboriginality, with 1 = "No" and 2 = "Yes."

Data Analysis

Unlike data collected from a simple random sample, the WAACHS sample was selected in three stages: census CDs, families, and children. CDs were selected with probabilities of inclusion in the survey proportional to the number of Aboriginal and Torres Strait Islander children living in the CD. As a result multilevel, or hierarchical, modeling was used to account for the hierarchical structure of the survey data. Hierarchical logistic regression modeling using SAS4.2 was then used to compare the influence of proposed protective factors on the likelihood of resilient emotional or behavioral functioning.

Results

Descriptive Analyses

There was an estimated population of 2,390 Aboriginal young people exposed to high family-risk. Of these high risk exposed young people nearly 57% were at low risk of emotional or behavioral difficulties. The estimated 2,390 young people were distributed across three age groupings of 12–13 years (40.4%), 14–15 years (31.1%), and 16–17 years (28.4%), with 50.1% being male. The proportion of Aboriginal young people affected by each of the five family-level risks associated with poor social or emotional well-being was as follows: 49.1% were in sole carer households; 12.9% had an unemployed primary carer; using a parenting scale, 42.6% of these young people reported parenting classified as "harsh parenting"; 45.2% reported parenting classified as "low nurturing"; and 91.3% reported exposure to family violence.

The majority of primary carers of high family-risk exposed young people had less than 10 years of formal schooling, with 44.3% completing 10 years of formal schooling, and only 6.9% completing 13 or more years. Geographically, nearly one-third lived in areas of no isolation such as the capital city of Perth, one-half (52.2%) in low to moderate areas of isolation, and the remainder in

high or extremely isolated parts of the State (18.8%). With respect to the socioeconomic status of the neighborhood or community as derived from Census data, a relatively small minority of young people (10.8%) lived in more advantaged areas ranked in the top 50% of relative socioeconomic disadvantage.

There was no significant difference between the proportions of males and females at low risk of emotional or behavioral difficulties. However, when examining emotional and behavioral difficulties separately, a significantly lower proportion of females were at low risk of emotional difficulties (62.6%) than males (83.0%), but no significant difference by sex was found for low risk of behavioral difficulties.

Bivariate Comparisons of Resilient and Less Resilient Young People

In bivariate analyses (see Table 33.2), the only statistically significant variables distinguishing resilient from less resilient young people were three single items from the Prosocial friend variable. These items indicated that a significantly higher proportion of resilient young people reported their special friend did not use drugs (76.4%) compared to less resilient young people (49.9%), did not get drunk (69.4 vs. 44.3%), and did not get into trouble with police (81.9 vs. 62%).

Although not statistically significant, there was a tendency for a higher proportion of resilient young people to be in the younger age group (12–13 years, 46.8%) than less resilient young people (32.3%), to have a special friend who supports and encourages them (79.4%) compared to 65.4% of less resilient young people and whose special friend does not get into fights (69.4%) compared to 53.7% of less resilient young people. More than double the proportion of less resilient young people (16.2%) lived in the top 50% of socioeconomic ranked areas compared to 6.6% of resilient young people.

There was no statistically significant difference between resilient and less resilient young people on any of the five single family-level contextual risks.

Table 33.2 Descriptive characteristics of resilient and less resilient young people

	Aboriginal young people 12–17 years at high family risk (N=2,390, 95% CI 2,340, 2,390)	
	Resilient (high family risk exposed, low risk of emotional or behavioral difficulties) N=1,350 (95% CI 1,200, 1,490)	Less resilient (high family risk exposed, high risk of emotional or behavioral difficulties) N=1,050 (95% CI 900, 1,200)
Sample characteristics		
Sex		
Male	53.1 (42.9–62.5)	46.4 (37.6–54.7)
Female	46.9 (37.5–57.1)	53.6 (45.3–62.4)
Age group		
12–13 years	46.8 (37.1–56.1)	32.3 (24.4–41.6)
14–15 years	26.0 (18.3–34.6)	37.7 (29.8–46.4)
16–17 years	27.2 (19.8–35.9)	30.0 (22.4–38.6)
Family environment		
Primary carer educational status		
Did not attend school	6.1 (2.0–13.3)	2.6 (0.5–6.5)
1–9 years education	25.8 (18.2–34.8)	26.0 (19.3–34.0)
10 years education	40.1 (30.6–50.0)	49.6 (40.8–59.2)
11–12 years education	21.2 (14.6–28.6)	14.6 (7.4–24.1)
13+ years education	6.7 (2.4–16.1)	7.1 (3.0–14.3)
Parental encouragement		
To get good marks at school		
Not at all/none	7.5 (3.0–14.7)	10.3 (5.5–17.4)
A little	9.5 (5.6–15.6)	13.1 (7.9–20.4)
Some	21.9 (14.0–30.8)	18.8 (13.2–25.7)
Quite a lot	23.5 (16.5–32.3)	21.9 (15.1–30.0)
Very much	37.6 (28.5–47.1)	35.8 (27.1–44.6)
To attend school		
Not at all/none	8.7 (4.0–16.9)	12.8 (7.4–21.2)
A little	6.6 (2.9–12.6)	6.8 (4.3–10.5)
Some	8.0 (4.1–14.8)	12.6 (6.5–21.5)
Quite a lot	26.2 (18.8–34.6)	21.4 (14.8–29.0)
Very much	50.6 (41.0–59.8)	46.4 (37.3–55.6)
To finish year 12		
Not at all/none	24.9 (17.1–33.8)	24.1 (16.9–32.3)
A little	5.6 (2.2–12.6)	8.8 (5.6–13.2)
Some	10.6 (5.0–18.0)	8.1 (3.6–15.3)
Quite a lot	16.1 (10.6–23.5)	19.3 (12.4–27.1)
Very much	42.8 (33.5–52.9)	39.7 (31.6–48.5)
Culture and language		
Knowledge of culture?		
Not at all/none	7.7 (3.0–14.7)	3.5 (0.6–8.7)
A little	24.0 (17.0–33.1)	26.4 (19.2–34.9)
Some	43.2 (33.7–53.0)	39.8 (31.0–48.5)
Quite a lot	18.3 (12.4–25.8)	20.8 (15.0–28.1)
Very much	6.9 (3.3–13.0)	9.4 (4.2–16.4)
Do you speak an aboriginal language?		
No	22.0 (15.2–30.3)	18.4 (12.1–26.5)
Yes, a few words	63.5 (53.4–72.7)	66.6 (57.5–75.0)
Yes, a conversation	14.4 (8.0–24.7)	15.1 (9.1–22.5)
Alcohol causes problems at home	33.2 (24.9–43.3)	38.0 (29.6–46.7)
Either of parents use drugs	10.2 (5.0–16.9)	9.2 (4.9–15.8)
Forced separation		
Family affected by forced separations of children from family	47.7 (38.2–58.1)	46.2 (36.7–56.2)

(continued)

Table 33.2 (continued)

Not affected by forced separations	52.3 (41.9–61.8)	53.8 (43.8–63.3)
Living in overcrowded accommodation		
Low household occupancy	64.8 (54.6–73.5)	68.8 (60.1–77.3)
High household occupancy	35.2 (26.5–45.4)	31.2 (22.7–39.9)
Single risk exposures		
Sole parent	48.4 (38.9–58.4)	50.0 (40.8–59.2)
Unemployed	11.4 (5.9–18.6)	14.8 (8.2–23.3)
Harsh parenting	37.7 (28.8–48.1)	49.0 (40.4–58.1)
Low nurturing parenting	42.1 (31.9–51.8)	49.2 (39.7–58.0)
Exposure to family violence	92.0 (84.4–96.4)	90.3 (83.9–94.7)
Number of total risk exposures for young people in high family-level risk (excluding "low risk exposed" of 0 and 1)		
2	72.1 (62.1–80.0)	56.1 (47.1–64.5)
3	24.2 (16.4–33.3)	36.1 (28.3–44.4)
4	3.7 (0.8–11.0)	6.2 (3.1–10.8)
5	0.0 (0.0–4.1)	1.6 (0.3–7.3)
Social ecology of the community		
Socio-economic index for areas (SEIFA)		
Bottom 5%	29.9 (20.8–40.6)	16.8 (9.5–25.7)
5–10%	15.0 (8.9–24.2)	12.6 (7.9–19.2)
10–25%	20.5 (13.8–29.0)	27.6 (19.6–36.1)
25–50%	27.9 (19.7–37.9)	26.8 (18.5–37.1)
Top 50% (above median)	6.6 (2.5–14.1)	16.2 (9.7–24.7)
Level of relative isolation (LORI)		
None (capital city)	26.3 (19.7–33.5)	32.5 (24.8–40.8)
Low	22.1 (15.8–29.5)	25.5 (18.7–33.8)
Moderate	26.3 (17.7–35.7)	31.7 (23.5–40.3)
High	11.8 (6.2–20.6)	3.5 (0.7–10.1)
Extreme	13.6 (6.7–23.5)	6.8 (2.9–12.6)
Has special friend or really close mate		
Prosocial friend		
Low prosocial special friend	34.5 (25.9–44.8)	65.1 (56.1–73.0)
High prosocial special friend	65.5 (55.2–74.1)	34.9 (27.0–3.9)
Prosocial friend: has a special friend who		
Takes an active part in school or community sports, clubs, activities	67.3 (56.7–76.2)	59.6 (50.6–68.6)
Does not use drugs (other than alcohol)®	76.4 (66.7–84.1)	49.9 (41.1–58.9)
Does not get drunk®	69.4 (60.1–78.3)	44.3 (35.5–52.9)
Likes to spend lots of time with their own family	73.2 (63.6–81.9)	62.5 (53.5–70.4)
Does not get into fights®	69.4 (59.7–78.3)	53.7 (44.4–63.1)
Goes to church	31.9 (23.3–41.4)	19.7 (13.5–27.9)
Does not get into trouble with police®	81.9 (72.4–89.0)	62.0 (52.5–70.2)
Supports and encourages me	79.4 (69.9–87.6)	65.4 (56.6–73.1)
Total prosocial friend (mean score of eight summed items, where 1 = not applicable i.e., has no special friend or mate, 2 = antisocial response, 3 = prosocial response)	13.7 (12.8, 14.7)	11.9 (12.3, 13.6)
® = items reverse coded so a higher score indicates prosocial activity		
Participation in organized sport		
Yes	63.4 (53.8–72.3)	59.4 (50.7–68.2)
Have done exercise requiring strong exertion in last week		
Yes	70.8 (61.8–79.2)	67.6 (58.7–75.3)
Have been treated badly because of race	14.5 (8.8–23.1)	27.3 (19.7–36.7)

Modeling Emotional or Behavioral Resilience Using Hierarchical Logistic Regression

A set of 18 predictor variables (see Table 33.2) were included in the model. These related to the young person (sex and age group); their primary carer (primary carer's level of education, youth reports of the extent to which they were encouraged by their parents to get good marks at school, to attend school, or to finish Year 12, whether alcohol causes problems in the family, whether either of their parents use drugs, young person's knowledge of Aboriginal culture, young person's use of an Aboriginal language), their family envi-

ronment (whether family affected by forced separations, and household overcrowding), and the social ecology of the community (socioeconomic disadvantage of the area LORI, Prosocial friend, participation in organized sport, recent vigorous physical activity, and experiences of racism).

We undertook logistic regression using SAS 4.2 (SAS Institute, 2006–2008). The goodness-of-fit of each model was assessed by convergence being achieved using Predicted Quasi-Likelihood Estimation, and model statistics (parameter estimates, standard errors, degrees of freedom, t-values, probabilities, and 95% confidence intervals) as reported in Table 33.3. Odds-ratios of less than 1.0 indicate a reduced likelihood of emotional or

Table 33.3 Modeling likelihood of emotional or behavioral resilience by individual, family, friend and community characteristics

Parameter	Estimate	SE	Df	T	p	Odds ratio	95% CI
Intercept	2.3164	1.4154	163	1.64	0.104		
Sex							
Female	Ref.					1.00	
Male	0.07509	0.3598	59	0.21	0.835	1.08	(0.53–2.18)
Adolescent age groups							
Younger	Ref.					1.00	
Middle	−0.8589	0.3791	59	−2.27	**0.027**	**0.42**	**(0.20–0.89)**
Older	−0.4212	0.4500	59	−0.94	0.353	0.66	(0.27–1.59)
Primary carer – level of educational attainment							
10 years education	Ref.						
Did not attend school	0.8988	1.0101	163	0.89	0.375	2.46	(0.30–17.80)
1–9 years education	−0.2315	0.3794	59	−0.61	0.544	0.79	(0.38–1.67)
11–12 years education	0.5828	0.4900	56	1.19	0.239	1.79	(0.69–4.68)
13+ years education	−0.00908	0.5473	56	−0.02	0.987	0.99	(0.34–2.90)
Encouraged for good marks						1.00	
Not at all/none	Ref.					1.00	
A little	−1.3951	1.0737	59	−1.30	0.199	0.25	(0.03–2.03)
Some	−0.4714	1.1076	59	−0.43	0.672	0.62	(0.07–5.47)
Quite a lot	−0.6681	1.0919	59	−0.61	0.543	0.51	(0.06–4.36)
Very much	−0.6484	1.1194	59	−0.58	0.565	0.52	(0.06–4.69)
Encouraged to attend school							
Not at all/none	Ref.						
A little	1.1412	1.0702	59	1.07	0.291	3.13	(0.40–25.50)
Some	0.5055	1.0032	59	0.50	0.616	1.66	(0.20–11.80)
Quite a lot	1.0218	0.9283	59	1.10	0.275	2.78	(0.50–17.10)
Very much	0.6607	0.9418	59	0.70	0.486	1.94	(0.30–12.30)
Encouraged to complete year 12							
Not at all/none	Ref.					1.00	
A little	−1.2171	0.6499	59	−1.87	0.066	0.30	(0.08–1.06)
Some	−0.7136	0.6173	59	−1.16	0.252	0.49	(0.15–1.64)
Quite a lot	−0.9788	0.5444	59	−1.80	0.077	0.38	(0.13–1.09)

(continued)

Table 33.3 (continued)

Very much	−1.0557	0.5490	59	−1.92	0.059	0.35	(0.12–1.02)
Parental use of drugs							
Yes	Ref.						
No	−0.7204	0.6169	59	−1.17	0.248	0.49	(0.15–1.63)
Alcohol causes problems at home							
Yes	Ref.						
No	0.2849	0.3856	59	0.74	0.463	1.33	(0.62–2.83)
Family affected by forced separation							
Yes	Ref.						
No	0.3522	0.3272	56	1.08	0.286	1.42	(0.75–2.70)
Level of household occupancy							
High household occupancy	Ref.						
Low household occupancy	−0.2220	0.4128	59	−0.54	0.593	0.80	(0.36–1.80)
Categories of socio-economic disadvantage							
Bottom 5%	Ref.					1.00	
5–10%	−0.2346	0.6109	163	−0.38	0.701	0.79	(0.24–2.62)
10–25%	−0.6795	0.5054	163	−1.34	0.181	0.51	(0.19–1.36)
25–50%	−0.2354	0.4917	163	−0.48	0.633	0.79	(0.30–2.07)
Top 50%	−1.5298	0.7442	163	−2.06	**0.041**	**0.22**	**(0.05–0.93)**
Level of relative isolation							
None	Ref.					1.00	
Low	0.1433	0.3684	163	0.39	0.698	1.15	(0.56–2.38)
Moderate	0.3635	0.5379	163	0.68	0.500	1.44	(0.50–4.13)
High	2.0277	1.2361	163	1.64	0.103	7.60	(0.70–85.70)
Extreme	0.7356	0.7737	163	0.95	0.343	2.09	(0.46–9.51)
Knowledge of aboriginal culture							
Not at all/none	Ref.					1.00	
A little	−1.0885	0.7894	59	−1.38	0.173	0.34	(0.07–1.58)
Some	−0.8202	0.7326	59	−1.12	0.267	0.44	(0.10–1.85)
Quite a lot	−0.8534	0.8732	59	−0.98	0.332	0.43	(0.08–2.36)
Very much	−1.7556	0.8824	59	−1.99	**0.051**	**0.17**	**(0.03–0.97)**
Speak or understand an aboriginal language							
No	Ref.					1.00	
A few words	−0.04482	0.4620	59	−0.10	0.923	0.96	(0.39–2.36)
A conversation	−0.8053	0.7677	59	−1.05	0.298	0.45	(0.10–2.01)
Prosocial special friend							
No special friend	Ref.					1.00	
Low prosocial friend	−0.2201	0.5573	59	−0.39	0.694	0.80	(0.27–2.39)
High prosocial friend	1.3040	0.5434	59	2.40	**0.020**	**3.68**	**(1.30–10.70)**
Organized sport							
No	Ref.					1.00	
Yes	0.03546	0.3171	59	0.11	0.911	1.04	(0.56–1.93)
Not applicable	−0.6639	0.8448	56	−0.79	0.435	0.52	(0.10–2.70)
Strong exercise							
No	Ref.					1.00	
Yes	−0.3403	0.3913	59	−0.87	0.388	0.71	(0.33–1.53)
Treated badly because of your race							
Yes	Ref.						
No	0.2279	0.4197	59	0.54	0.589	1.26	(0.55–2.86)

behavioral resilience, and where greater than 1.0, an increased likelihood of emotional or behavioral resilience, relative to a preset reference category.

We modeled the likelihood of resilient emotional or behavioral functioning in the context of high family risk with the 18 potentially protective variables, previously described (Table 33.2). Results showed resilient emotional or behavioral functioning to be independently and significantly associated with three variables:

1. *Prosocial friend.* Having a close friend with prosocial skills is associated with resilience. Young Aboriginal people with a "high" prosocial friend were more than 3 times more likely (OR 3.68, $p=0.020$, 95% CI 1.30, 10.70) to have resilient emotional or behavioral functioning than those with a "low" prosocial friend.
2. *SEIFA.* Higher area level socioeconomic status was associated with decreases in the proportion of young Aboriginal people who were resilient. The findings show that the ranking of geographic areas or neighborhoods by socioeconomic disadvantage was significantly associated with decreased resilient emotional or behavioral functioning. Relative to those young people living in geographic areas ranked in the bottom 5% of socioeconomic disadvantage, those young people in the top 50% were significantly *less* likely to show resilient emotional or behavioral functioning (OR 0.22, $p=0.041$, 95% CI .05, 0.93).
3. *Knowledge of culture.* Perhaps surprisingly, young people reporting that they know "very much" about Aboriginal culture and heritage were significantly *less* likely (OR 0.17, $p=0.051$, 95% CI 0.03, 0.97) to have resilient emotional or behavioral functioning.

Discussion

At the outset we underscore again the defining characteristics of our high family-risk sample. That is, nearly the entire sample self-reported that they were exposed to family violence, with many reporting harsh and low nurturing parenting, and many living in sole parent households where the primary carer was unemployed. Despite high exposure to these well documented threats to development, more than half of this sample (56.2%) of Aboriginal young people showed resilience in the domain of emotional or behavioral functioning.

We have identified only 3 factors out of 18 potentially protective factors that are independently associated with resilient emotional or behavioral functioning: area socioeconomic disadvantage, having a prosocial friend, and knowledge of Aboriginal culture and heritage. Each is discussed in turn.

Area disadvantage and resilience. Our findings revealed that lower levels of area socioeconomic disadvantage were associated with increasing levels of resilient emotional or behavioral functioning. This is counterintuitive and contrary to the often documented beneficial effects of living in more affluent neighborhoods, particularly where these concern improved academic achievement (e.g., Brooks-Gunn, Duncan, & Aber, 1997; Leventhal & Brooks-Gunn, 2003).

With nearly 90% of Aboriginal young people living in neighborhoods ranked in the bottom 50% of socioeconomic disadvantage, being part of the minority 10% living in *less* disadvantaged socioeconomic areas may pose risks to the extent that young people may feel threatened by negative stereotypes of disadvantage and race and feel a very identifiable minority, relative to the majority of Aboriginal youth living in less advantaged neighborhoods. Both the potential increased exposure to actual discrimination and racism, combined with an individual heightened sensitivity to perceive and interpret interactions as racist (Szalacha et al., 2003), may increase risk exposure for young Aboriginal people living in higher socioeconomic neighborhoods. The association observed here may signal that for young Aboriginal Australians, upward social mobility and its attendant resources carry very real stresses. This may entail becoming more aware of social stratification and its associated socioeconomic differences (McLoyd et al., 2009). Certainly this finding suggests that upward social mobility may impose sufficient burden to lower individual adaptive functioning in this vulnerable population.

The implications of this finding should not be construed as a rationale for perpetuating the current structural inequalities but points instead to the need for continued and deliberate qualitative and quantitative study of young Aboriginal people in social transition.

Prosocial friendships. The importance of having one special friend with prosocial skills who is engaged with their family, is a source of encouragement and support, and involved in a range of prosocial activities, was identified as a significant protective factor in the context of high family risk. This is consistent with a body of research undertaken in Canada on Aboriginal youth, which emphasizes the importance of supportive friends especially in high family-risk contexts when families are not able to provide the necessary support (Andersson & Ledogar, 2008).

The resilient young people in our study have a significantly higher proportion of prosocial friends (65.5%), compared to the less resilient young people (34.9%, Table 33.2). However, it is not possible to determine whether young people already with emotional or behavioral difficulties and in high family-risk contexts are attracted to more socially deviant peers, or whether there is a reverse influence – that having antisocial friends increases the risk of emotional or behavioral difficulties through involvement in antisocial activities. In this study, resilient young people report a significantly higher proportion of their prosocial friends do not use drugs or alcohol, and do not get into fights or into trouble with police. However, the direction of this association is not tested in the cross-sectional design of the survey.

Increasing opportunities for young people exposed to harsh and violent family life to engage in activities that connect them to prosocial youth, and that further provides opportunities for exposure to positive adult role models and mentors, should be seen as a priority for prevention and intervention in pathways to poor social and emotional well-being of Aboriginal young people. There are examples of good programs already in existence that could be tailored to the needs of high risk youth – for example, the Western Australian Bush Ranger Cadet program operates through schools and links young people to their communities through land-based conservation and restoration activities, which particularly resonate with Aboriginal traditional values of caring for land and country.

Knowledge of Aboriginal culture and heritage. Relative to young people who reported knowing nothing about Aboriginal culture and heritage, those reporting they knew "very much" were significantly *less* likely to have resilient emotional or behavioral functioning. This is contrary to the beneficial effects we expected to find based on the extant research showing cultural continuity or persistence to be important for a range of Aboriginal adolescent outcomes (e.g., suicide; Chandler, Lalonde, Sokol, & Hallett, 2003; Kirmayer et al., 2007). The reasons for this association are not clear – however, the general trend in the association suggests diminishing emotional and behavioral resilience as cultural knowledge increases. This finding suggests a broader question: Given the Australian history of colonization and dispossession, who are the young Aboriginal Australians who have maintained greater cultural knowledge? It may be that these young people carry a particular burden owing to their status as the carriers of cultural knowledge and that this has onward consequences for emotional and behavioral resilience. Alternately, it is possible that young Aboriginal people with good knowledge of their Aboriginal heritage and culture, and with a critical mass of other protective factors including functional and supportive families, are not represented in our high family-risk sample. In ordinary family-life circumstances, the knowledge of culture and heritage may be a necessary protective factor for psychosocial adjustment, but in high family-risk circumstances, it is not only not sufficient to act as a protective factor, but also the increased knowledge of culture could feasibly be associated with a heightened awareness of the loss of Aboriginal culture and heritage more generally. There has been no research to test our speculation, of which we are aware, although Andersson and Ledogar (2008) report that the instruments they used to measure culture and resilience in Canadian Aboriginal young people "were unable to detect clear associations between culture or spirituality and resilience" (p.11). These findings invite further research.

Finally any overview of the findings here should note the marked absence of significant associations between the selected predictors and emotional and behavioral resilience. Many of the associations that might have been expected are absent in this analysis. This finding is congruent with the broader analyses based on the WAACHS showing persistently diminished developmental effects across a range of social and environmental influences. Where resilience is observed in Australian Aboriginal young people, these findings suggest that we also consider those characteristics of resilient Aboriginal young people that are internal to the individual. Many of these young people are adapting in the face of persistent and pervasive challenge with very little outward manifest support.

Conclusion

This study seeks to contribute to the resilience literature by (1) empirically quantifying contextually specific risks for the domain of emotional or behavioral developmental in a high-risk Aboriginal youth population; and by (2) adding to our understanding of contextually specific protective factors operating at the highest level of risk in the lives of Aboriginal young people.

The findings provide empirical evidence for the role of supportive and prosocial friends in protecting the emotional or behavioral development of at-risk Aboriginal youth, and by extension, also supports a wider body of literature emphasizing the importance of having *someone* who cares and can provide the support required when family capacity is limited (e.g., Andersson & Ledogar, 2008; Werner, 1989). Implications for strategies to support positive mental health outcomes for young people with high family risk exposure are suggested for those factors amenable to intervention. Providing a variety of opportunities for young people to engage with and befriend prosocial young people and/or mentors via out of school activities has been demonstrated as directly protective for young people with antisocial friends (see \Wyman, 2003).

Finally, this research yielded surprisingly few statistically significant predictors of resilient emotional or behavioral functioning. This suggests that other factors not included in this current study, such as those pertaining to the individual's biogenetic predisposition, may be sources of resilience just as important as those provided by the external social ecology, in circumstances when the primary protective mechanism of the family is functioning poorly.

Acknowledgments   Funding for this research was provided through Australian Postgraduate Scholarships, Curtin University Postgraduate Scholarships, the Stan and Jean Perron Scholarship fund, and the Telethon Institute for Child Health Research. Cultural guidance was provided by the Aboriginal Collaborative Council Advising Research and Evaluation.

We acknowledge with deep respect the resilience of the Aboriginal and Torres Strait Islander peoples of Australia and their continuing connection to and responsibility for their land and culture. The authors acknowledge with gratitude the 1,999 families who participated in the WAACHS.

References

Adler, N. E., & Rehkopf, D. H. (2008). U.S. Disparities in Health: Descriptions, causes, and mechanisms. *Annual Review of Public Health, 29*(1), 235–252. doi: 10.1146/annurev.publhealth.29.020907.090852.

Anderson, P., & Wild, R. (2007). *Ampe Akelyeyernemane Meke Mekarle "Little children are sacred"*. Darwin: Northern Territory Government.

Andersson, N., & Ledogar, R. L. (2008). The CIET aboriginal youth resilience studies: 14 years of capacity building and methods development in Canada. *Pimatisiwin, 6*(2), 65–88.

Australian Bureau of Statistics. (2006). *An introduction to socio-economic indexes for areas (SEIFA), Cat. No. 2039.0*. Canberra: Commonwealth of Australia.

Australian Royal Commission into Aboriginal Deaths in Custody, & Dodson, P. (1991). *Regional report of inquiry into underlying issues in Western Australia*. Canberra: Australian Government Publishing Service.

Bolger, K. E., & Patterson, C. J. (2003). Sequelae of child maltreatment: Vulnerability and resilience. In S. S. Luthar (Ed.), *Resilience and vulnerability: Adaptation in the context of childhood adversities*. New York: Cambridge University Press.

Bronfenbrenner, U., & Evans, G. W. (2000). Developmental science in the 21st century: Emerging questions, theoretical models, research designs and empirical findings. *Social Development, 9*(1), 115–125.

Bronfenbrenner, U., & Morris, P. (2006). The bioecological model of human development. In R. M. Lerner (Ed.), *Handbook of child psychology: Theoretical models of human development* (Vol. 1, pp. 793–828). Hoboken: Wiley.

Brooks-Gunn, J., Duncan, G. J., & Aber, J. L. (Eds.). (1997). *Neighborhood poverty: Context and consequences for children* (Vol. 1). New York: Russell Sage.

Bryant, C., & Willis, M. (2008). Risk factors in indigenous violent victimisation. In Australian Institute of Criminology (Ed.), *Technical and Background Paper No. 30*. Canberra: Australian Institute of Criminology.

Chandler, M. J., Lalonde, C. E., Sokol, B. W., & Hallett, D. (2003). Personal persistence, identity development, and suicide: A study of native and non-native North American adolescents. *Monographs of the Society for Research in Child Development, 68*(2 273), 1–130; 139; vii.

Cripps, K. (2010). Indigenous Family Violence: Pathways Forward. In N. Purdie, P. Dudgeon, & R. Walker (Eds.), *Working together: Aboriginal and Torres Strait Islander mental health and wellbeing principles and practice*. Barton: Commonwealth of Australia.

Cripps, K., & McGlade, H. (2008). Indigenous family violence and sexual abuse: Considering pathways forward [Paper in special issue: Innovative Approaches to Family Violence. Schofield, Margot J. and Walker, Rae (eds.).]. *Journal of Family Studies, 14*(2–3), 240–253.

De Maio, J. A., Zubrick, S. R., Silburn, S. R., Lawrence, D. M., Mitrou, F. G., & Dalby, R. B. (2005). *The Western Australian aboriginal child health survey: Measuring the social and emotional wellbeing of aboriginal children and intergenerational effects of forced separation*. Perth: Curtin University of Technology and Telethon Institute for Child Health Research.

Department of Health and Aged Care. (2001). *Measuring remoteness: Accessibility/remoteness Index of Australia (ARIA) Occasional Papers New Series Number 14*. Canberra: Commonwealth Department of Health and Aged Care.

Evans, G. W., Gonnella, C., Marcynyszyn, L. A., Gentile, L., & Salpekar, N. (2005). The role of chaos in poverty and children's socioemotional adjustment. *Psychological Science, 16*(7), 560–565.

Fergusson, D. M., & Horwood, L. J. (2003). Resilience to childhood adversity: Results of a 21-year study. In S. S. Luthar (Ed.), *Resilience and vulnerability: Adaptation in the context of childhood adversities* (pp. 130–155). New York: Cambridge University Press.

Gapen, M., Cross, D., Ortigo, K., Graham, A., Johnson, E., & Evces, M. (2011). Perceived neighborhood disorder, community cohesion, and PTSD symptoms among low-income African Americans in an Urban health setting. *American Journal of Orthopsychiatry, 81*(1), 31–37. doi: 10.1111/j.1939-0025.2010.01069.x.

Goodman, R., Ford, T., Simmons, H., Gatward, R., & Meltzer, H. (2000). Using the strengths and difficulties questionnaire (SDQ) to screen for child psychiatric disorders in a community sample. *The British Journal of Psychiatry, 177*(6), 534–539. doi: 10.1192/bjp.177.6.534.

Greenberg, M. T. (2006). Promoting resilience in children and youth. Preventive interventions and their interface with neuroscience. *Annals of the New York Academy of Sciences, 1094*(1), 139–150.

Holt, S., Buckley, H., & Whelan, S. (2008). The impact of exposure to domestic violence on children and young people: A review of the literature. *Child Abuse & Neglect, 32*(8), 797–810.

Homel, R., Lincoln, R., & Herd, B. (1999). Risk and resilience: Crime and violence prevention in aboriginal communities. *Australian and New Zealand Journal of Criminology, 32*, 182–196.

Hopkins, K. D., Taylor, C. L., & Zubrick, S. R. (under review). The differential influence of contextual risks on psychosocial functioning and participation in education or work in 12–17 year old Australian Aboriginal youth.

Hudjashov, G., Kivisild, T., Underhill, P. A., Endicott, P., Sanchez, J. J., & Lin, A. A. (2007). Revealing the prehistoric settlement of Australia by Y chromosome and mtDNA analysis. *Proceedings of the National Academy of Sciences, 104*(21), 8726–8730. doi: 10.1073/pnas.0702928104.

Human Rights and Equal Opportunity Commission. (1997). *National inquiry into the separation of aboriginal and Torres Strait Islander children from their families*. Sydney: Commonwealth of Australia.

Jaffee, S. R., Caspi, A., Moffitt, T. E., Polo-Tomás, M., & Taylor, A. (2007). Individual, family, and neighborhood factors distinguish resilient from non-resilient maltreated children: A cumulative stressors model. *Child Abuse & Neglect, 31*(3), 231–253.

Jamieson, L. M., Harrison, J. E., & Berry, J. G. (2008). Hospitalisation for head injury due to assault among Indigenous and non-Indigenous Australians, July 1999 – June 2005. *Medical Journal of Australia, 188*(10), 576.

Kirmayer, L. J., Brass, G. M., Holton, T., Paul, K., Simpson, C., & Tait, C. (2007). *Suicide among aboriginal people in Canada*. Ottawa: Aboriginal Healing Foundation.

Lansford, J. E., Dodge, K. A., Pettit, G. S., Bates, J. E., Crozier, J., & Kaplow, J. (2002). A 12-year prospective study of the long-term effects of early child physical maltreatment on psychological, behavioral, and academic problems in adolescence. *Archives of Pediatric & Adolescent Medicine, 156*(8), 824–830. doi: 10.1001/archpedi.156.8.824.

Leventhal, T., & Brooks-Gunn, J. (2003). Moving to oppurtunity: An experimental study of neighborhood effects on mental health. *American Journal of Public Health, 93*(9), 1576–1582.

Luthar, S. S. (2003). *Resilience and vulnerability: Adaptation in the context of childhood adversities*. New York: Cambridge University Press.

Margolin, G., & Gordis, E. B. (2000). The effects of family and community violence on children. *Annual Reviews in Psychology, 51*(1), 445–479.

Margolin, G., & Vickerman, K. A. (2007). Posttraumatic stress in children and adolescents exposed to family violence: I overview and issues. *Professional Psychology: Research and Practice, 38*(6), 613–619.

McLoyd, V. C. (1998). Socioeconomic disadvantage and child development. *American Psychologist, 53*(2), 185–204.

McLoyd, V. C., Kaplan, R., Purtell, K. M., Bagley, E., Hardaway, C. R., & Smalls, C. (2009). Poverty and socioeconomic disadvantage in adolescence. In R. M. Lerner & L. Steinberg (Eds.), *Handbook of adolescent psychology: Contextual influences on adolescent development* (Vol. 2). Hoboken: Wiley.

Owens, E. B., & Shaw, D. S. (2003). Poverty and early childhood adjustment. In S. S. Luthar (Ed.), *Resilience and vulnerability: Adaptation in the context of childhood adversities*. New York: Cambridge University Press.

Riley, R. (1997). *From exclusion to negotiation: The role of psychology in Aboriginal Social Justice. Vol. 1/1997*. Perth: Curtin University of Technology.

Silburn, S., Zubrick, S., De Maio, J., Shepherd, C., Griffin, J., & Mitrou, F. (2006). *The Western Australian aboriginal child health survey: Strengthening the capacity of aboriginal children, families and communities*. Perth: Curtin University of Technology and Telethon Institute for Child Health Research.

Stanley, J., Kovacs, K., Tomison, A., & Cripps, K. (2002). *Child abuse and family violence in Aboriginal communities – exploring child sexual abuse in Western Australia. Australian Institute of Family Studies & National Child Protection Clearing House*. Canberra: Australian Government Canberra.

Steering Committee for the Review of Government Services Provision. (2009). *Overcoming indigenous disadvantage: Key indicators 2009*. Canberra: Australian Government.

Szalacha, L. A., Erkut, S., Garcia-Coll, C., Fields, J. P., Alarcon, O., & Ceder, I. (2003). Perceived discrimination and resilience. In S. S. Luthar (Ed.), *Resilience and vulnerability: Adaptation in the context of childhood adversities* (pp. 414–435). New York: Cambridge University Press.

Ungar, M. (2005). *Handbook for working with children and youth: Pathways to resilience across cultures and contexts*. Thousand Oaks: Sage.

Ungar, M. (2008). Resilience across cultures. *British Journal of Social Work, 38*(2), 218–235. doi: 10.1093/bjsw/bcl343.

Ungar, M. (2010). The social ecology of resilience: Addressing contextual and cultural ambiguity of a nascent construct. *American Journal of Orthopsychiatry, 81*(1), 1–17. doi: 10.1111/j.1939-0025.2010.01067.x.

Werner, E. E. (1989). High-risk children in young adulthood: A longitudinal study from birth to 32 years. *American Journal of Orthopsychiatry, 59*(1), 72–81. doi: 10.1111/j.1939-0025.1989.tb01636.x.

Wyman, P. A. (2003). Emerging perspectives on context specificity of children's adaptation and resilience: Evidence from a decade of research with urban children in adversity. In S. S. Luthar (Ed.), *Resilience and vulnerability: Adaptation in the context of childhood adversities*. New York: Cambridge University Press.

Yexley, M., Borowsky, I., & Ireland, M. (2002). Correlation between different experiences of intrafamilial physical violence and violent adolescent behavior. *Journal of Interpersonal Violence, 17*(7), 707–720.

Zubrick, S. R., Lawrence, D. M., Silburn, S. R., Blair, E., Milroy, H., & Wilkes, T. (2004). *The Western Australian aboriginal child health survey: The health of aboriginal children and young people* (Vol. 1). Perth: Telethon Institute for Child Health Research.

Zubrick, S. R., Silburn, S. R., De Maio, J. A., Shepherd, C., Griffin, J., & Dalby, R. B. (2006). *The Western Australian aboriginal child health survey: Improving the educational experiences of aboriginal children and young people* (Vol. 3). Perth: Telethon Institute of Child Health Research.

Zubrick, S. R., Silburn, S. R., Lawrence, D. M., Mitrou, F. G., Dalby, R. B., & Blair, E. M. (2005). *The Western Australian aboriginal child health survey: The social and emotional wellbeing of aboriginal children and young people* (Vol. 2). Perth: Telethon Institute of Child Health Research.

Zubrick, S. R., Silburn, S. R., & Prior, M. (2005). Resources and contexts for child development: Implications for children and society. In M. Prior & S. Richardson (Eds.), *No Time to Lose: The Wellbeing of Australia's Children* (pp. 161). Carlton: Melbourne University Press.

Biography

Editor's Biography

Michael Ungar is a Killam Professor of Social work at Dalhousie University in Halifax, Canada. He is currently the Principal Investigator of the Resilience Research Centre (www.resilienceresearch.org) that coordinates more than five million dollars in funded research in more than a dozen countries focused on how children, youth, and families thrive in culturally specific ways. He has published over 75 peer-reviewed articles and book chapters on this topic and is the author of ten books including his latest, *Counseling in Challenging Contexts: Working with Individuals and Families Across Clinical and Community Settings*, and *Strengths-Based Counseling with At-Risk Youth*. His novel, *The Social Worker*, was released in 2011. Michael also writes for parents and educators. Among his best known works are *The We Generation: Raising Socially Responsible Children and Teens* and *Too Safe For Their Own Good*. In addition to his research and writing, Michael maintains a family therapy practice in association with Phoenix Youth Programs, a prevention program for street youth and their families, is a board member of the American Family Therapy Academy, and is cochair of the Nova Scotia Mental Health Strategy. In 2010, he was the recipient of the Canadian Association of Social Workers Distinguished Service Award for Nova Scotia.

M. Ungar (ed.), *The Social Ecology of Resilience: A Handbook of Theory and Practice*, DOI 10.1007/978-1-4614-0586-3, © Springer Science+Business Media, LLC 2012

Index

443

Druck: KN Digital Printforce GmbH · Schockenriedstraße 37 · 70565 Stuttgart